Applied Computational Electromagnetics Society Symposium (ACES 2020-Monterey)

Held online due to COVID-19

Monterey, California, USA
22 – 26 March 2020

ISBN: 978-1-7138-2077-2

Printed from e-media with permission by:

Curran Associates, Inc.
57 Morehouse Lane
Red Hook, NY 12571

Some format issues inherent in the e-media version may also appear in this print version.

Printed with permission by Curran Associates, Inc. (2021)

The Applied Computational Electromagnetics Society (ACES)
www.aces-society.org

Additional copies of this publication are available from:

Curran Associates, Inc.
57 Morehouse Lane
Red Hook, NY 12571 USA
Phone: 845-758-0400
Fax: 845-758-2633
Email: curran@proceedings.com
Web: www.proceedings.com

2020 International Applied Computational Electromagnetics Society Symposium – (2020 ACES-Monterey) Virtual Conference

Conference Proceedings Table of Contents

Session 4: Printed, Flexible and Reconfigurable Antenna Implementations

Session 5: Recent Advances in Finite Difference Time Domain Methods

Session 6: Antennas and Sensors Applications

Session 7: Time Domain Modeling of Switchable and Tunable Devices in Photonics

Session 8: Advances in Finite Difference and Other Numerical Methods for Computational Electromagnetics and Photonics

Fast Antenna Optimization Using Gradient Monitoring and Variable-Fidelity EM Models

Slawomir Koziel[1] and Anna Pietrenko-Dabrowska[2]

[1] School of Science and Engineering, Reykjavik University, Reykjavik, Iceland, koziel@ru.is
[2] Faculty of Electronics, Telecommunications and Informatics, Gdansk University of Technology, 80-233 Gdansk, Poland

***Abstract*—Accelerated simulation-driven design optimization of antenna structures is proposed. Variable-fidelity electromagnetic (EM) analysis is used as well as the trust-region framework with limited sensitivity updates. The latter are controlled by monitoring the changes of the antenna response gradients. Our methodology is verified using three compact wideband antennas. Comprehensive benchmarking demonstrates its superiority over both conventional and surrogate-assisted algorithms.**

Keywords—antenna optimization, EM-driven design, trust-region framework, variable-fidelity EM simulations.

I. Introduction

Adjustment of geometry parameters is a necessary yet challenging stage of the antenna design process. Due to the complexity of contemporary structures, numerical optimization is recommended, and more and more widely used by the researchers [1]. Its major bottleneck, which is high CPU cost, can be alleviated by various means, e.g., utilization of adjoints sensitivities [2], surrogate modeling techniques [3], or by developing more efficient numerical routines [4]. This paper proposes a modification of the trust-region gradient search procedure aimed at improving the computational efficiency. Its two major components include variable-fidelity EM simulations (to speed up sensitivity estimation), as well as antenna response gradient monitoring (to reduce the number of expensive finite-differentiation-based sensitivity updates). Both mechanisms lead to a considerable reduction of the overall cost of the optimization process as demonstrated through examples. Furthermore, the proposed technique is shown competitive to both traditional and multi-fidelity algorithms.

II. Variable-Fidelity Gradient Search with Sparse Sensitivity Updates

For illustration purposes, the task of antenna matching improvement is considered, which can be formulated as:

$$x^* = \arg\min\{x : U(x)\}. \tag{1}$$

Here, $\boldsymbol{x}$ is a vector of antenna parameters, whereas the objective function is defined as $U(\boldsymbol{x}) = \max\{f \in F : |S_{11}(\boldsymbol{x},f)|\}$, where f is the frequency within the range of interest F (e.g., 3.1 GHz to 10.6 GHz for UWB antennas). The reflection characteristic $S_{11}(\boldsymbol{x},f)$ is obtained through a high-fidelity EM analysis.

The core of the proposed framework is the conventional trust-region (TR) gradient-based algorithm [5] solving (1) by producing approximations $\boldsymbol{x}^{(i)}$, $i = 0, 1, \ldots$, to $\boldsymbol{x}^*$ as:

$$\boldsymbol{x}^{(i+1)} = \arg \min_{x;\, -d^{(i)} \le x - x^{(i)} \le d^{(i)}} U_S(\boldsymbol{x}), \tag{2}$$

where $U_s(\boldsymbol{x}) = \max\{f \in F : S_L^{(i)}(\boldsymbol{x},f)\}$, and $S_L^{(i)}$ is defined as:

$$S_L^{(i)}(\boldsymbol{x},f) = S_{11}(\boldsymbol{x}^{(i)},f) + \boldsymbol{G}_S(\boldsymbol{x}^{(i)}) \cdot (\boldsymbol{x} - \boldsymbol{x}^{(i)}). \tag{3}$$

In (2), $\boldsymbol{d}^{(i)}$ is the TR size at the ith iteration, adjusted using the standard rules [5]. The gradient $\boldsymbol{G}_S$ is normally evaluated using finite differentiation (FD), which is the major contributor to the CPU cost of the process.

Here, we employ two mechanisms to reduce the cost of solving (1). The first one is utilization of a coarse-mesh EM antenna model $S_{11.c}(\boldsymbol{x},f)$ for the purpose of sensitivity estimation. As indicated in Fig. 1, despite noticeable discrepancies between the high- and low-fidelity models, the gradients are well aligned which makes the use of $S_{11.c}$ a reasonable (and, of course, cheaper) option.

The second technique is monitoring of the antenna response gradients aimed at detecting their stable patterns and, consequently, suppressing unnecessary FD updates. Here, we deal with the antenna reflection $S_{11}(\boldsymbol{x},f)$, for which the gradient $\boldsymbol{G}_S = [G_1 \ \ldots \ G_n]$ is a $1 \times n$ vector. The components G_k are compared between the algorithm iterations using a metric:

$$d_k^{(i+1)} = \underset{f \in F}{mean}\left(2\left[\left|G_k^{(i)}(f)\right| - \left|G_k^{(i-1)}(f)\right|\right] \Big/ \left[\left|G_k^{(i)}(f)\right| + \left|G_k^{(i-1)}(f)\right|\right]\right), \tag{4}$$

where $G_k^{(i)}(f)$ and $G_k^{(i-1)}(f)$ refer to the ith and $(i-1)$th iteration, respectively. The averaging is over the frequency range F. We also define a vector $\boldsymbol{d}^{(i)} = [d_1^{(i)} \ \ldots \ d_n^{(i)}]^T$ of the gradient difference factors used in the i-th iteration, $d_{\min}^{(i)} = \min\{k = 1,\ldots,n : d_k^{(i)}\}$, and $d_{\max}^{(i)} = \max\{k = 1,\ldots,n : d_k^{(i)}\}$. Furthermore, in the i-th iteration, a vector $\boldsymbol{N}^{(i)} = [N_1^{(i)} \ \ldots \ N_n^{(i)}]^T$ will stand for the numbers of subsequent iterations without FD. Its components are computed according to the conversion function:

$$N_k^{(i)} = \left[\!\left[N_{\max} + a^{(i)}(d_k^{(i)} - d_{\min}^{(i)}) \right]\!\right], \tag{5}$$

where $a^{(i)} = (N_{\max} - N_{\min})/(d_{\min}^{(i)} - d_{\max}^{(i)})$ and [[.]] is the nearest integer function. The function (5) establishes a relation between $N_k^{(i)}$ and $d_k^{(i)}$, which is based on the minimum and the maximum number of iterations without FD (algorithm control parameters). Given $N_k^{(i)}$, $N_k^{(i+1)}$ is obtained from (%) if FD was executed for the kth parameter in the ith iteration, otherwise $N_k^{(i+1)} = N_k^{(i)} - 1$. The maximum number of omissions is $N_{\max}$. The values of the difference factors $d_k^{(i)}$ retained through all the iterations without FD. They are utilized to determine $d_{\min}^{(i)}$ and $d_{\max}^{(i)}$ as well as to compute $N_k^{(i)}$ for other parameters.

In the proposed optimization framework, the gradient $\boldsymbol{G}_S$ is estimated using FD only in the first two iterations. Further, the gradient is exclusively computed using the low-fidelity EM model. In the remaining iterations, the components G_k are obtained based on $\boldsymbol{N}^{(i+1)}$: if $N_k^{(i)} = 1$, FD is performed, otherwise the most recent value estimated with FD is kept. This allows for a significant reduction of the computational cost of the optimization process.

III. Verification Examples

The test set consists of three antennas shown in Fig. 2. Antenna I, [6] is implemented on Taconic RF-35 substrate ($\varepsilon_r = 3.5$, $h = 0.762$ mm). It is described by parameters $\boldsymbol{x} = [l_0\ g\ a\ l_1\ l_2\ w_1\ o]^T$; $w_0 = 2o + a$, and $w_f = 1.7$ mm. Antenna II [7] is also implemented on RF-35; geometry parameters are $\boldsymbol{x} = [L_0\ dR\ R\ r_{rel}\ dL\ dw\ L_g\ L_1\ R_1\ dr\ c_{rel}]^T$. Antenna III [8] is implemented on FR4 ($\varepsilon_r = 4.3$, $h = 1.55$ mm); design parameters are $\boldsymbol{x} = [L_g\ L_0\ L_s\ W_s\ d\ dL\ d_s\ dW_s\ dW\ a\ b]^T$. All antennas are to operate within the UWB frequency range of 3.1 GHz to 10.6 GHz. The EM models are implemented in CST. The models incorporate the SMA connectors.

The antennas have been optimized for best matching, using the proposed algorithm with $N_{\min} = 1$ and $N_{\max} = 5$. Three other algorithms were also tested for comparison: (i) the TR algorithm (2), (3) working with the high-fidelity model only, (ii) the reference algorithm working with variable-fidelity models, and (iii) the algorithm of Section II working with the high-fidelity model only. To test the robustness, ten runs have been executed for each algorithm using random initial designs. Table I gathers the numerical data (see also Fig. 3).

The low-fidelity model simulation time is shorter by a factor of around 2.5 as compared to the high fidelity ones. For the algorithms using variable-fidelity models (Algorithms 2 and 4), the high-fidelity model was evaluated only around 13 times for all cases. As shown in Table I, the variable-fidelity approach allows for achieving good design quality and significant cost savings by a factor of around two. For Algorithm 4 (proposed in this work), the savings are also due to limiting the amount of FD, and the reduction of the overall cost is as high as four times for the Antenna II. The design quality is almost the same for Algorithms 2 and 3 for all benchmark cases. Combining both mechanisms as implemented in Algorithm 4 leads for certain quality degradation (by 0.8 dB and 0.7 dB, for Antennas I and II, respectively). For Antenna III, the degradation is higher, and it equals 2 dB. Note that such a considerable cost reduction was achieved despite the fact that the time evaluation ratio between the high- and low-fidelity model is less than three. In many cases, that ratio can be made much higher, consequently implying even more significant cost savings.

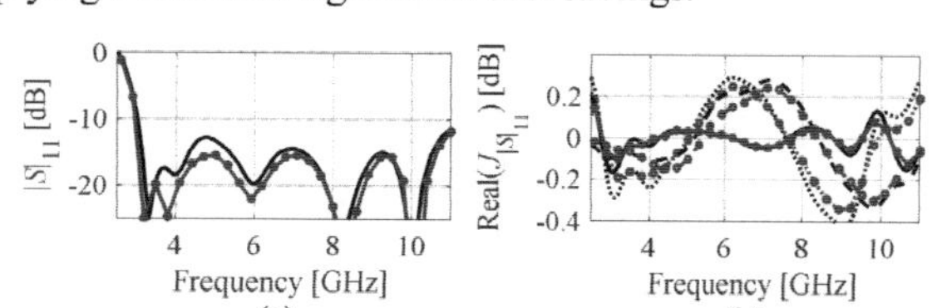

(a) (b)

Fig. 1. Example $|S_{11}|$ and sensitivity thereof of Antenna I of Section III: (a) high-fidelity EM model reflection response (-o-o) and low-fidelity EM model response (—); (b) sensitivity w.r.t. selected antenna parameters: high-fidelity EM model (··o··o··, - o - o, —o—o)) and low-fidelity model (·····, - - -, —).

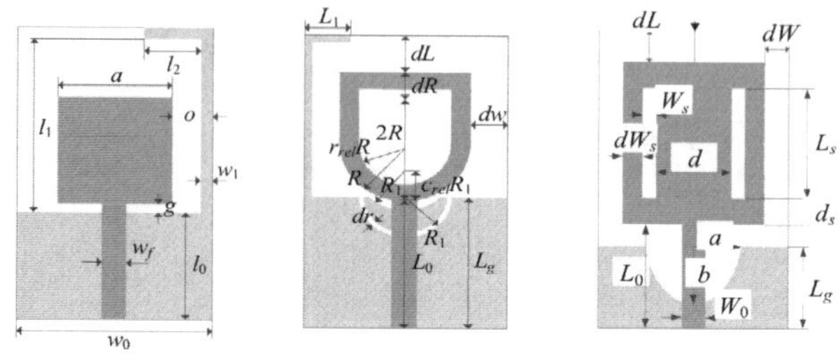

(a) (b) (c)

Fig. 2. Benchmark antennas: (a) Antenna I [6], (b) Antenna II [7], and (c) Antenna III [8]. Ground plane marked using light gray shade.

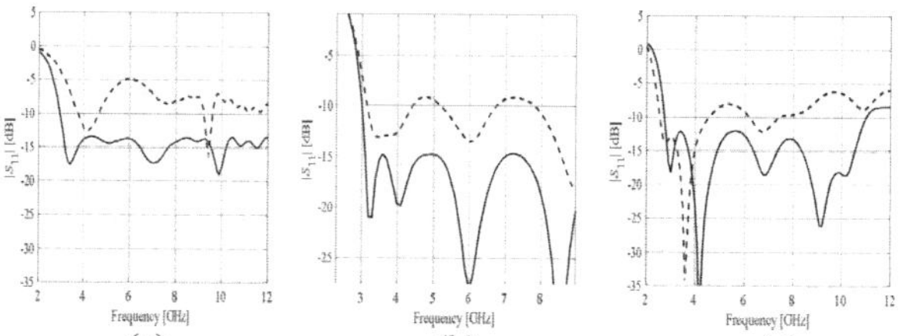

(a) (b) (c)

Fig. 3. Initial (- - -) and optimized (—) responses of the antennas found using the proposed variable-fidelity algorithm, shown for the representative runs of the procedure: (a) Antenna I, (b) Antenna II, and (c) Antenna III. Horizontal lines mark the design specifications.

TABLE I. Optimization Results and Benchmarking

Algorithm		Antenna I			Antenna II			Antenna III		
		Cost[$]	max $\lvert S_{11}\rvert$ [dB][*]	Time[#] [min]	Cost[$]	max $\lvert S_{11}\rvert$ [dB][*]	Time[#] [min]	Cost[$]	max $\lvert S_{11}\rvert$ [dB][*]	Time[#] [min]
1	Fine	97.6	–11.9	277.5	111.2	–14.9	389.2	111.0	–13.9	455.1
2	Coarse Fine	60.0 13.9	–11.8	119.8	97.2 13.4	–14.8	199.5	109.2 14.4	–13.7	199.2
3	Fine	46.1	–11.4	135.2	58.6	–14.7	205.0	68.7	–13.5	281.7
4	Coarse Fine	36.4 14.5	–11.1	90.5	45.4 12.7	–14.2	96.4	58.6 14.3	–11.9	133.9

Algorithms: 1 – reference (high-fidelity model only), 2 – reference (variable-fidelity models), 3 – gradient monitoring (high-fidelity model only), 4 – proposed framework.
[$] Number of EM simulations averaged over 10 algorithm runs (random initial points);
[*] Maximum |S11| within UWB frequency range (averaged over 10 algorithm runs).
[#] Overall optimization time.

Acknowledgment

This work is partially supported by the Icelandic Centre for Research (RANNIS) Grant 174114051, and by National Science Centre of Poland Grant 2015/17/B/ST6/01857.

References

[1] J. Wang, X. Yang, and B. Wang, "Efficient gradient-based optimisation of pixel antenna with large-scale connections," IET Microwaves, Antennas & Propag., vol. 12, no. 3, pp. 385-389, 2018.

[2] S. Koziel and A. Bekasiewicz, "Rapid design optimization of antennas using variable-fidelity EM models and adjoint sensitivities," Eng. Comp., vol. 33, no. 7, pp. 2007-2018, 2016.

[3] S. Koziel and S. Ogurtsov, Antenna Design by Simulation-driven Optimization. Surrogate-based Approach. Springer, New York, 2014.

[4] J. P. Jacobs, "Characterization by Gaussian processes of finite substrate size effects on gain patterns of microstrip antennas," IET Microwaves Ant. Prop., vol. 10, no. 11, pp. 1189-1195, 2016.

[5] A. R. Conn, N. I. M. Gould, and P. L. Toint, Trust Region Methods, MPS-SIAM Series on Optimization, 2000.

[6] S. Koziel and A. Bekasiewicz, "Low-cost multi-objective optimization of antennas using Pareto front exploration and response features," *IEEE Int. Symp. Ant. Prop.*, Fajardo, Puerto-Rico, 2016.

[7] M. G. N. Alsath and M. Kanagasabai, "Compact UWB monopole antenna for automotive communications," IEEE Trans. Ant. Prop., vol. 63, no. 9, pp. 4204-4208, 2015.

[8] M. A. Haq, S. Koziel, and Q. S. Cheng, "EM-driven size reduction of UWB antennas with ground plane modifications," Int. Applied Comp. Electromagnetics Society (ACES China) Symposium, 2017.

Low-Cost Surrogate Modeling of Miniaturized Microwave Components Using Nested Kriging

Anna Pietrenko-Dabrowska[1] and Slawomir Koziel[1,2]

[1] Faculty of Electronics, Telecommunications and Informatics, Gdansk University of Technology, 80-233 Gdansk, Poland
[2] School of Science and Engineering, Reykjavik University, Reykjavik, Iceland, koziel@ru.is

***Abstract*—In the paper, a recently reported nested kriging methodology is employed for modeling of miniaturized microwave components. The approach is based on identifying the parameter space region that contains high-quality designs, and, subsequently, rendering the surrogate in this subset. The results obtained for a miniaturized unequal-power-split rat-race coupler and a compact three-section impedance transformer demonstrate reliability of the method even for highly-dimensional parameter spaces, as well as its superiority over conventional modeling methods.**

Keywords— design optimization, microwave design, miniaturized structures, nested kriging, surrogate modeling.

I. INTRODUCTION

Full-wave electromagnetic (EM) analysis plays an important role in design closure of microwave structures, especially compact devices [1]. Yet, solving EM-driven design tasks is CPU intensive due to massive simulations involved. Computational savings can be obtained by using fast surrogate models of the structure under design. Conventional modeling methods, e.g., neural networks [2], or kriging [3], are limited by the curse of dimensionality to handling circuits described by small numbers of parameters.

In [4] and [5], constrained modeling of microwave structures was presented with the model domain confined to a region containing a set of pre-existing reference designs, optimized for problem-specific figures of interest. The advantage is a remarkable reduction of the domain volume, which mitigates the problem of excessive number of training data samples required by the traditional setup. A recent nested kriging approach [6] brings further improvements over [4], [5] by enabling uniform sampling and model optimization in a straightforward manner. Here, we demonstrate the feasibility of this method for modeling of compact microwave components.

II. NESTED KRIGING MODELING FORMULATION

In this paper, we apply the nested kriging approach of [6] to cost-efficient modeling of compact microwave components. A brief formulation of the framework is provided in this section, followed by demonstration case studies discussed in Section III.

A. First-Level Model

We denote by f_k, $k = 1, \ldots, N$, the figures of interest relevant to the design process (e.g., coupler operating frequency and/or power split ratio). We assume the existence of the reference designs $\boldsymbol{x}^{(j)} = [x_1^{(j)} \ldots x_n^{(j)}]^T$, $j = 1, \ldots, p$, optimized w.r.t. the performance vectors $\boldsymbol{f}^{(j)} = [f_1^{(j)} \ldots f_N^{(j)}]$. The objective space F is defined by the ranges $f_{k.\min} \leq f_k^{(j)} \leq f_{k.\max}$, $k = 1, \ldots, N$, to be covered by the surrogate. The first-level model $\boldsymbol{s}_I(\boldsymbol{f})$ maps F into the design space X. It is implemented using kriging [3], where $\{\boldsymbol{f}^{(j)},\boldsymbol{x}^{(j)}\}$ are the training points. Figure provides a graphical illustration of these concepts.

B. Domain Definition

The model domain X_S is constructed by "fattening" the set $\boldsymbol{s}_I(F) \subset X$ which approximates the region containing the designs that are optimum w.r.t. all $\boldsymbol{f} \in F$. This is realized by an orthogonal extension of $\boldsymbol{s}_I(F)$ towards its normal vectors $\{\boldsymbol{v}_n^{(k)}(\boldsymbol{f})\}$, $k = 1, \ldots, n - N$. Let $\boldsymbol{x}_{\max} = \max\{\boldsymbol{x}^{(k)}, k = 1, \ldots, p\}$, $\boldsymbol{x}_{\min} = \min\{\boldsymbol{x}^{(k)}, k = 1, \ldots, p\}$, and $\boldsymbol{x}_d = \boldsymbol{x}_{\max} - \boldsymbol{x}_{\min}$ (parameter variations within $\boldsymbol{s}_I(F)$). We also define:

$$\boldsymbol{\alpha}(\boldsymbol{f}) = [\alpha_1(\boldsymbol{f}) \ldots \alpha_{n-N}(\boldsymbol{f})]^T = 0.5T\left[|\boldsymbol{x}_d \boldsymbol{v}_n^{(1)}(\boldsymbol{f})| \ \ldots \ |\boldsymbol{x}_d \boldsymbol{v}_n^{(n-N)}(\boldsymbol{f})| \right]^T . \quad (1)$$

Here, T is a thickness parameter; α_k determine the boundaries of the domain X_S, located between the manifolds M_+ and M_-:

$$M_{\pm} = \left\{ \boldsymbol{x} \in X : \boldsymbol{x} = \boldsymbol{s}_I(\boldsymbol{f}) \pm \sum\nolimits_{k=1}^{n-N} \alpha_k(\boldsymbol{f}) \boldsymbol{v}_n^{(k)}(\boldsymbol{f}) \right\} . \quad (2)$$

Formally, we have:

$$X_S = \left\{ \begin{array}{l} \boldsymbol{x} = \boldsymbol{s}_I(\boldsymbol{f}) + \sum\limits_{k=1}^{n-N} \lambda_k \alpha_k(\boldsymbol{f}) \boldsymbol{v}_n^{(k)}(\boldsymbol{f}) : \boldsymbol{f} \in F, \\ -1 \leq \lambda_k \leq 1, k = 1, \ldots, n-N \end{array} \right\} . \quad (3)$$

The actual (second-level) surrogate is a kriging interpolation model set up in X_S, using a set of training data samples $\{\boldsymbol{x}_B^{(k)}, \boldsymbol{R}(\boldsymbol{x}_B^{(k)})\}_{k = 1, \ldots, N_B}$, where $\boldsymbol{R}$ is the EM-simulation model of the compact structure of interest.

C. Design of Experiments

The data sampling can be readily implemented by exploiting (3) and an appropriate two-stage mapping H from the unit interval $[0,1]^n$ onto X_S. Let $\{\boldsymbol{z}^{(k)}\}$, $k = 1, \ldots, N_B$, be the set of uniformly distributed data points obtained using LHS [6], with $\boldsymbol{z}^{(k)} = [z_1^{(k)} \ldots z_n^{(k)}]^T$. The mapping h_1:

$$\begin{array}{l} \boldsymbol{y} = h_1(\boldsymbol{z}) = h_1([z_1 \ldots z_n]^T) = [f_{1.\min} + z_1(f_{1.\max} - f_{1.\min}) \ \ldots \\ \ldots \ f_{N.\min} + z_N(f_{N.\max} - f_{N.\min})] \times [-1 + 2z_{N+1} \ \ldots \ -1 + 2z_n] \end{array} , \quad (4)$$

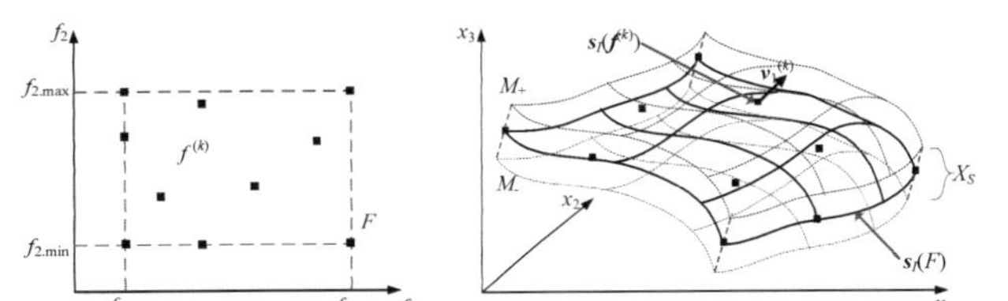

(a) (b)

Fig. 1. The concept of nested kriging modeling: (a) reference designs and objective space F; (b) the image $\boldsymbol{s}_I(F)$ of the first-level surrogate model and the normal vector $\boldsymbol{v}_1^{(k)}$ at $\boldsymbol{f}^{(k)}$; the manifolds M_- and M_+ as well as the surrogate model domain X_S defined as the orthogonal extension of $\boldsymbol{s}_I(F)$.

transforms the hypercube onto $F \times [-1,1]^{n-N}$ (here, $\times$ denotes a Cartesian product). Subsequently, the function h_2 defined as:

$$\boldsymbol{x} = h_2(\boldsymbol{y}) = h_2([y_1 \dots y_n]^T) = \boldsymbol{s}_I(\boldsymbol{y}) + \sum\nolimits_{k=1}^{n-N} y_{N+k}\alpha_k(\boldsymbol{y})\boldsymbol{v}_n^{(k)}(\boldsymbol{y}), \quad (5)$$

maps $F \times [-1,1]^{n-N}$ onto X_S. Uniformly distributed samples $\boldsymbol{x}_B^{(k)} \in X_S$ are then obtained as:

$$\boldsymbol{x}_B^{(k)} = H(\boldsymbol{z}^{(k)}) = h_2(h_1(\boldsymbol{z}^{(k)})). \quad (6)$$

The mapping H can also be used for optimization within X_S: regardless of the geometry of X_S, it is sufficient to operate within $F \times [-1,1]^{n-N}$ and apply (6) for EM evaluation purposes.

III. Microwave Modeling Using Nested Kriging

We consider two compact microstrip structures, a rat-race coupler (RRC) shown in Fig. 2 (a) and the 50-to-100 Ohm impedance matching transformer shown in Fig. 2 (d), composed of the CMRCs of Fig. 2 (c). Both structures are implemented on RF-35 substrate ($\varepsilon_r = 3.5$, $h = 0.762$ mm, $\tan\delta = 0.018$). The RRC parameters are: $\boldsymbol{x} = [l_1\ l_2\ l_3\ d\ w\ w_1]^T$, with relative variable $d_1 = d + |w - w_1|$ and dimensions $d = 1.0$, $w_0 = 1.7$, $l_0 = 15$ fixed (all in mm). The parameters of the transformer are $\boldsymbol{x} = [l_{1.1}\ l_{1.2}\ w_{1.1}\ w_{1.2}\ w_{1.0}\ l_{2.1}\ l_{2.2}\ w_{2.1}\ w_{2.2}\ w_{2.0}\ l_{3.1}\ l_{3.2}\ w_{3.1}\ w_{3.2}\ w_{3.0}]^T$.

The goal is to model the RRC within the region covering optimum designs corresponding to the operating frequencies f_0 from 1 GHz to 2 GHz and the power split ratios K from –6 dB to 0 dB (equal power split). The transformer model is supposed to cover the operating bands $[f_1\ f_2]$ for 1.5 GHz $\leq f_1 \leq$ 3.5 GHz, and 4.5 GHz $\leq f_2 \leq$ 6.5 GHz. The allocation of the reference designs for both structures are shown in Figs. 2 (b) and 2 (e), respectively. The lower and upper bounds for design variables are based on the reference designs. These are $\boldsymbol{l} = [2.0\ 7.0\ 12.5\ 0.2\ 0.7\ 0.2]^T$, and $\boldsymbol{u} = [4.5\ 12.5\ 22.0\ 0.65\ 1.5\ 0.9]^T$ for the RRC and $\boldsymbol{l} = [2.0\ 0.15\ 0.65\ 0.35\ 0.30\ 2.70\ 0.15\ 0.44\ 0.15\ 0.30\ 3.2\ 0.15\ 0.30\ 0.15\ 0.30]^T$, and $\boldsymbol{u} = [3.4\ 0.50\ 0.80\ 0.55\ 1.90\ 4.00\ 0.50\ 0.67\ 0.50\ 1.55\ 4.5\ 0.26\ 0.46\ 0.27\ 1.75]^T$ for the transformer.

The nested kriging surrogate has been constructed for various training data sets listed in Table I, using the thickness parameter $T = 0.05$. The model error was estimated with 100 independent test points. The results for the conventional kriging model set up in the interval $[\boldsymbol{l}, \boldsymbol{u}]$ are reported as well (see also Figs. 3 and 4). A considerable improvement of the modeling accuracy offered by the nested kriging surrogate over the conventional one can be observed. The comparable predictive power is obtained for much smaller training data sets, by a factor of four and higher. Note that in the case of the transformer, the accuracy of the conventional model is poor even for the largest data set consisting of 800 samples. This example is challenging due to a large number of parameters (fifteen) as well as wide parameter ranges.

Acknowledgment

This work is partially supported by the Icelandic Centre for Research (RANNIS) Grant 174114051, and by National Science Centre of Poland Grant 2017/27/B/ST7/00563.

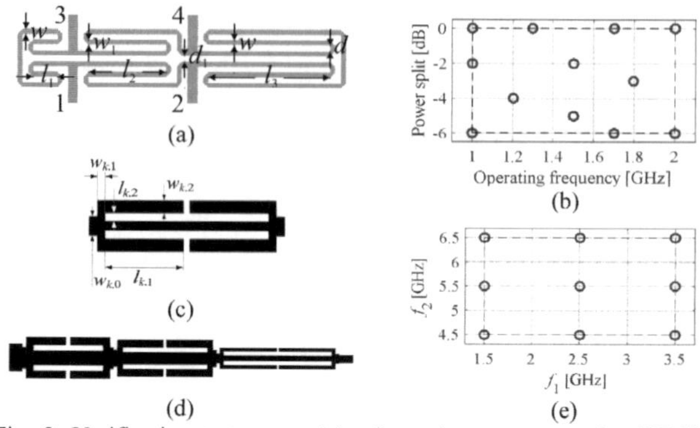

Fig. 2. Verification test cases: (a) microstrip rat-race coupler (RRC) [20], (b) allocation of the reference designs for the RRC, (c) compact cell (CMRC), (d) CMRC-based miniaturized three-section impedance transformer, and (e) allocation of the reference designs for the transformer.

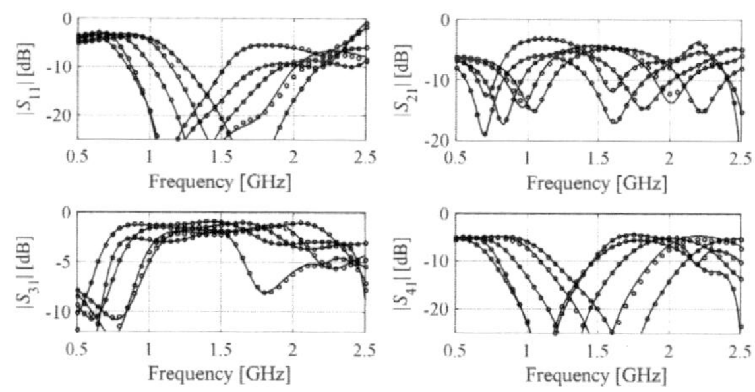

Fig. 3. Responses of the compact RRC of Fig. 2 (a) at the selected test designs for $N = 800$: EM model (—), nested kriging surrogate (o).

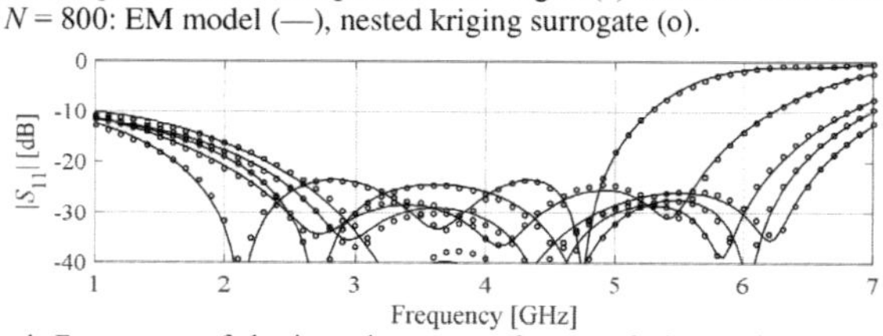

Fig. 4. Responses of the impedance transformer of Fig. 2 (d) at the selected test designs for $N = 800$: EM model (—), nested kriging surrogate (o).

Table I. Modeling Results For RRC and Transformer

Number of Training Samples	Relative RMS Error for Compact RRC		Relative RMS Error for Impedance Transformer	
	Conventional Kriging Model	Nested Kriging Model [This Work]	Conventional Kriging Model	Nested Kriging Model [This Work]
50	25.7%	6.9%	49.1%	17.3%
100	17.9%	5.7%	31.1%	13.9%
200	13.5%	3.8%	25.9%	10.3%
400	9.9%	3.5%	20.4%	7.4%
800	8.0%	3.1%	15.7%	6.1%

References

[1] J. Zhang, C. Zhang, F. Feng, W. Zhang, J. Ma, and Q. J. Zhang, "Polynomial chaos-based approach to yield-driven EM optimization," IEEE Trans. Microw. Theory Tech., vol. 66, no. 7, pp. 3186-3199, 2018.

[2] W. Liu, W. Na, L. Zhu, J. Ma, and Q. J. Zhang, "A Wiener-type dynamic neural network approach to the modeling of nonlinear microwave devices," IEEE Trans. Microwave Theory Tech., vol. 65, no. 6, pp. 2043-2062, 2017.

[3] D. I. L. de Villiers, I. Couckuyt, and T. Dhaene, "Multi-objective optimization of reflector antennas using kriging and probability of improvement," Int. Symp. Ant. Prop., pp. 985-986, San Diego, USA, 2017.

[4] S. Koziel and A. Bekasiewicz, "Accurate simulation-driven modeling and design optimization of compact microwave structures," Int. Microwave Symp., San Francisco, CA, 2016, pp. 1-3.

[5] S. Koziel and A. T. Sigurðsson, "Performance-driven modeling of compact couplers in restricted domains," Int. J. RF Microwave CAE, vol. 28, no. 6, 2018.

[6] S. Koziel and A. Pietrenko-Dabrowska, "Performance-based nested surrogate modeling of antenna input characteristics," IEEE Trans. Ant. Prop., vol. 67, no. 5, pp. 2904-2912, 2019.

Nonlinear Schrödinger Equation-Based Adjoint Sensitivity Analysis

Mahmoud M. T. Maghrabi
Dept. of Elec. and Comp. Engineering
McMaster University
Hamilton, Ontario, L8S 4K1, Canada
maghrabm@mcmaster.ca

Mohamed H. Bakr
Dept. of Elec. and Comp. Engineering
McMaster University
Hamilton, Ontario, L8S 4K1, Canada
mbakr@mcmaster.ca

Shiva Kumar
Dept. of Elec. and Comp. Engineering
McMaster University
Hamilton, Ontario, L8S 4K1, Canada
kumars@mcmaster.ca

***Abstract*—A general nonlinear adjoint sensitivity analysis (ASA) approach for the time-dependent nonlinear Schrödinger equation (NLSE) is presented. The proposed algorithm estimates the sensitivities of a desired objective function with respect to all design parameters using only one extra adjoint system simulation. We show the approach efficiency here through a numerical example.**

I. Introduction

Optical fibers play a vital role in telecommunication systems and networks [1]. The light wave propagation in optical fiber communication systems is described by the time-dependent NLSE. Accurate sensitivity analysis for the NLSE is essential in gradient-based design optimization of optical fiber systems. ASA approaches has been recently emerged as a low-complexity alternative to the classical finite-differences approaches [2]. Regardless of the number of design parameters, an ASA approach estimates the full gradient of the desired objective function or response using at most one extra system simulation. This is contrasted with the computationally expensive finite-differences approximations whose complexity scales linearly with the number of parameters. The need for an ASA algorithm significantly raises in case of design problems with large number of parameters, such as fiber-optic design problems.

Several ASA algorithms based on Maxwell's equations or wave equation have been developed for high frequency structures [2]. ASA approaches are also introduced for the linear Schrödinger equation, to evaluate the sensitivities of the semiconductor quantum structures in their static [3] and dynamic [4] cases. Recently, we proposed an ASA approach for the linear Schrödinger equation to evaluate the sensitivities of short-reach optical fiber communication systems [5]. In this paper, we extend our linear ASA approach for the general time-dependent nonlinear Schrödinger equation. Using only one extra adjoint simulation, the proposed nonlinear ASA approach estimates the sensitivities for a general long-reach fiber-optic communication system with respect to all design parameters of the fiber.

II. Adjoint Sensitivity Analysis Approach

The propagation of light through an optical fiber link is described by the normalized NLSE, given by [1]:

$$-\frac{\beta_3}{6}\frac{\partial^3 q}{\partial t^3}+\frac{i\beta_2}{2}\frac{\partial^2 q}{\partial t^2}+\beta_1\frac{\partial q}{\partial t}+\frac{\partial q}{\partial z}+\left(\frac{\alpha}{2}-i\gamma|q|^2\right)q=q_{Tx}\delta\left(z\right), \tag{1}$$

where $q\left(z,t\right)$ is the complex envelope of the propagated optical field, β_1 is the inverse group speed, β_2 and β_3 are the second- and third-order dispersion coefficients, α is the fiber loss coefficient, and γ is the nonlinear coefficient of the fiber. The signal $q_{Tx}\left(t\right)$ is the optical field transmitted signal and $i=\sqrt{-1}$. We discretize the computational domain into M spatial cells. Expressing $q=q_{re}+iq_{im}$, substituting in equation (1), separating the real and imaginary terms, and approximating the spatial derivatives using finite differences, Equation (1) for the whole domain can be casted as follows:

$$\boldsymbol{B}_3\frac{\partial^3 \boldsymbol{V}}{\partial t^3}+\boldsymbol{B}_2\frac{\partial^2 \boldsymbol{V}}{\partial t^2}+\boldsymbol{B}_1\frac{\partial \boldsymbol{V}}{\partial t}+\boldsymbol{K}_c\boldsymbol{V}+\boldsymbol{A}\boldsymbol{V}+\boldsymbol{\Gamma}\left(\boldsymbol{V}\right)\boldsymbol{V}=\boldsymbol{Q}_{in}, \tag{2}$$

where $\boldsymbol{V}=\left[\boldsymbol{q}_{re}^T\ \boldsymbol{q}_{im}^T\right]^T$ is the system state vector, $\boldsymbol{Q}_{in}\left(t\right)=\left[Re\left\{q_{Tx}\right\}\boldsymbol{e}_1^T\ \ Im\left\{q_{Tx}\right\}\boldsymbol{e}_1^T\right]^T$ is the excitation vector, and $\boldsymbol{e}_1$ is the 1st elementary column vector. The system matrices are given by: $\boldsymbol{B}_3=-\frac{\beta_3}{6}\boldsymbol{I}_{2M}$, $\boldsymbol{B}_2=\frac{\beta_2}{2}\begin{bmatrix}\boldsymbol{0} & -\boldsymbol{I}_M\\ \boldsymbol{I}_M & \boldsymbol{0}\end{bmatrix}$, $\boldsymbol{B}_1=\beta_1\boldsymbol{I}_{2M}$, $\boldsymbol{A}=\frac{\alpha}{2}\boldsymbol{I}_{2M}$, and $\boldsymbol{\Gamma}\left(\boldsymbol{V}\right)=\begin{bmatrix}\boldsymbol{0} & \tilde{\boldsymbol{\gamma}}\\ -\tilde{\boldsymbol{\gamma}} & \boldsymbol{0}\end{bmatrix}$, where $\boldsymbol{I}_M$ is an identity matrix of size M and $\tilde{\boldsymbol{\gamma}}$ is a diagonal matrix whose j^{th} entry is given by: $\gamma\left[q_{re}^2\left(jh\right)+q_{im}^2\left(jh\right)\right]$, $j=0,\ 1,\dots M-1$. Eq. (2) is solved numerically using the split-step Fourier-scheme method [1].

After a lengthy derivation, it can be shown that the adjoint problem corresponding to the original simulation (2) is given by:

$$-\boldsymbol{B}_3\frac{\partial^3 \boldsymbol{\lambda}}{\partial t^3}-\boldsymbol{B}_2\frac{\partial^2 \boldsymbol{\lambda}}{\partial t^2}-\boldsymbol{B}_1\frac{\partial \boldsymbol{\lambda}}{\partial t}-\boldsymbol{K}_c\boldsymbol{\lambda}+\boldsymbol{A}\boldsymbol{\lambda}+\boldsymbol{\Gamma}^{\lambda}\left(\boldsymbol{V}\right)\boldsymbol{\lambda}=\boldsymbol{Q}_{in}^{\lambda}, \tag{3}$$

where $\boldsymbol{\lambda}=\left[\boldsymbol{\lambda}_{re}^T\ \boldsymbol{\lambda}_{im}^T\right]^T$ is the adjoint state vector, $\boldsymbol{Q}_{in}^{\lambda}=\left[\partial\psi/\partial\boldsymbol{q}_{re}^T\ \ \partial\psi/\partial\boldsymbol{q}_{im}^T\right]^T$ is the adjoint excitation vector, and ψ is the kernel of the objective function integral [5]. The nonlinear matrix of the adjoint problem $\boldsymbol{\Gamma}^{\lambda}$ is given by: $\boldsymbol{\Gamma}^{\lambda}\left(\boldsymbol{V}\right)=\begin{bmatrix}\boldsymbol{a} & \boldsymbol{b}\\ \boldsymbol{c} & -\boldsymbol{a}\end{bmatrix}$, where $\boldsymbol{a}$, $\boldsymbol{b}$ and $\boldsymbol{c}$ are diagonal

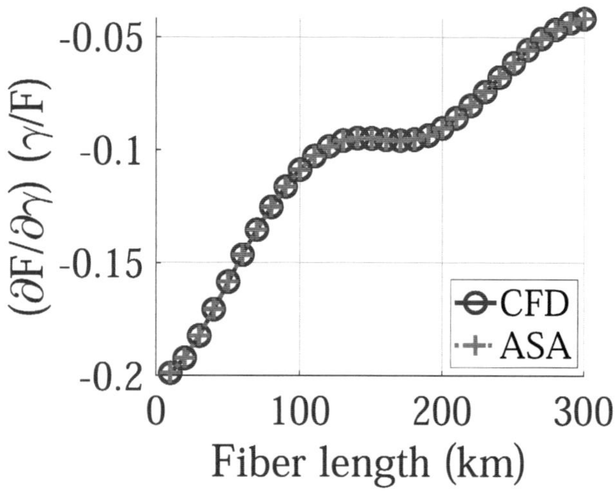

(a)

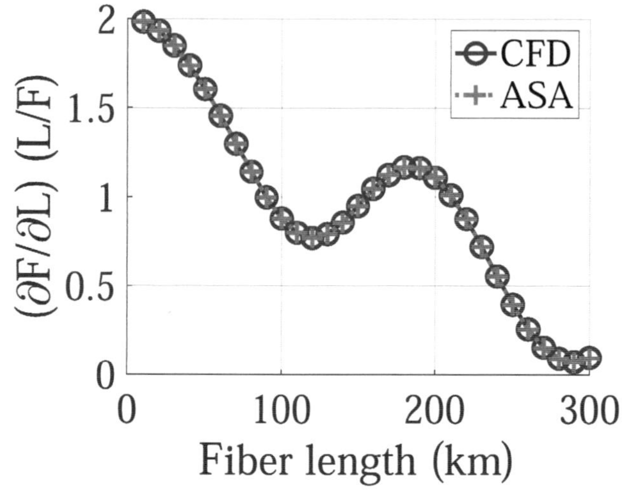

(b)

Figure 1. Normalized ASA sensitivities of objective function (4) with respect to the fiber nonlinear coefficient γ, and the fiber length L, for a sweep of L, as compared to the computationally expensive CFD.

matrices whose j^{th} diagonal elements are given as follows: $a_{jj}= 2\gamma q_{re}\,(jh)\, q_{im}\,(jh)$, $b_{jj}= -\gamma\left[3q_{re}^2\,(jh) + q_{im}^2\,(jh)\right]$, and $c_{jj}=\gamma\left[q_{re}^2\,(jh) + 3q_{im}^2\,(jh)\right]$, $j= 0,\ 1, \ldots M-1$.

Once the original and adjoint fields are determined, through solving (2) and (3), the sensitivities of the desired objective function with respect to all design parameters are estimated.

III. Results

To illustrate the efficiency of our ASA algorithm, we consider an example of an optical fiber communication system operating at 10 Gbaud. The transmitted data have a Gaussian pulse shape with 50% duty cycle. The on-off keying format is used. The transmitted pulse peak power is 2 dBm, and the number of transmitted bits is 32. The fiber parameters are [1]: $\beta_1 = 1.6$ ns/km, $\beta_2 = -21$ ps^2/km, $\beta_3 = 0.1$ ps^3/km, $\alpha = 0.2$ dB/km, and $\gamma = 1.1$ W^{-1}km^{-1}. A noise-free amplifier is inserted at the end of the fiber to compensate for the loss.

Our objective is to estimate the sensitivities of an objective function of the form:

$$F = \int_{-T_m}^{T_m} \left| q_{Rx} - q_{Ref} \right|^2 dt, \qquad (4)$$

where q_{Rx} is the complex envelope field of the received signal, $q_{Ref} = q_{Tx}\,(t - \beta_1 L)$ is a time delayed version of the transmitted complex envelope field, and T_m is half the computational time window size. This objective function measures the signal distortion due to fiber dispersion and nonlinear effects. We estimate the sensitivities of (4) with respect to 6-design parameters $\boldsymbol{x} = [\beta_1\ \beta_2\ \beta_3\ \alpha\ \gamma\ L]^T$.

Fig. 1 shows the normalized sensitivities of F with respect to the parameters γ and L. Due to space limitation, we only show a subset of the obtained sensitivities. Good agreement is achieved with central finite differences (CFD) for all parameters. The ASA algorithm requires only one extra system simulation per gradient evaluation, while the CFD requires 12 extra simulations. The ASA algorithm estimates the sensitivities in 2.45 s, as opposed to 10.74 s taken by the CFD algorithm, i.e., the ASA is 4.4 times faster than the CFD in this example.

IV. Conclusion

We presented a computationally efficient nonlinear adjoint sensitivity analysis approach for the general time-dependent nonlinear Schrödinger equation. As compared to the computationally expensive central finite-difference approach, the proposed algorithm estimates accurate sensitivities of the desired objective function with respect to all the design parameters but with a much lower computational cost.

References

[1] S. Kumar and M. J. Deen, Fiber optic communications: fundamentals and applications. John Wiley & Sons, 2014.

[2] M. Bakr, V. Demir, and A. Elsherbeni, Adjoint sensitivity analysis of high frequency structures with matlab. The Institution of Engineering and Technology (IET), 2017.

[3] M. A. Swillam, M. H. Bakr, X. Li, and M. J. Deen, "Efficient sensitivity analysis of the time independent schrödinger equation with application to quantum lasers," Optics Communications, vol. 281, no. 17, pp. 4459–4463, 2008.

[4] M. A. Ayad, S. S. Obayya, and M. A. Swillam, "Modelling of quantum confinement in optical nanostructures," Journal of Optics, vol. 18, no. 1, p. 015201, 2015.

[5] M. M. T. Maghrabi, M. H. Bakr, and S. Kumar, "Linear adjoint sensitivity analysis of the time-dependent schrödinger equation," in 2019 International Applied Computational Electromagnetics Society Symposium (ACES). IEEE, 2019, pp. 1–2.

The Design of a Switchable Infrared Hybrid Plasmonic Metasurface Absorber for Energy Harvesting Applications

Ayman Negm
Department of Electrical and Computer Engineering
McMaster University
Hamilton, Canada
negma1@mcmaster.ca

Mohamed Bakr
Department of Electrical and Computer Engineering
McMaster University
Hamilton, Canada
mbakr@mcmaster.ca

Matiar Howlader
Department of Electrical and Computer Engineering
McMaster University
Hamilton, Canada
mrhowlader@ece.mcmaster.ca

Shirook Ali
School of Mechanical and Electrical Engineering Technology
Sheridan College
Brampton, Canada
shirook.ali@ieee.org

***Abstract*—A plasmonic switchable polarization-insensitive metasurface absorber is proposed. The design provides two modes of operation by employing phase-change material in semiconductor and metallic phases. In this paper, we study the switchable absorption behavior of the metasurface operating in a dual-band and single-band modes targeting the mid-infrared range suitable for energy harvesting applications such as thermophotovoltaics. The design is optimized using a global optimization technique.**

***Index Terms*—energy harvesting, metasurface, plasmonic, polarization-insensitive, switchable.**

I. Introduction

The interest in using metasurfaces as electromagnetic absorber dramatically increased after the realization of the first perfect absorber metasurface by Landy et al. in 2008 [1]. Metasurfaces can behave as perfect absorbers because they can satisfy impedance matching with air at the resonating wavelengths [1]. One of the most popular metasurface designs is the metal-insulator-metal (MIM) configuration [1].

Active tuning of metasurfaces using phase-change materials (PCMs) is an interesting approach to change the response of the structure without modifying the design or repeating the fabrication. A PCM is switched from semiconductor to metallic phase by applying an external stimulus such as electric field, light, or heat [2]. Vanadium dioxide (VO_2) is a PCM that experiences transition from semiconductor to metallic phase at around 67°C [2]. It was used to design tunable metasurfaces for applications such as filters [3], thermal switches [4], and temperature sensors [5].

In this work, we propose a switchable, polarization-insensitive metasurface absorber for operation at single or dual-band mode using the phase transition property of VO_2. Based on the design introduced in [6], VO_2 is embedded within the gaps of a gold resonator. The structure provides dual-band absorption when operated at 30°C, and single-band absorption when operated at 90°C. The proposed absorber operates in the mid-infrared range, which is suitable for energy harvesting applications such as thermophotovoltaics.

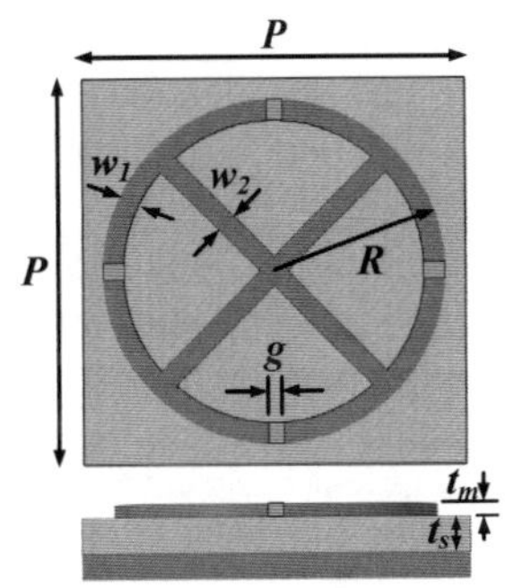

Fig. 1. Top and side views of the unit cell of the proposed absorber (t_m = 50 nm, t_s = 280 nm, P = 2780 nm, R = 1120nm, w_1 = 120 nm, w_2 = 420 nm, and g = 100 nm).

II. Proposed Structure

Fig. 1 shows the geoemtry of the switchable absorber suggested in this work. A circular gold resonator of radius R and width w_1 includes four gaps each of width g, and is combined with an inner cross of width w_2. The gaps are filled with patches of VO_2 to achieve the switchable operation. A thick gold layer is placed at the bottom to suppress wave transmission. A silicon dioxide layer separates the upper and bottom gold layers to complete the MIM configuration.

A practical realization of the structure can be achieved by following the approach in [7], where the VO_2 is deposited first based on a pattern by a lithography technique followed by overlaying of the gold resonator. The gold regions touching

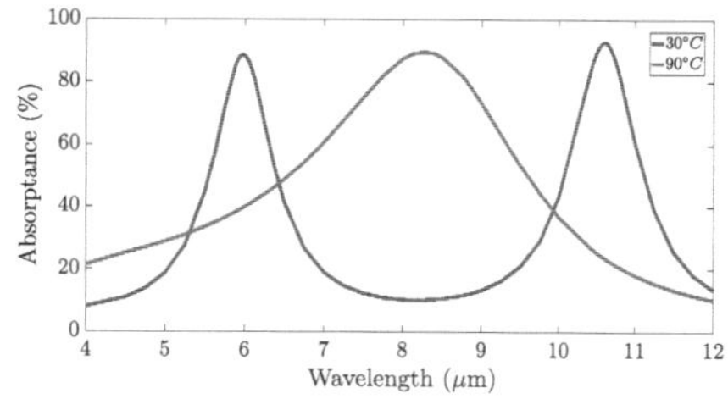

Fig. 2. Absorptance versus wavelength for the proposed metasurface at 30°C and 90°C.

the VO_2 patches can be used as joule heating elements to control the operating temperature [7].

To find the absorption characteristics of the structure, a normally incident transverse electromagnetic plane wave is excited upon the metasurface. The absorptance A can be calculated as:

$$A = 1 - R - T, \quad (1)$$

where R and T are the reflectance and transmittance of the structure respectively. Since the bottom gold layer blocks the transmission, T can be ignored in the calculation of A. Full-wave simulations were carried out using finite-element method in COMSOL Multiphysics 5.3. Periodic boundary conditions are applied to model a metasurface with periodicity P. The refractive index of gold was obtained from [8], while that of silicon dioxide is set to 1.5. Temperature-dependent permittivity models of VO_2 were obtained from [9].

Optimization is initialized with the values of the parameters reported in [6]. We target dual-band resonance at 6 μm and 10.6 μm suitable for ambient energy harvesting [10]. Adaptive wind-driven optimization (AWDO) is employed as a global optimization technique [11].

III. Results and Discussion

Fig. 2 shows the absorption spectra of the optimized absorber at different operating temperatures. At 30°C, the absorber exhibits a dual-band absorption with absorptance values of 88.4% and 92.85% at 6 μm and 10.6 μm respectively. At 90°C, single-band absorption at 8.25 μm with absorptance of 89.64% is achieved. This means that dynamic switching between single and dual-band absorption modes can be achieved without modifying the absorber geometry.

Fig. 3 shows the electric field distribution over the structure at the resonant wavelengths at 30°C. Electric field is highly confined within the semiconductor VO_2 patches at 6 μm and 10.6 μm, while there is no confinement at 8.25 μm. At 90°C, the VO_2 patches attain metallic properties, and the field confinement vanishes at 6 μm and 10.6 μm. New single-mode resonance is obtained at 8.25 μm, where high field is concentrated at the edges due to coupling between neighboring elements of the metasurface as shown in Fig. 4.

IV. Conclusion

A switchable plasmonic metasurface absorber for energy harvesting in the mid-infrared range is proposed. The symmetry of the design provides a polarization-insensitive response, and the phase transition property of VO_2 provides the switching mechanism. The dimensions of the structure are optimized using a global optimization technique.

References

[1] T. Lu, D. Zhang, P. Qiu, J. Lian, M. Jing, B. Yu, and J. Wen, "Ultrathin terahertz dual-band perfect metamaterial absorber using asymmetric double-split rings resonator," Symmetry, vol. 10, no. 7, p. 293, 2018.

[2] M. Liu, H. Y. Hwang, H. Tao, A. C. Strikwerda, K. Fan, G. R. Keiser, A. J. Sternbach, K. G. West, S. Kittiwatanakul, J. Lu, *et al.*, "Terahertz-field-induced insulator-to-metal transition in vanadium dioxide metamaterial," Nature, vol. 487, no. 7407, p. 345, 2012.

[3] D. Bouyge, A. Crunteanu, O. Massagué, J.-C. Orlianges, C. Champeaux, A. Catherinot, A. Velez, J. Bonache, F. Martin, and P. Blondy, "Applications of vanadium dioxide (vo 2)-loaded electrically small resonators in the design of tunable filters," in The 40th European Microwave Conference, pp. 822–825, IEEE, 2010.

[4] X. Li, S. Tang, F. Ding, S. Zhong, Y. Yang, T. Jiang, and J. Zhou, "Switchable multifunctional terahertz metasurfaces employing vanadium dioxide," Scientific Reports, vol. 9, no. 1, p. 5454, 2019.

[5] M. Baqir and P. Choudhury, "On the vo 2 metasurface-based temperature sensor," JOSA B, vol. 36, no. 8, pp. F123–F130, 2019.

[6] A. Negm, M. Bakr, M. Howlader, and S. Ali, "A dual band plasmonic metasurface absorber for energy harvesting applications," in 2019 International Applied Computational Electromagnetics Society Symposium (ACES), pp. 1–2, IEEE, 2019.

[7] Z. Zhu, P. G. Evans, R. F. Haglund Jr, and J. G. Valentine, "Dynamically reconfigurable metadevice employing nanostructured phase-change materials," Nano Letters, vol. 17, no. 8, pp. 4881–4885, 2017.

[8] A. D. Rakić, A. B. Djurišić, J. M. Elazar, and M. L. Majewski, "Optical properties of metallic films for vertical-cavity optoelectronic devices," Applied Optics, vol. 37, no. 22, pp. 5271–5283, 1998.

[9] H. Wang, Y. Yang, and L. Wang, "Wavelength-tunable infrared metamaterial by tailoring magnetic resonance condition with vo2 phase transition," Journal of Applied Physics, vol. 116, no. 12, p. 123503, 2014.

[10] A. Y. Elsharabasy, A. S. Negm, M. H. Bakr, and M. J. Deen, "Global optimization of rectennas for ir energy harvesting at 10.6 μm," IEEE Journal of Photovoltaics, vol. 9, no. 5, pp. 1232–1239, 2019.

[11] Z. Bayraktar and M. Komurcu, "Adaptive wind driven optimization," in Proceedings of the 9th EAI International Conference on Bio-inspired Information and Communications Technologies (formerly BIONETICS), pp. 124–127, ICST (Institute for Computer Sciences, Social-Informatics and Telecommunications Engineering), 2016.

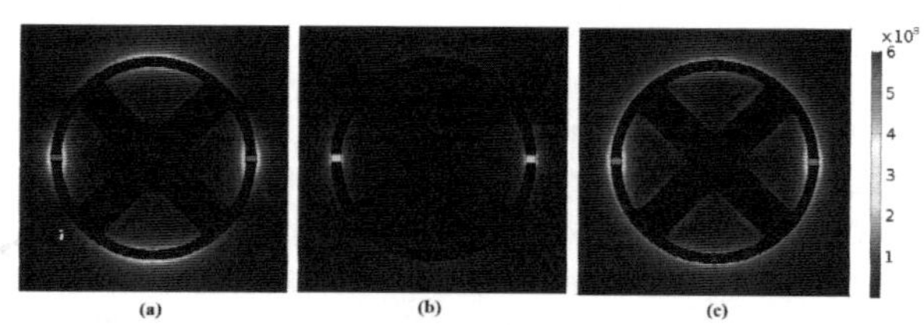

Fig. 3. Distribution of electric field at (a) 6 μm, (b) 8.25 μm, and (c) 10.6 μm when the operating temperature is 30°C.

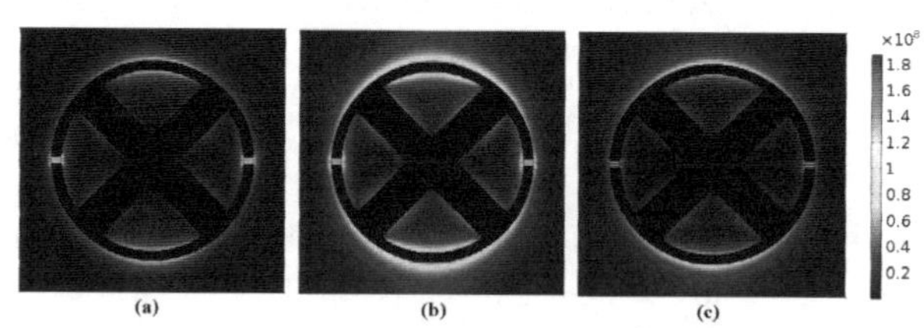

Fig. 4. Distribution of electric field at (a) 6 μm, (b) 8.25 μm, and (c) 10.6 μm when the operating temperature is 90°C.

Nested Kriging Surrogates for Rapid Multi-Objective Optimization of Compact Microwave Components

Anna Pietrenko-Dabrowska[1] and Slawomir Koziel [1,2]

[1] Faculty of Electronics, Telecommunications and Informatics, Gdansk University of Technology, 80-233 Gdansk, Poland
[2] School of Science and Engineering, Reykjavik University, Reykjavik, Iceland, koziel@ru.is

***Abstract*—A procedure for rapid EM-based multi-objective optimization of compact microwave components is presented. Our methodology employs a recently developed nested kriging modelling to identify the search space region containing the Pareto-optimal designs, and to construct a fast surrogate model. The latter permits determination of the initial Pareto set, further refined using a separate surrogate-assisted process. As an illustration, a three-section impedance transformer is designed for the best matching and minimum size. The set of trade-off designs is produced at the low computational cost of only a few hundred of high-fidelity EM simulations of the transformer circuit despite a large number of its geometry parameters.**

Keywords—Microwave optimization, multi-objective design, simulation-driven design, surrogate modelling.

I. Introduction

Circuit miniaturization has become a common trend in the design of microwave components [1]. Unfortunately, size reduction normally stays in conflict with ensuring desired electrical performance. Finding available design trade-offs can be realized through multi-objective optimization (MO) [2]. MO is a computationally expensive task, because reliable evaluation of compact structures requires full-wave electromagnetic (EM) analysis [3]. At the same time, the most popular MO techniques (population-based metaheuristics, e.g., particle swarm optimizers [4]) are computationally inefficient.

In this paper, a novel technique for MO of compact microwave components is presented, capitalizing on a recently reported nested kriging modeling paradigm [5]. The latter permits identification of the search space region containing the Pareto set and to set up, therein, a fast surrogate further utilized to yield an initial approximation of the trade-off designs. The procedure is supplemented with a surrogate-assisted refinement routine. Despite of using a single-level (high-fidelity) EM model only throughout the process and handling a large number of parameters, our framework is demonstrated to render the Pareto set at a low CPU cost.

II. Multi-Objective Design By Nested Kriging

A goal of MO is to determine a set of globally non-dominated designs representing the best possible trade-offs w.r.t. the objectives F_k, $k = 1, \ldots, N$ [2], all to be minimized. The MO process may be sped up by optimizing directly a faster surrogate model $\boldsymbol{R}_s$, instead of the EM-simulated (fine) model $\boldsymbol{R}(\boldsymbol{x})$ ($\boldsymbol{x}$ denotes the parameter vector), being the primary way of system evaluation. Due to a limited accuracy of the surrogate, the initial Pareto-optimal designs $\boldsymbol{x}_s^{(k)}$ have to be refined as follows:

$$\boldsymbol{x}_f^{(k)} = \arg \min_{\substack{\boldsymbol{x},\, F_2(\boldsymbol{x}) \le F_2(\boldsymbol{x}_s^{(k)}) \\ \vdots \\ F_N(\boldsymbol{x}) \le F_N(\boldsymbol{x}_s^{(k)})}} F_1\left(\boldsymbol{R}_s(\boldsymbol{x}) + [\boldsymbol{R}(\boldsymbol{x}_s^{(k)}) - \boldsymbol{R}_s(\boldsymbol{x}_s^{(k)})]\right), \quad (1)$$

where the last term represents output space mapping correction [7]. In this work, the surrogate is constructed using a recently reported nested kriging modelling approach [5], here, adopted to represent the system responses in the region containing the Pareto set. Let $\boldsymbol{x}^{(j)}$, $j = 1, \ldots, p$, denote the reference designs optimized w.r.t. the performance vectors $\boldsymbol{F}^{(j)} = [F_1^{(j)} \ldots F_N^{(j)}]$, with $\boldsymbol{x}^{(j)} = [x_1^{(j)} \ldots x_n^{(j)}]^T$. The objective space $\mathcal{F}$ is defined by the ranges $F_{k.\min} \le F_k^{(j)} \le F_{k.\max}$, $k = 1, \ldots, N$. The reference designs need to include the extreme designs $\boldsymbol{x}^{*(k)} = \mathrm{argmin}\{\boldsymbol{x} : F_k(\boldsymbol{R}(\boldsymbol{x}))\}$ (and other designs from the Pareto front if more detailed information is needed). These are obtained by solving:

$$\boldsymbol{x}^{w} = \arg\min_{\boldsymbol{x}} F_1\left(\boldsymbol{R}(\boldsymbol{x})\right), \quad (2)$$

subject to $F_j(\boldsymbol{x}) \le \sum_l w_l F_j(\boldsymbol{x}^{*(l)})$, $j = 2, \ldots, N$; $\boldsymbol{w} = [w_1 \ldots w_N]^T$ is a vector of weights; $0 \le w_j \le 1$ and $\sum_j w_j = 1$. The objective vector $\boldsymbol{F}(\boldsymbol{w})$ refers to the reference design $\boldsymbol{x}^{w}$; $\boldsymbol{w} = [0 \ldots 1 \ldots 0]^T$ (with 1 on the k-th position) corresponds to a single-objective design $\boldsymbol{x}^{*(k)}$. To handle the objective space region spanned by the reference designs an auxiliary mapping h_0 from a unit $N-1$ simplex $S^{N-1} = \{z = [z_1 \ldots z_{N-1}]^T : 0 \le z_k \le 1$ and $\sum_{k=1,\ldots,N-1} z_k \le 1\}$ onto the space of the weights $\boldsymbol{w}$ is used. If $N = 2$ (the case considered in the paper), the mapping h_0 is defined as (generalization for $N > 2$ is straightforward):

$$h_0(z) = \begin{bmatrix} 1 \\ 0 \end{bmatrix} + \begin{bmatrix} -1 & -1 \\ 1 & 0 \end{bmatrix} \cdot z\,. \quad (3)$$

Figure 1 provides a graphical illustration of the above concepts for $N = 2$. The nested kriging model is to be established in the marked part of the objective space. As the number of available reference designs is in practice limited, these designs merely approximate the Pareto front geometry. Hence, a certain extension is necessary. The extended region O is defined as the set of all points $\boldsymbol{w} = h_0(z)\cdot(1 + d)$ with $z \in S^{N-1}$ and $-d_w \le d \le d_w$, where d_w is the extension factor (here, $d_w = 0.05$ is used).

The actual modelling procedure involves two surrogates. The first-level model $\boldsymbol{s}_I(\mathcal{F}) \subset X$ (kriging model [6]; with $\{\boldsymbol{F}^{(j)}, \boldsymbol{x}^{(j)}\}$ being the training points) maps $\mathcal{F}$ into the design space X, and it is the first approximation of the surrogate model domain. The $\boldsymbol{s}_I(\mathcal{F})$ is then orthogonally extended towards its normal vectors [5] $\boldsymbol{v}_n^{(k)}(\boldsymbol{F})$, $k = 1, \ldots, n-N$, to ensure that all designs optimal w.r.t. F_k, are comprised in the model domain. Let us define: $\boldsymbol{x}_{\max} = \max\{\boldsymbol{x}^{(k)}, k = 1, \ldots, p\}$, $\boldsymbol{x}_{\min} = \min\{\boldsymbol{x}^{(k)}, k = 1, \ldots, p\}$, $\boldsymbol{x}_d = \boldsymbol{x}_{\max} - \boldsymbol{x}_{\min}$, along with the extension coefficients:

$$\boldsymbol{\alpha}(\boldsymbol{F}) = \left[\alpha_k(\boldsymbol{F})\right]_{k=1,\ldots,n-N}^T = 0.5\tau\left[\,|\,\boldsymbol{x}_d \boldsymbol{v}_n^{(k)}(\boldsymbol{F})\,|\,\right]_{k=1,\ldots,n-N}^T, \quad (4)$$

where τ is a user-defined thickness parameter. The surrogate model domain X_S is located between the manifolds M_+ and M_-, determined by the coefficients α_k:

$$M_{\pm} = \left\{ \boldsymbol{x} \in X : \boldsymbol{x} = \boldsymbol{s}_I(\boldsymbol{F}) \pm \sum_{k=1}^{n-N} \alpha_k(\boldsymbol{F}) \boldsymbol{v}_n^{(k)}(\boldsymbol{F}) \right\}. \quad (5)$$

Using (5), we define X_S as (cf. [5]):

$$X_S = \left\{ \begin{array}{c} \boldsymbol{x} = \boldsymbol{s}_I(\boldsymbol{F}) + \sum_{k=1}^{n-N} \lambda_k \alpha_k(\boldsymbol{F}) \boldsymbol{v}_n^{(k)}(\boldsymbol{F}) : F \in \Phi, \\ -1 \le \lambda_k \le 1, k = 1,\ldots,n-N \end{array} \right\}. \quad (6)$$

The first-level surrogate comprises two transformations: (i) the mapping h_0 from the Cartesian product of $S^{N-1} \times [-d_w, d_w]$ onto the objective space region O and (ii) the mapping $\boldsymbol{s}_I$ from O into X (merely used for the sake of convenience, as it is easier to implement uniform data sampling on $S^{N-1} \times [-d_w, d_w]$ rather than directly on O). The second-level surrogate is then set up in the orthogonally extended domain $\boldsymbol{s}_I(O)$.

III. Verification Examples

The optimization framework is illustrated using a CMRC-based three-section transformer [7] of Fig. 2, implemented on Taconic RF-35 substrate ($\varepsilon_r = 3.5$, $h = 0.762$ mm), and described by the parameters $\boldsymbol{x} = [l_{1.1}\ l_{1.2}\ w_{1.1}\ w_{1.2}\ w_{1.0}\ l_{2.1}\ l_{2.2}\ w_{2.1}\ w_{2.2}\ w_{2.0}\ l_{3.1}\ l_{3.2}\ w_{3.1}\ w_{3.2}\ w_{3.0}]^T$. The operating range is 1.75 GHz to 4.25 GHz. The figures of interest are: minimization of the in-band reflection (F_1) and minimization of the footprint area (F_2). The computational model $\boldsymbol{R}$ is simulated in CST Microwave Studio (~280,000 mesh cells, simulation time 2.5 min). Four reference designs are used, corresponding to the two single-objective designs and two more for $z = 0.33$ and $z = 0.66$ (cf. (3)).

The nested kriging surrogate was set using only 200 data samples. Its average RMS error is only 4.1%. For comparison, the surrogate was constructed within the reduced interval $\boldsymbol{l}^* = \min\{\boldsymbol{x}^{*(1)}, \boldsymbol{x}^{*(2)}\}$ and $\boldsymbol{u}^* = \max\{\boldsymbol{x}^{*(1)}, \boldsymbol{x}^{*(2)}\}$, typically containing the vast majority of the Pareto front [2]. Although 1600 training samples were used, the model error is 10.4%. The initial Pareto set was obtained by multi-objective evolutionary algorithm (MOEA) [7]. The selected Pareto-optimal designs, before and after refinement are shown in Fig. 3 (a). The reflection characteristics for the selected designs are presented in Fig. 3 (b). Table I contains the breakdown of the optimization cost. The presented approach offers several advantages: (i) the optimization cost, mostly incurred by training data acquisition for setting up the surrogate model, is considerably reduced (by around 65 percent), (ii) the overall MO cost is just 745 EM simulations, and (iii) more precise identification of the initial Pareto set can be obtained (owing to a considerably smaller domain of the nested kriging model and better predictive power of the surrogate).

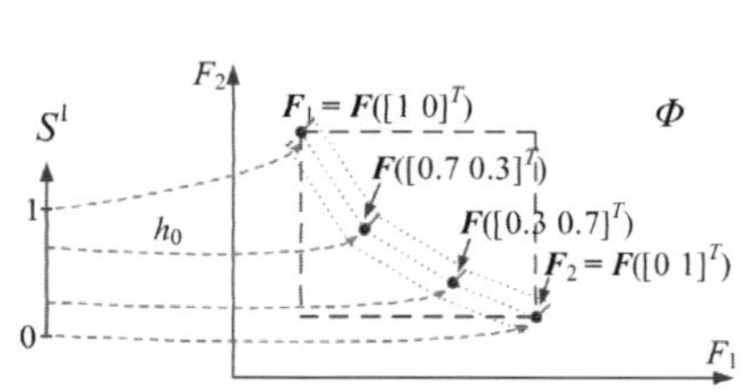

Fig. 1. Objective space Φ and the objective vectors representing selected reference designs; the region of the objective space for setting up the second-level model is marked using dotted lines; the mapping h_0 maps the unity simplex onto the relevant portion of the objective space region (two-objective case).

Fig. 2. CMRC-based three-section impedance matching transformer: (a) compact microstrip resonant cell (CMRC) cell, (b) transformer geometry.

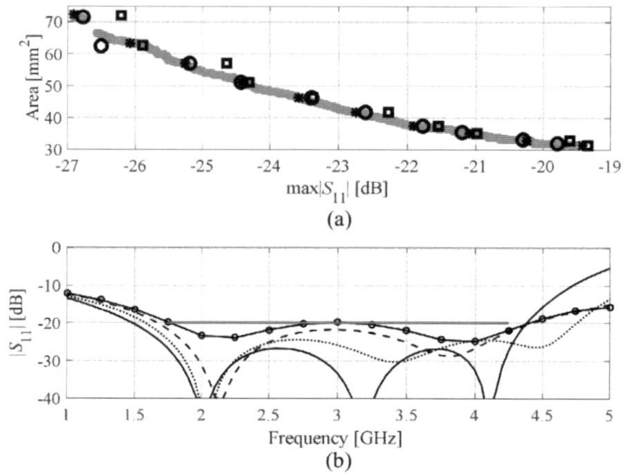

Fig. 3. (a) Pareto-optimal solutions: (o) initial set obtained with MOEA, (*) selected designs for refinement, ( ) EM-simulated selected designs, (O) EM-simulated refined designs; (b) reflection characteristics of the transformer for selected Pareto-optimal designs.

TABLE I. Optimization Cost Breakdown

Cost Item	Surrogate Model Domain	
	X_S (this work)	Hypercube $[\boldsymbol{l}^*, \boldsymbol{u}^*]$
Extreme points	$515 \times \boldsymbol{R}$	$515 \times \boldsymbol{R}$
Data acquisition for kriging surrogate	$200 \times \boldsymbol{R}$	$1600 \times \boldsymbol{R}$
MOEA optimization*	N/A	N/A
Refinement	$30 \times \boldsymbol{R}$	$30 \times \boldsymbol{R}$
Total cost#	$745 \times \boldsymbol{R}$ (31 h)	$2145 \times \boldsymbol{R}$ (89 h)

* The cost of MOEA optimization is negligible compared to other stages of the process.
# The total cost (equivalent number of EM simulations; CPU time shown in brackets).

Acknowledgment

This work is partially supported by the Icelandic Centre for Research (RANNIS) Grant 174114051, and by National Science Centre of Poland Grant 2018/31/B/ST7/02369.

References

[1] M. Cariou, B. Potelon, C. Quendo, E. Schlaffer, W. Pessl, and A. Le Fevre, "Compact X-band filter based on substrate integrated coaxial line stubs using advanced multilayer PCB technology," IEEE Trans. Microwave Theory Techn., vol. 65, no. 2, pp. 496-503, 2017.

[2] S. Koziel, A. Bekasiewicz, and P. Kurgan, "Rapid multi-objective simulation-driven design of compact microwave circuits," IEEE Microwave Wireless Comp. Letters, vol. 25, no. 5, pp. 277–279, 2015.

[3] J. Zhang, C. Zhang, F. Feng, W. Zhang, J. Ma, and Q. J. Zhang, "Polynomial chaos-based approach to yield-driven EM optimization," IEEE Trans. Microwave Theory Tech., vol. 66, no. 7, pp. 3186-3199, 2018.

[4] S. K. Goudos and J. N. Sahalos, "Pareto optimal microwave filter design using multiobjective differential evolution," IEEE Trans. Ant. Prop., vol. 58, no. 1, pp. 132-144, 2010.

[5] S. Koziel and A. Pietrenko-Dabrowska, "Performance-based nested surrogate modeling of antenna input characteristics," IEEE Trans. Ant. Prop., vol. 67, no. 5, pp. 2904-2912, 2019.

[6] T. W. Simpson, J. D. Pelplinski, P. N. Koch, and J. K. Allen, "Metamodels for computer-based engineering design: survey and recommendations," Eng. with Computers, vol. 17, pp. 129-150, 2001.

[7] S. Koziel and A. Bekasiewicz, "Rapid simulation-driven multi-objective design optimization of decomposable compact microwave passives," IEEE Trans. Microwave Theory Techn., vol. 64, pp. 2454-2461, 2016.

Multi-objective Optimization of Linear Proportional Solenoid Actuator

Shi Jie Wang
State Key Laboratory of Fluid Power and Mechatronic Systems
Zhejiang University
Hang Zhou, China
wsj19900210@zju.edu.cn

Zhi Dan Weng
Ningbo HOYEA Machinery Manufacture Co.Ltd.
Ningbo, China
derek.weng@hoyea.com

Bo Jin
State Key Laboratory of Fluid Power and Mechatronic Systems
Zhejiang University
Hang Zhou, China
bjin@zju.edu.cn

***Abstract*—This paper employed a multi-objective Genetic Algorithm(GA) process to optimize the structure parameters of Linear Proportional Solenoid(LPS). And designed objectives include magnitude of static push force, stability of push force with displacement in working range and push force to mass ratio. A two-dimensional finite element analysis model is presented to reduce the large calculation time generated by GA process. The optimization process result of LPS shape parameters is obtained and the optimal LPS is manufactured. Through using a high-precision measuring device in the static push force test, a comparison result between conventional shape and optimal shape shows that the proposed optimization strategy is feasible.**

Keywords—Multi-objective, Linear Proportional Solenoid, Genetic Algorithm, magnetostatic.

I. Introduction

Electro Magnetic Actuators as the core component are widely employed in vehicle suspension system and engine, Inverter Compressor and many other pneumatic/hydraulic control systems. Meanwhile, due to the simple structure, high reliability, low cost and long stroke, Linear Proportional Solenoid(LPS) is the most essential electro-magnetic actuator. This paper aims to optimize the LPS used in proportional control valve. Generally, the optimization strategies of LPS are usually implemented by shifting the shape parameters [1-2]. With the improvement of computing power, the iterative algorithm become a growing interest of computational electromagnetics field, especially in industrial application. Plavec and Wu considered the dynamic performance as an important object of on/off Electro-magnetic actuators optimization [3-4]. Since the volume of Electro-magnetic actuators is an important condition, five main shape parameters are optimized to obtain the maximum electro-magnetic force in a specific valve volume [5].

In this paper, a shape design optimization process of LPS is presented by GA and finite element analysis method. To optimize the static push force and decrease the impact on linearity and output efficiency, three objectives : static push force, stability of push force with displacement in working range and push force to mass ratio are proposed. Through the comparison of measurement result, the proposed multi-objective optimization process is adopted to optimize the static force of LPS.

II. Simulation Structure

Generally, three-dimensional model can obtain a high accuracy magnetostatic simulation result. The three-dimensional simulation model and geometry structure definition of LPS is shown in Fig. 1. Assuming that the magnetic flux density in soft magnetic material yoke is not fully saturated, the cubic three-dimensional structure LPS can be simplified by a two-dimensional axial symmetry shape model. In this two-dimensional model, we proposed a hypothesis that the yoke of simulation model has an equivalent radial cross-sectional area with actual LPS. In this paper the working stroke design of LPS is fixed at 3mm, the simulation sampling interval is 0.2mm and sampling range from 0.2mm to 3mm. Therefore, there are 16 different magnetostatic simulation model need to be calculated in one shape design sample. For reducing the computation time, it is necessary to employed this two-dimensional simulation model instead of three-dimensional model. In Fig. 2, it shows the parameterized simulation model by armature parameters a_1, a_2, a_3, a_4, coil parameters c_1, c_2, yoke parameters y_1, y_2, y_3,y_4, y_5, y_6 and other fixed parameters f_1, f_2, f_3, f_4, f_5, f_6.

III. Multi-Objective Optimization Method

LPS shape optimization is a multi-objective issue, it focused on push force output efficiency, magnitude and stability of static push force in working stroke. To solve this optimization issue, a genetic algorithm tool is employed to obtain optimal shape parameters and a finite element model is established to calculate the magnetostatic force at each sampling position in working stroke. All these work are accomplished by ANSYS MAXWELL. And the following equation (1) shows the optimization fitness function:

$$fitness= (F_{ex} - F_{AVG})/ F_{ex} + F_D/F_{AVG} + (K_{ex} - F/m)/ K_{ex} \quad (1)$$

Equation (1) include three normalized objects and each factor: average electromagnetic force-F_{AVG}, standard deviation of static electromagnetic force-F_D and average electromagnetic force to mass ratio of moving parts-F/m. In this paper, F_{AVG} is calculated by the average push forces of each sampling position in working stroke. It is used to evaluate the excitation force performance in coil rated current. And

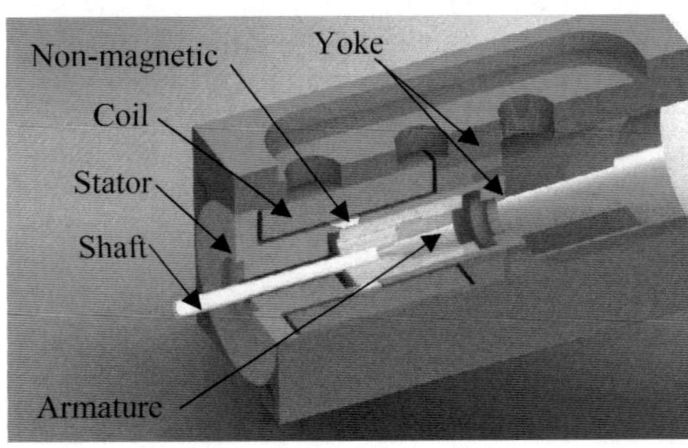

Fig. 1. Geometry structure definition of LPS three-dimensional simulation model.

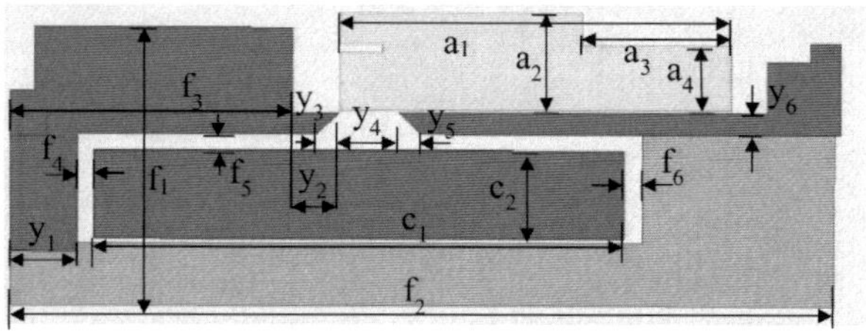

Fig. 2. Simplified LPS simulation two-dimensional model and design parameters.

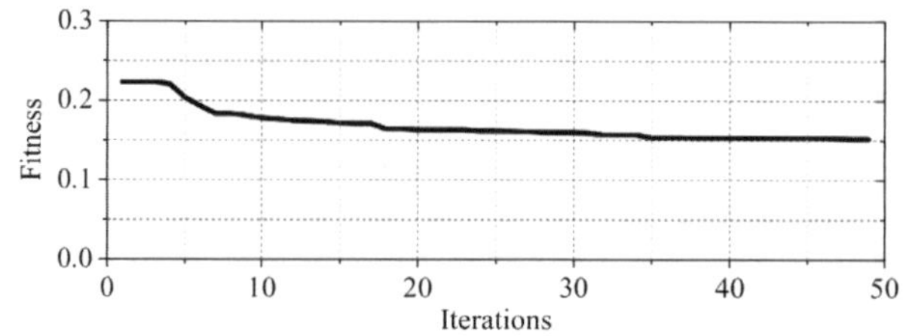

Fig. 3. Multi-objective GA optimization iteration result of LPS shape parameters.

F_{ex} =170N is the expectation average force. F_D is used to evaluate the deviation degree of the push force at each sampling position. *F/m* represents the push force output efficiency. K_{ex} =1.8 N/g is the expectation force to mass ratio.

A genetic algorithm, which is 100 population size and 49 generations, is employed to solve this optimization problem and obtain the optimal shape design parameters. The iteration result is shown in Fig. 3. And the shape design parameter array can be defined by P{a1, a2, a3, a4, y1, y2, y3, y4, y5, y6, c1, c2 }. The conventional shape design parameter array is {31.4, 7.40, 16.9, 3.55, 5.50,3.70, 3.10, 3.90, 0.83, 2.30, 42.80,8.20 }, and the optimal shape design parameter array is {32.3, 7.65, 4.70, 5.15, 5.50, 3.75, 3.11, 4.12, 1.06, 2.32, 43.48, 7.36}. The unit of shape parameter is millimeter. The mass of conventional shape LPS is 50.7g and the optimal shape LPS is 64.3g.

IV. Result

To ensure the accuracy of measurement results, ZLDS100 (ZSY GROUP LTD) laser displacement sensor and U9C(HBM) force transducer are employed in LPS's static performance test device in Fig. 4. For actual usage, the working stroke start from 3mm point and stop to 0.4mm. This paper measured several static posh force versus displacement curve in different coil excitation current, and the test result is shown in Fig. 5. In rated excitation current (total 1980 ampere turns), the numerical simulation calculation error result is increasing with the change of magnetic saturation phenomenon. In all excitation current, the optimal shape LPS shows the advantage of push force magnitude. Meanwhile in light load usage, the optimal LPS shows a better push force stability than the conventional LPS.

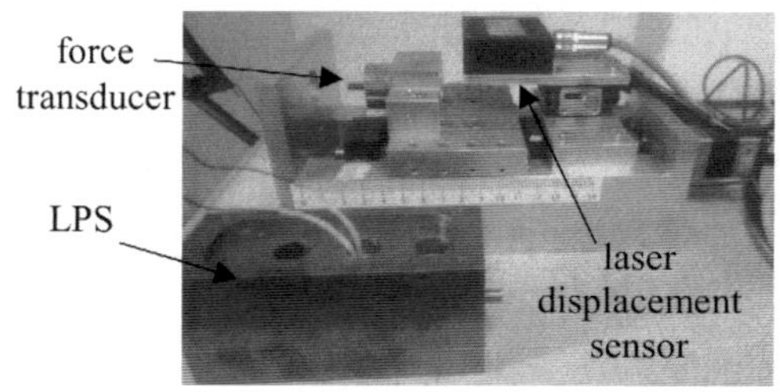

Fig. 4. Static performance test device of LPS and manufactured optimal shape LPS.

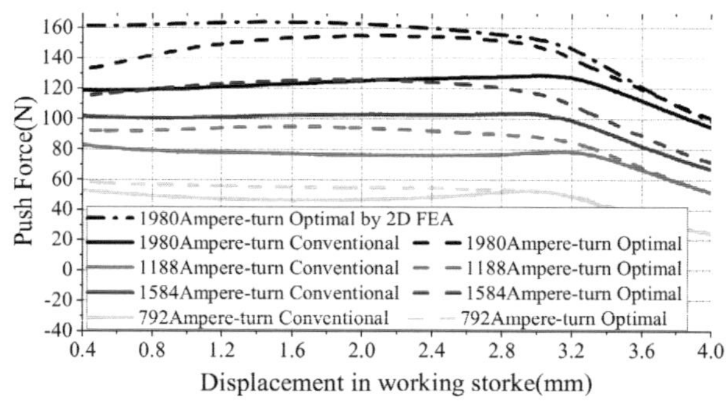

Fig. 5. Static push force measument in spesific coil exciting current.

V. Conclusion

Above all, a multi-objective GA optimization process of LPS is presented and the optimal shape design parameters in this process is manufactured. By the comparison of optimal LPS and conventional LPS in rated excitation current, average electromagnetic force is improved by 21.8%. But force to mass ratio is decreased by 9.4% and standard deviation of static electromagnetic force is decreased by 41%. Therefore, the above results can verify the validation of proposed optimization strategy. And next research step is to make a further comprehensive study on optimization fitness design part and optimization iteration algorithm part.

Acknowledgment

This work is supported by Ningbo major project of Science and Technology Innovation 2025(2019B10052).

References

[1] S. B. Yoon, J. Hur, Y. D. Chun, and D. S. Hyun, "Shape optimization of solenoid actuator using the finite element method and numerical optimization technique," IEEE Trans. Ind. Electron., 1997, 33(5), 4140-4142.

[2] S. N. Yun, Y. B. Ham, and J. H. Park, "New approach to design control cone for electro-magnetic proportional solenoid actuator," In Proceedings of the IEEE/ASME International Conference on Advanced Intelligent Mechatronics, Kaohsiung, Taiwan, 11-14 July 2012.

[3] E. Plavec, I. Uglesic, and M. Vidovic, "Genetic algorithm based shape optimization method of dc solenoid electromagnetic actuator," Appl. Comput. Electrom., 2018, 33(3) 325-334.

[4] S. Wu, X. Zhao, C. Li, Z. Jiao, and Y. Qu, "Multi-objective optimization of a hollow plunger type solenoid for high speed on/off valve," IEEE Trans. Ind. Electron., 2017, 65(4), 3115-3124.

[5] B. Cai, Y. Liu, X. Tian, Z. Wang, and R. Ji, "Optimization of submersible solenoid valves for subsea blowout preventers," IEEE Trans. Magn., 2010, 47(2), 451-458.

Nonlocal Hydrodynamic Models for the Optical Response of Plasmonic Nanostructures

Mario Kupresak
Department of Electrical Engineering (ESAT-TELEMIC)
KU Leuven
Leuven, Belgium
mario.kupresak@esat.kuleuven.be

Xuezhi Zheng
Department of Electrical Engineering (ESAT-TELEMIC)
KU Leuven
Leuven, Belgium
xuezhi.zheng@esat.kuleuven.be

Guy A. E. Vandenbosch
Department of Electrical Engineering (ESAT-TELEMIC)
KU Leuven
Leuven, Belgium
guy.vandenbosch@esat.kuleuven.be

Victor V. Moshchalkov
Institute for Nanoscale Physics and Chemistry (INPAC)
KU Leuven
Leuven, Belgium
victor.moshchalkov@fys.kuleuven.be

***Abstract*—In order to model the interaction between light and plasmonic structures at deep-nanometer scale, which is governed by non-classical effects, a nonlocal hydrodynamic approach has been extensively studied. Several hydrodynamic models have been proposed, solving the coupled equations: the linearized hydrodynamic equation of motion and the electrodynamic Maxwell's equations, by employing additional boundary conditions. This work compares four hydrodynamic models: the hard wall hydrodynamic model (HW-HDM), the curl-free hydrodynamic model (CF-HDM), the shear forces hydrodynamic model (SF-HDM), and the quantum hydrodynamic model (Q-HDM). The analysis is conducted for a metallic spherical nanoparticle, as an example. The above hydrodynamic models are also compared with experiments available in literature. It is demonstrated that HW-HDM and Q-HDM outperform the other two hydrodynamic models.**

***Keywords*— additional boundary condition, deep-nanometer scale, nonlocal hydrodynamic model, plasmonics.**

I. Introduction

Many conventional microwave topologies, such as a sphere, dipole, microstrip patch antenna, etc., have been successfully treated by using Maxwell's equations. However, the optical counterparts of these topologies, particularly the ones with deep-nanometric features, e.g., a metallic particle with a size of only a few nanometers, nanoparticle-on-mirror structure with a sub-nanometer gap, cannot be fully characterized by the abovementioned approach, due to the non-classical effects [1]. Notably, these effects may greatly affect the electromagnetic (EM) properties of the structure-under-study, which has been demonstrated in several plasmonic applications [2].

In order to study the non-classical effects, several semiclassical models, such as the hydrodynamic model (HDM) [3], have been introduced. HDM essentially investigates a multiphysics problem, namely the interaction between the mechanical motion of the free electron gas in metals and external EM fields. Metals are described by spatially dispersive (nonlocal) material parameters, meaning that the material response at a specific spatial point depends on the field in close vicinity of that point. On top, the material model introduces an additional wave, namely the longitudinal wave. In order to account for the longitudinal wave, HDM requires an additional boundary condition (ABC), in this way bridging the computational gap between the classical and *ab initio* quantum mechanical approaches.

However, the choice of HDM and ABC is not universal. Based on different physical approximations, several hydrodynamic models and ABCs have been proposed. Additionally, it has been demonstrated that different hydrodynamic models and ABCs may drastically modify the response of metallic nanotopologies [4,5].

This work reports on a comparison of the following hydrodynamic models: the hard wall hydrodynamic model (HW-HDM) with the Sauter ABC, the curl-free hydrodynamic model (CF-HDM) with the Pekar ABC, the shear forces hydrodynamic model (SF-HDM) with the specular reflection ABC, and the quantum hydrodynamic model (Q-HDM) with the corresponding ABC. The study is performed for a metallic nanosphere. For detailed discussion of the hydrodynamic models and ABCs, we refer the readers to our previous work [4].

II. Theoretical Framework

The studied structure and excitation are depicted in Fig. 1 (a). Gold is used as a constitutive metal, and glass as a surrounding medium. First, a hydrodynamic Drude model is employed, considering the contribution of free electrons. Then, the Drude model is extended by including the contribution of bound electrons. This is particularly important at optical frequencies, where bound electrons may considerably affect the response of noble metals [6]. The nanosphere is illuminated by an x-polarized plane wave, propagating along the z-axis.

In order to tackle the associated scattering problem, we implemented Mie's theory with spatial dispersion [7,8] for all hydrodynamic models. This approach expands the fields outside and inside the sphere into vector spherical harmonics. By applying the classical boundary conditions, which are augmented by ABCs, one may calculate the scattering coefficients [4].

III. Numerical Results

The following parameters for the permittivity of gold are used in the simulations: the plasma frequency $\hbar\omega_P$=9 eV, the damping frequency $\hbar\gamma$=0.05 eV, and the Fermi velocity v_F=1.4·10^6 m/s. The permittivity of the surrounding medium is 2.3.

The response of the nanoparticle is studied for both Drude and experimentally measured material models. The results for the extinction cross section are depicted in Figs. 1 (b) and (c).

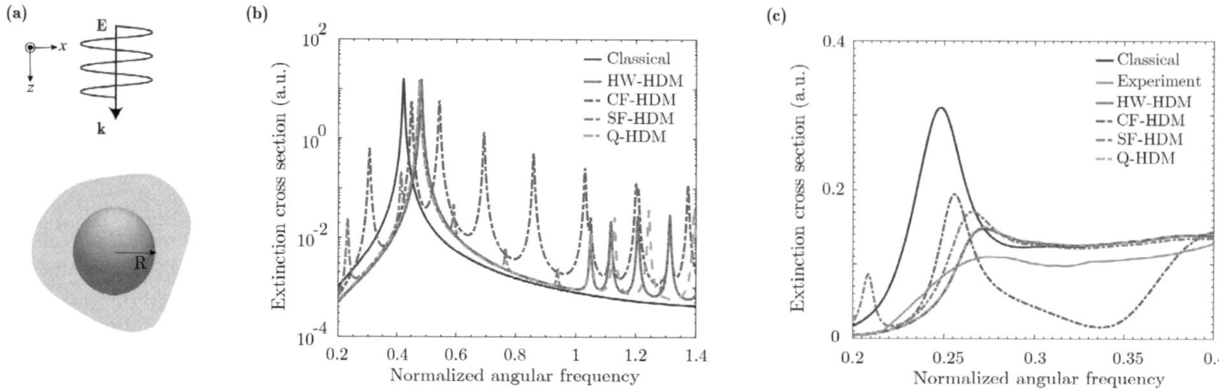

Fig. 1. Hydrodynamic analysis of a gold nanosphere: (a) the nanosphere with the radius R=1.45 nm embedded in glass and a plane wave excitation. Extinction cross section, normalized to the geometrical cross section of the sphere, is shown for (b) Drude and (c) experimentally measured material models. The results of the classical approach (no nonlocal effects) and experiments are employed as references [4].

IV. Discussion

Considering the response of free electrons, the main hydrodynamic surface plasmon resonances are blueshifted with respect to the classical one. As depicted in Fig. 1 (b), CF-HDM introduces the greatest blueshift, deviating from the other three hydrodynamic models. Moreover, above the plasma frequency, one may observe the propagating longitudinal wave modes. Four longitudinal resonances at spectral positions 1.05, 1.12, 1.21, and 1.31, may be clearly distinguished for HW-HDM. These resonances are identical to the ones of SF-HDM and are in good agreement with CF-HDM. Note that Q-HDM generates the greatest displacement of the longitudinal peaks, due to the fact that this model considers both quantum pressure and diffraction effects. Apart from the abovementioned resonances, CF-HDM and SF-HDM yield several other spurious resonances both below and above the plasma frequency, which appear more strikingly for CF-HDM. Such resonances occur since CF-HDM and SF-HDM consider, on top of the nonlocal longitudinal response (as for the other two hydrodynamic models), the nonlocal transverse response [4].

Compared with the abovementioned Drude case, the response of both free and bound electrons in the studied frequency range, described by an experimental material model [5], yields the following two differences: 1) the classical and nonlocal hydrodynamic surface plasmon resonances have been redshifted and 2) their magnitudes have been significantly attenuated, as illustrated in Fig. 1 (c). The results of HW-HDM and Q-HDM are almost the same, while the other two hydrodynamic models deviate considerably. Compared with HW-HDM and Q-HDM, SF-HDM generates a nearly identical nanoparticle's response above a spectral position of 0.3. However, it predicts a slightly lower blueshift of the surface plasmon resonance, and more surprisingly, this model reveals another distinguishable resonance peak at approximately 0.23. CF-HDM clearly introduces the greatest discrepancy in the spectrum.

Finally, the results of hydrodynamic models are compared with experiments available in literature for the studied topology. As it can be seen in Fig. 1 (c), the reported experimental results in general agree closely with HW-HDM and Q-HDM, and do not show spurious components generated by the other two hydrodynamic models.

V. Conclusion

This work performed a comparison of four nonlocal hydrodynamic models, namely HW-HDM, CF-HDM, SF-HDM, and Q-HDM. This was done by investigating the response of a metallic nanosphere with a spatially dispersive material parameter, under a plane wave excitation. First, a Drude material model was employed, considering the response of only free electrons. Second, an experimentally measured material model was employed, in order to include the response of both free and bound electrons. It was shown that different hydrodynamic models may predict the particle's response differently. CF-HDM and SF-HDM display anomalous features in the extinction spectrum, which do not show up for the other two hydrodynamic models. Additionally, the results of hydrodynamic models were compared with experimental results reported in literature, yielding a good agreement with HW-HDM and Q-HDM.

Acknowledgment

The authors gratefully acknowledge the financial support from the Fund for Scientific Research Flanders (FWO) under the contract numbers 3E151025 and G090017N, and the C2 Project (C24/15/015) of KU Leuven.

References

[1] K. J. Savage, et al., "Revealing the quantum regime in tunelling plasmonics," Nature, vol. 491, pp. 574-577, November 2012.

[2] P. Berini and I. De Leon, "Surface plasmon-polariton amplifiers and lasers," Nature Phot., vol. 6, pp. 16-24, January 2012.

[3] F. Forstmann and R. R. Gerhardts, Metal Optics Near Plasma Frequency, vol. 109, Berlin Heidelberg: Sprinder-Verlag, pp. 6-19, 1986.

[4] M. Kupresak, X. Zheng, G. A. E. Vandenbosch, and V. V. Moshchalkov, "Comparison of hydrodynamic models for the electromagnetic nonlocal response of nanoparticles," Adv. Theory and Simulations, vol. 1, 1800076, September 2018.

[5] S. Raza, G. Toscano, A.-P. Jauho, M. Wubs, and N. A. Mortensen, "Unusual resonances in nanoplasmonic structures due to nonlocal response," Phys. Rev. B, vol. 84, 121412, September 2011.

[6] P. B. Johnson and R. W. Christy, "Optical constants of the noble metals," Phys. Rev. B, vol. 6, 4370, December 1972.

[7] R. Ruppin, "Optical properties of small metal spheres," Phys. Rev. B, vol. 11, pp. 2871-2876, April 1975.

[8] V. V. Datsyuk and O. M. Tovkach, "Optical properties of a metal nanosphere with spatially dispersive permittivity," J. Opt. Soc. Am. B, vol. 28, pp. 1224-1230, May 2011.

Compressing H^2 Matrices for Translationally Invariant Kernels

R. J. Adams and J. C. Young
Electrical & Computer Engineering
University of Kentucky
Lexington, KY, USA
rjadams@uky.edu, john.c.young@uky.edu

S. D. Gedney
Electrical Engineering
University of Colorado Denver
Denver, CO, USA
stephen.gedney@ucdenver.edu

***Abstract*— H^2 matrices provide compressed representations of the matrices obtained when discretizing surface and volume integral equations. The memory costs associated with storing H^2 matrices for static and low-frequency applications are $O(N)$. However, when the H^2 representation is constructed using sparse samples of the underlying matrix, the translation matrices in the H^2 representation do not preserve any translational invariance present in the underlying kernel. In some cases, this can result in an H^2 representation with relatively large memory requirements. This paper outlines a method to compress an existing H^2 matrix by constructing a translationally invariant H^2 matrix from it. Numerical examples demonstrate that the resulting representation can provide significant memory savings.**

Keywords*— *integral equations, sparse matrices.

I. Introduction

Integral equations provide a useful method for formulating both linear and nonlinear electromagnetic problems. In most cases, discretized integral equations yield matrix equations having the following form,

$$\mathbf{Z}\,\mathbf{x} = \mathbf{f}\,, \tag{1}$$

where $\mathbf{Z}$ is the N-by-N system matrix, $\mathbf{f}$ is the N-by-1 source vector, and $\mathbf{x}$ is the vector of unknowns. The elements of $\mathbf{Z}$ are obtained from samples of an underlying kernel. Although the kernel, denoted G below, is often translationally invariant, the geometry usually is not. Consequently, the matrix $\mathbf{Z}$ seldom exhibits translational invariance.

The matrix in (1) is dense, and it is necessary to use compressed representations for large simulations. H^2 matrices provide one such representation [1, 2]. In this paper, the specific H^2 representation described in an appendix of [3] is used (the representation described in [3] was therein referred to as an MLSSM representation; it has since been determined that the MLSSM is equivalent to an H^2 matrix). In an H^2 representation, $\mathbf{Z}$ is decomposed using an octree as $\mathbf{Z} = \mathbf{Z}_{\text{near}} + \mathbf{Z}_{\text{far}}$, where $\mathbf{Z}_{\text{near}}$ contains only those source/field interactions that occur between touching groups at the finest level of the tree. All other interactions are included in $\mathbf{Z}_{\text{far}}$.

The matrix $\mathbf{Z}_{\text{far}}$ is decomposed by levels in the L-level octree (here, l=1 is the root level),

$$\mathbf{Z}_{\text{far}} = \mathbf{Z}_{\text{far}}^{(L)} + \mathbf{Z}_{\text{far}}^{(L-1)} + \cdots + \mathbf{Z}_{\text{far}}^{(3)}\,. \tag{2}$$

This work was supported in part by Office of Naval Research Grant N00014-16-1-3066 and NASA Grant NNX16AO88G.

$\mathbf{Z}_{\text{far}}^{(l)}$ is the portion of $\mathbf{Z}_{\text{far}}$ corresponding to interactions between non-touching groups at level-l of the tree that are not represented at a parent level.

Each matrix on the right side of (2) has the following form,

$$\mathbf{Z}_{\text{far}}^{(l)} = \mathbf{U}\,\mathbf{T}\,\mathbf{V}^{h}\,, \tag{3}$$

where $\mathbf{U}$ and $\mathbf{V}$ are orthonormal block-diagonal matrices that map from the original sources/observers in each level-l group to the minimum source/field interaction bases used by each level-l group. As in the fast multipole method (FMM), $\mathbf{U}$ and $\mathbf{V}$ are themselves a multilevel product of change-of-basis operators from the finest level of the octree to the basis used at level-l. This detail is omitted since only $\mathbf{T}$ is considered in the following.

As discussed in [3], the H^2 representation of (1) is obtained from sparse samples of $\mathbf{Z}$. Thus, $\mathbf{T}$ in (3) does not exhibit any translational invariance possessed by the kernel. This is in contrast to an FMM, which preserves a kernel's translational invariance. For this reason, the storage requirements associated with an H^2 representation can be larger than those required by an equivalent FMM. The remainder of this paper outlines a method for compressing $\mathbf{T}$ by developing a translationally invariant H^2 representation for translationally invariant kernels.

II. Translationaly Invariant H^2 Matrices

At each level, given $\mathbf{T}$, we seek an alternative representation with the form,

$$\mathbf{T} = \mathbf{L}\mathbf{T}_{\text{SI}}\mathbf{R}^{h}\,. \tag{4}$$

The following structure is imposed on the matrices on the right-side of (4). $\mathbf{L}$ and $\mathbf{R}$ are non-square, block-diagonal matrices, with one diagonal block per level-l group. The number of rows in each diagonal block of $\mathbf{L}$ and $\mathbf{R}$ must match the corresponding column dimensions of the blocks of $\mathbf{U}$ and $\mathbf{V}$; this value is denoted as n_g in the following. The number of columns in each block of $\mathbf{L}$ and $\mathbf{R}$ is discussed below. The translation matrix $\mathbf{T}_{\text{SI}}$ in (4) has the same structure as $\mathbf{T}$; $\mathbf{T}_{\text{SI}}$ has a nonzero interaction block (specified below) for each nonzero interaction block in $\mathbf{T}$, and the other blocks are zero. Unlike $\mathbf{T}$, $\mathbf{T}_{\text{SI}}$ is constructed to preserve any translational invariance present in the underlying kernel.

The procedure used to construct the representation on the right side of (4) consists in first specifying $\mathbf{T}_{\text{SI}}$, and then solving for the diagonal blocks of $\mathbf{L}$ and $\mathbf{R}$.

A. Constructing $\mathbf{T}_{SI}$

At level-l of the octree, $\mathbf{T}_{SI}$ is obtained as follows. A set of m random points, $\{\bar{\mathbf{r}}_i\}_{i=1}^{m}$, is uniformly distributed within a cube that is centered on the origin and has a size equal to a level-l octree box. Shifted copies of these points serve as both source and observer points within each non-empty group at this level; the shift is equal to the translation vector from the origin to the center $\bar{\mathbf{r}}_c$ of each non-empty octree box, $\{\bar{\mathbf{r}}_i - \bar{\mathbf{r}}_c\}_{i=1}^{m}$. If there are M groups, this procedure yields a square matrix, $\mathbf{T}_{SI}$, that preserves a kernel's translational invariance. The size of $\mathbf{T}_{SI}$ is (mM)-by-(mM). The value of m is determined dynamically, as discussed in the next section.

B. Solving for L and R

The diagonal blocks of **L** and **R**, as well as the value of m, are obtained using the following procedure, which uses Matlab notation. In this procedure, $\mathbf{L}_g$ and $\mathbf{R}_g$ denote the diagonal blocks of **L** and **R**, the subscript "g" implies a loop over the level-l groups, and "LS" denotes least-squares.

- m=0; err=1; $\mathbf{R}_g$ = zeros(n_g, 0)
- while $err > tol$
  - $m = m + m_{inc}$
  - retaining any previously computed portions of each $\mathbf{T}_{SI}$ block, fill in the new portion (which is due to incrementing m)
  - $\mathbf{L}_g$ = zeros(n_g, m); $\mathbf{R}_g$ = [$\mathbf{R}_g$, rand(n_g, m_{inc})];
  - for k = 1 : n_steps (n_steps=20 here)
    - fix **R**, and compute a LS solution for $\mathbf{L}_g$
    - fix **L**, and compute a LS solution for $\mathbf{R}_g$
  - $err = \| \mathbf{T} - \mathbf{L}\,\mathbf{T}_{SI}\,\mathbf{R}^h \| / \|\mathbf{T}\|$

At the termination of this procedure, the right side of (4) matches **T** with relative accuracy tol. For the following examples, tol = 1e-5, which is the same tolerance that will be used to approximate $\mathbf{Z}_{far}$ in (2) in the following examples.

III. Numerical Examples

The compression scheme (4) is illustrated for the kernel, $G(\mathbf{r}\text{-}\mathbf{r}') = 1/|\mathbf{r}\text{-}\mathbf{r}'|$, and three **Z** matrices using this kernel are considered below. In Example-1, $\mathbf{Z}_{far}$ consists of point-to-point samples of G, corresponding to interactions between a cluster of 2e4 points randomly distributed in a 1-by-1-by-1 meter cube; the matrix **T** is constructed at level-3 of the octree using the algorithm outlined in the appendix of [3]. Example-2 is similar to Example-1, except the 2e4 points are randomly located along a 1 meter line; the matrix **T** is constructed at level-6 of the tree. Finally, for Example-3, $\mathbf{Z}_{far}$ is obtained from a locally corrected Nyström discretization of the magnetostatic integral equation for a thin spherical steel shell [4] with N=18738; **T** is obtained at level-3 of the octree and is shown in Fig. 1.

Table I reports the compression ratio, ρ, obtained using the right side of (4) instead of **T**. In all three examples, the matrix $\mathbf{T}_{SI}$ is constructed using only point samples of the scalar kernel, G. The table also reports the number of nonempty groups, M, as well as m, the number of random points used in each nonempty level-l group (l=3 for Example-1 and Example-3, l=6 for Example-2). The final value of m is different for each geometry.

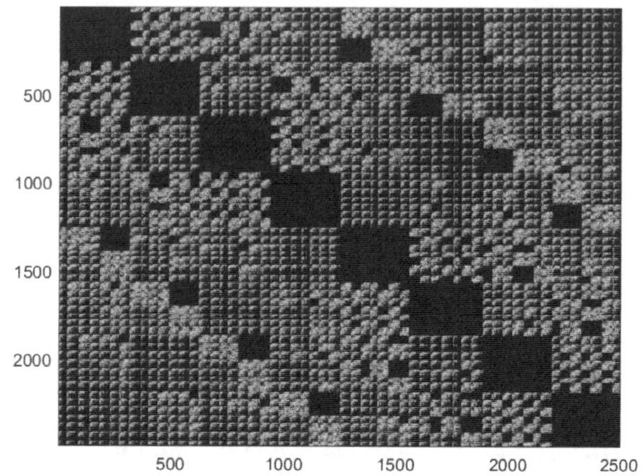

Fig. 1. Absolute value of the elements of **T** for Example-3 (log scale, dark blue colors indicate zeros). There are 56 nonempty level-3 groups; 56 column blocks and 56 row blocks are seen in the image.

TABLE I. Compression Ratios for the Three Examples.

	M	m	ρ
Example-1	64	56	5.95
Example-2	32	12	1.01
Example-3	56	75	4.21

IV. Summary

A method to compress the **T** matrix of an H^2 representation has been reported. The method works directly with **T** and samples of the underlying scalar kernel, G. It has been shown that the method provides significant memory savings in some cases. The presentation will discuss ways to further improve the compression ratios reported in Table I. It will also be shown that the proposed method provides super-algebraic convergence with increasing m, and methods for reducing the costs associated with computing **L** and **R** will be discussed.

References

[1] S. Börm, "Construction of data-sparse H2-matrices by hierarchical compression," *SIAM Journal on Scientific Computing,* vol. 31, no. 3, pp. 1820-1839, 2009.

[2] W. Hackbusch, *Hierarchical Matrices: Algorithms and Analysis* (Springer Series in Computational Mathematics). Berlin: Springer-Verlag, 2015.

[3] X. Xu and R. J. Adams, "Sparse matrix factorization using overlapped localizing LOGOS modes on a shifted grid," *IEEE Transactions on Antennas and Propagation,* vol. 60, no. 3, pp. 1414-1424, 2012.

[4] J. C. Young and S. D. Gedney, "A Locally Corrected Nystrom Formulation for the Magnetostatic Volume Integral Equation," *IEEE Transactions on Magnetics,* vol. 47, no. 9, pp. 2163-2170, Sep. 2011.

Balanced Wideband Impedance Transformer (BWIT) for Common-Mode Resonance Cancellation in UWB Dipoles over a Ground Plane

Alexander D. Johnson, Satheesh Bojja Venkatakrishnan, Elias A. Alwan, and John L.Volakis
RFCOM Laboratory, College of Engineering and Computing
Florida International University, Miami, Florida, 33174

***Abstract*— Within the context of modern radios, differential Radio Frequency (RF) front-ends provide much greater immunity to noise and distortion by suppressing second order harmonics. Recent advancements in differential RF front-ends offer high dynamic range, high linearity, and low noise in the transceiver chain. However, a major bottleneck with differential systems is the presence of common-mode resonances when scanning to low angles across large bandwidths. In this paper, we present a novel wideband differential feed for ultra-wideband (UWB) dipoles like the Tightly Coupled Dipole Array (TCDA). Our Balanced Wideband Impedance Transformer (BWIT) feed is developed for the UHF-S band (*viz.* 0.4 GHz to 3.2 GHz) with emphasis on resonance-free wide-angle scanning in the E-plane.**

***Index Terms*—Antenna arrays, differential geometry, phased arrays, ultra-wideband antennas.**

I. Introduction

Low profile wideband antennas and arrays are essential for high data rate communications and software defined radios (SDRs). An ultra-wideband (UWB) array replaces several narrowband antennas to reduce power, cost, and space requirements. UWB phased arrays are often hindered by their size, bandwidth, and scanning capabilities. Within this class, Tightly Coupled Dipole Array (TCDA) have been employed using single-ended feeds for low angle scanning over wide bandwidths for more than a decade. Unfortunately, these feeds introduce the possibility of broadside common-mode currents. Conversely, differential feeds inherently cancel common-mode currents at broadside, but exhibit common-modes when scanning to low angles in the E-plane. Notably, common-modes arise for particular scan angles and frequencies in the differential feed lines due to destructive mutual coupling between neighboring elements in presence of a third conductor (i.e., ground plane). If not addressed properly, these common-modes radiate in a manner that significantly reduces total efficiency and impedance bandwidths of balanced antenna structures [1]. For instance, the UWB differential feeds in [2]-[5] were plagued by common-mode resonances when scanning in the E-plane nearing angles down to 45°. Hence, the major challenge in the design of full differential radios is the reduction of these common-mode currents present in the feed-lines when scanning. The most prevalent way to suppress these scan-dependent common-modes is to employ a balanced-to-unbalanced feed (i.e., balun), thereby avoiding differential feeding altogether [6], [7]. Other methods have been explored to remove such modes by employing conductive E-Plane walls to disrupt the fields [2], [3], [8], or by using resistive terminations to attenuate the common-modes [4], [5].

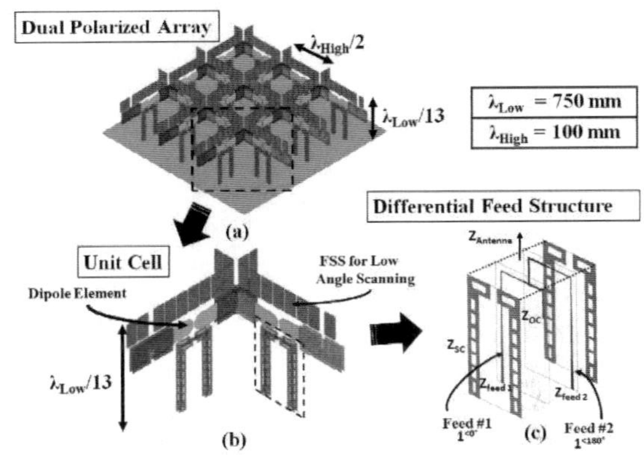

Fig. 1. Pictorial representation of a (a) dual polarized differential TCDA (D-TCDA) array with (b) unit cell of dual offset D-TCDA design, along with (c) the novel BWIT differential matching network.

Despite these challenges, differential feeding has the following benefits 1) direct compatibility with existing wideband differential components that enable high dynamic range and linearity, 2) differential signals provide inherent lower distortion in response to noise and interference from power supplies, and 3) distortions due to even order harmonics from nonlinear devices can be suppressed by differential feeds [9]. In this paper, an UWB differential feed that enables wide-angle scanning capability for a TCDA is presented (see Fig. 1). The presented feed structure, referred to as the Balanced Wideband Impedance Transformer (BWIT) [10], (see Fig. 1 (c)) is an improvement of [11], where the concept was shown to operate without common-modes across 3 GHz to 18 GHz (6:1 bandwidth) in full-wave simulations. The differential feed presented here achieves resonance-free scanning down to 45° from boresight in the principal E and H planes with a dipole array, from 0.4 GHz to 3.2 GHz (8:1 bandwidth).

II. Cancellation of Common-Mode Resonance

The balanced feed here improves on [11]. The BWIT feed was first simulated without the dipoles in ANSYS HFSS v.19, and found to have very good amplitude and phase balance with practically no amplitude variation and only ±1.5° phase imbalance, resulting in a common-mode-rejection ration (CMRR) of -27 dB. Further, the insertion loss of the full-wave EM model was < 0.8 dB an average over the band. Next, to show its effectiveness in cancelling common-modes while scanning, it was used to excite a TCDA. Fig. 2 depicts the surface current distribution on the feed with the dipoles from an HFSS infinite array simulation, showing clear cancellation of common-mode currents along the mirrored feed lines when scanning in the E-plane. As seen, the currents on the feed are

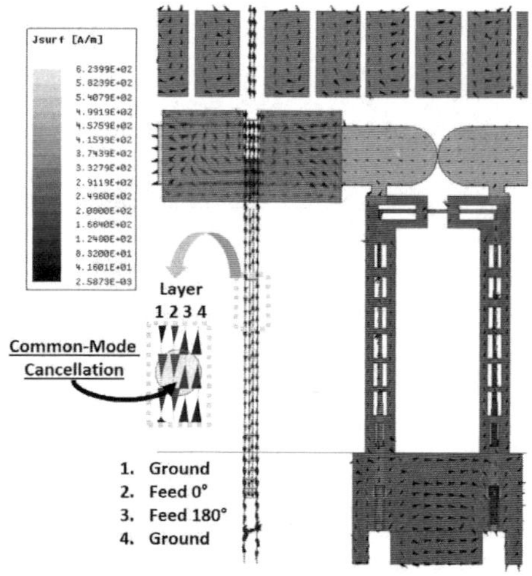

Fig. 2. HFSS screen capture showing cancellation of common-mode currents in the BWIT feed while scanning to 45°.

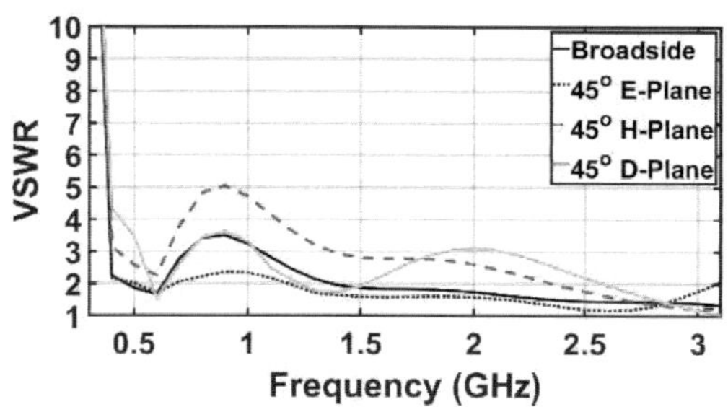

Fig. 3. Simulated infinite array VSWR in the E, H, and D-planes of the array at broadside and scanning to 45°.

directed in a balanced manner (propagating in opposite directions), due to the symmetry of the BWIT feed network, with fields confined by the via fence and two outer shielding conductor along the edges of the feed lines. This allows for resonance-free scanning down to 45° in the E-plane over the band, as seen in Fig. 3. The impedance matching here can be optimized in future iterations, but this plot shows the continuous resonance-free nature of the BWIT feed structure while scanning in the E-plane.

III. Conclusion

We presented a novel dual-polarized differential feed operating across the UHF to S bands (*viz.* 0.4 GHz to 3.2 GHz). When used in conjunction with differential RF components this array enables high dynamic range, high linearity, and low noise differential radio receivers. A key application of the novel Balanced Wideband Impedance Transformer (BWIT) feed is in UWB TCDA, to allow continuous scanning to low angles across large bandwidths with a balanced input.

References

[1] S. G. Hay and J. D. O'Sullivan, "Analysis of Common-mode Effects in a Dual Polarized Planar Connected-Array Antenna,"Radio Science RS6S04, vol. 43, Dec.2008.

[2] J.-P. R. Bayard, D. H. Schaubert, and M. E. Cooley, "E-plane Scan Performance of Infinite Arrays of Dipoles Printed on Protruding Dielectric Substrates: Coplanar Feed line and E-plane Metallic Wall Effects," IEEE Transactions on Antennas and Propagation, vol. 41, no. 6, pp. 837–841, Jun. 1993, ISSN: 0018-926X.

[3] S. Edelberg and A. Oliner, "Mutual Coupling Effects in Large Antenna Arrays II: Compensation Effects," IRE Transactions on Antennas and Propagation, vol. 8, no. 4, pp. 360–367, Jul. 1960, ISSN: 0096-1973.

[4] J. J. Lee, S. Livingston, and R. Koenig, "Performance of a Wideband (3-14 GHz) Dual-pol Array," in IEEE Antennas and Propagation Society Symposium, 2004, Jun. 2004, vol. 1, pp. 551–554.

[5] E. de Lera Acedo, E. Garcia, V. Gonzalez-Posadas, J. L. Vazquez-Roy, R. Maaskant, and D. Segovia, "Study and Design of a Differentially-Fed Tapered Slot Antenna Array," IEEE Transactions on Antennas and Propagation, vol. 58, no. 1, pp. 68–78, Jan. 2010, ISSN:0018-926X.

[6] J. P. Doane, K. Sertel, and J. L. Volakis, "A Wideband, Wide Scanning Tightly Coupled Dipole Array With Integrated Balun (TCDA-IB)," IEEE Transactions on Antennas and Propagation, vol. 61, no. 9, pp. 4538–4548, Sep. 2013.

[7] J. Zhong, A. Johnson, E. A. Alwan, and J. L. Volakis, "Dual-Linear Polarized Phased Array With 9:1 Bandwidth and 60° Scanning Off Broadside," IEEE Transactions on Antennas and Propagation, vol. 67, no. 3, pp. 1996–2001, Mar. 2019, ISSN: 0018-926X.

[8] J. T. Logan, R. W. Kindt, M. Y. Lee, and M. N. Vouvakis, "A New Class of Planar Ultrawideband Modular Antenna Arrays With Improved Bandwidth," IEEE Transactions on Antennas and Propagation, vol. 66, no. 2, pp. 692–701, Feb. 2018, ISSN: 0018-926X.

[9] D. M. Pozar, "Microwave Engineering Education: from Field Theory to Circuit Theory," in 2012 IEEE/MTT-S International Microwave Symposium Digest, Jun. 2012, pp. 1–3.

[10] A. D. Johnson, E. A. Alwan, and J. L. Volakis, "Balanced Wideband Impedance Transformer," U.S. Patent 10320088B1, 2019.

[11] A. D. Johnson, J. Zhong, M. Livadaru, E. A. Alwan, and J. L. Volakis, "Tightly Coupled Dipole Array with Wideband Differential Feeding Network," in 2018 IEEE International Symposium on Antennas and Propagation USNC/URSI National Radio Science Meeting, Jul. 2018, pp. 1987–1988

Field-based Model of Flux Compression Generators

Nicholas Klugman*†, James Vedral†, and Jeffrey Lang*
*Department of Electrical Engineering and Computer Science
Massachusetts Institute of Technology
nklugman@mit.edu, lang@mit.edu
†Charles Stark Draper Laboratory
nklugman@draper.com, jvedral@draper.com

***Abstract*—This paper provides a field-based model of flux compression generators, capturing the effects of magnetic diffusion and pressure. A set of differential-algebraic-equations are derived to describe the magnetic dynamics. The electromechanical dynamics of the cylindrical implosion generator, accounting for magnetic pressure, are also demonstrated.**

***Index Terms*—cylindrical implosion generator, explosive pulsed power, flux compression generator, magnetic pressure, magnetocumulative generator.**

I. Introduction

Flux compression generators (FCGs) are used in pulsed power to provide gain in both current and internal magnetic field strength. FCGs are commonly modeled via an equivalent circuit [1]. To provide a more thorough treatment of flux losses to diffusion than the commonly employed skin depth approximation [1] and to account for the effects of magnetic pressure, we develop an average-field-based model of FCG dynamics in long, open, single-loop generators, as shown in Fig. 1, e.g., plate, cylindrical implosion, loop, and strip generators. Calculation of the magnetic pressure in the device, enabled by a field-based model, can better predict system evolution and mechanical failure. A link between the magnetic field and the current is also considered.

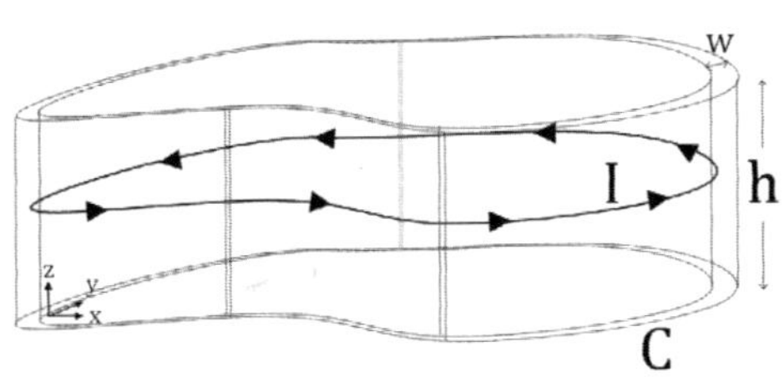

Fig. 1. Geometry of the FCG. The FCG is represented by the extrusion of area — lying in the x-y plane, bounded by a planar curve C, with width w — by a long distance h in the $\hat{\mathbf{z}}$ direction. (For compactness, h is pictured short, though assumed long.) A current, I, runs around the device parallel to the x-y plane.

II. Magnetic Diffusion

We first consider the magnetic diffusion problem that arises in solving for the flux lost from the cavity into the conductor. For simplicity, we zoom in close to the surface, as in Fig. 2 (a). We then have a temporally-varying magnetic field, $\mathbf{B} = -B_c(t)\hat{\mathbf{z}}$, within the cavity, diffusing into a yz-infinite plate conductor (curvature is negligible close enough to the surface), with finite width w, conductivity σ, a permeability μ_0 equal to that of free space, and moving with velocity $\mathbf{u} = u_0\hat{\mathbf{x}}$. Since the device is tall, the field at the non-cavity surface is zero. Fig. 2 (b) shows the problem in the frame of reference of the plate (transformed by $\xi = x - u_0t$), here denoting the field by $\mathbf{B}'$. In the quasi-static regime, this transformation leaves the magnetic field unaltered, so $\mathbf{B}' = -B_c(t)\hat{\mathbf{z}}$ inside the cavity [2]. From the quasi-static form of Maxwell's equations [2] and since the field inside the conductor is $-\hat{\mathbf{z}}$-directed and independent of y and z, the field diffuses into the conductor according to the following boundary value problem:

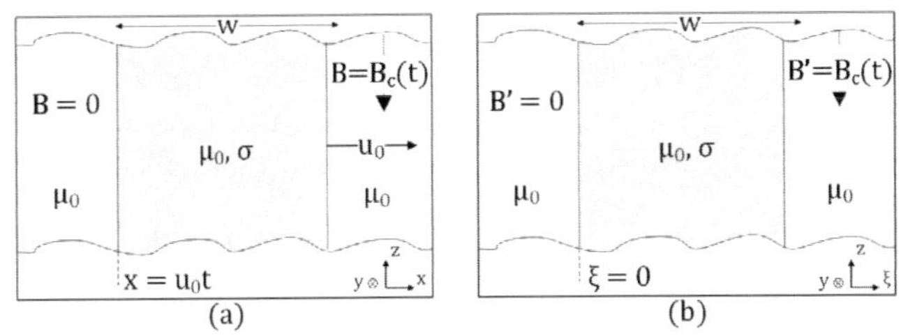

Fig. 2. Diffusion problem set-up. A plate of conductivity σ, permeability μ_0 (equal to that of free space), and width w is infinitely tall and long into the page. In (a), the plate moves with velocity $\mathbf{u} = u_0\hat{\mathbf{x}}$. On one side the magnetic field is $\mathbf{B}(x = u_0t) = 0$ and on the other it is given by $\mathbf{B}(x = u_0t + w) = -B_c(t)\hat{\mathbf{z}}$. In (b), the plate is stationary, with magnetic field $\mathbf{B}'(\xi = 0) = 0$ and $\mathbf{B}'(\xi = w) = -B_c(t)\hat{\mathbf{z}}$.

$$\frac{\partial B_z'}{\partial t} = \frac{1}{\mu_0\sigma}\frac{\partial^2 B_z'}{\partial \xi^2}, 0 < \xi < w; \tag{1}$$

$$B_z'(\xi = 0, t) = 0, t > 0; \tag{2}$$

$$B_z'(\xi = w, t) = -B_c(t), t > 0; \tag{3}$$

$$B_z'(\xi, t = 0) = -\frac{\xi}{w}B_c(0), 0 < \xi < w. \tag{4}$$

These initial conditions assume the worst-case scenario for diffusive losses from the seed current.

This boundary value problem is solved by:

$$B_z'(\xi, t) = -\frac{\xi}{w}B_c(t) + \frac{2}{\pi}\sum_{n=1}^{\infty} \left(\frac{(-1)^{n+1}}{n}\int_0^t e^{-\frac{n^2\pi^2}{\mu_0\sigma w^2}(t-\tau)}\dot{B}_c(\tau)d\tau \sin\left(\frac{n\pi\xi}{w}\right)\right). \tag{5}$$

III. Flux Dynamics

Now that we have an expression for the field within the conductor (which is the same in both reference frames), we can calculate the evolution of the flux lost to the conductor and the total flux in the device.

Flux is defined by $\lambda(t) = \iint_S \mathbf{B} \cdot \mathbf{dS}$. So, the flux in the conductor is given by $\lambda_c(t) = p(t) \int_{u_0 t}^{u_0 t + w} -B_z(x,t)dx$, where the perimeter, $p(t)$, is time-varying in general. Thus,

$$\lambda_c = \frac{p(t)w}{2}\left(B_c(t) - 8\sum_{\substack{n=1 \\ n \text{ odd}}}^{\infty} \int_0^t e^{\frac{n^2\pi^2(\tau - t)}{\mu_0 \sigma w^2}} \frac{\dot{B}_c(\tau)}{\pi^2 n^2} d\tau\right), \quad (6)$$

$$\approx \frac{p(t)w}{2}\left(B_c(t) - \frac{8}{\pi^2}\int_0^t e^{-\frac{\pi^2}{\mu_0\sigma w^2}(t-\tau)} \dot{B}_c(\tau) d\tau\right). \quad (7)$$

We now differentiate, truncate the series, and substitute,

$$\dot{\lambda}_c = \frac{\dot{p}}{p}\lambda_c + \frac{4p(t)}{\mu_0 \sigma w}\sum_{n=0}^{\infty}\int_0^t e^{-\frac{(2n+1)^2\pi^2}{\mu_0\sigma w^2}(t-\tau)}\dot{B}_c(\tau)d\tau, \quad (8)$$

$$\approx \frac{\dot{p}}{p}\lambda_c + \frac{4p(t)}{\mu_0\sigma w}\int_0^t e^{-\frac{\pi^2}{\mu_0\sigma w^2}(t-\tau)}\dot{B}_c(\tau)d\tau, \quad (9)$$

$$\approx \frac{\pi^2 p(t)}{2\mu_0\sigma w}B_c(t) + \left(\dot{p}/p - \pi^2/\left(\mu_0\sigma w^2\right)\right)\lambda_c. \quad (10)$$

Truncating λ_c overestimates the flux losses to the conductor and truncating $\dot{\lambda}_c$ underestimates growth of these losses.

Let the total flux be given by $\lambda_{tot}(t) = A(t)B_c(t) + \lambda_c(t)$, where $A(t)$ is the area of the cavity. Applying Faraday's Law to a loop, C', surrounding the device, we have $\dot{\lambda}_{tot} = -\oint_{C'} \mathbf{E} \cdot \mathbf{ds}$, where $\mathbf{E}$ is the electric field. Utilizing Ohm's Law — current density, $\mathbf{J} = \sigma(\mathbf{E} + \mathbf{u} \times \mathbf{B})$; the fact that the magnetic field is zero outside the device; and quasistatic Ampere's Law [2], $\nabla \times \mathbf{B} = \mu_0 \mathbf{J}$, we can conclude:

$$\dot{\lambda}_{tot}(t) \approx \frac{-p(t)}{\mu_0\sigma w}\left(B_c(t) + 2\int_0^t e^{\frac{\pi^2}{\mu_0\sigma w^2}(\tau - t)}\dot{B}_c(\tau)d\tau\right), \quad (11)$$

$$\approx \left(\pi^2\lambda_c - p(t)w(4+\pi^2)B_c(t)\right)/(4\mu_0\sigma w^2). \quad (12)$$

Here, the series truncation overestimates total flux losses.

Collecting our results, we have the following set of differential-algebraic-equations:

$$\dot{\lambda}_{tot} = \left(-p(t)w(4+\pi^2)B_c + \pi^2\lambda_c\right)/(4\mu_0\sigma w^2), \quad (13)$$

$$\dot{\lambda}_c = p(t)\pi^2 B_c/(2\mu_0\sigma w) + \left(\dot{p}/p - \pi^2/(\mu_0\sigma w^2)\right)\lambda_c, \quad (14)$$

$$\lambda_{tot} = A(t)B_c + \lambda_c. \quad (15)$$

To add the effects of magnetic pressure, rather than prescribing $A(t)$ and $p(t)$, one would add equations relating the magnetic field to these geometric quantities. The current can be calculated from this model during post-processing, since the total flux in the cavity is given by $i(t)L(t) = B_c(t)A(t)$, where $i(t)$ is the total current in the device and $L(t)$ is what the inductance would be if the metal were perfectly conducting. Keeping with our assumption of a long device, the inductance is approximately given by $L(t) = \mu_0 A(t)/h$, where h is the height of the device.

IV. Magnetic Pressure in a Cylindrical Implosion Generator

Since the exact relation between the field, the perimeter, and the area is geometry dependent, we here only consider the simple, but illustrative, example of the cylindrical implosion generator. The uniform magnetic field provides a uniform pressure of $B_c^2/(2\mu_0)$ over the surface of the conductor, so Newton's second law gives, $m\ddot{r} = 2\pi r h \cdot B_c^2/(2\mu_0)$ where m is the mass of the conductor (assumed constant) and r is the radius. So, accounting for magnetic pressure and diffusion, a long cylindrical implosion generator follows:

$$\dot{\lambda}_{tot} = \left(-2\pi r w(4+\pi^2)B_c + \pi^2\lambda_c\right)/(4\mu_0\sigma w^2), \quad (16)$$

$$\dot{\lambda}_c = \pi^3 r B_c/(\mu_0\sigma w) - \left(v/r + \pi^2/(\mu_0\sigma w^2)\right)\lambda_c, \quad (17)$$

$$\lambda_{tot} = \pi r^2 B_c + \lambda_c,\ \dot{r} = -v,\ \dot{v} = -\pi h B_c^2 r/(m\mu_0), \quad (18)$$

where the additional state variable, v, represents the inward radial velocity of the conductor.

Using this model to simulate a brass generator with initial radial velocity 2.5 $mm/\mu s$, thickness 1/8", radius 3", and initial magnetic field 5 T yields the results shown in Fig. 3. As the magnetic field peaks, the flux in the cavity dips significantly below the initial total flux.

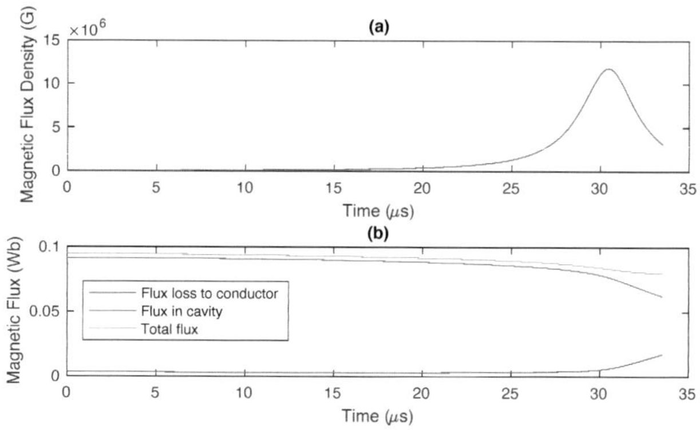

Fig. 3. Results of Simulation of Cylindrical Implosion Generator. Plot (a) shows the evolution of the magnetic flux density (B_c). It reaches a maximum value of 11.8 MG and the pulse has a full width at half max of 3.8 μs. Plot (b) shows the flux in the cavity ($B_c \cdot A$), in the conductor (λ_c), and in total in the device (λ_{tot}).

V. Conclusion

We have thus generated a set of differential-algebraic-equations to determine the magnetic field and/or current in a long flux compression generator, accounting for flux losses from diffusion, with the option of extension with the effects of magnetic pressure. We have also considered the specific case of the cylindrical implosion generator, accounting for magnetic pressure, capturing the electromagnetic and mechanical dynamics of the system.

References

[1] Fowler and Altgilbers, "Magnetic Flux Compression Generators: A Tutorial and Survey Contents," LANL, PACS №: 84.70+p, 2003.

[2] Woodson and Melcher, Electromechanical Dynamics. Krieger Publishing Company, 1968.

Microwave Non-Destructive Testing Technique for Material Characterization of Concrete Structures via Electromagnetic Waves with FDTD

Ummu Sahin Sener
Department of Mathematical Engineering
Yıldız Technical University
Istanbul, Turkey
ummusahin@klu.edu.tr

Sebahattin Eker
Informatics Institute
Istanbul Technical University
Istanbul, Turkey
ekerseb@itu.edu.tr

***Abstract*—** Concrete is a nonhomogeneous medium that contains coarse aggregate, sand (fine aggregate), cement powder, water and porosity. Microwave non-destructive testing (NDT) technique is used to simulate three layered media that contains air gap, coarse aggregate and a two layered media that contain rebar and void is modeled as closest to the reality. Interaction of electromagnetic wave and the concrete pile is utilized for numerical simulation. A Finite-Difference Time-Domain (FDTD) method with Perfectly Matched Layer (PML) Absorbing Boundary Condition (ABC) is proposed to simulate electromagnetic wave propagation in FRP tube and composite pile. 2D simulation of a wave generated from a point source at microwave frequencies is obtained by using MATLAB®.

Keywords*— *cement-based samples, layered media, rebar, finite-difference time-domain simulation, perfectly matched layer

I. INTRODUCTION

In the compositions obtained by mixing different materials, it is important for the quality of the composition to be obtained to maintain a certain level of each component quantity. The determination of the curing time in the structures that require a certain chemical activity to occur is also a condition that affects its mechanical properties [1, 2]. Compressive strength decreases if cement based samples (concrete and mortar blocks) are not cured properly. During the production of cement-based structures, the use of vibrators also is important to prevent the formation of porosity in the interior. There may be defects in concrete and mortar structures due to faults during production and improper curing, as well as disbands, delamination and interior defects due to use and external factors after a certain period of time. Cement-based structures may contain defects due to the reasons mentioned they should be inspected at regular intervals. Non-destructive testing (NDT) techniques are of great importance, as they do not affect the integrity of the structure to be inspected [1, 2]. Since microwave signals can easily penetrate into dielectric environments to a certain depth and are sensitive to the geometric and dimensional properties of a medium or a defect microwave NDT technique is used for simulation. In order to determine the thickness of concrete and mortar parts, coarse aggregates in the concrete part, air gaps between the masonry blocks on the surface, rebar and voids, the interaction of these environments and microwaves has been used for simulation with FDTD technique. For numerical application using difference equations, Maxwell curl equations and three scalar equations at the component level are given in the following section. Two dimensional geometric model to be simulated and samples that prepared according to this physical model are introduced.

II. THEORY AND NUMERICAL SIMULATION EXPERIMENTS

The Maxwell curl equations for linear, isotropic, nondispersive and lossy medium are used to understand how the electromagnetic wave interact with the cement-based environment.

In cases where the incident wave is the same in the z-direction, since all partial derivatives of fields relative to z are equal to zero, the Maxwell's equations are reduced to two-dimensional form. The two-dimensional forms containing E_x, E_y and H_z components are called TE mode and the mode containing H_x, H_y and E_z components are called TM mode. Since only TE mode waves will be used in this study, components of TE mode are given. In Cartesian coordinate system TE waves has three components as follows:

$$\frac{\partial E_x}{\partial t} = \frac{1}{\varepsilon}\left[\frac{\partial H_z}{\partial y} - \left(J_{source_x} + \sigma E_x\right)\right] \tag{1}$$

$$\frac{\partial E_y}{\partial t} = \frac{1}{\varepsilon}\left[-\frac{\partial H_z}{\partial x} - \left(J_{source_y} + \sigma E_y\right)\right] \tag{2}$$

$$\frac{\partial H_z}{\partial t} = \frac{1}{\mu}\left[\frac{\partial E_x}{\partial y} - \frac{\partial E_y}{\partial x} - \left(M_{source_z} + \sigma^* H_z\right)\right] \tag{3}$$

Thanks to FDTD the Maxwell's curl equations are discretized both space and time domains based on the Yee's algorithm [3, 4]. Central differences are applied for time and space derivatives in (1-3). Thus, the equations that will be used in the algorithm are attained and then the algorithm is implemented for 2D simulations in MATLAB®.

In numerical wave propagation computations, an artificial boundary must be defined to restrict the computation domain and absorb the outgoing waves. In PML boundary condition the waves, which have arbitrary incidence angle, frequency and polarization, are matched at the boundary [5].

The three-dimensional samples are simulated in two-dimensions and two-dimensional geometry is divided into cells of much smaller size than the wavelength. The physical models presented in Fig. 1 have 0.5 m in the x-axis and 0.25 m in the z-axis. The computational domain is a rectangular region of 0.5 m × 0.25 m. The numerical domain is obtained by dividing into 200 grids in the x-axis and 100 grids in the z-axis, $\Delta x = \Delta z = 0.0025$ m. In the first numerical experiment, namely in Case A, a three-layered rectangular computational domain is presented. The calculation domain includes masonry, mortar and concrete which contains coarse aggregate respectively from top to bottom. In the second experiment in a word Case B two-layered rectangular specimen that contain mortar and concrete layer is investigated. The second sample includes a void and three rebar, two of which are of the same radius and the other one is thicker. Physical structure and numerical model of computational domains are given respectively in Fig. 1 and Fig. 2.

(a) (b)

Fig. 1. Physical structure of specimens: a- Case A, b- Case B

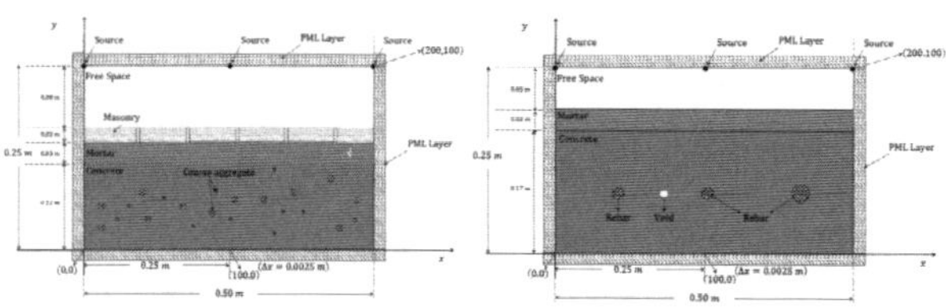

(a) (b)

Fig. 2. Numerical model of computation domain: a- Case A, b- Case B

III. SIMULATION RESULTS

Since the structures are excited by TE plane wave only E_x, E_y and H_z components are calculated. 1.5 GHz, 3.0 GHz and 6.0 GHz pointwise H hard sources in one dimension is used for simulation. The dielectric constants of concrete, mortar, masonry, void and rebar in Fig. 2 are $\varepsilon_{concrete} = 7.6$, $\varepsilon_{mortar} = 6.5$, $\varepsilon_{masonry} = 5.4$, $\varepsilon_{void} = 1.0$, $\varepsilon_{rebar} = 1.0$ and the conductivity of concrete, mortar, masonry, void and rebar are $\sigma_{concrete} = \sigma_{mortar} = \sigma_{masonry}\, 0.1\ (S/m)$, $\sigma_{void} = 0.0\ (S/m)$ and $\sigma_{rebar} = 10^7\ (S/m)$ respectively.

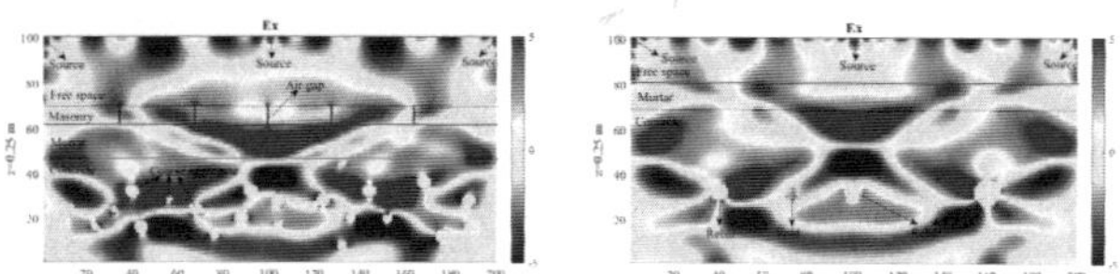

(a) (b)

Fig. 3. Simulation result for E_x at 1.5 GHz frequency: a- Case A, b- Case B

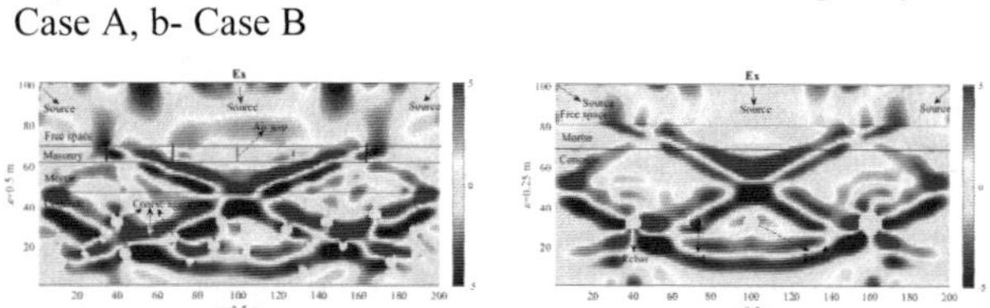

(a) (b)

Fig. 4. Simulation result for E_x at 3.0 GHz frequency: a- Case A, b- Case B

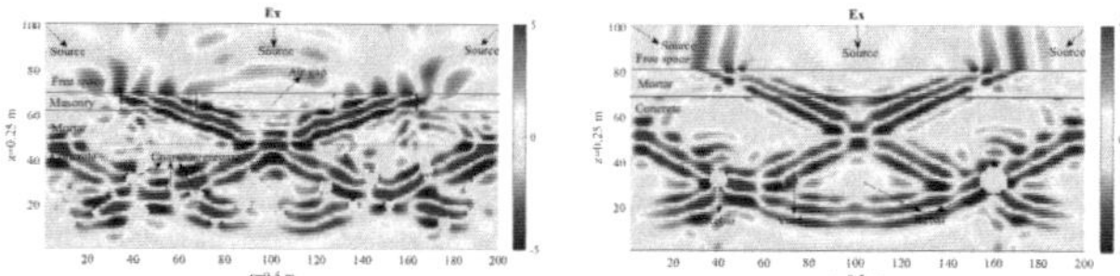

(a) (b)

Fig. 5. Simulation result for E_x at 6.0 GHz frequency: a- Case A, b- Case B

In Fig. 3 (a)-(b) E_x field distributions at 1.5 GHz for Case A and Case B are obtained, the layers of masonry, mortar and concrete can be seen clearly and even air gaps between masonries and coarse aggregates in Case A can be seen. In Fig. 3 (b) rebars and void can be seen transparently. In Fig. 4 (a) even though the coarse aggregates are visible, the layers are almost indistinguishable so 1.5 GHz frequency is more suitable for material characterizatin than 3.0 GHz and in Fig. 4 (b) everything is seen seamlessly. In Fig. 5 (a) layers are no longer fully distinguishable but aggregates are slightly visible. In Fig. 5 (b) the mortar layer is completely blurred but the rebars remains clearly visible and thickness differences between them can be observed in all results. At all frequencies that numerical models are simulated the rebar can be clearly but higher frequency namely at 6.0 GHz rebar is more clear.

IV. CONCLUSIONS

The two different examples of civil engineering studies are designed as a numerical simulation experiment. The capability of the FDTD method for simulation of the three-layered model containing air gap and coarse aggregates and two layered media that contain rebar are investigated. The layers of the numerical model, coarse aggregate, air gap, rebar and void inside the concrete and the rebar inside it are successfully viewed. Also, rebar in the reinforced concrete is observed in such a way that the thickness of the rebar is noticeable, and the best simulation result is obtained at 1.5 GHz frequency for microwave radar NDT technique.

REFERENCES

[1] K. J. Bois, A. D. Benally, R. Zoughi, "Microwave near-field reflection property analysis of concrete for material content determination," IEEE Transactions on Instrumentation and measurement, 49(1), 49-55, 2000.

[2] W. Wei, Z. Shao, Y. Zhang, R. Qiao, J. Gao, "Fundamentals and Applications of Microwave Energy in Rock and Concrete Processing-A Review," Applied Thermal Engineering, 113751, 2019.

[3] K. Yee, "Numerical solution of initial boundary value problems involving Maxwell's equations in isotropic media," IEEE Transactions on Antennas and Propagation, 14(3), 302-307, 1966.

[4] A. Taflove, S. C. Hagness, "Computational Electrodynamics: The Finite-Difference Time-Domain Method," Artech house, 2005.

[5] J. P. Berenger, "A perfectly matched layer for the absorption of electromagnetic waves," Journal of computational physics, 114(2), 185-20,1994

IMPATT Efficiency Extraction Using On-Chip Antenna Radiation

Talal Al-Attar
Computer, Electrical and Mathematical Science & Engineering Division
King Abdullah University of Science and Technology, Thuwal, Saudi Arabia
Talal.Attar@kaust.edu.sa

Abstract— **IMPATT diodes were designed and integrated with microstrip patch antenna on–chip in standard CMOS technology to extract the efficiency beyond avalanche frequency. By comparing the on-chip simulations and measurements of an IMPATT diode integrated in a CPW to an integrated one with a microstrip patch antenna at the same biasing conditions, the results demonstrated an efficiency ranging from ~ 0.01% to 0.016% without and with the added surface roughness losses, respectively. Such variation is strongly associated with the uncertainty provided by the increase of conduction losses ranging between 40%~80% beyond the avalanche frequency.**

Keywords— ***avalanche frequency, coplanar waveguide, high frequency, IMPATT diode, microstrip patch antenna, skin depth, surface roughness, transmission line.***

I. Introduction

The demand for precise and robust on-chip efficiency measurements of (Impact Avalanche Transit Time) IMPATT diodes is increasing due to the recent developments in IMPATT-Antenna integration for monolithic millimeter-wave applications in standard CMOS technology [1]. This accuracy affects the design and the optimization of the oscillation frequency and the radiated power.

IMPATT diode is a solid state device that converts the DC power into RF one by generating negative resistance beyond avalanche frequency [2-3]. CMOS IMPATT diodes demonstrated the capabilities of generating avalanche frequency beyond 30 GHz and negative resistance up to 80GHz [1-5]. The generation of the negative resistance and the capacitive reactive part at frequencies beyond the avalanche frequency is affected by controlling the breakdown voltage and the operating current [1-5].

In this paper, we demonstrate a robust on-chip integration and extraction methodology for the IMPATT diode efficiency beyond avalanche frequency.

II. The Antenna Integration

The on-chip lateral IMPATT diodes have been monolithically integrated with microstrip patch antenna in standard CMOS technology and successfully de-embedded and characterized [1]. With such configuration, the antenna can serve as a resonator and radiator simultaneously.

Using a patch antenna driven by a lateral IMPATT diode, the 4 mm^2 transmitter was DC biased at 11V with measured current of 30mA (Fig. 1). The modeled antenna with different levels of generated and radiated power is shown in Fig. 2, while the measured power at the spectrum analyzer is -62dBm at 77GHz (Fig. 3). By using this particular configuration, area requirements and several antenna losses including dielectric, conduction [6], radiation, surface wave and surface roughness losses [7] of the integrated transmitter are reduced.

III. Results and Discussion

The test setup includes an Anritsu ME7220A Radar Test System (RTS), WR12 E-band horn Antenna, and MS2663C 9K-8.1GHz spectrum analyzer (Fig. 3). The frequency band of the transmitter is initially down-converted by the RTS from 76-77GHz to an IF band of 4.7-5.7GHz before the radiated signal is characterized [1].

Initially, the supply is maintained at zero volts, and slowly increased (to avoid any surges), up to the operating voltage of the diode. At the nominal breakdown voltage of ~10V, a current of 2mA flows. As the supply voltage is gradually increased, the current drawn by the circuit also increases. When the on-chip transmitter is biased at 11V, the corresponding quiescent current is 30mA, and a signal is detected with an oscillation frequency of 77GHz, as shown in Fig. 3.

The Sonnet simulated results for the Directivity and the Gain of the patch antenna are 11dB and -23dB, respectively (Fig. 4). Once the surface roughness factor is included the Gain drops to -26dB. This indicates that the total losses of the antenna are 34dB and 37dB without and with the surface roughness impact, respectively. More simulated results are summarized in Table I for different dielectric thickness. It is clear that the dielectric thickness, is our main contributor to the low radiated power and the large simulated losses.

Based on the measured radiated power, the system losses, and the shift of the avalanche frequency [6-8], the calculated diode efficiency ranges between – 38dB to -41dB. This low efficiency is largely a result of the high capacitive loading from the depletion region [9]. Table II summarizes the generated and the radiated power at different stages.

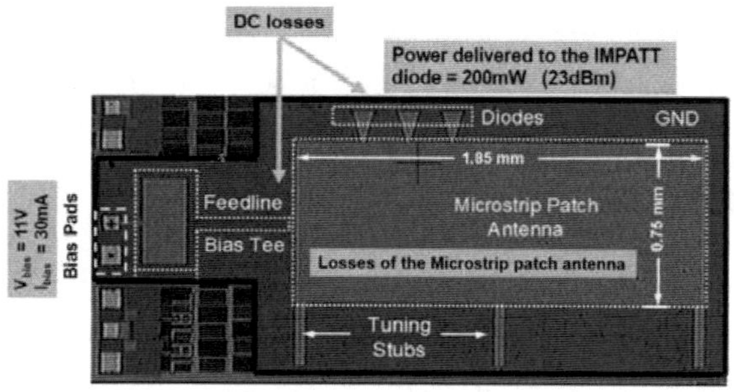

Fig. 1. Die photo of integrated IMPATT diode with microstrip patch antenna on-chip [1].

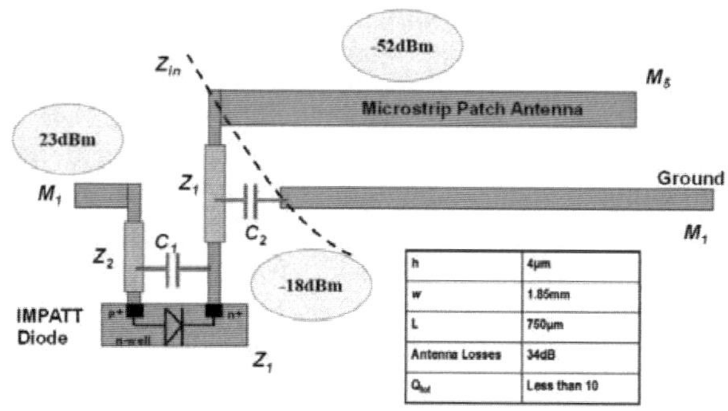

Fig. 2. The modeled antenna with the different power levels (the case with excluded surface roughness [7]).

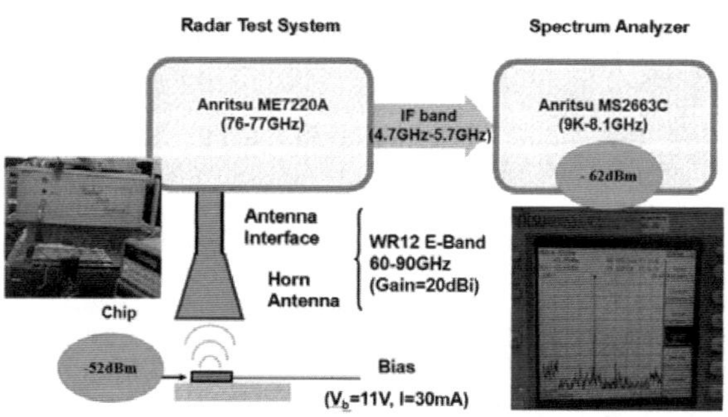

Fig. 3. Measurement setup, which includes Anritsu ME7220A Radar Test System (RTS), WR12 E-band horn Antenna, and Anritsu MS2663C 9K-8.1GHz spectrum analyzer.

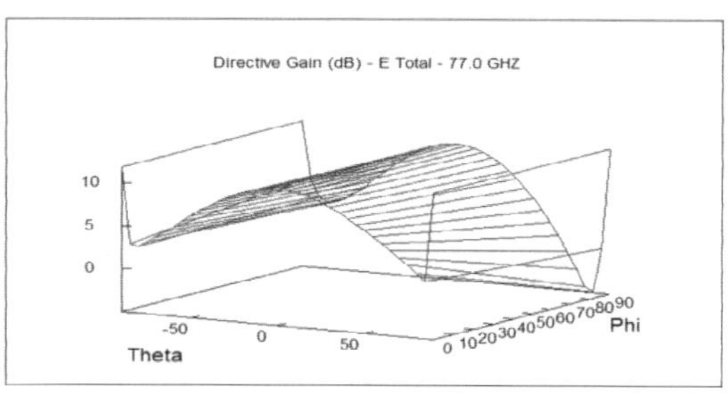

Fig. 4. The simulated directive gain of the CMOS microstrip patch antenna using Sonnet.

Table I: Simulated losses of on-chip antenna with different dielctric thickness (exluding the surface roughness) [7]

Dielectric Thickness (h) (μm)	Total Losses (dB)
100	8
30	14
10	20
4	34

Table II: Power measured at different levels with extracted IMPATT effeciency.

DC power delivered to the transmitter	330mW (25dBm)
DC losses including:	2dB
Power delivered to the IMPATT diode	200mW (23dBm)
Losses of the Microstrip patch antenna: (Without Surface Roughness) (With Surface Roughness)	34dB 37dB
Losses of the measurement setup (from the horn antenna to the spectrum analyzer)	10dB
Calculated power generated by the diode (Without Surface Roughness) (With Surface Roughness)	-18dBm -15dBm
Extracted diode efficiency (First lateral IMPATT efficiency 0.03% (-35dB) [9]) (Without Surface Roughness) (With Surface Roughness)	-41dB (0.01%) -38dB (0.016%)

IV. Conclusion

The realized integration of IMPATT diodes and on-chip microstrip patch antenna demonstrated considerable changes in the extracted IMPATT efficiency beyond avalanche frequency. This paper revealed the robustness of the methodology proposed despite the present impact of the surface roughness on the IMPATT efficiency. Based on the measured radiated power and the system losses, the extracted diode efficiency is ranging between -41dB to -38dB without and with the surface roughness, respectively. Because of the cost-efficiency and the robustness of standard CMOS manufacturing, this type of monolithic integrated transmitter may be well suited for use in IMPATT diode efficiency extraction beyond avalanche frequency.

References

[1] T. Al-Attar and T. H. Lee, "Monolithic integrated millimeter-wave IMPATT transmitter in standard CMOS technology," IEEE Transactions on Microwave Theory and Techniques, vol. 53, pp. 3557-3561, 2005.

[2] W. T. Read Jr. "A proposed high-frequency negativeresistance diode," Bell Syst. Tech. J., vol. 37, pp. 401- 446, Mar. 1958.

[3] T. Al-Attar, M. D. Mulligan, and T. H. Lee, "Lateral IMPATT Diodes in Standard CMOS Technology," IEEE International Electron Devices Meeting, IEDM, Dec., 2004.

[4] T. Al-Attar, "CMOS diodes operating beyond avalanche frequency," 12th International Symposium on Quality Electronic Design, pp. 1-6, 2011.

[5] M. C. A. M. Koolen, J. A. M. Geelen, and M. P. J. G. Versleijen, "An Improved De-embedding Technique for On-wafer High Frequency Characterization," Proceedings of the Bipolar Circuits and Technology Meeting, pp. 188-191, 1991.

[6] T. Al-Attar, A. Alshehri, A. Almansouri, and A. Alturki, "Critical parameters affecting the design of high frequency transmission lines in standard CMOS technology," Applied Computational Electromagnetics Society Symposium-Italy (ACES), pp. 1-2, Mar. 2017.

[7] T. Al-Attar, "The Impact of Surface Roughness on Avalanche Frequency," Applied Computational Electromagnetics Society Symposium (ACES), Apr. 2019.

[8] W. Zhang, E. Kasper, and J. Schulze, "An 82-GHz 14.6-mW Output Power Silicon Impact Ionization Avalanche Transit Time Transmitter With Monolithically Integrated Coplanar Waveguide Patch Antenna," IEEE Transactions on Microwave Theory and Techniques, vol. 67, no. 1, 2019.

[9] P. J. Stabile and B. Lalevic, "Lateral IMPATT Diodes," IEEE Electron Devices Letters, vol. 10, no. 6, June 1989.

New Features in Feko / WinProp 2019

Marlize Schoeman, Renier Marchand, and Johann van Tonder
Altair Development S.A. (Pty) Ltd
Stellenbosch, South Africa
schoeman@altair.co.za, rmarchand@altair.co.za, jvtonder@altair.co.za

Ulrich Jakobus and Andrés Aguilar
Altair Engineering GmbH
Böblingen, Germany
jakobus@altair.de, aguilar@altair.de

Taha Alwajeeh
Altair Engineering France
Meylan, France
talwajeeh@altair.com

Kitty Longtin and Martin Vogel
Altair Engineering, Inc.
Hampton, VA, USA
klongtin@altair.com, mvogel@altair.com

***Abstract*—This paper describes some of the latest features in the commercial electromagnetic software Feko (including WinProp). These include the modeling of non-ideal cable shield connections, the parallel direct adaptive cross approximation (ACA) solver, edge and wedge diffraction for the ray launching geometrical optics (RL-GO) solver, and several new features related to automotive radar.**

***Keywords*—adaptive cross approximation, automotive radar, cable shield connections, diffraction, Feko, RL-GO, WinProp.**

I. Introduction

Altair Feko [1] is a popular computational electromagnetics code widely used for academic research and commercial applications. Due to continuous improvements and extensions, it remains an industry leader in this field. This paper highlights some of the recent extensions made in the 2019 release.

II. Modeling of Non-Ideal Cable Shield Connections

Earlier, the Feko team developed the combined MoM/MTL method [2] as a solution approach to modeling shielded cable harnesses that do not run near a conducting installation surface. By using the method of moments (MoM) to model the outside of the harness within its environment, the frequency or so-called height limitation of the multiconductor transmission line (MTL) formulation can be relaxed.

The combined MoM/MTL method relies on the assumption that the exterior (structure and shield) and interior (cable bundle) problems only couple weakly through the shield transfer impedance, thereby limiting terminating connectors to be included as ideal in the model. In practice, however, not all connectors are manufactured with such high quality and coupling of currents and voltages through imperfect connectors should be considered.

Two new circuit components (a transformer and a voltage-controlled voltage source) were introduced to include connector leakage as a one- or bi-directional coupling effect in the model. In Fig. 1 an RG217 coaxial cable with double shield was modeled to illustrate the change in shielding effectiveness due to the inclusion of coupling effects (ideal versus non-ideal connection) at the harness terminations.

The harness was also modeled with an additional 50 mm pigtail at each connector to illustrate how the combined MoM/MTL method (different to the MTL) would take the additional line length (resulting in a downward resonant frequency shift) of the pigtail connections at the terminations into account.

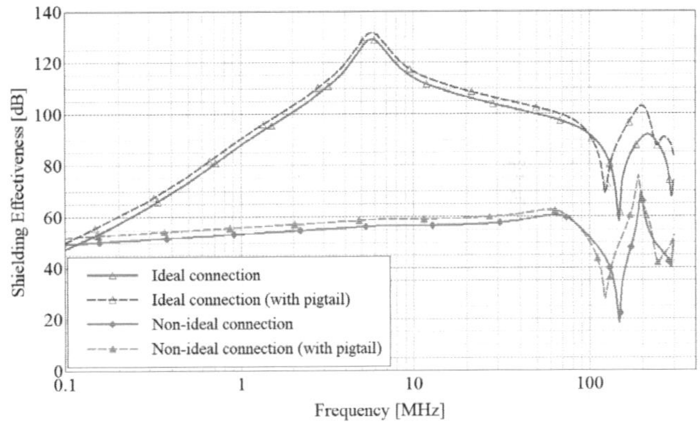

Fig. 1. Shielding effectiveness of an RG217 coaxial cable illustrating the effect of different terminal connections.

III. Parallel Direct ACA Solver

The adaptive cross approximation (ACA) available in Feko is a well-known technique for approximating a large dense matrix, like the MoM matrix, as the product of two much smaller matrices, saving memory and computational time. In a previous paper we have discussed the direct ACA solver [3]. This solver, however, is highly recursive due to the tree-like structure of the ACA matrix representation and is therefore not straightforward to parallelize.

We have extended the direct ACA solver to run in parallel in shared memory environments. This was accomplished by traversing the sequence of operations in the direct ACA solver and, rather than executing the operations, recording the basic operations on the leaves of the ACA tree one by one in a list of tasks to be executed later. These tasks can then be sent to multiple threads for execution.

Some tasks depend on the results of other tasks and cannot be executed until the tasks on which they depend are executed. As the number of threads increases the efficiency of the parallel calculation may suffer due to this dependency tree.

Fig. 2 shows some initial efficiency results for a sample Feko ACA calculation with 27464 unknowns. Using 8 threads the efficiency is still high at 89%.

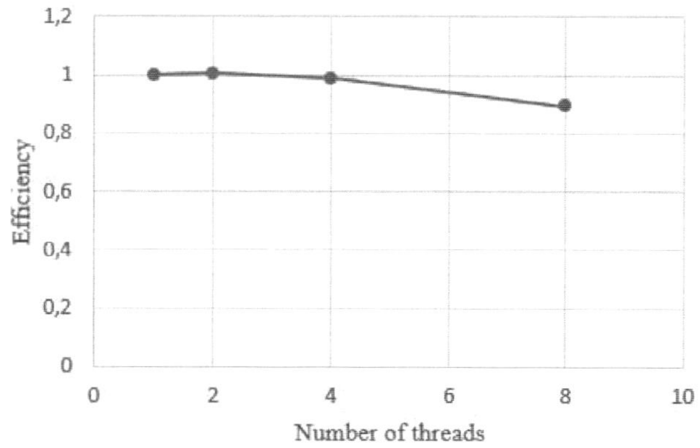

Fig. 2. ACA parallel efficiency versus the number of threads.

IV. RL-GO Edge and Wedge Diffraction

The RL-GO solver in Feko calculates high frequency specular reflection effects using a shooting-and-bouncing ray (SBR) type algorithm. Edge and wedge diffraction are often dominant in objects such as fins on aircraft. The calculation of these edge and wedge effects following [4] has recently been added to our existing RL-GO high frequency approximation.

Fig. 3 demonstrates the importance of edge diffraction for a simple canonical plate. High frequency results agree much better with the full wave multilevel-fast-multipole-method (MLFMM) results, especially when the plate is illuminated from an edge on direction. Improvements to results for general structures with dominant edge and wedge reflections are evident.

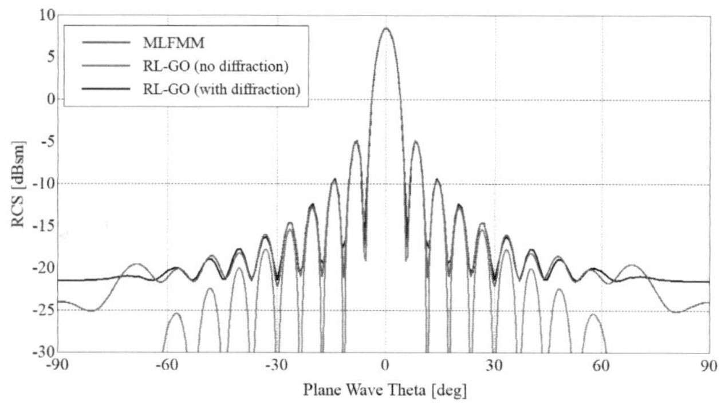

Fig. 3. Full wave MLFMM versus RL-GO results comparing the monostatic RCS (HH Polarization) of a 15cm x 15cm square plate at 10 GHz.

V. Automotive Radar

WinProp is the simulation tool bundled with Feko for electromagnetic propagation and wireless network planning, including 5G. Its computational methods range from empirical via proprietary semi-empirical to rigorous uniform theory of diffraction (UTD). One recent new WinProp application is automotive radar. For this, several new features have been added such as the ability to have both the transmitting and the receiving antenna moving with a car in a time-variant simulation, as well as the output of Doppler shift.

The analysis of the traffic scenario in Fig. 4 with UTD brings a challenge: the trade-off of accuracy and simulation time. The (simplified) car models consist of flat panels. An analysis with UTD includes specular reflections, diffuse scattering around the reflections, and edge diffractions. The simulation frequency is typically 77 GHz. At this high frequency, specular reflections rarely hit the receiver, while edge diffractions, which have a 1/sqrt(f) dependence, will under-estimate the received signal. The remaining contribution, diffuse scattering, depends on an un-scientific parameter set by the user.

The solution is to enhance the car models in WinProp by monostatic radar cross section (RCS) information determined with one of the full wave or asymptotic solvers in Feko. Feko can easily determine the RCS of a much more detailed car model and export it to WinProp. WinProp will then know, for every ray that hits the (possibly even more-simplified) car model, what the contribution will be to the signal received by the radar. The monostatic RCS is, for every snapshot in time, corrected for the finite distance. With this new approach, the simulation of automotive radar in WinProp gains both accuracy and speed.

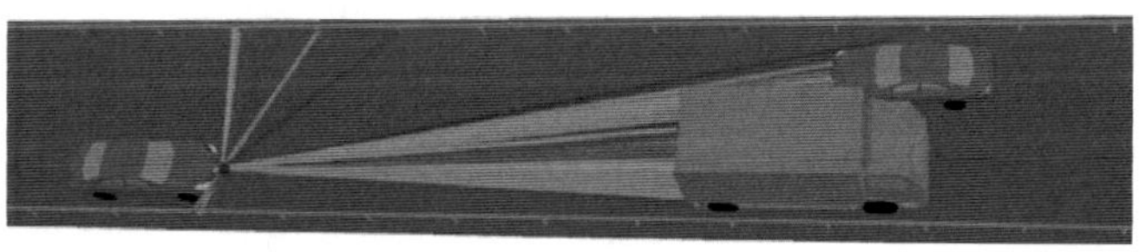

Fig. 4. Automotive radar simulation with traffic.

References

[1] Altair Feko, Altair Engineering, Inc., www.altairhyperworks.com/feko

[2] M. Schoeman and U. Jakobus, "Numerical solution of complex EMC problems involving cables with combined field / transmission line approach," Interference Technology, EMC Directory & Design Guide, pp. 78-88, 2011.

[3] U. Jakobus, A. Aguilar, E. Attardo, M. Schoeman, J. van Tonder, and K. Longtin, "Review of selected new features in Feko 2018," International Applied Computational Electromagnetics Society Symposium, 25-29 March 2018.

[4] P. M. Johansen "Uniform physical theory of diffraction equivalent edge currents for truncated wedge strips," IEEE Transactions on Antennas and Propagation, vol. 44, no. 7, July 1996.

FEKO™ Simulation of Radar Scattering from Objects in Low Earth Orbit for ISAR Imaging

Aaron Brandewie and Robert J. Burkholder
The Ohio State University ElectroScience Lab
Dept. of Electrical and Computer Engineering
Columbus, OH U. S. A.
burkholder.1@osu.edu

Abstract—**Objects in low earth orbit such as CubeSats and the International Space Station (ISS) move with constant velocity along a linear trajectory when viewed from a ground-based radar. The small change in attitude of the object as it flies overhead permits the generation of an inverse synthetic aperture radar (ISAR) image. In this paper, Altair's FEKO™ software is used to model the monostatic radar scattering from the ISS as a function of frequency and aspect angle. The computed data is used for generating a simulated ISAR image from a ground-based radar. The system design requirements for the radar are calculated from the radar equation.**

Keywords—electromagnetic scattering, inverse synthetic aperture radar, physical optics, radar imaging.

I. Introduction

Quantification of the radar cross-section (RCS) of objects in low earth orbit (LEO) is needed for the design of ground-based radars that can detect, track and image these objects [1]. Keeping track of LEO objects is becoming especially challenging with the proliferation of CubeSats, not to mention the growing presence of space junk [2]. Historically, large dedicated ground-based radars have been used to track orbital objects, including the Goldstone radars, Haystack radars, and the USAF Space Surveillance Network [3]. These aging systems are in need of upgrade or replacement by new systems such as the IoSiS (Imaging of Satellites in Space) under development at the Microwaves and Radar Institute of German Aerospace Center [4], for example.

Objects in low earth orbit (LEO) follow linear trajectories with constant velocity with respect to a fixed ground-based radar staring up into space, as illustrated in Fig. 1. As the object flies overhead through the field of view of the radar, its attitude changes. This small rotation relative to the ground radar permits the generation of an inverse synthetic aperture radar (ISAR) image [5]. This is demonstrated here by simulation of the International Space Station (ISS) modeled in FEKO™ for a UHF radar system. Results for CubeSats will be presented at the conference for higher frequency bands.

Section II describes the FEKO™ model of the ISS and shows the simulated image of the ISS generated from FEKO™ data. Section III investigates the requirements for the ground-based radar using the radar equation. Section IV discusses conclusions and additional work that will be presented at the conference.

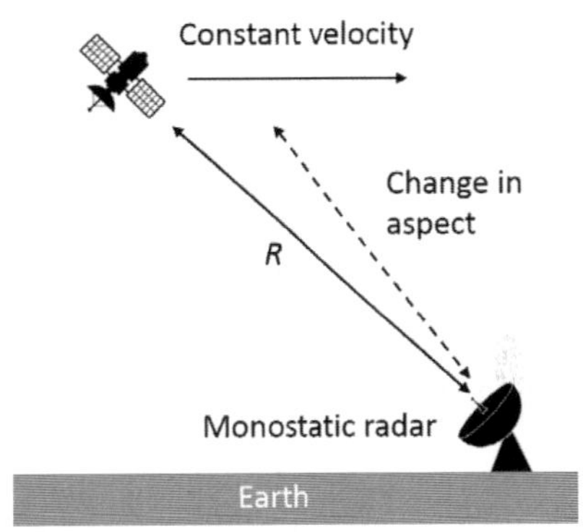

Fig. 1. Ground-based radar tracking a LEO object flying overhead. The change in aspect allows an ISAR image to be generated.

II. FEKO™ Model of the ISS

Fig. 2 (a) shows a graphic of the ISS and Fig. 2 (b) shows the FEKO model used here. There have been many variations and modules associated with the ISS over the years, so a basic configuration was chosen to capture the dominant scattering features. The overall dimensions are roughly 108 m x 73 m.

Due to its large size, a UHF radar should be able to easily track and image the ISS. A frequency band of 500-560 MHz with 121 points is chosen for the simulations. Monostatic scattering data is generated over azimuth angles 60° to 70° with 41 points. The downrange resolution is 2.5 m, and the cross-range resolution is 1.6 m for the 10° aspect range. The elevation angle is 10° with respect to the *x-y* plane. The scattered field is computed using large element physical optics with full ray tracing in the FEKO solver. The total computation time was about 1 minute on a laptop computer.

Fig. 2 (c) shows the ISAR image of the ISS computed using back-projection of the backscatter data with a Hamming window over both frequency and angle [5]. The image is projected into the *x-y* plane from the 10° slant plane. The dominant features are clear in the image, although the large flat surfaces of the solar panels are not seen because the aspect is far from broadside. The average RCS is around 10 dBsm over this range of aspects.

(a) www.gettyimages.com

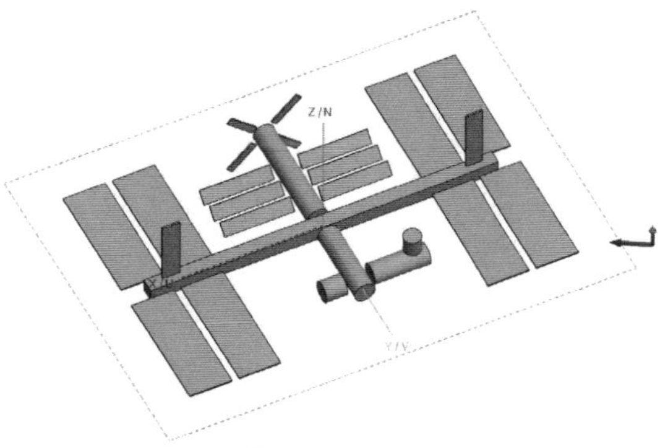

(b) FEKO™ model

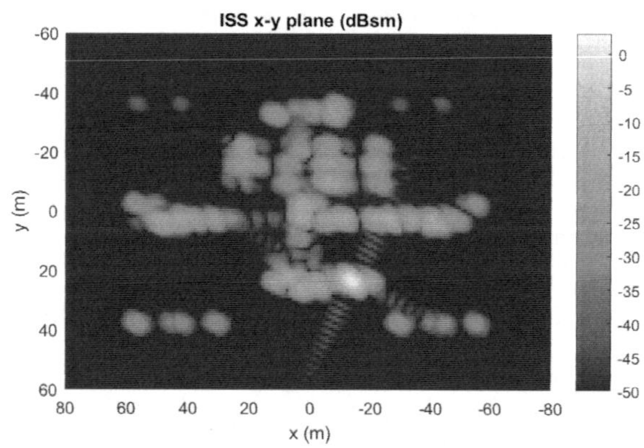

(c) ISAR image

Fig. 2. International Space Station (ISS). (a) ISS in orbit. (b) FEKO model. (c) UHF ISAR image projected in the *x-y* plane seen from an elevation slant plane of 10° (dBsm). A 10° azimuth window is used to generate the image.

III. Radar System Requirements

To understand the trade-offs involved with the design of a ground-based radar for tracking LEO objects, we begin with the monostatic radar equation [1]. Neglecting atmospheric attenuation, the received power is given by,

$$P_r = \frac{P_t G^2 \lambda^2 \sigma}{(4\pi)^3 R^4}, \quad (1)$$

where P_t is the transmitted power, G is the gain of the antenna, λ is the wavelength, σ is the RCS, and R is the distance. The ISS orbits at approximately 400 km, and the RCS is conservatively 10 dBsm away from broadside according to the FEKO simulation. The noise power of the receiver at room temperature for our 60 MHz bandwidth is -126 dB. For a signal-to-noise ratio of at least 10 dB we require $P_r > -116$ dB. Using (1) we find that $P_t G^2 > 136$ dB. This is achievable with a 40 dB antenna and 0.5 MW transmitted power. However, a UHF antenna with 40 dB gain is very large and 0.5 MW radiated power is challenging to obtain. The presentation will discuss ways to greatly reduce this requirement by taking advantage of the constant velocity of LEO objects, enabling long integration times.

IV. Conclusions

It has been demonstrated through FEKO simulation that ISAR imaging of LEO objects is possible using a ground-based radar. Specifically, the ISS was simulated for a UHF radar, and the radar equation was invoked to calculate the ground-based antenna and power requirements. The presentation will demonstrate imaging of much smaller CubeSats using a higher frequency band. It will be shown how a more modest ground-based radar system may be designed that trades off power and antenna gain for a larger time-bandwidth product.

References

[1] M. I. Skolnik, Introduction to Radar Systems, 3rd Edition, McGraw Hill, Boston, 2001.

[2] NASA Orbital Debris Program Office, https://orbitaldebris.jsc.nasa.gov/

[3] https://orbitaldebris.jsc.nasa.gov/measurements/

[4] S. Anger, M. Jirousek, S. Dill, and M. Peichl, "IoSiS – A high performance experimental imaging radar for space surveillance," 2019 IEEE Radar Conference, April 22-26, Boston, MA.

[5] D. Mensa, High Resolution Radar Imaging, 3rd ed., vol. 2. Oxford: Clarendon, 1892, pp. 68–73.

Open-Source Antenna Pattern Validation using FEKO

Christian W. Hearn
Deparment of Electrical and Computer Engineering
Weber State University
Ogden, UT - USA
christianhearn@weber.edu

***Abstract*— An open-source antenna pattern measurement system comprised of software-defined radios (SDRs), standard PVC tubing, and 3-D printer components measures the radiation patterns of student-built prototype antennas. Position control is realized using an Arduino microcontroller. Measured principal plane gain patterns for two antenna prototypes are compared to (FEKO) simulated results. The low-cost, open-source nature of the measurement system is ideal for undergraduate-level investigation of antenna theory and measurement.**

Keywords*—*Antenna measurements, antenna radiation patterns, microcontrollers, software-defined radios.

I. Description of System

An antenna pattern measurement system developed at Weber State University (WSU) was inspired by the published work of Picco and Martin [1]. Their practical system utilized commercially-available 2.4 GHz Wi-Fi routers to transmit and receive a single-frequency wireless signal. Open-source firmware accessed the received signal strength indicator (RSSI). Antenna position control, RF signal measurement, and write-to-file functions were realized using National Instruments LabVIEW.

The WSU prototype shown in Fig. 1 utilizes two GNU Radio Companion driven software-defined radios (SDRs) for the link between the source antenna and antenna-under-test (AUT). The AUT position control is achieved using an Arduino microcontroller with open-source software (GRBL) developed for 3-D printer systems. Low-cost, commercially-available three-dimensional printer hardware (e.g., gears, synchronous belts) and software are utilized for position-control.

Fig. 1. Principal plane pattern measurement setup for the Yagi-Uda prototype.

II. Antenna Pattern Validation

Complete developments of pattern, directivity, and gain discussed are available in numerous texts. Two popular examples include [2] and [3]. An approximation of the gain from the measured pattern of a lossless antenna may be determined by scaling the measured data to a calculated gain. FEKO is used to model the prototype and calculated maximum gain values. Comparisons of measured pattern data are straightforward once the measured pattern data is normalized and scaled to the maximum calculated gain. The method described is limited to a qualitative check, but it is a highly relevant demonstration of validation in an educational setting.

It is anticipated the majority of future student-built prototypes will be designed for Wi-Fi band ($f \approx 2.4\ GHz$) with a free-space wavelength of approximately $\lambda \approx 12.5cm$. Prototypes of three Wi-Fi band antennas were constructed to evaluate an antenna design and development process for undergraduate students. Comparisons of measured versus theoretical results are shown for the quarter-wave monopole and Yagi prototypes.

A. *Quarter-Wave Monopole on Finite Ground Plane*

A monopole above a $D=1\lambda$ ground plane shown in Fig. 2 was simulated for comparison to a physical prototype. Fig. 3 is a principal plane pattern comparison for one monopole prototype. The symmetry and close agreement above the ground plane are evident. Some deformation on the right-side behind the ground plane is due to the presence of the antenna feed.

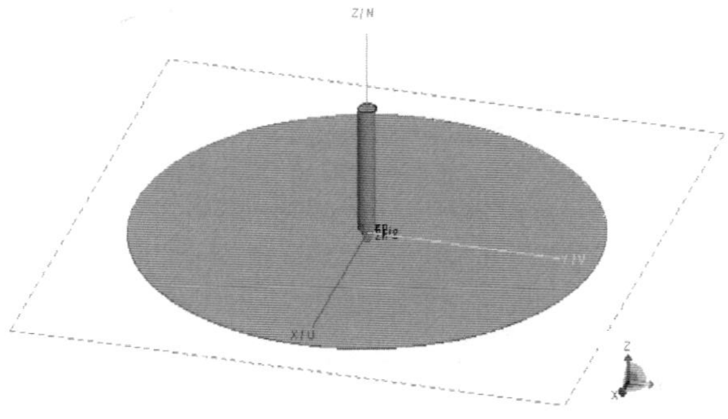

Fig. 2. CAD rendering of quarter-wave monopole prototype over finite ground plane.

Utah NASA Space Grant Consortium.

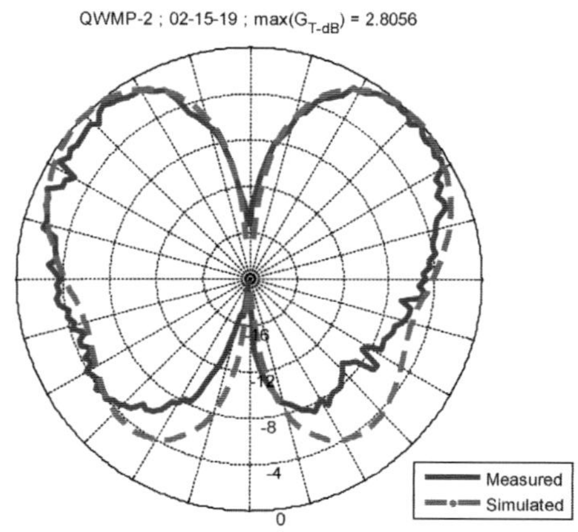

Fig. 3. Measured versus simulated results for principal plane pattern of λ/4 monopole over finite ground plane.

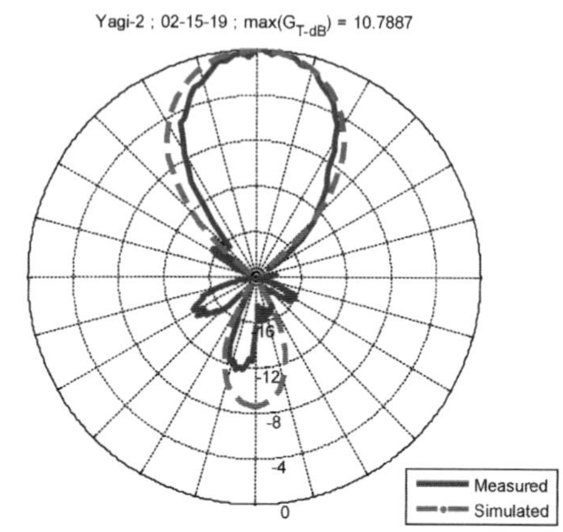

Fig. 5. Measured versus simulated results for principal plane pattern of the Yagi antenna prototype.

B. *Yagi Antenna*

Fig. 4 is a CAD rendering of the Yagi-Uda antenna model generated for comparison to constructed prototypes. Fig. 5 plots the scaled measured pattern to the simulated pattern. Front lobe agreement was observed for both prototypes. Feed interference seen previously with the monopole is also apparent with the Yagi-Uda measured pattern. Sidelobe levels behind boresight are 10 dB below the main beam levels and may be investigated when additional absorber is available.

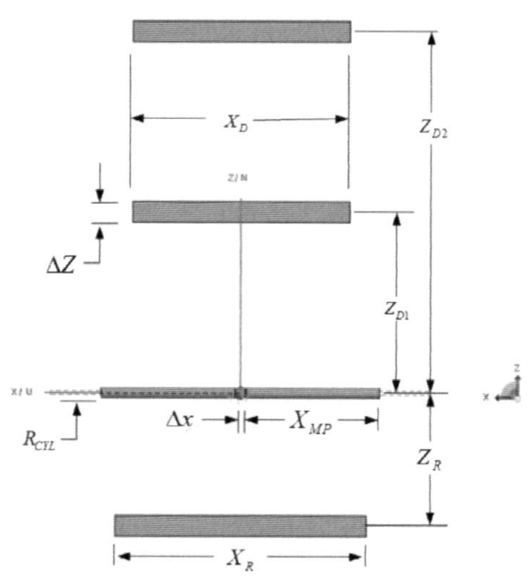

Fig. 4. CAD rendering of Yagi-Uda prototype.

III. Conclusions and Future Work

An antenna pattern measurement system based upon the Picco and Martin concept was modified to incorporate software-defined radios and commercially-available 3-D printer hardware. Examples of commercially-available hardware include low-cost synchronous gears and matching belts. Additional components were constructed using 3-D printer technology. Examples include both the base and head connecting the PVC mast to the azimuth and elevation synchronous gears.

Comparisons of simulated and measured gain patterns for the two antenna prototypes shown indicate the measurement system will be a valuable resource for laboratory exercises and student projects.

The current measurement system employs a 'noise subtraction' method at each sample point. An ambient noise measurement is taken before the transmitter signal is applied. A second receiver measurement of the transmitted signal plus noise is recorded. At each position, the ambient noise signal is subtracted from the transmitted signal measurement to obtain a pattern signal amplitude.

Future research with the pattern measurement system will incorporate modulation methods with noise-mitigation characteristics. Open-source SDRs permit the investigation of cellular phone signal processing techniques developed to mitigate noise, multipath and fading. Examples include analog Frequency Modulation and digital Binary-Phase Shift Key modulation to potentially improve pattern measurements made in non-anechoic environments. Narrow and Wide Band noise interferers will be introduced to evaluate measurement fidelity for different modulation techniques.

References

[1] V. Picco and K. Martin, "An automated antenna measurement system utilizing Wi-Fi hardware," IEEE A&P Magazine, vol. 53, Dec. 2011, pp 179-183.

[2] W. L. Stutzman and G.A. Thiele, Antenna Theory and Design, 2nd ed., Wiley & Sons, 1998.

[3] C. A. Balanis, Antenna Theory-Analysis and Design, 2nd ed., Wiley & Sons, 1997.

Fast and Intelligent Antenna Design Optimization using Machine Learning

Gopinath Gampala
Altair Engineering, Inc.
Phoenix, AZ, USA
gopi@altair.com

C. J. Reddy
Altair Engineering, Inc.
Hampton, VA, USA
cjreddy@altair.com

***Abstract*—Traditional antenna optimization solves the modified version of the original antenna design for each iteration. Thus, the total time required to optimize a given antenna design is highly dependent on the convergence criteria of the selected algorithm and the time taken for each iteration. The use of machine learning enables the antenna designer to generate trained mathematical model that replicates the original antenna design and then apply optimization on the trained model. Use of trained model allows to run thousands of optimization iterations in a span of a few seconds.**

Keywords—antenna optimization, design of experiments, machine learning, regression.

I. Introduction

In recent times, industries working with large amount of data have recognized the value of machine learning (ML) technology. Thus, it is widely used in financial services to prevent fraud, in health care to assess a patient's health in real time, in oil and gas to find new energy sources, in government services to minimize identity theft, in retail industry to personalize shopping experience, in transportation to make routes more efficient, and many more such applications. However, machine learning has not gained much attention in computer aided antenna design. With the advent of clever design exploration methods such as space filling Design of Experiments (DOE) approaches, machine learning can be used to speed up the antenna design optimization process tremendously. In addition, machine learning can also accelerate other related simulations such as tolerance studies using stochastic methods.

This paper presents how to use DOE and machine learning for fast and intelligent antenna design optimization with an example. Trained Mathematical model is generated using the multi-disciplinary design exploration and optimization software Altair HyperStudy [1] and numerical electromagnetic field simulations are done with Altair Feko [2].

II. Machine Learning

Machine learning is a method of data analysis that automates analytical model building. The machine learning algorithms on a broader scale can be classified into *unsupervised learning* and *supervised learning*.

A. Unsupervised Learning

To understand unsupervised learning, one should first understand what a dataset is: a collection of examples without a specific desired outcome or correct answer – just data. The machine learning algorithm attempts to automatically find structure in the data by extracting useful features and analyzing its structure.

B. Supervised Learning

Supervised learning is best suited to problems where there is a set of available reference points a.k.a. data with labels with which to train the algorithm. The data is generated by extensible sampling or by running simulations in our case of computer-aided antenna design. The two main types of supervised learning are *classification* and *regression*. This paper is focused on the regression method.

Regression models allow us to predict a continuous output variable Y based on the value of one or multiple predictor variables x,

$$Y = f(x_1, x_2, x_3, x_4, x_5, \ldots). \quad (1)$$

The goal of the regression model is to build a trained mathematical model a.k.a. machine learning model that defines Y as a function of the x variables. As such, (1) can be used to predict the outcome Y based on new values of the predictor variables x. Though there are several approaches to build the machine learning model Y, some of the typical methods are Least Square Regression (LSR), Moving Least Square Method (MLSM) and Radial Basis Functions (RBF). Regression methods are extremely useful to speed up the optimization process as the evaluation on the trained machine learning model is tremendously faster than the numerical solution of a physical simulation model. Data required to generate the trained model via regression can done by DOE methods as explained in the next section.

III. Design of Experiments [1]

DOE is a series of tests in which purposeful changes are made to input design variables to investigate their effect on the output responses and to get an understanding of the global behavior of a design problem. There are two types of DOE methods:

A. Screening Methods

These methods are mainly used to determine which input design variables and which variable interactions are most influential on the output responses of a given design. Some examples of the screening methods are, fractional factorial, full factorial, Plackett Burman and Taguchi.

B. Space Filling Methods

These methods can do screening to determine which factors are most influential on the output response and generate data that can be used by a machine learning algorithm to come up with a trained mathematical model that can be used as a surrogate in place of the original design. Box Behnken, Central Composite Design, Hammersley, Latin HyperCube and Modified Extensible Lattice Sequence (MELS) are the examples of some of the space filling methods.

IV. Antenna Optimization Using Machine Learning

Machine learning approaches presented in this paper can be applied to any type of antenna design with any number of design variables. The complete workflow of the machine learning approach for antenna design optimization is detailed in the below steps:

- Generate training and test data with an appropriate DOE study and numerical simulation.
- Build a machine learning model based on the generated training data.
- Validate the machine learning model using the generated test data.
- If the validation is not successful, generate additional training data or use a more appropriate machine learning approach.

A slotted patch antenna designed for the GPS application is chosen to demonstrate the above workflow. Fig. 1 shows the design of the square patch whose initial reflection coefficient is illustrated in Fig. 2. The reflection coefficient data clearly illustrates that the initial design has a resonance around the GPS operating frequency of 1575 MHz, but there is ample scope to improve the matching of this antenna by further optimizing this design.

Fig. 1. Slotted patch antenna designed for GPS applications.

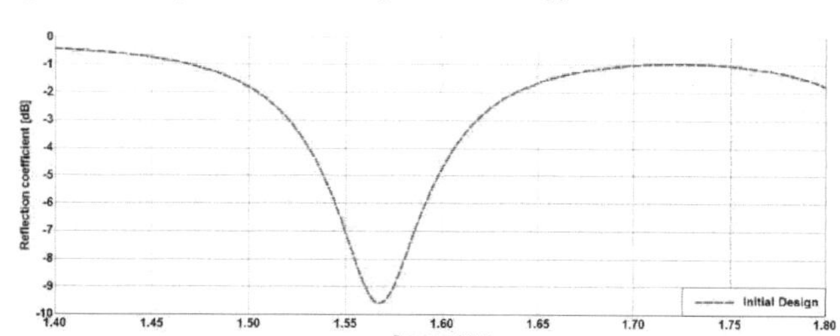

Fig. 2. Reflection coefficient of the initial patch antenna design.

The patch antenna is fully parametric with respect to the patch size, slot length, slot width, slot to edge length and the feed position. To understand the benefits of optimization using machine learning, this approach is compared with the traditional optimization using numerical field simulations. For a fair comparison between the two approaches, the Global Response Search Method (GRSM) optimization algorithm is used in both the optimization approaches. The traditional optimization ran for 250 iterations for a total of 810 seconds.

The first step in the machine learning approach is generating the test data and the space filling MELS method is used for this design exploration. This DOE study will also give a pareto chart illustrating the influence of each design variable on the output response, as shown in Fig. 3.

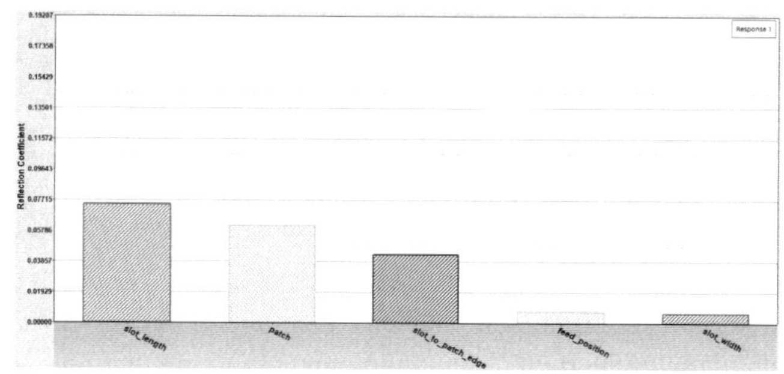

Fig. 3. Pareto chart illstrating the influence of each design variable on the output response.

The test data from the DOE study is then used by the Altair proprietary regression algorithm Fit Automatically Selected by Training (FAST) to generate a trained machine learning model. Optimization is then performed on the trained model rather than using the physical antenna design. Fig. 4 shows the comparison of the optimum reflection coefficient obtained using the traditional optimization and machine learning. The overall time required for the machine learning approach is 168 seconds (as compared to 810 secs) of which a total of 162 seconds is spent in DOE study. This clearly is orders of magnitude faster than traditional optimization.

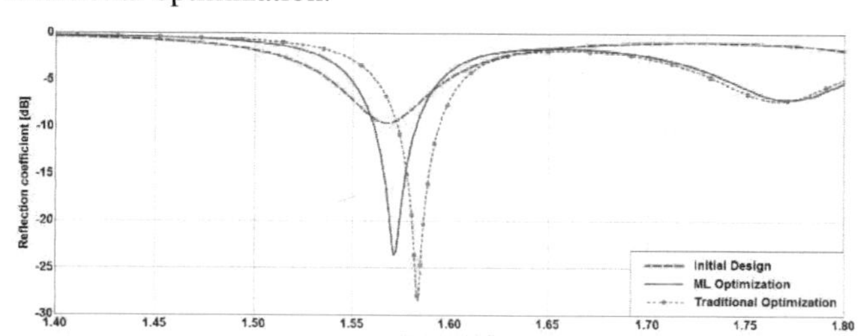

Fig. 4. Comparing the optimum design achieved via machine learning approach to the optimum from traditional optimization.

References

[1] Altair HyperStudy, Altair Engineering, Inc., www.altairhyperworks.com/product/HyperStudy

[2] Altair Feko, Altair Engineering, Inc., www.altairhyperworks.com/product/Feko

Simultaneous Transmit and Receive with Shared-Aperture Arrays

Aman Samaiyar, Dong-Chan Son, Mohamed A. Elmansouri, and Dejan S. Filipovic
Department of Electrical, Computer, and Energy Engineering
University of Colorado, Boulder, CO 80309-0425, USA
{Aman.Samaiyar, Dong-Chan.Son, Mohamed.Elmansouri, Dejan.Filipovic}@Colorado.EDU

***Abstract*—An approach based on shared aperture antenna array is researched for simultaneous transmit and receive (STAR) applications. The proposed configuration is a 10×10 antenna array of circularly-polarized (CP) elements with 50 elements, somewhat sparsely distributed, dedicated for Tx while the remaining elements dedicated for Rx. The high isolation is achieved between Tx and Rx elements at the expense of higher sidelobe levels, which is an inherent property of sparse antenna arrays. To demonstrate the performance of the proposed STAR configuration, numerical modelling is conducted using multilevel fast multipole method (MLFMM) solver in Altair FEKO.**

***Keywords*—Altair FEKO, dual-pol patch antenna, isolation, self-interference, sparse arrays, STAR.**

I. Introduction

The demand-driven modern wireless RF systems are required to maintain high data transfer rates to meet the increasing need for greater bandwidth and larger data streams. Simultaneous transmit and receive (STAR) is an emerging technology that is capable of transmit and receive with a single RF carrier at the same frequency and time, hence doubling the capacity of wireless network. A major challenge with STAR systems is the strong in-band self-interference (SI) at the receiver(s). Depending on the TX power and bandwidth, a Tx/Rx isolation in order of 110–140 dB is required to cancel the detrimental SI [1]. Several recent studies have demonstrated that >50dB of isolation can be achieved at the aperture layer by re-routing the coupled TX signals away from the RX port in beamformer networks (BFN), near-field cancellation, and modes multiplexing to mention few [2]–[3]. However, most of these approaches are not feasible to large planar arrays due to the complexity of the required BFN. In this paper, a simple bistatic shared-aperture approach relying on uniformly distributing and separating the CP Tx/Rx elements within the array (Fig. 1 (a)) is used to realize a conventional STAR array. Redistribution of Tx/Rx elements of the topologically the same aperture (Fig. 1 (b)) is investigated then and utilized to enhance the system isolation. The unique combination of sparsely and symmetrically distributed Tx and Rx coupling coefficients results in better SI cancelation, hence providing high isolation values compared to the baseline case. By controlling the number of elements, their positions and relevant weights in amplitude and phase, it becomes possible to ensure adequate far-field and isolation performances at the aperture level.

This research is supported by the Office of Naval Research (ONR) award # N00014-17-1-2882.

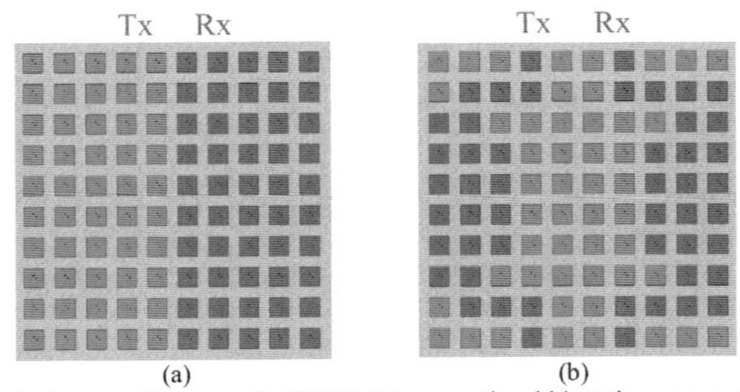

Fig. 1. Array architectures for STAR: (a) conventional bi-static array, and (b) proposed array topology.

To prove the concept, an air-loaded dual-pin-fed circularly polarized patch antenna is used because of its simple design and low computational demand. The 10×10 array consists of 50 elements each for Tx and Rx, distributed in the aperture as shown in Fig. 1. The STAR array is computationally studied using the commercial multilevel fast multipole method (MLFMM) solver in Altair FEKO. The performance of the proposed architecture is compared to that of uniform array.

II. Array Element

The unit cell element used for the proposed study is a dual-polarized, single layer, air-loaded, dual-pin fed, patch with 90° phasing between the feeds to achieve circular polarization. MLFMM is used to solve the full 10×10 array. To make

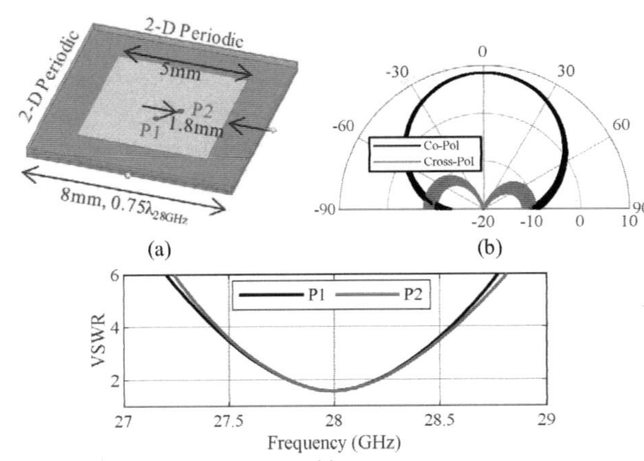

Fig. 2. Unit cell used in proposed array architecture. (a) Unit cell dimensions, (b) far-field radiation patterns, and (c) VSWRs at ports P1, P2.

computational problem reasonable in memory and running time demands [4], the unit cell is designed on an air substrate. Unit cell dimensions are shown in Fig. 2 (a). For demonstration purposes, substrate height is chosen as 0.16mm. To avoid any grating lobes, unit cell size is set to be 0.75 λ (< λ). Unit element is modeled in infinite array setup by applying the 2-D periodic boundary conditions. Fig. 1 (c) shows the impedance match at the input ports in the broadside (i.e., no scan) case. The antenna has VSWR < 2.1 over 27.75–28.25 GHz bandwidth. Embedded element gain for broadside operation is 8.5 dBic and axial ratio is < 0.1 dB at 28 GHz.

III. Array Architecture and Performance

Full 10×10 antenna array antenna system is modeled in FEKO as shown in Fig. 1. For baseline (conventional) case, half of the elements are used as transmitting elements and the other half as receiving. The isolation between Tx/Rx in above antenna array system can be calculated using (1),

$$\begin{bmatrix} b_1 \\ b_2 \\ \vdots \\ b_{200} \end{bmatrix} = \begin{bmatrix} S_{1,1} & \cdots & S_{1,200} \\ \vdots & \ddots & \vdots \\ S_{N,1} & \cdots & S_{200,200} \end{bmatrix} \begin{bmatrix} a_1 \\ a_2 \\ \vdots \\ a_{200} \end{bmatrix} \quad (1)$$

where $a_i = a_1, a_2, \ldots a_{200}$ are the input signals phased with $e^{i\cdot 0^\circ}$ and $e^{i\cdot 90^\circ}$ to form desired CP, $b_i = b_1, b_2, \ldots b_{200}$ are the output signals, and $[S]$ is the S-matrix of the proposed array. Total input power is normalized to 1 W. Total received power in Rx ports can be calculated using (2),

$$SI = \frac{1}{\sqrt{N}} \sum_{1}^{N} b_i \cdot C_i \cdot P_i \quad (2)$$

where N is total number of elements, C_i is phasing factor for circular polarization ($C_i = e^{i\cdot 0^\circ}$ when i is odd, $C_i = e^{i\cdot 90^\circ}$ when i is even), and P_i indicates Tx/Rx elements ($0 = Tx, 1 = Rx$). To determine which elements should be used for Tx and Rx, a random-search is performed on P_i with the goal to minimize SI over the frequency band. Values chosen for P_i are constrained to ensure symmetry across principle planes to preserve beam symmetry and low axial ratio. Fig. 1 (b) shows the configuration that provides significant improvement in isolation over desired bandwidth. As seen in Fig. 3, isolation > 63 dB is obtained over the band with average isolation improvement of 20 dB compared to the baseline case. Co-pol

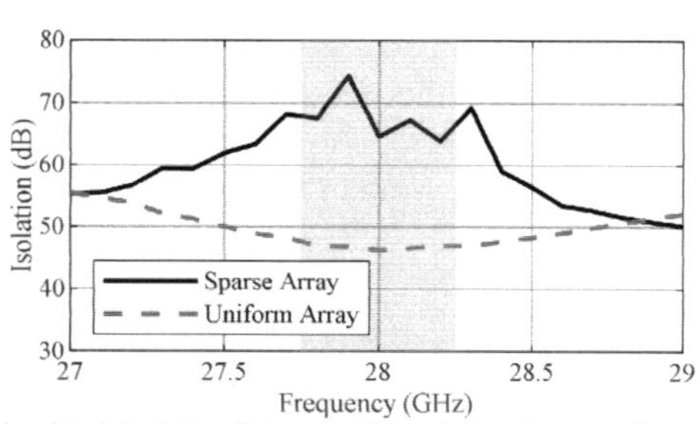

Fig. 3. Simulated isolation between Tx and Rx elements for uniform and proposed array configurations.

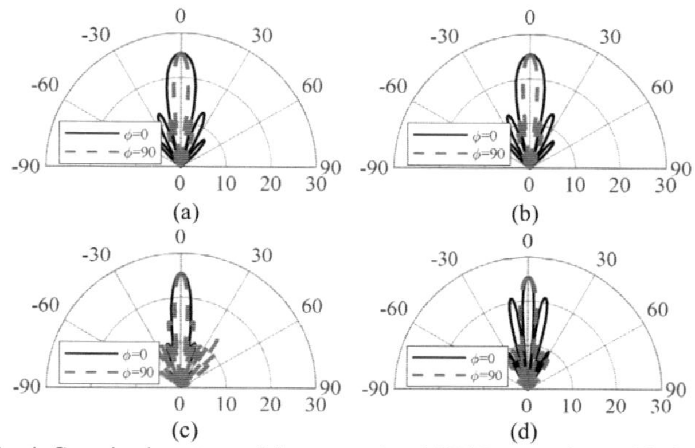

Fig. 4. Co-pol gain pattern of the conventional STAR array along with that of the proposed architecture. (a) Uniform array (Tx), (b) uniform array (Rx), (c) proposed array (Tx), and (d) proposed array (Rx).

Tx/Rx far-field patterns of the proposed array configuration is compared to the uniform array performance in Fig. 4. Cross-pol level remains > 30 dB below Co-pol. The peak directivity of both Tx and Rx beams in the proposed array configuration remains similar to the uniform array (25.53 dBic and 25.51 dBic, respectively). However, the side lobe level (SLL) increases particularly in the Rx case. Since the peak directivity remains the same as that of the uniform array, there is no degradation in the aperture efficiency of Tx and Rx. Reducing SLL in the proposed STAR array along with realizing a scan operation is currently being researched.

IV. Conclusion

A STAR antenna array configuration with isolation > 63 dB for broadside beam is proposed. The proposed array shows an isolation improvement of 20dB and more when compared to the conventional configuration. High isolation values are realized at the cost of higher SLLs, which is an inherent property of similar arrays. No degradation in aperture efficiency is observed for both Tx and Rx beams. High isolation characteristics and adequate far-field performances make shared aperture sparse antenna arrays a feasible candidate for full-duplex applications that require high gain and multifunctional operation.

References

[1] J. Choi, M. Jain, K. Srinivasan, P. Levis, and S. Katti, “Achieving single channel, full duplex wireless communication,” The 16th Annual Int. Conf. on Mobile Comp. Net., Chicago, IL, July 2010, pp. 1-12.

[2] J. Ha, M. A. Elmansouri, and D. S. Filipovic, “Monostatic co-polarized full-duplex antenna with left- or right-hand circular polarization,” IEEE Trans. Antennas and Propag., vol. 65, no. 10, Oct. 2017, pp. 5103–5111.

[3] E. A. Etellisi, M. A. Elmansouri, and D. Filipovic, “Wideband monostatic co-polarized co-channel simultaneous transmit and receive (C-STAR) broadside circular array antenna,” in IEEE Trans. Antennas and Propag., vol. 67, no. 2, Nov. 2018.

[4] J. J. van Tonder and U. Jakobus, "Fast multipole solution of metallic and dielectric scattering problems in FEKO," IEEE/ACES International Conference on Wireless Communications and Applied Computational Electromagnetics, 2005, Honolulu, HI, 2005, pp. 511-514.

Systematic CMA of the U-slot Patch with FEKO

John J. Borchardt
Sandia National Laboratories
Albuquerque, NM, USA
jjborch@sandia.gov

***Abstract*—Since its introduction 25 years ago, the probe-fed U-slot patch antenna has remained popular. Recently, Characteristic Mode Analysis (CMA) revealed these devices are governed by Coupled Mode Theory (CMT). Although this principle is conceptually simple, achieving this understanding is only possible through a systematic analysis using CMA. This paper uses the U-slot patch to illustrate a general process for analyzing electrically small antennas using CMA with the software package FEKO.**

Keywords—characteristic mode analysis, coupled mode theory, FEKO, U-slot patch antenna.

I. Introduction

Over the past 25 years, the probe-fed U-slot patch antenna [1] has remained popular in government and academia. Recently, CMA revealed these devices are governed by CMT; coupling between the conventional TM_{01} patch mode and the "uncoupled slot resonator" (a lumped LC resonator involving the slot and the probe) results in stagger-tuned in-phase and anti-phase modes that together produce broad impedance bandwidth and stable radiation pattern [2]. Although conceptually simple, achieving this understanding is only possible via a systematic analysis using CMA. This paper illustrates such a process for the U-slot patch using the software package FEKO [3].

CMA is a modal decomposition based on the method of moments (MoM) [4]. Within CMA, a set of real orthogonal basis currents J_n result from $[X]\,J_n = \lambda_n\,[R]\,J_n$ where $[Z] = [R] + j[X]$ is the MoM impedance matrix and λ_n is the eigenvalue. A mode is resonant when $\lambda_n = 0$ [4]. Currents driven by a source $E^{\mathrm{i}}_{\mathrm{tan}}$ may be represented as a sum of modes: $J_{\mathrm{total}} = \sum_n \alpha_n J_n$ where the modal weighting coefficient (MWC) $\alpha_n = \langle J_n, E^{\mathrm{i}}_{\mathrm{tan}} \rangle / (1 + j\lambda_n)$ [4]. Thus, the driven admittance of a structure is the sum of all modal admittances.

II. CMA Process

The usual steps of entering the geometry, meshing, and solving the structure are performed. It is important to mesh the probe and provide an excitation in these geometries, not only because the probe can affect the characteristic modes (CMs) but also because having an excitation gives clues (e.g., admittance & MWC) as to what modes are important. Note that CMA often benefits from a finer mesh than is required for solving a driven problem (for this analysis, triangle edge lengths were between $\lambda/25$ and $\lambda/50$). In FEKO, a driven MoM solve (i.e., using a 1V excitation) can be performed alongside a CMA solve.

Sandia National Laboratories is a multimission laboratory managed and operated by National Technology & Engineering Solutions of Sandia, LLC, a wholly owned subsidiary of Honeywell International, Inc., for the U.S. Department of Energy's National Nuclear Security Administration under contract DE-NA0003525. This paper describes objective technical results and analysis. Any subjective views or opinions that might be expressed in the paper do not necessarily represent the views of the U.S. Department of Energy or the United States Government.

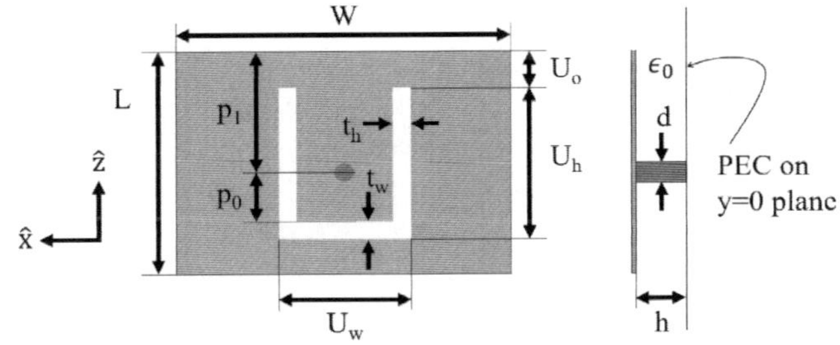

Fig. 1. U-slot patch geometry of [1]; (W, L, h, U_w, U_h, U_0, t_h, t_w, d, p_0) = (220, 124, 26.9, 68.6, 82.2, 22.9, 10.2, 8.89, 3.05, 33.9) mm.

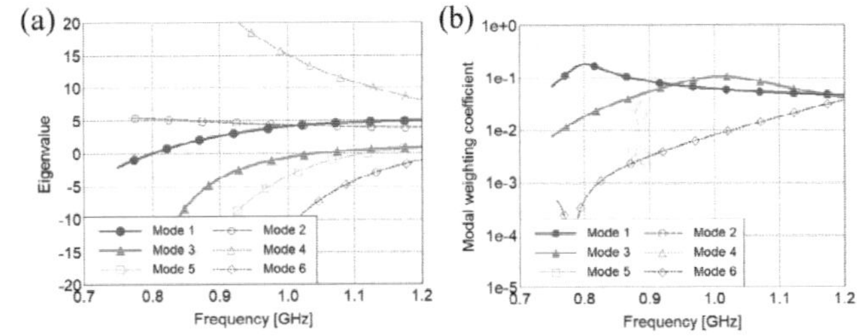

Fig. 2. Eigenvalues (a) and modal weighting coefficient α_n (b) of the first 6 modes of the Fig. 1 geometry calculated by FEKO.

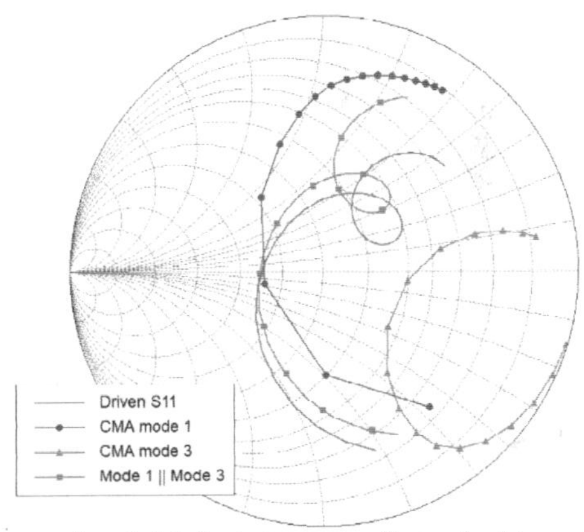

Fig. 3. The sum of mode 1 & 3 admittances replicates the driven admittance.

Data interpretation begins by viewing the eigenvalue spectrum shown in Fig. 2(a). The eigenvalue traces are inspected for mode-tracking errors (which greatly complicate data interpretation) and other phenomena such as eigenvalue crossing avoidance. Modes that are not resonant within the band of interest are often of secondary (if any) interest. We see that of six modes requested of FEKO, only modes 1, 3, 5 and 6 are resonant. For a 1V gap source excitation at the base of the probe, FEKO calculates α_n as seen in Fig. 2(b). Only modes 1, 3 and 6 are excited significantly and warrant further study.

We next seek to replicate the driven input admittance by a

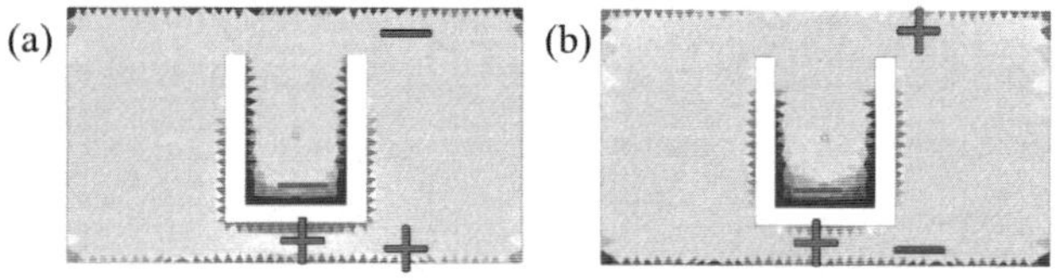

Fig. 4. Mode 1/in-phase (a) and Mode 3/anti-phase (b) charge distributions.

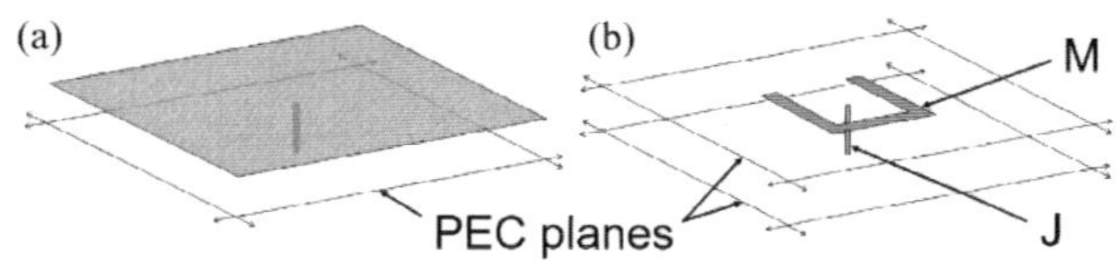

Fig. 5. Uncoupled patch (a) and uncoupled slot (b) resonator geometries.

sum of modal admittances. We find the mode 6 admittance is much lower than 1/50Ω, but that the sum of mode 1 and 3 admittances (calculated using a POSTFEKO Lua script) replicates the driven admittance locus well, as seen in Fig. 3. If the driven admittance cannot be adequately represented by the sum of mode admittances, then more CMs should be requested of FEKO, and the above process repeated.

We turn to physical interpretation of modes 1 and 3. FEKO plots the modal charge distributions (at phase angle $\phi = 90°$) near resonance; these are much simpler than current distributions and greatly aid in physical interpretation. We note in-phase and anti-phase charge accumulations on the patch and slot edges for modes 1 and 3, respectively, as seen in Fig. 4(a) and Fig. 4(b). This suggests that CMT underlies the U-slot patch, which was demonstrated rigorously in [2]; coupling is due to the mutual inductance of the slot.

At this point, the modal far-fields are compared to those of the driven problem to ensure the selected modes appropriately capture the radiation behavior of the driven structure.

With the important modes identified, we enquire about the nature of the *uncoupled* resonators (i.e., the isolated patch and slot); this process often requires some ingenuity. For example, it is simple to remove the *slot from the patch* and identify the conventional TM_{01} patch mode resonant near the full U-slot patch structure center frequency, however it is less obvious how to remove the *patch from the slot*. Increasing W and L to infinity, as shown in Fig. 5(b), gives results useful for design purposes [2].

FEKO can calculate CMs of the Fig. 5(b) structure using the planar multilayer Green's function and the planar Green's function aperture features (to represent magnetic currents on the U-slot), resulting in a mode resonant near the full U-slot patch structure center frequency. Infinite conducting planes are accounted for analytically; this is of critical importance, as large meshed ground planes supporting current explicitly as MoM unknowns result in low-frequency CMs that are of no interest (i.e., modes of the ground plane plates, rather than of the slot-probe structure). To avoid a FEKO error, the dielectric between the infinite conducting planes is set to $\epsilon_r = 1.01$ as seen in Fig. 6; in our experience, the numerical solution remains stable and the difference from the case where $\epsilon_r = 1$ is negligible. Of course, U-slot patches on dielectric substrates with $\epsilon_r > 1$ are

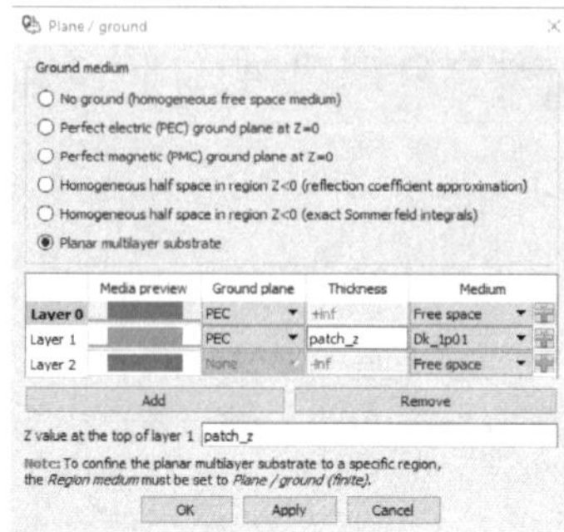

Fig. 6. FEKO planar multilayer Green's function configuration for Fig. 5(b).

easily addressed by FEKO.

To explain the uncoupled slot resonator behavior, CMA and CMT are utilized once again. The geometry of Fig. 5(b) is mirrored through the y=0 plane; one resulting CM satisfies a PEC boundary condition on y=0 and another a PMC boundary condition. The CM resonant frequencies and interpretation of the modal nearfields lead to a simple, four element LC equivalent circuit for the uncoupled slot resonator [2].

A volumetric grid of resonant modal near-fields $E_{1,2}$ and $H_{1,2}$ encompassing the uncoupled slot and patch resonators may be used to calculate the coupling between them via [5]:

$$\kappa = \frac{\int \epsilon E_1 \circ E_2 \, dV}{\sqrt{W_{e1} W_{e2}}} + \frac{\int \mu H_1 \circ H_2 \, dV}{\sqrt{W_{m1} W_{m2}}} \tag{1}$$

where $W_{e1,2} = \int \epsilon |E_{1,2}|^2 \, dV$ and $W_{m1,2} = \int \mu |H_{1,2}|^2 \, dV$, giving $|\kappa| = 0.19$—similar to that calculated via the coupled resonances $\omega_\pm$ as $\kappa = (\omega_+^2 - \omega_-^2)/(\omega_+^2 + \omega_-^2) = 0.26$ in [2].

III. Conclusion

A systematic approach to applying CMA to electrically small antenna problems was presented using FEKO and the U-slot patch: (1) include the excitation/mesh the probe and run driven MoM problem alongside CMA, (2) select resonant modes, (3) select modes with significant MWCs, (4) replicate driven admittance with sum of selected modal admittances, (5) check modal far-fields, (6) use CM current and charge distributions to obtain physical insight, and, for multi-modal antennas, (7) establish uncoupled resonator geometries and calculate coupling using near-fields.

References

[1] T. Huynh and K. F. Lee, "Single-layer single-patch wideband microstrip antenna," in Electronics Letters, vol. 31, no. 16, pp. 1310-1312, 3 Aug. 1995.

[2] J. J. Borchardt and T. C. Lapointe, "U-Slot Patch Antenna Principle and Design Methodology Using Characteristic Mode Analysis and Coupled Mode Theory," in IEEE Access, vol. 7, pp. 109375-109385, 2019.

[3] Altair Engineering, Inc. FEKO [Online] Available: https://altairhyperworks.com/product/FEKO

[4] R. Harrington and J. Mautz, "Theory of characteristic modes for conducting bodies," in IEEE Transactions on Antennas and Propagation, vol. 19, no. 5, pp. 622-628, Sep. 1971.

[5] J. Hong, "Couplings of asynchronously tuned coupled microwave resonators," in IEE Proceedings - Microwaves, Antennas and Propagation, vol. 147, no. 5, pp. 354-358, Oct. 2000

Using Near Field Equivalent Sources in Combination with Large Element Physical Optics to Model a Slant 45 Degree Omni Directional Antenna over Ground

Keith Snyder
Staff Electronics Engineer
Northrop Grumman
San Diego, USA
Snyder_kas@mindspring.com

***Abstract*—This paper compares the theoretical and measured antenna patterns of a slant 45-degree antenna on a rolled edge ground plane. Advantages of using sampled nearfield currents in combination with large element physical optics in determining the reflected far fields will be described.**

Keywords—Feko, MoM, PO, Slant 45, Multipath, Antenna, Equivalent Sources

I. Introduction

The purpose of this report is to demonstrate the behavior of a commercial slant 45 degree omni-directional when the antenna is mounted on a ground plane and show how one can predict the patterns using near field current distributions in conjunction with regular and large element physical optics approximations in Altair Feko [1]. .

There is a need in the antenna community for antennas that pick up both vertical and horizontal antenna patterns (as well as RCP and LCP) with the required field of view being 360 degrees in azimuth. In addition, the frequency band required may be over a broad range of frequencies. The antenna type that is often recommend for this application is a bi-conical antenna with a multi-layer polarizer composed of wire grids that are designed to tilt the polarization from pure vertical pole to slant 45 degree polarization. See Figure 1.

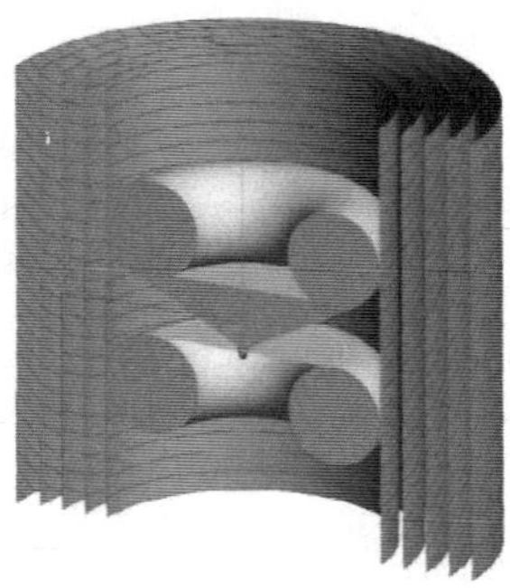

Figure 1. Broadband Discone Inside Slant 45 Polarizer

II. Sample Antenna Pattern no Ground Plane

A sample of the predicted antenna pattern for 8 GHz is shown in Figure 2. The plot shows both vertical and horizontal response and is a figure of revolution about the vertical axis.

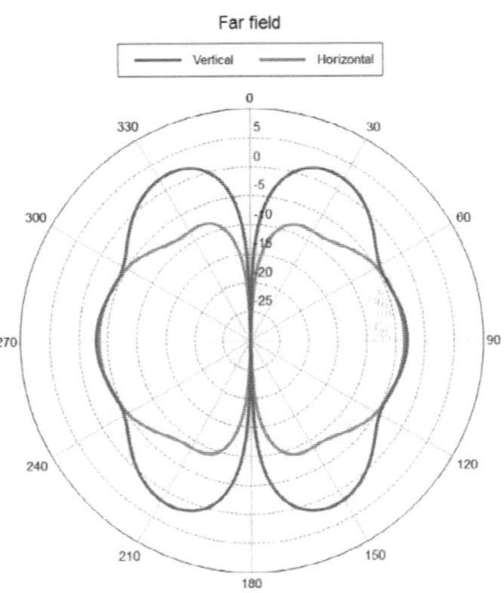

Figure 2. MoM Calculated Antenna Pattern at 8 GHz

III. Modeling the Ground Plane

The ground plane that will be used for antenna measurements on this antenna is a rolled edge circular ground plane. In order to calculate the antenna patterns at higher frequencies there are two steps. First calculate the Near Fields and Sample Currents on a volume that fully encloses the antenna using an infinite ground plane. This is a quick calculation. An example for the model at 6 GHz is shown in Figure 3.

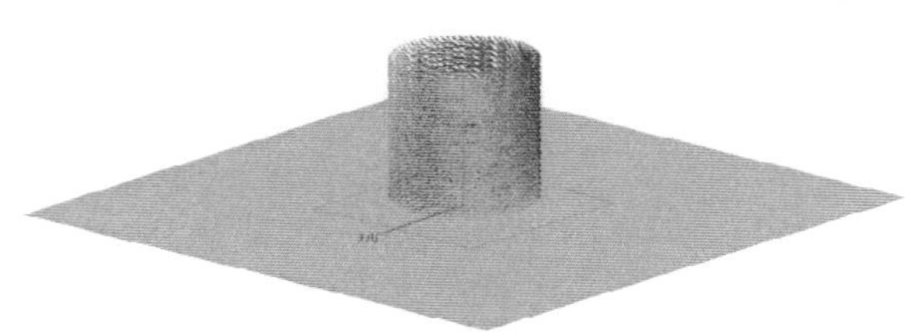

Figure 3. Method of Moments Model at 6 GHz over Infinite Ground

Both the Electric and Magnetic Near Fields are stored in separate files and then can be imported into Feko to simulate the actual rolled edge ground plane using physical optics. Figure 4 shows the intensity of the sampled near fields for 6 GHz.

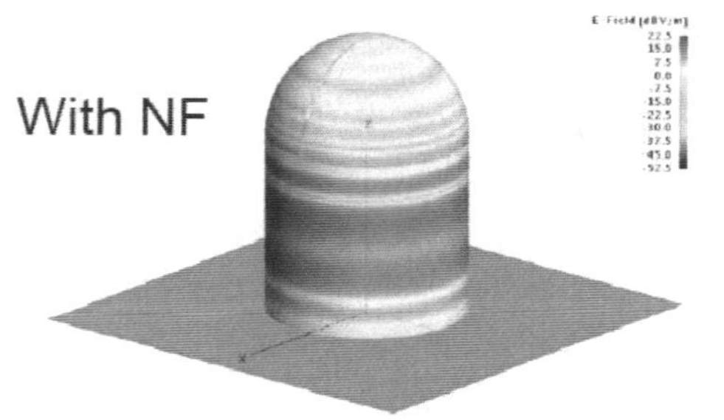

Figure 4. Electric Near Field

At this point the sample currents are placed slightly above the ground plane that the antenna will be mounted on. The ground plane is a 5 ft diameter rolled edge circular surface of revolution as shown in Figure 5.

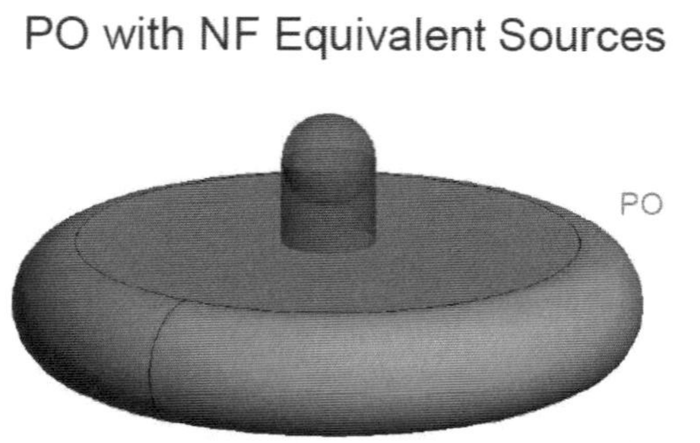

Figure 5. Near Field Equivalent Sources combined with Physical Optics

There is a great time savings by using PO with the Near Field Equivalent Surfaces to calculate the antenna patterns. The Antenna patterns calculated at 6 GHz for vertical polarization are shown in Figure 6 for several calculation options. Equivalent NF sources combine with Large Element PO [2] gives accurate results in a very short amount of time.

Note that because of reflections on the flat surface the vertical polarized signal now has nulls at elevation angles of 7.5, 18 and 34 degrees.

An off the shelf model of the antenna was measured on the same shape ground plane and the vertical antenna patterns are shown in Figure 7. Note that the measured antenna patterns agree with the calculated results with nulls at 7.5, 18 and 34 degrees elevation.

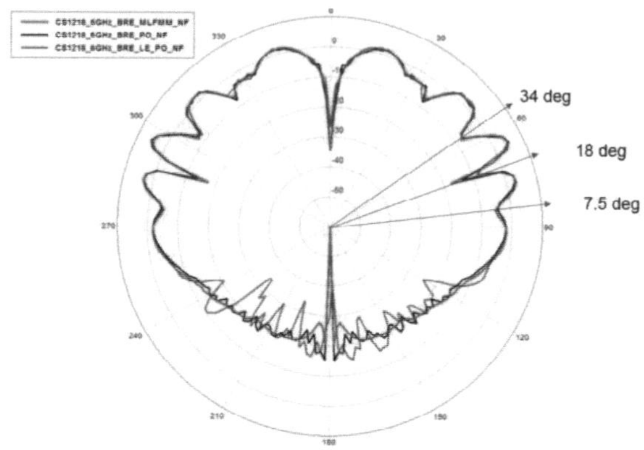

Figure 6. Calculated Vertical Pol at 6 GHz on Rolled Edge Ground Plane

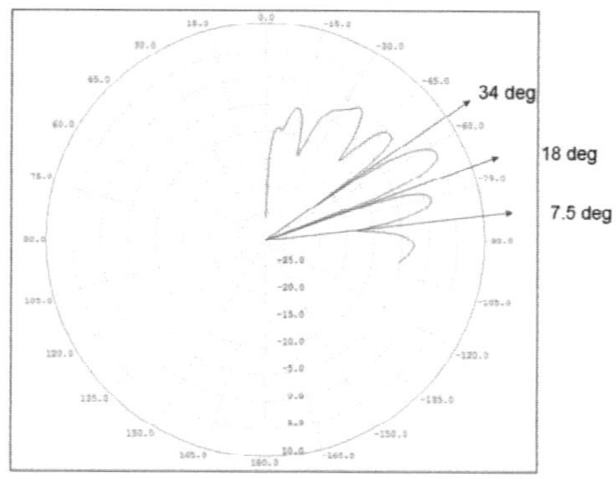

Figure 7. Measured Antenna Pattern of Slant 45 Degree Antenna On Rolled Edge Ground Plane at 6 GHz.

IV. Conclusion

Feko has been used combining NF Equivalent Sources and Physical Optics to predict antenna patterns on a rolled edge ground plane. Measured results confirm that there will be reflections in the resultant vertically polarized antenna patterns. This also occurs for horizontal polarization.

Acknowledgment

Persons to acknowledge are Scott Burnside, Dr. C. J. Reddy and Duff Weatherington.

References

[1] Altair Feko, https://altairhyperworks.com/product/FEKO

[2] Ulrich Jakobus, Marlize Schoeman, Johann van Tonder, Danie Ludick, and Willem Burger, "Selection of New Features in the Electromagnetic Solution Kernel of FEKO Suite 6.0", 27th Annual Review of Progress in Applied Computational Electromagnetics, March 27-31, 2011 - Williamsburg, Virginia.

Impact of Blood Environment on Integrated Antenna Performance

Ololade Sanusi, Langis Roy, and Ying Wang
Dept. of Electrical, Computer and Software Engineering
University of Ontario Institute of Technology
Oshawa, Canada
ololade.sanusi@uoit.ca, langis.roy@uoit.ca, ying.wang@uoit.ca

Farhan Ghaffar
Dept. of Electrical Engineering
Lakehead University
Barrie, Canada
fghaffar@lakeheadu.ca

***Abstract*—Emerging wireless applications call for flexible antenna designs that operate efficiently regardless of their host structures. A study of the performance of an inkjet printed dipole antenna for blood irradiation applications is presented. Simulations and measurements show that a blood environment can significantly impact antenna performance. The radiation pattern of the dipole antenna is significantly degraded when placed on a host blood bag, with a simulated maximum gain of -18 dBi at 2.45 GHz. To isolate the antenna from the host structure, the dipole antenna is integrated with an AMC structure operating at 2.45 GHz. In spite of the presence of the lossy host, simulations and measurements show a significant improvement in the antenna gain. Simulated and measured gains of 6.4 dBi and 4.1 dBi are attained by integrating the AMC ground plane.**

***Index Terms*—Artificial magnetic conductor (AMC), blood, dosimetry, flexible antennas, inkjet printing.**

I. Introduction

With rising applications of wireless technologies in the area of wearable technology [1], [2], internet of things [3], [4] and sensors, the need for low cost, lightweight and conformal microwave devices becomes prominent. Over the years, literature has also reported antenna designs for biomedical applications such as hearing instruments [5], and medical diagnosis [6]. Such applications have inspired the use of rapid prototyping techniques like inkjet printing to achieve flexible designs. More specifically, an emerging antenna application in blood irradiation procedures has been reported in [7].

Prior to transfusion, blood and blood products are irradiated in chambers containing X-ray or gamma ray to prevent infections and diseases like Transfusion Associated Graft-Versus Host Disease (TA-GVHD) [8]. Blood and blood products need to receive 25 Gy to 50 Gy of irradiation to be considered safe for use. A visual indicator called RadTag is currently used to confirm that the minimum dose has been received by the blood bag [8]. However, this method lacks an accurate reading of the radiation dosage received by the blood. Hence, a sensor that can accurately read and communicate the dosage received by blood under irradiation has been proposed in [9].

This paper presents a review of the 2.45 GHz inkjet printed artificial magnetic conductor(AMC)-backed antenna in [7] for dosimetry applications. The influence of blood on the antenna gain performance without and with an AMC ground plane is studied.

This work was supported in part by the Natural Sciences and Engineering Research Council (NSERC) and in part by Best Medical Canada Ltd.

II. Antenna Design and Performance

A 2.45 GHz dipole antenna with dimensions of 38.5×3.75 mm^2 is inkjet printed on a Kapton substrate using silver ink of conductivity, $\sigma = 1\times10^7$ S/m. The 0.12 mm-thick Kapton sheet has a dielectric constant, $\epsilon_r = 3.5$, and loss tangent, tan $\delta = 0.002$ [10].

To study the effects of blood on the antenna performance, the dipole antenna (without and with an AMC ground plane, depicted in Fig. 1 below) adhered to a blood bag is simulated using ANSYS HFSS and measured using the Satimo StarLab anechoic chamber. The dielectric properties of blood - $\epsilon_r = 58.3$, tan $\delta = 0.321$, and $\sigma = 2.545$ S/m at 2.45 GHz - are also taken into account in the simulations and measurements [11].

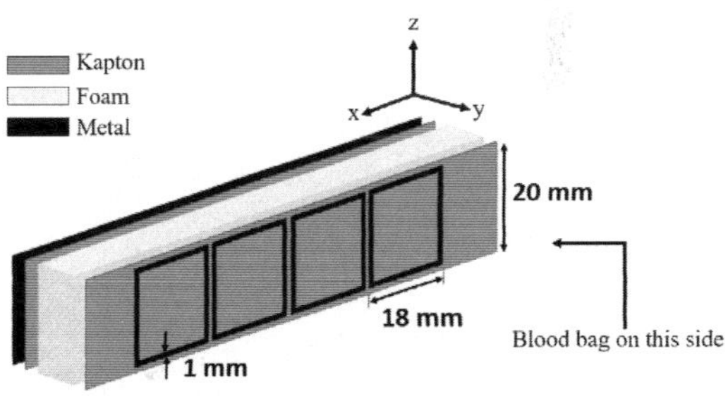

Fig. 1. 3D stackup of the AMC ground plane (full structure shown in [7]).

The simulated and measured radiation patterns of the dipole antenna are presented in Fig. 2 (a). Based on Fig. 2 (a), it is observed that the dipole antenna has an omnidirectional pattern with a simulated gain of 2.4 dBi in the absence of a blood bag. On the other hand, when the dipole antenna is attached to a filled blood bag, the maximum antenna gain is reduced to -18 dBi.

To isolate the blood from the antenna, the dipole antenna is then placed over the 100×20 mm^2 AMC ground plane, shown in Fig. 1 above. The AMC ground plane is based on a

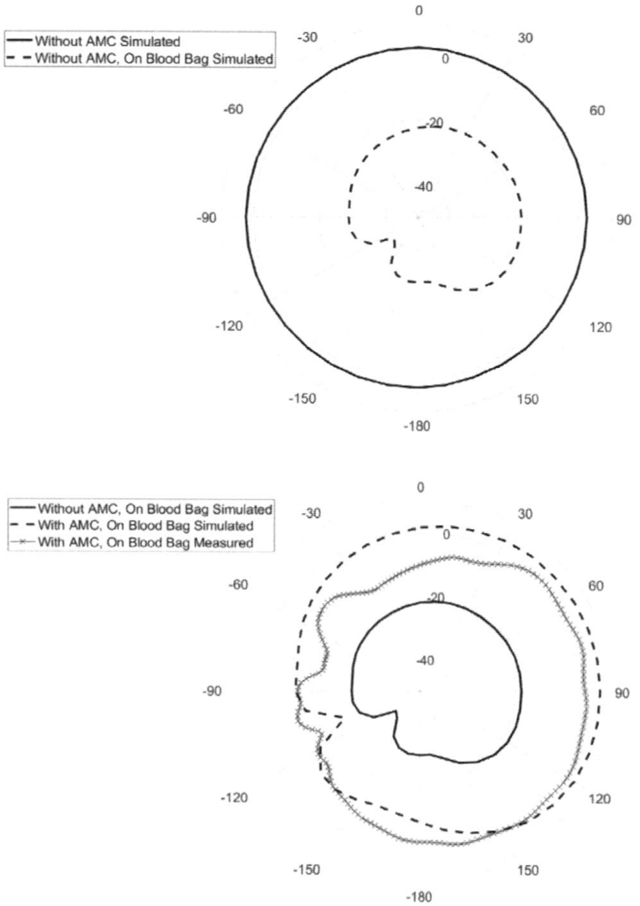

Fig. 2. Radiation patterns of the inkjet printed antenna in the H-plane (YZ) at 2.45 GHz.

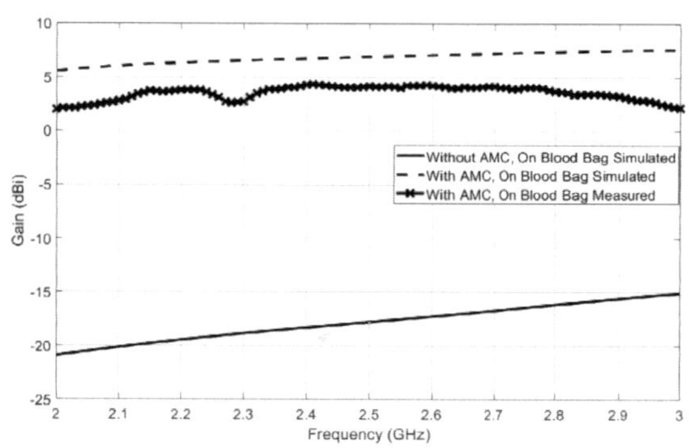

Fig. 3. Broadside gain versus frequency plot of the inkjet printed antenna.

square loop geometry and has a simulated reflection magnitude of -0.21 dB and reflection phase of 0.16^0. It comprises three layers - four metallic square loops inkjet printed on a 0.12 mm-thick Kapton substrate make up the top layer, a 9-mm thick foam spacer, and a ground plane.

The simulated antenna performance on the blood bag with and without the AMC ground plane are shown in Fig. 2 (b). The measured radiation pattern of the AMC-backed antenna in the H plane is also presented in Fig. 2 (b). The simulated and measured antenna gains as a function of frequency are also shown in Fig. 3. In the presence of the blood bag, the measured and simulated radiation patterns show that the antenna has a directional pattern. Without the AMC backing, the antenna has a simulated broadside gain of -18 dBi. Conversely, the antenna gain is significantly improved when backed by an AMC even in the presence of the blood. The AMC-backed antenna has a simulated broadside gain of 6.8 dBi and measured gain of 4.1 dBi at 2.45 GHz.

III. Conclusion

In this paper, the performance of a 2.45 GHz AMC-backed dipole antenna in a blood environment is studied. Results reveal that blood can significantly degrade antenna performance; simulations show the dipole antenna attains a gain of -18 dBi at 2.45 GHz when placed on a blood bag. However, simulated gain results of the AMC-backed dipole antenna show an improvement from -18 dBi to 6.8 dBi in the presence of the blood bag. Therefore, the integration of the AMC with the dipole antenna adequately isolates the influence of the blood (or lossy host structure) from the antenna; preventing degradation of the antenna gain.

References

[1] Q. H. Abbasi, M. U. Rehman, X. Yang, A. Alomainy, K. Qaraqe, and E. Serpedin, "Ultrawideband Band-Notched Flexible Antenna for Wearable Applications," in IEEE Antennas and Wireless Propagation Letters, vol. 12, pp. 1606-1609, 2013.

[2] G. Gao, C. Yang, B. Hu, R. Zhang, and S. Wang, "A Wearable PIFA With an All-Textile Metasurface for 5 GHz WBAN Applications," in IEEE Antennas and Wireless Propagation Letters, vol. 18, no. 2, pp. 288-292, Feb. 2019.

[3] G. Li, Y. Huang, G. Gao, X. Wei, Z. Tian, and L. Bian, "A Handbag Zipper Antenna for the Applications of Body-Centric Wireless Communications and Internet of Things," in IEEE Transactions on Antennas and Propagation, vol. 65, no. 10, pp. 5137-5146, Oct. 2017.

[4] A. Bekasiewicz and S. Koziel, "Compact UWB monopole antenna for internet of things applications," in Electronics Letters, vol. 52, no. 7, pp. 492-494, Apr. 2016.

[5] A. Ruaro, J. Thaysen, and K. B. Jakobsen,"Wearable Shell Antenna for 2.4 GHz Hearing Instruments," in IEEE Transactions on Antennas and Propagation, vol. 64, no. 6, pp. 2127-2135, June 2016.

[6] M. Rokunuzzaman, A. Ahmed, T. C. Baum, and W. S. T. Rowe, "Compact 3-D Antenna for Medical Diagnosis of the Human Head," in IEEE Transactions on Antennas and Propagation, vol. 67, no. 8, pp. 5093-5103, Aug. 2019.

[7] O. M. Sanusi, F. A. Ghaffar, A. Shamim, M. Vaseem, Y. Wang, and L. Roy, "Development of a 2.45 GHz Antenna for Flexible Compact Radiation Dosimeter Tags," in IEEE Transactions on Antennas and Propagation, vol. 67, no. 8, pp. 5063-5072, Aug. 2019.

[8] The Royal Children's Hospital Melbourne. (2011, January). Blood Transfusion: Irradiation of Blood Products. [Online]. Available: https://www.rch.org.au/bloodtrans/about_blood_products/Irradiation_of_blood_products/

[9] B. Yadegari, O. Sanusi, F. A. Ghaffar, S. McGarry, and L. Roy, "An Efficient and Compact Wireless Solution for Blood Sterilization Apparatus," 2018 18th International Symposium on Antenna Technology and Applied Electromagnetics (ANTEM), Waterloo, ON, 2018, pp. 1-3.

[10] DuPont. "DuPont™ Kapton® Summary Of Properties," 2017. [Online]. Available: http://www.dupont.com/content/dam/dupont/products-and-services/membranes-and-films/polyimde-films/documents/DEC-Kapton-summary-of-properties.pdf. Accessed on: July 18, 2018.

[11] D. Andreuccetti, R. Fossi, and C. Petrucci, "An Internet resource for the calculation of the dielectric properties of body tissues in the frequency range 10 Hz - 100 GHz," IFAC-CNR, Florence (Italy), 1997. Based on data published by C. Gabriel, et al. in 1996. [Online]. Available: http://niremf.ifac.cnr.it/tissprop/

A Thick Origami Traveling Wave Antenna

Gian P. Carrara, Muhammad Hamza, Constantinos L. Zekios, and Stavros V. Georgakopoulos
Department of Electrical and Computer Engineering
Florida International University
Miami, FL, USA
gcarr049@fiu.edu, mhamz005@fiu.edu, kzekios@fiu.edu, georgako@fiu.edu

***Abstract*—This paper presents a thick origami foldable traveling wave antenna. A typical microstrip rampart-line antenna is appropriately modified to enable folding/unfolding capability using a surrogate hinge. This antenna is designed on a 1.5 mm-thick FR4 substrate circularly polarized at 3.4 GHz and exhibits a peak gain of approximately 2.85 dB at broadside.**

***Index Terms*—antenna, circular polarization, hinge, thick origami, travelling wave antenna.**

I. Introduction

The concept of physically reconfigurable antennas has been recently introduced with origami antennas e.g., [1], [2]. Specifically, origami antennas can transform 2D structures into a 3D ones with a prescribed way. This capability has been extensively used in numerous applications, where efficiently packing and easy deployment are needed, [3]. Also, origami antennas have used the shape deformation of origami designs to provide several reconfigurable characteristics, [4], [5]. Recently the first thick origami array was introduced in [6]. This array was a monolithic design (i.e., the antenna and its hinges were fabricated using one PCB), which also exhibited better performance compared to the corresponding design. Here, we propose the first thick origami travelling wave antenna based on a microstrip-line array.

Circularly polarized microstrip arrays are extensively used in communication, remote sensing, navigation and radar systems because of their low-profile. They are classified into three main categories: a) circularly polarized microstrip patches, b) composite elements of electric and magnetic current source elements, c) traveling wave arrays that utilize radiation due to suitable discontinuities in traveling wave transmission lines. Here, we use the third type of array and a hinge that allows the array to fold/unfold while maintaining its electromagnetic characteristics.

II. Antenna Design

A. Circularly Polarized Microstrip Array Unit Cell

A circularly polarized $4x1$ microstrip line array is designed. Fig. 1 shows the unit cell used for the microstrip array initially proposed by Hall, [7]. The unit cell is composed of four right-angle bends as well as three lengths represented as $a = 3/8\lambda_g$, $b = 1/2\lambda_g$, and $c = 1/4\lambda_g$. When these lengths are appropriately chosen with respect to the guiding frequency, the radiated fields from the four right angle bends produce circular polarization. At the four right angle bends, miters are introduced in order to mitigate the susceptance resulting from these discontinuities. To make the array foldable a surrogate hinge (Fig. 2) is introduced between the two middle elements (Fig. 3).

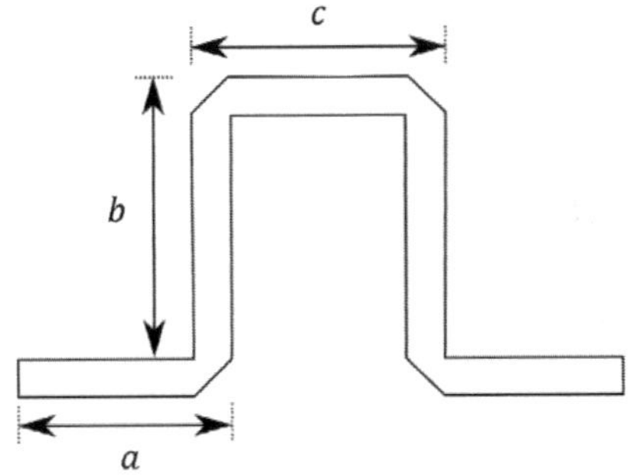

Fig. 1. Array Unit Cell.

B. Surrogate Hinge

The hinge used in this work was originally proposed by De Figueiredo, [8]. Shown in Fig. 2, the hinge allows the array to bend in either the clockwise or counter-clockwise direction minimizing the stress on the antenna components. A main advantage of this type of hinge is that both the array conductive layout and the hinge can be fabricated using a milling machine and a single PCB. Thus, a monolithic design can be fabricated without the need of any additional manufacturing processes. Results showing the impact of bending the hinge will be shown at the conference.

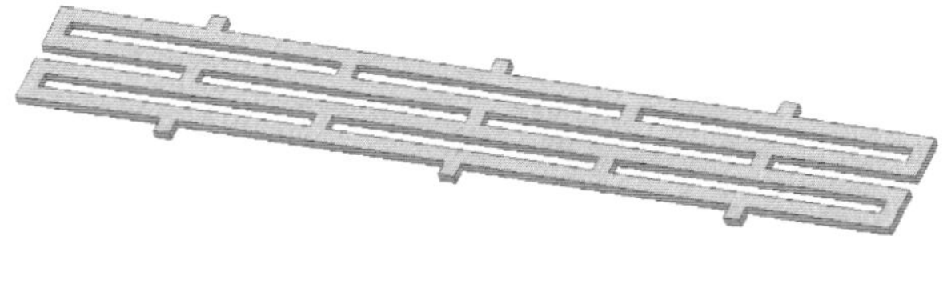

Fig. 2. Surrogate Hinge.

This work was supported by the Air Force Office of Scientific Research under grants FA9550-18-1-0191 and FA9550-19-1-0290, and the National Science Foundation under Grant EFRI 1332348.

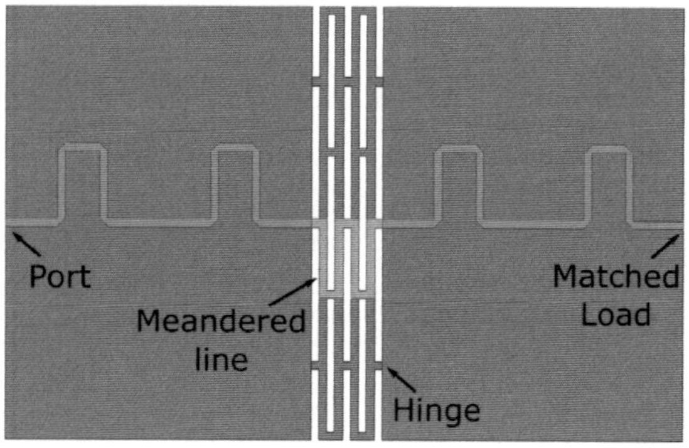

Fig. 3. 4 × 1 Traveling Wave Antenna.

C. Final Structure

The final design, shown in Fig. 3, encompasses the electromagnetic properties of the microstrip array and the flexibility of the hinge, all on a single PCB. The 4-element array is separated along the center of the array and is placed on the two opposing sides of the hinge. The array is then connected together with the use of a meandered line, which is guided along the length of the hinge. Both electromagnetic and mechanical analyses are performed for the optimal incorporation of the hinge. The corresponding results are not presented here for brevity and they will be presented at the conference.

III. Results

Fig. 4 shows the gain of the microstrip array with and without the hinge employed. It can be seen that the array without the hinge has a slightly wider beam, and also the level of its side lobes is significantly lower. This is expected since both dielectric and ground plane have been removed due to the introduction of the hinge. However, the array with the hinge radiates at the desired frequency of 3.5 GHz, with a maximum gain of approximately 2.8 dB. Both arrays with and without the hinge are circularly polarized. As shown in Fig. 5 the proposed design shows an axial ratio ≤ 3 dB at a wider bandwidth (3.19 GHz - 3.54 GHz) compared to the design without the hinge (3.09 GHz - 3.34 GHz). The shift of the circularly polarized bandwidth can be also attributed to the modifications done on the hinge portion of the design.

IV. Conclusion

A thick origami traveling wave antenna with a hinge is presented. The proposed design performs equivalently to the standard non-origami design. Also, more sections can be easily added in this configuration thereby creating a foldable array that can be stowed in an area as large as its unit cell. This provides significant savings in the antenna volume needed to stow this antenna.

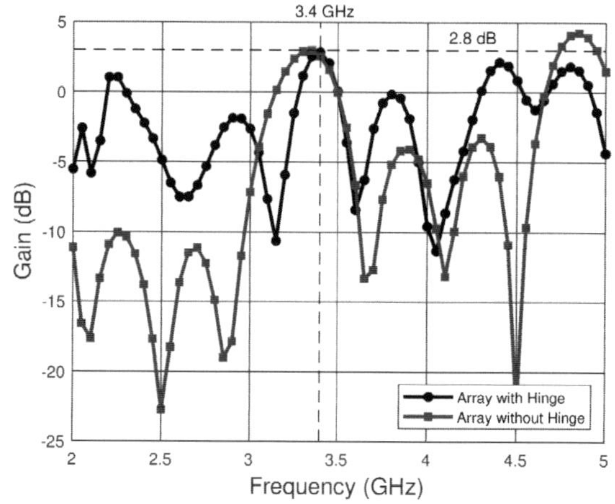

Fig. 4. Gain vs Frequency.

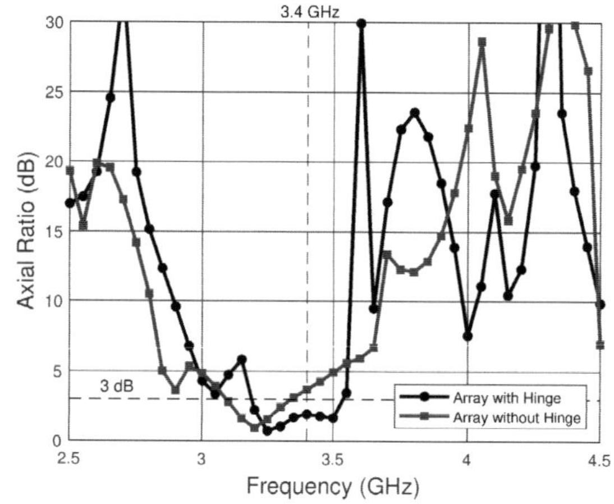

Fig. 5. Axial Ratio vs Frequency.

References

[1] W. Su, S. A. Nauroze, B. Ryan, and M. M. Tentzeris, "Novel 3D printed liquid-metal-alloy microfluidics-based zigzag and helical antennas for origami reconfigurable antenna 'trees'," 2017 IEEE MTT-S International Microwave Symposium (IMS), Honololu, HI, 2017, pp. 1579-1582.

[2] X. Liu, C. L. Zekios, and S. V. Georgakopoulos, "Analysis of a Packable and Tunable Origami Multi-Radii Helical Antenna," in IEEE Access, vol. 7, pp. 13003-13014, 2019.

[3] K. Miura, "Method of packaging and deployment of large membranes in space," The Inst. Space Anstronauit. Sci reportm, vol. 618, pp. 1709-1719, 1985.

[4] D. Sessions, K. Fuchi, S. Pallampati, D. Grayson, S. Seiler, G. Bazzan, G. Reich, P. Buskohl, and G. H. Huff, "Investigation of Fold-Dependent Behavior in an Origami-Inspired FSS Under Normal Incidence," Progress In Electromagnetics Research M, vol. 63, pp. 131-139, 2018.

[5] S. Yao, X. Liu, and S. V. Georgakopoulos, "Morphing Origami Conical Spiral Antenna Based on the Nojima Wrap," in IEEE Transactions on Antennas and Propagation, vol. 65, no. 5, pp. 2222-2232, May 2017.

[6] M. Hamza, C. L. Zekios and S. V. Georgakopoulos, "A Thick Origami Reconfigurable and Packable Patch Array with Enhanced Beam Steering," in IEEE Transactions on Antennas and Propagation. doi: 10.1109/TAP.2020.2963922.

[7] P. S. Hall, "Rampart microstrip line antennas," European Patent Application 79301340.0, 1979.

[8] De Figueiredo and B. Parker, "Developing New Classes of Thick-Origami-Based Mechanisms: Conceal-and-Reveal Motion and Folding Printed Circuit Boards" (2017). Theses and Dissertations. 6646.

SIW like Bull-Eye Antenna

Chao Ma, Zhiyi Tang, Zhouyi Wu, Peiying Lin, Ran Li, Huan Li and Jiangtao Huangfu*
Laboratory of Applied Research on Electromagnetics (ARE) Zhejiang University, Hangzhou 310027, China.
Email: huangfujt@zju.edu.cn

***Abstract*—In this paper, a novel low-profile, planar Bull-Eye antenna is proposed. Different from metal structure, the classical Bull-Eye ring structure is replaced by the substrate integrated waveguide (SIW) like structure. The antenna is made up of several piled-up PCB board and fed by slot. Based on PCB, by adjusting layers of substrates, far-field gain at desired frequency could be improved and could also adjust the band flexibly. This SIW like bull-eye antenna has lower profile than the classical antenna and is easy to integrate with RF circuit design, useful for high-directional integrated design. From the simulation results, far-field gain at desired frequency is over 15dB. This design gives the adjustment ability, compared to the classical design.**

Keywords—Bull-Eye antenna; substrate integrated waveguide (SIW); low profile

I. INTRODUCTION

High far-field gain antenna design is a challenging work due to the demand of aperture efficiency. The common high gain antenna design methods include antenna array design, traditional aperture antenna design, such as horn antenna, reflector antenna, lens antenna and so on [1]. The profiles of these aperture antennas is some high. Among new scheme antennas, the corrugated Bull-Eye antenna has advantages of

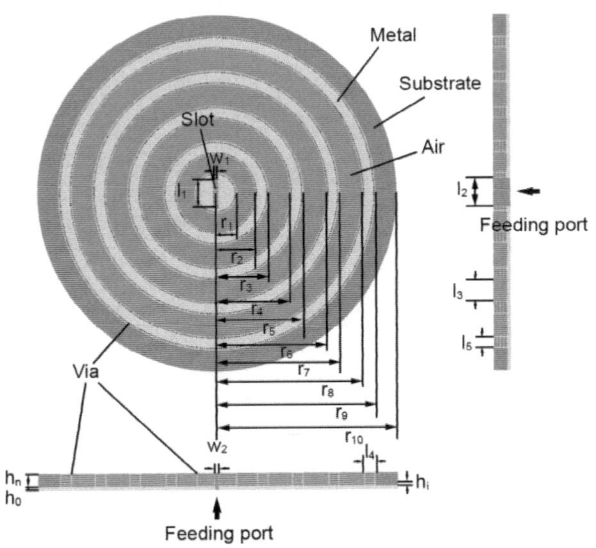

Fig. 1 SIW like Bull-Eye antenna setup.

high gain, low profile and so on, which is an interesting solution for wireless communication demand [2]-[4]. The common Bull-Eye antenna, which is usually metallic structure with a fixed design, and is hard to adjust [5]. By introducing layer structures, working band could be modified. Using PCB structures, by piling up boards, the profile of antenna could be modified easily, which could adjust high gain frequency. And by introducing substrate integrated waveguide (SIW) design method, using metalized via holes to create the electric sidewalls to replace metallic grooves [6], a metal-like groove based on PCB board generates. Thus, the machined metal structure changes to PCB board structure, which is convenient to adjust to adjust and modify.

The antenna proposed in this paper is a corrugated Bull-Eye antenna with SIW like structure. Compared to the traditional one, this antenna has lower profile due to the permittivity of the substrate, displaying a high gain and low side lobe level.

II. ANTENNA SETUP AND SIMULATION

Fig. 1 indicates a setup of the SIW like Bull-Eye antenna, the ground is made up of circular metal board with radius r_{10} = 120mm and thickness h_0 = 1mm. There is a slot in the middle of the ground, which length is l_1 = 18.64mm and width is 1.84mm. Above the ground there exist several layers of PCB board, the number is represented by n, and the thickness of each board is hi, which could vary with different layers. Each board contains concentric air grooves, with same height as the thickness of the board and same width, which cut off the substrate, and thus the substrate splits into a circular substrate in the center and several concentric substrate grooves. Two circular metal patches cover central substrate. And several pairs of metal grooves, with same radius and width, cover every substrate groove on both sides. Refer to the size of a typical metallic Bull-Eye antenna [5], we design a SIW like Bull-Eye antenna through simulation optimization. The radius of center substrate and two patches is r_1 = 11.48mm. From inside out, the sizes of the concentric substrate grooves are r_2 = 26.26mm, r_3 = 34mm, r_4 = 50.7mm, r_5 = 58.5mm, r_6 = 75.1mm, r_7 = 82.9mm, r_8 = 99.5mm, r_9 = 107.3mm. Thus, the width of air groove is l_3 = 12.2mm, and the width of the substrate and metal grooves is l_4 = 7.8mm.

There exist slots at the center of both circular patches, with width w_1 = 1.84mm and length l_1 = 18.64mm. A same slot is also at the center of the ground, and is used to feed. The sizes of the slot determine the impedance matching frequency. There are a round of via holes around the slot, which connect the top and the bottom patches, generating SIW like structure. These via holes create electric sidewalls, which could replace metallic sidewalls. The radius of the via holes is 0.3mm. Calculated from the centers of the via holes, the width of the square area generated by via holes is w_2 = 2.7mm, having 4 via holes, and the length is l_2 = 19.6mm, with 21 via holes, which means that the distance between neighbor via holes on the wide side is 0.9mm, and the length side distance is 0.98mm.

There is a round of via holes on every edge of the substrate grooves, connecting top and bottom metallic grooves, with same radius 0.5mm. These rounds of via holes are 1mm away from the nearest edges, i.e., l_5 is 5.8mm and the distance between neighbor via is about 2.4mm. Two rounds of via holes, with same connected pair of grooves, form an electric metallic

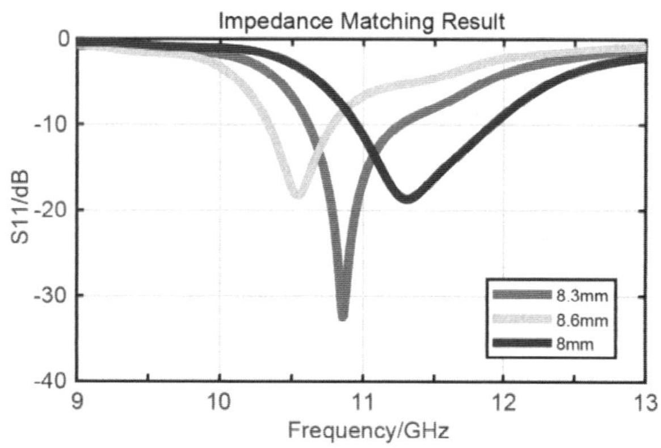

Fig. 2 Impedance Matching Simulation Result of the SIW like Bull-Eye antenna with different h.

groove, just as a metal groove.

Several layers of substrates pile up, expected grooves generate. The thickness of layers of substrates is $h_n = \sum_{i=1}^{n} h_i = h/\sqrt{\varepsilon_r}$, where h_n is the final height of the PCB groove, h is the height of the metallic groove [7], ε_r is the relative permittivity of the substrate. With different combinations of the thicknesses of PCB substrates, if the sum is the same, the effect is almost the same. From the equation, this method could lower the profile of the antenna. And the combination of different layers is set to adjust the height, which could overcome the fixed metallic Bull-Eye antenna's limitation. In this design, the working band is set at 10.8GHz, setting substrate F4B-255 with $\varepsilon_r = 2.55$ and h_i = 2.07mm, by piling up 4 layers, h = 8.3mm, and a SIW like Bull-Eye antenna generates. The feeding method can be microstrip slot feed or waveguide feed. For example, using a standard waveguide WR-90 connecting to the slot on the ground plane, this Bull-Eye antenna is fed by horizontal polarization wave, then the antenna radiates TM wave.

Fig. 2 indicates the impedance matching simulation result of the antenna with different substrate thicknesses. The center frequency of the antenna is around 10.8GHz, it would be tuning and move lower with thicker substrates.

Fig, 3 is the far-field gain results. From the figure, the maximum gain of the antenna is over 15dB. On E-plane, the beamwidth is about 15.3°. and the H-plane's beamwidth is

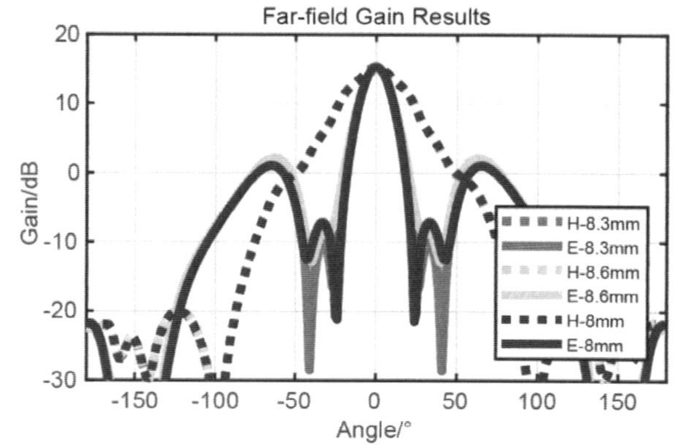

Fig. 3 Far-field Gain Results with different h.

about 33.8°. The height change of grooves mainly affect the far-field gain and has small impact on impedance matching, which means that grooves generated by the SIW like structure mainly affect he surface plasmon resonance. By changing the resonance quality factor, the working performance can be tuned to meet the variety of large bandwidth or high gain.

CONSLUSION

A SIW like Bull-Eye antenna is proposed in this paper. By using SIW structure to replace metallic structure, the Bull-Eye antenna could be generated by PCB boards, remaining high gain, low profile, adjustment and so on, which is easier to integrate with RF circuit design. By optimizing the structure, this antenna has wide use in wireless communication.

ACKNOWLEDGMENT

This work was supported by the NSFC under Grants No. 61675013 and U19A2054, the Zhejiang Provincial Natural Science Foundation of China under Grant No. LY18F010003.

REFERENCES

[1] C. A. Balanis, Antenna Theory: Analysis and Design, 3rd ed., NJ: John Wiley & Sons, Inc., 2005.

[2] U. Beaskoetxea, S. Maci, M. Navarro-Cía and M. Beruete, " 3-D-Printed 96 GHz Bull's-Eye Antenna With Off-Axis Beaming," IEEE Trans. Antennas Propag., vol. 65, n. 1, pp. 17-25, Jan. 2017.

[3] S. K. Podilchak, et al., "Optimization of a Planar "Bull-Eye" Leaky-Wave Antenna Fed by a Printed Surface-Wave Source," IEEE Antennas Wireless Propag. Lett., vol. 12, pp. 665–669, 2013.

[4] U. Beaskoetxea and M. Beruete, "High aperture efficiency Bull's-Eye Antenna," in Antennas and Propagation (EuCAP), 2017 11th European Conference on, 2017.

[5] M. Beruete, I. Campillo, J. S. Dolado, J. E. Rodríguez-Seco, E. Perea, F. Falcone, and M. Sorolla, "Very Low-Profile 'Bull's Eye Feeder Antenna," IEEE Antennas Wireless Propag. Lett., vol. 4, pp. 365–368, 2005.

[6] Z. N. Chen, D. Liu, H. Nakano, X. Qing and T. Zwick, Handbook of Antenna Technologies, Springer Singapore, 2016.

[7] H. J. Lezec, A. Degiron, E. Devaux, R. A. Linke, L. Martín-Moreno, F. J. García-Vidal, and T. W. Ebbesen, "Beaming of light from a subwavelength aperture," Science, vol. 297, pp. 820–820, 2002.

Novel Multi-frequency Vehicle Antenna

Zhiyi Tang[(1)] ,Chao Ma[(1)], Zhouyi Wu [(1)], Peiying Lin [(1)] , Xiaoxing Feng[(2)] and Jiangtao Huangfu[*(1)]

[(1)]Laboratory of Applied Research on Electromagnetics (ARE) Zhejiang University, Hangzhou 310027, China

[(2)]Atech Automotive (Wuhu) Co., Ltd

huangfujt@zju.edu.cn

***Abstract*—A novel multi-frequency vehicle antenna is proposed, which can work at 0.433 GHz, 2.83 GHz, 5 GHz by resonance simultaneously. It makes use of the vehicle's metal shell for signal radiation and collection. At the same time, its performance can be immune to the vehicle body structure. This antenna consists of Printed Circuit Board (PCB) excitation structure, matching circuit and metal shell of the vehicle. The trapezoidal PCB excitation structure has a hole in the middle, which cooperates with the matching circuit to excite the resonance of the required frequencies. The metal layers of the PCB connect the metal shell of the vehicle to achieve radiation, and they also connect transceiver through matching circuit. The excitation structure can be mounted on any place on the metal shell of the vehicle especially on the top. This vehicle antenna has the advantages of convenient installation and wide application range, and has the potential to replace some existing vehicle communication antennas.**

Keywords—Excitation structure, Multiple frequencies, Vehicle antenna.

I. Introduction

With the popularity of vehicles in the life and the rapid development of wireless communication, the demand for vehicle antennas is increasing. Not only are there strict requirements on its size and performance, but it is also required to be suitable for more wireless services, such as radio and TV broadcasting, cell-phones (GSM, UMTS), global positioning systems (GPS), satellite phones (Globalstar) [1]-[3]. [4]-[6] review on antenna designs for automotive applications [7]. The antenna used in the vehicle should consider the smallest occupation of the vehicle space, and can be better integrated with the vehicle. On the other hand, the impact of the vehicle structure on the antenna to a minimum need be considered[8].

The antenna proposed in this paper is like a shark fin antenna mounted on the outside of the vehicle body (as shown in Fig. 1), not occupying the space of the vehicle. Compared with the traditional shark fin antenna, it has a simpler structure to achieve multi-frequency. Moreover, the trapezoidal shape excitation structure reduces the wind resistance caused by the protruding antenna to some extent. The antenna excitation structure is perpendicular to the surface of the metal shell of the vehicle and its metal plate is used as part of the effective radiation of the antenna to minimize the impact of the vehicle itself on the performance of the antenna.

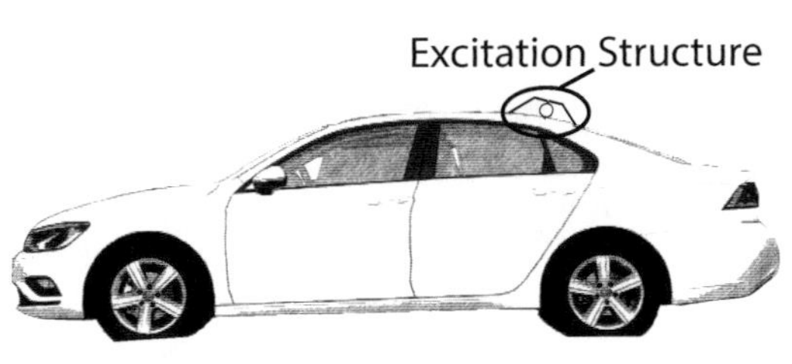

Fig. 1. The antenna mounted on vehicle.

II. Design and Simulation

The antenna proposed in this paper (shown in Fig. 2) includes PCB excitation structure, matching circuit and metal shell. The PCB excitation structure (with the size: L_1 =40mm, L_2 =140mm and 1mm thickness) is placed on the metal shell (with the size: L_3 =600mm, L_4 =300mm), which is an isosceles trapezoid with a hole (with the radius: r=15mm) in the middle and the metals on both sides of the PCB excitation structure are connected by vias on the outside of the hole. The hole extends to the edge of the isosceles trapezoid through the upper and lower notches (with the size of 5mm × 2mm). The PCB excitation structure is connected to the RF transceiver via the matching circuit which includes three capacitors and an inductor. The first capacitor(C_1=3pF) linking the transceiver is connected with the third capacitor via the second capacitor(C_2=0.3pF) and metal lines(with 2mm width and 2mm space). What's more, the third capacitor(C_3=1pF) and the inductor(L=400nH) are connected to the metal layers of excitation structure on both sides of the upper and lower notches respectively. With the signal passing through, the matching circuit, the excitation structure and the metal shell form radiation circuits, working at several frequencies simultaneously. At the same time, these resonances allow the signal to radiate through the surface current along metal shell of the vehicle.

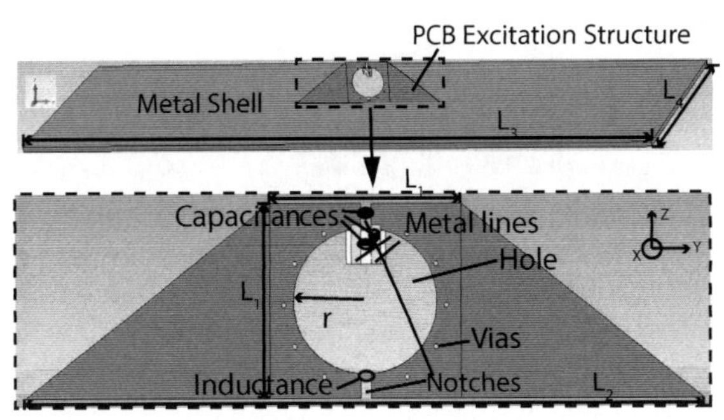

Fig. 2. Antenna structure.

When the signal is transmitted to the matching circuit, the inner and outer edge of the excitation structure and the metal shell are regarded as an inductor with the lumped capacitors and the lumped inductor forming a LC resonant circuit to work at several frequencies. The S_{11} parameter curve obtained by electromagnetic model simulation is shown in Fig. 3. It can be seen that the antenna will work around 0.433 GHz, 2.83 GHz, 5 GHz and the return loss is less than -10 dB, indicating that the antenna can generate effective radiation at these three frequency points simultaneously. Especially, the Bandwidth around 0.433GHz is 9MHz when S11 is less than −10dB. This is suitable for general communication protocols.

The three bands 0.433GHz, 2.83GHz and 5GHz are close to general frequency range of vehicle communication and positioning. This is just to show the working capacity of the multi frequency antenna with octave band, and its specific frequency can be adjusted when it is used in engineering.

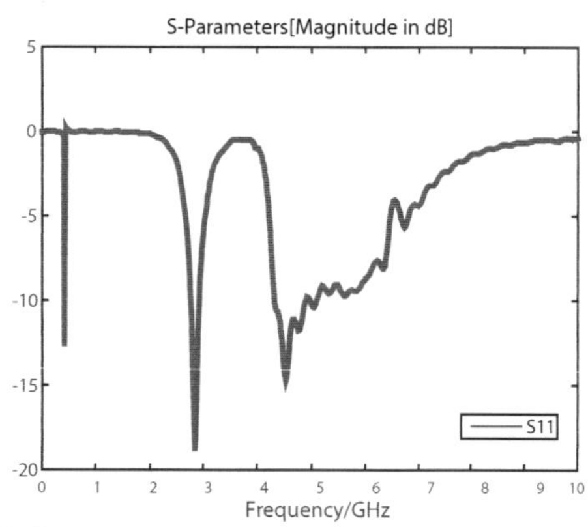

Fig. 3. S_{11} parameter curve.

The radiation characteristics of the antenna are also simulated. The far-field results of simulating Y-Z plane/X-Y plane are shown in Fig. 4. Fig. 4 (a) and Fig. 4 (b) show the Y-Z plane and X-Y plane pattern of f = 0.433 GHz with a maximum gain of 0.35 dB. Fig. 4 (c) and Fig. 4 (d) show the Y-Z plane and X-Y plane pattern of f = 2.83 GHz with a maximum gain of 2.14 dB. Fig. 4 (e) and Fig. 4 (f) show the Y-Z plane and X-Y plane pattern of f = 5 GHz with a maximum gain of 4.71 dB

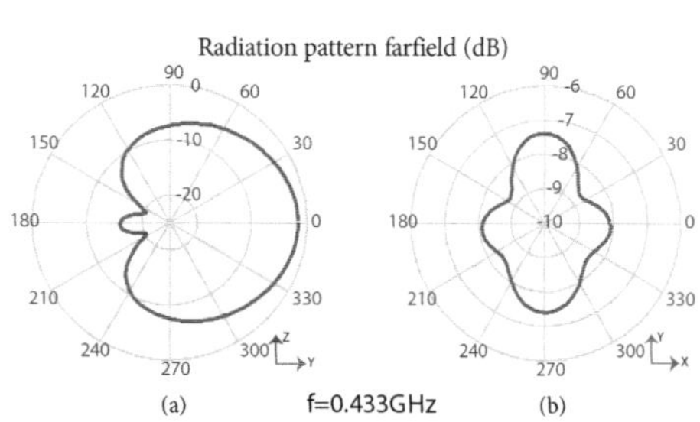

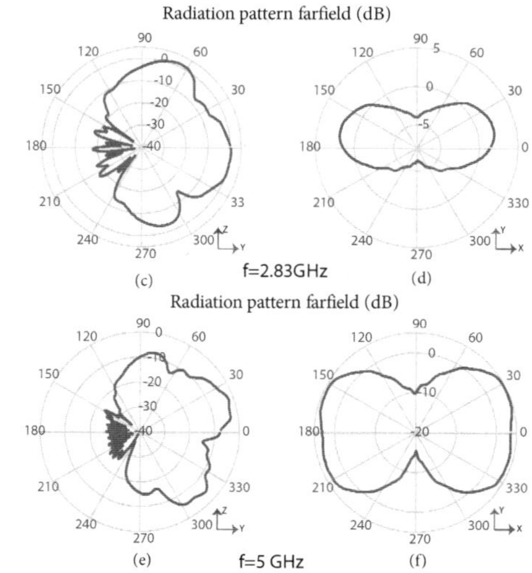

Fig. 4: Antenna pattern at:
(a), (b) 0.433 GHz; (c), (d) 2.83 GHz;(e), (f) 5 GHz.

III. Conclusion

This paper shows a vehicle antenna which can operate at three frequencies simultaneously and generate effective radiation to provide signals in multiple frequencies. With the design, the occupation of the vehicle space can be reduced through integrating antenna excitation structure and vehicle metal shell. It has great potential for vehicle-mounted 5G and various wireless applications.

Acknowledgment

This work was supported by the NSFC under Grant No. 61675013 and U19A2054, the Zhejiang Provincial Natural Science Foundation of China under Grant No. LY18F010003

References

[1] Y. Ma, "System Embedded Antenna for Portable TVWS Cognitive Radio Transceiver," in *IEEE Antennas and Wireless Propagation Letters*, vol. 14, pp. 265-268, 2015.

[2] D. Psychoudakis and A. Foroozesh, "Small millimeter wave printed antenna arrays for 5G applications," *2017 IEEE International Symposium on Antennas and Propagation & USNC/URSI National Radio Science Meeting*, San Diego, CA, 2017, pp. 1805-1806.

[3] W. Li, W. Chung, H. Tsuji, and A. Miura, "Novel internal high gain loop handset phone antenna design for satellite and terrestrial integrated mobile communications system applications," *2015 International Symposium on Antennas and Propagation (ISAP)*, Hobart, TAS, 2015, pp. 1-4.

[4] L. L. Nagy, Vehicle Antennas, New York: McGraw-Hill, 2007.

[5] K. L. Wong, Planar Antennas for Wireless Communications, NJ, Hoboken: Wiley Interscience, 2003.

[6] V. Rabinovich, N. Alexandrov, and B. Alkhateeb, Automotive Antenna Design and Applications, FL, Boca Raton: CRC Press, Taylor & Francis, 2003.

[7] S. Arianos, G. Dassano, F. Vipiana, and M. Orefice, "Design of Multi-Frequency Compact Antennas for Automotive Communications," in *IEEE Transactions on Antennas and Propagation*, vol. 60, no. 12, pp. 5604-5612, Dec. 2012.

[8] S. Arianos, G. Dassano, F. Vipiana, and M. Orefice, "Multi-band compact antennas for vehicular communications," 2011 IEEE International Symposium on Antennas and Propagation (APSURSI), Spokane, WA, 2011, pp. 2039-2042.

Design of Dual-Polarized Pyramidal Log-Periodic Antenna with Integrated Feed for Additive Manufacturing

Gaeron R. Friedrichs, Jake A. Cazden, and Dejan S. Filipovic
Department of Electrical, Computer, and Energy Engineering
University of Colorado Boulder, CO 80309-0425, USA
{Gaeron, Jake.Cazden, Dejan}@Colorado.EDU

***Abstract*—A dual-polarized log-periodic antenna with 5:1 bandwidth is considered for wideband, amplitude only direction-finding applications. The proposed system is comprised of two identical, orthogonal, sets of trapezoidal log-periodic arms. The arms' inclination from planar facilitates reduced back lobe radiation to improve directivity and efficiency once absorber is introduced. One arm of each polarization set contains a variable radius coaxial shell to achieve impedance matching such that the system impedance at the base of the antenna is matched to 50 ohms. Analysis and design for the 3d printed direction-finding antenna system is accomplished using a commercial off the shelf (COTS) finite element method (FEM) solver.**

Keywords— ***3d printing, direction finding, integrated feed, log periodic, wideband.***

I. INTRODUCTION

The relevance of amplitude only (AO) direction finding (DF) was reasserted with the ascension of most recent ultra-wideband spectral power measurement technologies, such as one demonstrated in [1]. This technology facilitates the need for wideband apertures to enable spectrum monitoring and DF without any gaps in frequency. Antennas with frequency independent behavior are desired, ideally with wide field of view and low gain rippling through frequency. These facilitate the decisive power ratios that are needed for meaningful AO-DF. Several antenna classes are feasible for this application inclusive of sinuous antennas projected onto a pyramid [2]. An objectively difficult structure to manufacture, the impedance behavior required matching to 250 Ω, without consideration of a balun. In [3], a balun was demonstrated; however, the increased integration complexity and cost to the manufacturing process, make the entire system cumbersome to produce.

Rectifying these shortcomings yields the proposed antenna system, Fig. 1. The trapezoidal log-periodic antenna in the pyramidal configuration is drastically simpler to manufacture, support, and feed. The addition of an integrated coaxial feed housed within the boom eliminates the need for a balun, effectively reducing the additional space, time, and cost resources a balun demands. The structure also lends itself to 3d printing technology, which can then be complemented with a metal plating process. Overall, this drastically reduces cost, duration, and complexity of manufacturing for the entire system.

The system is designed for operation from 1.67 GHz to 8.525 GHz using ANSYS HFSS. The patterns in both, the E-, and H-plane need a wide field of view with minimal gain rippling. The reduction of the back lobe is desired to maximize the efficiency payoffs precipitated by the pyramidal structure, and to reduce the impact of surrounding radiators on patterns' smoothness.

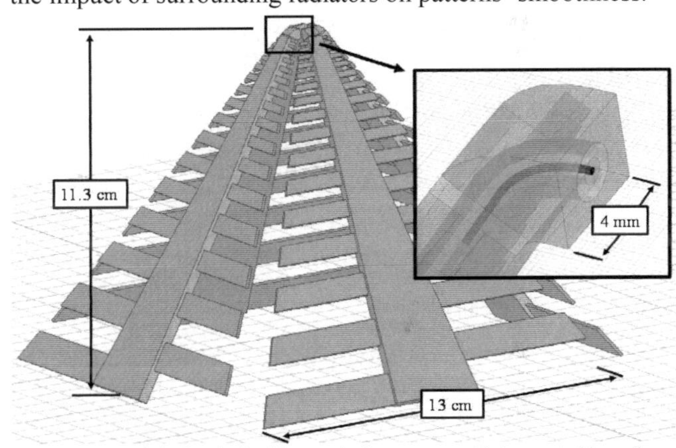

Fig. 1. Proposed dual-polarized log-periodic antenna with integrated impedance transforming feed.

II. DUAL POLARIZED LOG-PERIODIC ANTENNA

The proposed configuration is comprised of two orthogonal two-arm log-periodic structures. In order to reduce the back lobe and minimize the impact the eventual absorber has on efficiency and pattern smoothness; the arms are placed at an incline. The system parameter ψ is the angle between the two arms, such that a planar structure has a ψ of 180°. This, and the other parameters referenced in the design of this structure were summarized by DuHamel and Ore in [4]. The structure's outer angle is the angle prescribed by the tips of the elements on either side of the boom, and the tip of the pyramid. This parameter, α, becomes coupled with ψ in the dual-polarized case; the outer angle of one structure dictates the minimum angle of incline for the other. An increase in α shrinks the height of the structure, but disallows aggressive inclination, increasing the back lobe. The width of the boom is also dictated by an angle, β, which has some pertinence to the stability of the device's impedance. Element widths are

This research is sponsored by the S2 Corporation under the contract S2-1004-17-01.

described with a growth factor, τ, and selected based on a compromise between manufacturability and performance. The feed is a hollowed-out tunnel with a variable radius (to perform an impedance taper) that, after plating, serves as the outer conductor of a coaxial line. A dielectric and conductor from a COTS coax are modelled within the boom tunnel. However, to maximize efficiency of computational resources, the implemented system has a tip-located lumped port with reference impedance of 105 Ω, which represents the output port impedance of the internal transformer. Detailed parametric study resulted in antenna parameters shown in Table I.

Table I. Chosen log-periodic parameters for system implementation

α	β	ψ	τ
50°	10°	65°	0.85

III. Performance

VSWR < 2 was obtained across the band at both the lumped port (with respect to 105 Ω) and at the input of the integrated impedance transformer (with respect to 50 Ω), shown in Fig. 2.

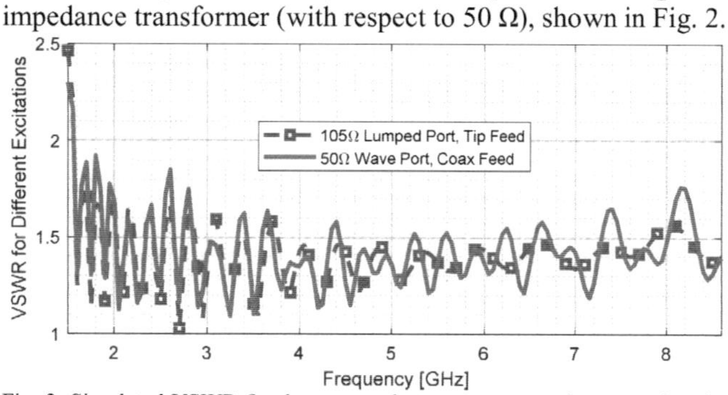

Fig. 2. Simulated VSWR for the proposed antenna system, demonstrating the impact of the integrated, impedance transforming feed.

The gain at boresight and half-power beamwidth (HPBW) of the system are shown in Fig. 3. The gain is stable throughout the band of interest, whereas HPBW changes ±8° across bandwidth. While not demonstrated herein, the addition of an absorber reduces the back lobe, improves pattern stability, but decreases radiation efficiency. This reemphasizes the importance of the pyramidal nature (α-ψ tradeoff) to extract as much radiation efficiency from the system as possible by improving main beam efficiency, while not compromising the performance or overall system size.

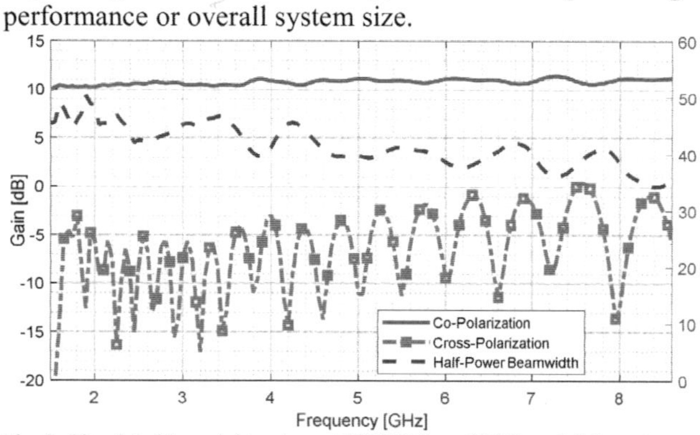

Fig. 3. Simulated boresight gain and HPBW from HFSS model featuring a tip-located lumped port.

To determine the behavior of the system as a direction-finding subsystem, a custom numerical subroutine, implemented in MATLAB, was used. The system function, a combination of two duplicate radiation patterns, squinted at some angle, was generated. The ratio of powers at each angle was obtained, resulting in the direction-finding function. The slope of this function, shown in Fig. 4, demonstrates the system's resolution, and correlates to its robustness to noise. In this case, the field of view is clearly 40° in the H-plane with near 0.5 dB/° slope throughout the band. The practical implications of the additive manufacturing process, including surface roughness and surface impedance is part of the future work.

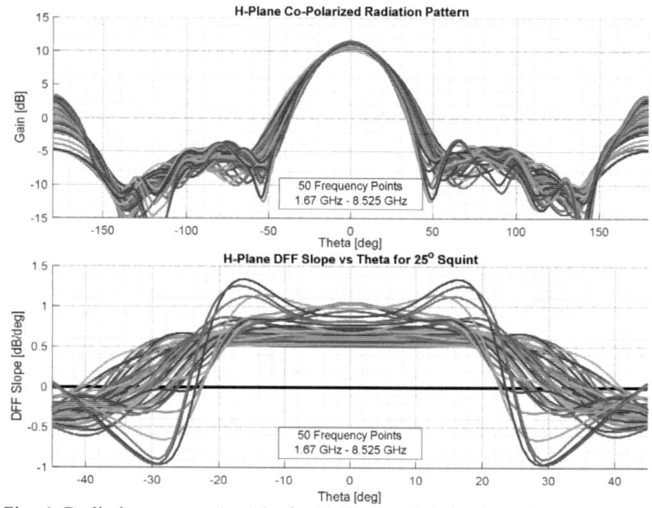

Fig. 4. Radiation pattern (top) in the H-Plane and derivative of the Direction-Finding Function (bottom) for the dual-polarized log-periodic antenna system squinted at 25°.

IV. Conclusion

A dual-polarized, log-periodic antenna in pyramidal configuration is proposed. The approach leveraged an integrated feed to perform impedance matching, improve integration ease with COTS components, and remove the need for a balun. Good performance over 5:1 bandwidth is obtained from simulations in ANSYS HFSS, while maintaining a structure that lends itself to additive manufacturing processes. The demonstrated field of view for the direction-finding function with 0.5 dB/° resolution is 40°.

References

[1] R. Mohan, T. Chang, et al., "Ultra-wideband spectral analysis using S2 technology," in The Journal of Luminescence., no. 127, March 2007, pp. 116-128.

[2] D. I. L. deVilliers, "Initial Study of a Pyramidal Sinuous Antenna as a Feed for the SKA Reflector System in Band-1," 2017 IEEE International Symposium on Antennas and Propagation & USNC/URSI National Radio Science Meeting, San Diego, CA, July 2017, pp. 555-556.

[3] M. Johnston, C. V. Niekerk, and D. I. L. deVilliers, "Ultra-wideband Planar Marchand Balun Design for the Pyramidal Sinuous Antenna," 2019 IEEE International Symposium on Antennas and Propagation & USNC/URSI Radio Science Meeting, Atlanta, GA, July 2019, pp. 735-736.

[4] R. H. DuHamel and F. R. Ore, "Logarithmically Periodic Antenna Designs," in 1958 IRE International Convention Record, New York, NY, March 1966, pp. 139-151.

Simulation of a Nonlinear Frequency Multiplier using the FDTD Technique

Joshua M. Kast
Department of Electrical Engineering
Colorado School of Mines
Golden, CO 80401 USA
jkast@mines.edu

Atef Z. Elsherbeni*
Department of Electrical Engineering
Colorado School of Mines
Golden, CO 80401 USA
aelsherb@mines.edu

***Abstract*— Nonlinear circuits are a key component in RF transceivers. Efficiency and power requirements for 5G communication are creating new challenges in simulation and modeling of nonlinear devices. An application of the finite-difference time-domain (FDTD) method to nonlinear circuits comprising diodes is demonstrated. A frequency multiplier is constructed from a diode and a low-pass filter. The diode is simulated in the context of this circuit to demonstrate the formation of harmonics.**

***Keywords*—FDTD, frequency multiplier, nonlinear.**

I. INTRODUCTION

Frequency multipliers are often employed in microwave communications devices operating at high frequencies, including those in the millimeter-wave region. Moreover, other devices share in the harmonic-generating property of a frequency multiplier, including nonlinear amplifiers and mixers. While harmonic-balance analysis has been a mainstay for the analysis of such devices, we demonstrate that the finite-difference time-domain (FDTD) simulation technique has merit for certain types of nonlinear problem.

A. Frequency Multiplier Theory of Operation

The voltage-current relationship for an ideal diode is [1]:

$$I_D(V_D) = I_s\left(e^{\frac{V_D}{\eta V_T}} - 1\right). \tag{1}$$

Where V_D is the voltage across the diode, I_s is the saturation current, V_T is the thermal voltage of the diode, and η is an ideality factor. This equation may be rewritten to remove the exponential, by:

$$I_D(V_D) = I_s \sum_{n=1}^{\infty} \frac{\left(\frac{V_D}{\eta V_T}\right)^n}{n!}. \tag{2}$$

If V_D is a sinusoidal signal given by $V_D = a\cos(\omega t)$, then (2) may be written as:

$$I_D(t) = I_s \sum_{n=1}^{\infty} \frac{\left(\frac{a\cos(\omega t)}{\eta V_T}\right)^n}{n!}. \tag{3}$$

*Adjunct Professor, Department of Elec. & Computer Eng., King Abdulaziz University, Jeddah, Saudi Arabia

Taking only the terms $n = (1,2,3)$, and using trigonometric identities to simplify the exponents [2], the current may be approximated as:

$$I_D(t) \approx I_s \left(\frac{a\cos(\omega t)}{\eta V_T} + \frac{a^2(\cos(2\omega t) + 1)}{4\eta^2 V_T^2} + \frac{a^3(\cos(3\omega t) - 3\cos(\omega t))}{24\eta^3 V_T^3} \right). \tag{4}$$

From this expression, it is possible to see how a sinusoidal voltage across a diode is transformed into both even and odd harmonics of the fundamental frequency. Thus, the diode may be used in this capacity as a frequency multiplier.

B. FDTD Simulation

Problems in this work are simulated using the well-known FDTD algorithm, based on discretizing the problem into a grid of Yee cells, and solving differential forms of Maxwell's equations in the time domain. All results presented here are generated based on the code developed in [3].

Simulation of the diode is performed by solving a modified form of (1) in order to update the values for electric fields in the region of the diode. This equation is solved iteratively using the Newton-Raphson method [3, Ch. 4].

II. SIMULATIONS AND RESULTS

To demonstrate FDTD simulation of a diode in the context of a frequency multiplier, we simulate two configurations. First, the diode is connected in series with a voltage source and a 50Ω resistor. Second, the diode is connected as a shunt device after a low pass filter. The configurations were simulated as circuit schematic models using the Transient simulation in Keysight's ADS software [4], with ADS results plotted alongside the FDTD results for comparison.

A. Diode in Series with Resistor

To test the diode updating equation in the context of a simple circuit, a diode was placed in series with a 50Ω resistor as shown in Fig. 1 (a). Conductors between lumped elements were modeled using thin-wire approximations. The voltage source was configured to produce a 5 GHz cosine wave with a peak-to-peak voltage of 3 V, and an internal resistance of 50Ω.

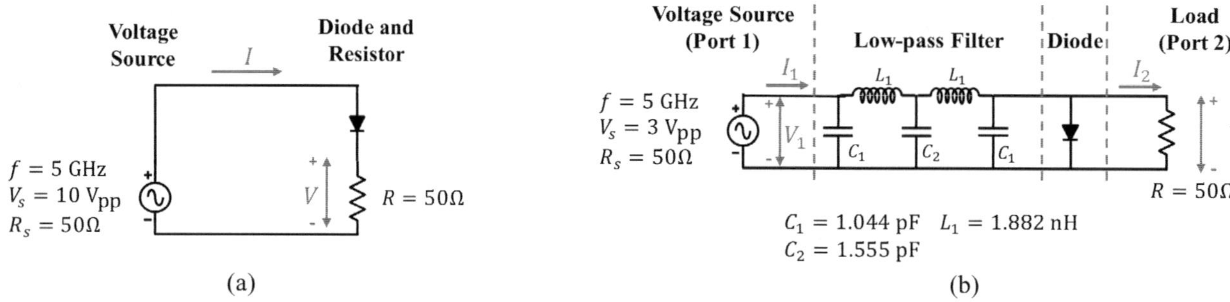

Fig. 1. Circuit schematics for diode simulations. (a) Diode in series with resistor, (b) diode with low-pass filter.

Time-domain results from this simulation are plotted in Fig. 2, where the diode is seen to rectify current traveling through the 50Ω resistor. The voltage across this resistor is plotted in the frequency domain in Fig. 3. In this plot, harmonics may be seen every 5 GHz, as a result of the diode's clipping effect.

B. Diode with Low-Pass Filter

From the previous results, we see that the diode produces numerous harmonics above 5 GHz. To make use of these harmonics for the function of frequency multiplication, it is necessary to place filters before and after the diode [5]. In this simulation, a low-pass filter is placed before the diode to prevent harmonics from reaching the source, as shown in Fig. 1 (b). Results from this simulation are plotted in Fig. 4: at port 1, only the excitation at 5 GHz may be seen. At port 2, following the diode, we see harmonics every 5 GHz as a result of the diode. Extension of this work to the FDTD simulation of transistors, as described in [6], is in progress.

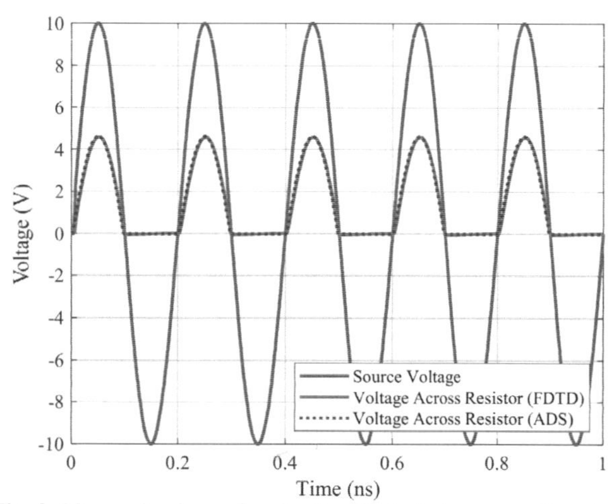

Fig. 2. Measured voltages for circuit with diode in series with resistor shown in Fig. 1 (a).

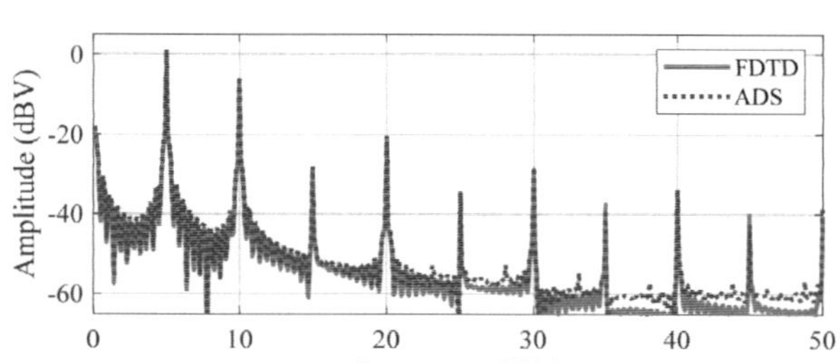

Fig. 3. Frequency domain plot of voltage measured across series diode and resistor from Fig. 1 (a).

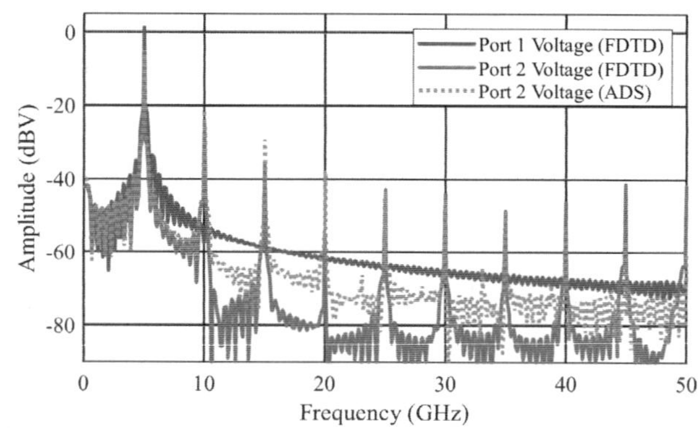

Fig. 4. Frequency-domain plot of voltages at port 1 and port 2 of network with low-pass filter shown in Fig. 1 (b).

III. CONCLUSIONS

As a proof-of-concept, we demonstrate an application of FDTD simulation to a circuit incorporating passive devices and a diode as a nonlinear circuit to analyze harmonics in microwave devices. From this result, we conclude that FDTD can be a useful method for modeling 3-D structures incorporating nonlinear devices.

REFERENCES

[1] W. Shockley, "The theory of p-n junctions in semiconductors and p-n junction transistors," *Bell Syst. Tech. J.*, vol. 28, no. 3, pp. 435–489, Jul. 1949.

[2] W. M. Haynes, Ed., *CRC Handbook of Chemistry and Physics, 92nd Edition*, 92 edition. Boca Raton, Fla.: CRC Press, 2011.

[3] A. Z. Elsherbeni and V. Demir, *The finite-difference time-domain method for electromagnetics with Matlab simulations*. Raleigh: The Institution of Engineering and Technology, 2016.

[4] Keysight, Santa Rosa, CA, USA. 2019. Advanced Design System 2019 [Online]. Available: http://www.keysight.comen/pc-1297113/advanced-design-system-ads?&cc=US&lc=eng

[5] S. A. Maas, *Nonlinear Microwave Circuits*. Artech House, 1988.

[6] K. ElMahgoub and A. Z. Elsherbeni, "FDTD Implementations of Integrated Dependent Sources in Full- Wave Electromagnetic Simulations," vol. 29, no. 12, p. 10, 2014

A Practical Fourth Order Finite-Difference Time-Domain Algorithm for the Solution of Maxwell's Equations

Antonio P. Thomson
Department of Electrical Engineering
Colorado School of Mines
Golden, CO 80401 USA
adesposito@mines.edu

Atef Z. Elsherbeni*
Department of Electrical Engineering
Colorado School of Mines
Golden, CO 80401 USA
aelsherb@mines.edu

Mohammed Hadi
Electrical Engineering Department
Colorado School of Mines
Golden, CO 80401 USA
mhadi@mines.edu

Abstract— **Implementing a practical fourth order accurate in time and second order accurate in space finite difference time domain simulation using MATLAB is the goal of this paper. The formulation presented for the fourth order approximation is simple to integrate into an existing second order accurate in time and second order accurate in space formulation and well-established code. The fourth order formulation has been verified and simulation accuracy is confirmed through the application of radiation from a single and an array of dipole antennas.**

Keywords— FDTD, finite difference time domain, higher order, fourth order approximation.

I. INTRODUCTION

The finite difference time domain (FDTD) method is a highly effective method of numerically solving Maxwell's equations in the time domain [1]. The standard derivative approximation is a second order accurate central differencing scheme for all derivatives in Maxwell's equations (second order) [1]. This paper will present the implementation for a practical FDTD scheme using fourth order accurate central differencing derivative approximations in space and second order accurate central differencing derivative approximations in time (fourth order). Fourth order FDTD simulations allow the cell size of the simulation to grow while maintaining necessary solution accuracy. Larger cell sizes are imperative when geometries become electrically large and the computational memory becomes too excessive. Many other papers have studied the benefits of fourth order FDTD, but none have simulated practical antenna problems with a simple formulation [2], [3], [4], [5]. The goal of this paper is to present a fourth order formulation that is straightforward and at the same time can simulate practical problems such as antenna arrays.

II. FOURTH ORDER FDTD FORMULATION

Fourth order FDTD can be simply derived by using fourth order accurate derivative approximations (equation 2) for spatial derivatives and using the second order accurate derivative approximation for the time derivative in Maxwell's equations. Consider, for example, the E_x component of Ampere's Maxwell equation as presented in [1]:

$$\frac{\partial E_x}{\partial t} = \frac{1}{\epsilon_x}\left(\frac{\partial H_z}{\partial y} - \frac{\partial H_y}{\partial z} - \sigma_x^e E_x - J_{ix}\right). \tag{1}$$

*Adjunct Professor, Department of Elec. & Computer Eng., King Abdulaziz University, Jeddah, Saudi Arabia

Upon using the fourth order accurate approximation for the spatial derivatives, that is:

$$f'\left(x - \frac{\Delta x}{2}\right) \approx \frac{-f(x+\Delta x) + 27f(x) - 27f(x-\Delta x) + f(x-2\Delta x)}{24\Delta x}, \tag{2}$$

the updating equation of the E_x component will take the following form:

$$E_x^{n+1}(i,j,k) = \begin{aligned} &+\frac{2\epsilon_x(i,j,k) - \Delta t\sigma_x^e(i,j,k)}{2\epsilon_x(i,j,k) + \Delta t\sigma_x^e(i,j,k)} E_x^n(i,j,k) - \frac{2\Delta t}{2\epsilon_x(i,j,k) + \Delta t\sigma_x^e(i,j,k)}\beta \\ &+\frac{2\Delta t}{2\epsilon_x(i,j,k) + \Delta t\sigma_x^e(i,j,k)}\alpha - \frac{2\Delta t}{2\epsilon_x(i,j,k) + \Delta t\sigma_x^e(i,j,k)} J_x^{n+\frac{1}{2}}(i,j,k) \end{aligned}, \tag{3}$$

where,

$$\alpha = \frac{-H_z^{n+\frac{1}{2}}(i,j+1,k) + 27H_z^{n+\frac{1}{2}}(i,j,k) - 27H_z^{n+\frac{1}{2}}(i,j-1,k) + H_z^{n+\frac{1}{2}}(i,j-2,k)}{24\Delta y},$$

and

$$\beta = \frac{-H_y^{n+\frac{1}{2}}(i,j,k+1) + 27H_y^{n+\frac{1}{2}}(i,j,k) - 27H_y^{n+\frac{1}{2}}(i,j,k-1) + H_y^{n+\frac{1}{2}}(i,j,k-2)}{24\Delta z}.$$

Note that based on the above representation, if the second order derivative approximation is anticipated, making this second order FDTD, all what is needed is to change the definitions of α and β. The other coefficients in equation (3) are the same for the second order and fourth order formulations. This makes the integration of this fourth order formulation into an existing second order code [1] rather simple. The updating equations for voltage and current sources as well as resistors and convolutional perfectly matched layer (CPML) can all be easily derived and integrated.

III. 1D VERIFICATION EXAMPLE

A simple 1D Gaussian wave propagating in free space was simulated with second order and fourth order formulations. The 1D domain is 1 meter long discretized with 300 cells of air. The source is an infinite sheet of J_z producing a Gaussian pulse with 5 cells per λ_{min}. For second order, 20 cells per λ_{min} is recommended [1] meaning this is a course grid.

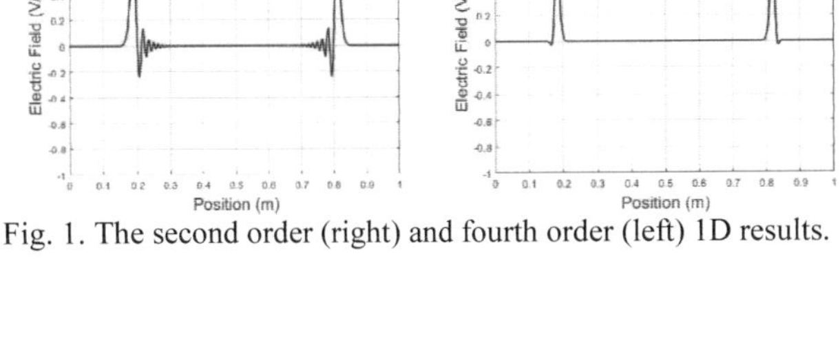

Fig. 1. The second order (right) and fourth order (left) 1D results.

As Fig. 1 shows the fourth order results have less dispersion than the second order results, showing the fourth order simulation is more accurate than the second order simulation.

IV. Practical Problem: Thin Wire Dipole

Although many papers have presented the formulation for fourth order FDTD, none have simulated practical problems such as antenna problems complete with CPML boundaries, and sources and loads in terms of voltage sources, resistors, and other circuit elements [2], [3], [4], [5]. A thin wire dipole antenna simulation using the developed fourth order FDTD is presented here. The improved thin wire formulation from [1, Ch. 10] is used with the necessary modifications to implement fourth order FDTD. The length of the dipole is 20mm oriented in the Z-direction, with a center gap of 1 cell length for the voltage source. The cell size is defined by dx=dy=dz=0.25mm. The voltage source supports a Gaussian waveform with a max frequency when 20 cells are used per λ_{min} and an internal impedance of 50Ω. A theoretical dipole transmits best when acting as a half wavelength dipole antenna [6]. Based on the length of this dipole, the minimum S_{11} reflection coefficient is predicted to be at 7.5 GHz.

The minimum reflection coefficient in Fig. 2 (left) occurs at 7.52 GHz which shows a difference of 0.27% when compared to the analytical expected value of 7.5 GHz. Additionally, the directivity in the x-y plane matches the expected isotropic radiation pattern for a half wavelength dipole antenna.

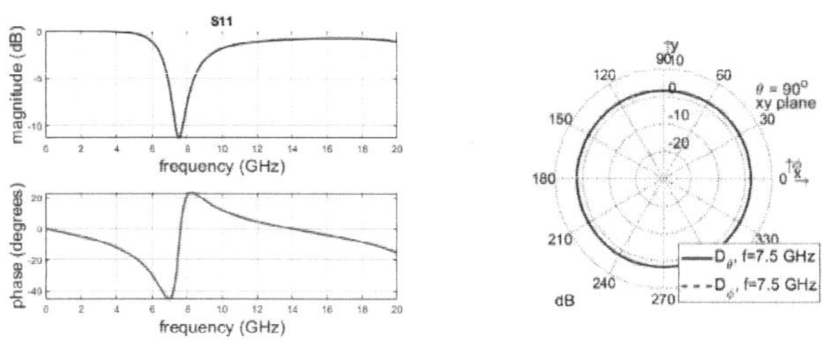

Fig. 2. The simulation results for a dipole antenna, (left) is the amplitude and phase of the reflection coefficient for a wide frequency band, (right) is the directivity pattern in the x-y plane.

V. Practical Problem: Thin Wire Dipole Array

The real benefit of using fourth order FDTD is evident when simulating electrically large problems, such as antenna arrays. For simplicity and ease of comparison to analytical solutions a simple two element array of thin wire dipole antennas is simulated. The array is in the x-direction with a spacing of $\lambda/2$ = 20mm. The problem space setup and each antenna geometry match that of the antenna simulated in Fig. 2.

Note that Fig. 2 (left) and Fig. 3 (left) do not match exactly because FDTD is a full wave solution technique and takes into account the coupling between the two antennas.

As this is a simple two element uniform linear array, the normalized array factor without coupling can be written as follows [6]:

$$(AF)_N = \cos\left(\frac{1}{2}(kd\cos\phi + \beta)\right). \tag{5}$$

The polar plot of the array factor has maximums at $\phi = 90^o$ and $\phi = 270^o$ and minimums at $\phi = 0$ and at $\phi = 180^o$.

Since the single element dipole directivity is isotropic in the x-y plane, the total directivity pattern of the array should match the shape of the array factor. Fig. 3 (left) demonstrates this fact, providing evidence that the fourth order FDTD produced good results for an antenna array problem. Fig. 3 (left) also demonstrates that larger arrays can be simulated using the presented fourth order FDTD implementation. The larger the array, the more computational advantage the fourth order formulation will have over the second order formulation.

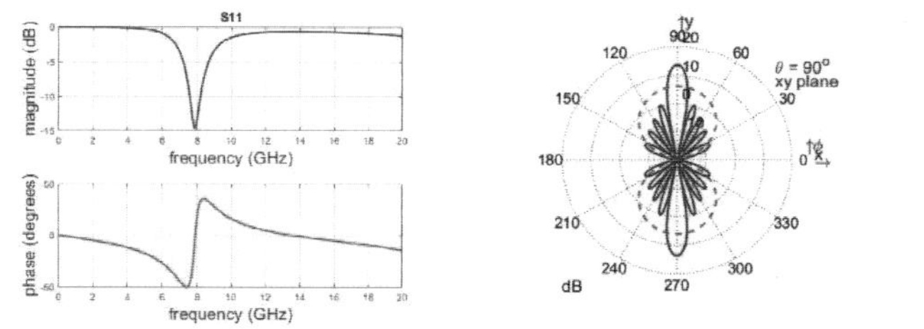

Fig. 3. The simulation results for an array of dipole antennas, (left) is the amplitude and phase of the reflection coefficient of the center element, (right) is the directivity pattern in the x-y plane for a ten-element array (solid blue) and the two-element array (dashed red).

VI. Conclusions

This paper demonstrates a practical and straightforward implementation of a fourth order FDTD formulation. The formulation allows for the integration of thin wire, active and passive circuit elements, CPML, and other special formulations as presented in a second order formulation. In order to confirm the validity and accuracy of the developed formulation the radiation from a single element and arrays of dipole antennas are performed leading to the expected results.

Future work will include implementing fourth order simulations of circuit elements such as inductors, capacitors, and diodes. Additionally, fourth order handling of perfect electric conductor (PEC) objects will be explored.

Aknowledgment

This project is partially supported by a gift fund from Futurewei Technology Inc., New Jersey Research Center, Bridgewater, NJ, USA.

References

[1] A. Z. Elsherbeni and V. Demir, The Finite-Difference Time-Domain Method for Electromagnetics with MATLAB® Simulations, 2nd edition, Edison, New Jersey: SciTech Publishing, 2015.

[2] M. Hadi and M.Piket-May, "A Modified FDTD (2, 4) Scheme for Modeling Electrically Large Structures with High-Phase Accuracy," IEEE Trans. Antennas Propagat., vol. 45, no. 2, Feb. 1997.

[3] J. Fang, "Time-domain finite difference computations for Maxwell's equations," Ph.D. dissertation, EECS Dept., Univ. California, Berkeley, 1989.

[4] K. Hwang and A. C. Cangellaris, "Computational Efficiency of Fang's Fourth-Order FDTD Schemes," Electromagnetics, vol. 23, 2003.

[5] N. V. Kantartzis and T. D. Tsiboukis, Higher Order FDTD Schemes for Waveguide and Antenna Structures, 1st edition, Morgan & Claypool Publishers, 2006.

[6] C. A. Balanis, Antenna Theory Analysis and Design, 3rd edition, Hoboken, New Jersey: A John Wiley & Sons, Inc., 2005.

IMPLEMENTATION OF PASSIVE AND ACTIVE CIRCUIT ELEMENTS IN CYLINDRICAL FINITE-DIFFERENCE TIME-DOMAIN FORMULATION

Abdullah M. Algarni*
Department of Electrical Engineering
King Fahd Univ. of Petru. & Min.
Dhahran, Saudi Arabia
algarnia@kfupm.edu.sa

Atef Z. Elsherbeni**
Department of Electrical Engineering
Colorado School of Mines
Golden, Colorado, USA
aelsherb@mines.edu

Mohammed Hadi
Department of Electrical Engineering
Colorado School of Mines
Golden, Colorado, USA
mhadi@mines.edu

***Abstract* — The implementation of passive and active linear circuit elements.in cylindrical finite-difference time-domain technique (CFDTD) is developed. The updating equations for active element such as a voltage sources and passive elements such as resistors, capacitors and inductors are represented for elements located along one of the cylindrical coordinate's independent parameters. The analytical solutions for simple circuit configurations are computed and used as a reference to verify and confirm the accuracy of the developed CFDTD formulation and numerical results.**

Keywords—cylindrical finite-difference time-domain, passive and active linear circuit elements.

I. INTRODUCTION

Finite-difference time-domain (FDTD) is a technique which is used to solve Maxwell's equations in time domain EM by using numerical approximation of the derivatives, mainly in the cartesian coordinates system [1]. The FDTD is an easy technique since it does not require some complicated functions such as the Green's functions to find the solution. Also, it handles complex geometries without further complications. In addition to these advantages, by using a source waveform like a Gaussian pulse, the solution of a wide spectrum of frequencies will be covered by solving the problem only one time. For cylindrical structure problems and especially near to the axis of rotation the FDTD formulation in cylindrical coordinates system (CFDTD) is required to yield high accuracy [2]. There are applications in which the CFDTD can be used such as in geophysics and petroleum engineering. One of these applications is the wireline logging which is a process of recording the formation's rock properties [3].

This summary introduces the formulation and verification of integrating passive and active circuit elements in the CFDTD formulation to facilitate the simulation of the radiating elements such as dipoles and loops excited with voltage sources required for such applications.

II. CFDTD UPDATING EQUATIONS

Field components where circuit elements are present in the computational domain needs special updating equations. Here, only the E_z updating equation will be modified for a circuit element located between the nodes carrying this E_z component. Starting with the E_z updating as shown below:

$$\begin{aligned}E_z^{n+1}(i,j,k) &= C_{eze}(i,j,k)\times E_z^{n}(i,j,k)\\ &+(C_{ezh\phi 1}(i,j,k)\times H_\phi^{n+\frac{1}{2}}(i,j,k)\\ &-C_{ezh\phi 2}(i,j,k)\times H_\phi^{n-\frac{1}{2}}(i-1,j,k))\\ &+C_{ezh\rho}(i,j,k)\times(H_\rho^{n+\frac{1}{2}}(i,j,k)-H_\rho^{n+\frac{1}{2}}(i,j-1,k))\\ &+C_{ezj}(i,j,k)\times J_{iz}^{n+\frac{1}{2}}(i,j,k),\end{aligned} \tag{1}$$

where

$$C_{ezj}(i,j,k) = -\frac{2\Delta t}{2\varepsilon_z(i,j,k)+\Delta t\sigma_z^e(i,j,k)},$$

and all other coefficients can be expressed from (3) in [2]. The parameters i, j, k represent the nodes in the ρ, ϕ, and z directions, respectively, while $\Delta\rho$ and $\Delta\phi$ are the step size in the ρ and ϕ directions, respectively. The time step Δt is given by (28) in [2]. All other fields updating equations can be expressed using the same methodology applied for E_z.

III. UPDATING EQUATIONS FOR PASSIVE AND ACTIVE ELEMENTS

The passive elements such as resistors, inductors and capacitors and active elements such as voltage sources are important components in any electromagnetics simulation. Here, any of these elements will be placed between nodes in z direction. Fig. 1 shows a general form of a simple circuit diagram where V_S and Z_S are placed between two nodes and Z_L is placed one node a way in the ρ direction. In this paper, three cases will be presented. The first case, Z_S is a resistor with a sinusoidal waveform as a voltage source. The second case, Z_S is a resistor with a capacitor in series and in the third case Z_S is a resistor with an inductor in series where a unit-step function

*Ph.D. student at Colorado School of Mines, Golden, CO, US.
**Adjunct Professor, Department of Elec. & Computer Eng., King Abdulaziz University, Jeddah, Saudi Arabia.

uses as a voltage source in the second and third cases. The Z_L for all cases is a resistor. For any of these cases, the updating equation for E_z in (1) can be modified with the help of term $J_{iz}^{n+\frac{1}{2}}(i,j,k)$.

For the first case, we have:

$$J_{iz}^{n+\frac{1}{2}}(i,j,k) = \frac{\Delta z}{2A_i R_S}\left(E_z^{n+1}(i,j,k) + E_z^{n}(i,j,k)\right) + \frac{V_S}{A_i R_S}, \quad (2)$$

for the second case, we used the recursive convolution method [1] and we get:

$$\begin{aligned} Q_{iz}^{n+\frac{1}{2}}(i,j,k) &= Q_{iz}^{n-\frac{1}{2}}(i,j,k)\times e^{-\frac{\Delta t}{CR_S}} \\ &\quad + \left(\Delta z E_z^{n}(i,j,k) + V_S\right), \\ J_{iz}^{n+\frac{1}{2}}(i,j,k) &= \frac{1}{A_i R_S}\left(\Delta z E_z^{n}(i,j,k) + V_S\right) \\ &\quad + (e^{-\frac{\Delta t}{CR_S}} - 1)\times Q_{iz}^{n+\frac{1}{2}}(i,j,k), \end{aligned} \quad (3)$$

and for the third case we get:

$$J_{iz}^{n+\frac{1}{2}}(i,j,k) = \frac{2L - R_S\Delta t}{2L + R_S\Delta t} J_{iz}^{n-\frac{1}{2}}(i,j,k) + \frac{2\Delta z\Delta t}{A_i(2L + R_S\Delta t)} E_z^{n}(i,j,k) + \frac{2\Delta z\Delta t}{A_i(2L + R_S\Delta t)} V_S, \quad (4)$$

where A_i is the area normal to $E_z(i,j,k)$ is given by:

$$A_i = i\Delta\rho^2\Delta\phi. \quad (5)$$

For all cases, the resistors are $R_S = R_L = 50\Omega$, the capacitor is C=1nF and the inductor is L=2.5 μH. In Fig. 2 and Fig. 3, the sampled voltage across the load using the CFDTD simulation of the circuit and the corresponding analytical solution show very good agreement.

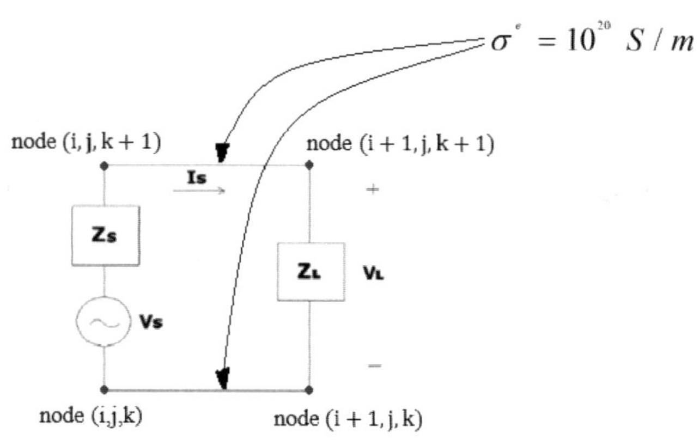

Fig. 1. Simple circuit diagram in CFDTD.

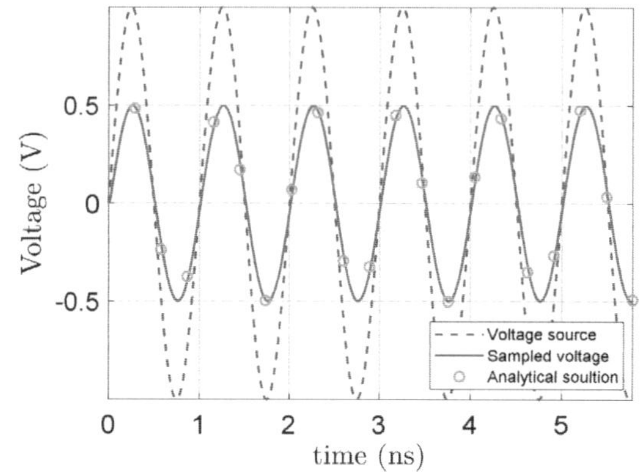

Fig. 2. Voltage across $Z_L = R_L$ using $Z_S = R_S$.

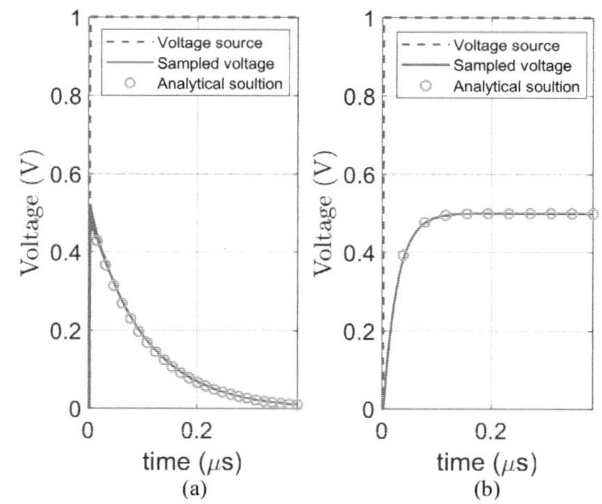

Fig. 3. Voltage across $Z_L = R_L$ using: (a) $Z_S = R_S + Z_{Cap}$ and (b) $Z_S = R_S + Z_{Ind}$.

IV. Conclusion

The validation of integrating passive and active circuit elements into the formulation and simulations using the cylindrical finite-difference time-domain is achieved. The developed code has been used to test other element positional possibilities in the CFDTD grid. Work is in progress to include nonlinear elements in this cylindrical formulation to address a larger array of electromagnetic problems.

References

[1] A. Elsherbeni and V. Demir, The Finite Difference Time Domain Method For Electromagnetics with MATLAB® Simulation, 2nd ed., SCITECH Publishing, 2015.

[2] M. F. Hadi and A. Z. Elsherbeni "Numerical Dispersion and Stability for Three-Dimensional Cylindrical FDTD near the Axis of Rotation," 11th European Conference on Antennas and Propagation (EUCAP), pp. 936-938, May 2017.

[3] D. V. Ellis and J. M. Singer, Well Logging for Earth Scientists, 2nd ed., Springer, pp. 3, 2007.

Arrow Patch-Slot Antenna for 5G Lower Frequency Band Communications

Yuhao Feng [1]
yuhaofeng@mymail.mines.edu

Yiming Chen [1]
yimingchen@mymail.mines.edu

Atef Z. Elsherbeni [1, 2, *]
aelsherb@mines.edu

Khalid Alharbi[2]
khalharbi@kau.edu.sa

[1] Department of Electrical Engineering
Colorado School of Mines
Golden, CO 80401 USA

[2] Department of Electrical and Computer Engineering
King Abdulaziz University
Jeddah, 21589, Saudi Arabia

Abstract— A compact size arrow shaped patch in a rectangular slot antenna is designed for 5G communications in the lower 3 to 6 GHz band. The antenna element is fed through a coplanar waveguide with partial ground plane for better impedance matching with 50 Ohms across the entire band. The maximum gain of a single element is 3.8 dB at 3.7 GHz, while for linear arrays of 5 and 15 elements with uniform excitation the maximum gains are 10.9 dB and 16 dB, respectively. The 5 and 15 elements arrays provide scanning range with no significant degradation of the main beam up to 30° and 45°, respectively. The properties of this antenna element makes it suitable for 5G wireless mobile devices and miniaturized base stations antenna arrays.

Keywords— *5G antenna, compact size, FDTD, wide-band.*

I. Introduction

In recent years, the establishment of the fifth-generation communication systems (5G) are getting more and more attentions [1], in which the antenna working as the wireless signal receiver and transmitter are facing the challenges of updating systematically due to the new licensed frequency band for 5G. The 5G frequency announced by the FCC in 2018 has the sub-6 bands like 3.55-3.7 GHz band and 3.7-4.2 GHz band, and higher frequency bands as 24.25-24.45 GHz band, 24.75-25.25 GHz band, 27.5-28.35 GHz, 37-38.6 GHz, etc. [2]. Initially, 5G antenna designs are mainly focus on the sub-6 bands due to the lower cost and lower manufacturing accuracy requirements. However, the wide-ranging bands at the sub-6 range are enforcing the need for antennas covering these bands in a configurable mechanism. Reconfigurable antennas are usually consisting of other circuit elements that introduces losses and complications to the design [3]. An alternative approach is to design an antenna that support the entire sub-6 GHz band with miniaturization and low cost in mind [4].

In order to achieve a compact size antenna working at different bands within the 3 to 6 GHz range using single feeding port, an arrow-like patch/slot type antenna with partially grounded coplanar waveguide (CPW) feed is considered. CPW feeding configuration has several advantages such as low profile, low cost, and broader bandwidth relative to traditional microstrip line configuration [5].

*Adjunct Professor, Department of Elec. & Computer Eng., King Abdulaziz University, Jeddah, Saudi Arabia

The finite difference time domain (FDTD) method is used for the current design simulation [6] and the numerical results for one element antenna is compared with the corresponding measured results of a fabricated prototype and simulated results using commercially available Ansys High Frequency Structure Simulator (HFSS). A linear array with 30° and 45° scanned beams are also simulated to show the future capabilities of this element in array configurations.

II. Antenna Design & Structure

The top view of the proposed antenna element is shown in Fig. 1 along with the fabricated prototype using an FR4 substrate, with thickness of 1.6 mm, relative permittivity of 4.4, and loss tangent of 0.02. The footprint size of this antenna is 35 (W) × 30 (H) mm^2, which are 0.43λ × 0.37λ at 3.7 GHz. The dash line in Fig. 1 (a) represents a partial metal ground plane at the bottom side of the substrate with dimensions of 35 (W) × 3 (H_b) mm^2. The above dimensions are optimized using the full wave simulation software CEMS [8] which is based on the FDTD method [6], but running on GPU. The other dimensions of the antenna element in millimeters are: $W = 35$, $H = 30$, $W_1 = 23$, $H_1 = 13$, $H_2 = 10$, Wp = 15.6, $H_p = 7.2$, $W_f = 3.6$, $H_f = 12.4$, s = 0.4, $H_b = 3$. Fig. 1 (b) presents the fabricated single element.

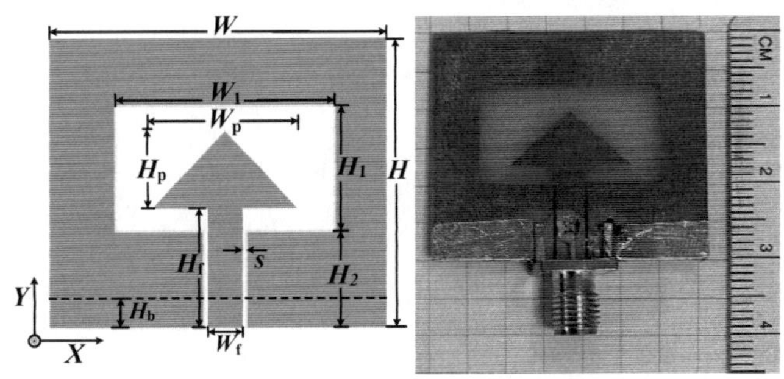

(a) (b)

Fig. 1. (a) The proposed arrow shaped patch/slot antenna element. (b) Fabricated prototype element.

To demonstrate the potential of this element in building a phased array base station antenna with miniaturized size and wide-band capabilities, a 5-elements and a 15-elements linear arrays were also simulated and sample results are presented. This design provides a good potential of multi-input and multi-output (MIMO) antenna designs for 5G applications.

III. Simulated And Measured Results

The major simulation parameters used in CEMS are: dx=0.1, dy=dz=0.2 mm and 50,000 time steps with 10 layers of convolutional perfectly matched layer (CPML) boundary.

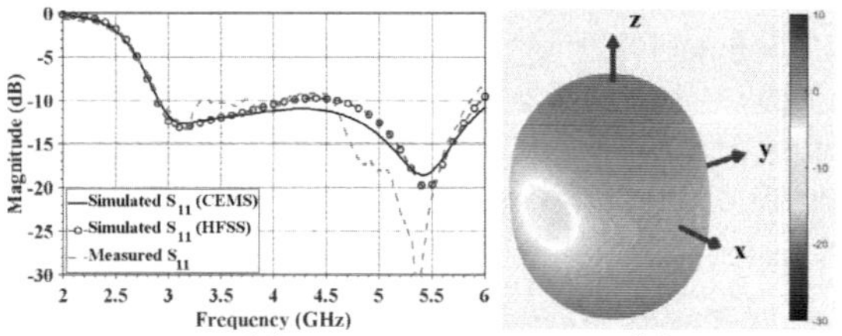

(a) (b)

Fig. 2. (a) Antenna element reflection coefficients, (b) far-field gain pattern at 3.7-GHz.

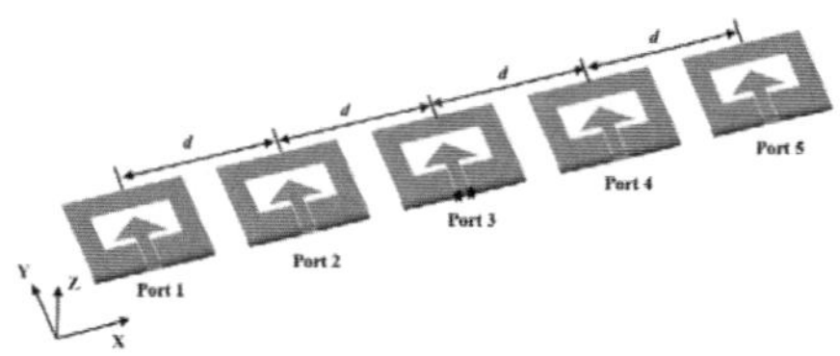

Fig. 3. A 5-elements linear array with size less than 2.65λ.

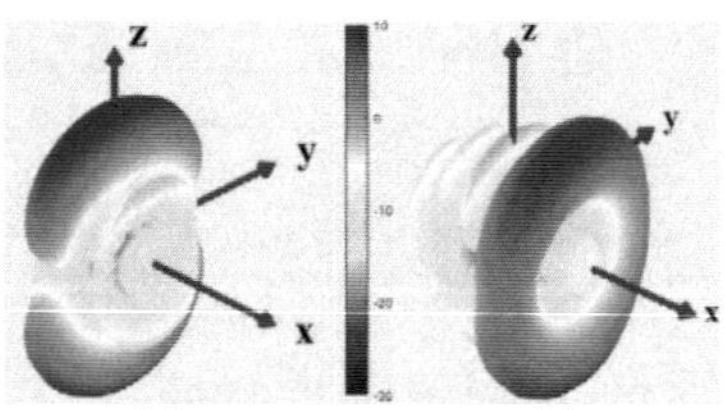

(a) (b)

Fig. 4. The 5-elements 3D far-field gain pattern at 3.7 GHz; (a) with uniform excitation, (b) with phase distribution for 30° scanned beam.

The comparison between the simulation based on CEMS and HFSS and measured reflection coefficient of a single element antenna yields good agreement from 2.9 GHz to 5.9 GHz as shown in Fig. 2 (a). The measured response covers two of the sub-6 bands for 5G: 3.55-3.7 GHz and 3.7-4.2 GHz. The far-field gain pattern of a single element at 3.7 GHz is shown in Fig. 2 (b) with maximum gain of 3.8 dBi at the broadside (θ=0°).

Fig. 3 shows the configuration of a 5-elements linear array which supports the operation in the sub-6 bands while maintaining coupling among the elements in the order or less than -20 dB. The 3D gain patterns for this configuration is shown in Fig. 4 for uniform and phased excitation with 0° and 30° main beam directions, respectively. Similarly, the gain patterns for a 15 elements array are shown in Fig. 5. The gain of 1 element, 5, and 15 elements with uniform and phased excitation for scanning at 30° and 45° are listed in Table I.

IV. Conclusions

A miniaturized, low-cost design of patch/slot antenna element and the corresponding linear arrays supporting the sub-6 GHz frequency bands for 5G communications is presented. Higher gains and larger scanning range are achieved with the increase of number of elements in the linear array configuration without obvious deterioration in S-parameters or far-field characteristics. Good element to element isolation is observed, and scanning capabilities are predicted for larger number of elements. Future work will include the extension to two-dimensional arrays.

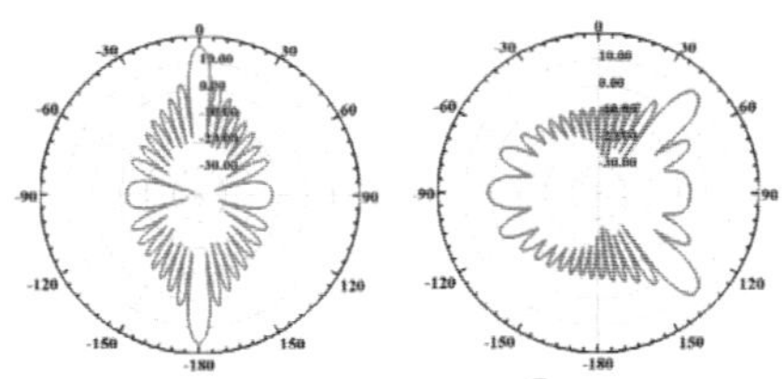

(a) (b)

Fig. 5. Far-field gain pattern of the 15-elements linear array in xz plane at 3.7 GHz with size less than 8.31λ; (a) with uniform excitation, (b) with phase distribution for 45° scanned beam.

Table I. Broadside Gain at 3.7GHz

Element Numbers (N)	*Main Beam Direction (degree)*	*Gain (dBi)*
N=1	0	3.8
N=5	0	10.9
N=5	30	9.4
N=15	0	16
N=15	45	12.4

Aknowledgment

This project is partially supported by a gift fund from Futurewei Technology Inc., New Jersey Research Center, Bridgewater, NJ, USA and by ANSYS gift of HFSS license.

References

[1] M. Agiwal, A. Roy, and N. Saxena, "Next Generation 5G Wireless Networks: A Comprehensive Survey," IEEE Communications Surveys & Tutorials, vol. 18, no. 3, pp. 1617-1655, August 2016.

[2] 5G Americas Spectrum Recommendations for the U.S. (2019, July 25). Retrieved from https://www.5gamericas.org/5g-americas-spectrum-recommendations-for-the-u-s/.

[3] A. Zaidi, A. Baghdad, W. A. Awan, Halima, A. Ballouk, and A. Badri, "CPW Fed Wide to Dual Band Frequency Reconfigurable Antenna for 5G Applications," 2019 International Conference on Wireless Technologies, Embedded and Intelligent Systems (WITS), Fez, Morocco, pp. 1-3, 2019.

[4] G. Gao, B. Hu, and J. Zhang, "Design of a Miniaturization Printed Circular-Slot UWB Antenna by the Half-Cutting Method," IEEE Antennas and Wireless Propagation Letters, vol. 12, pp. 567-570, May 2013.

[5] Y. Wang, Z. Ying, and G. Yang, "A compact CPW-fed wideband antenna design for 5G/WLAN wireless application," 2017 IEEE International Symposium on Antennas and Propagation Meeting, San Diego, CA, pp. 1775-1776, 2017.

[6] A. Z. Elsherbeni and V. Demir, The Finite-Difference Time-Domain Method for Electromagnetics with MATLAB® Simulations, New Jersey: SciTech Publishing, 2016.

[7] V. Demir and A. Elsherbeni, CEMS: A software package for electromagnetics simulations, Version 4, October 2019.

Debye Coefficients for Biological Tissues From 100 MHz to 100 GHz

Rachel Lumnitzer, Allison Tanner, and Atef Z. Elsherbeni
Electrical Engineering Department
Colorado School of Mines, Golden, CO, 80401

***Abstract*—Debye modeling of dispersive, biological tissues allows for the numerical analysis of electromagnetic waves in the vicinity of a human body using the FDTD method. Three-term Debye expansion coefficients for 55 human biological tissues are determined via a two-step numerical solver. The Debye coefficients obtained predict precisely the complex permittivity of the experimentally available tissue data.**

***Index Terms*—Debye, dispersive media, FDTD method, frequency domain.**

I. Introduction

Several methods have been used to evaluate the EM energy absorbed/penetration in biological tissues. Among these methods is the finite- difference time-domain (FDTD) which is considered the most useful for calculating specific absorption rate (SAR) and temperature rise in human tissues due to electromagnetic radiation at multiple frequencies [1]. The traditional FDTD formulation can easily be modified to include the dispersive type properties of the human tissues, provided their parameters are presented in a Debye form [2].

This paper focuses on providing Debye coefficient for 55 different human tissues for electromagnetic applications supporting frequencies up to 100 GHz. This is an extension of similarly presented work which was only applicable to 20 GHz [3]. Similar procedure to what was developed in [4] and [3] is applied here on tissues data obtained from [5] for a frequency range from 100 MHz to 100 GHz. The accuracy of the generated three-term Debye coefficients is verified by comparison with the original data at different frequency ranges.

II. Evaluation of Debye Coefficients

The Debye Model is best shown in the following compact form [6]:

$$\epsilon_r(\omega) = \epsilon_\infty + \sum_{k=1}^{N} \frac{\Delta\epsilon_k}{1+j\omega\tau_k} \; ; \; \Delta\epsilon_k = A_k(\epsilon_s - \epsilon_\infty)\,, \quad (1)$$

where:
N: Number of Debye terms
ϵ_∞: Permittivity at high frequency
$\Delta\epsilon_k$: Pole weight
τ_k: Relaxation time

The measured data of tissue parameters obtained from [5] are then used with equation (1) to calculate the Debye coefficients. Table I shows the relative permittivity and conductivity for a sample biological tissue within the range of 100 MHz to 100 GHz. The conductivity is converted to the corresponding imaginary part of the complex permittivity:

$$\epsilon_r(\omega) = \epsilon' - j\epsilon''\,. \quad (2)$$

Table I. Aorta parameters from [5]

Frequency (GHz)	Relative Permittivity ϵ'	Conductivity [S/m]
0.100	59.780	0.462
1	44.561	0.729
10	32.673	9.127
20	22.445	19.640
50	10.934	34.895
100	6.864	43.022

Since the number of data points obtained from [5] were limited for further numerical processing, an interpolation process to generate a larger number of points for each tissue is accomplished via the MATLAB function "pchip." Next, a two-step process is performed. First, the MATLAB function "invfreqs" is used to calculate the frequency transfer function from the data points,

$$\epsilon_r(\omega) = \frac{\sum_{k=1}^{N} b_{k-1}\omega^{k-1}}{\sum_{k=1}^{N+1} a_{k-1}\omega^{k-1}}\,, \quad (3)$$

where N is the number of poles that is desired to have in the numerical fit and the a_k and b_k coefficients are computed using the "invfreqs" function. Next, the transfer function can be used to calculate the poles and weights for the Debye coefficients using the "residue" function as was previously done in [4] and [3].

III. Results and Discussion

The large frequency range from 100 MHz to 100 GHz was divided into three sub-ranges, 100 MHz to 2 GHz, 2 GHz to 20 GHz, and 20 GHz to 100 GHz and Debye coefficients were computed for each sub-range. The computed three-term Debye coefficients for some sampled tissues are listed in Table II for frequency range from 20 GHz to 100 GHz.

The maximum percentage errors of these sampled tissues did not exceed 0.1% and 0.27% for ϵ' and ϵ'', respectively. The complete set of permittivity coefficients for the three frequency sub-ranges have been computed and will be presented. Fig. 1 shows excellent coincidence between the generated and original measured permittivity for the aorta.

IV. Conclusion

Three-term Debye coefficients for 55 biological tissues are determined from a small set of measured data for frequency range from 100 MHz to 100 GHz. With a three-term fit the maximum normalized errors related to the 55 tissue types was found to be 3.047% and 3.958% for ϵ' and ϵ'', respectively.

Table II. Three-term Debye parameters for frequency range of 20GHz-100GHz

Tissue	ε_∞	$\Delta\varepsilon_1$	$\Delta\varepsilon_2$	$\Delta\varepsilon_3$	τ_1 x10^9	τ_2 x10^9	τ_3 x10^9
Aorta	4.325	2.311	20.134	19.363	0.002	0.006	0.017
Bladder	2.635	0.969	8.610	7.917	0.002	0.006	0.019
Blood	4.498	3.684	32.111	26.674	0.002	0.006	0.021
Bone	2.565	0.335	1.158	1.407	0.001	0.005	0.016
Brain	4.428	3.123	25.887	20.355	0.002	0.006	0.019
Breast	2.513	0.074	0.555	2.391	0.002	0.007	0.021
Cartilage	4.371	2.030	11.251	25.934	0.001	0.006	0.020
Cervix	4.410	3.058	25.632	19.530	0.002	0.006	0.018
Colon	4.477	3.485	28.886	22.688	0.002	0.006	0.019
Cornea	4.465	3.452	28.828	22.807	0.002	0.006	0.022
Dura	4.602	3.754	19.037	19.513	0.002	0.006	0.019
Eye	4.460	3.447	28.933	22.031	0.002	0.006	0.019
Fat	2.566	0.339	1.182	1.424	0.001	0.005	0.016
Bladder	4.246	2.373	42.606	16.075	0.002	0.007	0.024
Heart	4.499	3.591	29.594	23.813	0.002	0.006	0.020
Kidney	4.491	3.497	28.628	24.139	0.002	0.006	0.022
Lens	4.376	2.803	23.427	18.053	0.002	0.006	0.017
Liver	4.345	2.401	20.938	20.001	0.002	0.006	0.019
Lung	4.418	3.061	25.394	19.870	0.002	0.006	0.018
Lymph	4.494	3.673	30.674	23.645	0.002	0.006	0.017
Muscle	4.490	3.793	29.742	19.355	0.002	0.006	0.017
Nail	2.647	0.695	2.683	6.163	0.001	0.006	0.019
Nerve	4.251	1.827	15.117	11.972	0.002	0.006	0.019
Ovary	4.618	3.608	19.036	24.768	0.002	0.006	0.022
Pancreas	4.494	3.673	30.674	23.645	0.002	0.006	0.017
Prostate	4.504	3.766	31.554	24.101	0.002	0.006	0.019
Retina	4.460	3.447	28.933	22.031	0.002	0.006	0.019
Skin	4.030	0.125	32.419	22.833	0.001	0.007	0.161
Intestine	4.506	3.796	31.520	28.688	0.002	0.006	0.027
Stomach	4.542	4.036	33.756	25.919	0.002	0.006	0.018
Tendon	4.251	1.611	14.119	27.539	0.002	0.007	0.018
Testis	4.504	3.766	31.554	24.101	0.002	0.006	0.019
Thymus	4.494	3.673	30.674	23.645	0.002	0.006	0.017
Thyroid	4.494	3.673	30.674	23.645	0.002	0.006	0.017
Tongue	4.451	3.348	27.925	21.646	0.002	0.006	0.017
Tooth	2.647	0.695	2.683	6.163	0.001	0.006	0.019
Uterus	4.511	3.804	31.844	24.425	0.002	0.006	0.019

With three-term Debye coefficients along with the FDTD formulations for dispersive type material, it is now possible to address many applications at high frequencies such as biomedical imaging and effect of radiation from 5G devices on human body.

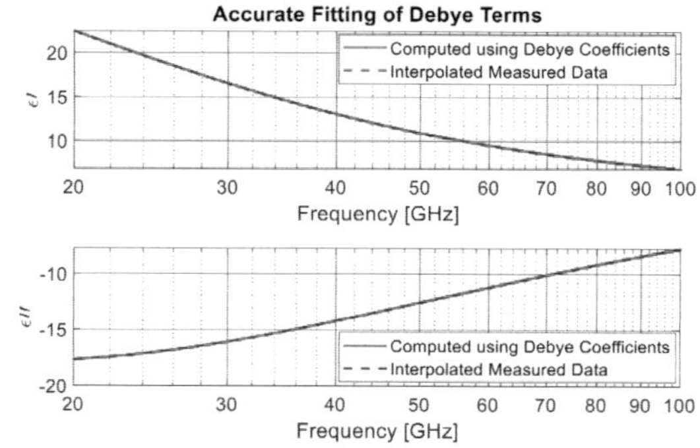

Fig. 1. Permittivity vs. frequency using Debye three-term fit and interpolated raw data for the human aorta tissue from 20 to 100 GHz.

REFERENCES

[1] F. Kaburcuk and A. Z. Elsherbeni, "Temperature Rise and SAR Distribution at Wide Range of Frequencies in a Human Head due to an Antenna Radiation," ACES Journal, vol. 33, no. 4, pp. 367–372, April 2018.

[2] A. Z. Elsherbeni and V. Demir, "The Finite-Difference Time-Domain Method for Electromagnetics with MATLAB Simulations," second edition, ACES Series on Computational Electromagnetics and Engineering, SciTech Publishing, an Imprint of IET, Edison, NJ, 2015.

[3] M. A. Eleiwa and A. Z. Elsherbeni, "Debye Constants for Biological Tissues from 30 Hz to 20 GHz," ACES Journal, vol. 18, no. 3, November 2001.

[4] M. Mrozowski and M. A. Stuchly, "Parameterization of Media Dispersive Properties for FDTD," IEEE Transactions on Antennas and Propagation, vol. 45, no. 9, September 1997.

[5] http://niremf.ifac.cnr.it/tissprop/ [Online website 2019].

[6] A. Velasco, M. F. Hadi, A. Z. Elsherbeni, and J. E. Diener, "Debye Coefficients for Low Frequency FDTD Dispersive Soils Analysis," ACES Conference, Nanjing, China, 2019.

Quantifying Sub-gridding Errors in Standard and Hybrid Higher Order 2D FDTD Simulations

Madison Le
Electrical Engineering Department
Colorado School of Mines
Golden, USA
madisonle@mines.edu

Mohammed Hadi
Electrical Engineering Department
Colorado School of Mines
Golden, USA
mhadi@mines.edu

Atef Elsherbeni
Electrical Engineering Department
Colorado School of Mines
Golden, USA
aelsherb@mines.edu

***Abstract*—Sub-gridding errors for a 2D Finite-Difference Time-Domain (FDTD) simulation are compared for both the standard FDTD and Hybrid higher order FDTD cases. Sub-gridding contrast ratios of 1:3, 1:9, 1:15, and 1:27 are considered and analyzed. A correlation is seen between the increase of contrast ratio with the increase of sub-gridding errors for both standard and hybrid cases. However, a trend of errors reduction when using hybrid formulations over standard formulations. is apparent for each contrast ratio.**

Keywords—Finite-Difference Time-Domain Method, High Order FDTD, Numerical Error Analysis, Sub-gridding.

I. Introduction

Due to increased development in 5G and IoT technologies, FDTD sub-gridding methods are necessary for these electrically large simulation domains. A standard FDTD [1] requires the minimum number of Yee cells to be at least 10 within the minimum wavelength [2]. Sub-gridding methods prove useful in accurately and efficiently analyzing electrically large domains with relatively low allocations of resources and memory. Sub-gridding consequently can lead to the appearance of errors caused by dispersion and stability [3-5]. Electrically large subgrid regions can also lead to errors [6], an example is when conducting full wave simulation of a large antenna array of multiple wavelengths. The relative error that arises with increased electrical sizes of sub-gridded regions, was previously discussed independently from the contrast ratio for 1D and 2D FDTD simulations [7].

This paper extends the work presented in [7] and will investigate the errors of 2D simulations with higher contrast ratios of 1:9, 1:15, and 1:27 using traditional 2nd order formulations as well as higher order FDTD methods.

II. Two-Dimensional FDTD Domain

The 2D FDTD setup, as shown in Fig. 1, involves a Gaussian pulse propagating through a domain of 308 by 243 cells in the x and y direction, respectively. Additionally, there is a subgrid region of 143 by 30 cells surrounding the source corresponding to about 7λ by 1.5λ. The considered Perfectly Matched Layer (PML) boundary consists of 10 coarse cells in all four directions.

The outer dimensions of the domain in Fig. 1 is static for all considered contrast ratios with the size of the course grid remains constant. As the contrast ratio increases, the fine cell size (dx_{fine}) decreases and thus creates a denser subgrid region. The parameters for each contrast ratio are outlined in Table I.

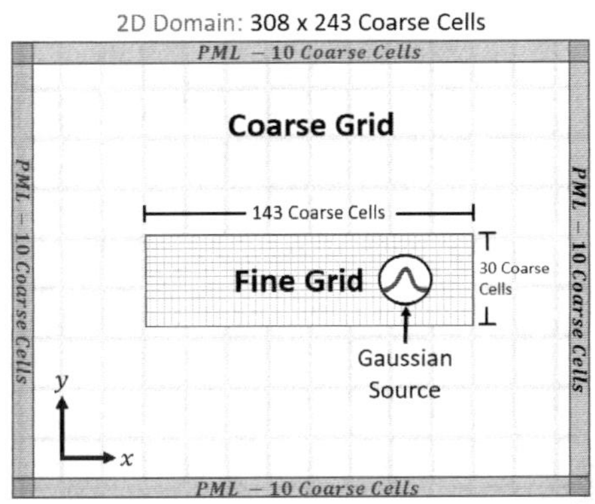

Fig. 1. Example from [1, Section 7.5.2]: Line source simulated with a 2D FDTD code. Striped box respresents physical location of fine grid region.

All previously mentioned parameters hold true for both traditional 2nd order formulations (S22) as well as for the hybrid cases of 4th and 2nd order FDTD formulations (HS24). Specifically, for the hybrid case, a 2nd order approximation will be used in the subgrid region (fine grid) and a 4th order approximation will be utilized in the remaining outer domain, including the PML (course grid). This hybrid case will aim to reduce errors when comparing to a reference domain. This reference domain will consist of a uniform mesh with cell sizes corresponding to cell size of the sub grid region, i.e., dx_{fine} and dy_{fine}. This reference domain will be calculated with the traditional 2nd order approximation throughout based on the formulation in [1].

TABLE I. 2D Domain Parameters

Contrast Ratio	Coarse Cell Size ($dx = dy$)	Fine Cell Size ($dx_{fine} = dy_{fine}$)	Time Step Size (dt)	# of Time Steps
1:3	3 *mm*	1 *mm*	2.1 *ps*	3,000
1:9	3 *mm*	0.33 *mm*	0.7 *ps*	9,000
1:15	3 *mm*	0.2 *mm*	0.42 *ps*	15,000
1:27	3 *mm*	0.11 *mm*	0.24 *ps*	27,000

III. Error Analysis

The normalized error for each S22 and HS24 case will be calculated by comparing to the reference domain described in Section II using the expression:

$$\frac{max(|E_{z,reference}(i,j,t)-E_{z,subgrid}(i,j,t)|)}{max(|E_{z,reference}(i,j,t)|)} \times 100\% , \quad (1)$$

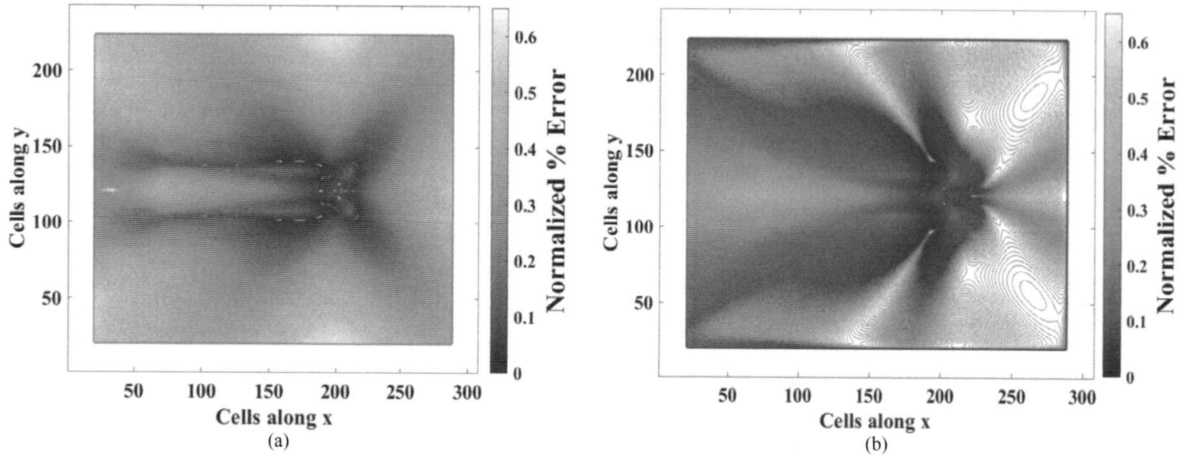

Fig. 2. Normalized percentage errors for the 2D FDTD as described in Fig. 1 and Table I for 1:3 contrast ratio: (a) S22 errors and (b) HS24 errors.

where the maximum absolute difference between the reference and the subgridded domain are compared for every time step at every location within the domain.

IV. Results & Analysis

The S22 and HS24 errors are depicted in Fig. 2 for a 1:3 contrast ratio. As shown, the errors for S22 are heavily concentrated outside of the fine grid region where the errors are increasing as they propagate outside of the fine grid region. In contrast, the error from the HS24 case is significantly lower outside of the fine grid region. The results for other contrast ratios are summarized in Table II.

TABLE II. 2D Domain Parameters

Contrast Ratio	S22 Errors	Hybrid Errors	Hybrid Improvement $\frac{\lvert Error_{S22} - Error_{Hybrid} \rvert}{\lvert Error_{S22} \rvert} \times 100\%$
1:3	0.6168 %	0.4202 %	32%
1:9	0.6971 %	0.1803 %	74%
1:15	0.7036 %	0.1614 %	77%
1:27	0.7061 %	0.1550 %	78%

The purpose of using higher contract ratio is to be able to conduct simulations where certain areas of the domain have fine geometrical details. It is apparent that there is a trend of increasing errors for the S22 case as the contrast ratio increases. However, the use of proposed hybrid formulation reduces maximum errors to an acceptable level due to better matching of the numerical phase velocities between the subgrid region and the free space region while allowing for higher contrast ratio.

V. Conclusion

The presented numerical results show strong improvement with the use of the hybrid formulations for 2D domains when fine discretization in sub areas, are required. This hybrid formulation becomes increasingly necessary when the contrast ratios increase as the sub-gridding using the standard S22 formulation yields increasingly worse errors. Further investigations will involve larger contrast ratios and extension to 3D simulation domains.

Acknowledgments

This project is partially supported by Futurewei Technology Inc., New Jersey Research Center, Bridgewater, NJ, USA.

References

[1] A. Z. Elsherbeni and V. Demir, The Finite-Difference Time-Domain Method for Electromagnetics with MATLAB® Simulations, 2nd edition, Edison, New Jersey: SciTech Publishing, 2015.

[2] M. W. Chevalier, R. J. Luebbers, and V. P. Cable, "FDTD local grid with material traverse," IEEE Trans. Antennas Propagat., vol. 45, no. 3, Mar. 1997.

[3] S. Wang, "Numerical examinations of the stability of FDTD sub-gridding schemes," ACES Journal, vol. 22, no. 2, Jul. 2007.

[4] F. L. Teixeira, "A summary review on 25 years of progress and future challenges in FDTD and FETD techniques," ACES Journal, vol. 25, no. 1, Jan. 2010.

[5] M. F. Hadi and R. K. Dib, "Eliminating interface reflections in hybrid low-dispersion FDTD algorithms," ACES Journal, vol. 22, no. 3, Nov. 2007.

[6] J. Nehrbass and R. Lee, "Optimal finite-difference sub-gridding techniques applied to the Helmholtz equation," IEEE Transactions on Microwave Theory and Techniques, vol. 48, no. 6, pp. 976–984, Jun. 2000.

[7] M. Le, M. Hadi, and A. Elsherbeni, "Quantifying sub-gridding errors when modeling multiscale structures with FDTD," 2019 International Applied Computational Electromagnetics Society (ACES), Miami, FL, USA, pp. 1-2, 2019.

Ku-Band Dual Linear Polarized Parabolic-Cylindrical Reflector Antenna with Beam Steering Performance

Ghanshyam Mishra
Dept. of Electrical and Computer Engineering
San Diego State University
San Diego, CA 92182
gmishra-sw@sdsu.edu

Satish K. Sharma
Dept. of Electrical and Computer Engineering
San Diego State University
San Diego, CA 92182
ssharma@sdsu.edu

Jia-Chi Chieh and Randall Olsen
Adv. Integrated Circuits Tech. and Tactical Networks Branch
Naval Info. Warfare Center Pac.
San Diego, CA 92152
sam.chieh@navy.mil and randall.olsen@navy.mil

Philip Nguyen
Dept. of Electrical and Computer Engineering
San Diego State University
San Diego, CA 92182
ptnguyen6-w@sdsu.edu

***Abstract*— A hybrid reflector-phased array antenna system for high data rate wireless network is proposed at *Ku*-band (12 - 15 GHz). The proposed hybrid antenna system uses an 8 × 4 dual linear-polarized stacked patch phased array antenna as the feed source to illuminate the 50 cm parabolic-cylindrical reflector of *f*/*D* = 0.4. The parabolic-cylindrical reflector has the property of a wide-angle beam steering along the cylindrical axis as compared to a conventional parabolic reflector. The multilevel fast multipole method (MLFMM) is used along with the method of moments (MoM) in TICRA GRASP to analyze the finite thickness effect of the reflector. The peak directivity of the reflector pattern is around 26 dBi, and a beam scanning of ±30° is achieved along the cylindrical axis of the reflector for 3 dB reduction in the gain. Anokiwave AWMF-0117 integrated silicon core chips are used in the beamforming network for achieving beam steering. The parabolic-cylindrical reflector is 3D printed and metalized with copper using the vapor-deposition technique. The phased array antenna is assembled with the Anokiwave chips and is currently being integrated with the 3D printed parabolic-cylindrical reflector for experimental verification of the scan performance.**

Keywords*— *Beam steering, beamforming network, dual-polarization, parabolic-cylindrical reflector, phased array antenna.

I. Introduction

An ever-increasing demand for high data rate wireless communication has augmented the interest in the design of energy-efficient and cost-effective antenna systems. The advance of high gain electronically steered antennas can enable high data rate as well as improve communications in adverse conditions. Naval ships can use these high data rate antenna systems for ship-to-ship and ship-to-shore communications instead of the traditional maritime radios.

A hybrid reflector-phased array antenna system is proposed for *Ku*-band (12 – 15 GHz) for high data rate wireless network applications. The reflector is a parabolic-cylindrical reflector of *f*/*D* = 0.4 and a maximum dimension of 50 cm. The parabolic-cylindrical reflector provides a wide-angle beam steering along the cylindrical axis compared to a conventional parabolic reflector [1]-[3]. The feed source is an 8 × 4 dual linear-polarized stacked patch phased array antenna integrated with the Anokiwave AWMF-0117 silicon core chips. The proposed research is a cost-effective and energy-efficient alternative to conventional antenna technologies for high gain and beam steering applications.

The proposed hybrid reflector-phased array antenna attains four primary objectives: (1) dual linear-polarization for transmit and receive communications; (2) stable radiation pattern with low cross-polarization; (3) high antenna gain of at least 25 dBi; and (4) beam steering of at least ± 30°. An initial simulation study on the beam steering performance of the parabolic-cylindrical reflector with physical optics and physical theory of diffraction is presented in [4].

II. Proposed Hybrid Reflector-Phased Array System

A. Principle of Operation

The proposed antenna system is a parabolic-cylindrical reflector (cylindrically shaped with a parabolic cross-section) fed with a phased array antenna placed along the focal line, as shown in Fig. 1. The parabolic-cylindrical reflector provides high gain, and the phased array antenna provides wide-angle beam steering. The power requirement and cost of the proposed antenna system is reduced compared to a conventional stand-alone phased array antenna of similar antenna gain.

B. Proposed Dual Linear-Polarized Stacked Patch Antenna

The geometry and S-parameters of the proposed dual linear-polarized stacked patch antenna are shown in Fig. 2. The antenna is designed on Rogers RO-4350 substrate with $\varepsilon_r = 3.66$ and is analyzed using Ansys HFSS. The impedance matching bandwidth ($|S_{11}| < -10$ dB) is from 12.7 GHz to 14.75 GHz, and the isolation between the port ($|S_{21}|$) is more than 22 dB. The average peak realized gain is 5.5 dBi, and the cross-polarization isolation is 20 dB, as shown in the realized gain pattern of the two polarization at 13.5 GHz in Fig. 3.

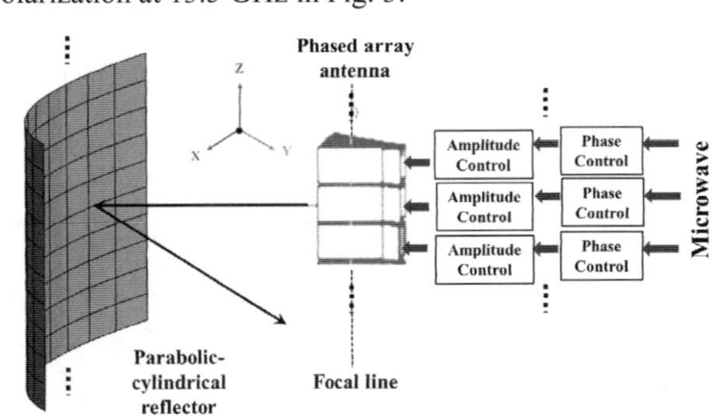

Fig. 1. Illustration of the proposed hybrid antenna architecture concept: parabolic-cylindrical reflector with phased array antenna as the feed source.

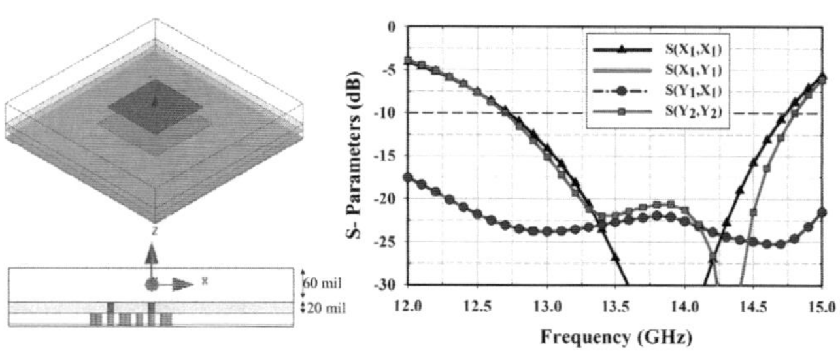

Fig. 2. Geometry and simulated S-parameters of the proposed dual linear-polarized stacked patch antenna at *Ku*-band.

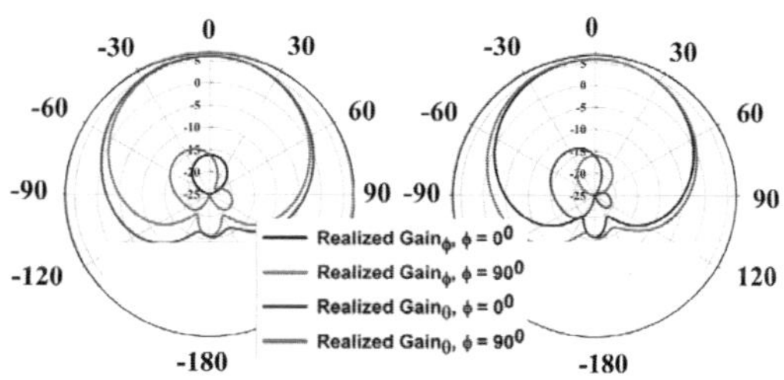

Fig. 3. Simulated realized gain pattern of the two polarization at 13.5 GHz.

C. Parabolic-cylindrical Reflector with Phased Array as Feed

The proposed stacked patch antenna is used as an element of 8 × 4 phased array antenna with the inter-element spacing of 12 mm, as presented in Fig. 4 (a). The phased array shows a peak gain of 20 dBi and beam scanning up to ± 45°, as shown in Fig. 4 (b). The phased array is used as a feed source to illuminate the parabolic-cylindrical reflector of f/D = 0.4 and maximum dimension of 50 cm as illustrated in Fig. 5. The multilevel fast multipole method (MLFMM) is used along with the method of moments (MoM) in TICRA GRASP to analyze the finite thickness effect of the reflector. The parabolic-cylindrical reflector provides gain of 26 dBi and beam steering of ±30° along the cylindrical axis of the reflector for 3 dB reduction in the gain as shown in Fig. 6 at 13.5 GHz. The beam steering range can be increased by increasing the dimension of the reflector.

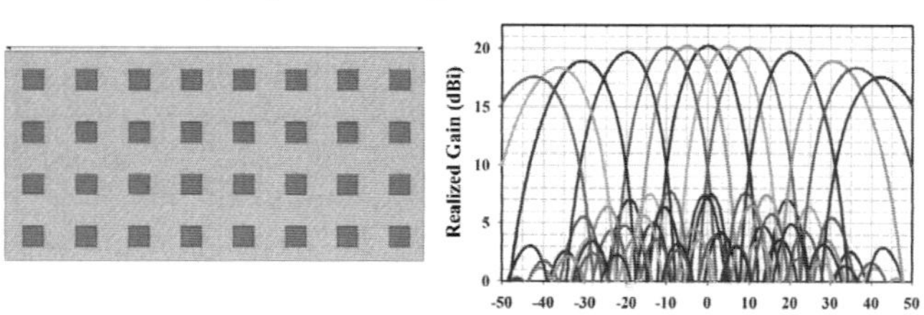

(a) (b)

Fig. 4. (a) Proposed 8 × 4 dual linear polarized stacked patch phased array antenna and (b) Simulated beam steering pattern of the phased array alone.

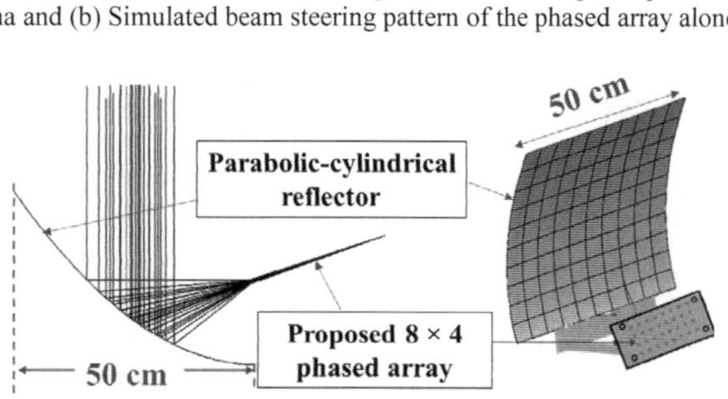

Fig. 5. Parabolic-cylindrical reflector with 8 × 4 phased array as a feed source.

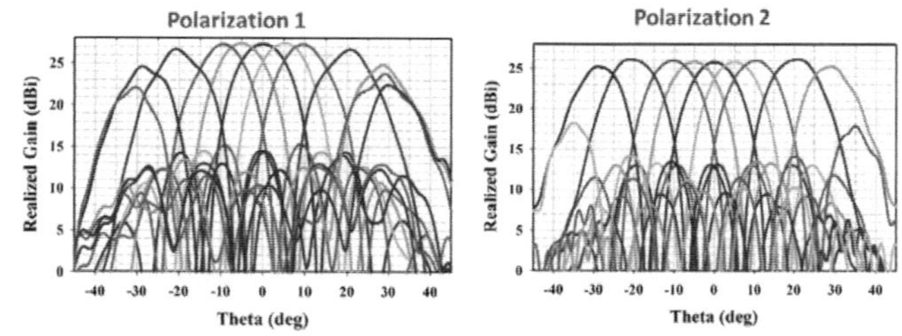

Fig. 6. Simulated beam steering radiation pattern of the parabolic-cylindrical reflector along the cylindrical axis for the two polarization at 13.5 GHz.

III. Conclusion and Future Work

An integrated reflector-phased array beam steering antenna system is proposed at *Ku*-band to provide a gain of about 26 dBi and a beam scanning of ±30° for 3 dB reduction in the gain. Anokiwave AWMF-0117 integrated silicon core chips are being used in the beamforming network for achieving beam steering. The chip size is 2.5 mm × 2.5 mm with the flip-chip package and features half-duplex operations with +20 dB transmit channel gain, +28 dB receive channel gain, 3 dB noise figure, 6-bit amplitude, and phase controls. The power consumption is 200mW on receive and 250mW on Transmit mode per chip. Fig. 7 (a) shows the fabricated 3D printed reflector metal plated with vapor-deposited copper and Fig. 7 (b) shows the fabricated phased array with the beamforming network. The integrated reflector and phased array beamforming board will be assembled and measured for experimental verification of gain and scan performance.

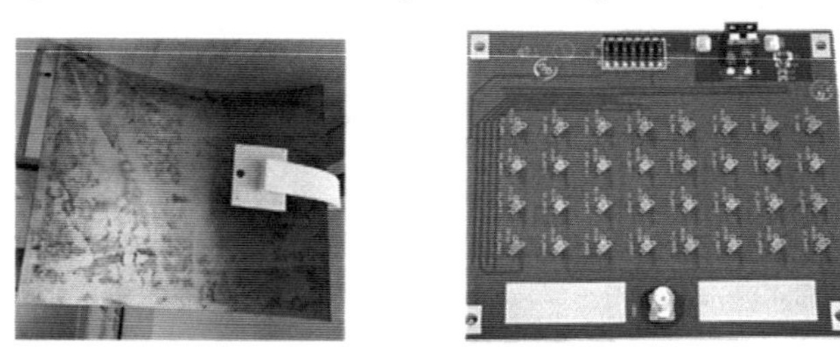

(a) (b)

Fig. 7. Photograph of (a) the fabricated 3D printed copper plated antenna and (b) fabricated complete phased array with beamforming network.

Acknowledgment

This work is supported by the Naval Information Warfare Center Pacific (NIWC-PAC).

References

[1] Y. Rahmat-Samii, et al., "Advanced precipitation radar antenna: array-fed offset membrane cylindrical reflector antenna," in *IEEE Transactions on Antennas and Propagation*, vol. 53, no. 8, pp. 2503-2515, Aug. 2005.

[2] Z. Hussein and J. Hilland, "Cylindrical antenna with partly adaptive phase-array feed," California Inst. Of Tech., Pasadena, CA, USA, NASA Tech Brief, Rep. NPO-30251, Dec. 2003.

[3] M. Cooley, "Phased Array Fed Reflector (PAFR) antenna architectures for space-based sensors," 2015 IEEE Aerospace Conference, Big Sky, MT, 2015, pp. 1-11.

[4] G. Mishra, S. K. Sharma, J. S. Chieh, and R. Olsen, "Wide Angle Beam Steering Cylindrical Parabolic Reflector with Phased Array as a Feed Source for Ku-Band Applications," IEEE International Symposium on Antennas and Propagation & USNC/URSI National Radio Science Meeting, Atlanta, GA, 2019, (Abstract).

Side-Frame Dual-Band MIMO Antennas for 5G Smartphone Applications

Guobo Wei
Information Science and Technology
Southwest Jiaotong University
Chengdu, China
zibai_wei@163.com

Quanyuan Feng*
Information Science and Technology
Southwest Jiaotong University
Chengdu, China
fengquanyuan@163.com

***Abstract*—A side-frame dual-band multi-input multi-output (MIMO) antenna system for fifth-generation (5G) mobile communication in smartphone applications is presented, operating in 3.5 GHz band (3400-3600 MHz) and 5 GHz band (4800-5000 MHz). The proposed four-element antenna array is placed at four corners of the circuit board and printed on the side edge frame. The height of the structure is only 4.1 mm, which is compatible for ultra-thin full screen smartphones. According to the verification of HFSS and CST, ideal impedance matching bandwidths (superior to 10dB) and excellent isolations (superior to 18 dB) are obtained over the 3.5 GHz band and 5 GHz band, with peak gain of 6.18 dB and 4.9 dB, respectively.**

***Keywords*—dual band; fifth-generation (5G); multi-input multi-output (MIMO); side frame.**

I. INTRODUCTION

In recent years, with the rapid development of 5G communication technology, multi-input multi-output (MIMO) antennas have become a hot topic [1-5], due to the advantages of low loss of signal, low co-channel interference and high data rate [1]. China have assigned 3.5 GHz band (3400-3600 MHz) and 5 GHz band (4800-5000 MHz) for 5G mobile phone communication. A dual-band antenna array is come up with 10 T-shaped slot elements, operating LTE 42/43/46 bands [5]. But antenna efficiencies of the system is not high. Nowadays, the side-edge frame antenna is a hot trend in current research, in order to satisfy the demand for ultra-thin and full-screen smartphones. Several side frame MIMO antennas have been proposed for 5G smartphones [6-8]. An eight-port side-edge frame printed antenna array is presented in [6], operating in 3.5 GHz band and 5 GHz band. However, the dimensions of the proposed antenna array is 15 mm × 7 mm. In [7], a ring-slot antenna system is put forward for metal-rimmed smartphones in 4G/5G communication. A reconfigurable 4G antenna is designed with a DC controlling circuit, covering 820–960 MHz and 1710–2690 MHz. And the 5G slot antenna array is designed for 3.5 GHz band (3400–3600 MHz) by utilizing single 2-mm-wide ring slot between the rim and metal ground.

In this paper, a MIMO antenna operating in the 3.5 GHz band and 5 GHz band for 5G ultra-thin full screen smartphones is proposed. The proposed four-port antennas are printed on the side frame with small requirements for clearance area. And 4.1 mm high is suitable for ultra-thin smartphones. The proposed mobile phone antenna was simulated by HFSS and CST. The representative parameters are given in the article, such as reflection coefficients, transmission coefficients, peak gain and antenna efficiency.

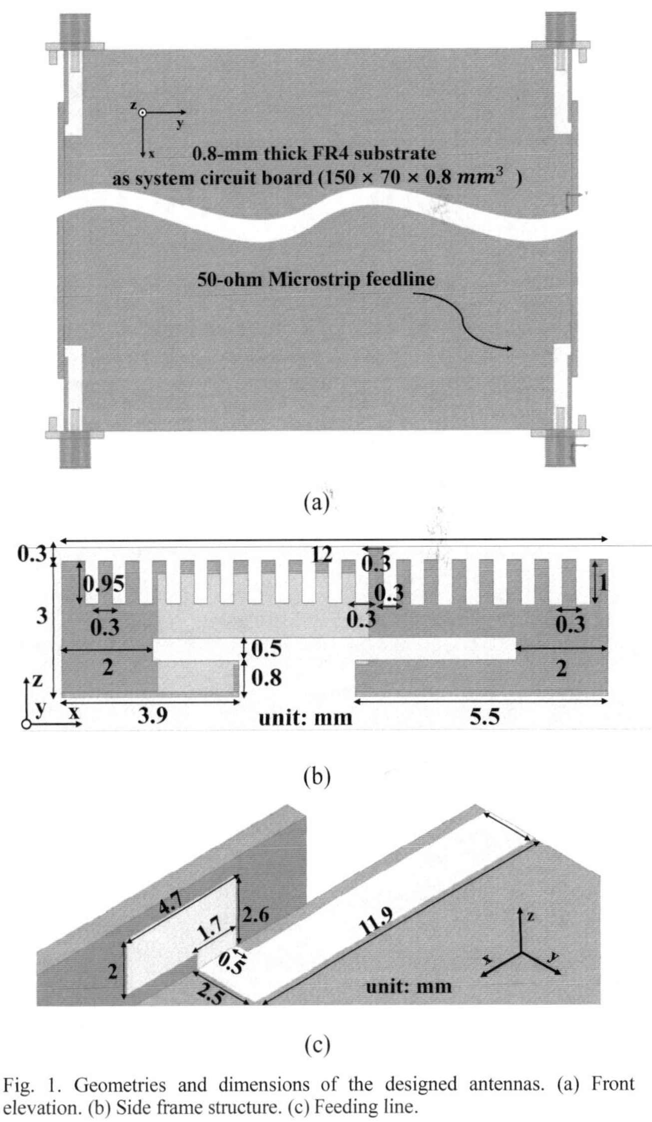

Fig. 1. Geometries and dimensions of the designed antennas. (a) Front elevation. (b) Side frame structure. (c) Feeding line.

This work is supported by Key Project of the National Natural Science Foundation of China (NNSF) under Grant [61531016], [61831017] and the Sichuan Provincial Science and Technology Important Projects under Grant [19ZDYF2904], [2018ZDZX0148] and [2018GZDZX0001]. (Corresponding author: Quanyuan Feng.)

II. ANTENNA DESIGN

The proposed MIMO antenna array is given in Fig. 1, which is composed of four similar elements. A 150 mm × 70 mm × 0.8 mm FR4 substrate (relative permittivity = 4.4, loss tangent = 0.02) is chosen for 5.5-inch smartphone system circuit board. Fig. 1 (a) exhibits the main view of the proposed antenna. The details of the radiating slot and 50-ohm feeding line are indicated in Figs. 1 (b) and (c). The pectinate strips and the prominent T-shaped structure in the gap of the ground plane are applied to realizing antenna miniaturization and adjust impedance matching, which can be observed in Fig. 2.

III. RESULTS AND DISCUSSIONS

Fig. 3 shows the simulated S Parameters of the designed antenna by HFSS and CST (commercial software). It is obvious that ideal impedance matching bandwidths and excellent isolations (superior to 18 dB) are obtained (superior to 10 dB) over the 3.5GHz band and 5GHz band. It can be observed that the antenna gains are approximately 4.89-6.18 dB and 4.65-4.90 dB over the desired bands in Fig. 4. The antenna total efficiencies are 62 – 72% and 72 – 80% over the 3.5GHz band and 5GHz band, respectively.

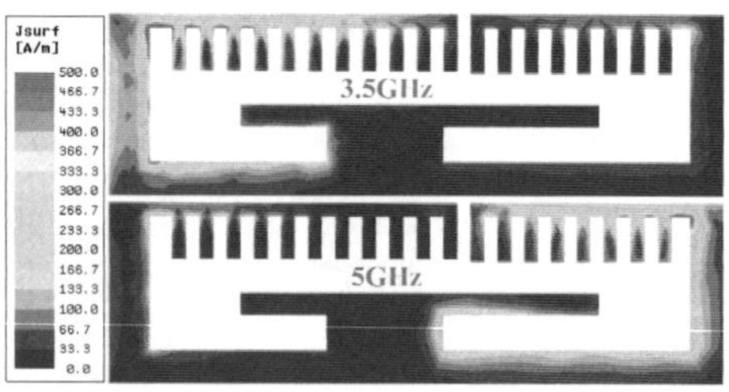

Fig. 2. Current distributions at 3.5GHz and 5GHz.

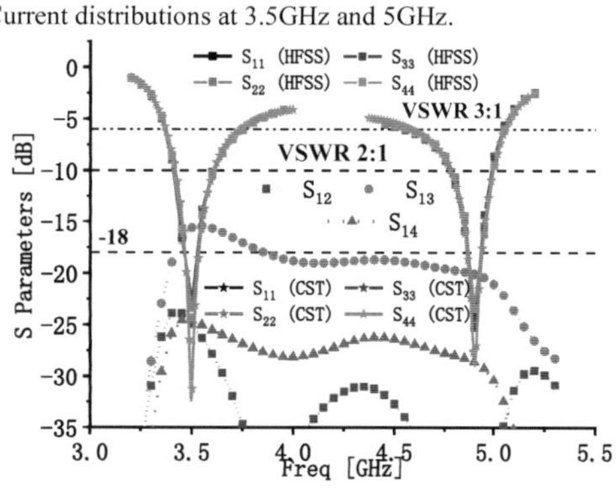

Fig. 3. Simulated S parameters by HFSS and CST.

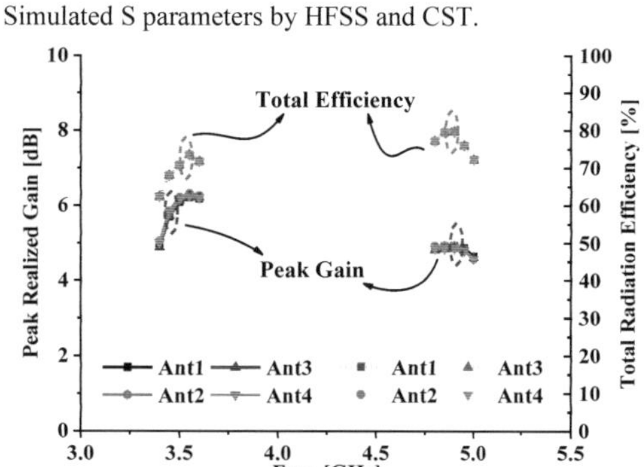

Fig. 4. Peak gains and total efficiencies of the designed antennas.

TABLE I. CONTRAST OF THE REFERENCED AND PROPOSED ANTENNA

Reference	Bandwidths (GHz)	Isolation (dB)	Dimensions (mm × mm)
5	3.4-3.8 and 5.1-5.9 (-6 dB)	>11	16.2 × 3
7	3.4-3.6 and 4.8-5.1 (-6 dB)	>11.5	15 × 7
The Proposed Antenna	3.35-3.75 and 4.45-5.1 (-6 dB) 3.40-3.60 and 4.80-5.0 (-10 dB)	>18	12 × 3.3

IV. CONCLUSION

Table I exhibits the comparison of the proposed antenna with the references. Compared to the references, it can draw a conclusion that the designed antenna performs better impedance matching bandwidth (better than 10 dB), low isolations (better than 18 dB), excellent antenna gains (superior to 4.65 dB and 4.89 dB, respectively) and good antenna efficiencies (62 – 72% and 72 –80 %). Particularly, due to printed on the side frame (4.1-mm high), the designed antenna system is an eligible candidate for 5G ultra-thin full screen smartphones.

REFERENCES

[1] J. G. Andrews, et al., "What will 5G be?,". IEEE J. Sel. Areas Commun., vol. 32, no. 6, pp. 1065–1082, Jun. 2014.

[2] Y.-X. Li, C.-Y.-D. Sim, Y. Luo, G.-L. Yang, "12-port 5G massive MIMO antenna array in sub-6 GHz mobile handset for LTE bands 42/43/46 applications," IEEE Access, vol. 6, pp. 344–354, Oct. 2017.

[3] M.-Y. Li, et al., "Eight-port orthogonally dual-polarized antenna array for 5G smartphone applications," IEEE Trans. Antennas Propag., vol. 64, no. 9, pp. 3820–3830, Sep. 2016.

[4] Z. Qin, W. Geyi, M. Zhang, and J. Wang, "Printed eight-element MIMO system for compact and thin 5G mobile handest," Electron. Lett., vol. 52, no. 6, pp. 416–418, 2016.

[5] Y.-X. Li, C.-Y.-D. Sim, Y. Luo, G.-L. Yang, "Multiband 10-Antenna Array for Sub-6 GHz MIMO Applications in 5G Smartphones," IEEE Access., vol. 6, pp. 28041–28053, May 2018.

[6] R. S. Aziz, A. K. Arya, and S.-O. Park, "Multiband full-metal-rimmed antenna design for smartphones," IEEE Antennas Wireless Propag. Lett., vol. 15, pp. 1987–1990, Mar. 2016.

[7] J.-L. Guo, L. Cui, C. Li, and B. Sun, "Side-Edge Frame Printed Eight-Port Dual-Band Antenna Array for 5G Smartphone Applications," IEEE Trans. Antennas Propag., vol. 66, no. 12, pp. 7412–7417, Dec. 2018.

[8] Q. Chen, J.-P. Wang, L. Ge, Y. Li, T.-Q. Pei, and C.-Y.-D. Sim, "Single Ring Slot Based Antennas for Metal-Rimmed 4G/5G Smartphones," IEEE Trans. Antennas Propag., vol. 67, no. 3, pp. 1476-1487, Mar. 2019.

Predicting Electromagnetic Interference to a Terminated Wire Using Characteristic Mode Analysis

Mohamed Z. M. Hamdalla
Department of Computer Science and Electrical Engineering
University of Missouri–Kansas City
Kansas City, MO, 64110, USA.
mhamdalla@mail.umkc.edu

Anthony N. Caruso
Dept. of Physics and Astronomy
University of Missouri–Kansas City
Kansas City, MO, 64110, USA.
carusoan@umkc.edu

Ahmed M. Hassan
Department of Computer Science and Electrical Engineering
University of Missouri–Kansas City
Kansas City, MO, 64110, USA.
hassanam@umkc.edu

***Abstract*—Electromagnetic coupling to realistic wire configurations exhibit large variations with respect to the frequency, incident angle, and polarization of the interfering signal. In this work, Characteristic Mode Analysis (CMA) is used to calculate the fundamental modes of a terminated wire above an infinite ground plane. Using the properties of the modes, the coupled currents to the wire's loads are predicted for different incident excitations. Using this simple but practical wire configuration, we show the versatility of CMA in practical electromagnetic interference and coupling applications.**

***Keywords*—Characteristic Mode Analysis, Field-to-wire Coupling, Interference.**

I. Introduction

In a highly congested wireless spectrum, electromagnetic interference poses a significant challenge in a wide range of applications. Therefore, predicting the coupling or interfering current to a particular load in a practical wiring system has received rising interest over the last decade [1], [2]. For a particular wire configuration, several simulations and/or measurements are needed to exhaustively quantify the variations in the coupled currents due to variations in the frequency, angle of incidence, and polarization of the interfering signal. In this work, Characteristic Mode Analysis (CMA) is applied to predict the coupling to a terminated wire above an infinite ground plane. CMA decomposes the currents induced on a scatterer in terms of a set of independent modes and quantifies the modal behavior such as the relative importance of each mode at the frequency of interest [3]. In this work, we show how this modal behavior can be used to guide coupling and interference to practical wire systems.

II. Computational Analysis

A. Wire Configuration

Fig. 1 shows a 1 m wire, 3 mm in radius, and at a height of 0.1 m above an infinite ground plane. The wire is terminated at both of its ends by 50 Ω loads labelled as Load 1 and Load 2, respectively. Moreover, a third 50 Ω load, Load 3, is attached to the middle of the wire. In spite of the simplicity of the configuration in Fig. 1, it has practical relevance in a wide range of studies [4]–[6]. In the next Sub-section, we show how CMA can be used to simplify the coupling analysis to the different loads in Fig. 1.

B. Characteristic Mode Analysis of the structure

The CMA of the wire configuration in Fig. 1 is performed using the commercial electromagnetic solver FEKO [7]. The components of the CMA are threefold: (*i*) the modal significance spectrum (Fig. 2), (*ii*) the modal current distribution (Fig. 3), and (*iii*) the modal fields or the radiation characteristics of each mode (Fig. 4) [8]. In the context of electromagnetic interference, the modes represent all possible pathways for the external electromagnetic radiation to couple to the wire configuration in Fig. 1. The modal current distribution and the modal significance are completely independent of the external excitation. The modal fields represent the coupling between the incident field and the modes. That is, the modal field patterns can be defined as the map of the electric field directions that minimize/maximize the coupling between the incident radiation and a particular mode.

III. Electromagnetic Interference Results

CMA provides the current distribution of the fundamental modes of the structure allowing the prediction of the response at different wire locations. For example, Fig. 3 shows that only the even modes, Modes 2, 4 and 6, have nonzero currents at the middle of the wire. Thus the middle load, Load 3, is immune to coupling from the odd modes. Starting with Mode 2, Fig. 4 shows that Mode 2 is more efficiently excited by an excitation at incidence angles of $\theta = 90^\circ$ and $\phi = 45^\circ$ (the green curve). Fig. 3 shows that Mode 2 resonates at 0.3 GHz. Therefore, Mode 3 should be strongly expressed in the coupled current to Load 3 at 0.3 GHz for an incident plane wave at angles of incidence $\theta = 90^\circ$ and $\phi = 45^\circ$. On the other hand, Fig. 2 shows that Mode 6 resonates at 0.9 GHz and Fig. 4 shows that Mode 6 can be most efficiently excited at angles of incidence $\theta = 50^\circ$ and $\phi = 0^\circ$. Therefore, at angles of incidence $\theta = 50^\circ$ and $\phi = 0^\circ$ maximum coupling should occur at 0.9 GHz which is the resonance frequency of Mode 6.

To test this hypothesis, Fig. 5 shows the coupled current to Load 3 for two different excitations. Clearly, the current coupled to Load 3 is maximum at 0.3 GHz when $\theta = 90^\circ$ and $\phi = 45^\circ$, due to the strong excitation of Mode 2, and the current coupled to Load 3 is maximum at 0.9 GHz when $\theta = 50^\circ$ and $\phi = 0^\circ$, due to the excitation of Mode 6.

For the terminal loads, Load 1 and Load 2, all the modes have high current values at the load locations as shown in Fig. 3. However, for frequencies below the resonance frequency of the first mode, i.e., frequencies below 0.15 GHz, only Mode 1 will contribute to the current coupled to the terminal loads because it will be the only mode that is significant as shown in Fig. 2. Fig. 4 shows that if the incident field is exerted at $\theta = 90^\circ$ and $\Phi = 90^\circ$, maximum coupling to Mode 1 will occur which will directly maximize

This work is sponsored by ONR grants # N00014-17-1-2932 and # N00014-17-1-3016, and University of Missouri-Kansas City, School of Graduate Studies Research Award.

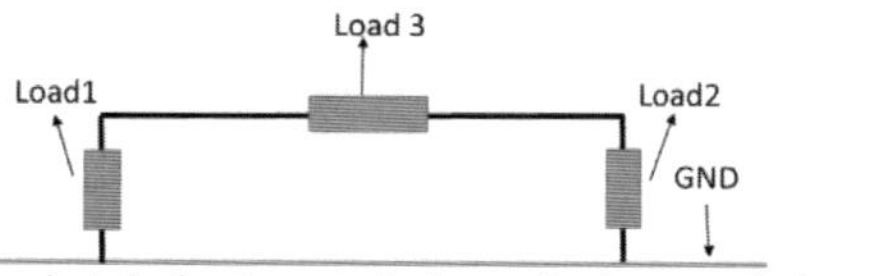

Fig. 1. Terminated wire above perfectly conducting ground plane.

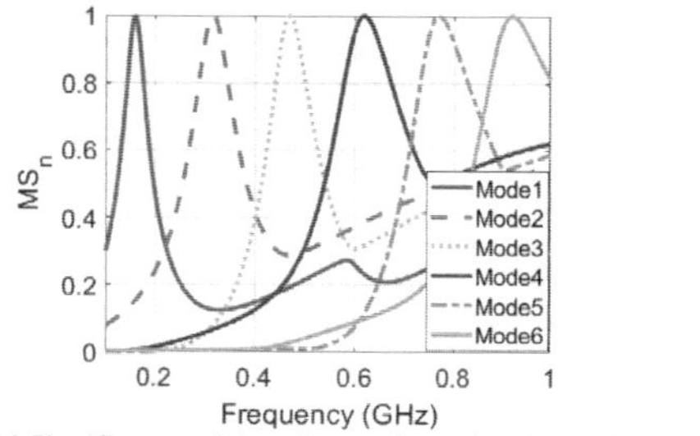

Fig. 2. Modal Significance of the wire configuration shown in Fig. 1.

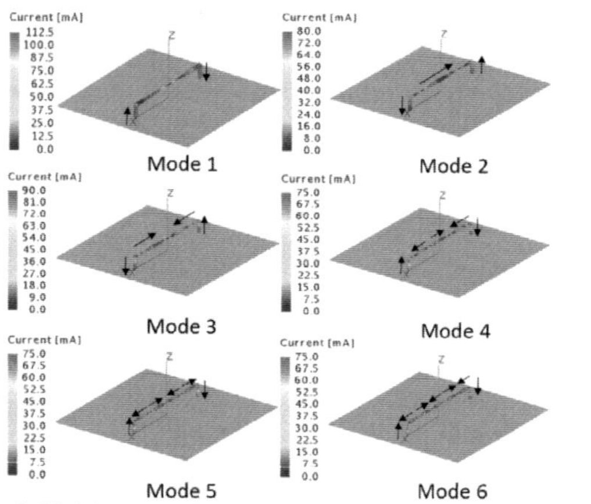

Fig. 3. Modal currents of the first 6 modes of the wire configuration.

the coupling to the terminal loads. For these angles of incidence, the maximum coupling to the terminal loads will occur at the resonance frequency of Mode 1, 0.15 GHz, as shown in Fig. 6. As the frequency increases, the higher-order modes, both odd and even, will start contributing to the current coupled to the terminal loads according to their modal significance shown in Fig. 2 and their modal fields in Fig. 4. The example studied in this paper shows the versatility of CMA in quantifying and predicting coupling. A similar CMA approach can be used to quantify and predict coupling to wire systems that are more complex than the one shown in Fig. 1 which will be presented at the conference.

IV. CONCLUSION

A simple wire configuration with three loads was studied to predict and control the coupling to each load individually at different frequencies. Characteristic Mode Analysis (CMA) was applied to identify all the modes of the structure and the possible ways to maximize/minimize coupling to each mode. This study will be extended in the future to study more complex wire systems and experimental validations of the CMA predictions will be presented.

REFERENCES

[1] X. Lu, G. Wei, X. Pan, L. Fan, and H. Wan, "Dual-port pulsed differential-mode current injection method for high-level electromagnetic pulse radiated susceptibility testing," IET Sci. Meas. Technol., vol. 10, no. 5, pp. 505–512, 2016.

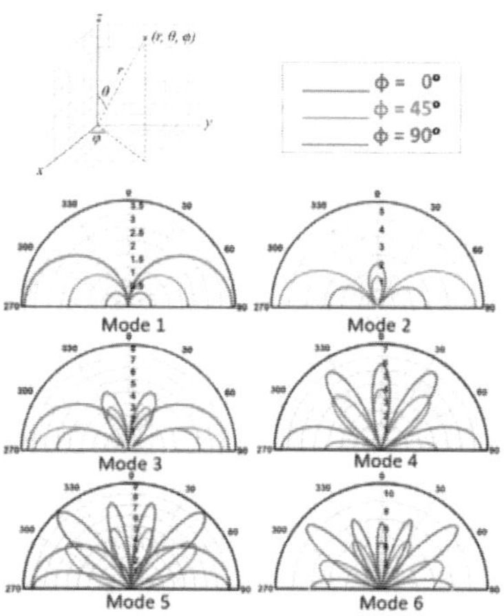

Fig. 4. Modal fields of the first 6 modes of the wire configuration shown in Fig. 1.

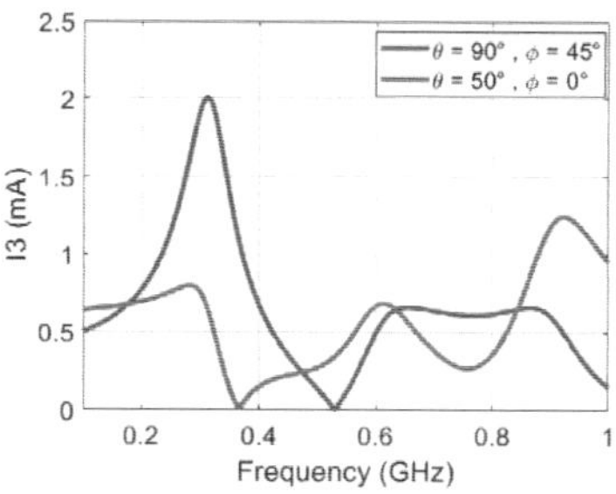

Fig. 5. Induced current on Load 3 for different field orientations.

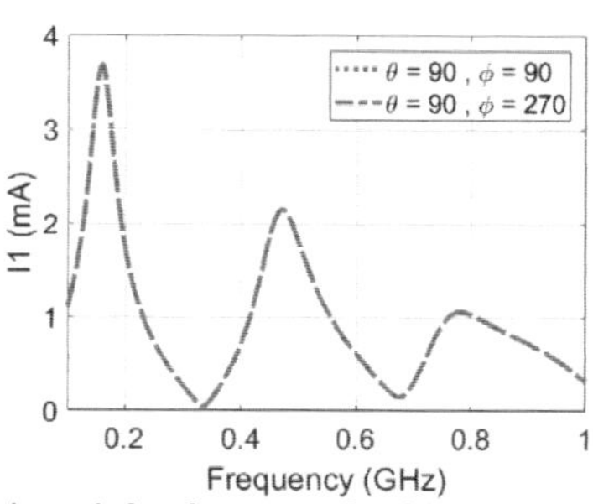

Fig. 6. Maximum induced current on Load 1.

[2] J. Jia, D. Rinas, and S. Frei, "Prediction of radiated fields from cable bundles based on current distribution measurements," in International Symposium on Electromagnetic Compatibility - EMC EUROPE, 2012, pp. 1–7.

[3] R. Harrington and J. Mautz, "Theory of characteristic modes for conducting bodies," IEEE Trans. Antennas Propag., vol. 19, no. 5, pp. 622–628, Sep. 1971.

[4] N. Toscani, G. Spadacini, F. Grassi, and S. A. Pignari, "Lumped and Distributed-Parameter Circuit Models of the Electromagnetic Clamp," IEEE Trans. Electromagn. Compat. , vol. 58, no. 4, pp. 1007–1015, Aug. 2016.

[5] L. Badini, G. Spadacini, F. Grassi, S. A. Pignari, and P. Pelissou, "A Rationale for Statistical Correlation of Conducted and Radiated Susceptibility Testing in Aerospace EMC," IEEE Trans. Electromagn. Compat. , vol. 59, no. 5, pp. 1576–1585, Oct. 2017.

[6] F. Grassi, H. Abdollahi, G. Spadacini, S. A. Pignari, and P. Pelissou, "Radiated Immunity Test Involving Crosstalk and Enforcing Equivalence With Field-to-Wire Coupling," IEEE Trans. Electromagn. Compat. , vol. 58, no. 1, pp. 66–74, Feb. 2016.

[7] https://altairhyperworks.com/product/FEKO. [Accessed: 07-Nov-2019].

[8] A. M. Hassan, F. Vargas-Lara, J. F. Douglas, and E. J. Garboczi, "Electromagnetic Resonances of Individual Single-Walled Carbon Nanotubes With Realistic Shapes: A Characteristic Modes Approach," IEEE Trans. Antennas Propag., vol. 64, no. 7, pp. 2743–2757, Jul. 2016.

Asymmetric Carbon Nanotube Dimers for Novel Sensing Applications

Sumitra Dey
Dept. of Computer Science and Electrical Engineering
University of Missouri–Kansas City
Kansas City, MO, 64110, USA
sumitra.dey@mail.umkc.edu

Ahmed M. Hassan
Dept. of Computer Science and Electrical Engineering
University of Missouri–Kansas City
Kansas City, MO, 64110, USA
hassanam@umkc.edu

***Abstract*—In this work, we study the use of asymmetric carbon nanotube (CNT) dimers for the contactless detection of foreign nano-particles. Asymmetric CNT dimers create a unique field distribution, through the electromagnetic coupling, which in turn generates two distinct resonances representing the bonding and anti-bonding modes. The presence of a foreign nano-particle (NP) in the vicinity of the CNT dimer perturbs the dimer's field distribution and causes the bonding and anti-bonding resonances to shift by unequal amounts depending on the NP location. By studying the difference in the shift of the bonding and the anti-bonding resonances, we show that the NP relative location can be reconstructed. The computational experiments performed in this work show how asymmetric CNT dimers can be used for novel sensing applications.**

Keywords—Anti-bonding modes, bonding modes, carbon nanotubes (CNTs), dimers, sensors.

I. Introduction

Carbon nanotubes (CNTs) are rolled versions of two-dimensional graphene sheets forming single-walled (SWCNT) or concentric multi-walled (MWCNT) tubes with high aspect ratios and exceptional mechanical, thermal and electrical properties [1]. Recent experimental and computational studies have demonstrated the existence of localized surface plasmon resonances (LSPR) in CNTs which vary depending on the CNT's length, shape, and environment [2]. This has paved the way for several potential applications of CNTs including nano-antennas, emitters, detectors, polarizers, and THz absorbers. [2]. In most of these applications, the CNTs are studied in bulk agglomerated form or in a large array. A CNT pair, termed as CNT dimer, has recently received rising interest [3]. If two CNTs of comparable dimensions are arranged in close proximity, they exhibit strong electromagnetic coupling and develop bonding and anti-bonding modes or resonances [3]. In the bonding resonance (BR), the currents of the two CNTs are in phase whereas in the anti-bonding resonance (ABR) the currents of the two CNTs are out of phase. This phenomenon exhibited by a CNT dimer is similar to the energy level splitting effect under optical illumination in plasmonic nano-particle assemblies [4].

We have re-investigated this dual-mode feature of CNT dimer and shown its potential in sensing applications. In order to get a strong expression from both the ABR and BR, we used length asymmetry in the CNT dimer assembly [3]. Each of these modes shows a unique near-field distribution that is sensitive to any external perturbations. Our analysis shows that the presence of an external nano-particle (NP) in the vicinity of the CNT dimer will perturb the near-field distribution and produce unequal shifts in the BR and ABR, depending on the particle location. The unequal shifts in the resonances can then be translated into a measure of the external NP's location.

This work was supported in part by the NIST "Multi-Scale Computational Modeling of Carbon Nanostructure Composites" under Grant 70NANB15H285 and in part by NSF CRI Award 1629908 "II-NEW: Experimental Characterization and CAD Development Testbed for Nanoscale Integrated Circuits."

II. Computational Modelling

The far-field electromagnetic response of the CNT dimer assemblies was calculated using our in-house full-wave Method of Moment (MOM) algorithm for Arbitrary Thin Wires (ATW) [3] and the near-field response was calculated using commercial electromagnetic solver FEKO [5]. The schematic configuration of the CNT dimer along with a foreign NP (a 50 nm long perfectly conducting nano-wire) is shown in Fig. 1 (a). Both the CNTs and the foreign NP are positioned in the *xy*-plane and aligned parallel to the *x*-axis. The assembly in Fig. 1 is excited with a normally incident plane wave with an *x*-polarized electric field. Both CNTs are single-walled, have an armchair (9, 9) chirality, and a radius $a = 0.61\ nm$. However, to create an asymmetric dimer, the CNTs are chosen of slightly different lengths, 96 nm and 86.4 nm separated by a constant gap of $20a = 12.2\ nm$. The position of the foreign NP is varied schematically over the five different locations as highlighted in Fig. 1 (b).

III. Isolated CNT vs Asymmetric CNT Dimer

In Fig. 2 (a), we compare the absorbed power of an isolated 96 nm long CNT1, in the absence of CNT2, versus that of an asymmetric CNT dimer. The asymmetric dimer exhibits two resonances whereas the single CNT exhibits only a single resonance. Fig. 2 (b) shows the *x*-component of the near electric field generated by a single CNT. Fig. 2 (c) and Fig. 2 (d) show the *x*-component of the near electric field generated by the asymmetric CNT dimer at the ABR and BR, respectively. Apart from the differences in magnitude, the near-field pattern changes considerably from the isolated CNT to the dimer case as shown in Fig. 2 (b) to Fig. 2 (d). These differences in the near-field distribution help in sensing the relative location of the foreign NP.

IV. Sensitivity to Foreign NP Location

Keeping all the previous parameters constant, we varied the *y*-location of the foreign NP symmetrically about the dimer axis

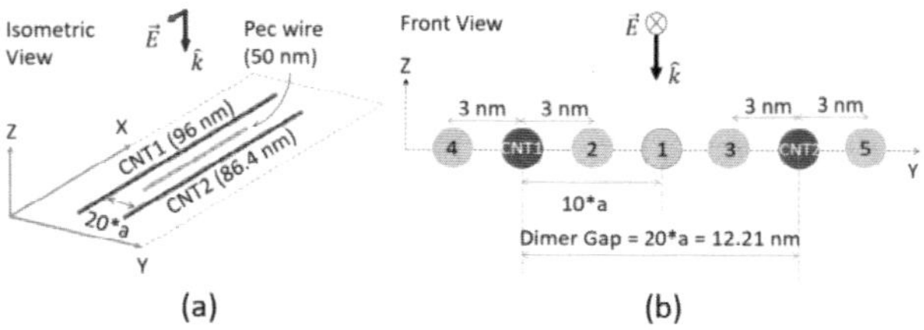

Fig. 1. (a) Asymmetric CNT dimer along with a PEC nano-wire placed at the center of the dimer gap excited with an x-polarized normally incident plane wave and (b) schematic view of five different y-locations of the PEC nano-wire on the same plane as the CNT dimer.

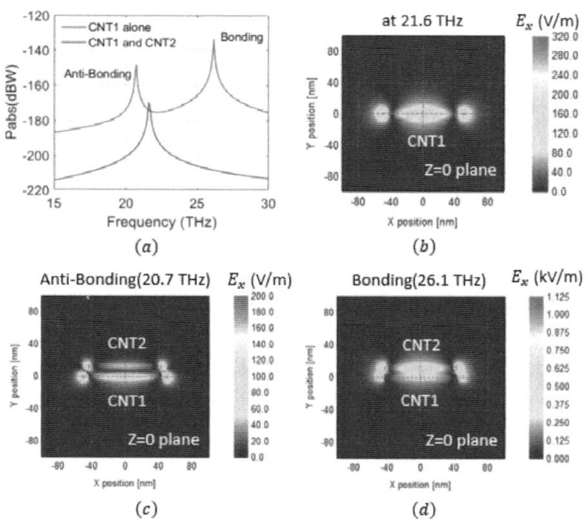

Fig. 2. (a) Absorbed power spectrums: CNT1 alone Vs CNT Dimer with 20a dimer gap (calculated by in-house algorithm). (b) Magnitude of E_x near-field component for CNT1 at 21.6 THz, (c) CNT-dimer at 20.7 THz (Anti-bonding mode), and (d) CNT-dimer at 26.1 THz (Bonding mode). (Simulated in FEKO 3D MOM solver [5]).

as shown in Fig. 1 (b), and calculated the corresponding absorbed power spectrums as shown in Fig. 3. The percentage shifts in resonances relative to unperturbed dimer configuration have been tabulated in Table I. When the foreign NP is placed in Position 1, it produces almost no shift in the ABR but a large shift in the BR. This is because, in the middle of the dimer, the anti-bonding mode has a vanishing near-field (Fig. 2 (c)) whereas the bonding mode has a strong near-field (Fig. 2 (d)). Moving the NP from Position 1 to Position 2, i.e., close to CNT1, where the anti-bonding near-field increases (Fig. 2 (c)) causes an increasing shift in ABR. The shift in BR remains the same since there is no relative change in the bonding mode near-field between Position 1 and 2 (Fig. 2 (d)). The opposite happens when we move NP from Position 1 to Position 3. If the NP is not in the dimer gap and is close to CNT1 (Position4) we see a comparatively bigger shift in ABR compared to BR. The opposite happens when we place NP at Position 5. Therefore, the main conclusion from Fig. 2., Fig. 3. and Table I is that the shifts in ABR and BR are proportional to their respective near-field intensity values at the location of the NP. However, due to the non-linear nature of the near-field variation (Fig. 2 (c)-(d)), the resonant frequency shifts will have a non-linear relationship with the NP position. There are many ways to control the near-field distribution of the dimer modes, such as by varying the

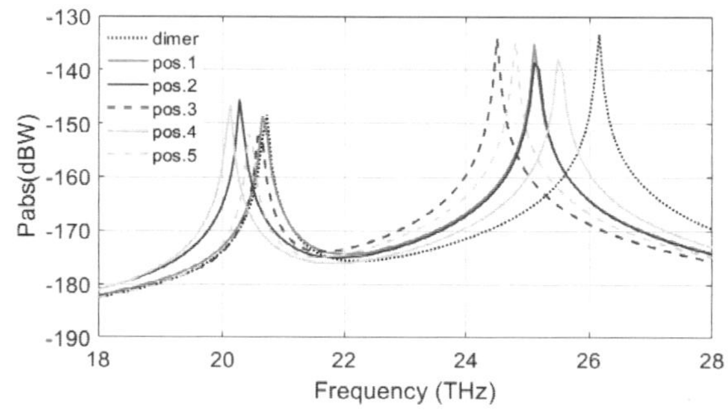

Fig. 3. Sensing foreign NP location by observing relative shifts in bonding and anti-bonding resonances of CNT dimer (calculated by in-house MOM algorithm).

TABLE I. Shift in Resonances Compared to Unperturbed Dimer

Position of NP	***Shift in Anti-bonding Resonance***	***Shift in Bonding Resonance***
1	-0.38%	-4.05%
2	-2.17%	-4.05%
3	-0.38%	-6.34%
4	-2.89%	-2.6%
5	-1.45%	-5.2%

CNT shape, orientation, conductivity, and dimer gap. The inclusion of these parameters can give extra degrees of freedom to the existing model.

V. Conclusion and Future Work

The unique sensing abilities of asymmetric CNT dimers have been presented with several computational experiments. This study reveals that the location of a foreign NP can be traced by mapping the relative frequency shifts of dimer anti-bonding and bonding mode resonances. However, the sensitivity and reliability of this mechanism may have a dependency on the geometrical and material properties of CNTs as well as target NP. A more detailed analysis is required to set the allowable tolerance levels for this mechanism to work precisely.

References

[1] G. W. Hanson, "Fundamental transmitting properties of carbon nanotube antennas," *IEEE Trans. Antennas Propag.*, vol. 53, no. 11, pp. 3426–3435, Nov. 2005.

[2] M. V. Shubha, *et. at.*, "Experimental evidence of localized plasmon resonance in composite materials containing single-wall carbon nanotubes," *Phys. Rev. B*, vol. 85. p. 16545, 2012.

[3] A. M. Hassan, F. Vargas-Lara, J. F. Douglas, and E. J. Garboczi, "Electromagnetic Scattering From Multiple Single-Walled Carbon Nanotubes Having Tumbleweed Configurations," in *IEEE Transactions on Antennas and Propagation*, vol. 65, no. 6, pp. 3192-3202, June 2017.

[4] P. K. Jain, S. Eustis, and M. A. El-Sayed, "Plasmon coupling in nanorod assemblies: Optical absorption, discrete dipole approximation simulation, and exciton-coupling model," *J. Phys. Chem. B*, vol. 110, no. 37, pp. 18243–18253, Sep. 2006.

[5] FEKO. EM Simulation Software V.18.0. [Online]. Available: https://www.feko.info

Circularly Polarized Log Periodic Dipole Antennas

Haruo KAWAKAMI[1], Masao TANIOKA[1], and Ryoji WAKABAYASHI[2]
[1]Kato Electric Industry Co., Ltd.
1-9-2-704 Haruno Minuma-ku
Saitama-city, Saitama Pref., JAPAN
[2] Tokyo Metropolitan College of Industrial Technology
8-17-1, Minami-Senju, Arakawa, Tokyo, 116-8523

Abstract- **This Modified Self-complementary LPDA [1] has a second array of dipoles so arranged that each dipole of the second array has a quarter-wavelength phase difference from that of the corresponding dipole of the standard LPDA array for the given radiation field. The cross-element LPDA does not need a broadband 90-degree hybrid junction to produce circular polarization.**

Index Terms- **Broadband , LPDA antennas.**

I. Introduction

In this paper we propose a LPDA. This LPDA, called a "cross-element LPDA," has a second dipole array which is orthogonal to that of the standard LPDA. Though a cross-element LPDA for EMC measurement has been manufactured by EMCO, this version of the antenna requires a discrete broadband 90-degree hybrid junction to produce the circular polarization. However, our version of an LPDA antenna does not require such a hybrid junction.

The cross-element LPDA antenna can radiate the horizontal and vertical components of the electric field with a polarization ratio of about only 1 dB for the vertical plane, and so the cross-element LPDA gives good circular polarization.

II. Cross Element of Theory and Mesurement Value

The geometry of a standard N-element LPDA [2]-[3] with associated parameters is shown in Fig. 1. An antenna length shows the length of the ith element, the distance between element i-1 and i and the wire radius of the ith element of a standard 16-element LPDA. These parameters are referred to the model 3146 (a product of EMCO). The parameters of the LPDA, di/li, scale factor (τ=di/di-1), the frequency of the half-wave resonance spacing factor (σ=di/li) and apex angle α. Then, it reasoned that the LPDA would have circular polarization if the LPDA had a set of cross elements perpendicular to the original elements and if each cross element was shifted from the original elements a distance equivalent to a phase shift of $\pi/4$ for the given radiation field.

The geometry of the cross-element LPDA with 2N elements is shown in Figs. 2 (a) and (b). Each N+ith cross element is lengthened to be 14.2/13=1.09 times longer than the corresponding i-th element so that α of the cross elements of the LPDA comes to the values of the original LPDA.

Fig. 3 shows the front view of the feed lines of the cross-element LPDA for the # i and # i+N elements. The characteristic impedance Z_0 of the feed line in Fig. 3 can be given as;

$$Z_0 = 138\log_{10}\frac{2\sqrt{2}D}{a},$$

It is found that $Z_0 \geq 62.3(\Omega)$, because D>a. In this paper, Z_0 is 75(Ω), for example, if a=10.0 mm, then D= 12.4 mm.

Figs. 4 (a) and (b) shows values calculated by the moment method [4] and the typical measured radiation pattern of the cross-element LPDA for a frequency of 1 GHz. The calculated patterns seem to be in close agreement to the measured patterns.

Figs. 5 (a) and (b) shows the measured an axial ratio of the cross-element LPDA for a frequency of 750MHz. An axial ratio of the cross-element LPDA is within 3 dB for the horizontal and 1 dB for the vertical plane in the forward direction. This shows that this type of antenna has circular polarization. Similar patterns are obtained for other frequencies from 300 MHz to 1000MHz. This antenna has a gain of about 5.8-5.0 dB at the frequency 300-1000MHz.

We consider that the two orthogonal components of the electric field, the E_φ component radiated from the original element and the E_θ component radiated from the cross element of the LPDA where maximum current is obtained, have a phase difference of $\pi/4$.

III. Conclusion

It has calculated the gain for the cross-element LPDA and has shown the characteristics of the cross-element LPDA clearly. The cross-element LPDA has an axial ratio of about 1 dB for the vertical plane. The cross-element LPDA has almost circular polarization.

References

[1] Y. Mushiake, Self-complementary Antennas. Springer, UK, 1996.
[2] R. Carrel, "The Design of Log-Periodic Dipole Antennas," Antenna Lab, University of Illinois, Urbana, Tech. Rep. 52, Sept. 1961.
[3] R. S. Elliott, Antenna Theory and Design. Prentice-Hall, Inc., pp. 382-384, 1981.
[4] R. F. Harrington, Field Computation by Moment Methods. Macmillan Co., Ltd. N.Y., 1968.

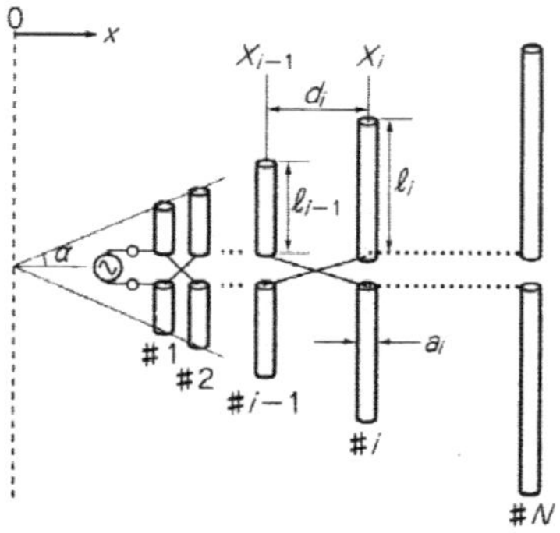

Fig. 1. Standard LPDA with associated parameters.

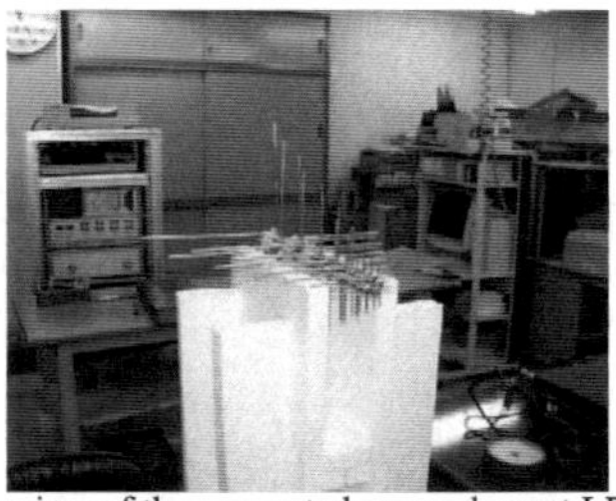

Fig. 2. (a) An exterior view of the suggested cross-element LPDA.

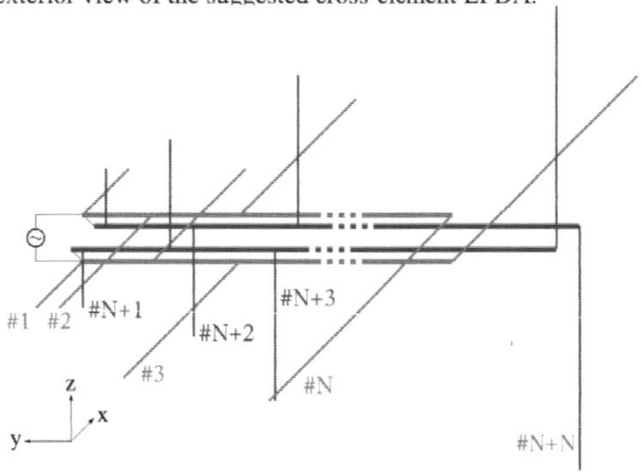

Fig. 2. (b) Suggested cross-element LPDA with associated parameters.

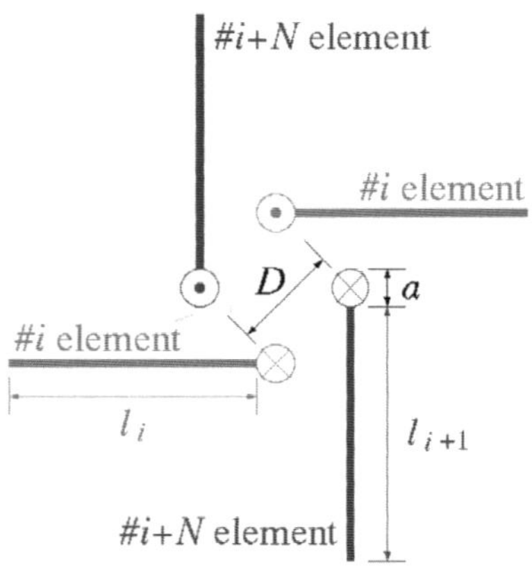

Fig. 3. A pair of feed lines with #ith and #i+Nth elements of the cross-element LPDA.

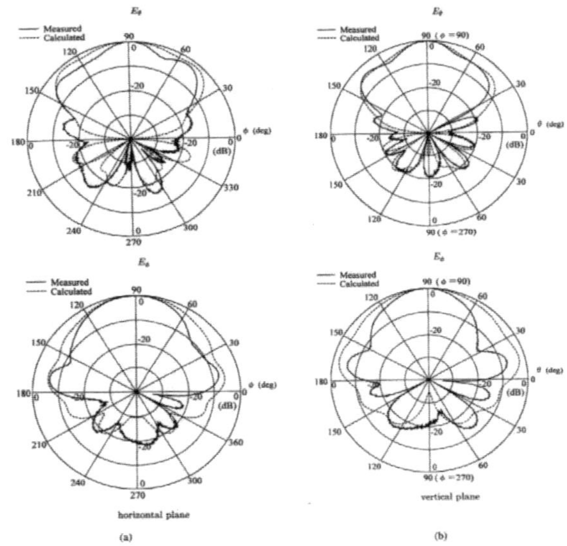

Fig. 4. Radiation pattern of the cross-element LPDA at 1000MHz, (a) horizontal plane, and (b) vertical plane.

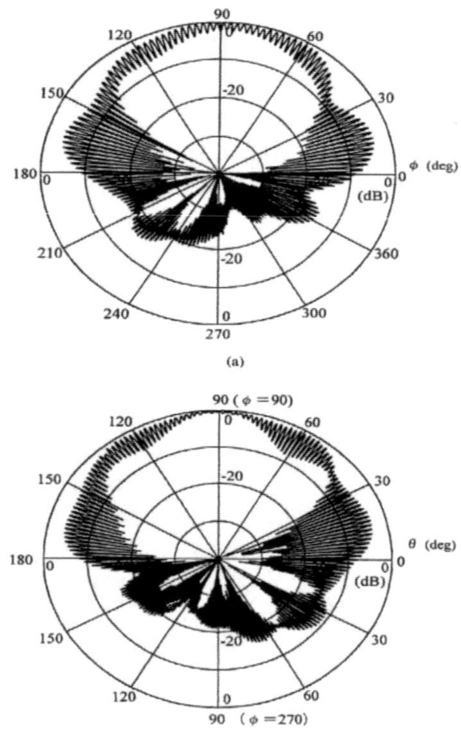

Fig. 5. Measured polarization ratio of the cross-element LPDA at 750MHz, (a) horizontal plane, and (b) vertical plane.

Mutual Coupling Compensation in Receiving Antenna Arrays

Sana Khan
Electrical Engineering
Istanbul Medipol University
Istanbul, Turkey
skhan@st.medipol.edu.tr

Hassan Sajjad
Electrical Engineering
Istanbul Medipol University
Istanbul, Turkey
hsajjad@st.medipol.edu.tr

Mehmet Kemal Ozdemir
Electrical Engineering
Istanbul Medipol University
Istanbul, Turkey
mkozdemir@medipol.edu.tr

Ercument Arvas
Electrical Engineering
Istanbul Medipol University
Istanbul, Turkey
earvas@medipol.edu.tr

***Abstract*—Mutual coupling compensation in uniform linear and circular receiving antenna arrays of thin wire dipoles is presented. It was observed that the mutual impedance is independent of the incident angle and depends solely on the geometry of the array. By using only one measurement, decoupling matrix is computed and direction of arrival is estimated.**

***Index Terms*—Direction of Arrival, Method of Moments, Mutual Coupling, Receiving Antenna Arrays, UCA, ULA.**

I. Introduction

Mutual Coupling is responsible for the degradation in antenna array performance, both in transmitting and receiving arrays [1–4]. In direction of arrival (DoA) estimation for receiving antennas, the received voltages must be decoupled in order to estimate the incoming signal DoA. In [5], mutual impedances are calculated when the array is in receiving mode. It has been shown experimentally [6], that this method works well for decoupling with a high resolution. However, measurements are required from various incident angles in order to compute the mutual impedances. This may not be practical for experimental purposes.

In this paper, an array of thin wire dipole antennas is illuminated by a plane wave. The received voltages are decoupled and the DoA is estimated. Examples for Uniform Linear Array (ULA) and Uniform Circular Array (UCA) are presented. Method of moments (MoM) is used to find the currents and voltages on the single mode antennas. Here, we show that the mutual impedance is constant for all angles and depends solely on the geometry of the antenna array. Furthermore, it can be calculated using only one measurement. This reduces the computation complexity and the physical labour in the experiments without degrading the accuracy of the mutual coupling compensation.

II. Formulation

Consider an N element array of thin wire dipoles where each element is terminated with a load Z_L. The received voltage at the antenna terminal V_i can be written as

$$V_i = I_i Z_L \tag{1}$$

The received voltage is the sum of two voltages, S_i and C_i. S_i is the voltage induced on the ith isolated antenna and C_i is the coupling effect from other elements. Thus (1) can be rewritten as,

$$V_i = S_i + C_i \tag{2}$$

C_i includes the re-radiation effects from all the other elements of the array on the ith antenna as

$$C_i = Z^{i,1}I_1 + Z^{i,2}I_2 + ... + Z^{i,i-1}I_{i-1} + Z^{i,i+1}I_{i+1} + ... + Z^{i,N}I_N \tag{3}$$

Here, $Z^{i,j}$ is the mutual impedance between elements i and j and I_j is the current induced at the jth port, given by

$$I_j = \frac{V_j}{Z_L} \quad \text{for} \quad j = 1, 2, ..., N. \tag{4}$$

To make the presentation simple, let us assume number of elements of the array $N = 4$. Then, from (2), (3) and (4) we get,

$$V_1 - Z^{1,2}\frac{V_2}{Z_L} - Z^{1,3}\frac{V_3}{Z_L} - Z^{1,4}\frac{V_4}{Z_L} = S_1 \tag{5}$$

$$V_2 - Z^{1,2}\frac{V_1}{Z_L} - Z^{1,2}\frac{V_3}{Z_L} - Z^{1,3}\frac{V_4}{Z_L} = S_2 \tag{6}$$

$$V_3 - Z^{1,3}\frac{V_1}{Z_L} - Z^{1,2}\frac{V_2}{Z_L} - Z^{1,2}\frac{V_4}{Z_L} = S_3 \tag{7}$$

$$V_4 - Z^{1,4}\frac{V_1}{Z_L} - Z^{1,3}\frac{V_2}{Z_L} - Z^{1,2}\frac{V_3}{Z_L} = S_4 \tag{8}$$

Due to the symmetry of the problems investigated, the mutual impedance matrix is Toeplitz. This property is used in the above equations. There are three unknowns, $Z^{1,2}$, $Z^{1,3}$ and $Z^{1,4}$ which can be solved by applying least square (LS) method to the above over-determined system for a single incident angle. Once the mutual impedances are found, the decoupling matrix can be found as follows.

$$\begin{bmatrix} 1 & -\frac{Z^{1,2}}{Z_L} & -\frac{Z^{1,3}}{Z_L} & -\frac{Z^{1,4}}{Z_L} \\ -\frac{Z^{1,2}}{Z_L} & 1 & -\frac{Z^{1,2}}{Z_L} & -\frac{Z^{1,3}}{Z_L} \\ -\frac{Z^{1,3}}{Z_L} & -\frac{Z^{1,2}}{Z_L} & 1 & -\frac{Z^{1,2}}{Z_L} \\ -\frac{Z^{1,4}}{Z_L} & -\frac{Z^{1,3}}{Z_L} & -\frac{Z^{1,2}}{Z_L} & 1 \end{bmatrix} \begin{bmatrix} V_1 \\ V_2 \\ V_3 \\ V_4 \end{bmatrix} = \begin{bmatrix} S_1 \\ S_2 \\ S_3 \\ S_4 \end{bmatrix} \tag{9}$$

III. Numerical Examples

In this section, examples of four-element ULA and UCA are presented. The computations are done using MoM as mentioned in[1], [7]. The mutual impedances calculated by the proposed method are compared with those of [5]. The DoA is estimated for two-coherent sources using the decoupled voltages.

A. Four-element ULA

A ULA with four dipole antennas at 2.4 GHz is considered with spacing $d = 0.2\lambda_0$, length $l = 0.48\lambda_0$ and $l/a = 100$, where a is the radius and λ_0 is the free space wavelength. Each antenna is terminated with $Z_L = 50\ \Omega$ load impedance. The array is excited by a plane wave with $\theta = 90°$ and $\phi = 90°$, where θ and ϕ are measured from positive z and positive x directions, respectively. These angles are chosen because coupling effect is maximum for the ULA. Using MoM, we find the received voltages at each antenna terminal, which is the coupled voltage. Then, the isolated voltages are computed by considering one antenna at a time in the absence of the others. Solving (5) to (8), we find the mutual impedances which are shown in Table I. It should be noted that in the proposed method, only one measurement angle (θ, ϕ) was used to compute the mutual impedances, whereas in [5] at least 10 angles were required to compute the same mutual impedances. It was observed that the mutual impedances found in the proposed method are more accurate than in [5]. Since mutual impedance is independent of the angle of arrival, the decoupling matrix of the proposed method can decouple any voltage irrespective of the incident angle, whereas [5] limits itself to a fixed elevation angle. The real and imaginary mutual impedances are shown in Fig. 1, which are constant for all angles (θ, ϕ).

B. DoA estimation of two sources

Here, two cases for DoA estimation are discussed. In case I, the ULA was excited by two plane waves, with fixed $\phi = 90^o$ and different elevation angles, $\theta_1 = 45^o$ and $\theta_2 = 75^o$. The uncoupled voltages were computed using the mutual impedances of Table I. The isolated, coupled and uncoupled voltages were given as an input to MUSIC algorithm [5] with forward-only spatial smoothing due to the coherent sources as plane wave. In case II, the plane waves were incident from a fixed $\theta = 90^o$ but different azimuth angles $\phi_1 = 45^o$ and $\phi_2 = 75^o$. As Fig. 2 shows, both of the DoAs are successfully detected.

C. Four-element UCA

The same dipole antennas are arranged in a UCA with a radius of $\lambda_0/8$ and excited by the plane wave with $\theta = 90°$, $\phi = 90°$. The coupled and isolated voltages are calculated and then the mutual impedances are computed which are compared in Table I.

TABLE I. RECEIVED MUTUAL IMPEDANCES

Comparison	ULA		
	$Z^{1,2}$	$Z^{1,3}$	$Z^{1,4}$
Proposed	$-19.26 + 11.13i$	$0.0675 + 15.38i$	$10.39 + 4.866i$
Ref [5]	$-18.47 + 10.94i$	$0.0263 + 15.61i$	$10.72 + 4.732i$
	UCA		
Proposed	$-21.56 + 9.238i$	$-14.52 + 14.12i$	$-21.74 + 9.371i$
Ref [5]	$-21.95 + 10.62i$	$-12.39 + 15.71i$	$-21.95 + 10.62i$

As an example, the UCA was excited by two incident plane waves with $\theta = 90^o$ and $\phi_1 = 35^o$ and $\phi_2 = 45^o$. The isolated, coupled and uncoupled voltages are shown in Table II. It can be seen that mutual coupling has been successfully compensated.

TABLE II. ISOLATED, COUPLED AND UNCOUPLED VOLTAGES

Ports	UCA		
	Isolated $[mV]$	*Coupled* $[mV]$	*Uncoupled* $[mV]$
V_1	$31.7\angle\ 14.0^o$	$29\angle 31.8^o$	$31.7\angle\ 14.0^o$
V_2	$31.7\angle -49.1^o$	$18\angle -101.2^o$	$31.7\angle -49.1^o$
V_3	$31.7\angle -43.6^o$	$16.6\angle -83.9^o$	$31.7\angle -43.6^o$
V_4	$31.7\angle\ 19.5^o$	$31.4\angle 39.7^o$	$31.7\angle\ 19.5^o$

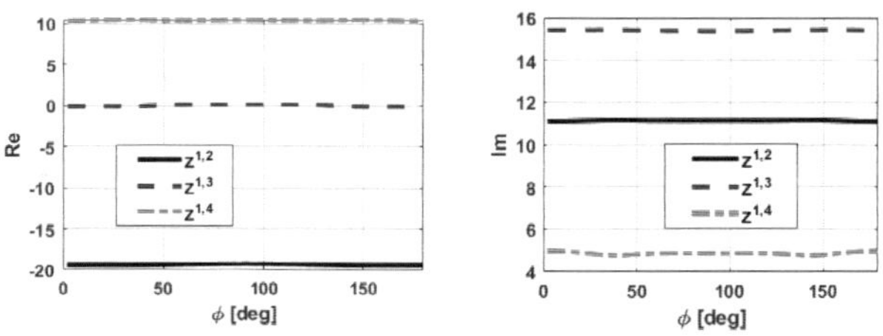

Fig. 1. Mutual impedance (*left*) real and (*right*) imaginary for four elements ULA, for all elevation angles.

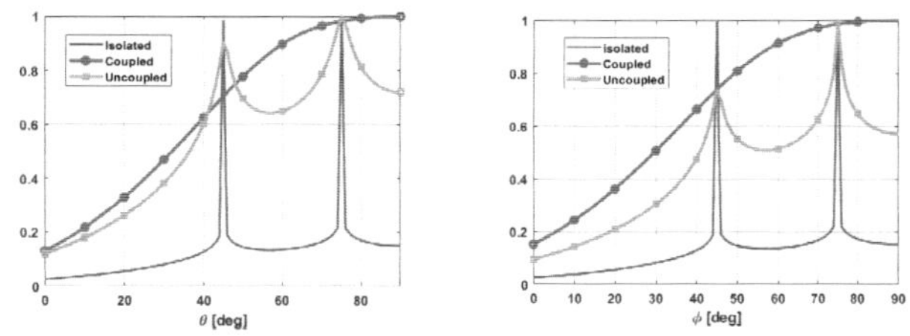

Fig. 2. Spatial spectrum of MUSIC algorithm for DoA detection of two coherent signals from. *(Left)*: $\phi = 90^o$, $\theta_1 = 45^o, \theta_2 = 75^o$. *(Right)*: $\theta = 90^o$, $\phi_1 = 45^o, \phi_2 = 75^o$.

IV. CONCLUSION

Mutual coupling in receiving antenna arrays of thin wire dipoles has been compensated by using only one measurement. It was observed that the mutual impedance depends only on the geometry of the structure and is independent of the incident angle.

ACKNOWLEDGMENT

This work has been partially supported by Tubitak project 215E316.

REFERENCES

[1] S. Khan, H. Sajjad, M. K. Ozdemir and E. Arvas, "Mutual Coupling Compensation in Transmitting Arrays of Thin Wire Antennas," ACES Journal, vol. 33, no. 11, pp. 1182-1189, Nov. 2018.

[2] M. K. Ozdemir, H. Arslan and E. Arvas, "Mutual coupling effect in multiantenna wireless communication systems," GLOBECOM '03. IEEE Global Telecommunications Conference (IEEE Cat. No.03CH37489), San Francisco, CA, vol. 2, pp. 829-833, 2003.

[3] H. Sajjad, S. Khan and E. Arvas, "Mutual coupling reduction in array elements using EBG structures," 2017 International Applied Computational Electromagnetics Society Symposium - Italy (ACES), Florence, pp. 1-2, 2017.

[4] X. Chen, S. Zhang and Q. Li, "A Review of Mutual Coupling in MIMO Systems," in IEEE Access, vol. 6, pp. 24706-24719, 2018.

[5] H. Lui and H. T. Hui, "Mutual coupling compensation of compact antenna array for direction-of-arrivals estimations," 2010 4th International Conference on Signal Processing and Communication Systems, Gold Coast, QLD, pp. 1-10, 2010.

[6] Y. Yu, H. Lui, C. H. Niow and H. T. Hui, "Improved DOA Estimations Using the Receiving Mutual Impedances for Mutual Coupling Compensation: An Experimental Study," IEEE Transactions on Wireless Communications, vol. 10, no. 7, pp. 2228-2233, July 2011.

[7] S. Khan and E. Arvas, "Compensation for the Mutual Coupling in Transmitting Antenna Arrays," IEEE APACE, pp. 84-88, Dec. 2016.

Circularly Polarized 5G Band MIMO Antenna Array for Future User Terminals

Sonika P. Biswal
[1]Electrical and Computer Eng.
[1]San Diego State University, CA, USA
[2]IIT (ISM), Dhanbad, India
Email: sbiswal@sdsu.edu

Satish K. Sharma
[1]Electrical and Computer Eng.
[1]San Diego State University, California, USA
Email: ssharma@sdsu.edu

Sushrut Das
[1]Electronics Engineering
Indian Institute of Technology (ISM), Dhanbad, India
Email: sushrut@iitism.ac.in

***Abstract*— A circularly polarized millimeter wave (*mm* wave) linear array antenna consisting of eight elements is demonstrated in this work. The mm-wave array antenna is designed to cover the currently used 5G band 27.5-28.35GHz for user terminal application. The antenna arrays can be also arranged together in a single platform to generate right- and left-hand circular polarization (LHCP). A directive pattern with a realized gain of 11dBic with scanning range of ±50⁰ is observed at the operating band. The simulated correlation coefficients over the operating band also satisfy the acceptable diversity criteria.**

***Keywords*—5G, circularly polarization, mm wave, MIMO.**

I. Introduction

The quest of high data traffic and enhanced channel capacity in modern wireless terminals has encouraged to explore 5G smart antenna solution. It is well known that the 5G bands will be a good solution, that could be utilized for improving the channel capacity and data-transfer rate that the user can realize [1]. When the number of MIMO antennas are comparable in both the handheld user terminals (UT) and the base station (BS), the channel capacity can be significantly improved. However, it is impractical to install an equal number of antenna elements in BS and handheld UTs. Owing to the very constrained space in handheld UTs, it is very challenging to deploy a comparable number of MIMO antennas as installed in the base station with good isolation and envelope correlation coefficient. It has been speculated that minimum 6 to 8 number of antennas are required to develop 5G massive MIMO for handheld UTs [2]. In both line of sight and multipath environments, circularly polarized radiators have the advantage of minimum polarization loss and less multipath interference over the linear polarization radiators. This also avoids the effect of polarization mismatch by uniform power distribution between the receiving radiators and provides the facility to receive the signal with equal strength despite the orientation of CP radiators. This attribute is suitable for the situation where the receiving antenna alters its position and orientation continuously with respect to the transmitter.

In literature, several works reported for *mm* wave MIMO antenna array design for user terminals are based on only linearly polarized radiators [3-5]. Based on author's best knowledge, circularly polarized enabled *mm* wave MIMO antenna array for user terminals is proposed here for the first time. The *mm* wave antenna array model with its antenna performances is demonstrated in Section-II followed by its beam steering performances in Section-III.

II. Antenna Design and Analysis

The schematic of the circular polarized radiator utilized in this work is shown in Fig. 1 (a). The antenna element is a printed rectangular slot-based loop radiator embedded on the ground plane, mounted on a 20mil thick Rogers 5880 dielectric substrate and fed by a microstrip feed line at the back. Circular polarization (CP) can be achieved due to the excitation of two uniform electric field components across the radiator which must be orthogonal to each other. Here, the CP behavior is achieved due to the separation of a horizontal branch of the loop by a gap. The length of the loop is chosen to be 0.95λ to operate at 28GHz. The slot is rotated with respect to Y- axis for a good CP behavior over the operating bandwidth. A rotated strip maintaining identical angle of rotation as the slot radiator is also connected at the top edge of microstrip feed line to maintain the CP behavior (3dB axial ratio bandwidth) over the operating range (10dB impedance bandwidth). The matching and axial ratio performances are shown in Fig. 1 (b). The antenna is right hand circularly polarized. The sense of polarization primarily depends on the rotation of the antenna element with respect to X-axis. An eight-element linear array is further designed by and is depicted in Fig. 2 (a).

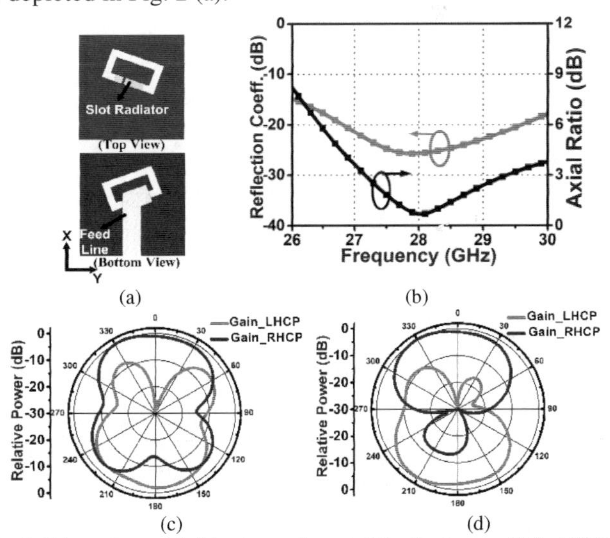

Fig. 1. Schematic model: (a) antenna element, (b) reflection coefficient (dB), (c) radiation pattern at phi = 0^0, and (d) radiation Pattern at phi = 90^0.

The inter-element spacing is kept as 0.6λ to avoid grating lobe generation over the beam scan range. The antenna performances such as impedance bandwidth, isolation, and axial ratio (AR) are shown in Figs. 2 (b-c). It can be observed that, the antenna covers the currently used 5G band (27.5-28.35GHz) with isolation greater than 20dB between the adjacent elements. The AR of the array is also less than 3dB over the operating bandwidth.

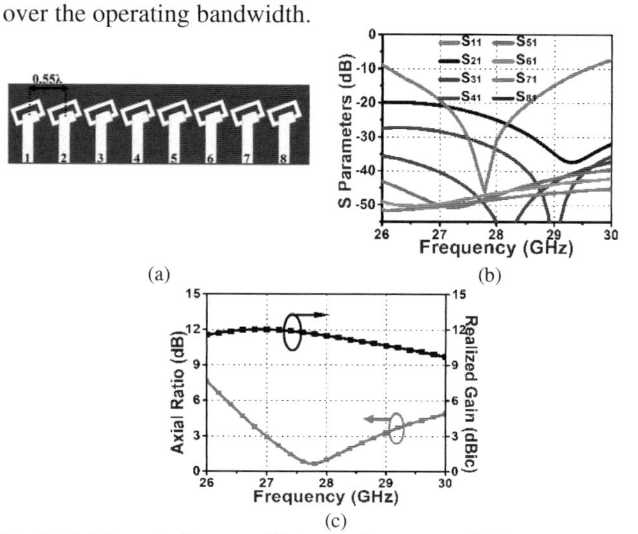

Fig. 2. (a) Schematic diagram of 8-element linear array, (b) S- parameters, and (c) axial ratio and gain.

III. Beam Steering Performances

The simulated beam steering performance of the array at ϕ =90 plane is shown in Fig. 3, where multiple lines represent steered beams while providing progressive phase shifts between elements. It can be seen that the array has a directive beam with wide beam-steering characteristic of ±50° for 3 dB reduction in the gain. The 3D radiation patterns of the array at 28 GHz when its beams are scanned at $\theta = 0°$, 25°, and 50° are also shown in Fig. 4, respectively.

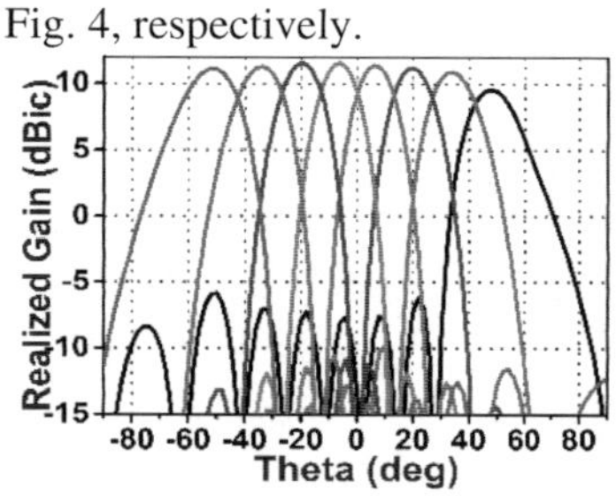

Fig. 3. Beam steering performance of the array.

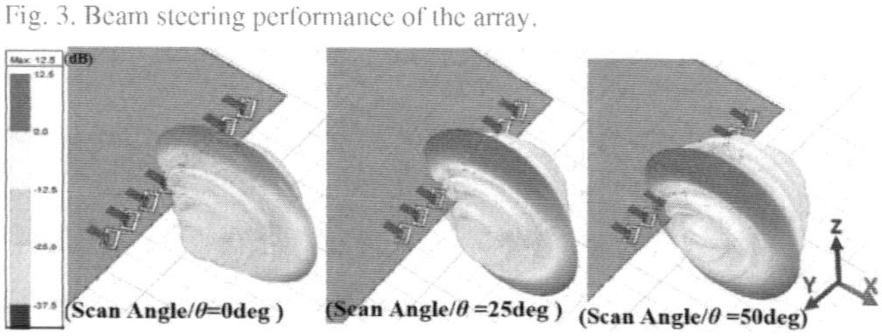

Fig. 4. 3D radiation patterns at three different scanning angles along ϕ =90 at $\theta = 0^0$, 30^0, and 60^0 respectively for 28GHz.

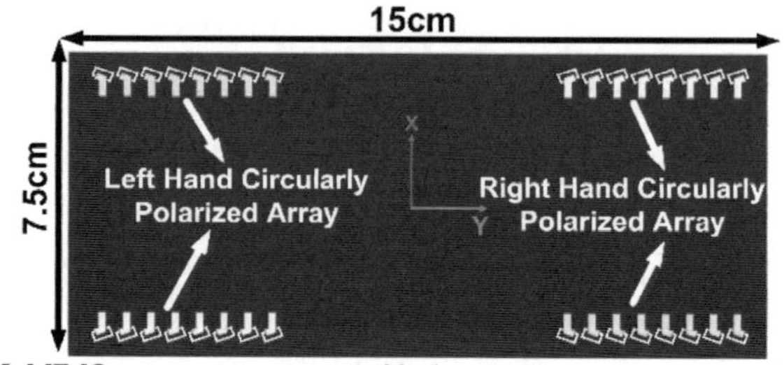

Fig. 5. MIMO antenna arrangement of 8-elements linear sub arrays on the host ground plane.

It can be observed that, the proposed antenna has a good beam steering property. The beam-steering performance of the linear array for both positive and negative scanning angles is comparatively symmetrical. For user terminals, although the coverage issue can be eliminated by steering the beam, it is still difficult to achieve a coverage range similar to the omnidirectional antenna by using one array. This can be resolved by bringing multiple sub arrays in a single host ground plane platform (Fig. 5). Multiple CP arrays can also be arranged together in a single platform to sense both right hand and left-hand circular polarization as illustrated in the figure.

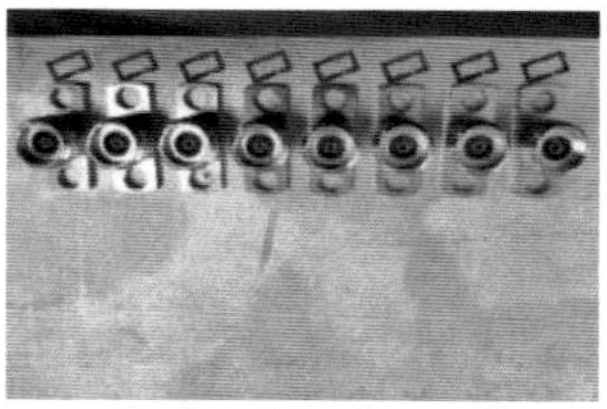

Fig. 6. Fabricated photograph of an eight element linear array.

IV. Conclusion and Future Study

A circularly polarized eight-element linear array is proposed here for 5G band, i.e., 27.5 - 28.35 GHz. A good beam steering performance between $\theta = \pm 50^0$ over the operating band is obtained. Multiple sub arrays can be arranged together in a single platform, e.g., hand held terminal to sense both the left- and right-hand circular polarization. The proposed antenna array can be a suitable candidate for future hand held terminals. The fabricated photograph is shown in Fig.6. Measurement results will be presented during the conference.

References

[1] M. Marcus, "5G and IMT for 2020 and beyond," [Spectrum Policy and Regulatory Issues}, IEEE Wirel. Commun., vol. 22, pp. 2-3, 2015.

[2] Y. Li , Y. Luo Y, and G. Yang, "12-port 5G massive MIMO antenna array in sub-6GHz mobile handset for LTE bands 42/43/46 applications," IEEE Access, vol. 6, pp. 344-54, 2018.

[3] N. Ojaroudiparchin, et al., "A switchable 3-D-coverage-phased array antenna package for 5G mobile terminals," IEEE Antennas and Wireless Propagation Letters, vol. 15, pp. 1747-50, 2016.

[4] M. Stanley, et al., "A capacitive coupled patch antenna array with high gain and wide coverage for 5G smartphone applications," IEEE Access. vol. 6, pp. 41942-54, 2018.

[5] B. Yu, et al., "A novel 28 GHz beam steering array for 5G mobile device with metallic casing application," IEEE Transactions on Antennas and Propagation, vol. 66, no. 1, pp. 462-6, Nov. 2017.

Time-modulated Coupled-cavity System for Optical Switching

(Invited Paper)

Adam Mock
School of Engineering and Technology
Central Michigan University
Mount Pleasant, MI, USA
mock1ap@cmich.edu

***Abstract*—The scattering parameters of a time-modulated two-coupled-cavity system are obtained using coupled mode theory and verified using the finite-difference time-domain method. We find that a suitably tailored time-modulation of the cavities allows for switching the output on and off. The proposed functionality can be used in direct amplitude modulation of an optical carrier from a frequency-modulated RF message.**

***Index Terms*—cavity resonators, finite-difference time-domain method, switch, time-varying circuits.**

I. Introduction

Linear time-invariant photonic systems form the backbone of many modern optical signal processing systems. However, material nonlinearities [1] and time-variation [2], [3] can be exploited to extend the design space of photonic device functionality. This presentation introduces a linear time-varying photonic switching device. We show how RF modulation of the refractive index of two coupled cavities can switch the output from on to off. This device functionality can be used for direct amplitude modulation of an optical signal using a phase or frequency modulated RF signal.

II. Coupled Cavities

Fig. 1 is a schematic depiction of two coupled resonant cavities each of which is coupled to a waveguide. The resonance frequency and loss rate of each cavity in isolation is ω_0 and γ, respectively. Temporal coupled mode theory (CMT) [4] can be used to obtain the resonances of the two-cavity coupled system by diagonalizing:

$$\frac{d}{dt}\begin{bmatrix} a_1(t) \\ a_2(t) \end{bmatrix} = -i\begin{bmatrix} \omega_0 & \kappa \\ \kappa & \omega_0 \end{bmatrix}\begin{bmatrix} a_1(t) \\ a_2(t) \end{bmatrix} - \begin{bmatrix} \gamma & 0 \\ 0 & \gamma \end{bmatrix}\begin{bmatrix} a_1(t) \\ a_2(t) \end{bmatrix}, \quad (1)$$

where $a_j(t)$ is the field amplitude in the jth resonator and κ is the coupling rate between the cavities. The coupled eigenstates are given by $a_\pm(t) = [a_1(t) \pm a_2(t)]/\sqrt{2}$ with frequencies $\omega_\pm = \omega_0 \pm \kappa$. Fig. 1 depicts the qualitative nature of the modes of the two-cavity system. Essentially $a_+(t)$ is an even combination of the isolated cavity modes, and $a_-(t)$ is an odd combination of the isolated cavity modes.

In this work, the effect of time-modulation of the refractive index of the cavities is investigated. The time-modulation is modeled as a perturbation to the cavity resonance frequency in the CMT analysis. Including the time-modulation term as well as coupling to the input and output waveguides, the CMT equations can be written as:

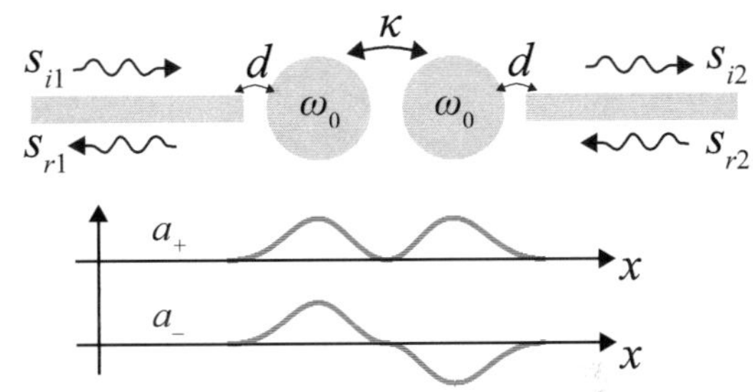

Fig. 1. Top: schematic depiction of two coupled resonant cavities each of which is coupled to a waveguide. Bottom: example depiction of the spatial part of the coupled-cavity fields.

$$\dot{\mathbf{a}} = [-i\mathbf{\Omega} - i\delta\mathbf{\Omega}(t) - \mathbf{\Gamma}]\mathbf{a} + \sqrt{2}\mathbf{D}^{\mathrm{T}}\mathbf{s}_{\mathrm{inc}}, \quad (2)$$

where $\mathbf{a} = \begin{bmatrix} a_+(t) & a_-(t) \end{bmatrix}^T$, $\mathbf{\Gamma}$ is a diagonal matrix with γ on the diagonal, $\mathbf{\Omega}$ is given by:

$$\mathbf{\Omega} = \begin{bmatrix} \omega_0 + \kappa & 0 \\ 0 & \omega_0 - \kappa \end{bmatrix}, \quad (3)$$

and

$$\mathbf{D} = \frac{1}{\sqrt{2}}\begin{bmatrix} d & d \\ d & -d \end{bmatrix}. \quad (4)$$

d is the coupling rate between the cavity and the waveguide. $\mathbf{s}_{\mathrm{inc}} = \begin{bmatrix} s_{i1} & s_{i2} \end{bmatrix}^{\mathrm{T}}$ is a vector describing the incident field amplitudes in ports 1 and 2. In the presence of waveguide coupling, the loss rate decomposes into $\gamma = \gamma_i + \gamma_c$ where γ_i is the intrinsic cavity loss rate, and γ_c is the loss rate due to cavity coupling. The loss rate is related to the waveguide coupling parameter d via $d^2 = 2\gamma_c$ [4].

In the isolated cavity basis we choose the time-modulation term to take the form:

$$\delta\mathbf{\Omega}_{iso}(t) = \begin{bmatrix} \delta\omega\cos(\omega_m t) & 0 \\ 0 & -\delta\omega\cos(\omega_m t) \end{bmatrix}, \quad (5)$$

where the refractive indices of the two cavities are modulated at a frequency ω_m and π out of phase. This time-modulation term introduces a spatial perturbation with odd parity. The result is coupling between the even and odd coupled-cavity modes. This can be seen by inspecting $\delta\mathbf{\Omega}_{iso}(t)$ in the coupled-cavity basis [3]:

$$\delta\mathbf{\Omega}(t) = \begin{bmatrix} 0 & \delta\omega\cos(\omega_m t) \\ \delta\omega\cos(\omega_m t) & 0 \end{bmatrix}. \quad (6)$$

Fig. 2 (a) shows how one could implement the schematic system of Fig. 1. We start with a one-dimensional photonic crystal consisting of air holes etched into an InP semiconductor waveguide. The cavities are formed by removing two sets of three holes. The coupling between the cavities (κ) is controlled by the number of holes between the cavities, and the waveguide coupling (γ_c) is controlled by the number of holes on either side of the cavities. The index modulation is performed by applying electrodes to either side of the cavity and applying a voltage. The applied voltage is sinusoidal with frequency ω_m. The applied signal is inverted when applied to cavity 2.

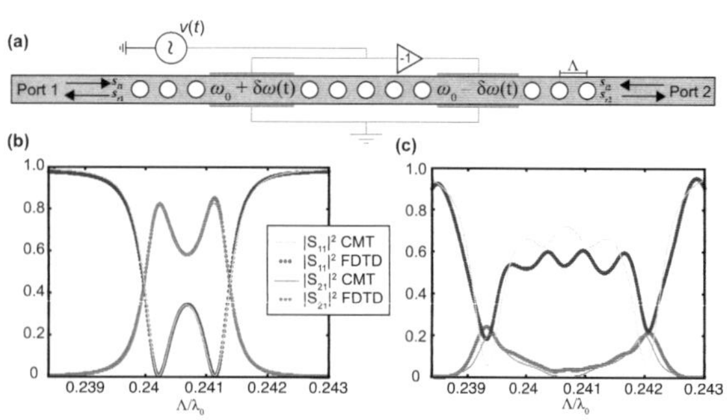

Fig. 2. (a) Schematic depiction of the two-coupled-cavity system modeled using two-dimensional FDTD. (b) The transmission ($|S_{21}|^2$) and reflection ($|S_{11}|^2$) coefficients of the cavity system in (a) when no modulation is applied. (c) The transmission and reflection coefficients of the cavity system in (a) when modulation is applied and chosen according to Eqs. 10 and 11.

The scattered wave amplitude into ports 1 and 2 is given by:

$$\mathbf{s}_{\text{ref}} = -\mathbf{s}_{\text{inc}} + \mathbf{D}\mathbf{a}, \quad (7)$$

where $\mathbf{s}_{\text{ref}} = \begin{bmatrix} s_{r1} & s_{r2} \end{bmatrix}^{\text{T}}$ represents the amplitudes of the outgoing waves in ports 1 and 2 [4]. Fig. 2 (b) displays the reflection and transmission spectra for incidence from port 1 calculated using CMT and simulated using the two-dimensional finite-difference time-domain (FDTD) method. The two reflection dips and transmission peaks resulting from the coupled-cavity resonances are clear. We chose the coupling rate so that the power throughput would be high ($> 80\%$) at the resonance frequencies $\omega_0 \pm \kappa$. The throughput power approaches 100% as $\gamma_i/\gamma_c \to 0$. There is good qualitative agreement between the CMT and FDTD simulation results.

III. Modulated Cavities

To solve the CMT equations when the modulation is turned on, one must introduce the ansatz $a_{\pm}(t) = \sum_n a_{\pm,n}e^{-i(\omega+n\omega_m)t}$ and solve for the Fourier series coefficients $a_{\pm,n}$. The equations governing $a_{\pm,n}$ are:

$$[-i(\omega + n\omega_m - w_0 - \kappa) + \gamma]a_{+,n} + \frac{\delta\omega}{2}(a_{-,n+1} + a_{-,n-1}) = ds_{i1}\delta_{n,0}, \quad (8)$$

and

$$[-i(\omega + n\omega_m - w_0 + \kappa) + \gamma]a_{-,n} + \frac{\delta\omega}{2}(a_{+,n+1} + a_{+,n-1}) = ds_{i1}\delta_{n,0} \quad (9)$$

assuming incidence from port 1. To solve these equations we keep only the $n = -1, 0, 1$ harmonics. More harmonics can be kept in the solution which will improve agreement between CMT and simulation and experimental results, but it becomes more difficult to obtain analytic design rules. With only zeroth and first order harmonics, we find that if ω_m and $\delta\omega$ are chosen as:

$$\omega_m = \sqrt{\frac{3\gamma^2 + 4\kappa^2}{5}}, \quad (10)$$

and

$$\delta\omega = \sqrt{8(\omega_m^2 + \gamma^2)}, \quad (11)$$

then the throughput power at $\omega_0 \pm \kappa$ (which was nominally above 80%) goes to zero. Fig. 2 (c) shows the output spectra when the modulation is applied and set according to Eqs. 10 and 11 which corresponds to $\omega_m = 0.0005$ and $\delta\omega = 0.0017$. Qualitatively, the transmitted and reflected spectra switch roles when the modulation is applied. In these simulation results, the output swings from above 0.8 without modulation to below 0.06 using the proposed modulation scheme. This represents a switching ratio of 11.2 dB. Because the throughput is proportional to ω_m around the set point Eq. 10, this device functionality would allow one-step amplitude modulation of an optical carrier wave from a frequency or phase modulated RF signal.

IV. Conclusion

This work shows how temporal CMT can be used to obtain design rules that leverage time-modulated coupled cavities to perform novel optical signal processing. We show how a truncated Fourier series provides acceptable comparison to FDTD simulation results. The presentation will also discuss a method by which we use Fourier analysis to obtain scattering spectra using FDTD simulations with time-varying refractive indices.

References

[1] G. P. Agrawal, Nonlinear Fiber Optics. Massachusetts: Academic Press, 2007.

[2] A. Mock, D. Sounas, and A. Alù, "Tunable orbital angular momentum radiation from angular-momentum-biased microcavities," Physical Review Letters, vol. 121, p. 103901, 2018.

[3] A. Mock, D. Sounas, and A. Alù, "Magnet-Free Circulator Based on Spatiotemporal Modulation of Photonic Crystal Defect Cavities," ACS Photonics, vol. 6, p. 2056–2066, 2019.

[4] W. Suh, Z. Wang, and S. Fan, "Temporal coupled-mode theory and the presence of non-orthogonal modes in lossless multimode cavities," IEEE Journal of Quantum Electronics, vol. 40, p. 1511–1518, 2004.

Artificial Synapse with Mnemonic Functionality using GSST-based Photonic Integrated Memory

Mario Miscuglio
Department of Electrical and Computer Engineering
George Washington University
Washington DC 20052, USA
mmiscuglio@gwu.edu

Jiawei Meng
Department of Electrical and Computer Engineering
George Washington University
Washington DC 20052, USA
mengjw93@gwu.edu

Omer Yesiliurt
Birck Nanotechnology Center
School of ECE, Purdue University,
West Lafayette, IN 47907, USA,
oyesilyu@purdue.edu

Yifei Zhang
Department of Materials Science & Engineering
Massachusetts Institute of Technology
Cambridge, MA, USA
yzhang94@mit.edu

Ludmila J. Prokopeva
Birck Nanotechnology Center
School of ECE, Purdue University,
West Lafayette, IN 47907, USA,
lprokop@purdue.edu

Armin Mehrabian
Department of Electrical and Computer Engineering
George Washington University
Washington DC 20052, USA
armin@gwu.edu

Juejun Hu
Department of Materials Science & Engineering
Massachusetts Institute of Technology
Cambridge, MA, USA
hujuejun@mit.edu

Alexander V. Kildishev
Birck Nanotechnology Center
School of ECE, Purdue University,
West Lafayette, IN 47907, USA,
kildishev@purdue.edu

Volker J. Sorger
Department of Electrical and Computer Engineering
George Washington University
Washington DC 20052, USA
sorger@gwu.edu

***Abstract*—Here we present a multi-level discrete-state non-volatile photonic memory based on an ultra-compact (<4µm) hybrid phase change material GSST-silicon Mach Zehnder modulator, with low insertion losses (3dB), to serve as node in a photonic neural network. Emulating an opportunely trained 100 × 100 fully connected multilayered perceptron neural network with this weighting functionality embedded as photonic memory, shows up to 92% inference accuracy and robustness towards noise when performing predictions of unseen data.**

Keywords—Phase change memories, photonic memories, GSST

I. Introduction

Computing AI-systems and machine-learning (ML) tasks, while transferring and storing data exclusively in the optical domain, is highly desirable because of the inherently large bandwidth, low residual crosstalk, and short-delay of optical information transfer. [1] However, the functionality of memory for storing the trained weights is not straightforwardly achieved in optics [2], [3], or at least in its non-volatile implementation, and therefore requires additional circuitry and components (i.e. DAC, memory) and related consumption of static power, sinking the overall benefits (energy efficiency and speed) of photonics. The non-volatile retention of information in integrated photonics can be provided by the light-matter interaction in phase change memory (PCM)[4]–[8]. Here, we leverage on a recently engineered class of optical PCMs, based on Ge–Sb–Se–Te (GSST) alloy[9], whose amorphous state is not characterized by high absorption coefficient, like the commonly used Ge–Sb–Te, and upon phase change, its refractive index is still subjected to unitary modulation. The optimized alloy, $Ge_2Sb_2Se_4Te_1$, combines broadband transparency (1–18.5 µm), large optical contrast ($\Delta n = 2.0$), and significantly improved glass forming ability. Thence, we design a low loss non-volatile multilevel photonic memory, using a balanced GSST-based Mach Zehnder Modulator and develop a numerical framework for optimizing the heaters configuration and evaluating the temporal switching response of such GSST-based photonic memory. Exploiting the low delay interconnectivity of photonic integrated chips and the non-volatile transitions of PCM, an all-optical (AO) trained NN, that effortlessly performs dot-product functionality, can be achieved, enabling intelligent computing functionality at the time-of-flight of the photon with an inference accuracy of 92% when used as MNIST classifiers of handwritten digits.

This work is supported by the Presidential Early Career Award for Scientist and Engineers (PECASE) nominated by AFOSR.

II. Results

Improvements in the field of non-volatile photonic memory pertains the engineering of processes aimed at synthetizing more effective and efficient films based on phase change alloys, in which a concurrent minimization of the losses and maximization of the modulation between amorphous and crystalline state allows to keep information longer in the optical-domain, i.e. avoids cumbersome O-to-E-to-O conversions[7], [10]. This, however, requires a wisely engineered material process, e.g. interfacial PCM ($GeTe/Sb_2Te_3$)[7] and optimized alloys[9]. Contrary to regularly used GST (**Fig. 1a**), $Ge_2Sb_2Se_4Te_1$ [GSST] exhibits a 3 orders of magnitude lower absorption coefficient while preserving a large Δn of 2.1 to 1.7 across the near- to mid-IR bands. Additionally, the GSST film is characterized by a high index ratio, $\Delta n/\kappa = 5$, due to its low index contrast and relatively small κ, even without any metal-insulator transition. Electro-refractive modulators based on hybrid GSST-Silicon waveguide operating at 1550 nm would allow to fabricate photonic memory devices with remarkably large contrast and contained insertion losses. Refractive index of GSST used in our model are taken from [9], however a full multivariate time-domain model can be built using the generalized dispersive material model[10]. When the network is trained offline using emulators, such as TensorFlow, which accounts for the physics of the devices and their functionalities[12], [13], the extracted weights are set by selectively 'writing' portions of the GSST deposited on the waveguides, by heat induced laser irradiation, or local electrothermal heating, which promotes crystallization, and consequently modifies the waveguide modal refractive index in a reversible process (**Fig. 2**).

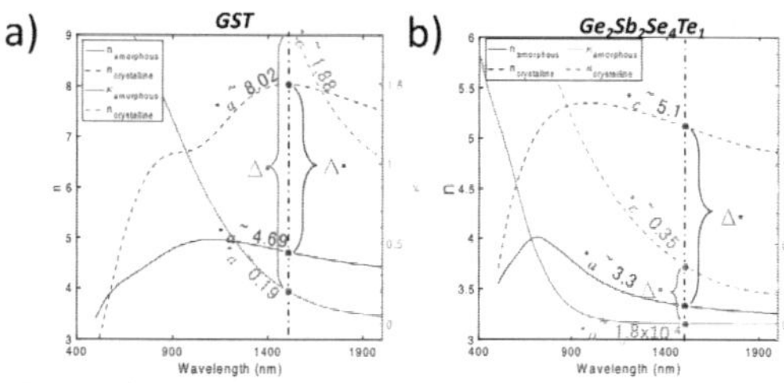

Figure 1. Experimentally obtained (ellipsometry) optical properties of phase change material (PCM) films: GST (**a**), and Ge2Sb2Se4Te1(**b**). Real (n, left y-axis) and imaginary (κ, right y-axis) parts of the refractive indices of the amorphous (solid line) and crystalline alloys. (dashed line). For our study, we consider GSS4T1

A PCM film of 30 nm of GSST is considered to be deposited atop of a planarized waveguide and a phase transition is induced by local heaters. We proceed to designing a balanced passive push-pull Mach Zehnder modulator (MZM) configuration (**Fig. 2a**), in which on one side the GSST material is deposited in the amorphous condition (aGSST). To modulate the intensity of the signal at its output, the MZI is purposely unbalanced by thermally writing a portion of the GSST film deposited in the "programmable arm" of the MZI. For a TM mode (**Fig. 2b**), for instance, the length of the active part of the modulator is just 3.8 μm short for achieving a π phase shift, when the entire film on the 'recordable' branch has changed to its crystalline phase. To our knowledge, the device is one order of magnitude smaller than one of the most compact MZM ever reported[13], with positive effects on the electrical capacitance improving both response time and power consumption. The lateral section of the written part of the material corresponds to a "quantized weight", and assuming a stabile writing resolution of about 500 nm[8], same achieved by optical writing, which would avoid crosstalk among multiple states, the total amount of available discrete resolution is given by 8 distinct states (3-bit). This condition on the resolution can be relaxed by extending the device length by multiple of L_π (**Fig.2d-e**) or by physically separating portions of the film. Additionally, this is a reversible process, which allows to update the weights after many execution times. Interestingly, this solution is not hindered by insertion losses, which are negligible due to the rather low absorption coefficient of GSST at 1550 nm, and the total losses (~3dB) are mainly caused by the balancing mechanism (in this first analysis straightforwardly obtained achieved by placing a gold contact on the balancing arm). The GSST needs to be locally written according to the weights obtained during the training phase. For performing this function, we consider using electro-thermal local switching using heaters. 3D time-dependent multi-physics simulations, including model for heat transfer in solids coupled with the electric currents model, have been carried out. Preliminary thermal characterization conducted by our group shows that the conductivity of GSST is 0.17±0.02 W/m/K for amorphous phase and 0.43±0.04 W/m/K for crystalline phase, while the heat capacity in amorphous and crystalline phase for GSST film are 1.45±0.05 MJ/m^3/K and 1.85±0.05 MJ/m^3/K, respectively. The heating element (**Fig. 2a**) considered is tungsten shaped in a circuitous serpentine (10 μm length, 20 folds), and properly biased dissipate energy in the form of Joule heat in the surrounding media. The temperature at which the GSST reaches the amorphous state is considered around 900 K, whereas for inducing re-crystallization, the GSST needs to be heated above the crystallization temperature (~523 K) but below the melting point, for a critical amount of time, therefore multiple pulses are needed [9]. Two tungsten resistive heaters placed directly in contact with the GSST film, 100 nm away from the waveguide, provides heat to the film locally (lowering the switching threshold), and storing heat for successive pulses. This configuration is affected by limited insertion losses due to the non-plasmonic properties of tungsten (additional ~0.1dB/μm for a propagating TM mode) and reversible amorphization by applying a 15 V pulse of 2 μs and crystallization using 20 pulses of 1 μs for a low threshold voltage (5 V) (**Fig. 2c**). A resistive heater optimized for efficient and low-loss switching, can be made in doped silicon, ITO [14] or in silicide, currently used in p-n modulator, positioned next to the waveguide [15].

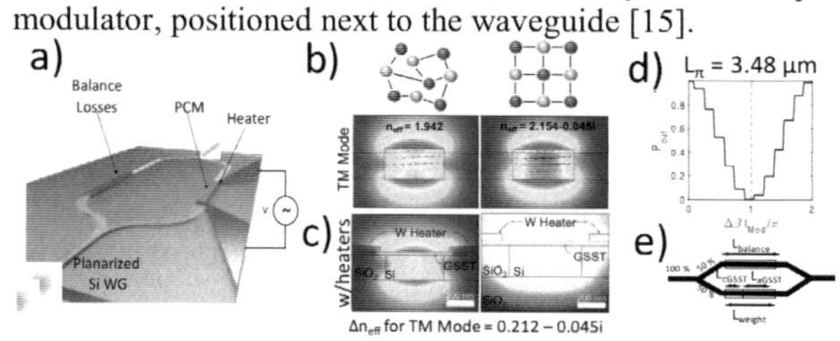

Figure 2. Photonic memory. (**a**) Schematic of an electro-optic modulator based on a balanced Mach Zehnder interferometer (MZI), such as used to program weights (dot-products) of a photonic NN. (**b**) Fundamental transverse magnetic mode profiles (normalized electric field) of the GSST-Silicon hybrid waveguide at 1550 nm for amorphous and crystalline GSST show a strong index (real-part) difference ~ 0.2, while incurring a relatively low loss $\Delta\kappa$ = 0.4. Black arrows represent the direction and intensity of the magnetic field (Hx,Hy). (**c**) Mode and heat profile produced by Joule heating of a hybrid waveguide with tungsten heating element, considering the aGSST (**d**) Normalized output power considering compensated losses for the MZI. The weighting is quantized since the resolution of the phase changing process is 500nm for altering the active arm of the MZI (**e**).

The NN architecture that exploits the proposed non-volatile weighed addition can be emulated on an open source ML framework, i.e. Tensorflow [16]. As preliminary study, we estimated the functionality of the proposed perceptron as main unit of the NN, by emulating its behavior in a 3-layer fully connected NN implemented in the Google Tensorflow (**Fig. 3a**) and, as an initial example, for the MNIST data set. Nonlinear activation functions (here considered as electro-optic[17]) are placed between two consecutive layers on each input connection. The network is trained both without and with noise of the weights and NLAF. Our hypothesis, confirmed in a recent publication[11] and from preliminary studies on the network is that, when we allow for a certain amount of noise during the training, the model during the inference stage becomes more robust; the effect of adding a noise equivalent to 0.01% of the maximum signal swing at the output of neurons significantly improves inference up to 92%, as shown in **Fig. 3b**.

III. CONCLUSIONS AND OUTLOOK

In summary, we have investigated a low losses programmable Mach Zehnder modulator, based on a hybrid

GSST-silicon waveguide, with a $L\pi$ <4μm, which showed a coherent quantized response as function of the portion of the phase change material that has been written by means of electrothermal switching (at sub MHz speed). Tested the quantized transfer function on a standardized neural network training set we show that the neural network reaches very high level of accuracy (>91%) in the inference phase and sufficiently robust.

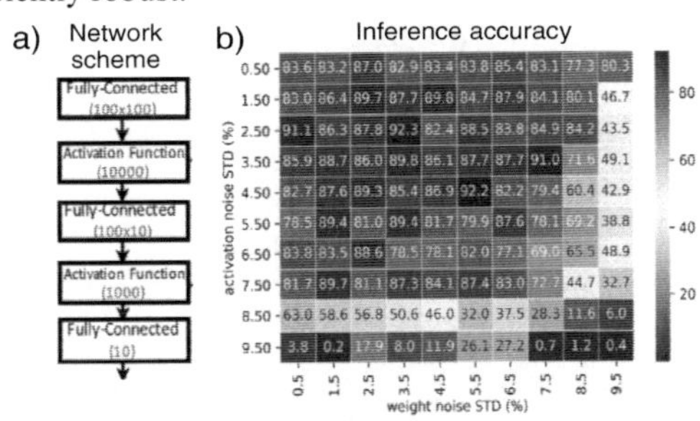

Figure 3 (**a**) Schematic of the fully connected network composed by 2 layers of 100 neurons. (**b**) Accuracy results for the inference on unseen data for NN trained with 2% of noise.

IV. ACKNOWLEDGMENT

V.S. is supported by the Presidential Early Career Award for Scientist and Engineers (PECASE) nominated by the Department of Defense (AFOSR).

V. REFERENCES

[1] D. A. B. Miller, "Optical interconnects to electronic chips.," *Applied optics*, vol. 49, no. 25, p. F59-F70, 2010.

[2] G. Heinze, C. Hubrich, and T. Halfmann, "Stopped Light and Image Storage by Electromagnetically Induced Transparency up to the Regime of One Minute," *Phys. Rev. Lett.*, vol. 111, no. 3, p. 033601, Jul. 2013.

[3] L. Ma, O. Slattery, and X. Tang, "Optical quantum memory based on electromagnetically induced transparency," *J Opt*, vol. 19, no. 4, Apr. 2017.

[4] M. Stegmaier, C. Ríos, H. Bhaskaran, C. D. Wright, and W. H. P. Pernice, "Nonvolatile All-Optical 1 × 2 Switch for Chipscale Photonic Networks," *Advanced Optical Materials*, vol. 5, no. 1, p. 1600346, Jan. 2017.

[5] P. Xu, J. Zheng, J. K. Doylend, and A. Majumdar, "Low-Loss and Broadband Nonvolatile Phase-Change Directional Coupler Switches," *ACS Photonics*, vol. 6, no. 2, pp. 553–557, Feb. 2019.

[6] L. Waldecker *et al.*, "Time-domain separation of optical properties from structural transitions in resonantly bonded materials," *Nature Materials*, vol. 14, no. 10, pp. 991–995, Oct. 2015.

[7] R. E. Simpson *et al.*, "Interfacial phase-change memory," *Nature Nanotechnology*, vol. 6, no. 8, pp. 501–505, Aug. 2011.

[8] M. Rudé *et al.*, "Optical switching at 1.55 μ m in silicon racetrack resonators using phase change materials," *Appl. Phys. Lett.*, vol. 103, no. 14, p. 141119, Sep. 2013.

[9] Y. Zhang *et al.*, "Broadband transparent optical phase change materials for high-performance nonvolatile photonics," *Nat Commun*, vol. 10, no. 1, pp. 1–9, Sep. 2019.

[10] L. J. Prokopeva *et al.*, "Time domain modeling of bi-anisotropic media and phase change materials with generalized dispersion (Conference Presentation)," in *Metamaterials, Metadevices, and Metasystems 2019*, 2019, vol. 11080, p. 1108006.

[11] A. Mehrabian, M. Miscuglio, Y. Alkabani, V. J. Sorger and T. El-Ghazawi, "A Winograd-Based Integrated Photonics Accelerator for Convolutional Neural Networks," in *IEEE Journal of Selected Topics in Quantum Electronics*, vol. 26, no. 1, pp. 1-12, 2020.

[12] C. Ríos *et al.*, "Integrated all-photonic non-volatile multi-level memory," *Nature Photon*, vol. 9, no. 11, pp. 725–732, Nov. 2015.

[13] R. Amin *et al.*, "0.52 V mm ITO-based Mach-Zehnder modulator in silicon photonics," *APL Photonics*, vol. 3, no. 12, p. 126104, Dec. 2018.

[14] Y. Gui *et al.*, "Towards integrated metatronics: a holistic approach on precise optical and electrical properties of Indium Tin Oxide," *Sci Rep*, vol. 9, no. 1, pp. 1–10, Aug. 2019.

[15] N. C. Harris *et al.*, "Efficient, compact and low loss thermo-optic phase shifter in silicon," *Opt. Express*, vol. 22, no. 9, p. 10487, May 2014.

[16] M. Miscuglio *et al.*, "All-optical nonlinear activation function for photonic neural networks [Invited]," *Optical Materials Express*, vol. 8, no. 12, p. 3851, Dec. 2018.

[17] R. Amin *et al.*, "ITO-based electro-absorption modulator for photonic neural activation function," *APL Materials*, vol. 7, no. 8, p. 081112, Aug. 2019.

Synthesizing High-performance Reconfigurable Meta-devices through Multi-objective Optimization

Sawyer D. Campbell, Yuhao Wu, Eric B. Whiting, Lei Kang, Pingjuan L. Werner, and Douglas H. Werner
Department of Electrical Engineering
The Pennsylvania State University
University Park, PA 16802, USA
sdc22@psu.edu

***Abstract*—Metasurfaces offer the potential to realize large SWaP (size, weight, and power) reduction over conventional optical elements for their ability to achieve comparable functionalities in ultrathin geometries. Moreover, metasurfaces designed with phase change materials offer the potential to go beyond what is achievable by conventional optics by enabling multiple functionalities in a single reconfigurable meta-device. However, designing a single metasurface geometry that simultaneously achieves multiple desired functionalities while meeting all bandwidth requirements and fabrication constraints is a very challenging problem. Fortunately, this challenge can be overcome by the use of state-of-the-art multi-objective optimization algorithms which are well-suited for the inverse-design of multi-functional meta-devices.**

Keywords—nanoantennas; optimization; inverse-design; metasurfaces; reconfigurable; metamaterials.

I. Introduction

Metasurfaces are the two-dimensional counterparts to metamaterials in that that they enable designers to engineer the behavior of electromagnetic waves at surfaces and interfaces as opposed to volumetric wave manipulation more commonly associated with bulk metamaterials [1]. Moreover, due to their ability to replicate traditional optical functionality in an ultrathin geometry [2], metasurfaces have the potential to disrupt optical system design by achieving massive SWaP (size, weight, and power) reduction and enabling applications not previously possible with heavy conventional systems [3]. To this end, phase-gradient metasurfaces have garnered tremendous interest for imaging applications due to their ability to exploit the generalized form of Snell's law [4] and bend electromagnetic waves in ways not possible with traditional spherical glass lenses. Such metasurfaces achieve their behavior through an intelligent pattering of nanoantennae (also known as "meta-atoms"), which are designed to achieve a desired complex transmission and/or reflection behavior. For imaging applications, the need for highly transmissive applications has necessitated that the nanoantennae be composed of dielectric materials due to their low loss [5]. However, most dielectric metasurface designs typically achieve only a single functionality which can limit their ability to supplant conventional lenses in the system design process. Meanwhile, phase change materials (PCMs) possess tunable dielectric permittivities which can be exploited to synthesize reconfigurable metasurface devices such as beam-steerers, optical shutters, spectral filters, and adaptive focal length lenses [6]–[9]. While PCMs offer the ability to realize multi-functional meta-devices, they bring with them a significant expansion of the degrees of design freedom available to the designer. Consequently, the inclusion of PCMs in the system can significantly increase the difficulty of the inverse-design process making more traditional optimization approaches intractable for optical designers. Fortunately, there exists a number of optimization techniques for meta-device optimization including recent developments such as topology optimization [10], deep learning [11], and multi-objective optimizers [12]. In fact, multi-objective optimization (MOO) algorithms are the natural choice for the inverse-design of multi-functional meta-devices since all functionalities can be each represented by a single objective and simultaneously optimized [13], [14]. This paper presents a brief introduction to multi-objective optimization and its potential for synthesizing high-performance multi-functional PCM-based metasurfaces.

The work is supported in part by DARPA contract no. HR00111720032.

II. Multi-functional Meta-device Optimziation

Unlike traditional single-objective optimizers which only find a single optimal solution, MOO algorithms generate a set of optimal solutions called the Pareto set. When visualized in objective space, these solutions can help designers understand

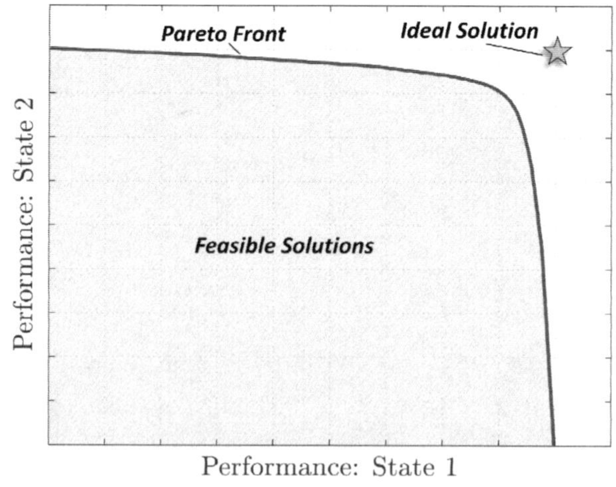

Fig. 1. Visualization of a hypothetical multi-objective optimization problem for a reconfigurable PCM-based meta-device.

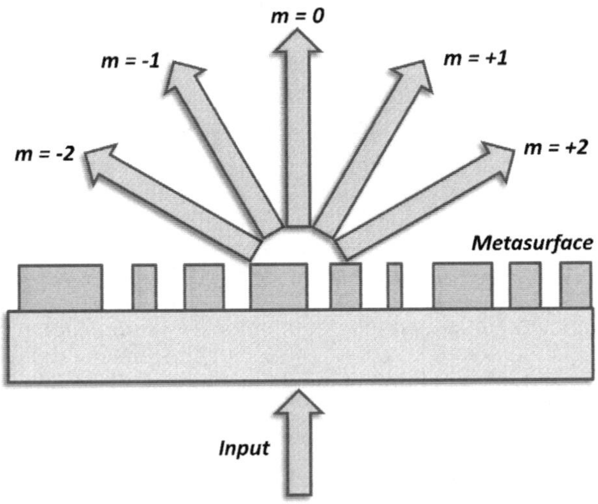

Fig. 2. Metasurface supercell concept with multiple pathways for the incident wave to couple into. Such a supercell is perfectly suited for a MOO algorithm as multiple performances can be simultaneously maximized.

the tradeoffs inherent between competing design objectives (*e.g.*, size versus efficiency or bandwidth). For reconfigurable meta-devices, these objectives can be the desired optical functionalities at various states of the PCM (*e.g.*, amorphous and crystalline). Figure 1 presents a hypothetical solution space for a reconfigurable PCM-based meta-device. The solid line is the Pareto front which is a continuous surface that contains all solutions in the Pareto set. In this example, there is a clear tradeoff between achievable performance in material states 1 and 2. While the ideal solution in which the device exhibits the maximum theoretical performance in both states is unachievable, the MOO algorithm is able to present the user with a range of solutions and their tradeoffs from which they can select the design that best attains their desired performances. When applied to optical metasurface design, the MOO algorithm can be assigned a unique cost function per available diffraction order allowing the user to simultaneously maximize the performance at each order while also providing tradeoffs for multi-diffraction order performance. For example, consider the metasurface supercell shown in Fig. 2. Due to the supercell periodicity the m = -2, -1, 0, +1, and +2 diffraction orders are available to couple into. When paired with PCM materials, such a supercell could steer into one order (*e.g.*, +1) in the amorphous state and into another order (*e.g.*, +2) in the crystalline state. In fact, switching between steering into single or multiple orders is possible if the optimizer is given an appropriate set of user-defined cost functions. Moreover, the supercell can also be optimized to switch between transmission and reflection modes which gives the designer tremendous flexibility in achieving functionalities that can disrupt conventional optical device design.

III. Future Work

Note that, while multi-objective optimization is a generic paradigm, there are a number of unique multi-objective algorithms designers can employ in their inverse-design procedure. Moreover, different algorithms can offer designers with unique functionalities or geometrical creation capabilities. For example, the Multi-Objective Optimization with TOLerance (MOTOL) algorithm can yield designs with robustness as an explicit objective [15] while the Multi-Objective Lazy Ant Colony (MOLACO) algorithm [16] can synthesize contiguous three-dimensional structures to realize true bi-anisotropic metamaterial unit cells.

References

[1] N. Engheta and R. W. Ziolkowski, Eds., *Metamaterials: Physics and Engineering Explorations*. Piscataway, NJ: IEEE Press, 2006.

[2] N. Yu and F. Capasso, "Flat Optics with Designer Metasurfaces," *Nat. Mater*, vol. 13, no. 2, pp. 139–150, Feb. 2014.

[3] H. Hogan, "For IR Imaging, Better SWaP Beckons," *Photonics Spectra*, vol. 49, no. 8, pp. 48–51, 2015.

[4] N. Yu, P. Genevet, M. A. Kats, F. Aieta, J.-P. Tetienne, F. Capasso, and Z. Gaburro, "Light Propagation with Phase Discontinuities: Generalized Laws of Reflection and Refraction," *Science, New Series*, vol. 334, no. 6054, pp. 333–337, 2011.

[5] A. Arbabi, Y. Horie, M. Bagheri, and A. Faraon, "Dielectric Metasurfaces for Complete Control of Phase and Polarization with Subwavelength Spatial Resolution and High Transmission," *Nat. Nanotechnol.*, vol. 10, no. 11, pp. 937–943, Nov. 2015.

[6] A. Karvounis, B. Gholipour, K. F. MacDonald, and N. I. Zheludev, "All-Dielectric Phase-change Reconfigurable Metasurface," *Applied Physics Letters*, vol. 109, no. 5, p. 051103, Aug. 2016.

[7] Q. Wang, E. T. F. Rogers, B. Gholipour, C.-M. Wang, G. Yuan, J. Teng, and N. I. Zheludev, "Optically Reconfigurable Metasurfaces and Photonic Devices Based on Phase Change Materials," *Nature Photonics*, vol. 10, no. 1, pp. 60–65, Jan. 2016.

[8] L. Liu, L. Kang, T. S. Mayer, and D. H. Werner, "Hybrid Metamaterials for Electrically Triggered Multifunctional Control," *Nature Communications*, vol. 7, p. 13236, Oct. 2016.

[9] L. Kang, R. P. Jenkins, and D. H. Werner, "Recent Progress in Active Optical Metasurfaces," *Adv. Opt. Mater.*, vol. 7, no. 14, p. 1801813, Apr. 2019.

[10] D. Sell, J. Yang, S. Doshay, and J. A. Fan, "Periodic Dielectric Metasurfaces with High-Efficiency, Multiwavelength Functionalities," *Adv. Opt. Mater.*, vol. 5, no. 23, p. 1700645, Dec. 2017.

[11] S. D. Campbell, D. Sell, R. P. Jenkins, E. B. Whiting, J. A. Fan, and D. H. Werner, "Review of Numerical Optimization Techniques for Meta-device Design [Invited]," *Opt. Mater. Express*, vol. 9, no. 4, pp. 1842–1863, Apr. 2019.

[12] K. Deb, *Multi-objective Optimization using Evolutionary Algorithms*, Paperback edition. Chichester: Wiley, 2008.

[13] S. D. Campbell, D. Z. Zhu, E. B. Whiting, J. Nagar, D. H. Werner, and P. L. Werner, "Advanced Multi-objective and Surrogate-assisted Optimization of Topologically Diverse Metasurface Architectures," in *Metamaterials, Metadevices, and Metasystems 2018*, vol. 10719, p. 107190U.

[14] S. D. Campbell, E. B. Whiting, D. H. Werner, and P. L. Werner, "High-Performance Metasurfaces Synthesized via Multi-Objective Optimization," in *2019 International Applied Computational Electromagnetics Society Symposium (ACES)*, pp. 1–2.

[15] J. A. Easum, J. Nagar, P. L. Werner, and D. H. Werner, "Efficient Multiobjective Antenna Optimization with Tolerance Analysis Through the Use of Surrogate Models," *IEEE Transactions on Antennas and Propagation*, vol. 66, no. 12, pp. 6706–6715, Dec. 2018.

[16] D. Z. Zhu, P. L. Werner, and D. H. Werner, "Design and Optimization of 3-D Frequency-selective Surfaces based on a Multiobjective Lazy Ant Colony Optimization Algorithm," *IEEE Transactions on Antennas and Propagation*, vol. 65, no. 12, pp. 7137–7149, 2017.

Reconfigurable All-dielectric Metasurfaces based on Optical Phase change Materials: Design Approaches

Mikhail Y. Shalaginov
Dept. of Materials Science & Engineering
Massachusetts Institute of Technology
Cambridge, MA, USA
mys@mit.edu

Sensong An
Dept. of Electrical & Computer Engineering
Univ. of Massachusetts Lowell
Lowell, MA, USA
sensong_an@student.uml.edu

Yifei Zhang
Dept. of Materials Science & Engineering
Massachusetts Institute of Technology
Cambridge, MA, USA
yzhang94@mit.edu

Fan Yang
Dept. of Materials Science & Engineering
Massachusetts Institute of Technology
Cambridge, MA, USA
yangf@mit.edu

Clayton Fowler
Dept. of Electrical & Computer Engineering
Univ. of Massachusetts Lowell
Lowell, MA, USA
clayton_fowler@uml.edu

Hualiang Zhang
Dept. of Electrical & Computer Engineering
Univ. of Massachusetts Lowell
Lowell, MA, USA
hualiang_zhang@uml.edu

Juejun Hu
Dept. of Materials Science & Engineering
Massachusetts Institute of Technology
Cambridge, MA, USA
hujuejun@mit.edu

Tian Gu
Dept. of Materials Science & Engineering
Massachusetts Institute of Technology
Cambridge, MA, USA
gutian@mit.edu

***Abstract*—Optical metasurface is a recently emerged paradigm for controlling light propagation, which enables implementation of ultra-compact optical devices with extended functionalities. Nowadays the main challenge in the field is to realize active metasurfaces with high quality, high efficiency, and large tuning range. Here we present a design approach for constructing a two-state reconfigurable metalens made of low-loss optical phase-change material (O-PCM). The metalens design is capable to produce diffraction limited focusing, large change in focal length (from 1.5 mm to 2mm), and decent focusing efficiency of about 20% in both states. The proposed design methodology is generic and can be easily extended towards constructing metasurfaces, which can switch between two or more arbitrary phase maps.**

Keywords— GSST, metasurface, metalens, phase change materials, PCM, reconfigurable optics

I. Introduction

Planar periodic arrays of subwavelength antennas, also termed as metasurfaces, open up new functionalities for light manipulation as well as lead to optical components with substantially reduced SWAP-C characteristics. Due to the small volumes of used material, metasurfaces are also a suitable platform for constructing optical devices which characteristics can be modulated or tuned after fabrication. Numerous approaches have been proposed to realize metasurface switching [1]. However, demonstated methods, especially non-mechanical ones, either suffer from low efficiency or have a tiny tuning range.

Recently we developed a new class of chalcogenide glasses, Ge-Sb-Se-Te (GSST) [2]. This material is a low-loss optical phase change material (O-PCM), which can switch between amorphous and crystalline states. In mid infrared the material transition causes drastic change in refractive index ($\Delta n > 1$) while still maintains low losses ($k \sim 0.02$) in both states.

DARPA Extreme Optics and Imaging (EXTREME) program under contract number HR00111720029.

II. Design of a Varifocal Metalens

The proposed metalens is composed of a patterned 1-µm thick GSST film on top of a low-index CaF_2 substrate [3]. Fig. 1 depicts the concept of the metalens operation. When meta-atoms are in amorphous state, collectively they focus the transmitted optical power to a focal spot f_1 = 1.5 mm. After GSST was transitioned to crystalline state, the primary focal spot moves to position f_2 = 2mm.

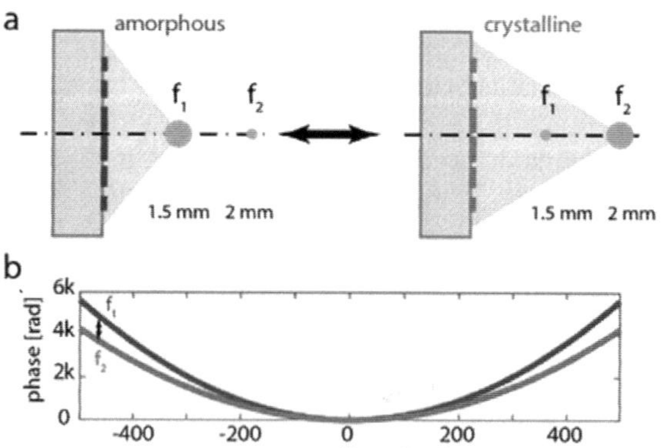

Fig. 1. (a) Operation principle of a reconfigurable bifocal metalens: in amorphous light is primarily focused at a distance f_1 = 1.5 mm, and in crystalline state – f_2 = 1.5 mm. (b) Modulation of focal spot position is driven by the change in the metasurface phase-profile shape: blue and red curves correspond to amorphous and crystalline states, respectively.

Metasurface focusing capability is dictated by the phase map pattern. For a standard metalens, spatial phase profile is a hyperbolic function. By modulating refractive index of the meta-atoms, we can change the shape of phase profile, hence switch the focal distance (Fig.1 (b), blue and red curves).

presented in Fig. 2 (c). The root-mean-square (RMS) phase errors are approximately 0.1 π. By considering these errors, the

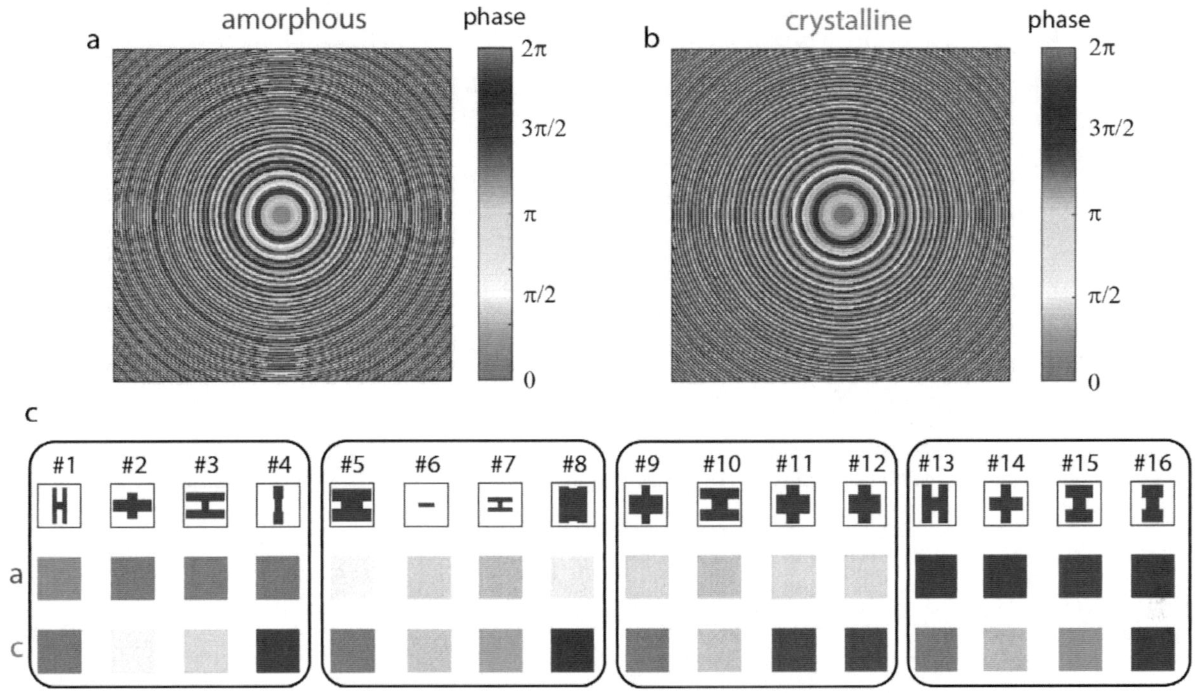

Fig. 2. 2D phase maps of the metalens in amorphous and crystalline states. Change of the focal length is associated with pixel-to-pixel phase pattern transformation. Each of the 16 meta-atoms serves as a phase-pixel switch. The geometry of meta-atoms was selected to enable the phase transitions between the 4 groups of colors: red, yellow, green, and blue, which correspond to the approximate phase-shift values of 0°, 90°, 180°, and 270°.

The final 2D phase maps corresponding to amorphous and crystalline states are shown in Figs. 2 (a) and (b), respectively. Initially we generated ideal (continuous) phase maps by employing Kirchhoff diffraction integral method, then the continuous phase maps were discretized into four phase-levels of 0°, 90°, 180°, and 270°. For achieving "pixel-by-pixel" transitioning between the two discretized phase maps, we searched for a group of 16 meta-atoms with specified responses in the two states. In a more general case, one would have to utilize a library of mn meta-atoms, where m is a phase-map discretization level and n is the number of metasurface states, in our example, $m = 4$ and $n = 2$. To identify the proper library of meta-atoms, we ran numerous FDTD simulations (CST Microwave Studio) with various shapes ("H", "I", "+") and geometrical parameters, and retrieved their phase/amplitude responses. Film thicknesses and permittivities of the GSST material in both states were measured in an experiment and used as a fixed parameter in the simulations. The best meta-atom candidates were selected from the database by maximizing a figure-of-merit (FOM), which encompasses meta-atom transmittance and its phase error (phase deviation from the desirable phase value). The final set of 16 meta-atoms is metalens in both states is expected to produce diffraction-limited focal spot with a Strehl ratio of > 0.96 and decent focusing efficiency exceeding 35%. The metasurface design can be further improved by increasing phase discretization level as well as by finding better geometries of meta-atoms. For instance, here we used a brute-force method to search for suitable meta-atom designs, however, with the help of neural network machinery it is possible to generate a vast library of unintuitive geometries with better performance metrics [3].

References

[1] L. Kang, R. P. Jenkins, and D. H. Werner, "Recent progress in active optical metasurfaces," Adv. Opt. Mater., vol. 7, no. 14, pp. 1–26, 2019.

[2] Y. Zhang, et al., "Broadband transparent optical phase change materials for high-performance nonvolatile photonics," Nat. Commun., vol. 10, no. 1, pp. 1–9, 2019.

[3] M. Y. Shalaginov, et al, "Reconfigurable all-dielectric metalens with diffraction limited performance," arXiv: 1911.12970 7014, 2019.

[4] S. An, et al., "A deep learning approach for objective-driven all-dielectric metasurface design," ACS Photonics, p. acsphotonics.9b00966, Nov. 2019.

Nonlinear Lorentz Model for Explicit Integration of Optical Nonlinearity in FDTD

Charles Varin
Département de physique
Cégep de l'Outaouais
Gatineau (QC) J8Y 6M4, Canada

Rhys Emms
Measurement Science and Standards
National Research Council Canada
Ottawa (On) K1A 0R6, Canada

Graeme Bart
Department of physics
University of Ottawa
Ottawa (ON) K1N 6N5, Canada

Thomas Fennel
Institut für Physik
Universität Rostock
18051 Rostock, Germany

Thomas Brabec
Department of physics
University of Ottawa
Ottawa (ON) K1N 6N5, Canada

***Abstract*—Including optical nonlinearity in FDTD software in a stable, efficient, and rigorous way can be challenging. Traditional methods address this challenge by solving an implicit form of Maxwell's equations iteratively. Reaching numerical convergence over the entire numerical space at each time step demands significant computational resources, which can be a limiting factor for the modeling of large-scale three-dimensional nonlinear optics problems (complex photonics devices, laser filamentation, ...). Recently, we proposed an explicit methodology based on a nonlinear generalization of the Lorentz dispersion model and developed example cases where it was used to account for both linear and nonlinear optical effects. An overview of this work is proposed here.**

***Index Terms*—FDTD modeling, nonlinear materials, photonics.**

I. Introduction

Including optical nonlinearity in the finite-difference time-domain (FDTD) framework is not straightforward. It is easily demonstrated with the Ampère's circuital law:

$$\nabla \times \mathbf{H} - \epsilon_0 \frac{\partial \mathbf{E}}{\partial t} = \frac{\partial \mathbf{P}}{\partial t}, \tag{1}$$

where the source term depends on a nonlinear susceptibility of the form:

$$\mathbf{P} = \epsilon_0(\chi^{(1)}\mathbf{E} + \chi^{(2)}\mathbf{E}^2 + \chi^{(3)}\mathbf{E}^3 + \ldots), \tag{2}$$

Yee discretization of (1) with (2) leads to a set of coupled nonlinear equations that are implicit in the electric field vector and whose solution is nontrivial. A formal solving approach, proposed by Greene and Taflove [1], uses a recursive Newton method to obtain an approximate solution for $\mathbf{E}$. To ensure numerical convergence, it has to be iterated over the entire numerical space a few times per time step, at minimum. This is a rigorous way to include optical nonlinearity into FDTD, but efficient implementation for solving three-dimensional problems is inherently complex. For that reason, FDTD developers typically rely, instead, on explicit tricks whose implementation is simpler and computationally more efficient (see, e.g., [2]). In a series of papers [3]–[5], we developed an explicit methodology based on a nonlinear generalization of the Lorentz dispersion model, providing a rigorous, flexible, efficient, and transparent approach to the nonlinear-FDTD problem.

NSERC CCIPE (517932-17); FRQNT (2019-CO-254385); PADRRC (10696); Deutsche Forschungsgemeinschaft (SPP1840); Heisenberg fellowship (ID FE 1120/4-1).

II. The Nonlinear Lorentz Model

Typical nonlinear optics scenarios are reasonably described by the two-level atom model (see, e.g., [6]). We have shown in [5] that when there is a negligible transition probability to the upper level (weak field, long wavelength), this quantum mechanical model can be reduced to the following second-order differential equation for the induced macroscopic polarization density $\mathbf{P}$:

$$\frac{d^2\mathbf{P}}{dt^2} + \gamma\frac{d\mathbf{P}}{dt} + \omega_0^2\mathbf{P} = \omega_0^2\epsilon_0(\bar{\chi}^{(1)}\mathbf{E} + \bar{\chi}^{(2)}\mathbf{E}^2 + \bar{\chi}^{(3)}\mathbf{E}^3 + \ldots). \tag{3}$$

The model is parametrized by an effective damping constant γ, the transition energy $\hbar\omega_0$, and the nth-order optical susceptibility parameters $\bar{\chi}^{(n)}$ (ϵ_0 is the electric constant). The overbar indicates that the $\bar{\chi}^{(n)}$'s are assumed to be constant, i.e., they do not vary much on the electronic time-scale (see III-B for further details). As emphasized in [4], (3) can be discretized using the leapfrog method to match the Yee discretization scheme (see, e.g., [7]), resulting in a fully explicit FDTD integration of Maxwell equations. The linear and nonlinear material responses are then introduced *via* the effective susceptibility parameters $\bar{\chi}^{(n)}$, while dispersion is set by ω_0 and γ (see [5] for further development on this topic).

III. Application Examples

A. Second Harmonic Generation

We considered quasi-phase-matched (QPM) second harmonic generation (SHG) in periodically poled lithium niobate (PPLN) and compared FDTD simulations using the nonlinear Lorentz model (3) (referred to as NL-FDTD below) to a conventional theoretical model for QPM SHG (see, e.g., (2.7.10)

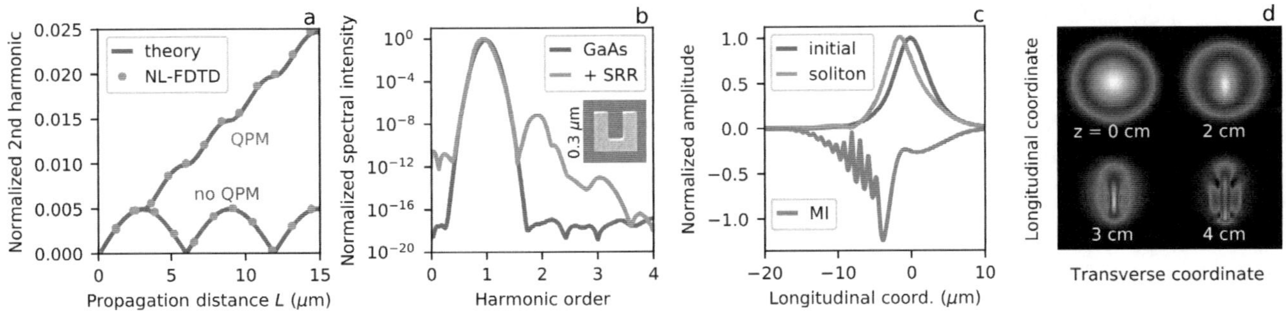

Fig. 1. Application examples of the nonlinear Lorentz model equation (3), combined with FDTD integration of Maxwell's equations (NL-FDTD, see also [3]–[5]). In (a), NL-FDTD simulations of quasi-phase matching (QPM) in periodically poled lithium niobate show exceptional agreement with traditional theoretical models. In (b), a GaAs crystal is aligned with the polarization of the electric field to give no second harmonic (GaAs). However, SHG emerges when a gold split-ring resonator is placed on top (+ SRR, see below legend for sketch). In (c), the propagation of a sech^2-shaped laser pulse in fused silica is modelled with NL-FDTD (the envelope is obtained by taking the absolute value of the Hilbert transform of the electric field). Depending on the input laser intensity, the pulse after travelling over 6 mm exhibits a solitonic behavior (compare the "soliton" and "initial" curves) or pronounced envelope distortion due to modulation instability (MI). Finally in (d), spatio-temporal structuring of a Gaussian laser pulse during self-focusing in air at propagation distance z.

and (2.7.11) in [6]). For the demonstration, we considered a plane wave moving along the axis of an infinite PPLN crystal, modelled with an homogeneous linear index and a second-order parameter $\bar{\chi}^{(2)}$ whose sign is switched periodically to achieve QPM (see [4] for details). The excellent agreement between theory and NL-FDTD in Fig. 1 (a) shows that the NL-FDTD analysis succeeds in reproducing quantitatively the dispersion, scattering, and wave mixing processes in SHG, as well as their interplay.

For rigorous modeling of three-dimensional (3D) optics in solids, it is often necessary to consider the tensorial nature of the susceptibility. This has to be added explicitly to (3). To test this procedure, we considered 3D vectorial NL-FDTD modeling of the SHG enhancement in a gallium arsenide (GaAs) substrate by a split-ring resonator (SRR) nano-antenna. The gold SRR was modelled with a Drude equation while GaAs was modelled with the nonlinear Lorentz equation that follows:

$$\frac{d^2\mathbf{P}_{\mathrm{GaAs}}}{dt^2} + \frac{d\mathbf{P}_{\mathrm{GaAs}}}{dt} + \omega_0^2\mathbf{P}_{\mathrm{GaAs}} = \omega_0^2\epsilon_0\bar{\chi}^{(1)}\mathbf{E} + \epsilon_0\bar{\chi}^{(2)}\left[(E_zE_z - E_yE_y)\,\mathbf{i} - 2E_xE_y\,\mathbf{j}\right], \tag{4}$$

where $\mathbf{i}$ and $\mathbf{j}$ are unit vectors along x and y, respectively. With the electric field polarized along x, there is no second-order effect with GaAs alone [see the "GaAs" curve in Fig. 1 (b)]. Nevertheless, when the SRR is present near-field components in y and z are created, which induces SHG in GaAs [see the "+ SRR" curve in Fig. 1 (b)].

B. Raman Nonlinearity

The nonlinear Lorentz equation (3) accounts for the fast (almost instantaneous) optical response on the electronic time scale. An accurate description of the nonlinear optical processes in centrosymmetric dielectrics must also include a delayed contribution associated with stimulated molecular Raman scattering. This can be done by complementing (3) with an equation that accounts for the modification of the nonlinear susceptibility on the "slow" molecular time scale. The complete model is then given by the following two equations [4]:

$$\frac{d^2\mathbf{P}}{dt^2} + \gamma\frac{d\mathbf{P}}{dt} + \omega_0^2\mathbf{P} = \omega_0^2\epsilon_0(\bar{\chi}^{(1)}\mathbf{E} + \alpha\bar{\chi}^{(3)}\mathbf{E}^3 + Q\mathbf{E}), \tag{5a}$$

$$\frac{d^2Q}{dt^2} + 2\gamma_R\frac{dQ}{dt} + \omega_R^2 Q = (1-\alpha)\bar{\chi}^{(3)}\omega_R^2\left|\mathbf{E}\right|^2, \tag{5b}$$

where α is a parameter that defines the balance between the instantaneous (Kerr) and delayed (Raman) contributions to the third-order susceptibility. The Raman response is itself parameterized by the angular frequency and damping constants ω_R and γ_R whose values are chosen to fit a given Raman-gain spectrum. An equation like (5b) is also used for the Greene-Taflove's implicit method [1], but here integration of both (5a) and (5b) with the leapfrog technique leads to a fully explicit nonlinear-FDTD scheme (see [4] for details). Examples of results obtained with this model are given in Figs. 1 (c-d).

ACKNOWLEDGMENT

CV acknowledges motivating discussions with James Pond (Lumerical Inc.) and precious help from Lumerical's support team.

REFERENCES

[1] J. H. Greene and A. Taflove, "General vector auxiliary differential equation finite-difference time-domain method for nonlinear optics," Optics Express, vol. 14, pp. 8305–8310, 2006.

[2] I. S. Maksymov, A. A. Sukhorukov, A. V. Lavrinenko, and Y. S. Kivshar, "Comparative Study of FDTD-Adopted Numerical Algorithms for Kerr Nonlinearities," IEEE Antennas and Wireless Propagation Letters, vol. 10, pp. 143–146, 2011.

[3] C. Varin, G. Bart, R. Emms, and T. Brabec, "Saturable Lorentz model for fully explicit three-dimensional modeling of nonlinear optics," Optics Express, vol. 23, pp. 2686–2695, 2015.

[4] C. Varin, R. Emms, G. Bart, T. Fennel, and T. Brabec, "Explicit formulation of second and third order optical nonlinearity in the FDTD framework," Computer Physics Communications, vol. 222, pp. 70–83, 2018.

[5] C. Varin, G. Bart, T. Fennel, and T. Brabec, "Nonlinear Lorentz model for the description of nonlinear optical dispersion in nanophotonics simulations [Invited]," Optical Materials Express, vol. 9, no. 2, pp. 771–778, 2019.

[6] R. Boyd, Nonlinear Optics, 3rd ed. Elsevier Science, 2008.

[7] A. Taflove and S. Hagness, Computational Electrodynamics: The Finite-Difference Time-Domain Method. Artech House, 2005.

Optical Isolation using Compact Time-modulated Cavity Array

Adam Mock
School of Engineering and Technology
Central Michigan University
Mount Pleasant, MI, USA
mock1ap@cmich.edu

***Abstract*—It is shown using coupled mode theory and verified using finite-difference time-domain simulations how a time-modulated three-cavity array can be designed to allow transmission from port 1 to port 2 but to prevent transmission from port 2 to port 1 thereby implementing optical isolation. The reciprocity of the system is broken by phase-shifting the modulation signal applied to each cavity by 120 degrees which gives the system a synthetic linear momentum.**

***Index Terms*—cavity resonators, finite-difference time-domain method, isolators, time-varying circuits.**

I. Introduction

Optical isolators allow propagation of electromagnetic waves in one direction and block them in the reverse direction. To implement this functionality, the Lorentz reciprocity inherent in most materials must be broken. Most existing optical isolators use Faraday rotation induced by the magneto-optic effect. However, these devices can be bulky and require specialized magneto-optic materials which can be difficult to process in integrated photonics applications [1]. This work presents a theoretical framework verified by finite-difference time-domain simulation of an isolator device made by time-modulating the refractive index of three coupled cavities.

II. Coupled Cavities

Fig. 1 (a) depicts a generic system comprised of two waveguides and three optical resonators with frequency ω_0, cavity-coupling rate κ and waveguide coupling rate d. Temporal coupled mode theory (CMT) [2] can be used to model the dynamics of the system according to:

$$\dot{\mathbf{a}} = [-i\mathbf{\Omega} - \mathbf{\Gamma}]\mathbf{a} + 2\mathbf{D}^{\mathrm{T}}\mathbf{s}_{\mathrm{inc}}, \tag{1}$$

where $\mathbf{a} = \begin{bmatrix} a_1(t) & a_2(t) & a_3(t) \end{bmatrix}^T$, $\mathbf{\Omega}$ is given by:

$$\mathbf{\Omega} = \begin{bmatrix} \omega_0 & \kappa & 0 \\ \kappa & \omega_0 & \kappa \\ 0 & \kappa & \omega_0 \end{bmatrix}, \tag{2}$$

$\mathbf{\Gamma}$ is given by:

$$\mathbf{\Gamma} = \begin{bmatrix} \gamma_i + \gamma_c & 0 & 0 \\ 0 & \gamma_i & 0 \\ 0 & 0 & \gamma_i + \gamma_c \end{bmatrix}, \tag{3}$$

and $\mathbf{D}$ is given by:

$$\mathbf{D} = \frac{1}{2}\begin{bmatrix} d & 0 & 0 \\ 0 & 0 & 0 \\ 0 & 0 & d \end{bmatrix}. \tag{4}$$

$a_j(t)$ is the field amplitude in the jth resonator, γ_i is the intrinsic loss rate of an isolated resonator and γ_c is the loss rate of a resonator due to waveguide coupling. d and γ_c are related according to $d^2 = 2\gamma_c$. $\mathbf{s}_{\mathrm{inc}} = \begin{bmatrix} s_{i1} & 0 & s_{i2} \end{bmatrix}^{\mathrm{T}}$ is a vector describing the incident field amplitudes in ports 1 and 2. The matrix $\mathbf{D}$ has only two non-zero values consistent with only the left and right cavities being coupled to waveguides. The presence of only two coupling loss terms γ_c in $\mathbf{\Gamma}$ also reflects this configuration.

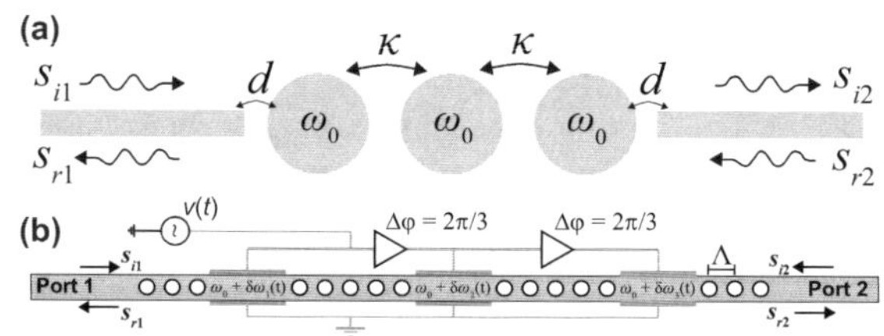

Fig. 1. (a) Schematic depiction of two coupled resonant cavities each of which is coupled to a waveguide. (b) Geometry of system modeled using FDTD. The index of the gray waveguide is set to 3.1. White areas are air. The time-variation of the refractive index was implemented within the FDTD algorithm rather than through an applied voltage as shown.

Fig. 1 (b) shows how the coupled-cavity system depicted in Fig. 1 (a) could be implemented in a compact integrated photonics platform. The gray region represents an InP rectangular waveguide. The cavities are defined by defects in a one-dimensional array of air holes etched into the semiconductor waveguide. The array of air holes creates a bandgap centered at the normalized frequency $\Lambda/\lambda_0 = 0.24$. When defects are introduced into the array, incident energy can couple into them, and the energy in the defects can then couple to output ports. Without modulation, the transmission spectra of this system would be the same for incidence from port 1 or 2.

Optical isolation is implemented by time-modulating the resonance frequency of each cavity via the electro-optic effect at a frequency ω_m which is much smaller than the optical carrier frequency. The sinusoidal signal applied to each cavity is phase shifted by $2\pi/3$ resulting in a synthetic forward linear momentum applied to the system. It is this directional momentum that breaks the reciprocity necessary for isolation.

In the presence of the proposed time-modulation, the CMT equation becomes:

$$\dot{\mathbf{a}} = [-i\mathbf{\Omega} - i\delta\mathbf{\Omega}(t) - \mathbf{\Gamma}]\mathbf{a} + 2\mathbf{D}^{\mathrm{T}}\mathbf{s}_{\mathrm{inc}}, \tag{5}$$

where $\delta\mathbf{\Omega}(t)$ is given by:

$$\delta\omega \begin{bmatrix} \cos(\omega_m t) & 0 & 0 \\ 0 & 2\cos(\omega_m t + 2\pi/3) & 0 \\ 0 & 0 & \cos(\omega_m t + 4\pi/3) \end{bmatrix}. \tag{6}$$

To obtain the scattered wave amplitude into ports 1 and 2 one solves Eq. 5 for a_j and substitutes the result into:

$$\mathbf{s}_{\mathrm{ref}} = -\mathbf{s}_{\mathrm{inc}} + \mathbf{D}\mathbf{a}, \tag{7}$$

where $\mathbf{s}_{\mathrm{ref}} = \begin{bmatrix} s_{r1} & 0 & s_{r2} \end{bmatrix}^{\mathrm{T}}$ represents the amplitudes of the outgoing waves in ports 1 and 2 [2].

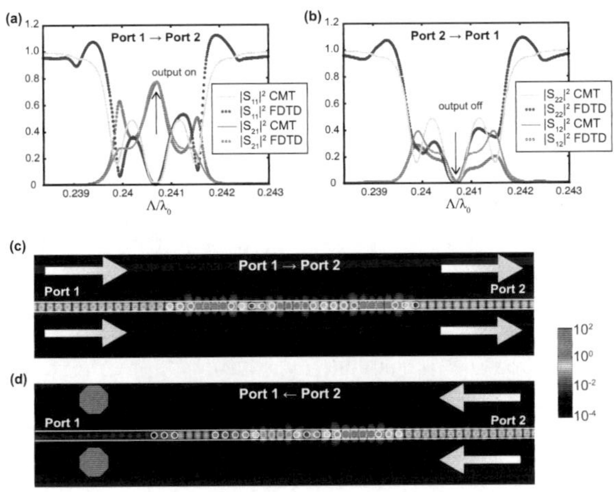

Fig. 2. (a) The scattering parameters calculated using CMT and simulated using FDTD for incidence from port 1. (b) The scattering parameters for incidence from port 2. (c) Depiction of $|H_z(x,y)|^2$ on a logarithmic scale for incidence from port 1 at the isolation frequency. The field is shown radiating into port 2. (d) Same as (c) except incident energy is from port 2, and the energy is blocked from reaching port 1.

Figs. 2 (a) and (b) depict the scattering spectra for incidence from ports 1 and 2, respectively, calculated using CMT and simulated via the two-dimensional finite-difference time-domain (FDTD) method. The resonance frequencies of the three-cavity system are ω_0 and $\omega_0 \pm \sqrt{2}\kappa$. The three peaks in the transmission spectra $|S_{21}|^2$ correspond to the three resonance frequencies. The system was designed to provide optical isolation at the middle resonance frequency (ω_0) at a normalized frequency $\omega_0\Lambda/(2\pi c) = \Lambda/\lambda_0 = 0.2407$. The modulation parameters were set to $\omega_m = 0.00082$ and $\delta\omega = 0.0046$ which were determined using a numerical optimization that simultaneously maximized (minimized) throughput in the forward (backward) direction based on the CMT equations [3]. The qualitative agreement between the theoretical predictions and the numerical simulation is good. Figs. 2 (a) and (b) show how the transmission is on in the forward direction and off in the backward direction. In both cases, the reflected energy is minimal at the isolation frequency. Figs. 2 (c) and (d) depict the fields in the cases of incidence in the forward and backward directions, respectively, and confirm the isolation behavior of the device. We found that with the phase-shifted spatio-temporal modulation scheme and appropriately chosen values of $\delta\omega$ and ω_m, the power transmission from port 1 to port 2 is 77%, and the power transmission from port 2 to port 1 is suppressed to 0.7% resulting in 20.4dB of isolation. Using intuition from our previous studies [3], [4], we believe the transmission can be further increased and the required modulation frequency and amplitude decreased by using cavities with lower intrinsic losses (γ_i). The intrinsic loss of the proposed cavities can be decreased using straightforward geometry modifications [5].

III. Analysis of Time-varying Systems

In the solution of the CMT equations in the presence of modulation, one must introduce the ansatz $a_j(t) = \sum_n a_{j,n}e^{-i(\omega+n\omega_m)t}$ and solve for the Fourier series coefficients $a_{j,n}$. In order to keep the analysis reasonable, we truncated the Fourier series and kept only the $n = -1, 0, 1$ harmonics. Even with this approximation, the qualitative agreement between the theoretical predictions and FDTD simulation is good.

The FDTD simulation is performed by exciting the system with a pulse centered at the frequency of interest. The incident, reflected and transmitted power spectra are recorded. $|S_{11}|^2$ and $|S_{21}|^2$ are obtained by dividing the reflected and transmitted power spectra by the incident power spectra ($|S_{12}|^2$ and $|S_{22}|^2$ are obtained analogously). This excitation energizes a range of frequencies simultaneously thereby producing entire scattering spectra with a single simulation. In the presence of time-varying materials, the scattering spectra will display frequency mixing. In Fig. 2(a) and (b) the reflected scattering parameter exceeds 1 due to overlapping of multiple sidebands. In another presentation [6], we discuss more details of time-domain modeling of time-varying materials.

References

[1] Y. Shoji, T. Mizumoto, H. Yokoi, I-W. Hsieh, and R. M. Osgood, "Magneto-optical isolator with silicon waveguide fabricated by direct bonding," Applied Physics Letters, vol. 92, pp. 071117, 2008.

[2] W. Suh, Z. Wang, and S. Fan, "Temporal coupled-mode theory and the presence of non-orthogonal modes in lossless multimode cavities," IEEE Journal of Quantum Electronics, vol. 40, pp. 1511–1518, 2004.

[3] A. Mock, D. Sounas, and A. Alù, "Magnet-Free Circulator Based on Spatiotemporal Modulation of Photonic Crystal Defect Cavities," ACS Photonics, vol. 6, pp. 2056–2066, 2019.

[4] A. Mock, D. Sounas, and A. Alù, "Tunable orbital angular momentum radiation from angular-momentum-biased microcavities," Physical Review Letters, vol. 121, pp. 103901, 2018.

[5] A. Zain, N. Johnson, M. Sorel, and R. De La Rue, "Ultra high quality factor one dimensional photonic crystal/photonic wire micro-cavities in silicon-on-insulator (SOI)," Optics Express, vol. 16, pp. 12084, 2008.

[6] A. Mock, "Calculating scattering spectra using time-domain modeling of time-modulated systems," submitted to 2020 International Applied Computational Electromagnetics (ACES) Symposium, Monterey, CA, USA, March 2020, paper 1140.

Adaptable Nonstandard FDTD Schemes for the Precise Evaluation of Electrostatic Fields

Tadao Ohtani
Asahikawa 070-0841, Japan
bytcg100@ybb.ne.jp

Yasushi Kanai
Engineering Department,
Niigata Institute of Technology
Kashiwazaki, 945-1195, Japan
kanai@iee.niit.ac.jp

Nikolaos V. Kantartzis
ECE Department,
Aristotle University of Thessaloniki
GR-54124 Thessaloniki, Greece
kant@auth.gr

***Abstract*—The reduction of the total computational overhead in the design of complex geometries, such as modern aircrafts, is a very challenging problem, particularly when electrostatic fields (ESF) for lightning protection, are considered. To this aim, an efficient ESF evaluation scheme, based on the nonstandard finite-difference time-domain (NS-FDTD) method, is proposed. Combining the total-field/scattered-field (TF/SF) concept with a distinct sine-wave form, the novel technique cancels the accumulative errors caused by the static field component. Numerical results reveal that the featured method enables the use of high-frequency discretization models to ESF problems, with notable accuracy and seriously decreased design costs.**

Keywords—FDTD methods, nonstandard (NS)-FDTD techniques, numerical analysis, radar cross section.

I. Introduction

There are many electric evaluation issues when it comes to the design of an aircraft. Amid them, lightning protection is a crucial safety factor [1]-[3]. So, to avoid the risk of lightning strikes, the electrostatic field (ESF) strength around airframe must be analyzed. Typically, the finite difference technique or the finite element method are employed for the static analysis [4], while, physical optics and the geometrical theory of diffraction [5] treat high frequency scenarios. On the other hand, for medium frequencies, the finite-difference time domain (FDTD) algorithm could be a solid choice [6], [7]. Thus, for wideband designs, several of the prior options should be combined, leading to rather inefficient implementations, explicitly for 3-D real-world applications. Not to mention that such combinations usually lead to excessively large numerical calculation models, i.e. discretized lattices, that can hardly be handled, even by contemporary computational systems.

In this paper, we present a rigorous ESF calculation technique via the 3-D NS-FDTD method, that is a high frequency analysis tool, to treat all the electrical design requirements of an aircraft. However, the NS-FDTD method is applicable to only one preset wave (and not a dc) [8]. Hence, we introduce an adaptable procedure utilizing the total-field/scattered-field (TF/SF) separation model [7] as a source of the ESF and a tuned input wave form which cancels the accumulative errors generated by the dc component. Our algorithm is validated via the analysis of a perfectly electric conductor (PEC) sphere [9]. It is shown that the proposed method can successfully extend the application of high-frequency discretized grids to ESF computations, reducing significantly the system resource costs in the electrical design of realistic problems.

II. The ESF Evaluation Methodology

A. Incorporation of the Input Wave Form

To embody the NS-FDTD method in the ESF analysis, we adopt a modified sine-wave form with a dc component as

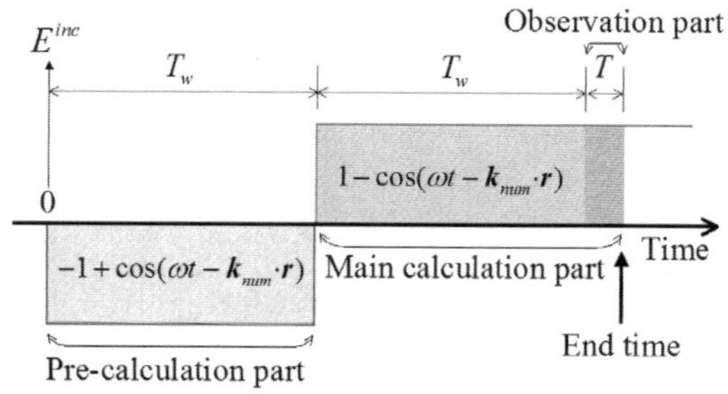

Fig. 1. Time diagram of the E^{inc} field for the proposed ESF evaluation.

$$\begin{cases} E^{inc}(t,\boldsymbol{r}) = 0 , & \omega t - \boldsymbol{k}_{\text{num}}\cdot\boldsymbol{r} \le 0 \\ E^{inc}(t,\boldsymbol{r}) = -1+\cos(\omega t - \boldsymbol{k}_{\text{num}}\cdot\boldsymbol{r}), & 0 < \omega t - \boldsymbol{k}_{\text{num}}\cdot\boldsymbol{r} \le \omega T_{\text{w}} \\ E^{inc}(t,\boldsymbol{r}) = 1-\cos(\omega t - \boldsymbol{k}_{\text{num}}\cdot\boldsymbol{r}), & \omega T_{\text{w}} < \omega t - \boldsymbol{k}_{\text{num}}\cdot\boldsymbol{r} \end{cases} \quad (1)$$

where t is the time, ω the angular frequency, $\boldsymbol{r}$ the TF/SF separation position vector, and $\boldsymbol{k}_{\text{num}}$ the numerical wavenumber. Furthermore, $T_w = m(2\pi/\omega)$ is set long enough for the incident wave E^{inc} to fully cover the TF/SF separation area, with m a natural number. The second and third branch in (1) correspond to $E_{\text{dc}} = -1$ and $E_{\text{dc}} = 1$ in the time average, respectively. In fact, the second E^{inc} term is the prior calculation part for the accumulative error owing to the dc-component in $0 < t \le 2T_w$. Its error is used to cancel the corresponding error in the third E^{inc} term of (1). The time diagram of E^{inc}, during the aforementioned procedure, is described in Fig. 1, which indicates that the ESF observation is performed after the period of $2T_w$, via

$$E^{\text{static}} = \frac{1}{T}\int_0^T E(t)\,dt \quad \text{with} \quad T = 2\pi/\omega . \quad (2)$$

So, the total amount of calculation time-steps in our scheme is $(2T_w + T)/\Delta t$, unlike in the usual pulse response analysis where end time-steps can not be set beforehand. Additionally, the use of the TF/SF separation model, as a field source, permits the generation of along arbitrary directions.

B. Verification of the ESF Calculation Scheme

The theoretical solution for a PEC sphere, of radius a and a smooth surface, placed in a uniform ESF, is given by [9]

$$E(r,\theta) = E_0\left(1+\frac{2a^3}{r^3}\right)\cos\theta \quad \text{for} \quad r \ge a , \quad (3)$$

where E_0 is the applied ESF, r the distance from the center of the sphere, and θ the angle in spherical coordinates. Note that the electric potential of the sphere is 0. Using (3), we examine the ability of our scheme to treat the specific problem. The sphere is discretized into cubic cells of width Δ and is set at the center of TF/SF separation area. Moreover,

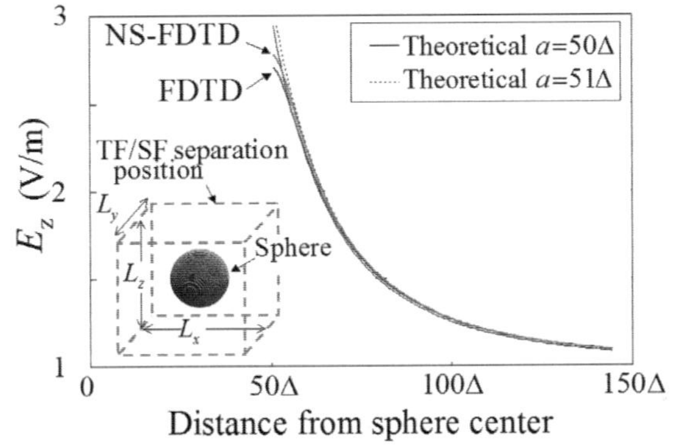

Fig. 2. Variation of the E_z component versus distance (along the z-axis) from the sphere center, derived by various methods. The applied field, with E_0 = 1 V/m, is parallel to z axis. The theoretical values via (3) are shown for the cases of a and $a + \Delta$, since a discretized cell model has an ambiguity of one Δ in the FDTD algorithm. The TF/SF separation area size is $L_{x,y,z}$ = 290Δ.

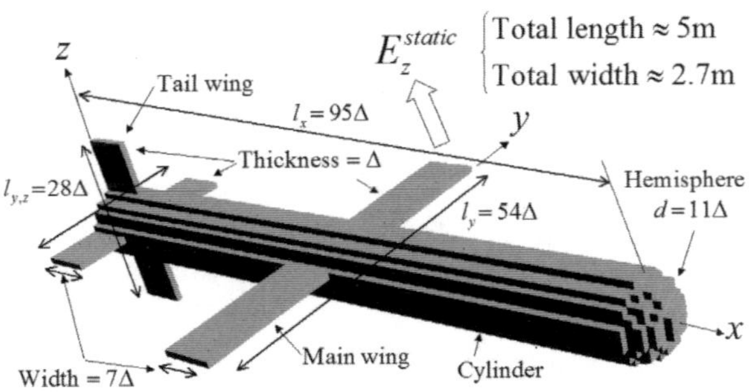

Fig. 3. A realistic aircraft model discretized by 9449 cubic PEC cells. The tail wing is placed at the center of the cylinder, while the main wing position is one Δ beyond the tail wing towards the z direction. The cylinder lies along the x axis and the main wing along the y axis.

the incident field of (1) propagates along the z axis with θ = 90°, φ = 0°, T_w = 3600Δt, and Δ = λ/10, with λ = 1 m and Δt = (ω/2π)/36. In this context, Fig. 2 illustrates the behavior of the E_z component, indicating that our ESF evaluation scheme, combined with the NS-FDTD method, is in excellent agreement with both the FDTD technique and the theoretical solution of (3), for $E(a,0)$ = 3 V/m. Moreover, the NS-FDTD approach is more accurate than the FDTD one in the vicinity of the sphere surface. This fact proves the superiority of the new formulation over existing methods, leading to the conclusion that the featured ESF evaluation scheme can be deemed a powerful tool for such problems.

III. Application to a Realistic Aircraft Design

Next, we apply our method to the ESF analysis of a real-world aircraft model, as depicted in Fig. 3. All lattice cells are PEC cubes with a width of Δ = λ/20 and λ = 1 m, whereas the applied ESF magnitude is $E_z^{\text{static}} = 1$ V/m. In this problem, we consider a TF/SF separation area with L_x = 210Δ and $L_{y,z}$ = 160Δ, illuminated by an incident field traveling along the x direction through (1) for T_w = 7200Δt and Δt = (ω/2π)/72. Numerical results are given in Fig. 4, together with the FDTD ones, for the sake of comparison. A very satisfactory coincidence may be promptly detected, while the demanding ESF concentration on the wingtips is simulated very well [10]. Also, as noted in Fig. 2, the NS-FDTD technique is more accurate than FDTD one, since $E_z^{\text{NS-FDTD}} > E_z^{\text{FDTD}}$. From

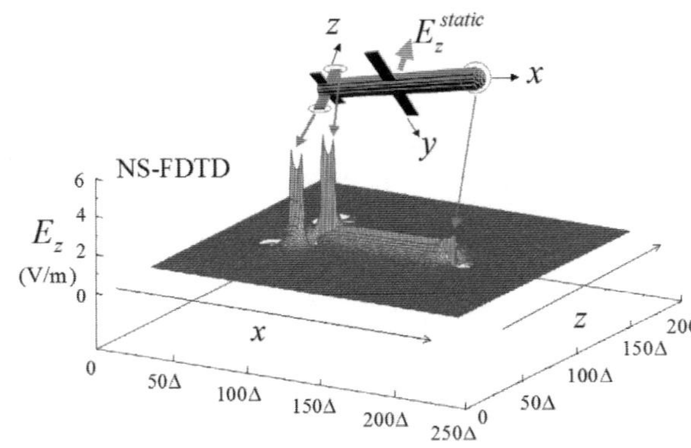

(a)

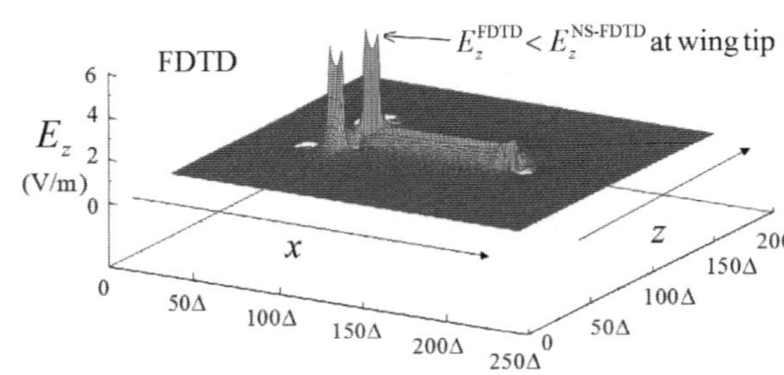

(b)

Fig. 4 Distribution of the ESF (E_z) magnitude along the central vertical cross-section of the aircraft, given in Fig. 3, caluclated in terms of (a) the NS-FDTD and (b) the FDTD method.

this fact, it is deduced that we can successfully obtain the ESF solution by means of our evaluation method using the high-frequency discretized cell model directly in the 3-D NS-FDTD method. Therefore, the proposed algorithm can drastically reduce the total computational cost of the design process, even for rather complex applications, such as the static field analysis of various aircrafts, with electrically large size, arbitrary shapes, ad diverse material properties.

References

[1] D. Morgan, C. J. Hardwick, S. J. Haigh, and A. J. Meakins, "The interaction of lightning with aircraft and the challenges of lightning testing," *J Aerospace Lab*, no. 5, art. no. AL05-11, 2012.

[2] R. Majkner, "Overview - Lightning protection of aircraft and avionics," *LI IEEE EMC*, no. 10, 2003 at https://www.ieee.li/pdf/viewgraphs/lightning_protection_aircraft_avionics.pdf.

[3] M. Eberle, R. Marcordes, D. Jaeger, R. A. Perala, A. Plumer, and H. Schwarz, "Lightning protection design methodology for a very large non rigid airship," *SAE*, art no. 2001-01-2931, 2001.

[4] R. Gordon, T. Arola, K. Wendel, O. Rynanen, and J. Hyttinen, "Accuracy of numerical methods by calculating static and quasistatic electric fields," in *Proc. Estonian Acad. Sci. Eng.*, 2006, no. 12, pp. 262-283.

[5] R. M. O'Donnell, "Radar systems engineering lecture 7 part 2 radar cross section," *IEEE New Hampshire Section Guest Lecturer*, 2010.

[6] J. Burke and A. Poggio, *Numerical Electromagnetic Code 2 (NEC2)*, 1981 at http://www.nec2.org/.

[7] A. Taflove and S. Hagness, *Computational Electrodynamics: The Finite-Difference Time-Domain Method.* Norwood, MA: Artech House, 2005.

[8] J. B. Cole, "High-accuracy Yee algorithm based on nonstandard finite differences: New developments and verifications," *IEEE Trans. Antennas Propag.*, vol. 50, no. 9, pp. 1185–1191, Sep. 2002.

[9] J. A, Stratton, *Electromagnetic Theory*. New York, NY: McGraw-Hill, 1941, ch. III, sec. 3.24 and ch. I, sec. 1.22.

[10] Space Propulsion Laboratory, *Aircraft Lightning Strike Research*, Massachusetts Institute of Technology, 2012 at http://spl.mit.edu/plasmas-aerospace.

Height and Angle Characteristics of Point Source Transmitting Power of Wireless Avionics Intra-Communication Systems Based on FDTD Analysis

Shunichi Futatsumori
Surveillance and Communications Department, Electronic Navigation Research Institute
National Institute of Maritime, Port and Aviation Technology
Chofu, Japan
futatsumori@mpat.go.jp

Kazuyuki Morioka
Surveillance and Communications Department, Electronic Navigation Research Institute
National Institute of Maritime, Port and Aviation Technology
Chofu, Japan
morioka@mpat.go.jp

Takashi Hikage
Graduate School of Information Science and Technology
Hokkaido University
Sapporo, Japan
hikage@wtemc.ist.hokudai.ac.jp

Tetsuya Sekiguchi
Graduate School of Information Science and Technology
Hokkaido University
Sapporo, Japan
t-sekiguchi@wtemc.ist.hokudai.ac.jp

Manabu Yamamoto
Graduate School of Information Science and Technology
Hokkaido University
Sapporo, Japan
yamamoto@wtemc.ist.hokudai.ac.jp

Toshio Nojima
Graduate School of Information Science and Technology
Hokkaido University
Sapporo, Japan
nojima@wtemc.ist.hokudai.ac.jp

***Abstract*—The equivalent isotopically radiated power (EIRP) of a wireless avionics intra-communication (WAIC) system is limited to 6 dBm/MHz at the geometrical center of the aircraft, to avoid interference with aircraft radio altimeters, which are operated at the same frequency band between 4,200–4,400 MHz. In this paper, the height and angle characteristics of the point source EIRP of a WAIC system are analyzed based on the large scale FDTD analysis. Firstly, the strength of the electric field (E-field) around the three-dimensional model of Airbus A320-200 is analyzed. Then, the point source EIRP is calculated based on the analyzed E-field strength. Finally, the height and angle characteristics are analyzed to estimate the electromagnetic field characteristics of the aircraft.**

Keywords—aircraft, large-scale finite-difference time-domain method, point source transmitting power, radio altimeter interference, wireless avionics intra-communication.

I. Introduction

A wireless avionics intra-communication (WAIC) system offers wireless connections between the various components in an aircraft. These systems are allocated the frequency band of 4,200–4,400 MHz [1]. However, conventional aircraft radio altimeters are already operated over the frequency band. Therefore, the condition of frequency coexistence between WAIC systems and radio altimeters are discussed at standardization organizations. The minimum aviation system performance standard (MASPS) of WAIC systems limit the equivalent isotopically radiated power (EIRP) of the WAIC transmitter to less than 6 dBm/MHz at the geometrical center of the aircraft [2]. We have been developing a method for a detailed estimation of the electromagnetic field (EMF) distribution, based on the large-scale finite-difference time-domain (FDTD) analysis method [3].

In this paper, the height and angle characteristics of the point source EIRP estimations based on FDTD analysis are discussed. Firstly, the electric field (E-field) strength around the Airbus A320-200 aircraft, in which the WAIC transmitting antenna is installed inside the cabin, are analyzed. Then, the point source EIRP is calculated based on the analyzed E-field strength. This procedure is the same as the measurement procedures for the WAIC MASPS [2]. Finally, the evaluation height and angle characteristics of the point source EIRP are discussed to determine the EMF characteristics.

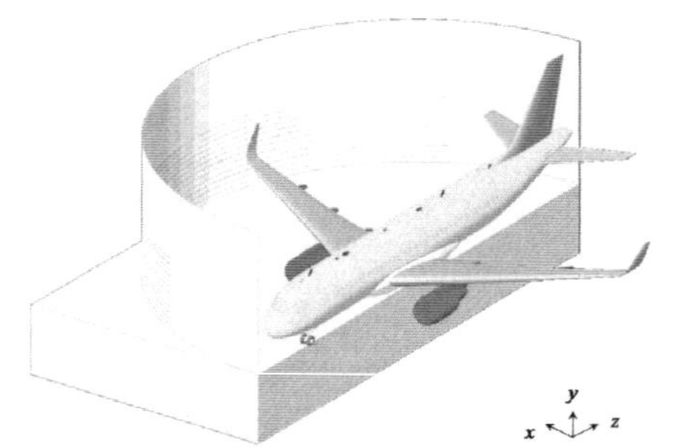

Fig. 1. Overview of the electric field strength evaluations on the circle around the aircraft based on the three-dimensional Airbus A320-200 model.

II. E-Field Estimation Based on FDTD Analysis

The strength of the E-field, which is converted to the point source EIRP, is obtained by using the large-scale FDTD analysis [3]. Fig. 1 shows the overview of the E-field strength evaluations at a radius of 20 m for a three-dimensional model of Airbus A320-200. The center of the circle is also the geometrical center of the aircraft. The strength of the E-field at the surface of the cylinder is evaluated. Fig. 2 shows the analysis model and the location of the transmitting antenna. The vertically polarized dipole antenna is located at the center of the aircraft and at 1.0 m from the floor. The frequency and transmitting power are 4,400 MHz and 20 dBm, respectively. The aircraft model possesses internal structures and electric constants such as the conductivity and the loss tangent [3]. The dry ground with a thickness of 10 cm (relative dielectric constant = 15 and conductivity = 0.001 S/m) is modeled.

The perfect magnetic walls are located at the center of the aircraft to reduce the required analysis memory. The total cell size of the analysis and the required memory are 66,800 M cells and 6,400 GB, respectively [3]. Fig. 3 shows the typical analyzed three axis combined E-field strength distributions along (a) the *xz*-plane at the antenna height (4.7 m from the ground), and along (b) the radius of 20 m.

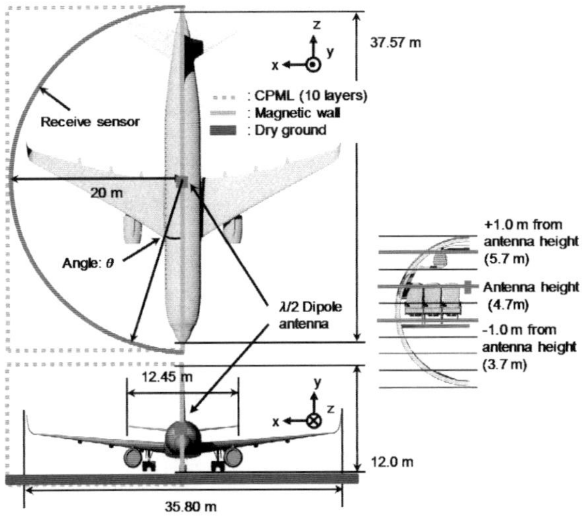

Fig. 2. Three-dimensional aircraft model based on Airbus A320-200 and the evaluation height.

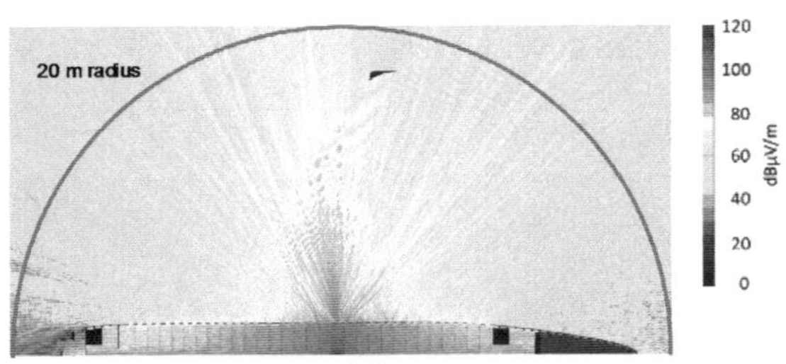

(a) E-field strength distributions along the *xz*-plane at the transmitting antenna height (4.7 m from the ground)

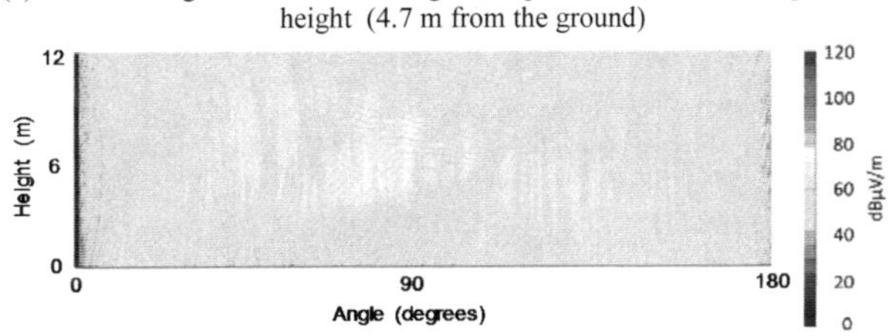

(b) E-field strength distributions along radius of 20 m

Fig. 3. Analyzed three axis combined E-field strength distributions along (a) the *xz*-plane at the antenna height and along (b) a radius of 20 m.

III. Point Source EIRP Evaluation

The point source EIRP is evaluated based on the analysis results. The point source EIRP P_T is calculated using the following equation:

$$P_T = \frac{P_R}{G_T G_R} \times \frac{(4\pi r)^2}{\lambda^2}, \quad (1)$$

where G_T and G_R are the transmitting and receiving antenna gains, respectively. In addition, P_R is the received power at each point on the measurement circle. The terms r and λ denote the radius of the measurement circle and the wavelength, respectively. Assuming point source radiation, G_T and G_R are equal to 0 dBi, and r and λ are equal to 20 m (i.e., the evaluation radius) and 0.068 m (4,400 MHz), respectively. Fig. 4 shows the analyzed point source EIRP angle characteristics along the circle around the aircraft, with respect to different evaluation planes. The estimated point source EIRP at 3.7 m (antenna height -1.0 m), 4.7 m (antenna height), and 5.7 m (antenna height +1.0 m) are shown. The point source EIRP between 0° and 60°, 120° and 180°, which corresponds to the noise and tail directions of the aircraft, exhibit identical trends for all evaluation heights. On the contrary, different EIRP height patterns are observed between 60° and 120°. This is mainly due to the reflection from the main wing, which includes the winglets. Table I lists the maximum point source EIRP at different evaluation heights and angles. The maximum EIRP value of -4.3 dBm is observed at a height of 5.7 m and between 90° and 120°. On comparing the 20 dBm transmitting power, it is confirmed that a minimum of approximately 24 dB additional pass loss is obtained at this antenna location.

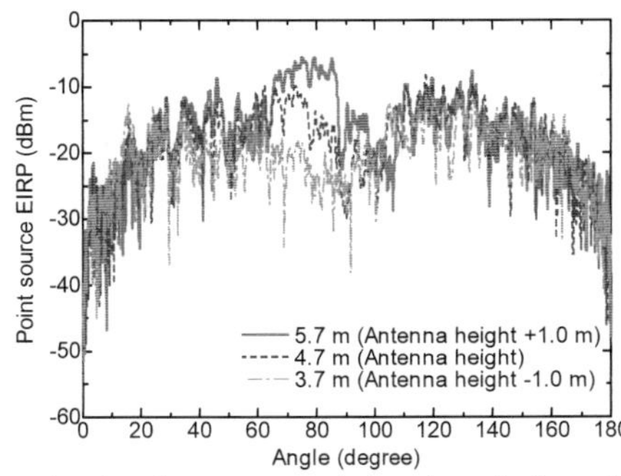

Fig. 4. Analyzed point source equivalent isotopically radiated power (EIRP) angle characteristics on the circle around the aircraft for different evaluation planes.

TABLE I. The Maximum Point Source EIRP at Different Evaluation Height and Angle

Evaluation Height/Angle	0°–30°	30°–60°	60°–90°	90°–120°	120°–150°	150°–180°
0.7 m	-19.1	-21.1	-23.2	-16.6	-12.9	-15.1
1.7 m	-14.6	-17.1	-20.7	-11.9	-12.7	-13.9
2.7 m	-12.5	-13.5	-15.8	-11.4	-11.2	-13.1
3.7 m	-11.6	-10.6	-9.8	-8.30	-9.6	-12.1
4.7 m	-11.6	-8.7	-5.5	-8.7	-7.8	-11.8
5.7 m	-12.7	-6.9	-4.6	-4.3	-11.4	-14.6

Unit: dBm

IV. Conclusions

The height and angle characteristics of the point source EIRP of a WAIC system was evaluated based on the large-scale FDTD analysis. The point source EIRP evaluation was performed on a developed three-dimensional model of Airbus A320-200. Then, the E-field strength around the aircraft was calculated along a radius of 20 m. Finally, the height and angle characteristics of the maximum point source EIRPs were calculated. These results can be used to estimate the transmitting power tolerance of WAIC systems.

References

[1] International Telecommunication Union, Resolution 424 of World Radiocommunication Conference 2015, "Use of wireless avionics intra-communications in the frequency band 4200-4400 MHz," Nov. 2015.

[2] Radio Technical Commission for Aeronautics, "DO-378 - Minimum Aviation System Performance Standard (MASPS) for Coexistence of Wireless Avionics Intra-Communication Systems within 4200-4400 MHz," Jul. 2019.

[3] S. Futatsumori, et. al, "Analysis of radar altimeter interference due to wireless avionics intra-communication systems by using large-scale FDTD method—Investigation on Airbus A320 class passenger aircraft," Proceedings of the 34th International Review of Progress in Applied Computational Electromagnetics, pp. 1–2, Mar. 2018.

THz Square Cross Section Smooth Spline Horns as a Competitive Alternative to Corrugated Horns

Yogesh Karandikar
Tantrayut Telecommunications Pvt Ltd
Ambernath, India
yk@tantrayut.in

Branko Kolundzija
WIPL-D
Belgrade, Serbia
branko.kolundzija@wipl-d.com

***Abstract*—This paper describes a novel design of smooth wall spline horn with square cross section throughout its length instead of circular. The paper further describes the design philosophy of such horn along with its simulated parameters. The simulated results from WIPL-D tool suggests that this horn has very high Gaussian Coupling efficiency (η_G) comparable to classical corrugated horns. As a case study the said horn is designed over frequency range of 110-170 GHz (D-band) with standard WR-06 rectangular waveguide as its input. The simulated results suggests a minimum η_G of $\approx 95\%$ over whole bandwidth with its value better than 98% over 140-150 GHz. Furthermore the said horn maintains a constant beam waist (ω_0) of 3.65 mm over full waveguide band. This feature shows the effectiveness of these horns as an alternative to classical corrugated horns for THz Quasi-optical systems. It is also worth to mention that with the absence of corrugations the fabrication of these horns using convectional split block technique as well as using modern additive manufacturing becomes very cost effective for mass production. The fabricated prototype of the said horn is also presented in this paper.**

***Index Terms*—Gaussian Coupling Efficiency, Spline Horn, THz Horns.**

I. Introduction

The corrugated horns are very widely used horns when it comes to performance in terms of side-lobes, cross-polar and coupling to Gaussian optics. However with large number of required corrugations makes these horn bulky and demands elaborate precision machining. To overcome these, it has been conclusively shown that the smooth wall spline profile horns are equally competitive alternative to corrugated horns [1]. Further it is shown that these can be pushed in THz regime and their fabrication can simply be achieved by a simple drilling process with spline profile custom drill [2]–[4].

However, all these horns are still using circular waveguide as its input mode launcher. So for THz electronics housed in classical split block assembly needs a transition from standard rectangular waveguide to circular. Recent advances in the field have shown modification of classical diagonal horn with spline profile in THz regime [5], [6]. However it still needs a spline profile at 45 deg angle with the input waveguide. Also the said papers [5], [6] does not comment on the wideband ability of these horns interms of coupling to fundamental Gaussian mode.

Therefore this paper focuses on properties of square cross section, spline profiled smooth wall such as Gaussicity (η_G), beamwaist (ω_0) and it's location (Z_0) inside the throat of the horn. These quantities will be used to estimate performance bandwidth of the said horn.

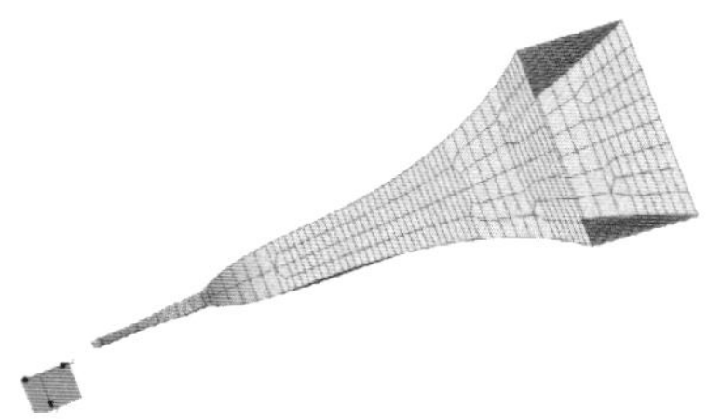

Fig. 1. Square cross section smooth spline horn.

Fig. 2. Fabricated prototype.

The section II of paper describes a test case of D-band ($110-170$ GHz) horn with WR-06 waveguide as its input. The simulated results of these horn are shown in section III and finally conclusions are made in section IV based on performance bandwidth interms of Gaussicity.

II. Modelling of Horn using WIPL-D

The said D-band horn is modeled using WIPL-D Pro tool [7] with WR-06 waveguide as its input port as shown in Fig.1. The horn has a quadratic aperture of 25×25 mm and its length is 60 mm. A linear taper 6 mm is used to transform rectangular WR-06 waveguide to 0.826×0.826 mm square waveguide and further this square waveguide is flared out to required aperture size. A 7th order Bezi´er curve is used as a profile of the smooth wall horn. The fabricated prototype of this horn using split block method is shown in Fig. 2.

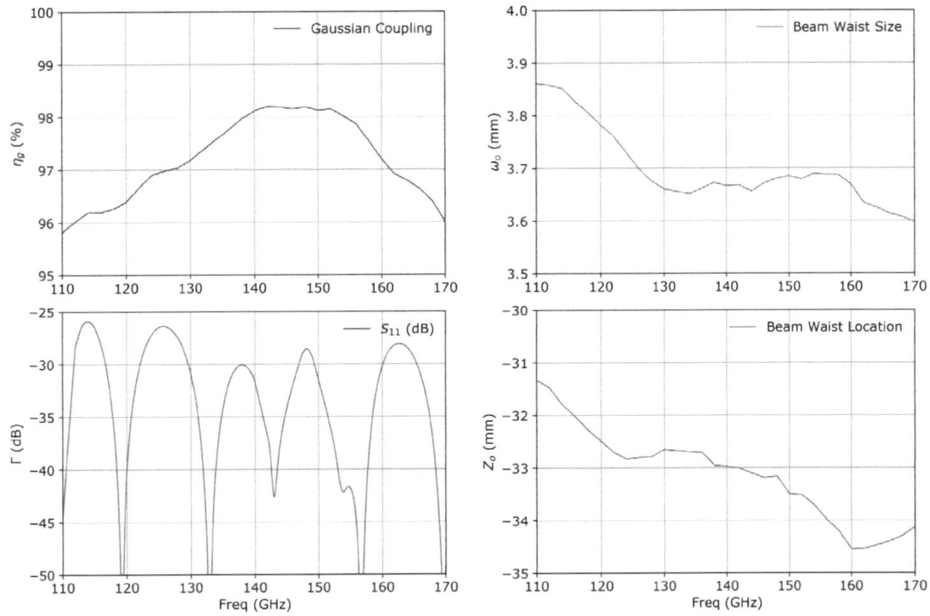

(a) Gaussicity and input matching (b) Beam waist and its location

Fig. 3. Gaussian beam parameters of sq. spline horn.

III. Simulated Results

This horn is simulated over $110-170$ GHz and for each 2 GHz step its far-field is evaluated and from far-field the key Gaussian beam parameters (η_G,ω_0,Z_0) are extracted using [8]. The computed Gaussian parameters are shown in Fig. 3(a) and Fig. 3 (b). It can be observed that the Gaussian Coupling efficiency of this horn stay above 95% over entire waveguide band. Also the beam waist of 3.65mm stay constant within ±0.2mm. This property makes this horn very attractive for quasi-optical system which often demands constant beam waist over required operational bandwidth. Furthermore this horn does not require any complex transition to circular waveguide. Thus making it very suitable for fabrication. A sample far-field of this horn at 144 GHz is shown in Fig. 4.

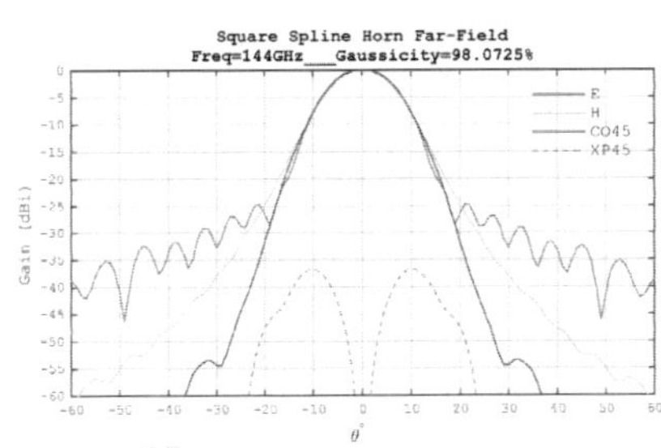

Fig. 4. E-, H- and $\phi = 45°$ plane patterns @ 144 GHz.

IV. Conclusions

It is shown by simulations that the square cross-section spline profile smooth wall horn could achieve 98% Gaussian Coupling over 10% bandwidth and over 95% for a full waveguide band. With elimination of corrugations as well as circular waveguide this horn gives an edge over classical corrugated horns in terms of performance as well as ease with fabrication.

References

[1] C. Granet, G. L. James, R. Bolton, and G. Moorey, "A smooth-walled spline-profile horn as an alternative to the corrugated horn for wide band millimeter-wave applications," IEEE Transactions on Antennas and Propagation, vol. 52, no. 3, pp. 848–854, March 2004.

[2] A. Hammar, Y. Karandikar, P. Forsberg, A. Emrich, and J. Stake, "A 340 ghz high gaussicity smooth spline horn antenna for the steamr instrument," in 2014 IEEE Antennas and Propagation Society International Symposium (APSURSI), July 2014, pp. 649–650.

[3] Y. Karandikar, A. Hammar, P. Sobis, P. Forsberg, A. Emrich, and J. Stake, "A 874 ghz mixer block integrated spline horn and lens antenna for the ismar instrument," in 2015 9th European Conference on Antennas and Propagation (EuCAP), April 2015, pp. 1–5.

[4] A. Hammar, D. Nyberg, Y. Karandikar, P. Sobis, O. Tropp, P. Forsberg, S. McCallion, A. Emrich, and J. Stake, "Thz smooth-walled spline horn antennas: Design, manufacturing and measurements," in 2016 IEEE International Symposium on Antennas and Propagation (APSURSI), June 2016, pp. 1341–1342.

[5] H. J. Gibson, B. Thomas, L. Rolo, M. C. Wiedner, A. E. Maestrini, and P. de Maagt, "A novel spline-profile diagonal horn suitable for integration into thz split-block components," IEEE Transactions on Terahertz Science and Technology, vol. 7, no. 6, pp. 657–663, Nov 2017.

[6] D. Montofré, R. Molina, A. Khudchenko, R. Hesper, A. Baryshev, N. Reyes, and F. P. Mena, "High-performance smooth-walled horn antennas for thz frequency range: Design and evaluation," IEEE Transactions on Terahertz Science and Technology, pp. 1–1, 2019.

[7] "Wipl-d pro," http://www.wipl-d.com.

[8] Y. Karandikar, "Factorization of gaussian coupling efficiency and algorithm to compute it," in 2012 6th European Conference on Antennas and Propagation (EUCAP), March 2012, pp. 868–872.

Design of Ultra Low Profile Inverted L Antenna Composed of CPW Printed on PET Sheet for IoT Application

Mitsuo Taguchi
Graduatae School of engineering
Nagasaki University
Nagasaki, Japan
mtaguchi@nagasaki-u.ac.jp

***Abstract*—The ultra low profile inverted L (ULPIL) antenna on a rectangular conducting plane is located above the lower conducting plane and numerically analyzed for the application of IoT. The coplanar waveguide is inserted within the antenna element. The antenna element is printed on the polyethylene terephthalate (PET) sheet. The shift of the resonant frequency of this antenna is small due to the existence of lower conducting plane. The influence of the existence of the lower conducting plane can be neglected when the distance between the ULPIL antenna and the lower conducting plane is longer than 6 mm (0.049 wavelength). Therefore the ULPIL antenna may be promising for the IoT application.**

***Keywords*— inverted L antenna, IoT, low profile antenna, printed antenna, polyethylene terephthalate sheet.**

I. Introduction

In the antennas closely located on a conducting body for the IoT application, the existence of conducting body near antenna affects to the antenna characteristics because it works as an antenna element. The authors have proposed the unbalanced fed ultra low profile inverted L (ULPIL) antenna on the rectangular conducting plane [1]. The inverted L antenna is composed of the semi-rigid coaxial cable. The inner conductor of the coaxial cable is extended from the end of outer conductor, that is, this antenna is excited at the end of outer conductor. The resonant frequency is adjusted by the horizontal length of antenna, and the impedance matching is adjusted by the length of outer conductor of coaxial cable. When the size of conducting plane is 0.245 λ (λ: wavelength) by 0.49 λ and the antenna height is $\lambda/30$, and the length of horizontal element is around a quarter wavelength, the input impedance of this antenna is matched to 50 Ω and its directivity becomes more than 4 dBi. In this antenna, the electromagnetic field concentrates on the inverted L element and the ground plane under it. Therefore, when this antenna is used for the IoT application, the existence of conducting body may not affect to the antenna characteristics. In [2], the coaxial cable of the antenna of the inverted L antenna is replaced by the planar conductor and it is fed by a delta-gap generator. Then the coplanar waveguide (CPW) is inserted within a planar conductor in order to realize the feed line on the conducting plane [3]. An off-center-fed printed dipole was proposed for the Machine-to-Machine (M2M) application [4]. This antenna is constructed from a polyethylene terephthalate (PET) sheet. The antenna element is printed by a inkjet printer. The authors proposed the ULPIL antenna on a rectangular conducting plane with its inverted L element printed on the PET sheet [5]. The end of center conductor of CPW is T shaped. Then, this antenna located on the lower conducting plane is studied as an example of antennas for IoT application [6].

In this paper, an ULIPL antenna closely located on the lower rectangular conducting plane is numerically analyzed and the antenna characteristics are studied by changing the geometry of lower conducting plane. In the numerical analysis, the electromagnetic simulator WIPL-D based on the Method of Moments is used [7].

II. Analytical Model

Fig. 1 shows the proposed ULPIL antenna with a built-in CPW mounted on the rectangular conducting plane. The size of conducting plane is (pxp + pxm) by (pyp + pym). This antenna is located above the lower conducting plane. The distance between the ULPIL antenna and the lower conducting plane is gh. The size of lower conducting plane is (pxp+pxm+2*gx) by (pyp+pym+2*gy). The design frequency

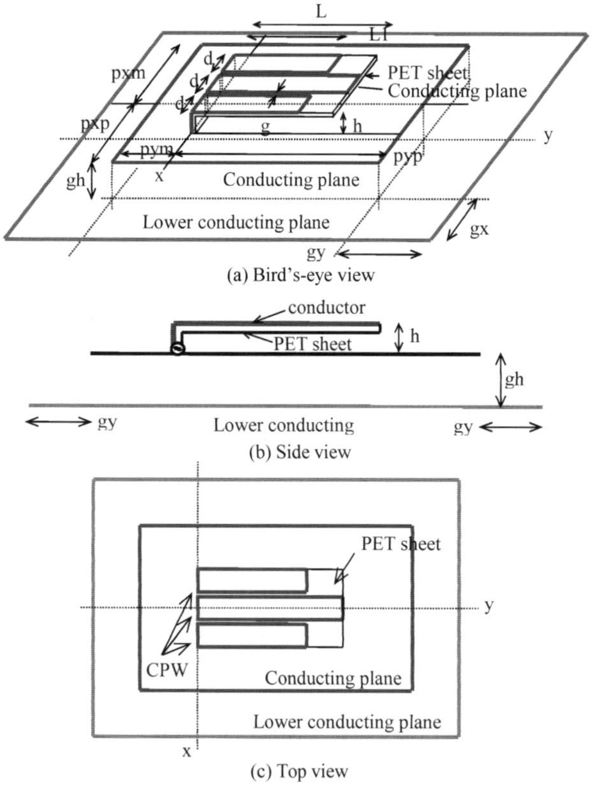

Fig. 1. ULPIL antenna located above a lower conducting plane.

is 2.45 GHz. The parameters of proposed antenna are as follows: L = 35.9 mm, L1 = 24.5 mm, pxp = pxm = 15 mm, pym = 10 mm, pyp = 50 mm, d = 4.6 mm, g = 0.3 mm, h = 2.4 mm. The relative permittivity of PET sheet = 3.0 and its thickness = 0.135 mm. The conductivity of conducting plane is assumed be infinite.

III. Results and Discussion

Fig. 2 shows the S11 characteristics of the antenna as a function of gh. The shift of resonant frequency is small by changing the size of lower conducting plane and the distance gh between the ULPIL antenna and lower conducting plane. When gh becomes longer than 6 mm, the influence of lower conducting plane to the antenna characteristics can be neglected. Fig. 3 shows the directivity characteristics in the z direction as a function of gx = gy. The distance gh between ULPIL antenna and the lower conducting plane is 2 mm. The directivity at the lower resonant frequency becomes small. Fig. 4 shows the current distribution on antenna at the lower resonant frequency of 2.33 GHz and the design frequency of 2.45 GHz. In the antenna in [6], the edge current of outer conductor of CPW becomes large. On the other hand, in the proposed antenna, the edge currents flow along the outer conductor and the top end of center conductor of CPW. The length of outer conductor L1 is small compared with the length, pym + pyp, of ground plane. Therefore the mutual coupling between ULPIL antenna and the lower conducting plane becomes small in the proposed antenna.

IV. Conclusion

The ultra low profile inverted L antenna on a rectangular conducting plane closely located above the lower conducting plane has been numerically analyzed. The CPW is installed within antenna element printed on the PET sheet. The shift of the resonant frequency of ULPIL antenna is small when the size of the lower conducting plane and distance to ULPIL antenna are changed. The second lower resonance occurs due to the coupling of ULPIL and the lower conducting plane. The influence of the existence of the lower conducting plane can be neglected when the distance between the ULPIL antenna and the lower conducting plane is longer than 6 mm (0.049 λ). Therefore the ULPIL antenna may be promising for the IoT antenna.

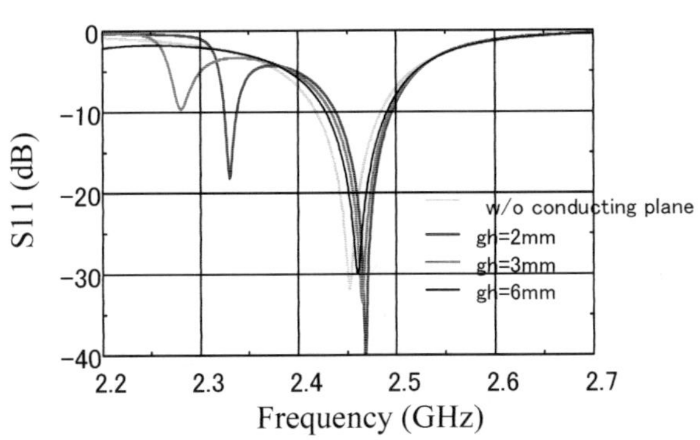

Fig. 2. S11 characteristics of proposed antenna. L = 35.9 mm, L1 = 24.5 mm, pxp = pxm =15 mm, pym =10 mm, pyp = 50 mm, d = 4.6 mm, g = 0.3 mm, h = 2.4 mm, gx = gy = 10 mm.

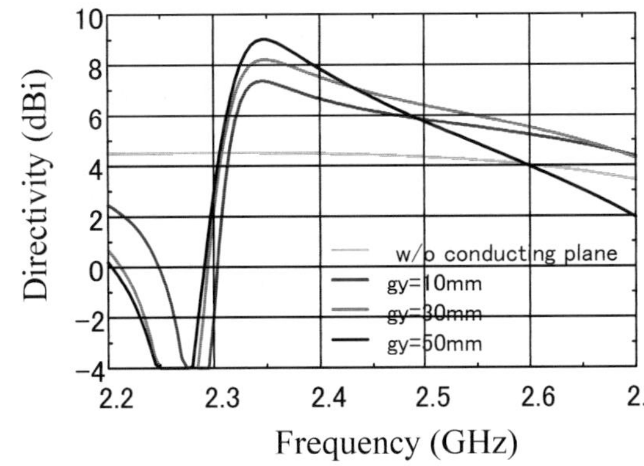

Fig. 3. Directivity characteristics of proposed antenna in z direction. L = 35.9 mm, L1 = 24.5 mm, pxp = pxm =15 mm, pym =10 mm, pyp = 50 mm, d = 4.6 mm, g = 0.3 mm, h = 2.4 mm, gh 2 mm.

(a) Resonant frequency of 2.33 GHz

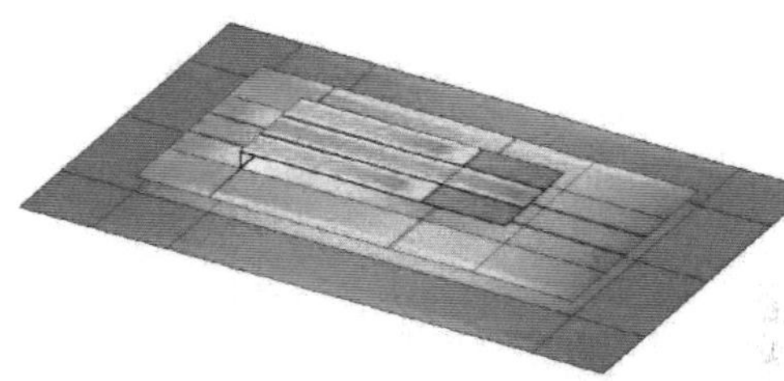

(b) Design frequency of 2.45 GHz

Fig. 4. Current distributions on proposed antenna. L = 30.9 mm, L1 = 24.8 mm, pxp = pxm =15 mm, pym =10 mm, pyp = 50 mm, d = 4.6 mm, g = 0.3 mm, h = 2.4 mm, gh = 2 mm, gx = gy = 10 mm.

References

[1] T. Yamashita and M. Taguchi, "Ultra Low Profile Inverted L Antenna on a Finite Conducting Plane", Proc. of ISAP 2009, pp. 361-364, 2009.

[2] K. Takata and M. Taguchi, "Offset Fed Inverted L Antenna with Planar Element," Proc. of 2016 IEICE General Conference, B-1-53, Mar. 2016 (*in Japanese*).

[3] M. Taguchi and K. Takata, "Offset Fed Planar Inverted L Antenna with Built-in Coplanar Waveguide," Proc. of IEEE APS 2017, pp. 1773-1774, July 2017.

[4] M. Sumi and J. Takada, "Multiband Antennas Comprising Off-Center-Fed Dipoles for M2M Applications," Proc. of IEEE CAMA 2018, 36.2, Sept. 2018.

[5] M. Taguchi, "Ultra low profile inverted L antenna composed of CPW printed on PET sheet," Proc. of IEEE APWC 2019, pp. 419-420, Sept. 2019.

[6] http://www.wipl-d.com/

[7] M. Taguchi, "Ultra low profile inverted L antenna composed of CPW printed on PET sheet for IoT application," Proc. of IEEE CAMA 2019, Oct. 2019.

Improvements in Insertion of Auxiliary Parity Segments in WIPL-D All-Quad Meshing Algorithm

Branko Lj. Mrdakovic[1,2], Branko M. Kolundzija[1]

[1] Dept. of Electrical Engineering
University of Belgrade, King Alexander Blvd 73, 11120 Belgrade, Serbia
branko.mrdakovic@gmail.com, kol@etf.rs

[2] WIPL-D d.o.o.
Gandijeva 7/32, 11073 Belgrade, Serbia
branko.mrdakovic@wipl-d.com

***Abstract*— This paper provides a new technique that improves the all-quad meshing algorithm implemented in the WIPL-D software. The technique allows for the insertion of required auxiliary segments to achieve parity of a number of segments over all closed loop faces. The aim of the improvement is to reduce the total number of mesh elements in the final mesh. The efficiency of the proposed technique is compared to the traditional one mentioned earlier. A reduction in the number of mesh elements of about 15% has been achieved when applied to a log-periodic antenna WIPL-D model.**

Keywords — All-Quad Mesh, Fully Connected Mesh, Parity of Closed Loops, WIPL-D

I. Introduction

In most cases, a CEM simulation starts with meshing of an appropriate CAD model. From the perspective of this paper, emphasis is placed on MoM SIE numerical engines that typically implement triangular or quadrilateral mesh elements. It is shown in [1] that the use of a quadrilateral mesh results in a more efficient analysis. According to [2], using higher order basis functions (HOBFs), rather than low-order ones, brings an additional effectiveness to the method since it reduces memory requirements and increases simulation speed even further [3].

A quadrilateral meshing algorithm, optimized for HOBFs and based on reducing the meshing of an arbitrary shaped surface to the meshing of a flat polygon, is presented in [4]. A problem occurring with the mesh described in [4] is how to minimize the number of auxiliary segments to be added to the polyline representation of the edges, in order to achieve parity of the total number of segments over the closed loops of the faces. The requirement to achieve a fully connected mesh implies that the addition of auxiliary segments on an edge cannot be performed independently from the meshing of its adjacent faces. A technique to eliminate redundant auxiliary parity segments is suggested in [4]. In this paper, an improvement to the meshing technique that enables further reduction of the number of auxiliary parity segments, and consequently, a reduction of the total number of mesh elements in the final mesh, is described.

The quadrilateral meshing algorithm implemented in WIPL-D is briefly described in Section II. Improvement to the technique of insertion of parity segments over closed loops is described in Section III. Finally, a comparison between the technique described in [4] and the new technique is provided in Section IV.

II. Description of Meshing Algorithm

The specific all-quad meshing algorithm of interest is described in detail in [4]. Only the basics will be repeated here. The algorithm is composed of 5 steps:

1. Division of all faces into sub-faces. At the completion of this procedure, the angle between the normal vectors of any two points of a sub-face is smaller than or equal to the predefined surface angle tolerance.
2. Polyline representation of edges. The edges of sub-faces, created in Step 1 are divided into polylines according to the predefined mesh size and the edge angle tolerance. The lengths of all the segments within these polylines are less than or equal to the maximum mesh size. The outer angle between adjacent segments is less than or equal to the predefined edge angle tolerance.
3. Face projecting on a plane. All polyline nodes created in Step 2 are projected to a plane that uniquely corresponds to the face. In this way, a face is mapped into a flat polygon that lies in the plane. The plane itself contains a parametric center of the face and its normal vector is parallel to the normal vector of the face in its parametric center.
4. Quadrilateral meshing of flat polygons. The algorithm used for meshing flat polygons is described in [5]. This algorithm has been modified in order to take into account the shape of the face mapped to the polygon. In order to maintain face connectivity in the final mesh, insertion of additional points to the polygon edges is forbidden.
5. Projecting flat polygon meshes onto corresponding faces. Once the flat polygon is meshed, the final mesh is created by projecting the flat quads to the face.

III. Insertion of Auxiliary Segments

After the second phase of the algorithm described in Section II is completed, all quasi-planar sub-faces are ready to be projected onto the polygons that lie in the corresponding planes. Meshing of these polygons and the projection of the mesh elements onto the original sub-faces will then result in the final mesh of the structure. Nevertheless, polygons whose number of segments over closed loops is an odd number cannot be divided into quads without leaving triangular gaps in the division. Therefore, auxiliary segments have to be added to the polyline representation of certain edges in order to achieve an even number of segments over the closed loops of all sub-faces.

In the proposed technique, it is assumed that auxiliary segments have to be added to the polyline representation of all edges initially represented by a polyline with an odd number of segments. In the technique proposed in [4], the additional segments are not required on the edges that satisfy certain conditions. The basic idea of the new technique is that auxiliary segments can be added not only to the polylines that initially possess an odd number of segments, but to all polylines. The following principles are applied in the new technique:

- Edges going out from one vertex or going out from two adjacent vertices, must have an all even or an all odd number of segments. The decision regarding the parity of the edges is based on the number of additional auxiliary segments that should be added to the analyzed group in its entirety, in order to achieve the mentioned condition. A minimal number of auxiliary segments is preferred.
- If an auxiliary segment is already added to some edge from the analyzed group (as defined above), no change is allowed to the other edges, i.e., the initial requirement that the auxiliary segments should be added to odd edges but not even edges remains.

IV. Numerical Example

A comparison of the new technique and the one proposed in [4] is provided for the WIPL-D Pro CAD [6] model of a log-periodic antenna, shown in Fig. 1.

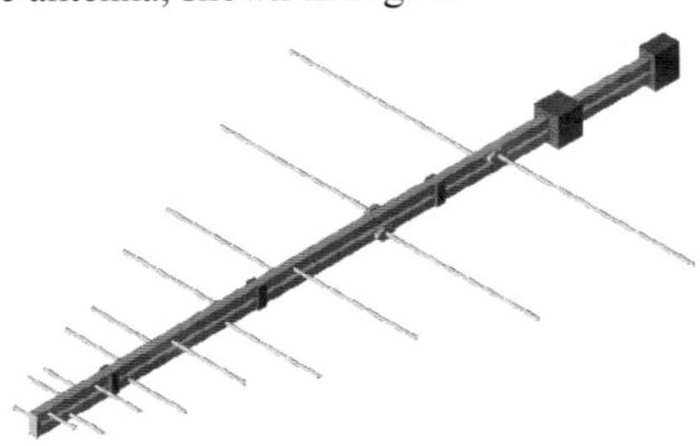

Fig. 1. WIPL-D Pro CAD model of a log-periodic antenna.

The antenna length is equal to 1.6 m. The longest dipole length is 1 m, and the shortest dipole length is 0.15 m. The antenna is simulated in the frequency range of 100 MHz to 1 GHz.

The number of mesh elements and number of unknown coefficients for the two techniques is provided in Table I. As can be seen, the new technique brings a reduction in both: number of mesh elements and number of unknown coefficients.

Table I. Number of Mesh Elements and Unknowns

Technique	Number of Mesh Elements	Number of Unknown Coefficients
Old technique	2056	7147
New technique	1764	6374

The mesh of the antenna obtained using the two techniques is shown in Fig. 2. The portions of the model where large differences in the meshes occurs are marked and magnified in the picture.

The meshes shown in Fig. 2 demonstrate that, in certain parts of the model, the number of mesh elements is reduced by a factor of 4 using the insertion of auxiliary parity segments technique proposed in this paper.

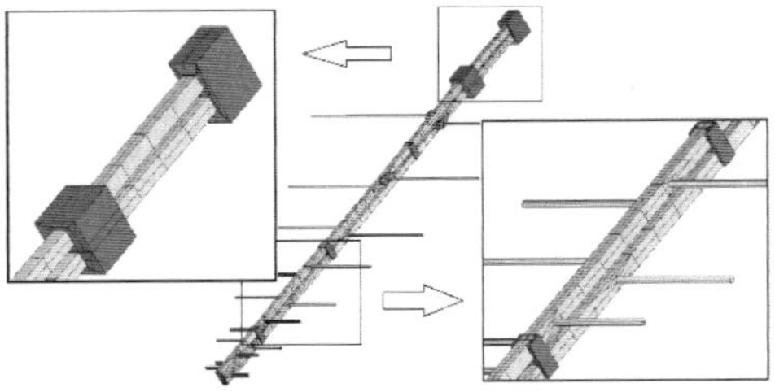

a) Old technique

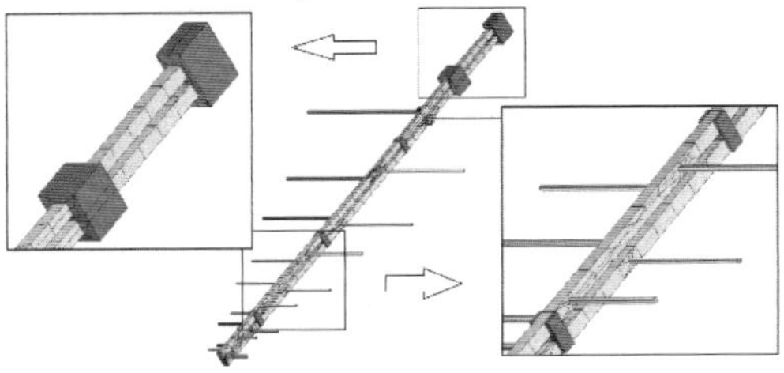

b) New technique

Fig. 2. All-quad mesh of log-periodic antenna.

V. Conclusion

The new technique of insertion of auxiliary segments, required to achieve parity of the total number of segments on the closed loops of the faces, has been introduced. The basic idea of the proposed method is that it allows the addition of auxiliary segments to all edges, and not only to those whose initial polyline representation contains an odd number of segments as previously proposed. Moreover, using the new technique significantly reduces the total number of mesh elements in the final mesh.

In this paper, the focus was solely on the number of mesh elements. Nevertheless, it is important to note that the new technique provides much more flexibility than its predecessor. Auxiliary segments can be added to edges represented by even and odd number of segments. Applying different criteria than the number of additional segments, such as minimal length of a segment or a number of segments over the analyzed edges, should also be considered in order to obtain a better mesh quality factor and further reduce the number of mesh elements.

References

[1] B. M. Kolundzija and A. R. Djordjevic, Electromagnetic Modeling of Composite Metallic and Dielectric Structures, Artech House, Norwood, 2002.

[2] B. M. Kolundzija and B. D. Popovic, "Entire- Domain Galerkin Method for Analysis of Metallic Antennas and Scatterers," IEE Proceedings-H, vol. 140, no. 1, pp. 1-10, Feb. 1993.

[3] B. M. Kolundzija, "Comparison of a class of subdomain and entire domain basis functions automatically satisfying KCL," IEEE Transactions on Antennas and Propagation, vol. 44. no. 10, Oct. 1996.

[4] B. Lj. Mrdakovic, et al., "A New Method for Quadrilateral Meshing of Arbitrary Shaped Geometry Based on Meshing of Flat Polygons," European Conference on Antennas and Propagation (EuCAP), The Hague, Netherlands, Apr. 6-11, 2014.

[5] M. S. Tasic and B. M. Kolundzija, "Efficient electromagnetic modeling based on automated quadrilateral meshing of polygons," Elsvier Science Proc., Eng. Analysis with Boundary Elements 27, pp. 361-373, 2003.

[6] WIPL-D Pro CAD 2019, WIPL-D d.o.o, Belgrade, 2019.

Rectangular Slot Array Antenna

Elvis J. Trinidad Garcia
NAWCAD
Radar, Antennas and Sensor Fusion Division
Patuxent River, MD, USA
elvis.j.garcia@navy.mil

Ruben P. Ortega
NAWCAD
Radar, Antennas and Sensor Fusion Division
Patuxent River, MD, USA
ruben.ortega1@navy.mil

Saad N. Tabet
NAWCAD
Radar, Antennas and Sensor Fusion Division
Patuxent River, MD, USA
saad.tabet@navy.mil

***Abstract*—Slot antenna elements are quite popular for use in flat-panel arrays, due to their compactness and relatively large bandwidth. According to Babinet's Principle, slots and dipoles are duals in performance. Therefore, a vertically placed slot is horizontally polarized and a horizontally placed slot is vertically polarized. A rectangular slot array lends itself to a broad range of applications, e.g., tactical and weather radar. Such arrays can be gimbaled to point their beam in any azimuth and elevation angle of interest. In this effort, a slot antenna element is designed in WIPL-D Pro to operate over the 7.5 - 8.5 GHz frequency range. The element is designed to resonate at 8 GHz. The slot element is used to generate a 6x12 slot array normal to the xy-plane. Separate Taylor tapers (nbar = 5) are applied to the 6-row and 12-column elements to provide 25 dB and 30 dB sidelobe level (SLL) suppression, respectively. The input impedance and pattern performance for a single slot, as well as the slot array's radiation performance show excellent broadband performance.**

Keywords*— *Array, Broadband, Sidelobe, Slot, Taylor Taper, WIPL-D.

I. Introduction

A slot antenna is a very useful type of antenna for specific applications. Its duality with respect to a dipole (Babinet's Principle) is one of its primary features, especially when a vertically oriented, horizontally polarized antenna is required. When a large number of half-wave dipoles is used to produce a horizontally polarized array, the width of the array may become physically untenable. On the other hand, a similar array built from half-wave slots would be vertically oriented, allowing for a much larger number of slot elements to be included in the same available space.

A common application for slot arrays is in horizontally polarized tactical and weather radar, where the array is positioned normal to the xy-plane. The need for a much narrow azimuth beamwidth (BW) relative to the elevation BW, lends itself quite well for the use of vertical slot arrays. In such a configuration, a large number of elements in each row and a much smaller number of elements in each column are used to produce a narrow azimuth beam and wider elevation beam (known as a fan beam), respectively.

According to Babinet's Principle, a center-fed half-wave thin slot placed in an infinite Perfect Electric Conductor (PEC) plane is the dual of a center-fed half-wave dipole of infinitesimal wire radius. The input impedance of the slot is related to that of the half-wave dipole as provided in [1]. The resulting input impedance is very high, hence poorly matched to 50 Ω. Moreover, in order for a slot to be useful in antenna array applications, a slot element must be confined to a finite space. Those elements can then be duplicated to form an array with properties unique to the application at hand.

In this effort, a self-contained slot antenna is designed in WIPL-D Pro [2]. The self-contained slot is then used to design a 6x12 vertical slot array. Separate Taylor tapers (nbar = 5; Number of nearly constant adjacent sidelobes) are applied to the 6-row and 12-column elements to provide 25 dB and 30 dB sidelobe levels (SLLs), respectively.

II. Modeling Effort Details

A. Slot Antenna and Array Design and Modeling

A self-contained slot antenna (antenna from hereon), as shown in Fig. 1, was designed in WIPL-D for an 8 GHz center frequency and a 7.5 - 8.5 GHz frequency range of operation. The slot length was set to half-wave at 8 GHz, while its width was set to 0.015λ. The slot feed location was swept from its center towards one end until a perfect match to 50 Ω at 8 GHz was achieved. The slot was designed to be self-contained in a rectangular box. The backplane of the box was set to 0.25λ at 8 GHz, for best boresight performance. The height and width of the box were arbitrarily chosen and each set to 1″.

The antenna input impedance and VSWR performance, from 7.5 – 8.5 GHz, are shown in Fig. 2. Principal azimuth and elevation cut overlays at 7.5, 8 and 8.5 GHz are shown in Figs. 3 and 4, respectively.

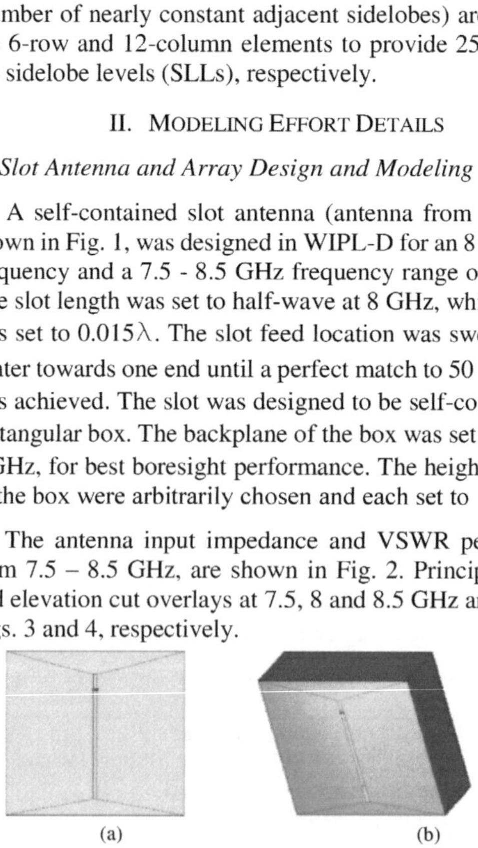

(a) (b)

Fig. 1. Slot Antenna Model. (a) Front View; (b) Isometric View.

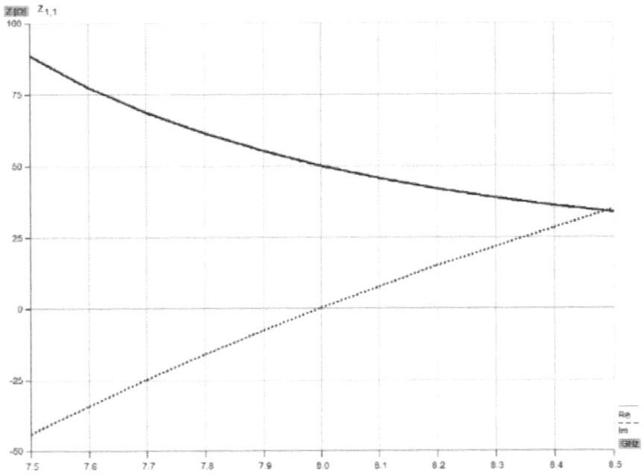

(a)

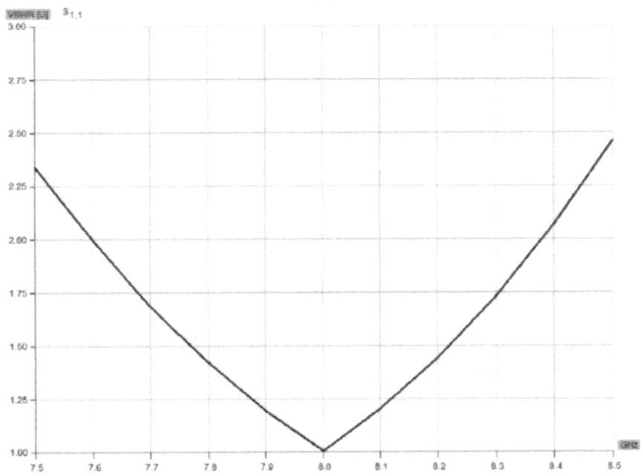

(b)

Fig. 2. Slot Antenna Parameters. (a) Input Impedance; (b) VSWR.

A slot array was then formed by copying the one slot element model five times to form one 6-element column sub-array. Then the entire 6-element column was grouped and copied 11 times to form the entire 6x12 (6″x12″) slot array, as shown in Fig. 3.

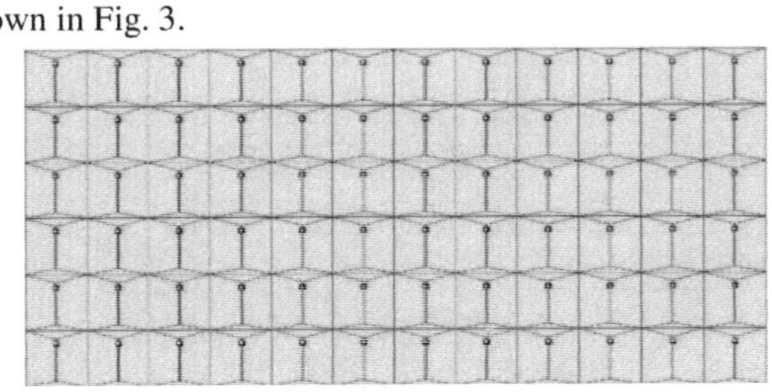

(a)

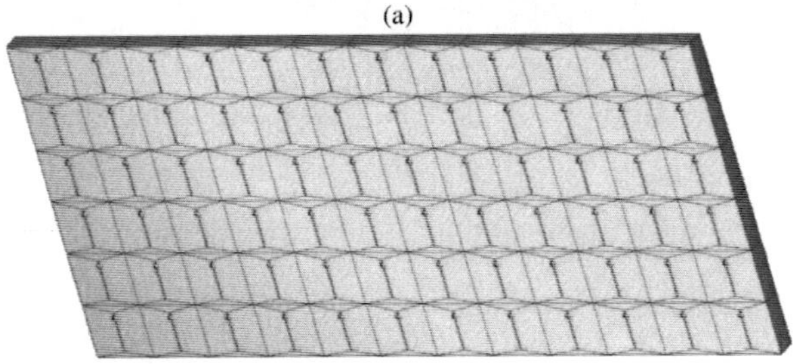

(b)

Fig. 3. Slot Antenna Array Model. (a) Front View; (b) Isometric View.

The slot array's Principal azimuth and elevation cut overlays at 7.5, 8 and 8.5 GHz are shown in Figs. 4 and 5, respectively.

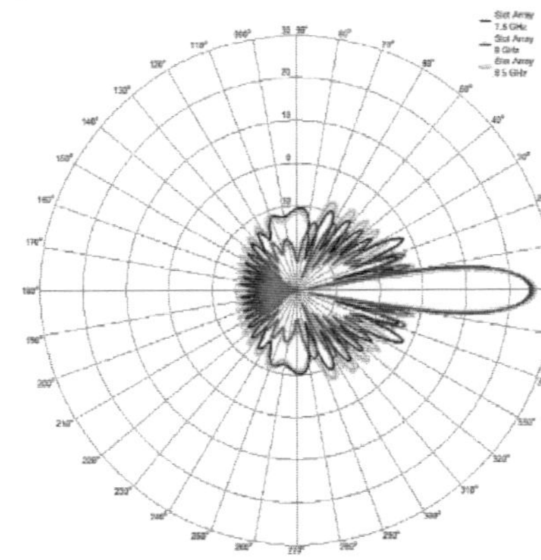

Fig. 4. Slot Array Principal Azimuth Cut Overlays.

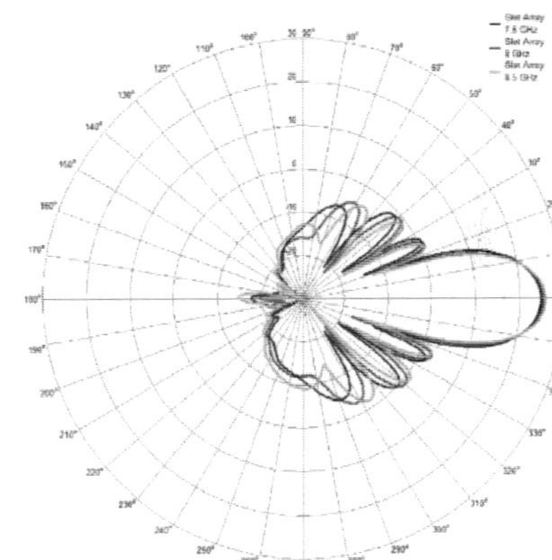

Fig. 4. Slot Array Principal Elevation Cut Overlays.

III. CONCLUSIONS

A compact self-contained slot antenna element is designed to provide directional boresight radiation and good impedance matching to 50 Ω, over a relatively broad range of frequencies. Due to its compact size, the slot element is used to produce a 6x12 element array that fit within a 6″x12″ space, respectively. The array exhibits consistent azimuth and elevation gain, BW and SLL performance relative to the design parameters, across the entire 7.5 – 8.5 GHz frequency range of operation.

REFERENCES

[1] C. A. Balanis, Antenna Theory– Analysis and Design, 4th Edition, Hoboken, NJ: John Wiley and Sons, 2016, pp. 680-684.

[2] WIPL-D Pro, Software and User's Manual, WIPL-D d.o.o., Belgrade, 2019.

Generation of Radiation Patterns Equivalent to In-Flight Measurements

Ruben P. Ortega
NAWCAD
Radar, Antenna, and Sensor Fusion Division
Patuxent River, MD, USA
ruben.ortega1@navy.mil

Lauren M. Jugler
NAWCAD
Radar, Antenna, and Sensor Fusion Division
Patuxent River, MD, USA
lauren.jugler@navy.mil

Yaseman Shiri
NAWCAD
Radar, Antenna, and Sensor Fusion Division
Patuxent River, MD, USA
yaseman.shiri4@navy.mil

Saad N. Tabet
NAWCAD
Radar, Antenna, and Sensor Fusion Division
Patuxent River, MD, USA
saad.tabet@navy.mil

***Abstract*—Comparison of in-situ measured antenna radiation patterns (RPs) to modeled ones is vital for validation of both. In-flight measured RPs do not always produce a standard conic or elevation cut (constant θ or ϕ angle, respectively), but rather Great Circle (GC) cuts at the aircraft bank angle of interest. WIPL-D's post-processing routines, on the other hand, do not produce GC cuts in normal setups. A manipulation of the aircraft orientation in xyz-coordinates is required to accomplish this task. Under standard conditions in WIPL-D, the fuselage is positioned parallel to the x-axis and the wings parallel to the y-axis. A model rotation of 90° with respect to the y-axis allows for the generation of GC cuts, where θ and ϕ swap roles. This makes comparison between in-flight measurements and computed data cumbersome. This paper investigates several options to produce non-standard RPs in WIPL-D and MATLAB (using WIPL-D results) that are equivalent to those of in-flight measurements.**

Keywords—Great Circle, In-flight measurements, Radiation Pattern, WIPL-D.

I. Introduction

In-flight Radiation Pattern (RP) measurements for in-situ antennas are normally collected by flying the aircraft in a circular flight path at a distance from the data collection tower. As the aircraft executes its flight path, collected points that are away from the aircraft's centerline will be above the aircraft's horizon on one side and below the aircraft's horizon on the opposite side. The collected data points form a great circle (GC) cut at a bank angle γ with respect to the aircraft's horizon, as shown in Fig. 1.

For a single simulation run, the WIPL-D Pro graphing utility provides the ability to plot standard conic and elevation cuts, assuming the aircraft is oriented in standard position (x-axis is parallel to the fuselage, y-axis is parallel to the wings, and positive z-axis towards zenith). Multiple runs would be required to produce both standard and non-standard cuts. A simple rotation of the aircraft along the x-axis for each γ angle will produce the desired data. However, this approach may be prohibitive if data sets for a large number of cases (frequencies and/or bank angles) are being analyzed. This is especially true for models with very large number of unknowns. This effort provides a description of how to achieve non-standard GC cuts, in WIPL-D, using various methods.

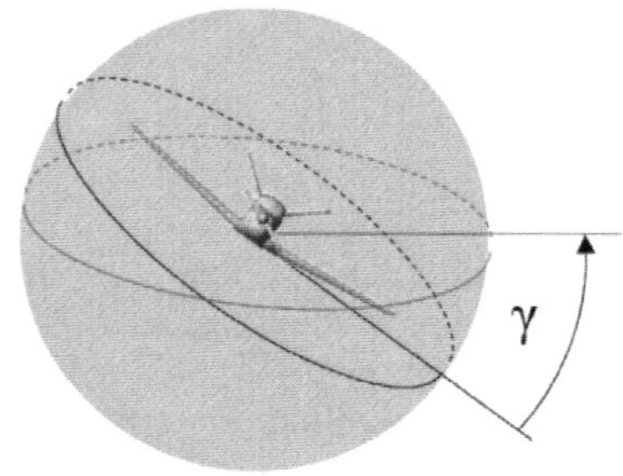

Fig. 1. Great Circle Illustration at Angle γ.

II. CEM Modeling Details

A half-wave cross-dipole antenna, arbitrarily designed to operate at 300 MHz, was constructed in WIPL-D. Its dipole elements were fed in quadrature, to produce right-hand circular polarization (RHCP). The antenna was then placed a quarter-wavelength above the surface of a Beechcraft Bonanza aircraft WIPL-D model, as shown in Fig. 2. The model was run at 300 MHz in WIPL-D using the standard position to produce standard elevation and conic cuts. The model was subsequently run in various orientations to generate GC cuts for each of the methods, as described below.

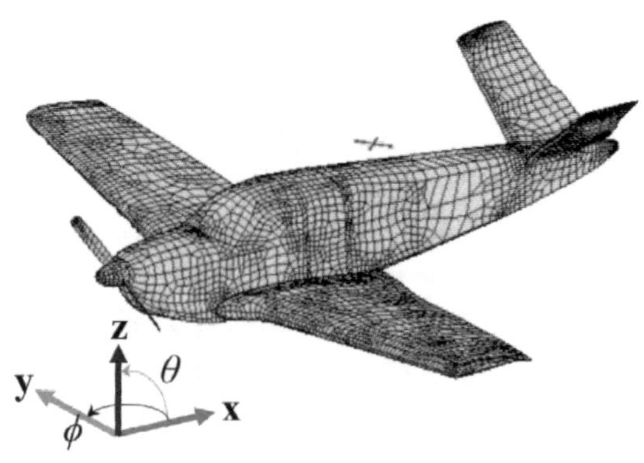

Fig. 2. Cross-Dipole Onboard Beechcraft Bonanza WIPL-D Model.

A. *Rotation about x-axis*

For each bank angle γ of interest, rotate the model about the x-axis accordingly and re-run the model individually. This is the reference case, since it emulates real world in-flight measurements.

B. *Sampling discrete points on full sphere*

Generate a dense three-dimensional (3-D) RP over the entire 4π steradian space. Rotate the $\gamma = 0°$ cut, [1], to the bank angle of interest. Run a MATLAB post-processing routine to interpolate the gain values from the original 3-D RP file to generate the GC cut of interest.

C. *Matrix inversion avoided*

Run the CEM model in the standard position and save a copy of the WIPL-D generated current distribution ".dis" file, as well as the WIPL-D input ".IWP" file, [2]. Open the ".IWP" and modify it by rotating the model by the bank angle γ. Turn on the "Matrix Inversion Avoided" option in WIPL-D. Set the RP output to provide only the principal azimuth cut, re-run the model to generate the corresponding GC cut quickly. This process is repeated to generate GC cuts for other bank angles of interest.

D. *Rotation about y-axis*

Rotate the standard position model by 90° along the y-axis, as shown in Fig. 3. Set up and run the model to generate elevation cuts that actually represent the GC cuts of interest. However, the equivalent θ–range must be -90° to 270°, to match the ϕ-range of 0° to 360° for the standard position, respectively.

Comparison of GC gain, for $\gamma = 20°$, in Method B to the reference case is provided in Fig. 4. Comparison of Methods C and D, for $\gamma = 20°$, to the reference case is provided in Fig. 5. Comparison of unwrapped GC phase in Method D, for $\gamma = 20°$, to the reference case is shown in Fig. 6.

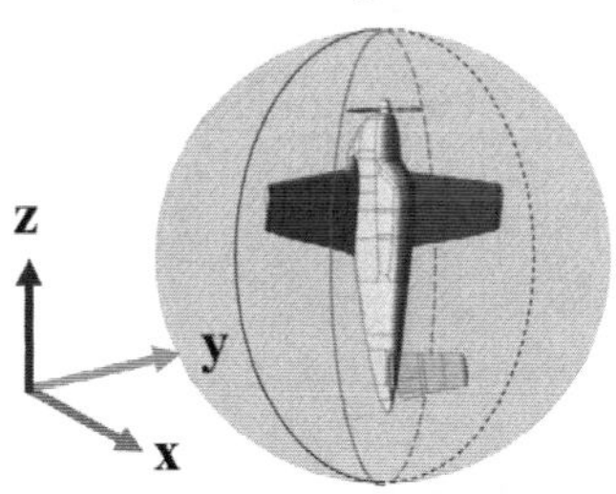

Fig. 3. Beechcraft Bonanza WIPL-D Model Rotated 90° about y-Axis.

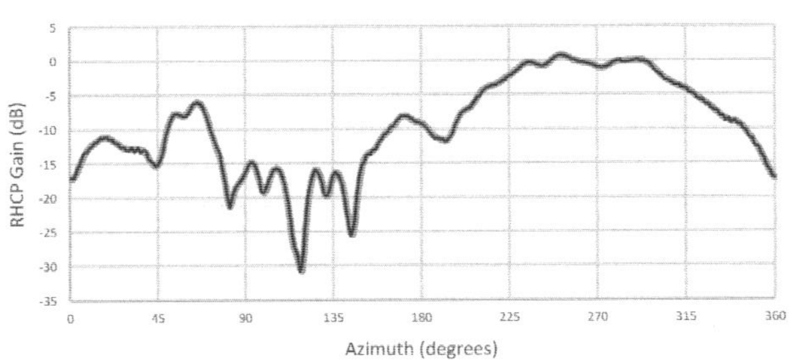

Fig. 4. Gain Comparison of Discrete Sampling to Reference Case.

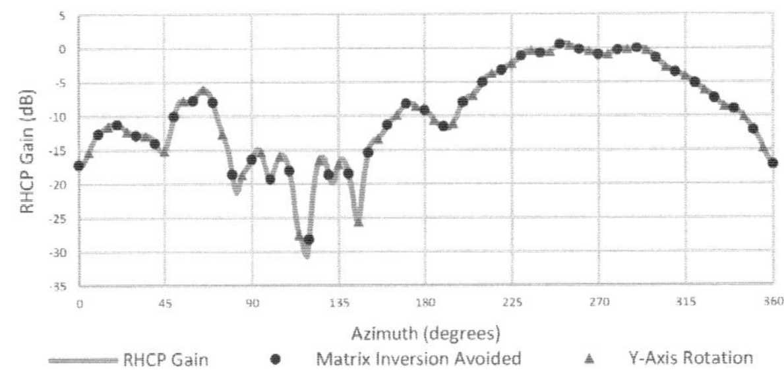

Fig. 5. Gain Comparison of Matrix Inversion Avoided and y-Axis Rotation to Reference Case.

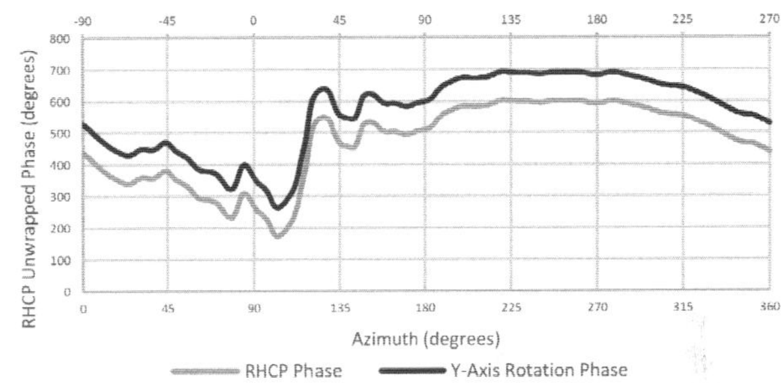

Fig. 6. Phase Comparison of y-Axis Rotation to Reference Case.

III. Conclusions

Even though it is equivalent to in-flight measurements, the reference case has the major drawback of having to run the model multiple times. This is not an issue when the WIPL-D model has a very low number of unknowns, and runs in a few minutes. However, that is not the case when there are many frequencies to study and the model grows into the hundreds of thousands of unknowns, taking hours to days to run each case individually.

The discrete sampling method, Method B, requires very small increments in θ and ϕ to yield acceptable results, especially for linear polarization components where the error increases with the increase in γ. This requires a significant amount of additional post-processing to overcome. The Matrix Inversion Avoided method (Method C) is ideally suited for this purpose. However, when WIPL-D automatically internally re-meshes the model, this could lead to a mismatch between the stored current coefficients and the respective surfaces to which they belong, thus producing erroneous results. The rotation about the y-axis method (Method D) generates identical GC gain results to the reference case. However, all the unwrapped GC phase results shifted by 90°, even though the RHCP feature of the cross-dipole is preserved. The root cause for this phase shift must be investigated further, but is suspected to mainly be due to the contrasting ways θ and ϕ are incremented.

References

[1] G. Strang, Linear Algebra and its Applications, 4th Edition, Belmont, CA: Thompson Corporation, 2006, pp. 130–132.

[2] WIPL-D Pro, Software and User's Manual, WIPL-D d.o.o., Belgrade, Serbia 2019.

Wide band antenna with Ultra-smooth spectral characteristics

Agaram Raghunathan, B.S. Girish, R.Somashekar, K.S. Srivani
Electronics Engineering Group
Raman Research Institute
Bangalore, India
raghu@rri.res.in , bsgiri@rri.res.in, som@rri.res.in, vani_4s@rri.res.in

Saurabh Singh, Ravi Subrahmanyan
Astronomy and Astrophysics Group
Raman Research Institute
Bangalore, India
saurabhs@rri.res.in, rsubrahm@rri.res.in

N.Udaya Shankar, Mayuri Sathyanarayana Rao, Jishnu Nambissan T
Astronomy and Astrophysics Group
Raman Research Institute
Bangalore, India
uday@rri.res.in, mayuris@rri.res.in,jishnu@rri.res.in

***Abstract*—Understanding the evolution of Universe is, in the forefront of, the modern day observational cosmology. It requires precise and accurate measurement of cosmological signal, orders of magnitude weaker than the bright sky background. Detection of such a signal having distinct spectral signature, needs an antenna with frequency independent characteristics over more than an octave bandwidth. A spherical monopole antenna has been designed to operate in the frequency range 50-200 MHz with a spectral smoothness of about few parts in 10^4. The structure has been modeled and optimized using WIPL-D, to minimize spectral features arising out of abrupt reflections of surface currents and frequency dependent radiation patterns. A prototype has been built to validate the design. This paper presents the methodology adopted in the overall antenna design, experiences in its prototyping and simulation and the measurement results.**

Keywords—Cosmic microwave background radiation, antenna.

I. INTRODUCTION

Continuous efforts are being made to get a better understanding of the thermal history of the Universe. Astrophysical evolution over cosmic times is predicted to distort the spectrum of the primordial cosmic microwave background radiation. In the evolutionary process of the Universe, Epoch of reionization (EoR) is considered as an important period during which the universe had a complete transformation from its neutral state to ionized state. Spin flip transition in neutral hydrogen during this era resulted in the generation of 21cm signal corresponding to 1420 MHz. This signal is predicted to distort the spectrum of cosmic microwave background radiation and appear today at red shifted frequency range of 50-200 MHz due to the cosmological expansion of the Universe[1]. The magnitude of the distortion (~20mK) is predicted to be orders of magnitude weaker than the bright sky background(~3000K) at these frequencies. Hence, detection of such a signal requires a wideband antenna free from spectral features.

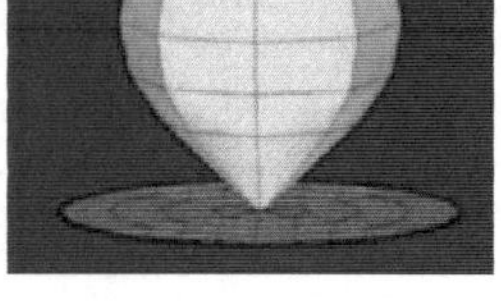

Fig.1.Simulated spherical Monopole antenna structure

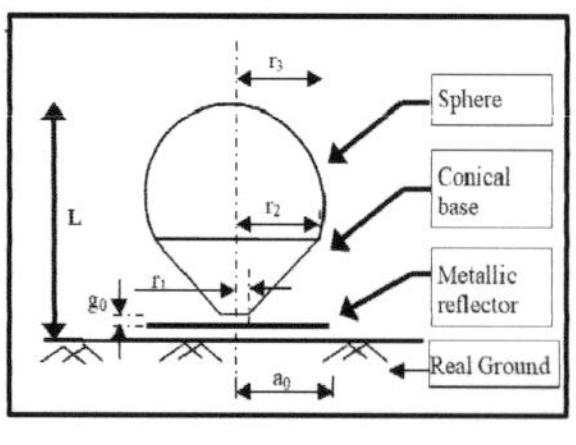

Fig.2. Schematic diagram of the antenna structure wit real earth below.

It is an engineering challenge to design an antenna of more than an octave bandwidth with frequency independent characteristics. Frequency dependent radiation and impedance characteristics and squint in the antenna pointing in the sky result in undesirable features similar to the cosmological signal of interest, in the antenna's spectral response. We have designed a spherical monopole antenna to operate in its non-resonant mode in the frequency range of 50-200 MHz. It has i) a return loss of more than 10 dB at the highest frequency and an acceptable 0.05 dB at the lowest frequency ii) frequency independent radiation patterns and iii) spectral response smooth to an extent of few parts in 10^4. Sections below describe design methodology adopted, fabrication details, measurement and simulation results and summary of work carried out.

II. DESIGN METHODOLOGY

Literature lists [2] as ultra wide band spherical monopole antenna. We have appropriately modified it to suit our requirement. While modifying it, it is i) made electrically small at the highest operating frequency to achieve frequency independent radiation patterns and ii) shaped to minimize reactive component of antenna impedance. Cone introduced at the feeding section for impedance match is made to intersect the sphere at the top tangentially to ensure smooth transition at their line of contact. The structural dimensions of the antenna are optimized in WIPL-D to reduce the undesirable features in the spectral response caused by the multiple reflections of the surface current. While this is carried out, the dielectric constant and conductivity are assumed to be 13 and 0.005 S/m. The simulated structure with real earth around and its schematic showing dimensions symbolically are shown in Figs.1-2. The optimized dimensions expressed as fractions of design wavelength of 1333mm are: i) radius of sphere($r3$)=0.11,ii)radius of feeding conic section at the top($r2$)=0.0765iii)radius of feeding conic section at the bottom($r1$)=0.0045 iv)gap at the feeding section(g_0)=0.001,v)=radius of metallic reflector(a_0)=0.3 and vi)length of monopole antenna(L)=0.26.

III. FABRICATION DETAILS

The fabricated antenna is shown in Fig.3. It has mainly two parts:i)conic section at the feeding point and ii) sphere on top as radiator. Conic section is fabricated by turning an aluminium cylinder block to the desired shape and spherical

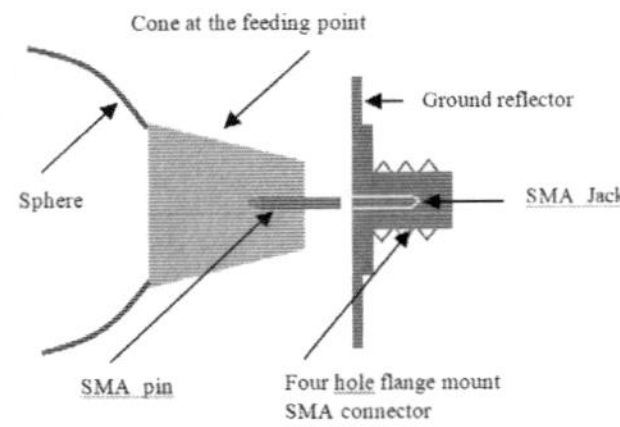

Fig.3 Antenna prototype fabricated

Fig.4 Mechanism adopted to excite the antenna

radiator is fabricated using metal spinning process. The metal spinning is a cold forming process of forming a blank metal sheet into the desired shape. The excitation of the antenna is done using SMA pin-jack arrangement as shown in Fig. 4. Pin is made part of the antenna and jack is inserted in the reflector. Styrofoam is used for supporting the antenna.

IV. MEASUREMENT AND RESULTS

The spherical monopole antenna was characterised by measuring its return loss and radiation patterns in the field. Since the moisture content in the ground was observed to influence the antenna characteristics significantly, all the measurements were carried out under dry ground conditions Fig.5 shows return loss characteristics. Both simulation and measurement results made by Agilent N9915A - Field fox microwave hand held analyser are observed to match closely within few percent. The residuals obtained after fitting the measured return loss data with maximally smooth function is shown in Fig. 6. We observe that the return loss characteristics has smoothness to a few parts in 10^4, but still an order poorer than the desired value.

The simulated and measured radiation patterns at several discrete frequencies are shown in Figs. 7 and 8. Measured patterns matched with the simulation within 10-12 % of their 3 dB beamwidths. The observed deviation in the peak position at low frequencies is attributed primarily to the near field effect and reflections from nearby objects. The total efficiency computed is shown in Fig.9. Poor efficiency observed at low frequencies is primarily due to loss of sky signal by the absorption of real earth and poor impedance match of the antenna respectively.

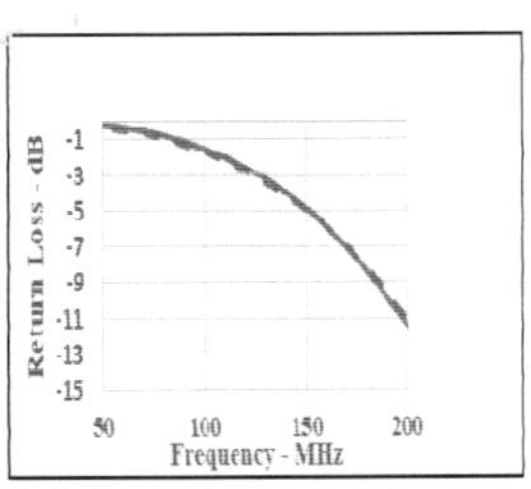

Fig.5. Return loss characteristics: Solid line is simulation and dotted is measurement

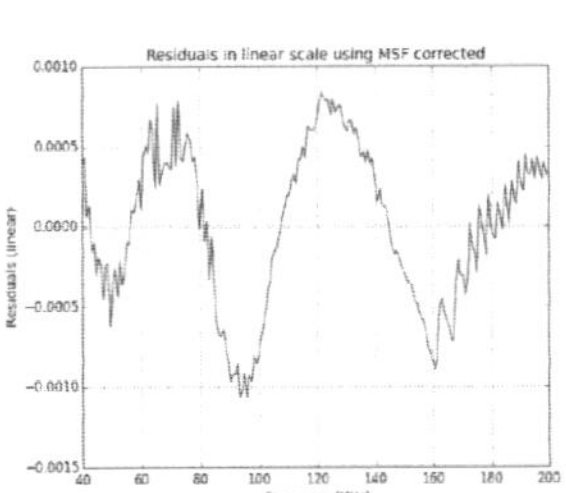

Fig.6. Residuals obtained after fitting the measured return loss data with maximally smooth function.

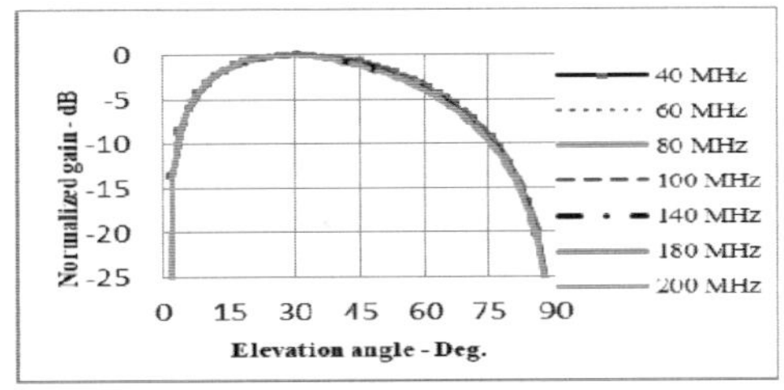

Fig.7. Simulated radiation patterns of the spherical monopole antenna at discrete frequencies in the range 40 -200 MHz

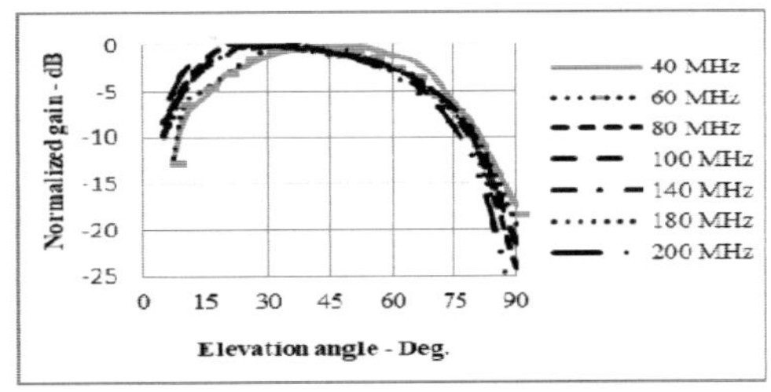

Fig.8. Measured radiation patterns of the spherical monopole antenna at discrete frequencies in the range 40 - 200 MHz

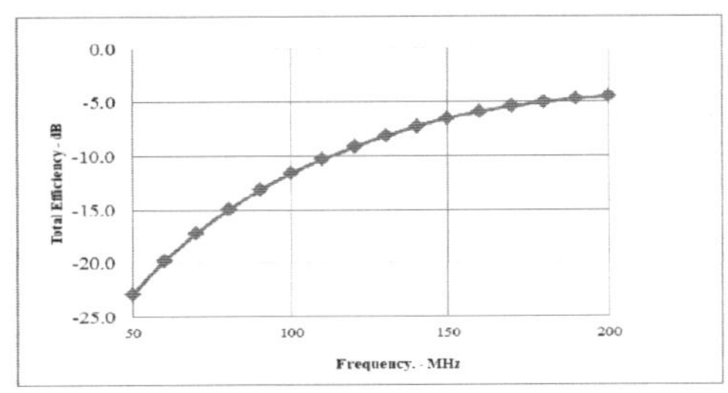

Fig.9. Total Efficiency computed from return loss and radiation efficiency

V. SUMMARY

We have designed a wide band spherical monopole antenna for detecting EoR signal in the freq. range 50-200 MHz. It has acceptable return loss of about 0.05 dB at 50 MHz and better than 10 dB at 200 MHz, However its spectral response is smooth to few parts in 10^4. The radiation patterns are frequency independent with a maximum deviation of 10-12% in their 3dB beamwidths. The total efficiency observed at low frequencies is inadequate for the detection of EoR signal. Work is in progress towards constructing one which is most suitable for the detection.

ACKNOWLEDGEMENT

We acknowledge all the people of Electronics Engineering Group, workshop and Gauribidanur observatory who have helped us build the antenna and do the measurements in the field.

REFERENCES

1. J. R. Pritchard, and A. Loeb, "21 cm cosmology in the 21st century", Reports on Progress in Physics, 75, 086901, 2012.
2. Cheolbok Kim; Kyoung Tae Kim; Yong-Kyu Yoon; Jong Kyu Kim., Spherical Super Wideband (SWB) Monopole Antenna With Micromachined Tapered Feeding Line., IEEE Antennas and Propagation Society International Symposium.,pg.226-227, 2013.

Frequency-Selective Planar Coil Architecture Modeling for WPT Access Control

Xinyue Zhou
Department of Electrical and Computer Engineering
Miami University
Oxford, OH
zhoux17@miamiOH.edu

Dmitriy Garmatyuk
Department of Electrical and Computer Engineering
Miami University
Oxford, OH
garmatd@miamiOH.edu

***Abstract*— In this paper, an approach to access control in wireless power transfer (WPT) systems via frequency-selective architecture is proposed. We perform modeling of planar square loop resonance behavior in GHz range using Ansys HFSS®. Power transfer efficiency is found from the accepted power and radiated power. Using a multi-coil design, where the transmitter and receiver switch between coils of different resonance frequencies in sync, can provide for effective access control. Modeling results for a prototype coil design that will lead to this functionality are presented and discussed.**

Keywords*— *Access control in WPT systems Ansys HFSS, power transfer efficiency, resonant coupling, wireless power transfer.

I. Introduction

Wireless power transfer (WPT) techniques have received considerable interest in recent years [1–3]. For the near-field (non-radiative) range, WPT can be achieved via inductive coupling and magneto-dynamic coupling. In [1], the authors have proposed to utilize resonant inductive coupling to achieve non-radiative mid-range energy transfer. By utilizing strong resonant coupling between the primary and secondary coils, the efficiency was shown to reach nearly 40% over the distance as great as 2 meters. However, with the growing interest in extending WPT range, access control may become problematic. The possibility of power theft will need to be addressed as mid-range WPT systems can proliferate as widely as Wi-Fi in the near future. Our previous work focused on experimental validation of one approach to implementing access control via multiple tunable coils [4]. In it, we have introduced both the frequency-selective tuned coil architecture and a method of pseudo-random frequency hopping. The experimental prototype was intended for the relatively low-frequency range of operations. In this work, we consider WPT access control for multiple GHz in frequency.

Frequency-selective WPT multi-receiver design has been investigated in [5], where different resonance frequencies were used to achieve selective power transfer. Resonant coupling naturally results in minimum interaction with nearby off-resonant objects and free space. With this well-established physical principle, access control can be achieved by utilizing multiple coils and switching between them in a fashion known to the authorized receiver only. WPT efficiency can then reach its maximum only if the primary and secondary coils are in resonance, while for other off-resonant receivers the power transfer efficiency (PTE) will be extremely low.

This project was supported by the 2019 Miami University Undergraduate Summer Scholar (USS) program.

II. Proposed Access-Controlled Architecture

A block diagram for the access-controlled multi-coil (ACMC) system is shown in Fig. 1. The transmitter (TX) can choose which oscillator and coil are enabled at each transmission interval. Only the authorized receiver (RX) can follow the switching pattern of the transmitter. An un-authorized single-coil device will be out of resonance for a significant duration of time, thus achieving much lower PTE. Synchronization between TX and RX is outside the scope of this paper and will be addressed in the future.

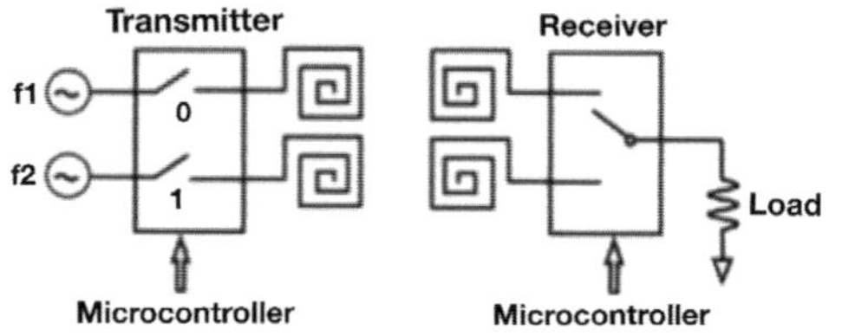

Fig. 1. ACMC system block diagram.

The simulation model of a single-loop primary coil is shown in Fig. 2. This single planar copper coil is modeled with Ansys HFSS® for a range of dimensions, with the coil length of 70 mm, 1 mm trace width and 0.1 mm trace height. The secondary coil is identical to the first one and is placed at distances from D to 5D, where D is the length of the loop diagonal.

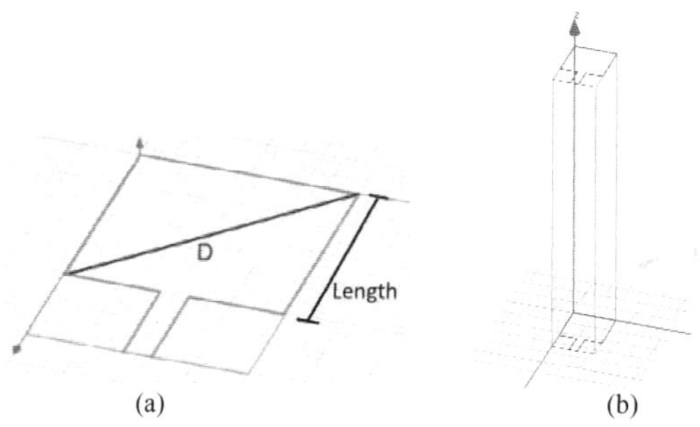

Fig. 2. Simulation model: (a) single planar coil; (b) two identical coils spaced by 5D.

III. Simulation Results

The HFSS® simulations were run for a frequency span from 1 GHz to 20 GHz. "Infinite Sphere" radiation option was set up to calculate the accepted and radiated power. Reflection loss, S_{11} and insertion loss, S_{21} were analyzed to ascertain the resonance frequency of a single coil, and the PTE between any two coils, respectively. Coil dimensions and distance between the coils were also varied. An example of S_{11} and S_{21} for the 70 mm-length coil is shown in Fig. 3.

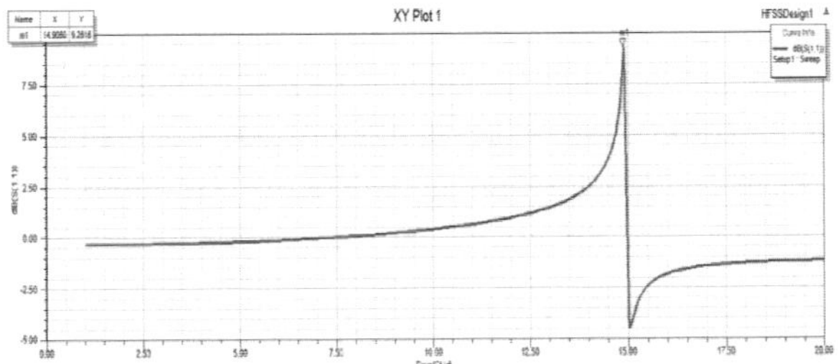

(a)

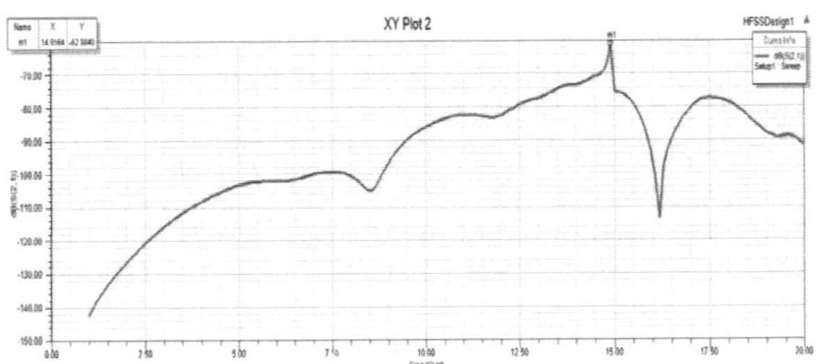

(b)

Fig. 3. S-parameters for the sample system: (a) S_{11}; (b) S_{21}.

To demonstrate the access control potential, two 70 mm-length coils were placed 396 mm apart and frequency sweep simulations were run from 2.5 GHz to 23 GHz. Results for ACMC system modeling are shown in Fig. 4. There were no other objects in the simulation; also, losses in loop material were not accounted for, leading to somewhat idealistic setup and results.

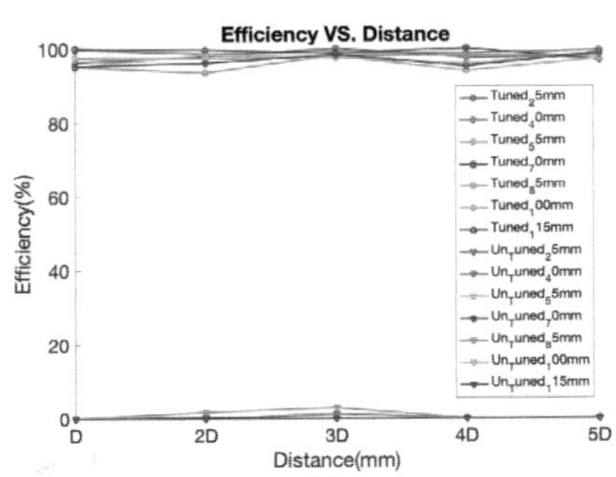

(a)

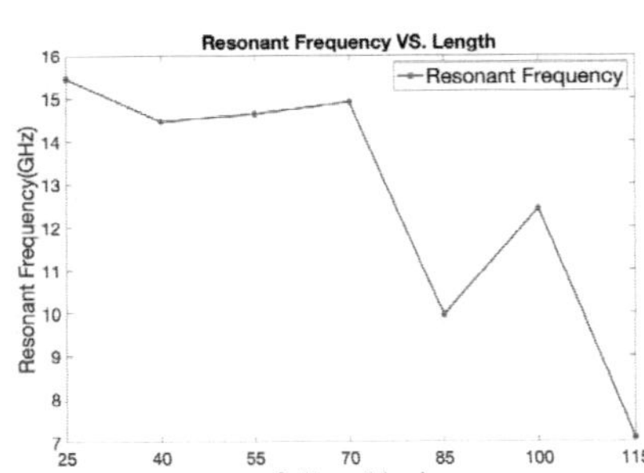

(b)

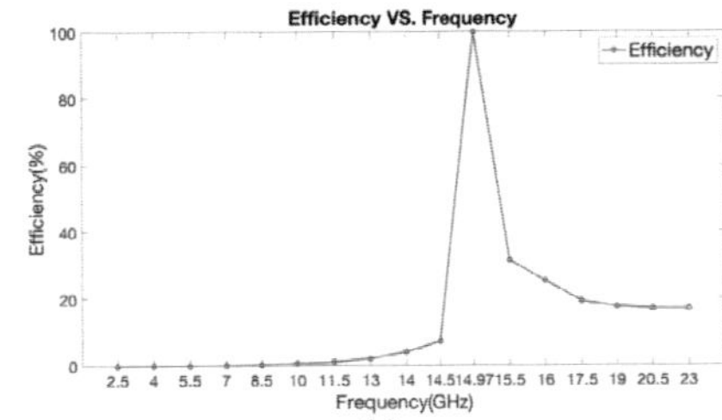

(c)

Fig. 4. HFSS® simulation results: (a) PTE vs. distance; (b) resonance frequency vs. coil length; (c) PTE vs. frequency.

Fig. 4 (a) shows PTE of tuned and untuned coils as a function of distance between them. Fig. 4 (b) shows dependence of the planar square coil's resonant frequency on its side length. Fig. 4 (c) shows PTE as function of frequency – e.g., PTE reaches nearly 100% at 14.97 GHz, while detuning results in 7.2% PTE at 14.5 GHz.

Our modeling confirms that the proposed approach is viable for creating ACMC systems. A diagram of an ACMC transmitter employing a frequency multiplier is shown in Fig. 5. Here, four different coils are connected to different outputs of the frequency multiplier, where e.g., "X2" stands for double the original frequency f0.

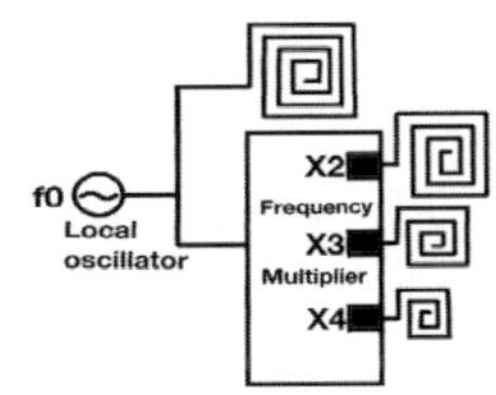

Fig. 5. Simplified design for multi-loop ACMC WPT system.

IV. Conclusion

In this work, we have modeled an approach to ACMC WPT system design based on resonance frequency selectivity for planar square coils in the GHz frequency range. Our findings confirm the feasibility of the approach in which an authorized receiver switches between its multiple coils in-sync with the transmitter, which leads to maximum PTE for the tuned systems and provides for much lower efficiency of an unauthorized single-coil interceptor. Our future work includes building an experimental ACMC WPT system based on a frequency multiplier and implementing synchronization strategies.

References

[1] A. Kurs, A. Kaalis, R. Moffatt, J. D. Joannopoulos, P. Fisher, and M. Soljačić, "Wireless power transfer via strongly coupled magnetic resonances," Science, vol. 317, no. 5834, pp. 83-86, Jul. 2007.

[2] S. Y. R. Hui, W. Zhong, and C. K. Lee, "A critical review of recent progress in mid-range wireless power transfer," IEEE Trans. Power Electron., vol. 29, no. 9, pp. 4500-4511, Sep. 2014.

[3] Ansys HFSS Blog: Wireless Power Transfer (website). Available: https://www.ansys.com/blog/wireless-power-transfer, 2019.

[4] T. Maschino, "Frequency-selective design of wireless power transfer systems for controlled access applications," M. S. Thesis, Miami University, 2016.

[5] Y. Zhang, T. Lu, Z. Zhao, et al., "Selective wireless power transfer to multiple loads using receivers of different resonant frequencies," IEEE Trans. Power Electron., vol. 30, no. 11, pp. 6001-6005, 2015.

Effects of the Human Body on Wearable Wireless Power Transfer Systems

Gianfranco Perez-Greco, Juan Barreto, Abdul-Sattar Kaddour, and Stavros V. Georgakopoulos
Department of Electrical and Computer Engineering
Florida International University
Miami, FL, USA
gpere227@fiu.edu, jbarr244@fiu.edu, akaddour@fiu.edu, georgako@fiu.edu

***Abstract*—In this paper, the effects of different parts of the human body on a wearable Wireless Power Transfer (WPT) system are examined. A Strongly Coupled Magnetic Resonators (SCMR) WPT system operating in the ISM band 40.68 MHz is used in this study. The results show that when the WPT system is placed directly on the human body its Power Transfer Efficiency (PTE) is reduced by 13% on average in both simulations and measurements. These losses are attributed to the material properties of the human body. Also, different parts of the human body cause different drops in PTE due to their different shapes and geometries.**

***Index Terms*—Human body, Wearable, Wireless power transfer, SCMR.**

I. Introduction

Wireless Power Transfer (WPT) was first introduced by Nikola Tesla in the early 1900s. Since that date, WPT has attracted significant attention by consumer electronics and biomedical applications [1] for implantable [2] and wearable devices [3]. It provides the advantage of supplying power to electronics inside or on the human body without restricting wires and batteries. Many methods have been used to power wearable devices, such as, inductive coupling [2] and Strongly Coupled Magnetic Resonance (SCMR) [4]-[5]. SCMR is typically preferred as it provides high efficiency and longer range. Hence, SCMR method is used in our study since its very well suited for wireless powering wearable devices. However, the human body, where the WPT receiver element (Rx) is placed, has significant influence on the WPT system performance, such as, the operation frequency and Power Transfer Efficiency (PTE). Therefore, these effects must be investigated in advance since the performance of a WPT system degrades when it is placed on the human body depending on its specific location.

II. Wireless Power Transfer System

A. SCMR Design

The SCMR is a wireless power transfer system that functions using an inner ring, which operates as either a source or load depending on its placement in the circuit, and an outer ring, which is the primary determinant of the resonant frequency of the SCMR. The size of the SCMR as well as other properties, such as the width of the outer ring, have an impact on the performance and the range at which the maximum efficiency is achieved. A larger SCMR operates at larger distance than a smaller one, but wearable and implantable applications impose strict limitations to the size of SCMR systems. In this work, the SCMR design is optimized to have peak performance at 40.68 MHz (ISM band) for a separation of 60mm. A capacitor (Cp= 198 pF) is added to the outre ring, as shown in Fig. 1, to tune the SCMR to the frequency where the structure exhibits maximum Q-factor. The geometry of our design and its measured and simulated PTE are presented in Fig. 1. Specifically, our WPT system exhibits 81% and 70% simulated and measured efficiencies, respectively. This difference between measurements and simulations is attributed to manufacturing imperfections and capacitor tolerances.

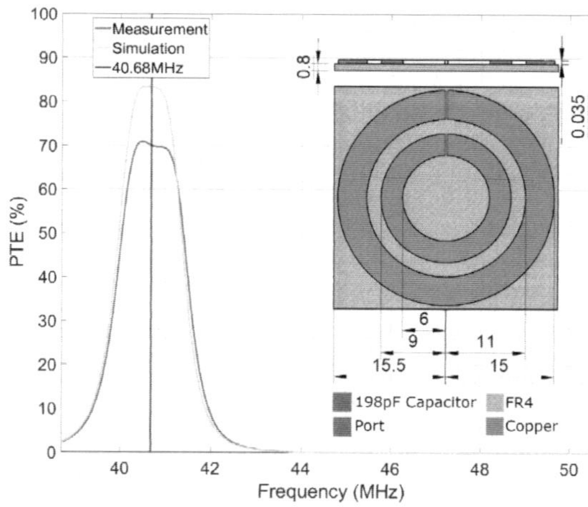

Fig. 1. Simulated and measured PTE versus frequency.

B. SCMR System on the Human Body

The performance of our SCMR is simulated and measured for 26 different locations organized into the following categories: head,neck/bicep, torso, arm and leg, as shown in Fig. 2 (a). Each category had 5 measurement points, except for the torso, which had 6. The simulations were performed in ANSYS HFSS using the ANSYS Human body model. A 3D printed support was used in measurements to maintain a 60mm separation as shown in Fig. 2 (b).

III. Results

The average of the PTE on the different sections at the operating frequency is listed in Table I along with a reference (SCMR operating in free space). These results are reported

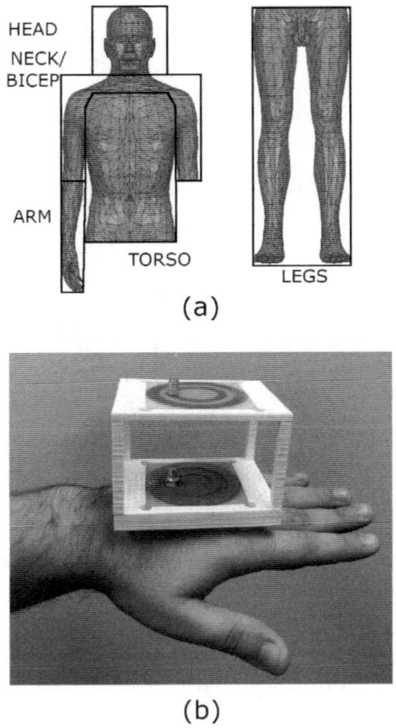

Fig. 2. (a) ANSYS human body model, (b) 10mm measurement setup on the hand.

TABLE I: PTE(%) on Human Body

Body Part/ Group	Power Transfer Efficiency			
	Simulated		*Measured*	
	0mm	*10mm*	*0mm*	*10mm*
REFERENCE	*83.4*		*70.4*	
INNER THIGH[a]	67.2	74.0	50.7	67.6
TOP OF WRIST[b]	72.1	80.0	62.5	69.5
HEAD	69.1	77.0	59.9	66.0
NECK/BICEP	66.0	75.7	57.6	66.0
TORSO	68.6	75.4	54.0	64.2
ARMS	70.5	76.2	60.7	67.4
LEGS	73.2	78.9	53.7	66.9

(a) High loss, (b) Low loss.

for two different distances from the human body (0mm and 10mm). The body parts group with the highest and lowest measured losses were the legs and the arms, respectively. The greatest and lowest losses were observed for the outer thigh and the top of the wrist, respectively, as shown in Table I.

Our results show that the PTE of SCMR systems mainly depends on the mass of the human body behind the receiver. When SCMR loops are placed on body parts that are smaller than their size, then the body does not completely influence the EM fields and in consequence the losses are smaller (i.e., less body absorption). This explains why our WPT system experiences the lowest losses on the arms. Also, this justifies the similarity between groups, such as, the torso and leg regions (which, besides the actual foot, had similar losses to the torso), as they both are larger in volume and area. Additionally, the materials present in different parts of the human body play a significant role in determining the losses of a wearable WPT system. For example, materials such as bone will have less conductivity compared to muscle or fat. Furthermore, organs may have different properties, leading to differences in PTE. This explain why the thigh measurements, neighboring the gluteus maximus and a particularly dense area of the body, have the greatest losses, surpassing the larger torso areas.

The model used in our simulations was an approximate model, and thus not perfectly representative of the human body and its several different components, all with varying electrical properties. This is why the higher and lower loss areas in simulation exhibit a difference of only 5% efficiency, while in measurements the maximum difference of the efficiency in these areas is 12% at 0mm.

Conclusion

In this paper, the effect of different parts of the human body on the PTE of a WPT system in both simulation and measurement were presented. The results showed a tangible difference in term of PTE on different parts of the human body.

Acknowledgement

This research was supported by the Air Force Office of Scientific Research under grant FA9550-16-1-0145.

References

[1] H. Hu, S. V. Georgakopoulos, and Kun Bao, "Wireless Power Transfer in Human Tissue via Conformal Strongly Coupled Magnetic Resonance," IEEE Wireless Power Transfer Conference, Boulder, Colorado, May 13-15, 2015.

[2] G. Wang, W. Liu, M. Sivaprakasam, M. Zhou, J. D. Weiland, and M. S. Humayun, "A Dual Band Wireless Power and Data Telemetry for Retinal Prosthesis," 28th EMBS Annual International Conference, New York, Aug. 2006.

[3] S. Xu, et al., "Soft microfluidic assemblies of sensors, circuits, and radios for the skin," Science, pp. 70-74, Apr. 4, 2014.

[4] K. Bao, C. L. Zekios and S. V. Georgakopoulos, "A Wearable WPT System on Flexible Substrates," in IEEE Antennas and Wireless Propagation Letters, vol. 18, no. 5, pp. 931-935, May 2019

[5] O. Jonah, S. V. Georgakopoulos, and M. M. Tentzeris, "Strongly coupled wireless power transfer with conformal structures," in Proc. 29th Annu. Rev. Progress Appl. Comput. Electromagn., Monterey, CA, USA, Mar. 24–28, 2013.

Two-dimensional Wireless Power Relay Plane based on Rectangular Switchable Units

Zhouyi Wu, Peiying Lin, Chao Ma, Zhiyi Tang, Ran Li, Jiangtao Huangfu*
Laboratory of Applied Research on Electromagnetics (ARE), Zhejiang University, Hangzhou 310027, China
email: huangfujt@zju.edu.cn

Abstract—In this paper a two-dimensional wireless relay plane consists of square resonant units is proposed. Power transfer between the transmitting coil and receiver above any unit can be achieved by resonance through the shortest routes on the plane. The self-resonant frequencies of units on the planned route are adjusted to be identical for efficient power transfer, while units beyond the route are isolated from power exchange due to frequency shift. Full wave electromagnetic simulation is executed and analysed. According to the simulation results, concentrated power transfer can be realized on the power relay plane, and the highest transmission efficiency is 73.93%.

Index Terms—wireless power transfer, resonance coupling, routing

I. Introduction

Wireless power transfer (WPT) has been an active research field in recent years. [1 - 3] focus on transmitter and receiver topology of WPT method in multi-load applications. [4 - 6] aim to extend power transmission distance by increasing number of relay coils. Here we consider the situation where receiver will appear in arbitrary locations of a two-dimensional plane with power requirement. A high-frequency wireless relay plane is proposed, which can deliver power directionally from transmitting coil to the receiver while avoiding excess power dissipation.

II. Analysis Model

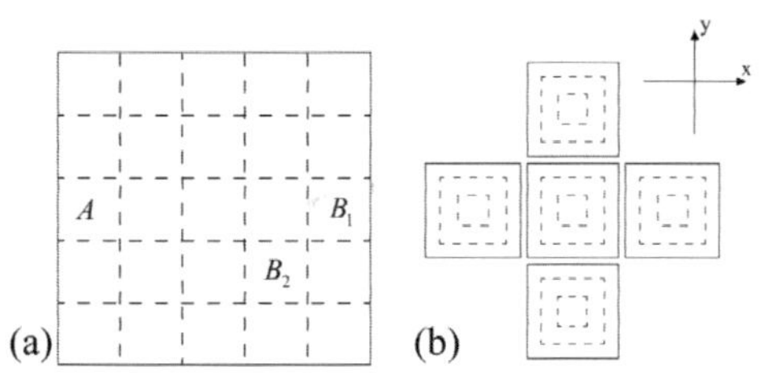

Fig. 1. (a) A two-dimensional power relay plane. A is the start unit, and B_1, B_2 are two locations of the receiver. (b) Each unit can transfer power to its adjacent units in x and y directions.

Considering a two-dimensional WPT plane in Fig. 1 (a), high frequency AC power is coupled to a start point A through a transmitting coil to power a receiver, of which B_1 and B_2 are two randomly selected positions. The plane is divided into small square power transfer units, all of which have their own circuit self-resonant frequency. As illustrated in Fig. 1 (b), power in each unit can be transferred to its adjacent units in x and y directions. The power transfer between two circuits with different self-resonant frequencies is weak. However, when some units have identical self-resonant frequency, magnetic coupling resonance occurs among these units and leads to an efficient power exchange. Take advantage of this principle, a concentrated propagation of power can be achieved along resonant units.

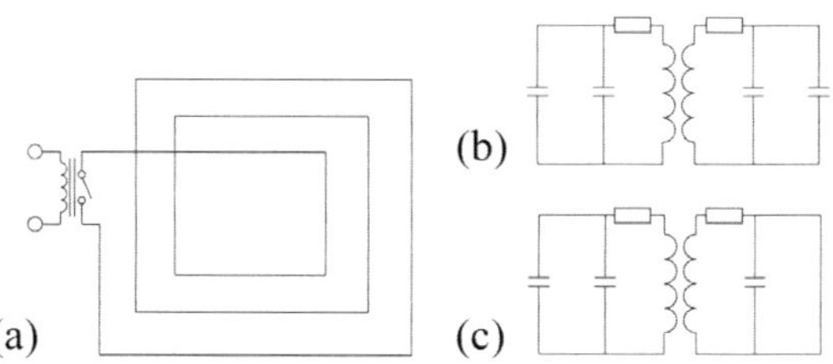

Fig. 2. (a) Circuit diagram of a unit, including a rectangular coil, a relay switch, and a control circuit. (b) Equivalent circuit of two activated units. (c) Equivalent circuit of an activated unit and a hibernated unit.

A planar rectangular coil is selected as the inductance of a unit, with two ends connected to a relay switch. The circuit diagram of each unit is shown in Fig. 2 (a). A control circuit is linked to each unit in parallel, responsible for switch on-off control. When both relay switches of two adjacent units are turned off, the circuit can be equivalent to Fig. 2 (b). Every unit consists of the coil equivalent inductance and resistance, and two parallel capacitors, the parasitic capacitance of the coil and the equivalent capacitance of the relay switch. Power can be efficiently transmitted between these two units through resonant coupling, and the state of these units is called activated state. On the contrary, when switch of one unit is turned on, its equivalent capacitance is short-circuited as shown in Fig. 2 (c). Change in circuit capacitance leads to an increase of unit resonant frequency compared to the activated units. This frequency divergence will destroy the resonance, which is equivalent to isolating the unit from

This work was supported by the NSFC under Grant No. 61675013 and U19A2054, the Zhejiang Provincial Natural Science Foundation of China under Grant No. LY18F010003.

power exchange. Therefore, this is called the hibernated state of unit.

Among all the power transfer routes from transmitting coil to the destination, those that pass through the least amount of units are defined as the shortest. Initially, all units are in hibernated state. The power source frequency is set to the resonant frequency of activated units. When a receiver enters the power relay plane, units on the shortest route are activated to power the receiver, while the other units remain in hibernated state. As the receiver changes its location, the shortest route is continuously recalculated, resulting in incessant state-switching of related units between activated and hibernated states.

III. Electromagnetic Simulation Results

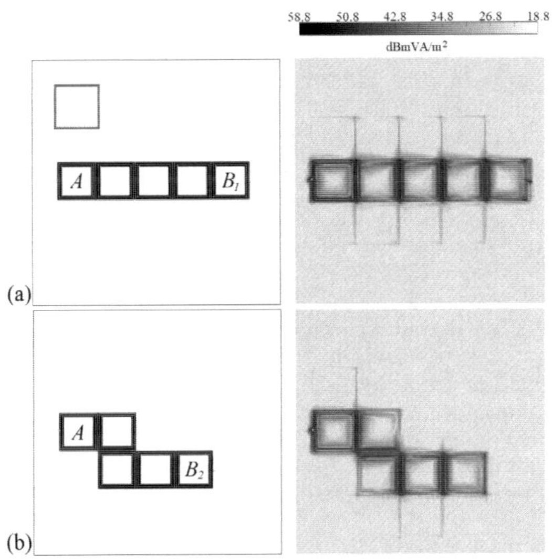

Fig. 3. (a)A 5×5 matrix model. Power transfer route from A to B_1 is high-lighted on the left. In the red box is the model of single unit. On the right is the power flow. (b) Power transfer route from A to B_2 on the left, and power flow on the right.

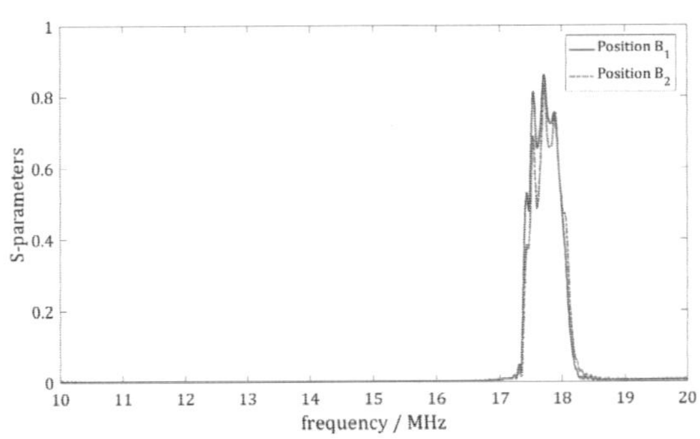

Fig. 4. S_{21} simulation results when the receiver is in position B_1 and B_2.

The design of a unit in simulation model is shown in the red box in left Fig. 3 (a). It's a rectangular 4-turn spiral copper coil with a size of $1016mm \times 1016mm \times 1.6mm$. The copper strip width and the gap between each turn are $16mm$. As illustrated in Fig. 3 (a), units are arranged together with a spacing of $18mm$ to form a 5×5 matrix as the model of power relay plane. Two $960mm \times 956mm \times 1.6mm$ single-turn copper coils are placed $13mm$ above the coils. Each coil is connected to a port of 50Ω impedance. One is located at position A as the transmitting coil, feeding power into the plane through coupling with the rectangular coil below. And the other one plays the role of the receiver, floating above positions B_1 and B_2. The shortest routes from position A to B_1 and B_2 are respectively high-lighted in left Fig. 3 (a) and (b). Coil beyond the power transfer route is short-circuited by connecting two ends with a short copper strip to simulate a hibernated unit, while the coil with both ends open is an activated unit as the switch in off state.

The S_{21} results of the receiver acquired from electromagnetic simulation at position B_1 and B_2 are drawn in Fig. 4, with a power transmission efficiency of 73.93% and 68.96% at $17.72MHz$. The power flow is specifically verified at resonant frequency $17.72MHz$ with $0.5W$ input power. The results are displayed on the right column in Fig. 3. It can be seen from the power distribution maps that the energy is concentrated in the power transfer route. Intuitively, the power exchange is interrupted when an activated unit is encountered with a hibernated coil, and hibernated coils have almost no access to the AC power.

References

[1] H. Han, Z. Mao, Q. Zhu, M. Su, and A. P. Hu, "A 3D Wireless Charging Cylinder with Stable Rotating Magnetic Field for Multi-Load Application," IEEE Access, 2019:1-1.

[2] W. Liu, K. T. Chau, C. H. T. Lee, C. Jiang, W. Han, and W. H. Lam, "Multi-Frequency Multi-Power One-to-Many Wireless Power Transfer System," IEEE Transactions on Magnetics, 2019:1-9.

[3] D. Ahn, S. M. Kim, S. W. Kim, J. I. Moon, and I. K. Cho, "Wireless Power Transfer Receiver with Adjustable Coil Output Voltage for Multiple Receivers Application," IEEE Transactions on Industrial Electronics, 2018:1-1.

[4] C. Cheng, F. Lu, Z. Zhou, W. Li, C. Zhu, et al. "Load-Independent Wireless Power Transfer System for Multiple Loads Over a Long Distance," IEEE Transactions on Power Electronics, 2018:1-1.

[5] C. Zhang, D. Lin, N. Tang, and S. Y. R. Hui, "A Novel Electric Insulation String Structure With High-Voltage Insulation and Wireless Power Transfer Capabilities," IEEE Transactions on Power Electronics, 2018.

[6] C. Cheng, Z. Zhou, W. Li, C. Zhu, Z. Deng and C. C. Mi, "A Multi-load Wireless Power Transfer System with Series-parallel-series (SPS) Compensation," IEEE Transactions on Power Electronics, 2019:1-1.

On the Design of a Multi-Frequency Wireless Power and Data Transfer System

Nunzia Fontana
DESTEC
University of Pisa, Italy
nunzia.fontana@unipi.it

Danilo Brizi
Dipartimento di Ingegneria dell'Informazione
University of Pisa, Italy

Sami Barmada
DESTEC
University of Pisa, Italy

Agostino Monorchio
Dipartimento di Ingegneria dell'Informazione
University of Pisa, Italy

***Abstract*—A methodology for the design of a multi-frequency Wireless Power transfer (WPT) and data transfer (DT) applications with reduced computational burden, is presented. The configuration is made by an array of passive resonant elements placed in the proximity of the driver coil of a common 2-coils system. The proposed methodology is well-known in phased array design and here adopted for WPT and DT applications. The method is based on one numerical full-wave evaluation of the scattering parameters matrix of a 2 -coils system together with a passive resonant array of (N-2) x (N-2) elements, made resonant by tuning capacitors. By a post-processing evaluation of the S_{NxN} matrix of the system, it can be possible obtaining the desired multiple frequencies tuning of the array by acting only on the tuning post-processed capacitors. We finally demonstrated that the proposed arrangement enhances the efficiency level of the simple 2-coils driver-receiver system at the multiple frequencies obtained by the chosen multi-tuning condition.**

Keywords—Data transfer, multi-frequency, multi-resonant coils, near-field array, scattering parameters, telemetry, Wireless Power Transfer.

I. Introduction

Inductive resonant Wireless Power Transfer and telemetry are commonly and simultaneously used in different areas, especially for biomedical implants, in which system powering and at least one channel for basic information transferring must co-exist [1], [2]. With this purpose, it would be desirable developing flexible systems showing multiple working frequencies to optimize efficiency and telemetry with respect to classical single frequency or narrowband systems (typically composed by two main coils, one adopted as driver and one as receiver). Moreover, considering the increasing usage of multi transmitters in WPT applications, the phenomenon of multiple interferences needs to be addressed. The challenge is realizing a broadband or multiband WPT or DT system, relying on a system by its own nature narrowband as a classical 2-coils system is. The antenna array theory [3] suggested us to propose the insertion of an array of passive resonant elements in between the driver and the receiver coils of a standard 2-coils system which principally influences the electromagnetic near field [4]. The array is positioned as close as possible to the driver loop, thus not affecting the useful working distance [5]. In this paper, we propose an array of spiral resonators (SRA) interposed between a driver and a receiver able to increase the number of working frequencies. Specifically, we here introduce a method for choosing the resonances of the SRA by acting on the tuning capacitors of each element without resorting to onerous simulations for frequency response estimation and nearfield extraction of the system. Finally, we demonstrated that a multi-frequency system can be obtained achieving good results in terms of efficiency.

II. Method

The proposed method aims to speed-up the procedure for designing a multi-resonant array with the purpose of creating a multi-frequency WPT system. Firstly, a full-wave numerical simulation of the entire 2-coils system with the presence of the resonators matrix must be performed: at this step (STEP 1), all the feeding ports (P) and all the lumped elements (L) are considered as 50Ohm ports. The aim of the last simulation is obtaining the S parameters matrix having NxN elements, where N=P+L, which completely describes the system: at this stage, the system can be interpreted as a black box. Therefore, a circuit design of the complete equivalent system (STEP 2) can be performed by feeding the actual ports and inserting all the tuning elements as shown in Fig.1 (b). An optimization of the values of tuning capacitors can be developed in order to enhance the performance of the array used in the WPT system in the desired frequency range. In order to validate the proposed methodology, one further full-wave simulation has been accomplished taking into account the tuning capacitors values obtained by the circuital simulation.

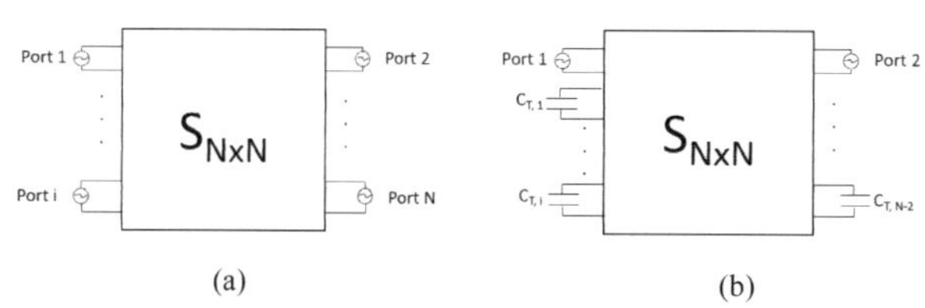

Fig. 1. Circuit model of the system: (a) circuital representation at STEP 1; (b) circuital representation at STEP 2.

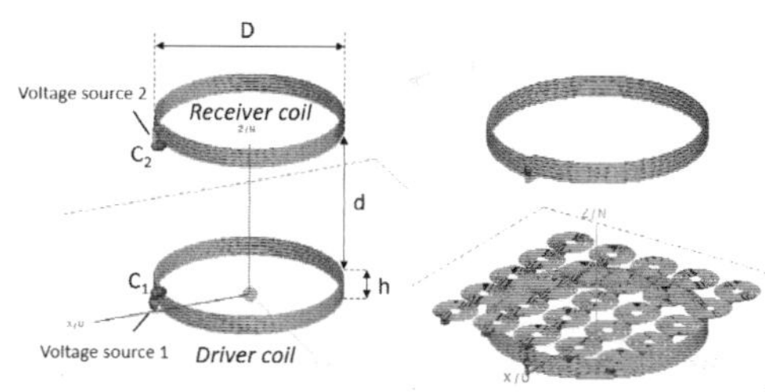

Fig. 2. CAD model representing: (a) a simple 2-coils WPT system; (b) the multi-resonant array placed in close proximity to the driver coil. The working distance is preserved with respect to the simple driver-receiver system (i.e., 18 cm).

III. Numerical Design and Validation

The numerical simulations were carried out with an electromagnetic solver based on the Methods of Moments

(Feko suite, Altair, Troy, MI, USA). The first step involved the design of a classical 2-coils system which represents the most common configuration used in WPT applications; then, we inserted the spiral resonator array between the driver and receiver coils, as depicted in Fig. 2 (b). The array was composed by a 5×5 matrix of passive resonant planar spirals: we placed the array as close as possible to the driver coil (1 mm away), in order to preserve the useful working distance (i.e., the available space between the array and the receiver coil). The geometry of the 2-coils WPT system we analyzed is well-described in [5]. At this stage, all the existing lumped elements are considered as ports. Then, the method has been validated by comparing the results in terms of S parameters obtained by numerical full-wave simulation and circuital post-processing evaluation on a specific tuning condition for the capacitors. Fig. 3, as expected, shows a very good agreement between the two results, suggesting that the two approaches are completely equivalent.

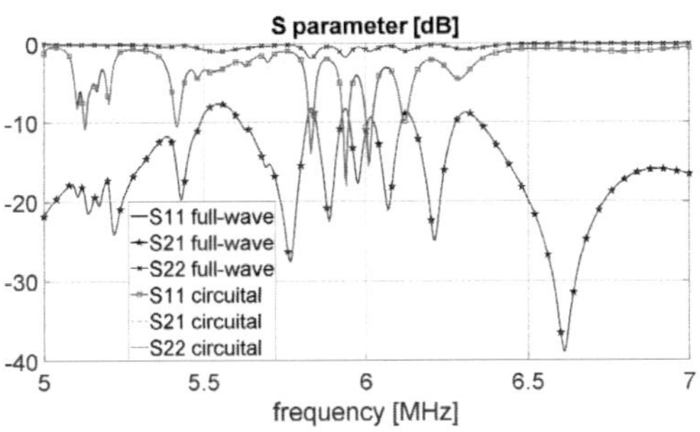

Fig. 3. S parameters comparison: full-wave analysis versus circuital analysis.

IV. Results

The method has been applied with the aim of enhancing the efficiency levels of the system in two tuning SRA conditions of use. In particular, for the same working distance (18 cm) and loading configuration of the receiver (50 Ω), we reported the efficiency levels comparisons between a simple two-coils WPT system, the case in which all the array tuning capacitors have the same value equal to 585pF and the case in which their values are chosen as a gaussian distribution having mean value equal to 585pF and a standard deviation equal to 50. For a gaussian distribution of capacitance values on the spiral resonators array (randomly placed among the matrix), we obtained an enhancing of efficiency at several frequencies of the observed bandwidth (5MHz - 7MHz) into respect to the simple 2-coils system (η = 6.5 %), reaching the value of η = 10% at the operative frequency of 5.54MHz. The corresponding values for the capacitors in the last configuration have been reported in Fig. 4. The results suggested us that a quick and easy prediction of the working frequency capability of the proposed system can be done just by acting on tuning capacitors in a post-processing evaluation. The methodology can be used for a fully systemic approach on the performance tuning of the spiral resonators array implemented in the system before the prototyping stage. Each capacitor can be optimized in order to obtain a desired frequency response defined from the specific application. Fig. 5 shows that the same system can be simultaneously used for WPT and DT purposes without losing of performances.

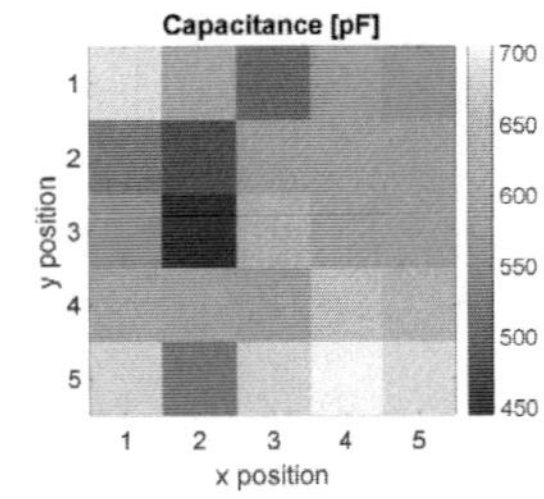

Fig. 4. Tuning capacitances in the 5x5 spiral resonators array. The values have been calculated as gaussian distribution with mean value equal to 585pF and standard deviation equal to 50.

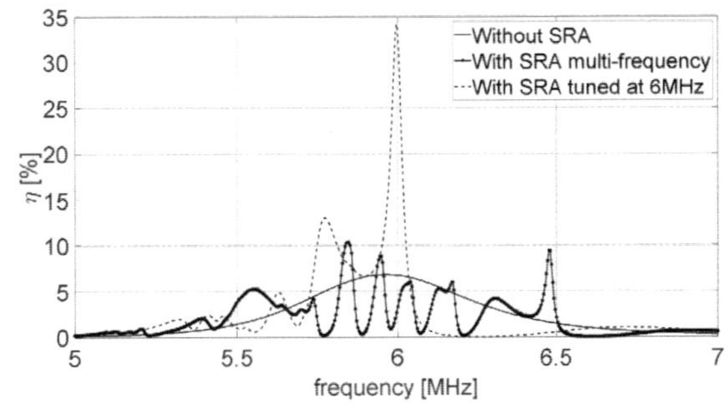

Fig. 5. Efficiency representation according to the frequency obtained by applying the proposed method in two tuning SRA conditions of use.

V. Conclusions

A methodology for the design of a multifrequency system for wireless power and data transfer applications has been presented. The system consists of 2-coils with the presence of a spiral resonators array (SRA) in the nearby of the driver coil. After the scattering parameters calculation by the means of one full-wave simulation, through a circuital post-processing procedure, an optimization of the working frequencies of the system can be very quickly accomplished. In this way a significant reduction of the computational burden by acting only on the circuital representation of the system for its tuning can easily lead to a multi-frequencies behavior, that can be extremely helpful in a number of different WPT applications.

References

[1] A. K. RamRakhyani and G. Lazzi, "On the Design of Efficient Multi-Coil Telemetry System for Biomedical Implants," IEEE Transactions on Biomedical Circuits and Systems, vol. 7, no. 1, February 2013.

[2] N. Fontana, A. Monorchio, M. O. Munoz Torrico and Y. Hao, "A numerical assesment of the effect of MRI surface coils on implanted pacemakers," IEEE Antennas and Propagation Society, AP-S International Symposium (Digest), 2012.

[3] D. Bianchi, et al., "Multi-objective optimization of wideband Spiral Arrays," IEEE Antennas and Propagation Society, AP-S International Symposium, Toronto, July 2010.

[4] S. Barmada, M. Tucci, N. Fontana, Wael Dghais and M. Raugi, "Design and Realization of a Multiple Access Wireless Power Transfer System for Optimal Power Line Communication Data Transfer Article," Energies, 12 (6), 988, March 2019.

[5] D. Brizi, N. Fontana, S. Barmada and A. Monorchio, "A Multi-Transmitter Configuration for High-Safety Wireless Power Transfer Applications," Applied Computational Electromagnetics Society (ACES) Symposium, Miami, April 2019.

Localization of a Discharge in Transmission Line Networks using Time Reversal with TLM

Wolfgang J. R. Hoefer
Dept. of Electrical and Computer Engineering
University of Victoria
Victoria, BC, Canada
w.hoefer@ieee.org

***Abstract*—The location of an electrical discharge in a transmission line network is found from its recorded transient response by means of a time reversal simulation. The accuracy of the localization procedure depends on how closely the simulator models the wave properties of the network that must be linear, reciprocal, and virtually loss-free. TLM simulations are presented.**

***Keywords*—electrical discharge, electromagnetic simulation, source reconstruction, time reversal, transmission line networks.**

I. INTRODUCTION

Finding the location of an electrical discharge is an important issue in electromagnetic compatibility and interference (EMI/EMC) [1]. A discharge in a complex transmission line network produces a transient signal that propagates and scatters through the entire system. As time moves forward, the signal becomes increasingly distorted due to multiple reflections, scatterings, and multipath transmission, looking less and less like the original excitation waveform. Nevertheless, this time response contains, at any point in the network, sufficient information to recover the discharge location, provided that the network is linear and reciprocal, and has negligible losses. All we need is an accurate computational space-time model of the network, such as a Transmission Line Matrix (TLM) or a Finite Difference Time Domain (FDTD) model, to reconstruct this location from the output signal picked up and recorded at one or more points in the original network. This procedure is based on the computational reversal of time and amounts to injecting the time-reversed output signal back into the model, yielding the origin of the disturbance.

The use of time reversal as a method for solving inverse problems, such as finding a unknown source from its known emitted field, dates back to the late 1950s and has been applied extensively in optics, acoustics, seismology, and electromagnetics. For a list of references and a general introduction to time reversal, see the recent article on "Time Reversal in Electromagnetics" by the author [2]. Inverse problem solutions such as time reversal procedures, can be mathematically and computationally complex. However, a time domain electromagnetic simulator is a powerful tool for solving such problems with ease, accuracy and speed, as demonstrated by the example presented below. The essence of the computational time reversal procedure will be summarized in terms of a correlation performed by the simulator.

II. THE EXAMPLE SCENARIO

A. Topology of a Transmission Line Network

Fig. 1 shows an arbitrary transmission line network example used to demonstrate the localization procedure. It consists of several interconnected TEM transmission lines, two of them matched, and the rest short-circuited. We assume that an electric discharge occurs at time $t=0$ at the position n, and the network response is picked up at two probes (nodes) $m1$ and $m2$. To facilitate the visualization of the electromagnetic events, the figure shows the 2D model of a real structure as it appears in the Editor window of the TLM simulator MEFiSTo-3D Pro. It is the top view of a network of parallel-plate transmission lines with magnetic side walls drawn in blue in the x,y-plane (H-plane), while the electric field is normal to the page.

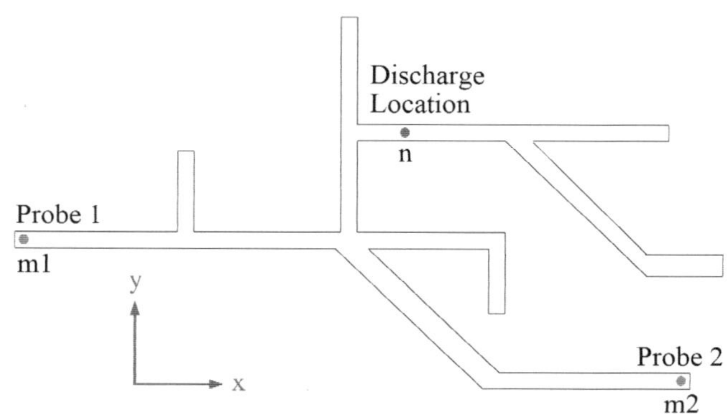

Fig. 1. Transmission line network consisting of TEM waveguides (top view).

B. Electromagnetic Response to a Discharge

The first step is to obtain the electromagnetic response of the network to a discharge at location n. In a real-world experiment, the response is physically recorded at $m1$ and $m2$, and stored for further processing. However, in order to derive a general discrete Green's formulation of the time reversal procedure for the problem, we shall generate this response with the same space-time discrete TLM model that will be used later for the recovery of the source location. Note that the time variable is now discretized into steps of Δt and defined as $t=k\Delta t$, where k is the integer time index. We assume at first that the discharge at $t=0$ $(k=0)$ is modeled by a unit impulse or Kronecker Delta function $\delta(k,k')$, which has the value *unity* at time step $k=k'$.

(We can later extend the solution by convolving the impulse response with a more realistic excitation waveform). The computed impulse response e_z at any output node m to a unit excitation $e_z(n,0)$ at input node n and at time $k'=0$ is then:

$$e_z(m,n,k) = g(m,n,k). \quad (1)$$

This response to a unit impulse is a discrete Green's function, shown in Fig. 2 as recorded at locations *m1* and *m2* for the first *3 ns* (*K=424* time steps) following the excitation event.

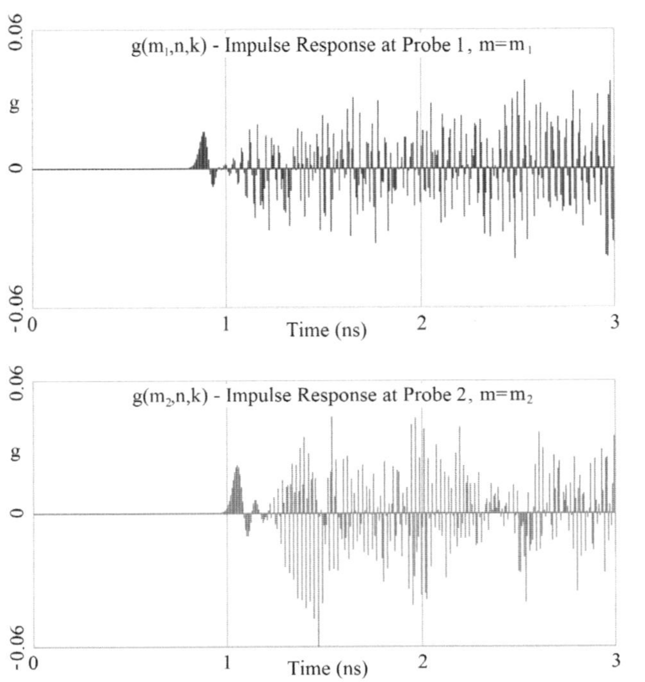

Fig. 2. The impulse responses *g(m,n,k)* at locations *m=m1* (top) and *m=m2* (bottom) are terms of the discrete Green's function of the network.

C. Time Reversal of the Impulse Responses

The source location is now recovered by flipping the above impulse responses in time and re-injecting them back into the TLM model at the probes where they have been initially recorded. These responses are essentially finite sequences of K real numbers, where K is the total number of time steps. The inverse of a response *g(m,n,k)* is written as *g(m,n,K-k)*. When it is injected back into the model as a source signal for a second simulation, the TLM simulator effectively convolves it with its own impulse response *g(m,n,k)* by virtue of its reciprocity property [3]. We can write this as:

$$A(n,k) = g(m,n,k) * g(m,n,K-k). \quad (2)$$

The symbol $*$ designates a numerical convolution. *A(n,k)* is defined in signal processing as the autocorrelation of *g(m,n,k)*. The signal computed at any location other than that of the original impulse excitation will be the cross-correlation of two different terms of the discrete Green's function, which will typically be an order of magnitude smaller than the auto-correlation product. Hence, we only need to inspect the final field distribution computed by the TLM solver at $k=K$ and look for the location at which the field has a maximum value.

III. Results of the Time Reversal Computation

Fig. 3 shows the distribution of the computed electric field e_z in the network at the end *(k=K)* of the inverse TLM simulation. It is essentially a map of correlation products of terms of its discrete Green's function. All are cross-correlation products, except for the autocorrelation term that occurs at the original source location and clearly stands out, revealing the location of the discharge with mesh resolution. Note that one impulse response recorded at a single probe is already sufficient for reconstructing the source.

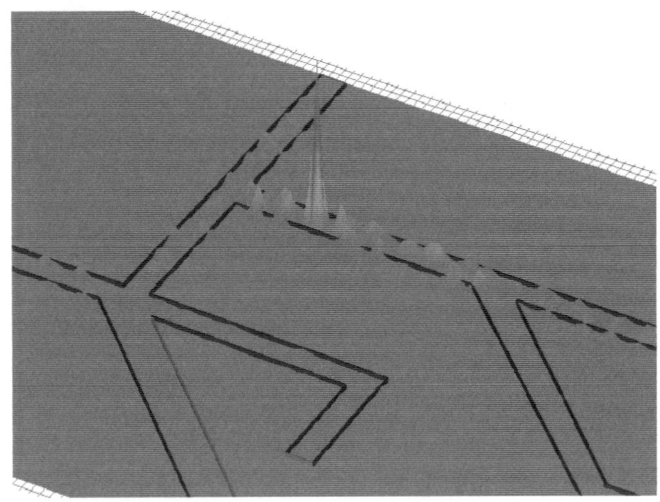

Fig. 3. The electric field distribution in the network at the end of the inverse simulation shows a clear maximum at the location of the original unit excitation. The impulsive excitation provides mesh resolution. (Mesh size $\Delta\ell = 1mm$.)

IV. Discussion and Conclusion

To achieve highly accurate results, it is essential to have a very good model of the transmission line network under investigation. In the above example this was guaranteed since we used the same TLM model to perform the forward and inverse simulation. However, in a practical surge localization problem the forward propagation occurs in a real structure, while the inverse source reconstruction is performed by simulation. Furthermore, the waveform produced by a real surge looks more like a double exponential pulse and has a narrower spectrum than the Kronecker Delta function, resulting in a reduction of spatial resolution.

References

[1] F. Rachidi, M. Rubinstein, and M. Paolone, "Electromagnetic time reversal: Application to EMC and Power Systems," John Wiley & Sons, Inc.: New York, 1917.

[2] W. J. R. Hoefer, "Time reversal in electromagnetics," Wiley Encyclopedia of Electrical and Electronics Engineering, John Wiley & Sons, New York, 2018, pp. 1-24. DOI: 10.1002/047134608X.W8366.

[3] W. J. R. Hoefer, "Computational time reversal - A frontier in electromagnetic structure synthesis and design," IEEE Trans. on Microwave Theory Techn, vol. MTT-63, no. 1, pp. 3-10, Jan. 2015. DOI: 10.1109/TMTT.2014.2373367.

The Diffraction by the Half-plane with the Fractional Boundary Condition

Vasil Tabatadze
Institute of Informatics
Istanbul Technical University
Istanbul, Turkey
vasilitabatadze@gmail.com

Eldar Veliyev
Institute of Informatics
Istanbul Technical University
Istanbul, Turkey
veliev51@gmail.com

Ertuğrul Karaçuha
Institute of Informatics
Istanbul Technical University
Istanbul, Turkey
karacuhae@itu.edu.tr

Kamil Karaçuha
Institute of Informatics
Istanbul Technical University
Istanbul, Turkey
kamoka.eee@gmail.com

***Abstract*— In this article, there is considered the electromagnetic plane wave diffraction by the half-plane with fractional boundary conditions. As a mathematical tool, the fractional calculus is used. The theoretical part is given based on which the near field, Poynting vector and energy density distribution are calculated. Interesting results are obtained for the fractional order between marginal values, which describes a new type of material with new properties. The results are analyzed.**

Keywords* — *electromagnetic waves, half-plane, integral boundary conditions.

I. INTRODUCTION

The problem investigated in the study is a new approach to the diffraction problem including a half-plane surface and the plane wave as an incidence wave. The new method is called as the fractional derivative method (FDM). The method yields to explain the continuous intermediate stages of the two canonical states of the electromagnetic field. The first studies related to the fractional approach for the electromagnetic theory and its applications are investigated by Engheta [1-3]. Then, Veliev developed the idea for the boundary condition which is called the fractional boundary condition (FBC) [4-6].

Fractional boundary condition describes the intermediate boundary condition between Dirichlet and Neumann boundary conditions. When the fractional order $\nu = 0$, this boundary condition corresponds to the perfect electric conductor (PEC). When $\nu = 1$, it stands for the perfect magnetic conductor (PMC). For fractional order between $0 < \nu < 1$, FBC corresponds to the intermediate case between the PEC and PMC [5, 6]. The solution to this problem for the marginal values of the fractional order is given in the book [7].

In this article, the fractional boundary condition is applied to the half-plane surface which describes the new type of material with interesting properties.

II. THE FORMULATION OF THE PROBLEM

In the formulation of the problem section, the main theoretical background is highlighted. In Fig. 1, the geometry of the problem is given.

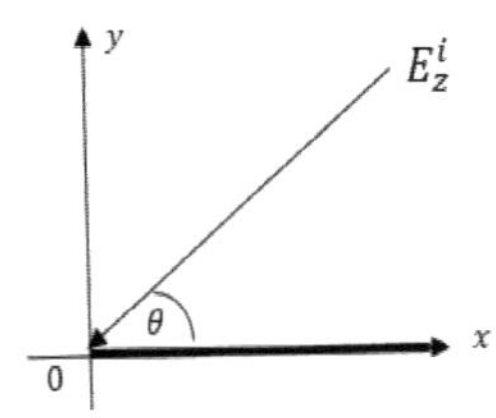

Fig. 1. The geometry of the problem

The incidence E-polarized electromagnetic wave can be denoted as $\vec{E}_z^i = e^{-ik(x\cos\theta + y\sin\theta)}\hat{e}_z$. Note that, the time dependency is $e^{-i\omega t}$, θ is the angle of incidence and $\hat{e}_z$ is the unit vector in the z-direction. The incidence wave is scattered by a half-plane located at $y = 0, x \epsilon [0, \infty)$. The total electric field $\vec{E}_z = \vec{E}_z^i + \vec{E}_z^s$ must satisfy the fractional boundary condition [6, 8]:

$$D_{ky}^{\nu} E_z(x, y) = 0, \quad y \to \pm 0, \quad x > 0. \tag{1}$$

Here, D_{ky}^{ν} denotes the operator of the fractional derivative. $\nu \in [0,1]$. The value $\nu = 0$ corresponds to the perfect electric conductor and the value $\nu = 1$ corresponds to the perfect magnetic conductor. The expression for the scattered field is:

$$E_z^s(x, y) = -i\frac{e^{\pm i\pi\frac{\nu}{2}}}{4\pi}\int_{-\infty}^{\infty} F^{1-\nu}(q)e^{ik\left(xq+|y|\sqrt{1-q^2}\right)}(1-q^2)^{\frac{\nu-1}{2}}dq \tag{2}$$

where, $F^{1-\nu}(q)$ is the Fourier transform of the fractional current density $\tilde{f}^{1-\nu}(\xi)$:

$$F^{1-\nu}(q) = \int_{-\infty}^{\infty} \tilde{f}^{1-\nu}(\xi)e^{-ikq\xi}d\xi. \tag{3}$$

The fractional current density is expanded as orthogonal series by Laguerre polynomials with unknown coefficients f_n^{ν}:

$$\tilde{f}^{1-\nu}\left(\frac{\varsigma}{k}\right) = e^{-\varsigma}\varsigma^{\nu-\frac{1}{2}}\sum_{n=0}^{\infty} f_n^{\nu} L_n^{\nu-\frac{1}{2}}(2\varsigma), \varsigma = kx. \tag{4}$$

After some mathematical operations the problem is reduced to the solution of the linear algebraic equation system (SLAE):

$$\sum_{n=0}^{\infty} f_n^{\nu} C_{nm}^{\nu} = B_m^{\nu}, \tag{5}$$

where,

$$C_{nm}^{\nu} = \frac{1}{k}\gamma_n^{\nu}(-1)^{n+m}\int_{-\infty}^{\infty}\frac{(1-iq)^{n-m-\nu-\frac{1}{2}}}{(1+iq)^{n-m+\nu+\frac{1}{2}}}(1-q^2)^{\nu-\frac{1}{2}}dq,$$

$$B_m^{\nu} = -4\pi e^{i\frac{\pi}{2}(1-3\nu)}sin^{\nu}(\theta)\frac{(icos(\theta)-1)^m}{(icos(\theta)+1)^{\nu+m+\frac{1}{2}}}.$$

After solving this SLAE, unknown coefficients f_n^{ν} is determined. This gives the ability to find the fractional current density $\tilde{f}^{1-\nu}$ with (4) and its Fourier transform with the (3) [8]. Then, the near scattered electric field distribution can be found with (2). Before ending the theoretical part, it is needed to mention that there exists the relationship between the fractional order and the impedance value for normal incidence (η) which is $\eta = -i \times tan\left(\frac{\pi}{2}\nu\right)$ [4].

III. Results of the Numerical Simulation

Based on the above mentioned mathematical algorithm the program package was created in MatLab which gives an ability to calculate near field distribution, Poynting vector distribution and Energy density distribution. Below there are given the obtained results and their analysis.

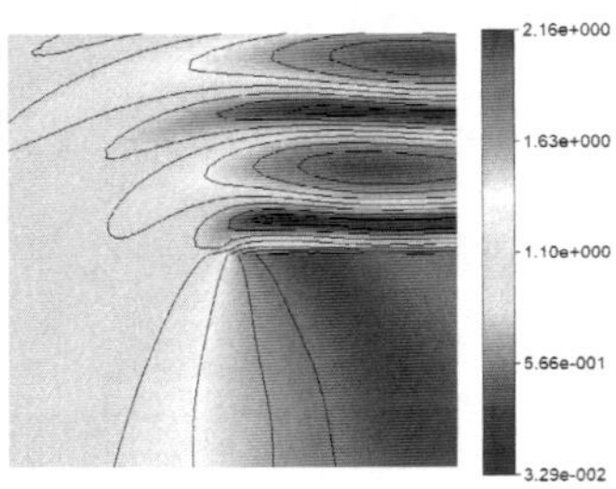

Fig. 2. Near E_z field distribution calculated with FDM at $\nu = 0.5, \theta = \frac{\pi}{2}$

Fig. 2 shows the near field distribution when fractional order, $\nu = 0.5$ as we see under the half-plane, the high field values are observed instead of shadow. This is not an ordinary behavior of the material. It seems that such material works like a capacitor for electromagnetic waves. It accumulates the energy and then radiates it below (this is also clearly seen in Fig. 3 and Fig. 4. Such behavior is known for resonators but usual resonators need a more complex structure. Also, antennas have such behavior when they direct energy in a certain direction. Fig. 3 shows the Poynting vector distribution. Here, we see that, in reality, the energy flow is in the lower part of the half-plane. This proves the idea given in the description of Fig. 3. Fig. 4 shows the energy density distribution and here also most of the energy is given in the lower part of the half-plane.

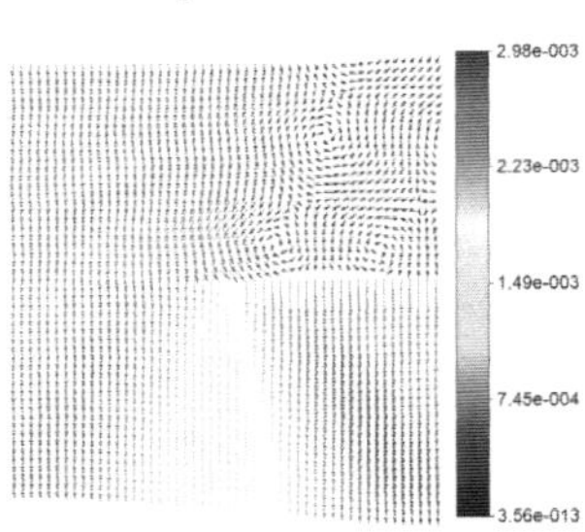

Fig. 3. Poynting vector distribution at $\nu = 0.5, \theta = \frac{\pi}{2}$

Fig. 5(a) gives the near field distribution obtained with our method and Fig. 5(b) gives the same distribution obtained with the analytical formula [7-8]. As it can be seen in Figures, the results are quite similar to each other.

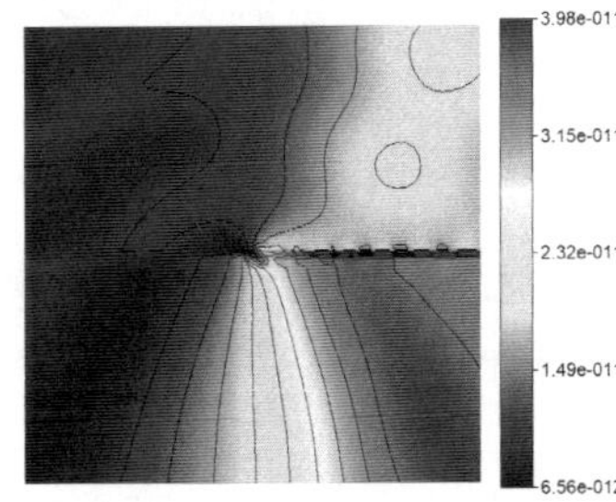

Fig. 4. The energy density distribution at $\nu = 0.5, \theta = \frac{\pi}{2}$

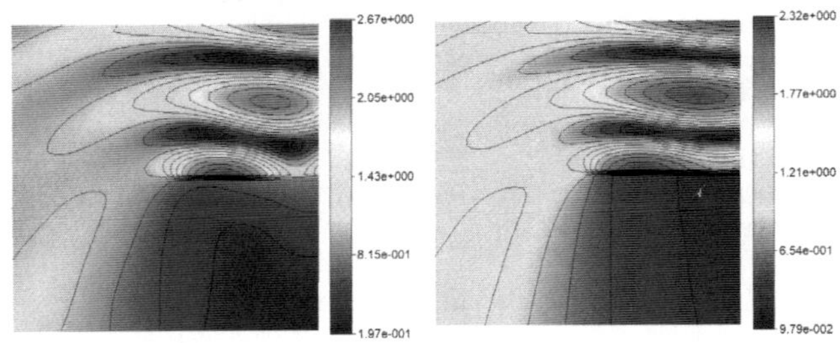

(a) (b)

Fig. 5. The near E_z field distribution calculated with FDM at $\nu = 1, \theta = \frac{\pi}{2}$ and analytical solution for PMC ($\nu = 1$)

Fractional order value $\nu = 0.5$ corresponds to the material for which the corresponding impedance is $\eta = -i$. Such material does not exist in nature but it has very interesting properties. If such a material can be made artificially, it would have a lot of useful applications such as high-quality resonators, waveguides, and antennas.

References

[1] N. Engheta, "Use of fractional integration to propose some``fractional''solutions for the scalar helmholtz equation," *Prog. Electromagn. Res.*, vol. 12, pp. 107–132, 1996.

[2] N. Engheta, "Fractional curl operator in electromagnetics," *Microw. Opt. Technol. Lett.*, vol. 17, no. 2, pp. 86–91, 1998.

[3] N. Engheta, "Phase and amplitude of fractional order intermediate wave," *Microw. Opt. Technol. Lett.*, vol. 21, no. 5, pp. 338–343, 1999.

[4] E. Veliev, T. Ahmedov, and M. Ivakhnychenko, "Fractional operators approach and fractional boundary conditions," *Electromagn. Waves*, p. 117, 2011.

[5] E. I. Veliev, M. V Ivakhnychenko, and T. M. Ahmedov, "Fractional boundary conditions in plane waves diffraction on a strip," *Prog. Electromagn. Res.*, vol. 79, pp. 443–462, 2008.

[6] M. V Ivakhnychenko, E. I. Veliev, and T. M. Ahmedov, "Scattering properties of the strip with fractional boundary conditions and comparison with the impedance strip," *Prog. Electromagn. Res.*, vol. 2, pp. 189–205, 2008.

[7] M. Born and E. Wolf, "Principles of Optics, 7th (expanded) edition," *United Kingdom Press Synd. Univ. Cambridge*, vol. 461, 1999.

[8] E. I. Veliyev, V. Tabatadze, K. Karaçuha, and E. Karaçuha, "The Diffraction by the Half-Plane with the Fractional Boundary Condition," *Progress In Electromagnetics Research M*, Vol. 88, 101-110, 2020..

Self-Inductance of an Extrusion of a Planar Curve

Nicholas Klugman*†, James Vedral†, and Jeffrey Lang*

*Department of Electrical Engineering and Computer Science
Massachusetts Institute of Technology
nklugman@mit.edu, lang@mit.edu

†Charles Stark Draper Laboratory
Cambridge, MA
nklugman@draper.com, jvedral@draper.com

***Abstract*—In this paper, we develop a formula for calculating the inductance of a perfectly conducting extrusion of a planar curve along an arbitrary line segment. We demonstrate agreement in the limiting case between this formula and the Neumann formula for self-inductance of a current loop. We also give special consideration to the case of a planar curve that is most naturally broken into segments, applying the concept of partial inductance.**

***Index Terms*—inductance, Neumann formula, partial inductance.**

I. Introduction

Inductors are often formed from wire loops, with an inductance defined by the flux of the magnetic fields piercing the surface bounded by the wire. Should an inductor be made from a surface, rather than an infintesimal wire, it becomes impossible to define a unique surface through which flux can be calculated. In this paper, we consider the self-inductance of such inductors, deriving a formula analagous to the Neumann formula. In particular we consider inductors formed by extruding a planar curve in an arbitrary direction out of its plane. We also demonstrate agreement between our formula and the Neumann formula in the limiting case of extruding zero distance. Finally, we generalize to partial self- and mutual-inductances of extrusions of open planar curves, simplifying calculations of loop inductance of extrusions of closed planar curves.

II. Inductance of Extrusion

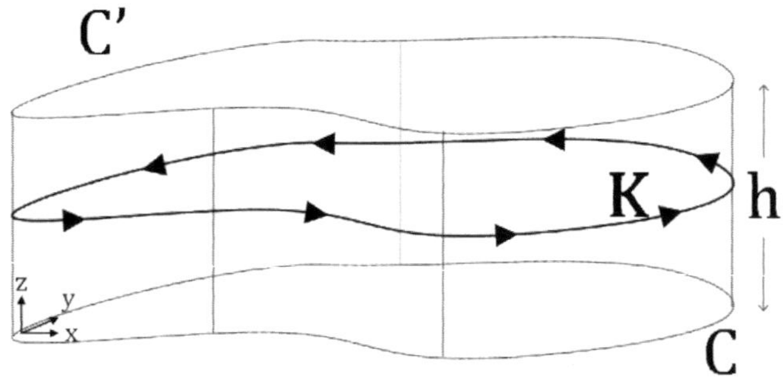

Fig. 1. Extrusion of the planar curve C into the 3D surface S of height h. Surface current density $\mathbf{K}$ flows around S parallel to the x-y plane.

In this paper we consider an inductor constructed by extruding a curve, C, along a line segment of length h perpendicular to the x-y plane in which C resides (as pictured in Fig. 1). We now have a perfectly conducting surface, S, such that each cross section parallel to the base is congruent to C.

Suppose there is a surface current density, $\mathbf{K}$, flowing around the surface ($\mathbf{K}\cdot\hat{\mathbf{z}} = 0$) with magnitude $\|\mathbf{K}\| = i/h$. Let the inductance, L, be defined by the potential energy, U, and the relation $U = \frac{1}{2}Li^2$.

We can calculate the potential energy from the formula $U = \frac{1}{2}\iint_S \mathbf{K}\cdot\mathbf{A}da$, where $\mathbf{A}$ is the magnetic vector potential ($\mathbf{B} = \nabla\times\mathbf{A}$). The magnetic vector potential at a point $\mathbf{r}$ is given by the superposition integral $\mathbf{A}(\mathbf{r}) = \frac{\mu_0}{4\pi}\iint_{\mathbf{r}'\in S}\frac{\mathbf{K}(\mathbf{r}')}{\|\mathbf{r}-\mathbf{r}'\|}da'$.

Rewriting each surface integral as a line integral around C and an integral over the height and substituting in the surface current, we have:

$$U = \frac{1}{2}\oint_C\int_0^h \frac{i}{h}\hat{\mathbf{s}}\cdot\mathbf{A}(\mathbf{s}+z\hat{\mathbf{z}})\,dz\,ds, \text{ and} \tag{1}$$

$$\mathbf{A}(\mathbf{r}) = \frac{\mu_0}{4\pi}\oint_C\int_0^h \frac{\frac{i}{h}\hat{\mathbf{s}}}{\left\|\mathbf{r}-(\mathbf{s}+z\hat{\mathbf{z}})\right\|}\,dz\,ds, \tag{2}$$

where the line integrals are around C and parameterized by $\mathbf{s} = (s_x, s_y, 0)$.

Combining the two gives a quadruple-integral formula for the inductance, solely dependent upon the geometry,

$$L = \frac{\mu_0}{4\pi h^2}\oint_C\oint_C\int_0^h\int_0^h \frac{\hat{\mathbf{s}}\cdot\hat{\mathbf{s}}'}{\left\|(\mathbf{s}'-\mathbf{s})+(z'-z)\hat{\mathbf{z}}\right\|}\,dz'\,dz\,ds'\,ds. \tag{3}$$

Substituting $\Delta z = z' - z$, splitting up the integral, and swapping the order of the inner two integrals gives:

$$L = \frac{\mu_0}{4\pi h^2}\oint_C\oint_C\int_{-h}^h \frac{h-|\Delta z|}{\left\|(\mathbf{s}'-\mathbf{s})+\Delta z\hat{\mathbf{z}}\right\|}\,d(\Delta z)\,ds'\cdot ds. \tag{4}$$

Since $(\mathbf{s}-\mathbf{s}') \perp \hat{\mathbf{z}}$, the denominator is given by Pythagorean theorem, $\left\|(\mathbf{s}'-\mathbf{s})+\Delta z\hat{\mathbf{z}}\right\| = \sqrt{\|\mathbf{s}'-\mathbf{s}\|^2+\Delta z^2}$.

Evaluating the innermost integral yields:

$$L = \frac{\mu_0}{2\pi h} \oint_C \oint_C \left(\log\left(\left(\Delta z + \sqrt{\|\mathbf{s}-\mathbf{s}'\|^2 + \Delta z^2} \right) / h \right) \right.$$
$$\left. - \sqrt{\|\mathbf{s}-\mathbf{s}'\|^2 + \Delta z^2} \Big/ h \right) \Bigg|_0^h d\mathbf{s}' \cdot d\mathbf{s}, \quad (5)$$

$$= \frac{\mu_0}{2\pi h} \oint_C \oint_C \hat{\mathbf{s}} \cdot \hat{\mathbf{s}}' \left(\log\left(\frac{h}{\|\mathbf{s}-\mathbf{s}'\|} + \sqrt{1 + \frac{h^2}{\|\mathbf{s}-\mathbf{s}'\|^2}} \right) \right.$$
$$\left. -h \Big/ \left(\|\mathbf{s}-\mathbf{s}'\| + \sqrt{\|\mathbf{s}-\mathbf{s}'\|^2 + h^2} \right) \right) ds'\, ds. \quad (6)$$

In this form, the effects of the finite height of the inductor have been completely accounted for in the integrand and the integration only occurs over the curve, considering the contribution of inductance from linkage between vertical strips at two positions (s and s') coming off the curve C.

III. Agreement with Neumann Formula

As a brief means of verification of the preceding inductance formula, we consider the limiting case of $h \to 0$, in which case we are considering the inductance of an arbitrary planar current loop along an infintesimal wire.

From L'Hospital's rule and since the paths of integration are independent of h, it suffices to differentiate the integrand with respect to h and evaluate at $h = 0$,

$$L = \frac{\mu_0}{2\pi} \oint_C \oint_C \frac{d}{dh} \left[\log\left(\frac{h}{\|\mathbf{s}-\mathbf{s}'\|} + \sqrt{1 + \frac{h^2}{\|\mathbf{s}-\mathbf{s}'\|^2}} \right) \right.$$
$$\left. - h \Big/ \left(\|\mathbf{s}-\mathbf{s}'\| + \sqrt{h^2 + \|\mathbf{s}-\mathbf{s}'\|^2} \right) \right] \Bigg|_{h=0} d\mathbf{s}' \cdot d\mathbf{s}, \quad (7)$$

$$= \frac{\mu_0}{4\pi} \oint_C \oint_{C^*} \frac{\hat{\mathbf{s}} \cdot \hat{\mathbf{s}}'}{\|\mathbf{s}-\mathbf{s}'\|} ds'\, ds, \quad (8)$$

where C is along the surface of the wire, as before, and C^* is along the center of the wire. The modification from C to C^* is necessary for this integral to converge; if both integrals were along C, the limit would diverge, a consequence of the faulty assumption of an infintesimal wire.

This inductance formula matches Neumann's self-inductance formula in [1]. Another possible correction for the Neumann formula would be to evaluate our extrusion inductance formula, setting h to the diameter of the wire, rather than 0. Our formula does not suffer the same trouble with a divergent integral, as the singularity occurs whenever $\mathbf{s}$ approaches $\mathbf{s}'$, which prevents integration in the case of a wire loop (in which case the integral diverges just as $\int_0^1 \frac{1}{x} dx$ diverges), but in the case of an extrusion, the integral is now in the form of $\int_0^1 \log(\frac{1}{x}) dx$, which does converge.

IV. Partial Inductance of Segmented Extrusion

In some cases, the curve C will most naturally be considered a combination of N segments, $\{C_n\}_{n=1}^N$. Each segment, C_n, is then extruded into a surface segment, S_n, which combined form the surface, S, mentioned previously. For such cases, it is useful to consider individually the contribution of each segment to the inductance. We can break up the surface integral for potential energy to integrate over the surface segments, $U = \frac{1}{2} \sum_{n=1}^N \iint_{S_n} \mathbf{K} \cdot \mathbf{A} da$, and the magnetic vector potential can be similarly broken up, $\mathbf{A}(\mathbf{r}) = \frac{\mu_0}{4\pi} \sum_{m=1}^N \iint_{\mathbf{r}' \in S_m} \frac{\mathbf{K}(\mathbf{r}')}{\|\mathbf{r}-\mathbf{r}'\|} da'$. Just as before, we can consider these surface integrals as the integral of a line integral and combine the two equations;

$$U = \frac{1}{2} i^2 \sum_{n=1}^N \int_{C_n} \frac{1}{h} \int_0^h \frac{\mu_0}{4\pi} \sum_{m=1}^N \int_{C_m} \frac{1}{h} \int_0^h \hat{\mathbf{s}}_n \cdot \hat{\mathbf{s}}_m$$
$$\|(\mathbf{s}_m - \mathbf{s}_n) + (z_m - z_n)\hat{\mathbf{z}}\|^{-1} dz_m\, ds_m\, dz_n\, ds_n. \quad (9)$$

We can now define the partial self-inductance, L_n, of each surface S_n and its partial mutual inductance, M_{mn}, with each other surface S_m such that:

$$L_n = \frac{\mu_0}{4\pi h^2} \int_{C_n} \int_0^h \int_{C_n} \int_0^h \frac{\hat{\mathbf{s}} \cdot \hat{\mathbf{s}}'}{\|(\mathbf{s}'-\mathbf{s}) + (z'-z)\hat{\mathbf{z}}\|}, \quad (10)$$
$$dz'\, ds'\, dz\, ds,$$

$$M_{mn} = \frac{\mu_0}{4\pi h^2} \int_{C_n} \int_0^h \int_{C_m} \int_0^h \frac{\hat{\mathbf{s}}_n \cdot \hat{\mathbf{s}}_m}{\|(\mathbf{s}_m - \mathbf{s}_n) + (z_m - z_n)\hat{\mathbf{z}}\|}$$
$$dz_m\, ds_m\, dz_n\, ds_n, \quad (11)$$

$$L = \sum_{n=1}^N L_n + 2 \sum_{n=1}^N \sum_{m>n} M_{mn}. \quad (12)$$

These expressions can be simplified in the manner of Section II, yielding formulas in the same form as Eq. (6), except that closed line integrals around C are replaced with line integrals along C_m and C_n in the case of M_{mn} and along C_n in the case of L_n. For more information on the interpretation and utility of partial inductance, see [1].

V. Conclusion

We have here developed a formula for the inductance of surface currents on generalized cylinders analagous to the Neumann formula for arbitrary wire paths. We have also demonstrated an agreement between these two formulas and shown how to apply partial inductance to break up such an inductance problem for easier computation. This double-integral formula is more easily computed than the general quadruple-integral formula in Eq. (3) and does not require explicit calculation of fields throughout the inductor (as some inductance codes are wont to do). Additionally, the integrand of Eq. (6) gives a weight function to evaluate where on the curve contributes most to the total inductance, which is useful in optimization of inductor design.

References

[1] Paul, Inductance: Loop and Partial. John Wiley & Sons, 2009.

Analysis of Spatiotemporal Field Modes of Particle-in-Cell Plasma Simulations via Proper Orthogonal Decomposition

Julio L. Nicolini and Fernando L. Teixeira
ElectroScience Laboratory, The Ohio State University
Columbus, OH 43212 USA
{delimanicolini.1, teixeira.5}@osu.edu

Abstract—**The Proper Orthogonal Decomposition (POD) is a data-driven technique that allows extraction of coherent structures from a set of data. The POD allows for the extraction of spatiotemporal modes that can be used for the construction of reduced order models. We showcase its use on a numerical particle-in-cell simulation of an accelerated electron beam in the presence of a transverse magnetic field.**

I. Introduction

The Proper Orthogonal Decomposition (POD) is a technique that decomposes a set of data into representative modes [1]–[5]. When the data represents a quantity that varies with both space and time, this allows for the extraction of spatiotemporal coherent modes [6], [7]. The POD has been used for creation of reduced-order models [8]–[10]; in [11] it was applied in that context on electromagnetic particle-in-cell (PIC) simulations of kinetic plasmas [12]. Here we briefly showcase the technique and its ability to extract spatiotemporal modes from the data of interest. In what follows the discussion is restricted to the modal extraction of the electric field due to space considerations, but it equally applies to magnetic fields and other quantities of interest.

II. Proper Orthogonal Decomposition

The POD allows the electric field to be written as:

$$\mathbf{E}(\mathbf{x},t) = \sum_{i=1}^{N_m} \sigma_i \Psi_i(\mathbf{x}) \Phi_i(t), \qquad (1)$$

where N_m is the total number of modes extracted from the data, σ_i is the spatiotemporal modal amplitude, Ψ_i are (vector-valued) spatial modes and Φ_i are (scalar-valued) temporal modes. This is achieved by sampling data-points from a numerical or practical experiment and arranging them in a "snapshot" matrix $[\mathbf{A}]$ such that its column space spans the spatial variation of the sampled field and its row space spans the temporal variation, i.e., each column of $[\mathbf{A}]$ consists of the values of the electric field at different spatial points, at a given time, in the domain of interest. The snapshot matrix can then be decomposed via singular value decomposition (SVD) as:

$$[\mathbf{A}] = [\mathbf{U}] \cdot [\mathbf{\Sigma}] \cdot [\mathbf{V}]^T. \qquad (2)$$

The columns of $[\mathbf{U}]$ provide a basis for the column space of $[\mathbf{A}]$, hence for the spatial distribution of the field, so they are the spatial modes Ψ_i. The columns of $[\mathbf{V}]$ provide a basis for the row space of $[A]$, hence for the temporal evolution of the field, so they are the temporal modes Φ_i. Lastly, the singular values present in $[\mathbf{\Sigma}]$ are the spatiotemporal amplitudes σ_i.

III. Numerical Results and Discussion

To showcase the ability of the POD to extract spatiotemporal field modes from a set of numerical data, a simulation using our PIC algorithm (for details on the algorithm see e.g., [11], [13], [14]) is performed. Consider a vacuum-filled square cavity with perfect electrical conductor (PEC) walls measuring 1 [m]. It is discretized with an irregular triangular mesh containing $N_0 = 1633$ nodes, $N_1 = 4768$ edges and $N_2 = 3136$ faces. Electrons are injected into the cavity at the lower boundary with velocity $v_0 = 5 \times 10^6$ [m/s] and absorbed at the upper boundary. There is an external voltage bias set to $V_{bias} = 1 \times 10^3$ [V] and an external magnetic field given by $\mathbf{B}_{ext} = \hat{\mathbf{z}} B_0 \sin(\omega_b t)$, with $B_0 = 6 \times 10^{-4}$ [T] and $\omega_b \approx 157 \times 10^6$ [rad/s]. Each computational particle represents 500,000 physical electrons, and five particles are injected every time-step according to a uniform random distribution at $y = 0$ between $x = 0.4$ and $x = 0.6$. The time step interval is $\Delta_t = 1 \times 10^{-11}$ [s]. The snapshot matrix is construed by harvesting values every 500 time steps until $n = 20,000$.

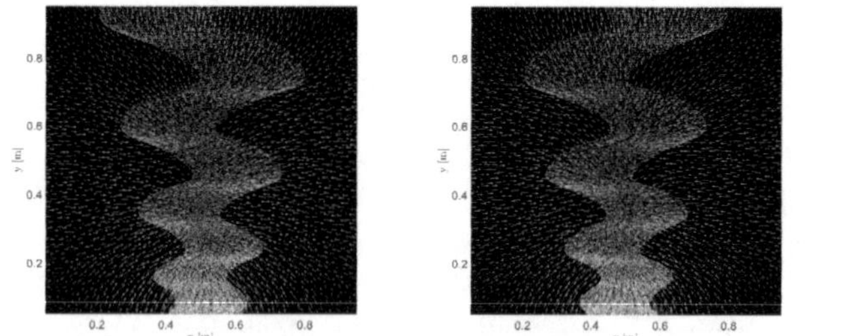

(a) $t = t_1$ (b) $t = t_2$

Fig. 1. Electric field and particle snapshot at two arbitrary times in steady-state for the numerical example. The yellow dots are the computational particles and the cyan arrows denote the electric field amplitude and direction at the points they are anchored to.

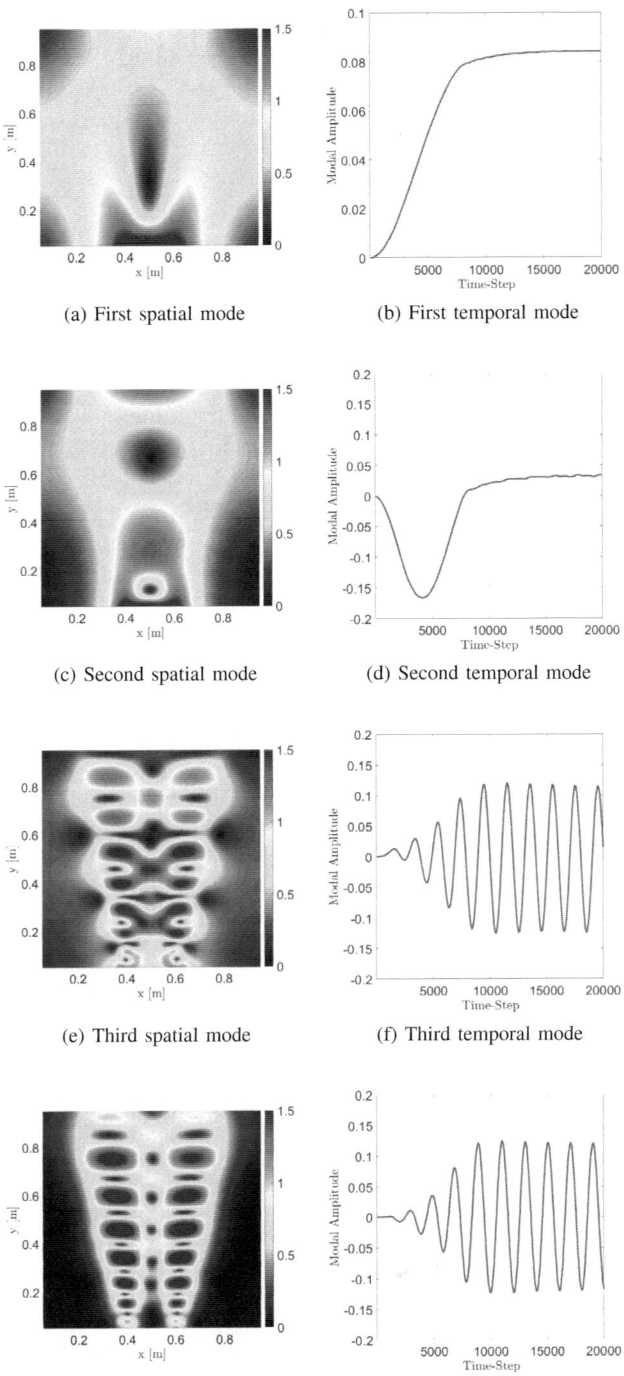

(a) First spatial mode (b) First temporal mode

(c) Second spatial mode (d) Second temporal mode

(e) Third spatial mode (f) Third temporal mode

(g) Fourth spatial mode (h) Fourth temporal mode.

Fig. 2. Spatial patterns (left) and their associated temporal evolutions (right) for the first four modes of the electric field in the numerical example. The colorbars denote the amplitude of spatial field distributions. Note that the modal amplitudes shown here (either spatial or temporal) do not take into account the actual spatiotemporal amplitudes σ_i.

Fig. 1 shows two snapshots of the electric field amplitude (cyan arrows) and electron particle positions (yellow dots) at arbitrary time points after the steady state has been reached. In particular, notice the oscillatory behavior of the beam induced by the external magnetic field. Fig. 2 showcases the distributions of the amplitudes of the first four spatial modes and the evolution of the associated four temporal modes extracted by the POD algorithm. It is clear from Fig. 2 that the first mode is a dominant, steady mode that represents the bulk behavior of the self-fields generated by the electron beam. In contrast, the second mode is mainly responsible for transient corrections (notice how the spatial distribution tends towards the bottom half of the domain and the temporal evolution dies down to near zero after some time steps). Modes 3 and 4 are higher-order spatial modes that represent the effect of the laterally oscillating beam particles, which can be seen by the "hot spots" in the spatial distributions and by the oscillatory behavior in the temporal evolution. Even higher order modes (not shown) alternate between higher-order corrections to either the oscillatory or the transient behavior, with decreasing importance due to smaller spatiotemporal amplitudes.

ACKNOWLEDGEMENT

This work was supported in part by NSF grant ECCS-1305838, DTRA grant HDTRA1-18-1-0050, and OSC grants PAS-0061 and PAS-0110.

REFERENCES

[1] Y. Liang, H. Lee, S. Lim, W. Lin, K. Lee, and C. Wu, "Proper orthogonal decomposition and its applications, Part I: Theory," J. Sound Vibration, vol. 252, no. 3, pp. 527–544, 2002.

[2] A. Chatterjee, "An introduction to the proper orthogonal decomposition," Current Sci., pp. 808–817, 2000.

[3] M. Rathinam and L. R. Petzold, "A new look at proper orthogonal decomposition," SIAM J. Num. Anal., vol. 41, pp. 1893–1925, 2003.

[4] W. Cazemier, Proper orthogonal decomposition and low dimensional models for turbulent flows. PhD thesis, Rijksuniversiteit Groningen, 1997.

[5] W. Cazemier, R. Verstappen, and A. Veldman, "Proper orthogonal decomposition and low-dimensional models for driven cavity flows," Phys. Fluids, vol. 10, no. 7, pp. 1685–1699, 1998.

[6] N. Aubry, R. Guyonnet, and R. Lima, "Spatiotemporal analysis of complex signals: Theory and applications," Journal of Statistical Physics, vol. 64, no. 3-4, pp. 683–739, 1991.

[7] N. Aubry, "On the hidden beauty of the proper orthogonal decomposition," Theor. Comp. Fluid Dyn., vol. 2.

[8] S. S. Ravindran, "A reduced-order approach for optimal control of fluids using proper orthogonal decomposition," Int. J. Num. Meth. Fluids, vol. 34, no. 5, pp. 425–448, 2000.

[9] H. V. Ly and H. T. Tran, "Modeling and control of physical processes using proper orthogonal decomposition," Math. Comp. Model., vol. 33, no. 1-3, pp. 223–236, 2001.

[10] A. Pierquin, T. Henneron, S. Clenet, and S. Brisset, "Model-order reduction of magnetoquasistatic problems based on pod and arnoldi-based krylov methods," IEEE Trans. Magn., vol. 51, no. 3, pp. 1–4, 2015.

[11] J. L. Nicolini, D.-Y. Na, and F. L. Teixeira, "Model order reduction of electromagnetic particle-in-cell simulations via proper orthogonal decomposition," IEEE Trans. Plasma Sci. In print.

[12] D.-Y. Na, H. Moon, Y. Omelchenko, and F. Teixeira, "Relativistic extension of a charge-conservative finite element solver for time-dependent maxwell-vlasov equations," Physics of Plasmas, vol. 25, no. 1, p. 013109, 2018.

[13] D.-Y. Na, H. Moon, Y. A. Omelchenko, and F. L. Teixeira, "Local, explicit, and charge-conserving electromagnetic particle-in-cell algorithm on unstructured grids," IEEE Trans. Plasma Sci., vol. 44, pp. 1353–1362, 2016.

[14] H. Moon, F. L. Teixeira, and Y. A. Omelchenko, "Exact charge-conserving scatter-gather algorithm for particle-in-cell simulations on unstructured grids: A geometric perspective," Comput. Phys. Commun., vol. 194, pp. 43–53, 2015.

Computational Performance of MATLAB and Python for Electromagnetic Applications

Alec Weiss
Department of Electrical Engineering
Colorado School of Mines
Golden, Colorado
aweiss@mines.edu

Atef Elsherbeni*
Department of Electrical Engineering
Colorado School of Mines
Golden, Colorado
aelsherb@mines.edu

***Abstract*—MATLAB and Python are two commonly used scripting languages for prototyping electromagnetic problems today. Each of these languages provides access to computationally efficient functions allowing a user to easily run many math heavy problems with minimal programming. In this paper we will discuss the usage of MATLAB and a variety of libraries in Python capable of running these efficient computations. Tests will be run in both languages to compare both CPU and GPU computations. The runtimes of a variety of problems using each of these platforms will also be compared for a variety of mathematical operations typically used in electromagnetic problems. Finally, a simple angle of arrival calculation using conventional beamforming will be performed to show these speeds on a realistic problem.**

Keywords— Computational Electromagnetics, GPU Programming, MATLAB, Python.

I. Introduction

Modern high-level programming languages such as MATLAB and Python provide an easy way to quickly create software for electromagnetic simulations and data processing. These languages excel by abstracting the difficulties and verbosity of lower level languages such as FORTRAN or C. This abstraction comes at the expense of computational efficiency. MATLAB and python libraries such as Numpy and Numba are designed specifically to increase the efficiency by calling more efficient C and FORTRAN subroutines.

Acceleration techniques in MATLAB for computational electromagnetic (CEM) problems has been previously studied in various papers [1,2]. Previous works have also compared MATLAB and Python in a variety of areas such as the usage for linear algebra [3] and general usability [4] in comparison to MATLAB. Previous work has not compared MATLAB and Python for usage with complex numbers with basic operators ranging from addition to complex exponentials which is important as these datatypes and operators are prevalent in a variety of CEM applications.

This work covers the comparison of MATLAB and Python for complex number calculations that may be seen in typical electromagnetic problems. Each language will be tested with variety of libraries and programming techniques. Initial tests run and compare speeds when performing a single operation such as (e.g., $a + b$) and a small collection of operations (e.g., $a * (b + c)$) on a set of data providing a basis for a large variety of electromagnetic problems. Results comparing a realistic angle of arrival (AoA) simulation using conventional beamforming will also be tested to provide a more realistic CEM application.

*Adjunct Professor, Department of Elec. & Computer Eng., King Abdulaziz University, Jeddah, Saudi Arabia

II. Introduction to Python and MATLAB for CEM

A. MATLAB

An inherent benefit of MATLAB is that all required commands are built in and do not require the importing of libraries. This can make the language easier to learn and implement for an inexperienced programmer but comes at the cost of flexibility. While many ways exist to perform computations in MATLAB, this work will focus on standard usage of built-in functions without any special optimizations. Code can also easily take advantage of graphics processing units (GPUs) using the gpuArray command. MATLAB Results were obtained using MATLAB R2018a.

B. Python

Unlike MATLAB, python libraries must be explicitly imported. While this adds an extra layer of difficulty to the language, it also provides the flexibility of using a variety of libraries. This work will test a few of the most popular libraries for vectorized computation on the CPU. These libraries are Numpy/Scipy and Numba. Numpy and Scipy are a set of commonly used libraries for performing many vectorized and linear algebra operations in a similar way to MATLAB where once the variables are declared, the multiplication operator will perform elementwise multiplication with optimized subroutines. Numba extends upon the capability of Numpy by allowing for user defined vector functions and precompiled sections of code. Like MATLAB, code can also easily be extended to a GPU using the CuPy library. Python Results were obtained with Python 3.7.3, Numpy 1.16.5, Scipy 1.3.1, and Numba 0.44.1.

III. Operator Testing

Initial speed comparisons were done with testing of single and multi-operator arithmetic. By testing these more generic situations, it is possible to estimate the runtimes of a variety of CEM problems. Each of these tests was run with both single and double precision complex data types.

Tests with a single operator were run for both single (using the single() command) and double precision complex values using MATLAB and Python. The tests were run for typical arithmetic operators (+,-,*,/) along with a complex exponential, matrix multiply, and summation. Additional testing was also performed with LU decomposition, FFT, sparse matrix multiplication, and the equation $c = a + b * exp(a)$ where a and b are complex matrices. All tests were run on a Intel Xeon E5-2620 processor with 128GB of RAM. The runtimes in seconds from these tests for double and single precision are shown in Table and II, respectively. It should be noticed that for most of the tested cases, using either Numba or Numpy provides very close runtimes to MATLAB. In some cases, such as FFT, combined computations, and sparse matrix multiplication Python outperforms the similar routines in MATLAB.

Table I. Double Precision Complex Operation Runtimes (seconds)

Operation	MATLAB	Python (Numpy)	Python (Numba)
Add	0.2249	0.2814	0.2774
Subtract	0.2280	0.2745	0.2847
Multiply	0.2281	0.2706	0.2927
Divide	0.2322	0.4667	0.2845
Matrix Multiply	8.0504	7.5575	N/A
Exponential	0.2974	3.1985	0.3177
Sum	0.0169	0.0515	N/A
LU Decomposition	2.9076	4.4278	N/A
FFT	0.2113	0.1345	N/A
Combined	0.5750	3.8899	0.3292
Sparse	4.2567	3.0242	N/A

Table II. Single Precision Complex Operation Runtimes (seconds)

Operation	MATLAB	Python (Numpy)	Python (Numba)
Add	0.1135	0.1459	0.1512
Subtract	0.1136	0.1481	0.1538
Multiply	0.1180	0.1504	0.1567
Divide	0.1275	0.4082	0.1538
Matrix Multiply	3.7282	3.5604	N/A
Exponential	0.2127	2.9446	0.1575
Sum	0.0086	0.0287	N/A
LU Decomposition	1.5741	2.6686	N/A
FFT	0.1218	0.0783	N/A
Combined	0.3639	3.2805	0.1609
Sparse	N/A	1.8862	N/A

IV. Realisitc AoA Example

Angle of arrival calculations are performed in a variety of EM applications to estimate the direction from which waves are impinging upon an antenna array. While many algorithms exist for this calculation (e.g., [5]), a basic example of conventional beamforming can be used for speed comparison because it contains complex elementwise multiplication, exponentials, matrix multiplication, and summations. The conventional beamforming equation with frequency domain data for AoA estimation can be written as:

$$\sum_{e=1}^{E} W(e)S(e,f)e^{k(f)\mathrm{r}(e)},$$

where E is our total number of elements, $W(e)$ is the weighting on each of the elements, and $e^{k(f)r(e)}$ is the steering vector. $S(e,f)$ is the received complex data at each element. For this problem incident plane waves were synthetically impinged upon a planar array allowing simulation of what an antenna array of that shape and size may measure. The runtimes in seconds for double and single precision beamforming on a 10x10 element planar array with a synthetic incident plane wave at 45 degrees show what MATLAB is having a slight performance advantage over Python using Numba as shown in Table III.

Table III. Beamforming Runtimes (Seconds)

Mean Runtime (Seconds)	MATLAB	Python (Numpy)	Python (Numba)
Double	0.6448	1.8860	0.7776
Single	0.2779	1.4079	0.3270

V. Conclusions

We have shown the runtime comparisons for a variety of operations on complex numbers in MATLAB and two Python libraries that are typically used in CEM applications using CPUs. Similar analysis conducted on GPUs will be presented at the conference. While in many of the cases MATLAB outperforms Python, Python comes very close in most operations and in some cases even outperforms MATLAB. Python comes with the added benefits of being completely free along with having many other libraries and acceleration techniques beyond Numpy and Numba to compete with the runtimes that MATLAB can achieve.

References

[1] A. J. Weiss, A. Z. Elsherbeni, V. Demir, and M. F. Hadi, "Using MATLAB's Parallel Processing Toolbox for Multi-CPU and Multi-GPU Accelerated FDTD Simulations," vol. 34, no. 5, p. 7, 2019.

[2] M. Capek, P. Hazdra, J. Eichler, P. Hamouz, and M. Mazanek, "Acceleration techniques in Matlab for EM community," in 2013 7th European Conference on Antennas and Propagation (EuCAP), 2013, pp. 2639–2642.

[3] J. Unpingco, "Some Comparative Benchmarks for Linear Algebra Computations in Matlab and Scientific Python," in 2008 DoD HPCMP Users Group Conference, 2008, pp. 503–505.

[4] J. Ranjani, A. Sheela, and K. P. Meena, "Combination of NumPy, SciPy and Matplotlib/Pylab -a good alternative methodology to MATLAB - A Comparative analysis," in 2019 1st International Conference on Innovations in Information and Communication Technology (ICIICT), 2019, pp. 1–5.

[5] P. Vouras, et al., "Gradient-Based Solution Of Maximum Likelihood Angle Estimation For Virtual Array Measurements," in 2018 IEEE Global Conference on Signal and Information Processing (GlobalSIP), 2018, pp. 1257–1261.

Dynamic Mode Decomposition for Prediction of Kinetic Plasma Behavior

Indranil Nayak and Fernando L. Teixeira
ElectroScience Laboratory, Department of Electrical and Computer Engineering
The Ohio State University
Columbus, OH 43212 USA
{nayak.77, teixeira.5}@osu.edu

***Abstract*—We present a reduced-order model based on the dynamic mode decomposition (DMD) for capturing the essential dynamics of kinetic plasma simulation. We apply the proposed methodology to the case of an accelerated electron beam propagation inside a cavity in the presence of a transverse magnetic field. The full order model utilizes a local and explicit finite-element time-domain (FETD) based electromagnetic particle-in-cell (EM-PIC) algorithm for simulating the beam. We employ DMD to extract dominant features that help us predict the future distribution of self electric field. The reduction achieved by this analysis can be instrumental in reducing the computation cost of complex plasma simulations.**

***Index Terms*—Finite elements, kinetic plasma, reduced order model, particle-in-cell, time domain.**

I. Introduction

The dynamic mode decomposition (DMD) is a powerful tool for data-driven modelling of complex dynamical systems. Since its introduction [1] DMD has gained popularity especially among the fluid dynamics community due to its "equation-free" character [1]–[3]. In a typical application, DMD models the time evolution of a complex dynamical system by finite approximation of the infinite dimensional Koopman operator [4]. The eigenvalues of this approximated finite operator along with the computed DMD modes describe the dominant spatio-temporal behavior of a system.

EM-PIC algorithms are powerful tool for solving the Maxwell-Vlasov system for kinetic plasma simulations [5], [6]. However, one of the drawbacks of EM-PIC algorithm is the high computation time and memory requirement for large number of particles. Reduced order models like DMD can be very useful in such cases to predict the solution in future time with no need to run the high-fidelity algorithm. DMD has been applied for plasma diagnostics in magnetohydrodynamics formulation [7], but to the best of the authors' knowledge, its application to EM-PIC is unprecedented. In this paper we apply DMD on EM-PIC simulation of oscillating plasma beam and show that the electric field (self-field) pattern can be accurately predicted until considerable time in future.

II. EM-PIC Simulation and DMD Algorithm

The EM-PIC algorithm updates the electric and magnetic field on the mesh and pushes the superparticles (coarse graining of phase space of electron density) in the solution domain through four consecutive operations at each time step: (1) field solver, (2) gather, (3) particle pusher, and (4) scatter [8]–[10]. We apply a local and explicit FETD based field solver which conserves energy and charge from first principle on unstructured grids [8], [11], [12].

In DMD, we first run the full order EM-PIC simulation until certain point in time (harvesting limit) to collect snapshots of degree of freedom (DoF) of electric field intensity at the mesh edges. Each snapshot is represented by a spatial vector $\mathbf{E^n} = [E_1^n \; E_2^n \; ... \; E_i^n ... \; E_{N_1-1}^n \; E_{N_1}^n]^T$, where E_i^n denotes the DoF of electric field intensity at i^{th} edge (total N_1 edges) at n^{th} time step. The basic algorithm is summarized in [2], [13]. We form two matrices using the snapshot vectors, $X = [\mathbf{E^{n_1}} \; \mathbf{E^{n_2}} \; ... \; \mathbf{E^{n_{p-1}}}]$ and $X' = [\mathbf{E^{n_2}} \; \mathbf{E^{n_3}} \; ... \; \mathbf{E^{n_p}}]$; where n_p is the harvesting limit and $n_{j+1} - n_j = m$, $(1 \leq j < p)$; m being the number of time steps between snapshots. DMD assumes $X' \approx A \cdot X$ and estimates the eigenvalues and eigenvectors of A. The singular value decomposition (SVD) of X produces $X \approx U\Sigma V^*$. A is approximated as $\tilde{A} = U_r^* X' V_r \Sigma_r^{-1}$, where U_r, Σ_r and V_r are formed by taking first r columns; first r columns, r rows and first r columns of U, Σ and V respectively. The DMD modes and corresponding frequencies are given by Φ_k, the columns of Φ and ω_k, i.e., $\Phi = X' V_r \Sigma_r^{-1} W$ and $\omega_k = ln(\lambda_k)/(m\Delta_t)$, where $\Delta_t = 10^{-11}$ [s] is the time step interval, λ_k are the diagonal entries of Λ, which we get along with W from the eigendecomposition of $\tilde{A}$, i.e., $\tilde{A}W = W\Lambda$. The reconstructed DoF of electric field intensity is given by:

$$\mathbf{E(t)} = \sum_{k=1}^{r} b_k \Phi_k e^{\omega_k t} \tag{1}$$

where the scaling factor for each mode b_k is computed in accordance with [14]. In our algorithm, we stack multiple time-shifted data matrices to form X and X' [2], [13].

III. Numerical Experiments and Discussion

Consider a square two-dimensional cavity with dimension $l \times l$ (see Fig. 1). Superparticles are injected randomly (uniform distribution) at the bottom of the cavity in the region $[l/2 - b, l/2 + b]$, where $b = 0.1$ [m] is the half-beam width. Assuming $l = 1$ [m], the square cavity is discretized using an irregular triangular mesh with number of nodes $N_0 = 1633$, edges $N_1 = 4768$ and triangles $N_2 = 3136$. All four sides of the cavity are assumed to be perfect electric conductors (PEC).

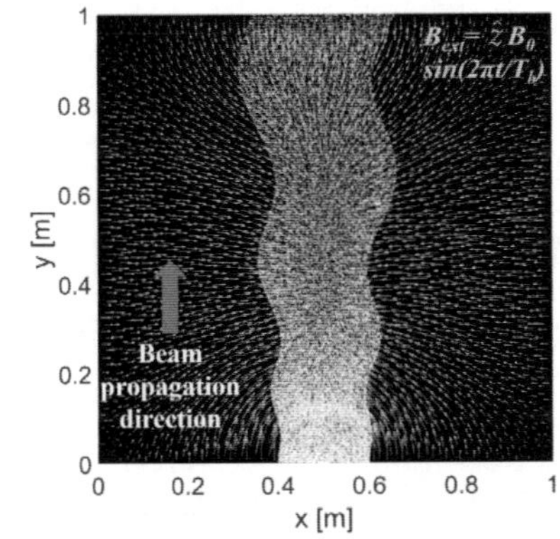

Fig. 1. Snapshot of oscillating electron beam at the middle ($n = 23921$) of the FETD-based EM-PIC simulation time window. The yellow dots represent the superparticles and the cyan arrows indicates the electric field (self-field) distribution.

Superparticles are injected with initial velocity $v_0 = 5 \times 10^6$ [m/s] along y direction with an injection rate of 40 superparticles per 5 time steps. Each superparticle represents of 5×10^5 electrons. The external voltage bias is set to $V_b = 2 \times 10^3$ [V] and external magnetic field to $B_{ext} = B_0 \, \sin(2\pi t/T_b) \, \hat{\mathbf{z}}$, with $B_0 = 4 \times 10^{-4}$ [T] and $T_b = 2 \times 10^{-8}$ [s]. The superparticles are absorbed as they hit the upper boundary. We set the harvesting limit to time step $n = 21761$, chosen in such a way that the system is in equilibrium state. Instead of collecting snapshots from $n = 1$, we start from $n = 161$ time steps. The harvesting region is divided in four sub-regions (see Fig. 2) with interval between snapshots (m values) $m_4 = 320$, $m_3 = 160$, $m_2 = 80$ and $m_1 = 80$ time steps in sub-region (iv),(iii), (ii) and (i) respectively. We apply DMD on these sub-regions separately. Fig. 2 shows the time variation of the $2-$norm error in $\mathbf{E}$. The error at n^{th} time step is given by, $\delta^n = ||\mathbf{E}^n_{\text{DMD}} - \mathbf{E}^n_{\text{FETD}}||_2/||\mathbf{E}^n_{\text{FETD}}||_2$. The secular growth in the error is very small and the overall error remains within acceptable bounds beyond the harvesting region. In Fig. 3 we see that DMD predicts the electric field (self-field) pattern in the extrapolated region with good accuracy. We stress that by using DMD no time-update is necessary in the extrapolated window as the time variation is captured by the term $e^{\omega_k t}$, as given by (1).

ACKNOWLEDGMENT

This work was supported in part by DTRA grant HDTRA 1-18-1-0050 and OSC grants PAS-0061 and PAS-0110.

REFERENCES

[1] P. J. Schmid, "Dynamic mode decomposition of numerical and experimental data," Journal of Fluid Mechanics, vol. 656, pp. 5–28, Aug 2010.

[2] J. H. Tu, C. W. Rowley, D. M. Luchtenburg, S. L. Brunton, and J. N. Kutz, "On dynamic mode decomposition: theory and applications," arXiv:1312.0041, Nov 2013.

[3] J. Kou and W. Zhang, "An improved criterion to select dominant modes from dynamic mode decomposition," European J. Mech. B - Fluids, vol. 62, pp. 109–129, Mar-Apr 2017.

[4] C. W. Rowley, I. Mezić, S. Bagheri, P. Schlatter, and D. S. Henningson, "Spectral analysis of nonlinear flows," Journal of Fluid Mechanics, vol. 641, pp. 115–127, Dec 2009.

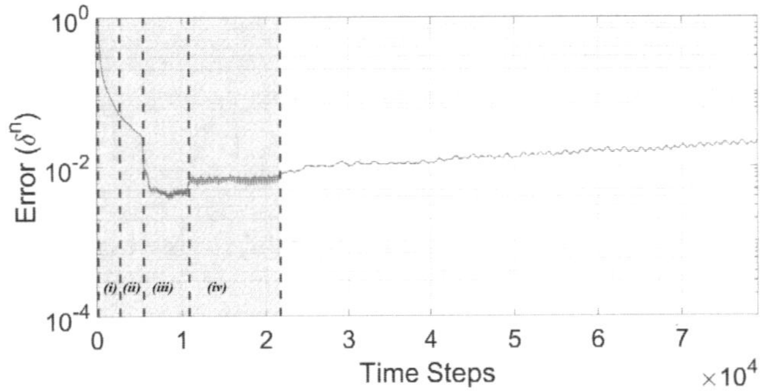

Fig. 2. The 2-norm error ($\delta^n = ||\mathbf{E}^n_{\text{DMD}} - \mathbf{E}^n_{\text{FETD}}||_2/||\mathbf{E}^n_{\text{FETD}}||_2$) in $\mathbf{E}$ inside the harvesting region (green shaded area) and in the extrapolated region, with $r = 16$ in each sub-region.

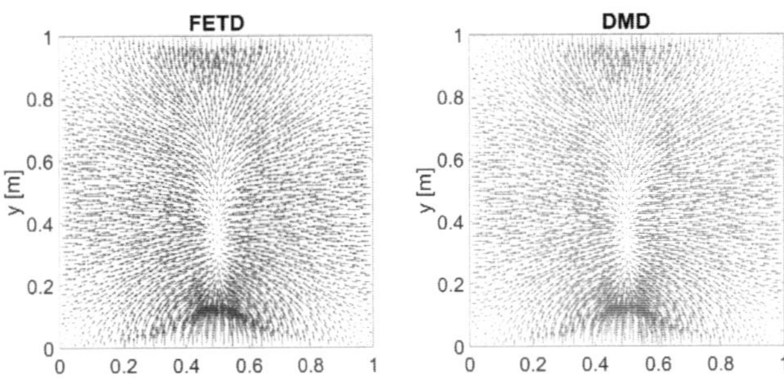

Fig. 3. Electric field (self-field) patterns in the extrapolated region. The blue arrows show the electric field pattern of FETD based EM-PIC simulation at time step $n = 63921$ and the red arrows show the electric field pattern predicted by the DMD at the same time.

[5] R. W. Hockney and J. W. Eastwood, Computer Simulation Using Particles. New York: CRC Press, Jan 1988.

[6] C. K. Birdsall and A. B. Langdon, Plasma Physics via Computer Simulation. New York: CRC Press, Oct 2004.

[7] R. Taylor, J. N. Kutz, K. Morgan, and B. A. Nelson, "Dynamic mode decomposition for plasma diagnostics and validation," Rev. Sci. Instr., vol. 89, no. 5, p. 053501, May 2018.

[8] D.-Y. Na, H. Moon, Y. A. Omelchenko, and F. L. Teixeira, "Local, explicit, and charge-conserving electromagnetic particle-in-cell algorithm on unstructured grids," IEEE Trans. Plasma Sci., vol. 44, pp. 1353–1362, Aug 2016.

[9] H. Moon, F. L. Teixeira, and Y. A. Omelchenko, "Exact charge-conserving scatter–gather algorithm for particle-in-cell simulations on unstructured grids: A geometric perspective," Comput. Phys. Commun., vol. 194, pp. 43–53, Sep 2015.

[10] D.-Y. Na, H. Moon, Y. A. Omelchenko, and F. L. Teixeira, "Relativistic extension of a charge-conservative finite element solver for time-dependent Maxwell-Vlasov equations," Phys. Plasmas, vol. 25, no. 1, p. 013109, Jan 2018.

[11] B. He and F. L. Teixeira, "Differential forms, Galerkin duality, and sparse inverse approximations in finite element solutions of Maxwell equations," IEEE Trans. Antennas Propag., vol. 55, pp. 1359–1368, May 2007.

[12] J. Kim and F. L. Teixeira, "Parallel and explicit finite-element time-domain method for Maxwell's equations," IEEE Trans. Antennas Propag., vol. 59, pp. 2350–2356, Jun 2011.

[13] J. N. Kutz, S. L. Brunton, B. W. Brunton, and J. L. Proctor, Dynamic mode decomposition: Data-driven modeling of complex systems. SIAM, Dec 2016.

[14] M. R. Jovanović, P. J. Schmid, and J. W. Nichols, "Sparsity-promoting dynamic mode decomposition," Physics of Fluids, vol. 26, no. 2, p. 024103, Feb 2014.

Multiple OAM Beams Design Using the Pattern Product Method

Ziyang Wang*, Fan Yang, Shenheng Xu, and Maokun Li
Beijing National Research Center for Information Science and Technology
Department of Electronic Engineering, Tsinghua University, Beijing, 100084, China
E-mail:wanziyang1@tsinghua.edu.cn*, fan_yang@tsinghua.edu.cn

***Abstract*—In this paper, vortex electromagnetic wave with multiple Orbital Angular Momentum (OAM) beams is designed based on the pattern product method, and demonstrated by using a 1-bit coding electromagnetic surface at 12.5 GHz. First, compensated phase distributions of the electromagnetic surface are derived to realize an OAM beam and multiple pencil beams, respectively. Next, using the pattern product method, a new phase distribution is obtained to realize the multiple OAM beams. Thereafter, numerical calculation results and full wave simulation results based on a 1-bit square-patch surface are presented, which verify the feasibility of the proposed method. It provides useful reference for the subsequent realization of multiple OAM beams with adjustable function in 3D space.**

Keywords—Coding Surface, OAM; 1-bit, Multiple Beams, Multiple OAM Beams, Pattern Product Method.

I. Introduction

Vortex electromagnetic wave carrying OAM may be a potential technology for future mobile communication. Hence, OAM has gradually become a hotpot [1], and be widely studied in academia. OAM is applied in optics firstly, and gradually extended to the field of radio frequency (RF). It has been reported that spiral phase plate, spiral reflector and antenna array are used to realize OAM beams in the RF field. As an important generating and modulation device for electromagnetic wave, the "artificial electromagnetic surface" has many advantages, such as easy processing and forming. In addition, it is also applied to the generating of OAM beams [2].

In most of the papers about the realization of vortex electromagnetic wave by using artificial electromagnetic surface, the beam is single and fixed. In another words, it has only one outgoing direction of beam. Then, multiple-antennas array is used to realize multiple pencil beams or multiple OAM beams. For which, it is necessary to increase the number of antenna elements to solve the problem of multiple pencil beams with different directions, which greatly increases the cost and complexity of the antenna design. There are also a few reports on the idea of realizing multiple pencil beams based on artificial electromagnetic surface. Thereafter, the introduction of digital coding electromagnetic surface [3] can reduce the design complexity of elements, since it contains only limited phase states of 0 and 1. So that the element does not need to strictly meet the requirement of 360° phase range full coverage. Moreover, it lays the foundation for the design of multiple OAM beams with the adjustable function of beam scanning and mode switch.

In this letter, an electromagnetic surface consists of 1-bit phase elements is briefly described to realize multiple OAM beams. First, the design and realization of an OAM beam based on 360° phase elements are introduced. Then, the design of multiple pencil beams is also shown in detail. Next, combining the above two designs, the implementation of multiple OAM beams based on 360° phase units by using the pattern product method is presented. Finally, the feasibility of multiple OAM beams by using 1-bit phase elements is verified, which provides a strong basis for the realization of multiple OAM beams with the function of dynamic regulation in future.

II. Analysis and Design of Multiple OAM Beams

A. Design and Implementation for a Vortex beam

The design and implementation of the vortex beam are introduced in this section. Firstly, a reflective surface is used to generate the OAM beam, in which a 360° phase range should be covered for a good radiation performance. Meanwhile, the compensation phase of each element on the electromagnetic surface can be calculated by Eq. (1), therefore OAM beams with:

$$\varphi(m,n)_{OAM} = k \times r_{fmn} - k \times r_{mn} \times u_0 + \Delta\varphi + l \times \Phi_{mn} \cdot \quad (1)$$

$$\text{While, } l = 0, \pm 1, \pm 2, \ldots \quad (2)$$

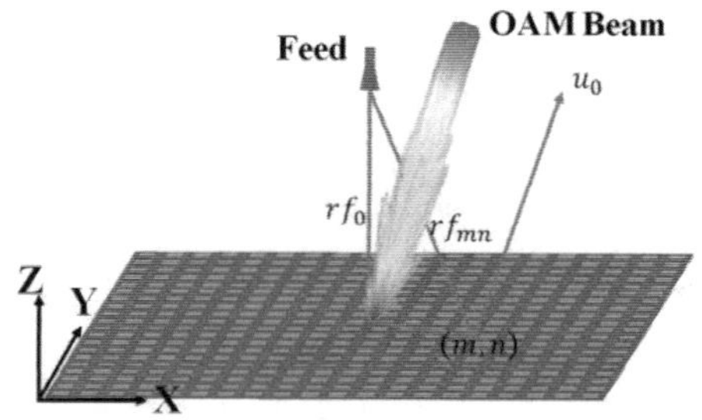

Fig. 1. Schematic diagram of OAM beam in reflectarray system.

different modes for vortex radiation can be obtained, such as l =1, l =-1, l =2 and so on. Reflective square patch units covering 360° phase range with different sizes are selected to verify the design of an OAM beam. In the end, the design of the OAM beam is simulated by full wave simulation software HFSS. Moreover, the diagrammatic sketch of the electromagnetic surface system with a 3D pattern for OAM radiation is presented in Fig. 1.

Project funded by China Postdoctoral Science Foundation (2019M650677).
fan_yang@tsinghua.edu.cn.wangziyang1@tsinghua.edu.cn, The authors declare that there are no conflicts of interest related to this article.
978-1-7335096-0-2 Â©2020 ACESâ

B. Design and Realization for Multiple Pencil Beams

The realization for a single OAM beam has been presented in the previous section. Next, the generating of multiple pencil beams based on reflective elements is discussed in this section. An algorithm with universal applicability is presented to realize a certain number multiple pencil beams when the number of array elements is large enough.

The compensation phase for multiple pencil beams on the metasurface can be calculated by Eq. (3). Next, the 2D and 3D radiation patterns are obtained by using the full wave electromagnetic simulation software HFSS to verify the feasibility of the proposed multiple pencil beams method. In this design, a reflective metasurface consists of 360° continuous phase elements is introduced with the size of 20×20 elements at 12.5 GHz.

$$\varphi_{Multiple} = k \times r_f + angle(\sum_{i=1}^{Num} e^{-jk \times ru_i}) . \quad (3)$$

C. Design and Realization for Multiple OAM Beams

Up to now, the methods for a single OAM beam and multiple beams have been delineated. Combining the two designs mentioned above, the design of multiple OAM beams is obtained by using the pattern product method. The formula for calculating the phase of multiple OAM beams on the surface is presented in Eq. (4). Meanwhile, the amplitude A_{mn} on:

$$\varphi_{need} = \varphi_{Multi} + \varphi_{vortex} . \quad (4)$$

the surface can be obtained by using Eq. (5) in the space-feed:

$$A_{mn} = \frac{FP \times EP \times |\Gamma_{mn}|}{r_{fmn}} . \quad (5)$$

system. In the end, the electric fields at the far field observation point can be calculated by Eq. (6).

$$E(\theta, \varphi) = \cos^{qe}\theta \sum_{m=1}^{M} \sum_{n=1}^{N} A_{mn} e^{(-jkr_{fmn} + j\varphi_{need} + jkr_{mn}u)} . \quad (6)$$

In order to clarify the phase design for two OAM beams more clearly, the three different phase distributions are presented in Figs. 2 (a-c), respectively, with the size of array about 20×20 elements. Finally, a simple explanation is displayed according to the method of pattern product for two OAM beams. The far-field 3D patterns corresponding to each cases in Fig. 2 are shown in Fig. 3 by the array theory method [4]. Therefore, as shown in Fig. 3, the two OAM beams can be obtained from single OAM beam and two pencil beams. Moreover, it is feasible that this scheme can be extended to three and four OAM beams.

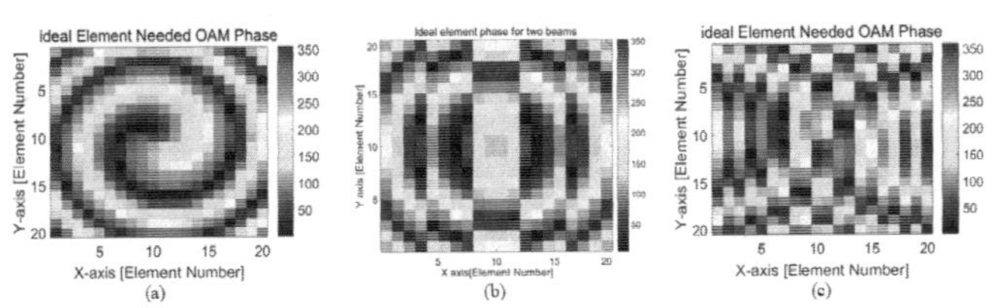

Fig. 3. Phase distributions for different cases: (a) single OAM beam, (b) two pencil beams at θ=±30°, and (c) two OAM beams at θ=±30°.

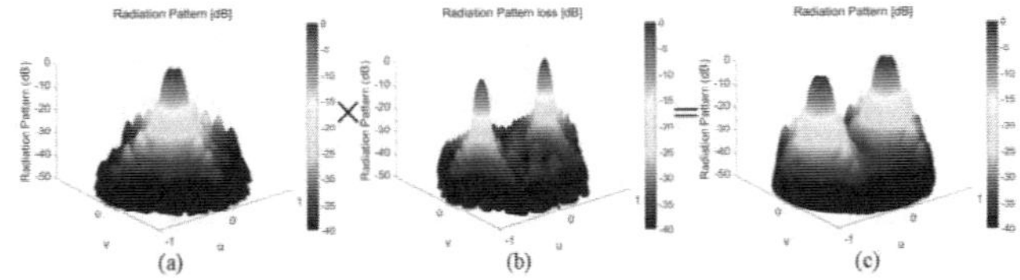

Fig. 3. Numerical results of the pattern product method: (a) single OAM beam, (b) two pencil beams, and (c) two OAM beams.

D. The Realization of Multiple OAM Beams by using 1-bit Phase Units

According to the method of pattern product, the multiple OAM beams is realized based on 360° continuous phase elements which has been verified clearly. Then, the realization of multiple OAM beams by using 1-bit phase elements is also investigated. The 1-bit quantization phase for the realization of multiple OAM beams is generated by Eq. (7). Then, the phase distribution on the coding surface and 3D pattern for two OAM beams are obtained based on the 1-bit phase element, as shown in Fig. 4. Therefore, the feasibility of realizing multiple OAM beams based on the 1-bit phase element has verified briefly:

$$\varphi_{1bitneed} = \begin{cases} 0, -\frac{\pi}{2} < \varphi(m,n)_{need} < \frac{\pi}{2} and \varphi(m,n)_{need} = \pm\frac{\pi}{2} \\ \pi, -\pi < \varphi(m,n)_{need} < -\frac{\pi}{2} and \frac{\pi}{2} < \varphi(m,n)_{need} < \pi \end{cases} . \quad (7)$$

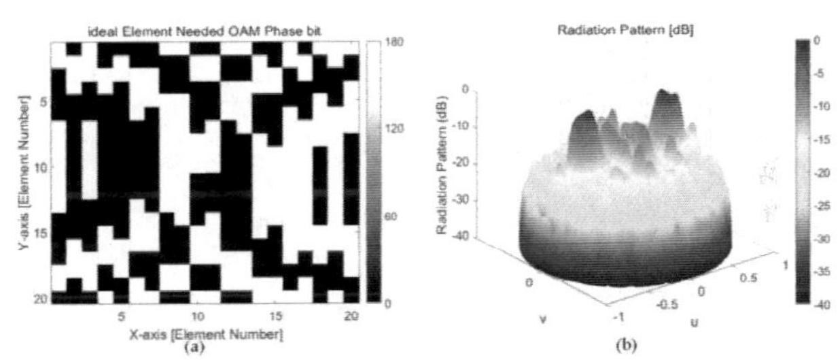

Fig. 4. Two OAM beams based on the 1-bit phase element for the mode of l=1 (a) phase distribution on the surface and (b) 3D pattern.

REFERENCES

[1] W. Park, L. Wang, H. D. Bruns, et al., Introducing a Mixed-Mode Matrix for Investigation of Wireless Communication Related to Orbital Angular Momentum (OAM)[J]. IEEE Transactions on Antennas and Propagation, 2018:1-1.

[2] S. Yu, L. Li, G. Shi, et al., Design, fabrication, and measurement of reflective metasurface for orbital angular momentum vortex wave in radio frequency domain[J]. Applied Physics Letters, 2016, 108(12):121903.

[3] T. J. Cui, S. Liu, L. L. Li, Information entropy of coding metasurface[J]. Light: Science & Applications, 2016, 5(11):e16172.

[4] P. Nayeri, F. Yang, and A. Z. Elsherbeni. Reflectarray Antennas: Theory, Designs and Applications. Wiley-IEEE Press, 2018.

Adaptive Interference Cancellation Using Atomic Norm Minimization

Shuang Li, Daniel Gaydos, Payam Nayeri, and Michael B. Wakin
Department of Electrical Engineering, Colorado School of Mines, Golden, CO, USA

***Abstract*—The rapid increase in number of wireless devices in modern communication networks has significantly increased the number of interference sources, which severely impacts communication reliability. With the projected further increase in the number of wireless devices, adaptive interference cancellation is quickly becoming a necessity for modern networks. During interference cancellation, a digital beamformer adaptively adjusts its weight vector using an array processing algorithm, which in turn shapes the radiation pattern in a manner that minimizes interference power and maximizes the desired signal power. In this work, we propose two atomic norm minimization-based methods to design a weight vector that can be used to simultaneously cancel the interference and remove the impact of frequency offset in both noiseless and noisy frameworks. Numerical simulations indicate that our proposed methods significantly outperform the classic SMI technique.**

***Index Terms*—Array signal processing, atomic norm minimization, beamforming, frequency offset, interference cancellation.**

I. Introduction

Adaptive beamforming is an array signal processing technique for directional signal transmission and reception [7, 6]. In the case of adaptive interference cancellation, a weight vector is designed to attenuate signals in the directions of interference sources and strengthen signals in the direction of the desired transmitter. Sample Matrix Inversion (SMI) [8, 6] is a common method for calculating such a weight vector. It relies on directly computing a pseudoinverse matrix, which makes it very simple. However, due to its reliance on a known pilot signal, it is very sensitive to frequency offsets in the received signal. Measuring and removing this frequency offset can be difficult in high-interference scenarios. Genetic algorithms (GAs) are one way to overcome the limitations of SMI with unknown frequency offset [1].

In recent years, atomic norm minimization (ANM) has been extensively studied in both line spectral estimation and array signal processing [5, 9, 3]. In this work, we highlight that the problem of interference cancellation with unknown frequency offset can be formulated as an ANM problem, which can be solved efficiently and used to exactly identify the frequency offset in the noiseless case. In particular, we propose two ANM-based methods (for the noiseless and noisy cases) to design a weight vector that can be used to cancel the interference when the signal frequency offset is unknown. This novel combination of ANM and SMI enables us to remove the impact of unknown frequency offset in beamforming directly and without a GA.

II. Problem Formulation and Main Results

In a conventional linear array, assume that we collect M snapshots on N sensors and obtain the data matrix:

$$\mathbf{X}^\star = \sum_{k=1}^{K} (\boldsymbol{s}_k \odot \boldsymbol{a}(f_k))\mathbf{asv}(\theta_k) \in \mathbb{C}^{M\times N}, \tag{1}$$

where $\boldsymbol{s}_1$ and $\{\boldsymbol{s}_k\}_{k=2}^K$ denote the desired signal and interferers, respectively. Assume that $\{\boldsymbol{s}_k\}_{k=1}^K$ are time samples of complex exponentials, i.e., $\boldsymbol{s}_k = [1 \; e^{j2\pi f_k^o} \; \cdots \; e^{j2\pi f_k^o(M-1)}]^\top$, where f_k^o denotes the frequency of the desired signal (if $k=1$) or the interferer (if $k>1$). Define $\boldsymbol{a}(f_k) \triangleq [1 \; e^{j2\pi f_k} \; \cdots \; e^{j2\pi f_k(M-1)}]^\top$ with f_1 and $\{f_k\}_{k=2}^K$ being the frequency offset of the signal and interferers, respectively. Finally, let θ_1 and $\{\theta_k\}_{k=2}^K$ denote the angle to the desired source and interferers, respectively, and let $\mathbf{asv}(\theta_k) \triangleq e^{j2\pi \sin(\theta_k)\boldsymbol{x}}$ be the array steering vector with $\boldsymbol{x} \in \mathbb{R}^{1\times N}$ being the element positions.

Given the data matrix $\mathbf{X}^\star$ and the desired signal $\boldsymbol{s}_1$, we aim at designing a weight vector $\boldsymbol{w} \in \mathbb{C}^N$ for an array such that the array output is $\mathbf{X}^\star \boldsymbol{w} = \boldsymbol{s}_1$, which implies that the interferers are completely cancelled and the output only contains the desired signal. This problem has been heavily studied in array signal processing. The SMI method [8, 6] minimizes the mean-squared error between the beamformer output and desired signal by directly applying the pseudoinverse matrix, i.e., $\boldsymbol{w} = \mathbf{X}^{\star\dagger}\boldsymbol{s}_1$. This and other classical interference cancellation methods work well when there is no frequency offset and $\boldsymbol{s}_1$ correctly represents the source signal.

Inspired by the SMI method, we propose to design the weight vector $\boldsymbol{w}$ as $\boldsymbol{w} = \mathbf{X}^{\star\dagger}(\boldsymbol{s}_1 \odot \boldsymbol{a}(f_1))$. To do this, note that we must first estimate the signal frequency offset f_1.

Observe that data matrix in (1) can be rewritten as:

$$\mathbf{X}^\star = \sum_{k=1}^{K} (\boldsymbol{s}_k \odot \boldsymbol{a}(f_k))\mathbf{asv}(\theta_k) = \sum_{k=1}^{K} \boldsymbol{a}(f_k^o + f_k)\mathbf{asv}(\theta_k),$$

with $\boldsymbol{a}(f_k^o + f_k) = [1 \; e^{j2\pi(f_k^o+f_k)} \; \cdots \; e^{j2\pi(f_k^o+f_k)(M-1)}]^\top$. It can be seen that the above data matrix can be represented with only a few atoms from the following *atomic set*:

$$\mathcal{A} = \{\mathbf{A}(f^o + f, \mathbf{asv}(\theta)) : f^o + f \in [0,1), \mathbf{asv}(\theta) \in \mathbb{C}^{1\times N}\},$$

with $\mathbf{A}(f^o+f,\mathbf{asv}(\theta)) \triangleq \boldsymbol{a}(f^o+f)\mathbf{asv}(\theta)$. The *atomic norm* of an arbitrary matrix $\mathbf{X}$ is then defined as:

$$\|\mathbf{X}\|_{\mathcal{A}} = \inf\left\{\sum_k c_k : \mathbf{X} = \sum_k c_k \boldsymbol{a}(f_k^o + f_k)\mathbf{asv}(\theta_k),\ c_k \geq 0\right\}.$$

Therefore, similar to the approach used in line spectral estimation problems [4, 3], we can solve the following ANM:

$$\min_{\mathbf{X}} \|\mathbf{X}\|_{\mathcal{A}} \text{ s.t. } \mathbf{X} = \mathbf{X}^\star, \tag{2}$$

to recover $\{f_k^o + f_k\}_{k=1}^K$ and thus get f_1. In particular, one can use the CVX software package [2] to solve the semidefinite program (SDP) corresponding to (2), namely,

$$\begin{aligned} \min_{\mathbf{X},\boldsymbol{u},\mathbf{V}} \quad & \frac{1}{2M}\mathrm{Tr}(\mathcal{T}(\boldsymbol{u})) + \frac{1}{2}\mathrm{Tr}(\mathbf{V}) \\ \text{s.t.} \quad & \begin{bmatrix} \mathcal{T}(\boldsymbol{u}) & \mathbf{X} \\ \mathbf{X}^* & \mathbf{V} \end{bmatrix} \succeq 0, \quad \mathbf{X} = \mathbf{X}^\star, \end{aligned}$$

which can return the dual solution $\mathbf{Q}$ of (2) directly. Here, $\mathcal{T}(\boldsymbol{u})$ is a Hermitian Toeplitz matrix with $\boldsymbol{u}$ as its first column. With the dual solution $\mathbf{Q}$, one can formulate the dual polynomial $\mathcal{Q}(f) = \mathbf{Q}^*\boldsymbol{a}(f)$ to identify the frequencies $\{f_k^o + f_k\}_{k=1}^K$ by localizing the places where the dual polynomial achieves $\|\mathcal{Q}(f)\|_2 = 1$ [4, Proposition 1]. We denote this method as ANM+SMI since it is inspired by both ANM and SMI.

In the case when the data matrix $\mathbf{X}^\star$ is contaminated by Gaussian noise, one can solve the atomic norm denoising (AND) problem:

$$\min_{\mathbf{X}} \frac{1}{2}\|\mathbf{Y} - \mathbf{X}\|_F^2 + \lambda\|\mathbf{X}\|_{\mathcal{A}},$$

to obtain the dual solution $\mathbf{Q}$. Here, $\mathbf{Y} = \mathbf{X}^\star + \mathbf{E}$ is the observed data, $\mathbf{E}$ is the noise matrix, and λ is a regularization parameter that depends on the noise variance and dimension of the problem [3]. We denote this method as AND+SMI.

III. Numerical Simulations

We test the proposed ANM-based methods on noiseless and noisy data and compare them with classic SMI. In particular, we work on a uniform linear array with half-wavelength element spacing and $N = 4$ elements, i.e., the element position vector $\boldsymbol{x} = -(N-1)d/2 : d : (N-1)d/2$ with $d = 0.5$. We use a complex exponential $e^{j2\pi f_1^o t}$ with $f_1^o = 1/20$ as the desired signal, and another two complex exponentials $2e^{j2\pi f_2^o t}$ and $3e^{j2\pi f_3^o t}$ with $[f_2^o\ f_3^o] = [1/40\ 1/50]$ as the interferers. The true frequency offsets are set as $[f_1\ f_2\ f_3] = [1/100\ 1/100\ 1/200]$. The angles to the desired signal and two interferers are set as $\theta_1 = -20°$, $\theta_2 = -60°, \theta_3 = 20°$. We take $M = 100$ snapshots from each sensor and formulate the data matrix $\mathbf{X}^\star$ in the noiseless case. Then, we apply the proposed ANM+SMI method to recover the frequencies $\{f_k^o + f_k\}_{k=1}^K$ and thus get the frequency offset f_1 and weight vector $\boldsymbol{w}$. The dual polynomial used to identify the frequency offset and the radiation pattern (array factor) are presented in Fig. 1. Next, we repeat the above experiment by adding complex Gaussian noise with variance $\sigma^2 = 0.05$ to the clean data $\mathbf{X}^\star$. We present the dual polynomial and radiation pattern obtained from AND+SMI in Fig. 2. It can be seen that the proposed ANM-based methods significantly outperform the classic SMI method in both the noiseless and noisy cases when the source frequency offset is unknown.

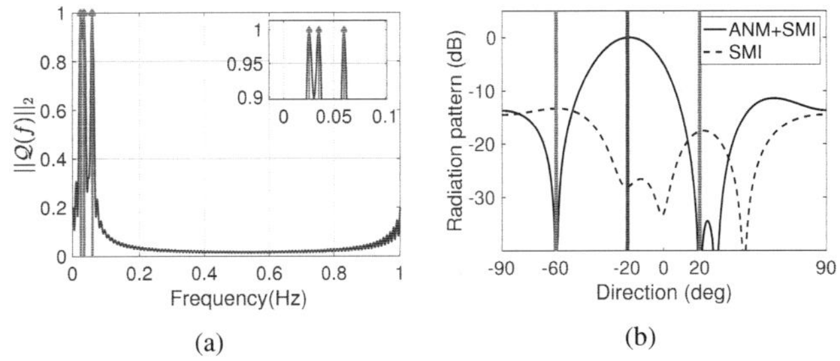

Fig. 1. ANM+SMI for (a) identifying frequency offset in order to (b) perform interference cancellation in the noiseless case.

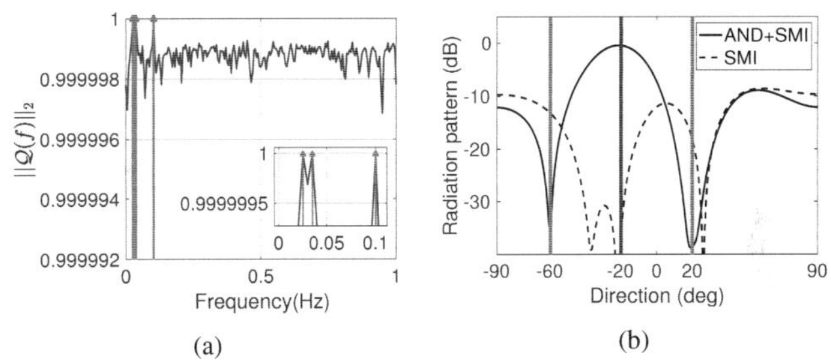

Fig. 2. AND+SMI for (a) identifying frequency offset in order to (b) perform interference cancellation in the noisy case.

IV. Conclusion

In this work, we proposed two ANM-based methods to address both interference cancellation and frequency drift problems in array signal processing. In particular, we improved the classic SMI method by combining it with the well-known ANM/AND used in line spectral estimation in order to remove the impact of frequency offset contained in the desired signal.

References

[1] D. Gaydos, P. Nayeri, and R. Haupt. Adaptive beamforming in high-interference environments using a software-defined radio array. In IEEE International Symposium on Antennas and Propagation and USNC-URSI Radio Science Meeting, July 2019.

[2] M. Grant, S. Boyd, and Y. Ye. Cvx: Matlab software for disciplined convex programming, 2008.

[3] S. Li, D. Yang, G. Tang, and M. B. Wakin. Atomic norm minimization for modal analysis from random and compressed samples. IEEE Transactions on Signal Processing, 66(7):1817–1831, 2018.

[4] Y. Li and Y. Chi. Off-the-grid line spectrum denoising and estimation with multiple measurement vectors. IEEE Transactions on Signal Processing, 64(5):1257–1269, 2015.

[5] G. Tang, B. N. Bhaskar, P. Shah, and B. Recht. Compressed sensing off the grid. IEEE Transactions on Information Theory, 59(11):7465–7490, 2013.

[6] H. L. Van Trees. Optimum Array Processing: Part IV of Detection, Estimation, and Modulation Theory. John Wiley & Sons, 2004.

[7] B. D. Van Veen and K. M. Buckley. Beamforming: A versatile approach to spatial filtering. IEEE ASSP Magazine, 5(2):4–24, 1988.

[8] B. Widrow, P. Mantey, L. Griffiths, and B. Goode. Adaptive antenna systems. Proceedings of the IEEE, 55(12):2143–2159, 1967.

[9] Z. Yang and L. Xie. Enhancing sparsity and resolution via reweighted atomic norm minimization. IEEE Transactions on Signal Processing, 64(4):995–1006, 2015.

Quantum Monopulse Radar

David Luong, Sreeraman Rajan, and Bhashyam Balaji

Department of Systems and Computer Engineering
Carleton University, Ottawa, Canada
david.luong3@carleton.ca

***Abstract*—We evaluate the feasibility of a quantum monopulse radar, focusing on quantum illumination (QI) radars and quantum two-mode squeezing (QTMS) radars. Based on their similarity with noise radar, for which monopulse operation is known to be possible, we find that QTMS radars can be adapted into monopulse radars, but QI radars cannot. We conclude that quantum monopulse radars are feasible.**

***Index Terms*—Monopulse, noise radar, quantum illumination, quantum radar.**

I. Introduction

Quantum radars are sensors which exploit quantum mechanical phenomena in order to improve detection efficiency over conventional radars operating at the same frequency and transmit power [1], [2]. One of the most important quantum mechanical phenomena is called *entanglement*, in which two signals share a very high correlation. Most quantum radar proposals exploit entanglement in order to improve the radar's ability to differentiate between signal and noise. An example of such a proposal is *quantum illumination* (QI) radar [3], [4], one of the most widely studied types of quantum radar.

Recently, a variation of QI radar called *quantum two-mode squeezing* (QTMS) radar was proposed [5]–[8] which is more practical to implement at microwave frequencies. A laboratory prototype that incorporates all of the components necessary in a QTMS radar has already been built. Preliminary results suggest that when a classical radar and a QTMS radar operate at the same frequency and power, the classical radar can achieve the same performance of the QTMS radar only when the coherent integration time is *eight times as long* as that of the latter [8].

In light of this large potential gain, one question which arises is whether quantum radars can support the same functions as conventional radars, e.g., SAR/ISAR imaging or interference suppression. Many such functions require an array of transmitters. We have shown that radar arrays based on certain types of quantum radars, such as QTMS radar, are indeed possible [9]. However, they require multiple quantum signal generators, which may not be practical in the short term. Then it is natural to ask the following question: is it possible to move beyond simple range-finding without the need for a quantum radar array? The central idea of this paper is to answer this question.

Monopulse radars use two or more antenna elements, slightly offset from each other either in beam direction or in phase, to determine both range and direction from a single pulse [10]. Because such radars require only one (specially-designed) transmit antenna, it does not require multiple signal generators. In this paper, we will show that QTMS monopulse radars are feasible.

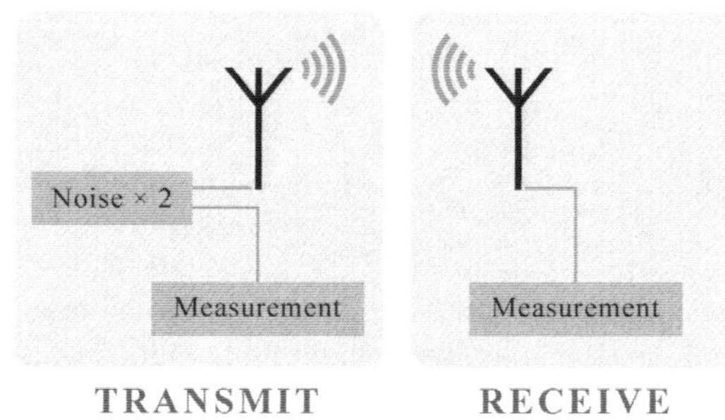

Fig. 1. Block diagram illustrating the basic idea behind noise radar.

II. Noise Radars, QTMS Radars, and QI Radars

Standard noise radars [11] use conventional equipment such as an arbitrary waveform generator to generate two copies of a Gaussian noise signal (Fig. 1), one of which is retained for correlation (matched filtering) with the received signal. It is commonly assumed that these copies are exactly the same. This is not exactly true: a type of noise called *quantum noise* is inherent in all electromagnetic signals and becomes significant when signal power is low, spoiling the correlation between the copies [8], [12].

QTMS radars [8] and QI radars (of the type described in [4]) overcome this by using an entangled signal generator. In this context, entanglement means that there exist correlations between the quantum noise components of the two Gaussian noise signals. The overall correlation between the pair of signals is thus higher than for a noise radar. From an electromagnetic perspective, all three types of radars emit the same *type* of signal; quantum entanglement only improves the *correlation* between the retained and transmitted signals. Classical electromagnetism as applied to antenna design still holds, at least to a first approximation.

The QTMS radar prototype described in [8] used a device called a *Josephson parametric amplifier* to generate the entangled Gaussian noise signals. The center frequencies of the signals were 7.5376 GHz and 6.1445 GHz; the bandwidth was 1 MHz; and the transmit power (after amplification) was -82 dBm. The 7.5376 GHz signal was transmitted through free space through a commercially-available horn antenna and was received at a similar antenna. This shows that the transmission of a quantum-enhanced signal does not require any special electromagnetic engineering.

Apart from the signal generation step, QTMS radars and noise radars are exactly the same. In particular, they employ standard heterodyne detection. Therefore, the received signal and the internally retained signal can be measured separately. QI radars, however, require a sophisticated joint measurement between the received and retained signals, so the latter must be *physically* preserved until the echo arrives from the target. In effect, while QTMS radars and noise radars measure the retained signal and use the resulting measurement record as a reference for matched filtering of the received signal, QI radars use the physical retained signal for "matched filtering".

III. Quantum Monopulse Radars

As we have seen in the previous section, all three types of radars emit Gaussian noise signals. QTMS radars and QI radars use entanglement to enhance the correlation between the retained and transmitted signals. QI radars also employ a sophisticated joint measurement to correlate the received and retained signals, while noise radars and QTMS radars perform matched filtering after conventional heterodyne detection. These similarities and differences have a strong bearing on the feasibility of a quantum monopulse radar.

One key insight is that noise monopulse radars have already been shown to be feasible [13], [14]. The question of the feasibility of quantum monopulse radar then reduces to whether the similarities between noise radars, QTMS radars, and QI radars are sufficient to apply this result to the quantum case.

We have already shown that all three types of radars transmit Gaussian noise; any "quantumness" lies not in the transmit signal itself, but in the correlation of that signal with a reference signal. Thus, the antennas used in a QTMS radar or QI radar need not possess any special electromagnetic characteristics beyond what is necessary in a conventional radar. This was experimentally demonstrated in [8]. There is no reason why either QTMS radar or QI radar would be incompatible with a transmit antenna designed for monopulse operation.

At receive, however, the situation is different. Since QI requires a complicated joint measurement of the received signal with the retained signal, it is not possible to form the sum and difference signals required in a monopulse radar. This is not an obstacle for QTMS radar, which receives and processes signals in exactly the same way as a noise radar and can therefore generate the sum and difference signals as required.

IV. Conclusion

There exists at least one type of quantum radar which can be adapted into a monopulse system, namely QTMS radar. At a conceptual level, all that is necessary is to replace the signal generator of a noise monopulse radar with an appropriate quantum signal generator. Compared to phased arrays, the monopulse solution is simple and inexpensive while still retaining good tracking capabilities. Therefore, a monopulse QTMS radar could be an important and inexpensive first step toward demonstrating that certain types of quantum radar can support functions beyond simple range finding.

However, not all types of quantum radar are similarly adaptable: quantum illumination radar is an example of a system which is incompatible with monopulse operation. This serves as a warning that quantum radar is not monolithic: statements made about one type of quantum radar cannot automatically be applied to another. We would suggest, also, that quantum radar proposals not be evaluated solely on target detection performance, but also on whether they are compatible with functions such as monopulse operation.

References

[1] M. Lanzagorta, *Quantum Radar*, ser. Synthesis Lectures on Quantum Computing. Morgan & Claypool Publishers, 2011.

[2] B. Balaji, "Quantum radar: Snake oil or good idea?" in *Proceedings of the 2018 International Carnahan Conference on Security Technology (ICCST)*, Oct. 2018, pp. 1–7.

[3] S. Lloyd, "Enhanced sensitivity of photodetection via quantum illumination," *Science*, vol. 321, no. 5895, pp. 1463–1465, 2008.

[4] S.-H. Tan, B. I. Erkmen, V. Giovannetti, S. Guha, S. Lloyd, L. Maccone, S. Pirandola, and J. H. Shapiro, "Quantum illumination with Gaussian states," *Physical Review Letters*, vol. 101, p. 253601, Dec. 2008.

[5] C. W. S. Chang, A. M. Vadiraj, J. Bourassa, B. Balaji, and C. M. Wilson, "Quantum-enhanced noise radar," *Applied Physics Letters*, vol. 114, no. 11, p. 112601, 2019.

[6] D. Luong, B. Balaji, C. W. S. Chang, A. M. Vadiraj, and C. Wilson, "Microwave quantum radar: An experimental validation," in *Proceedings of the 2018 International Carnahan Conference on Security Technology (ICCST)*, Oct. 2018, pp. 1–5.

[7] D. Luong, A. Damini, B. Balaji, C. W. S. Chang, A. M. Vadiraj, and C. Wilson, "A quantum-enhanced radar prototype," in *Proceedings of the 2019 IEEE Radar Conference*, Apr. 2019.

[8] D. Luong, C. W. S. Chang, A. M. Vadiraj, A. Damini, C. M. Wilson, and B. Balaji, "Receiver operating characteristics for a prototype quantum two-mode squeezing radar," *IEEE Transactions on AES (arXiv:1903.00101)*, accepted for publication, 2019.

[9] D. Luong, S. Rajan, and B. Balaji, "Are quantum radar arrays possible?" in *Proceedings of the IEEE International Symposium on Phased Array Systems and Technology*, accepted for publication, 2019.

[10] M. I. Skolnik, *Introduction to radar systems*. McGraw-Hill, 1962.

[11] M. Dawood and R. M. Narayanan, "Receiver operating characteristics for the coherent UWB random noise radar," *IEEE Transactions on Aerospace and Electronic Systems*, vol. 37, no. 2, pp. 586–594, Apr. 2001.

[12] D. Luong and B. Balaji, "Quantum two-mode squeezing radar and noise radar: covariance matrices for signal processing," *IET Radar, Sonar & Navigation*, vol. 14, no. 1, pp. 97–104, Jan. 2020.

[13] R. Narayanan, "Random noise monopulse radar system for covert tracking of targets," in *Unclassified Proceedings from the 11th Annual AIAA/MDA Technology Conference*, Jul. 2002.

[14] Y. Zhang and R. M. Narayanan, "Design considerations for a real-time random-noise tracking radar," *IEEE Transactions on Aerospace and Electronic Systems*, vol. 40, no. 2, pp. 434–445, Apr. 2004.

Effect of Sparse Array Geometry on Estimation of Co-array Signal Subspace

Mehmet Can Hücümenoğlu and Piya Pal

***Abstract*—This paper considers the effect of sparse array geometry on the co-array signal subspace estimation error for Direction-of-Arrival (DOA) estimation. The second largest singular value of the signal covariance matrix plays an important role in controlling the distance between the true subspace and its estimate. For a special case of two closely-spaced sources impinging on the array, we explicitly compute the second largest singular value of the signal covariance matrix and show that it can be significantly larger for a nested array when compared against a uniform linear array with same number of sensors.**

***Index Terms*—Davis Kahan, Difference co-arrays, Sparse arrays, Subspace Estimation.**

I. Introduction

Sparse array geometries have recently gained significant research interest [1]–[4] owing to several attractive benefits over traditionally used uniform linear arrays (ULA), such as the ability to identify $O(P^2)$ uncorrelated sources using only P sensors [1], [2], [5], as well as lower Cramér-Rao bounds and higher spatial resolution than ULAs with the same number of spatial and temporal measurements [4], [6]. These enhanced abilities are attributed to the fact that the difference co-arrays of these sparse arrays contain a ULA segment (consisting of consecutive lags around 0) of size $O(P^2)$ that can be exploited by algorithms such as co-array MUSIC [1], [4], [7] to resolve more sources than sensors. However, the performance of co-array based DOA estimation algorithms can potentially deteriorate when the so-called signal subspace is not identified properly. In this paper, we study how the geometry of sparse arrays can influence the distance between the true signal subspace and its estimate for the special case of two narrowband sources. We show that the second largest singular value of the signal covariance matrix controls the mismatch between the true and estimated subspaces. In general, larger the second largest singular value, smaller the mismatch. Given a sparse array and ULA with same number of sensors, we show that the second largest singular value of the sparse can be significantly larger than that of the ULA. We will use this result in future to understand non asymptotic performance of sparse arrays with closely spaced sources.

II. Effect of Sparse Array Geometry on Signal Subspace Perturbation

Consider a linear array of P antennas located at $\{d_p\lambda/2, p=1,2,\cdots,P\}$, where d_p belongs to an integer set $\mathbb{S}, |\mathbb{S}|=P$, and λ is the wavelength of far-field narrowband sources impinging on the array. In this paper we consider the special case of two narrowband sources with Direction-of-Arrival (DOA) $\theta_1,\theta_2 \in (-\pi/2,\pi/2]$. The data vector $\mathbf{y}\in\mathbb{C}^P$ consisting of measurements collected at the P antennas is given by:

$$\mathbf{y}=\mathbf{A}\mathbf{x}+\mathbf{n}.$$

Here $\mathbf{A}=[\mathbf{a}(\theta_1)\ \mathbf{a}(\theta_2)]$ is the array manifold matrix where $\mathbf{a}(\theta_i)=[e^{j\pi d_1 sin(\theta_i)}\ \ldots\ e^{j\pi d_M sin(\theta_i)}]^T$ represents the array steering vector corresponding to the direction θ_i. Furthermore $\mathbf{x}=[x_1,x_2]^T$ is the vector of complex amplitude of the two sources and $\mathbf{n}$ represents the additive noise at the P antennas.

Role of Difference Co-array: If we assume that the source amplitudes x_1,x_2 are zero-mean statistically uncorrelated random variables, and the noise is zero-mean white and statistically independent of $\mathbf{x}$, the correlation matrix of $\mathbf{y}$ is given by:

$$\mathbf{R}_{\mathbf{yy}}=\mathbf{APA}^H+\sigma_n^2\mathbf{I}_P,$$

where $\mathbf{P}=\text{diag}(p_1,p_2)$ is a diagonal matrix with $p_1=E(|x|_1^2), p_2=E(|x|_2^2)$ and $E\left(\mathbf{nn}^H\right)=\sigma_n^2\mathbf{I}$. Notice that the cross-correlation between the measurement at the mth and kth antennas is given by:

$$[\mathbf{R}_{\mathbf{yy}}]_{m,k}=\sum_{i=1}^{2}e^{j\pi\sin\theta_i(d_m-d_k)}p_i+\sigma_n^2\delta[m-k]. \tag{1}$$

In other words, the cross-correlation depends on the pairwise difference $\{d_m-d_k\}$ between the sensor locations. This naturally leads to the notion of a difference set [1].

Definition II.1. The difference set of a set of integers $\mathbb{S}$ is defined as $\mathbb{D}_\mathbb{S}=\{d_i-d_j|d_i,d_j\in\mathbb{S}\}$.

Given a sensor array $\mathbb{S}$, we can associate a "virtual difference co-array" whose element locations are given by the set $\mathbb{D}_\mathbb{S}$. We can also define an integer $N_{\max}$ as the largest integer such that $\{0,1,\ldots,N_{\max}\}\subset\mathbb{D}_\mathbb{S}$. In this case, the set $\mathbb{U}_\mathbb{S}=\{0,1,\cdots,N_{\max}\}$ is called the "Non-negative ULA segment" of the difference co-array. We can extract $N_{\max}+1$ entries $\mathbf{R}_{m,n}$ of the data correlation matrix such that $\{d_m-d_n\}\in\mathbb{U}_\mathbb{S}$ and collect them in a vector $\mathbf{z}\in\mathbb{C}^{N_{\max}+1}$. Using (1), it can be shown that:

$$\mathbf{z}=\mathbf{A}_{\mathbb{U}_\mathbb{S}}\mathbf{p}+\sigma_n^2\mathbf{e},$$

where $\mathbf{A}_{\mathbb{U}_\mathbb{S}}\in\mathbb{C}^{(N_{\max}+1)\times 2}$ is the array manifold matrix corresponding to a ULA with element locations given by the set $\mathbb{U}_\mathbb{S}$. It is well-known that for specially designed sparse arrays such as nested and coprime arrays [1], [2], $N_{\max}=\Theta(P^2)$ whereas for ULA, $N_{\max}=\Theta(P)$. The large difference set of sparse arrays can be utilized to localize more sources than sensors using the so-called co-array MUSIC algorithm [1], [4], [7]. In this paper, we investigate how the large difference co-array of nested arrays helps to characterize subspace estimation errors.

Work supported in parts by NSF CAREER Award 1700506, ONR N00014-19-1-2227 and the University of California, San Diego.

Distance between Perturbed and True Signal Subspaces: Let $\hat{\mathbf{z}}$ be an estimate of $\mathbf{z}$ obtained from the sample covariance matrix $\hat{\mathbf{R}}_{\mathbf{yy}}$. Then, we have:

$$\text{Toep}(\hat{\mathbf{z}}) = \mathbf{A}_{\mathbb{U}_S}\mathbf{P}\mathbf{A}_{\mathbb{U}_S}^H + \mathbf{H}, \tag{2}$$

where Toep$(\hat{\mathbf{z}})$ represents a Hermitian Toeplitz matrix whose first column is $\hat{\mathbf{z}}$ and $\mathbf{H} = \text{Toep}\left(\sigma_n^2\mathbf{e} + \hat{\mathbf{z}} - \mathbf{z}\right)$ captures the effect of noise and estimation error. The co-array signal subspace is defined as the span of the co-array steering vectors corresponding to the source directions θ_1 and θ_2 and is given by [4]:

$$\mathcal{S}_{\text{ca}} = \text{Range}\left(\mathbf{A}_{\mathbb{U}_S}\right). \tag{3}$$

Algorithms such as co-array MUSIC [1], [4] aim to obtain an estimate of this subspace, which is subsequently used for identifying the DOAs using similar principle as the classical MUSIC algorithm [8]. A popular practice is to use the following estimate of $\mathcal{S}_{\text{ca}}$:

$$\hat{\mathcal{S}}_{\text{ca}} = \text{Range}\left(\hat{\mathbf{U}}\right),$$

where the columns of $\hat{\mathbf{U}} \in \mathbb{C}^{(N_{\max}+1)\times 2}$ are the singular vectors of Toep$(\hat{\mathbf{z}})$ corresponding to the two largest singular values. It is obvious that the accuracy of DOA estimation crucially depends on the subspace estimation error, which in turn, depends on the array geometry. Let $\mathbf{U}$ be an orthogonal basis for $\mathcal{S}_{\text{ca}}$. Let σ_2 be the second largest singular value of $\mathbf{A}_{\mathbb{U}_S}\mathbf{P}\mathbf{A}_{\mathbb{U}_S}^H$. If $\sigma_2 > \|\mathbf{H}\|_2$, we can use Davis-Kahan theorem [9] to bound the distance between the true subspace and its estimate as:

$$\text{dist}(\mathbf{U}, \hat{\mathbf{U}}) = \|\mathbf{U}\mathbf{U}^H - \hat{\mathbf{U}}\hat{\mathbf{U}}^H\|_2 \le \frac{\|\mathbf{H}\|_2}{\sigma_2 - \|\mathbf{H}\|_2}. \tag{4}$$

Here, $\|\mathbf{H}\|_2$ is the spectral norm of the matrix $\mathbf{H}$. The condition $\sigma_2 > \|\mathbf{H}\|_2$ is also related to the assumption of "no subspace swap", which is crucial for analysis of co-array MUSIC [4]. We next explicitly characterize the role of co-array geometry in determining how large σ_2 can be by considering two array geometries: ULA and nested array. Let $L = N_{\max} + 1$ and $\beta = (\sin(\theta_1) - \sin(\theta_2))/2$ is the normalized angle distance. We explicitly compute the second largest singular value of $\mathbf{A}_{\mathbb{U}_S}\mathbf{P}\mathbf{A}_{\mathbb{U}_S}^H$ as:

$$\sigma_2 = \frac{L(p_1+p_2)}{2} - \sqrt{\left(\frac{L(p_1-p_2)}{2}\right)^2 + p_1p_2\frac{1-cos(2\pi L\beta)}{1-cos(2\pi\beta)}}. \tag{5}$$

Notice that σ_2 grows linearly with $L = N_{\max} + 1$, when other quantities are held constant. Recall that for a ULA, $N_{\max} = P - 1$ and for a nested array, $N_{\max} = \lfloor \frac{P}{2} \rfloor (\lceil \frac{P}{2} \rceil + 1)$ [1]. Therefore, for a nested array, σ_2 grows quadratically with the number of sensors P whereas for a ULA, it only grows linearly with P. This is illustrated in Fig. 1. In Fig. 2, we plot σ_2 as a function of β which is the normalized separation between source directions. For most values of the separation between sources, σ_2 for the nested array is significantly larger than that of a ULA.

III. Conclusion

We studied the effect of sparse array geometry on co-array signal subspace estimation. For the special case of two sources, we explicitly characterized the second largest singular value and how it controls the distance between the true signal subspace and any estimate. In future, we will use this results to characterize non-asymptotic performance of sparse array based DOA estimation algorithms.

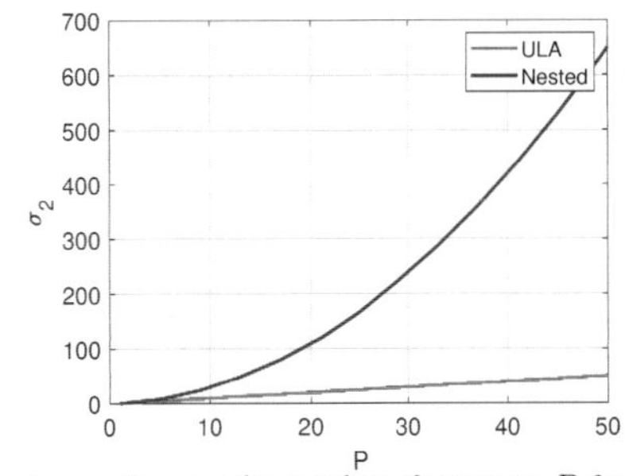

Fig. 1. Dependence of σ_2 on the number of antennas P for nested array and ULA. Here, $p_1 = p_2 = 1$ and $\beta = \frac{1}{2}$.

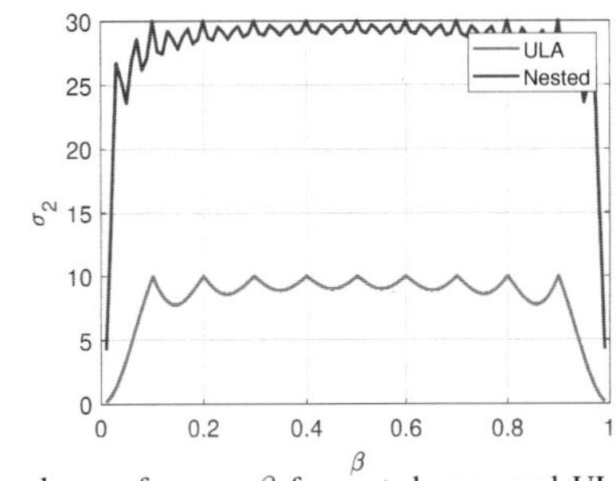

Fig. 2. Dependence of σ_2 on β for nested array and ULA. Here, $P = 10$ for both arrays and $p_1 = p_2 = 1$.

References

[1] P. Pal and P. Vaidyanathan, "Nested arrays: A novel approach to array processing with enhanced degrees of freedom," *IEEE Transactions on Signal Processing*, vol. 58, no. 8, pp. 4167–4181, 2010.

[2] P. P. Vaidyanathan and P. Pal, "Sparse sensing with co-prime samplers and arrays," *IEEE Transactions on Signal Processing*, vol. 59, no. 2, pp. 573–586, 2011.

[3] H. Qiao and P. Pal, "On maximum-likelihood methods for localizing more sources than sensors," *IEEE Signal Processing Letters*, vol. 24, no. 5, pp. 703–706, 2017.

[4] M. Wang and A. Nehorai, "Coarrays, music, and the cramér–rao bound," *IEEE Transactions on Signal Processing*, vol. 65, no. 4, pp. 933–946, Feb. 2017.

[5] Y. I. Abramovich, N. K. Spencer, and A. Y. Gorokhov, "Detection-estimation of more uncorrelated gaussian sources than sensors in nonuniform linear antenna arrays .I. fully augmentable arrays," *IEEE Transactions on Signal Processing*, vol. 49, no. 5, pp. 959–971, May 2001.

[6] A. Koochakzadeh and P. Pal, "Cramér–rao bounds for underdetermined source localization," *IEEE Signal Processing Letters*, vol. 23, no. 7, pp. 919–923, 2016.

[7] P. Pal and P. P. Vaidyanathan, "Coprime sampling and the music algorithm," in *2011 Digital Signal Processing and Signal Processing Education Meeting (DSP/SPE)*. IEEE, 2011, pp. 289–294.

[8] R. Schmidt, "Multiple emitter location and signal parameter estimation," *IEEE Transactions on Antennas and Propagation*, vol. 34, no. 3, pp. 276–280, 1986.

[9] C. Davis and W. M. Kahan, "The rotation of eigenvectors by a perturbation. iii," *SIAM Journal on Numerical Analysis*, vol. 7, no. 1, pp. 1–46, 1970.

DOA Estimation in Heteroscedastic Noise with sparse Bayesian Learning

1st Peter Gerstoft
NoiseLab, UCSD
La Jolla, USA

2nd Christoph F. Mecklenbräuker
Inst. of Telecommunications TU Wien
Vienna, Austria

3rd Santosh Nannuru
IIIT Hyderabad, SPCRC, IIIT Hyderabad
Hyderabad, India

4th Geert Leus
Dept. of Electrical Eng., Delft Univ. of Technology
Delft, Netherlands

***Abstract*—We consider direction of arrival (DOA) estimation from long-term observations in a noisy environment. In such an environment the noise source might evolve, causing the stationary models to fail. Therefore a heteroscedastic Gaussian noise model is introduced where the variance can vary across observations and sensors. The source amplitudes are assumed independent zero-mean complex Gaussian distributed with unknown variances (i.e., source powers), leading to stochastic maximum likelihood (ML) DOA estimation. The DOAs are estimated from multi-snapshot array data using sparse Bayesian learning (SBL) where the noise is estimated across both sensors and snapshots.**

***Index Terms*—Heteroscedastic noise, sparse reconstruction**

I. Introduction

With long observation times, parameters of weak signals can be estimated in a noisy environment. Most analytic treatments analyze these cases assuming Gaussian noise with constant variance. For long observation times the noise process is likely to change with time leading to an evolving noise variance. This is called a heteroscedastic Gaussian process. While the noise variance is a nuisance parameter, it still needs to be estimated or included in the processing in order to obtain an accurate estimate of the parameters of the weak signals.

We resolve closely spaced weak sources when the noise power is varying in space and time. Specifically, we derive noise variance estimates and demonstrate this for compressive beamforming [1]–[3] using multiple measurement vectors (MMV or multiple snapshots). We solve the MMV problem using sparse Bayesian learning (SBL) [2], [4], [5]. Further details is in the paper [6] and demonstrated on real data [7].

We base our development on our fast SBL method [4], [5] which simultaneously estimates noise variances as well as source powers. For the heteroscedastic noise considered here, there could potentially be as many unknown variances as the number of observations. We estimate the unknown variances using approximate stochastic ML [8], [9] modified to obtain noise estimates even for a single observation.

Let $\mathbf{X} = [\mathbf{x}_1, \ldots, \mathbf{x}_L] \in \mathbb{C}^{M\times L}$ be the complex source amplitudes, $x_{ml} = [\mathbf{X}]_{m,l} = [\mathbf{x}_l]_m$ with $m \in \{1, \cdots, M\}$ and $l \in \{1, \cdots, L\}$, at M DOAs (e.g., $\theta_m = -90^\circ + \frac{m-1}{M}180^\circ$) and L snapshots for a frequency ω. We observe narrowband waves on N sensors for L snapshots $\mathbf{Y} = [\mathbf{y}_1, \ldots, \mathbf{y}_L] \in \mathbb{C}^{N\times L}$. A linear regression model relates the array data $\mathbf{Y}$ to the source amplitudes $\mathbf{X}$ as:

$$\mathbf{Y} = \mathbf{A}\mathbf{X} + \mathbf{N}. \tag{1}$$

The dictionary $\mathbf{A}=[\mathbf{a}_1,\ldots,\mathbf{a}_M]\in\mathbb{C}^{N\times M}$ contains the array steering vectors for all hypothetical DOAs as columns, Further, $\mathbf{n}_l \in \mathbb{C}^N$ is additive zero-mean circularly symmetric complex Gaussian noise, which is generated from a *heteroscedastic* Gaussian process $\mathbf{n}_l \sim \mathcal{CN}(\mathbf{n}_l; \mathbf{0}, \mathbf{\Sigma}_{\mathbf{n}_l})$. We assume that the covariance matrix is diagonal and parameterized as:

$$\mathbf{\Sigma}_{\mathbf{n}_l} = \sum_{n=1}^{N} \sigma_{n,l}^2 \mathbf{J}_n = \operatorname{diag}(\sigma_{1,l}^2, \ldots, \sigma_{N,l}^2), \tag{2}$$

where $\mathbf{J}_n = \operatorname{diag}(\mathbf{e}_n) = \mathbf{e}_n\mathbf{e}_n^T$ with $\mathbf{e}_n$ the nth standard basis vector. Note that the covariance matrices $\mathbf{\Sigma}_{\mathbf{n}_l}$ are varying over the snapshot index $l = 1, \ldots, L$. The set of all covariance matrices are $\mathbf{\Sigma}_{\mathbf{N}} = \{\mathbf{\Sigma}_{\mathbf{n}_1}, \ldots, \mathbf{\Sigma}_{\mathbf{n}_L}\}$. We consider three cases for the a priori knowledge on the noise covariance model (2):

I: We assume wide-sense stationarity of the noise in space and time: $\sigma_{n,l}^2 = \sigma^2 =$ const. The model is homoscedastic.

II: We assume wide-sense stationarity of the noise in space only, i.e., the noise variance for all sensor elements is equal across the array, $\sigma_{n,l}^2 = \sigma_{0,l}^2$ and it varies over snapshots. The noise variance is heteroscedastic in time (across snapshots).

III: No additional constraints other than (2). The noise variance is heteroscedastic across both time and space (sensors and snapshots.)

We assume $M>N$ and thus (1) is underdetermined. In the presence of only few stationary sources, the source vector $\mathbf{x}_l$ is K-sparse with $K\ll M$. We define the lth active set $\mathcal{M}_l = \{m \in \mathbb{N}|x_{ml} \neq 0\}$, and assume $\mathcal{M}_l=\mathcal{M}=\{m_1,\ldots,m_K\}$ is constant across all snapshots l. Also, we define $\mathbf{A}_{\mathcal{M}}\in\mathbb{C}^{N\times K}$ which contains only the K "active" columns of $\mathbf{A}$.

We assume that the complex source amplitudes x_{ml} are independent both across snapshots and across DOAs and follow a zero-mean circularly symmetric complex Gaussian distribution with DOA-dependent variance γ_m, $m = 1, \ldots, M$,

$$p(x_{ml}; \gamma_m) = \begin{cases} \delta(x_{ml}), & \text{for } \gamma_m = 0 \\ \frac{1}{\pi\gamma_m} \mathrm{e}^{-|x_{ml}|^2/\gamma_m}, & \text{for } \gamma_m > 0 \end{cases}, \tag{3}$$

$$p(\mathbf{X}; \boldsymbol{\gamma}) = \prod_{l=1}^{L}\prod_{m=1}^{M} p(x_{ml}; \gamma_m) = \prod_{l=1}^{L} \mathcal{CN}(\mathbf{x}_l; \mathbf{0}, \mathbf{\Gamma}), \tag{4}$$

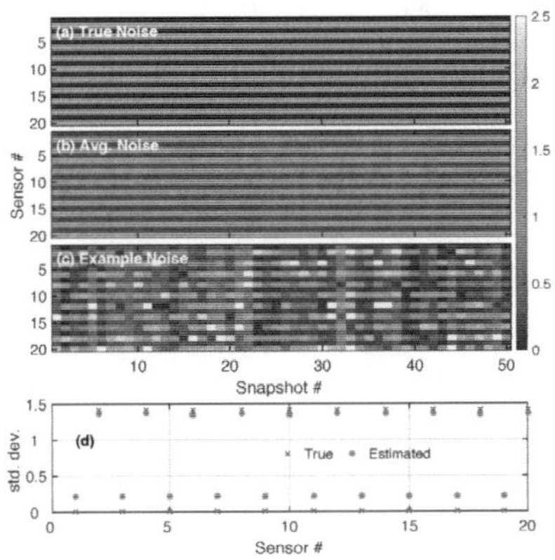

Fig. 1. Single source at DOA $-3°$, array SNR = 0 dB, noise standard deviation statistics: (a) true noise parameters, (b) average estimated noise parameters from SBL (100 simulations), (c) a typical SBL estimate, and (d) average across simulations and snapshots.

i.e., the source vector $\mathbf{x}_l$ at each snapshot $l \in \{1, \cdots, L\}$ is multivariate Gaussian with potentially singular covariance matrix,

$$\mathbf{\Gamma} = \mathrm{diag}(\boldsymbol{\gamma}) = \mathsf{E}[\mathbf{x}_l \mathbf{x}_l^H; \boldsymbol{\gamma}], \tag{5}$$

as $\mathrm{rank}(\mathbf{\Gamma}) = \mathrm{card}(\mathcal{M}) = K \leq M$ (typically $K \ll M$). Note that the diagonal elements of $\mathbf{\Gamma}$, i.e., $\boldsymbol{\gamma} \geq \mathbf{0}$, represent source powers. When the variance $\gamma_m = 0$, then $x_{ml} = 0$ with probability 1. This likelihood function is identical to the Type II likelihood function (evidence) in standard SBL [2], [4] which is obtained by treating $\boldsymbol{\gamma}$ as a hyperparameter. The estimates $\hat{\boldsymbol{\gamma}}$ and $\widehat{\mathbf{\Sigma}}_\mathbf{N}$ are obtained by maximizing the likelihood,

$$(\hat{\boldsymbol{\gamma}}, \hat{\mathbf{\Sigma}}_\mathbf{N}) = \underset{\boldsymbol{\gamma} \geq 0,\, \mathbf{\Sigma}_\mathbf{N}}{\arg\max} \log p(\mathbf{Y}; \boldsymbol{\gamma}, \mathbf{\Sigma}_\mathbf{N}). \tag{6}$$

The goal is thus to solve (6) and the active DOAs $\mathcal{M}$ is where $\hat{\boldsymbol{\gamma}} > 0$. The SBL algorithm solves (6) by iterating between the source power estimates $\hat{\boldsymbol{\gamma}}$ derived in this section and the noise variance estimates $\hat{\mathbf{\Sigma}}_\mathbf{N}$. Assuming γ_m^{old} and $\mathbf{\Sigma}_{\mathbf{y}_l}$ given (from previous iterations) we obtain the following fixed point iteration for the γ_m [4] ($b = 0.5$):

$$\gamma_m^{\text{new}} = \gamma_m^{\text{old}} \left(\frac{\sum_{l=1}^{L} |\mathbf{y}_l^H \mathbf{\Sigma}_{\mathbf{y}_l}^{-1} \mathbf{a}_m|^2}{\sum_{l=1}^{L} \mathbf{a}_m^H \mathbf{\Sigma}_{\mathbf{y}_l}^{-1} \mathbf{a}_m} \right)^b . \tag{7}$$

II. Example

An example statistic of the heteroscedastic noise standard deviation is shown in Fig. 1 for a 20 element array with a single source. The standard deviation for each sensor is either 0 or $\sqrt{2}$ (Fig. 1a). The estimates of the standard deviation are in Figs. 1b, 1c). Average of estimated noise (Fig. 1b) resembles well the true noise (Fig. 1a) whereas the sample standard deviation estimate (Fig. 1c) has high variability—each estimate is based on just one observation. Given many simulations and snapshots, however, the mean of the estimated standard deviation is close to the true noise (Fig. 1d). Three noise cases are simulated: (a) Noise Case I: constant noise standard deviation over snapshots and sensors, (b) Noise Case II: standard deviation changes across snapshots with $\log_{10}\sigma_l \sim \mathcal{U}(-1,1)$, and (c) Noise Case III: standard deviation changes across both snapshots and sensors with $\log_{10}\sigma_{n,l} \sim \mathcal{U}(-1,1)$.

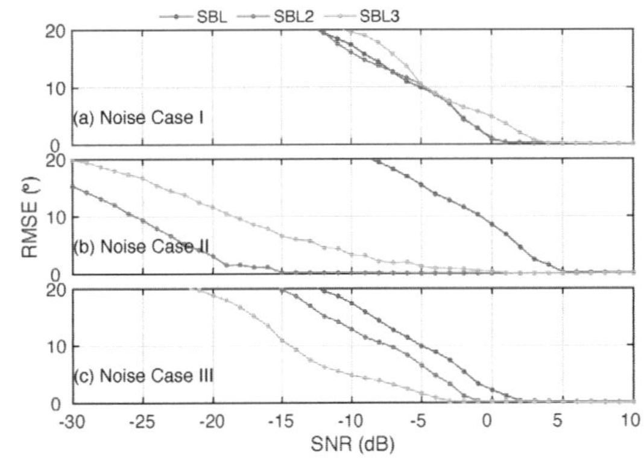

Fig. 2. RMSE vs. SNR with the three sources at $\{-3°, 2°, 50°\}$ and power $\{10, 22, 20\}$ dB.

In Fig. 2, we consider three sources located at $[-3, 2, 50]°$ with power $[10, 22, 20]$ dB. The complex source amplitude is stochastic and there is additive heteroscedastic Gaussian noise with SNR variation from -35 to 10 dB. The $N=20$ elements sensor array with half-wavelength spacing observe $L=50$ snapshots. The angle space grid $[-90 : 0.5 : 90]°$ ($M=360$). The single-snapshot array signal-to-noise ratio (SNR) is $\mathrm{SNR} = 10\log_{10}[\mathsf{E}\{\|\mathbf{A}\mathbf{x}_l\|_2^2\}/\mathsf{E}\{\|\mathbf{n}_l\|_2^2\}]$. The root mean squared error (RMSE) of the DOA estimates over 100 noise realizations is used for evaluating the algorithms.

The simulation shows that for Noise Case III (Fig. 2c) best results are obtained when estimating the full noise covariance matrix (green line, SBL3). Thus, the simulation demonstrates that estimating the noise carefully gives improved DOA estimation at low SNR.

References

[1] A. Xenaki, P. Gerstoft, and K. Mosegaard. Compressive beamforming. *J. Acoust. Soc. Am.*, **136**(1):260–271, 2014.

[2] D. P. Wipf and B.D. Rao. An empirical Bayesian strategy for solving the simultaneous sparse approximation problem. *IEEE Trans. Signal Process.*, **55**(7):3704–3716, 2007.

[3] P. Gerstoft, A. Xenaki, and C.F. Mecklenbräuker. Multiple and single snapshot compressive beamforming. *J. Acoust. Soc. Am.*, 138(4):2003–2014, 2015.

[4] P. Gerstoft, C. F. Mecklenbräuker, A. Xenaki, and S. Nannuru. Multisnapshot sparse Bayesian learning for DOA. *IEEE Signal Process. Lett.*, 23(10):1469–1473, 2016.

[5] S. Nannuru, K.L Gemba, P. Gerstoft, W.S. Hodgkiss, and C.F. Mecklenbräuker. Sparse bayesian learning with multiple dictionaries. *Signal Processing*, 159:159–170, 2019.

[6] P. Gerstoft, S. Nannuru, C. F. Mecklenbräuker, and G. Leus. DOA estimation in heteroscedastic noise. *Signal Processing*, 161:63–73, 2019.

[7] K. L. Gemba, S. Nannuru, and P. Gerstoft. Robust ocean acoustic localization with sparse bayesian learning. *IEEE Journal of Selected Topics in Signal Processing*, 2019.

[8] J.F. Böhme. Source-parameter estimation by approximate maximum likelihood and nonlinear regression. *IEEE J. Oceanic Eng.*, 10(3):206–212, 1985.

[9] P. Stoica and A. Nehorai. On the concentrated stochastic likelihood function in array processing. *Circuits Syst. Signal Process.*, 14(5):669–674, 1995.

Ground Penetrating Radar Radargram Filter using Singularity Expansion Method

Eder Fabian Ruiz[1*], Daniel Chaparro-Arce[1], John J. Pantoja[1,2], Felix Vega[1,2], Chaouki Kasmi[2], and Fahad Al Yafei[2]

[1]Departamento de Ingeniería Eléctrica y Electrónica, Universidad Nacional de Colombia - Sede Bogota
Bogota, Colombia

[2]Directed Energy Research Centre, Technology Innovation Institute
Abu Dhabi, United Arab Emirates

[*]edruiza@unal.edu.co

***Abstract*—In this paper, the singularity expansion method (SEM) is used to improve the signal-to-clutter ratio of radargrams obtained with a ground penetration radar (GPR). SEM allows to select the poles of the GPR signals corresponding to unwanted signals, clutter, and also reflections of specific buried objects. A highly reflective metallic material was used to assess the use of SEM as a tool to eliminate unwanted reflections and signals produced by a GPR. Selected clutter poles are eliminiated from each frame of the SAR image in order to keep only desired poles for analysis. Finally, the reconstructed radargram obtained applying SEM is compared with the image obtained using a well-known processing technique. Results show that the proposed technique can be used to straightforwardly remove undesired signals measured with GPRs.**

I. Introduction

Ground penetrating radar (GPR) is a widely used method for subsurface inspection through the analysis of reflected pulsed signals. In the last decades, it has been used for humanitarian demining in combination with metal detectors [1]. Although anti-personal mines can be detected with this technique, there are still challenges in detecting and identifying improvised explosive devices with low metallic content since similar scattered signals are measured from clutter [2]. Clutter includes unwanted signals due to antenna crosstalk, ground reflections, buried rocks reflections, among others.

Radargrams are images that are produced from scans of the GPR signals. A radargram is made up of impulse response functions (IRFs) taken in different physical positions around an axis, generating a synthetic aperture radar (SAR) image. For this reason, relevant information is not directly revealed in a radargram and mathematical processing is needed to highlight the information it generates. Clutter removal techniques include background removal, filtering, wavelet reconstruction, deconvolution, among others [4]. This variety of techniques shows that still there is not a clear tool to reduce the clutter from GPR images. In this work, singularity expansion method (SEM) is proposed for clutter removal. SEM allows the representation of a signal as a combination of exponentially damped and/or non-damped sinusoids with specific parameters (i.e., frequencies and damping factors) [3]. These singularities can provide information related to the physical characteristics of the soil and buried objects.

This work is supported by Universidad Nacional de Colombia under project No. 41771/2018.

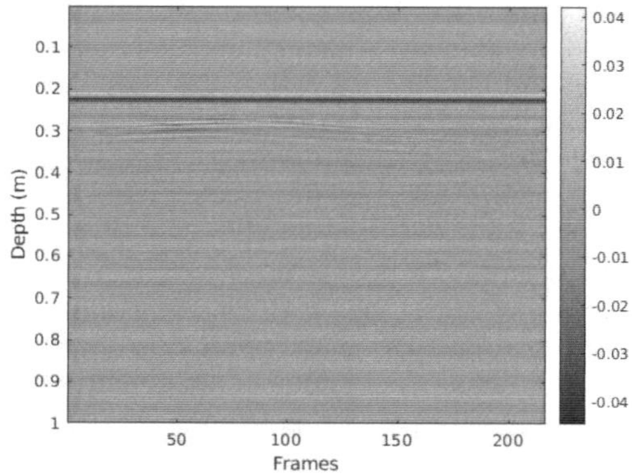

Fig. 1. Radargram obtained with raw data.

II. Experimental Setup

For the experiment, an aluminium pyramid-shaped object was placed over a floor formed of a layer of ceramic and steel. Both, the pyramid and the floor present high reflectivity and both are easily visible in the SAR image. The acquisition system is conformed by an Ultra-Wideband Ground Penetration Radar (GPR-UWB), a Vivaldi antenna with a bandwidth from 300 MHz to 3 GHz, and a computer. It was suspended in a XY positioning system which scans over a distance of 120 cm with a total of 216 frames during each sweep.

III. Data Processing

In Fig. 1 a raw radargram is presented. Since the same antenna is being used for transmitting and receiving, the transmitted pulse is first visualised in Fig. 1 (i.e. yellow and blue lines along the radargram). Then, lower intensity signals coming from the object and floor reflections are registered. However, the object cannot be easily appreciated in this raw data.

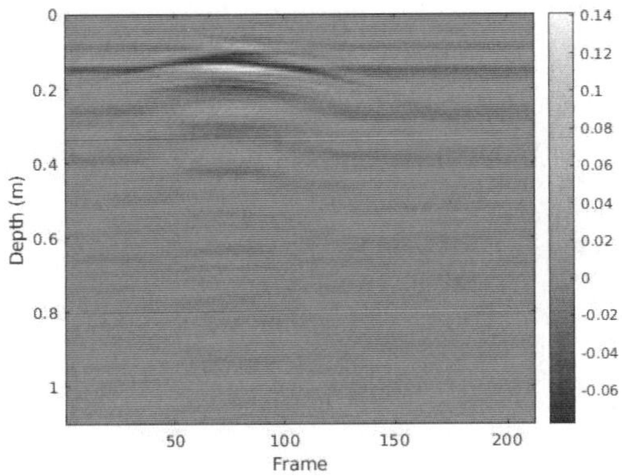

Fig. 2. Radargram using background removal as processing technique.

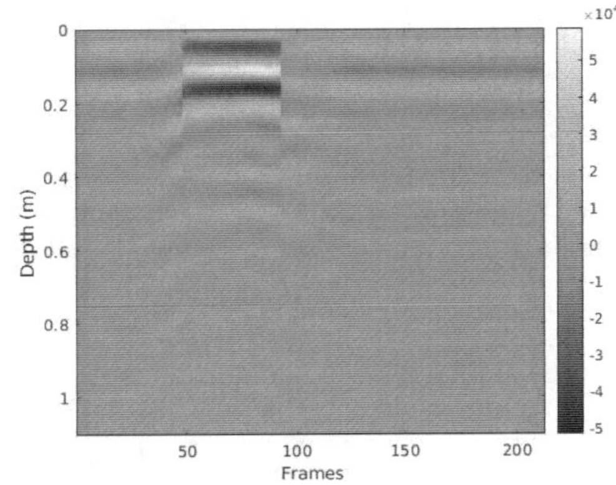

Fig. 3. Radargram using SEM and background removal.

A. Background Removal

Background removal, which is a commonly used technique, can be applied [4]. This technique subtracts from the image the average of all the frames, which mostly represent the background. As shown in Fig. 2, some details are highlighted. Although the object now can be identified, there are also strong reflections from the floor and collateral reflections that can difficult the reading of this image.

B. Application of SEM to the Radargram

As an alternative, the radargram was processed using SEM. A particular implementation of SEM called Matrix Pencil Method (MPM) was used [3]. This representation allows to have a set of poles that contain the signal of each frame in the complex plane. Then, the clutter poles can be identified and removed from the analysis. In our case, poles due to reflections of the laboratory floor are removed from each radargram frame. After removing undesired poles, the signal of each frame is reconstructed using 16 poles.

C. Pole Removal Method

To remove undesired poles from the signal, first unwanted poles are identified. Similar to the background removal technique, the average of all frames is calculated and its poles are taken as clutter. Then, these poles are removed from each frame. An explored alternative for pole removal is windowing the complex plane and eliminating undesired poles. This method can eliminate substantial characteristics of the signal and can produce singular matrices for closely spaced poles. Another assessed alternative is direct subtraction of poles. In this method, the average value of the complex poles of the clutter is directly subtracted from each frame. This is achieved defining the entire radargram as an A_{pm} matrix, where p is the number of poles and m the number of frames as follows:

$$\begin{bmatrix} a_{11} & \dots & a_{1n} \\ \vdots & \vdots & \vdots \\ a_{p1} & \dots & a_{pn} \end{bmatrix} - \begin{bmatrix} c_1 \\ \vdots \\ c_p \end{bmatrix} = \begin{bmatrix} a_{11} - c_1 & \dots & a_{1n} - c_1 \\ \vdots & \vdots & \vdots \\ a_{p1} - c_p & \dots & a_{pn} - c_p \end{bmatrix}.$$

Then, from the reconstructed signals with a lower number of poles, a new radargram is generated. As the removal is not clean, there are subtractions that make the clutter poles to concentrate on the origin, mitigating its effect and even generating positive poles. For this reason, an additional step of applying the classical background removal technique is still required. Fig. 3 shows the radargram obtained by applying poles removal and background removal, where $1 < p < \infty$ and $m = 223$. In the figure, the object is clearly highligted from the background and the floor reflections are almost deleted. After the processing few relevant poles are maintained (i.e., less than 10) producing a sparse matrix and loss of resolution in the image.

IV. Discussion

Results show that the proposed method can generate a selective filtered radargram if the complex poles of the image are properly manipulated. The method of direct substraction of poles has the issue that generates very large gain and also introduces virtual components in frequency. Although the results presented here are preliminary, promising features of this technique, such as the elimination of known reflections, were demonstrated in this paper.

References

[1] M. Sato, K. Kikuta, R. B. Miller, "Evaluation of ALIS GPR for Humanitarian Demining in Colombia and Cambodia," 2018 International Conference on Electromagnetics in Advanced Applications (ICEAA), Cartagena des Indias, 2018, pp. 114-117.

[2] F. Lombardi, H. D. Griffiths, and A. Balleri, "Bistatic radar signature of buried landmines," International Conference on Radar Systems (Radar 2017), Belfast, 2017, pp. 1-6.

[3] Y Hua and T. K. Sarkar, "Matrix Pencil Method for Estimating Parameters of Exponentially Damped/Undamped Sinusoids in Noise," IEEE Transactions on Acoustics, Speech and Signal Processing, vol. 38, no. 5, 1990.

[4] S. Gutierrez, F. Vega, F. A. González, C. Baer, and J. Sachs, "Application of Polarimetric Features and Support Vector Machines for Classification of Improvised Explosive Devices," in IEEE Antennas and Wireless Propagation Letters, vol. 18, no. 11, pp. 2282-2286, Nov. 2019.

Mutual Coupling Compensation in Receiving Arrays and Its Implementation on Software Defined Radios

Sana Khan
Electrical Engineering
Istanbul Medipol University
Istanbul, Turkey
skhan@st.medipol.edu.tr

Hassan Sajjad
Electrical Engineering
Istanbul Medipol University
Istanbul, Turkey
hsajjad@st.medipol.edu.tr

Mehmet Kemal Ozdemir
Electrical Engineering
Istanbul Medipol University
Istanbul, Turkey
mkozdemir@medipol.edu.tr

Ercument Arvas
Electrical Engineering
Istanbul Medipol University
Istanbul, Turkey
earvas@medipol.edu.tr

***Abstract*—Mutual coupling is compensated in a four element uniform linear receiving array using software defined radios. Direction of arrival (DoA) is estimated in real-time for the array with spacing $d = \lambda/4$. The decoupling matrix was measured using a VNA for only one incident angle. After compensation the error in DoA estimation was reduced to 5%. Comparing the DoA results with $d = \lambda/2$ spaced Uniform Linear Array (ULA), 1.2% error was observed. Although, the experiment was performed indoors with a low SNR, the results show a substantial improvement in the estimated DoA after compensation.**

***Index Terms*—Direction of Arrival, LabView, Mutual Coupling, Receiving Antenna Arrays, SDR.**

I. Introduction

Direction of Arrival is an important aspect when considering receiving antenna arrays. However, mutual coupling is a notorious problem in estimating the accurate angle of arrival, if the elements of the array are placed closer than $\lambda/2$ [1]. Using Software Defined Radios (SDR), Direction Finding (DF) can be accomplished using the high-speed FPGA of the SDR or doing the computation offline on a host computer using Matlab, LabView or GNURadio [3]. SDR and Universal Software Radio Peripheral (USRP) are often used analogous, however, USRP paired with a host computer creates a complete SDR system. In DoA estimation using SDR, the receiving ULA are spaced $\lambda/2$ or greater to avoid coupling [3–5]. The received voltages must be decoupled to estimate the DoA, for spacing less than $\lambda/2$. In this work, for the first time, mutual coupling has been compensated in real-time using SDRs for a four element ULA with inter-element spacing of $\lambda/4$ in receiving case and DoA is estimated. For this, the ULA is illuminated by a plane wave and mutual impedances are measured. After finding the decoupling matrix [1], the real-time received voltages acquired by the SDRs are decoupled. These voltages are then given as an input to MUSIC algorithm to detect the DoAs. The implementation is done using NI USRP and LabView.

II. Proposed System Design

The block diagram of the system is shown in Fig. 1. A total of six USRPs are used along with OctoClock-G CDA-2990 and a Gigabit Ethernet Switch (GbE) connected to a host computer. Here, we use four NI USRP 2930 as RF receivers and NI-USRP 2932 and Ettus USRP B210 as RF transmitters. NI-USRP 2932 is used for calibration as Reference (Ref) signal in order to synchronize the phase of all the RF receivers. The phase is calibrated by physically wiring a 10 kHz tone Ref signal from the USRPs TX1/RX1 port to each RX2 port of the four receiving USRPs using a 4 port Wilkinson Power Divider. Phase synchronization is the most important part of the setup since this is the basic assumption for many DF algorithms. Four antennas are attached to each RX1/TX1 port of the four RF receivers. Furthermore, an external high accuracy time and frequency reference (Octoclock) is used for RF local oscillator synchronization and ADC timestamp alignment for the RF receivers. This can be achieved by connecting the 10 MHz reference clock and 1 PPS signal generated by the Octoclock to the RF receivers. Since, we have used the NI USRP 2930 which is a combination of (N210+WBX+GPSDO), therefore, the GPSDO must be manually disconnected in order to connect the external reference clock and external PPS ports of the four receiving USRPs with those of Octoclock, respectively. The second transmitting USRP B210 is used as the incident target source which transmits a tone of 100 kHz. The measurements were taken for a fixed elevation angle $\theta = 90°$ and the distance between the transmitter (target) and receiving array was fixed at 1 m for optimum results[3]. The details of the equipment are mentioned in Table. 1. The complete system can be seen in Fig. 2. It should be noted that, all the measurements were taken indoors in the Istanbul Medipol University (IMU) campus building corridor which is a noisy atmosphere with multi-paths, standing waves, and interference. Hence, the readings are more realistic and the compensation in such a scenario shows the robustness of the applied method.

III. Mutual Impedance Measurements

The same ULA with four antennas at 2 GHz is considered with a spacing $d = \lambda/4$. In this section, we first measure the isolated voltages received by the four element ULA using a VNA by measuring the S-parameters (S_{21}) of the array [2]. A Log Periodic antenna was placed 1 m away to act as a plane wave source with $\theta = 90°$ and $\phi = 90°$. Using the method in [1], we find the decoupling matrix, which was used in LabView to decouple the received voltages at the RF receivers. These measurements were performed separately but in the same noisy environment as in Sec. II.

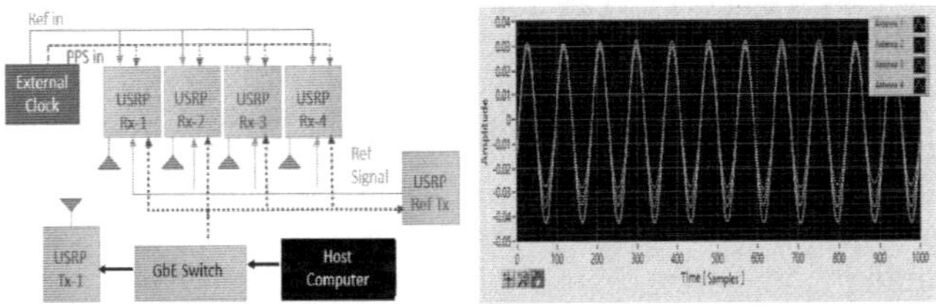

Fig. 1. Block diagram of DoA estimation system (*left*). Received signal amplitude after calibration (*right*).

TABLE I. EXPERIMENTAL SETUP

Item	Detail
SDR	NI USRP 2930 * 4, NI-USRP 2932*1, B210*1
Antenna	JCG401 GSM Antenna*4, LogPeriodic LP0965*1
Frequency-Time Module	OctoClock-G CDA-2990
Gigabit Ethernet Switch	Tplink TL-SG108
Carrier Frequency	2 GHz
Antenna Array Spacing	$\lambda/2$, $\lambda/4$
MUSIC snapshot	3000
Sampling Rate	1 MHz
Platform	LabView

IV. Experimental Results

At the receiver, two signals are received, Ref signal and target signal (Tx-1). These signals are separated using a digital filter. The Ref signal is used for phase synchronization by estimating the phase shift and then calibrating the phase and gain of all the four receivers. The received signal before and after phase synchronization is shown in Fig. 1 (right) and Fig. 3. The target signal is also calibrated and decoupled using the measured decoupling matrix before being given as an input to MUSIC algorithm. Two ULAs, with inter-element spacing $d{=}\lambda/2$ and $\lambda/4$, were used for measurements. First,

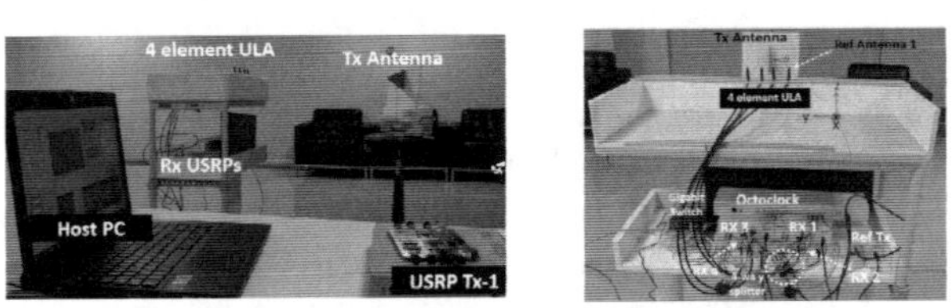

Fig. 2. Experimental setup for DoA estimation.

the general case of $d=\lambda/2$ was considered and DoA was calculated for angles 0 to 60° in steps of 5°. Without using a decoupling matrix, the target signal is directly fed to the MUSIC algorithm. Next, the ULA with $d{=}\lambda/4$ is used and DoA is estimated without using the decoupling matrix. Finally, the mutual coupling is compensated by using the decoupling matrix and the DoA is estimated. The results are shown in Fig. 4 (left). The percentage error for $d=\lambda/2$ is 3.52%. The results are highly erroneous when $d=\lambda/4$, with 9.81% error and after compensation of mutual coupling the error is reduced to 4.72%. The MUSIC spectrum for the case when DoA is from $\phi = 60^o$ is shown in Fig. 4 (right). It can be seen that the compensated results for $d{=}\lambda/4$ are in close proximity to those measured when ULA with $d{=}\lambda/2$ is used.

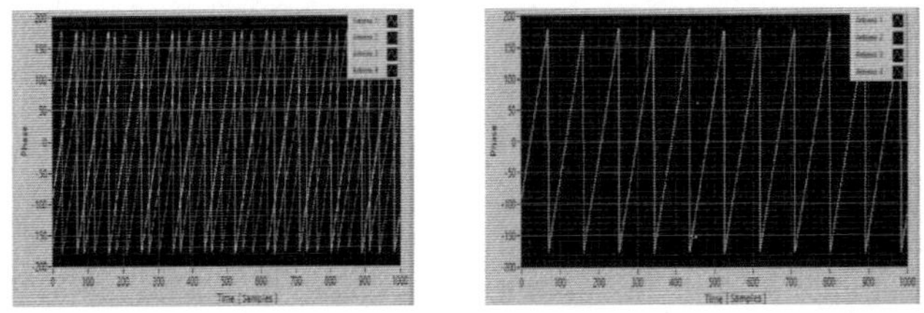

Fig. 3. Received signal. Before (*left*) and after (*right*) phase calibration.

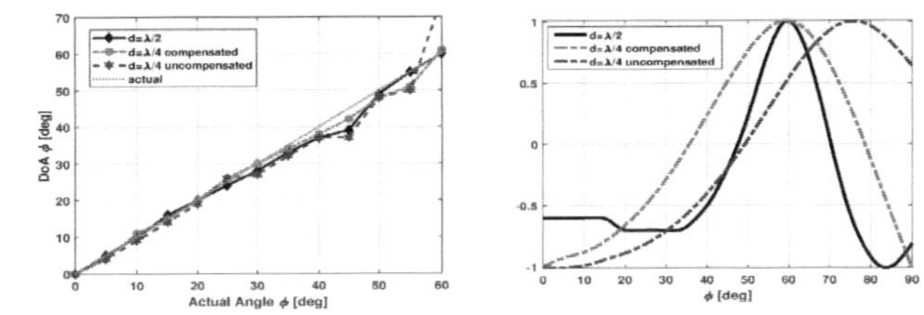

Fig. 4. DoA estimation for a four element ULA with $d{=}\lambda/2$ and $d{=}\lambda/4$ (with and without mutual coupling compensation). Estimated DoA vs Actual DoA for $\theta = 90^o$ (*left*). Spatial spectrum of MUSIC algorithm for DoA detection of signal from $\theta = 90^o$, $\phi = 60^o$ (*right*).

V. Conclusion

Mutual coupling is compensated in a four element receiving ULA using SDR. Two ULAs were studied to see the effect of coupling using a general case of $d = \lambda/2$ and coupled case of $d{=}\lambda/4$ inter-element spacing. The decoupling matrix was measured for the case of coupled ULA and then used to decouple the received voltages in real-time. The initial results show promising improvement in DoA estimation. Further testing using different arrays and experimental testbeds will be carried out in future work.

Acknowledgment

This work has been partially supported by Tubitak project 215E316.

References

[1] S. Khan, H. Sajjad, M. K. Ozdemir and E. Arvas, "Mutual Coupling Compensation in Receiving Antenna Arrays," 2020 International Applied Computational Electromagnetics Society Symposium (ACES), Monterey, USA, March 2020. (Submitted)

[2] Y. Yu, H. Lui, C. H. Niow and H. T. Hui, "Improved DOA Estimations Using the Receiving Mutual Impedances for Mutual Coupling Compensation: An Experimental Study," in IEEE Transactions on Wireless Communications, vol. 10, no. 7, pp. 2228-2233, July 2011.

[3] B. Rares et al., "Experimental Evaluation of AoA Algorithms using NI USRP Software Defined Radios," 2018 17th RoEduNet Conference: Networking in Education and Research, Cluj-Napoca, pp. 1-6, 2018.

[4] N. Tayem, "Real Time Implemenation for DOA Estimation Methods on Ni-Pxi Platform," Progress In Electromagnetics Research B, Vol. 59, 103-121, 2014.

[5] S. A. Alawsh et al., "Sparse direction of arrival estimation using sparse arrays based on software-defined-radio platform," 2017 10th International Conference on Electrical and Electronics Engineering (ELECO), Bursa, pp. 671-675, 2017.

Modelling Nonlinear Optics in Epsilon-Near-Zero Oxides Through Carrier Kinetics

Nathaniel Kinsey
Dept. of Electrical & Computer Engineering
Virginia Commonwealth University
Richmond, VA 23284
nkinsey@vcu.edu

Ray Secondo
Dept. of Electrical & Computer Engineering
Virginia Commonwealth University
Richmond, VA 23284
secondorr@vcu.edu

Dhruv Fomra
Dept. of Electrical & Computer Engineering
Virginia Commonwealth University
Richmond, VA 23284
fomrad@vcu.edu

Abstract — **Epsilon-near-zero materials such as the transparent conducting oxides have arisen as promising nonlinear materials due to enhanced light-matter interactions. However, loss plays a key role. Here we discuss these advances and develop phenomenological models to guide efforts, focusing on the role of loss.**

I. Introduction

The response of a material due to an incident electromagnetic field is described through the permittivity and permeability of a given material. The design of these properties, either through homogeneous growth methods or through engineered structures, enables the tailoring of the interaction between light and matter. In recent years, one of the intriguing areas of research has been Epsilon-Near-Zero (ENZ) materials [1] – a condition where the real permittivity of a material vanishes – as it has been shown to give rise to fascinating effects such as super-coupling, 'static-light', and extreme confinement. However, one area of impact for ENZ materials has been in the field of nonlinear optics [2–4]. Experiments have shown remarkable effects such as unity-order index tuning [5], metal-to-dielectric transitions, near unity frequency conversion [6], phase conjugation, and more. Despite the exciting experimental demonstrations for nonlinear effects in ENZ materials, the theoretical background has lagged. Here we present our models for refractive index tuning in ENZ materials through the intensity-dependent refractive index (IDRI). From the fundamental properties of the material (band structure, linear optical properties, thermal properties, etc.) and excitation conditions (irradiance, pulse-width, wavelength, etc.), we construct a physical model that predicts the nonlinear response of these materials through carrier kinetics without fitting parameters. Moreover, the physicality of the model enables us to explore the role of various parameters upon the nonlinear response, such as material loss, and highlight optimized excitation regions and trade-offs in performance. This work provides a foundation for the continued exploration of enhanced light-matter interaction in ENZ materials and provides new avenues to explore the additional material and excitation optimization for application-driven goals.

This work was supported by the Air Force Office of Scientific Research Grant FA9550-18-1-0151.

II. Intraband Nonlinearity Model

To derive the nonlinear change in ENZ materials we begin by establishing the condition for which ENZ exists through the Drude model of permittivity.

$$\varepsilon = \varepsilon_\infty - \frac{Nq^2}{\varepsilon_0}\frac{1}{\omega^2+i\omega\Gamma(I)}\frac{1}{\frac{1}{N}\sum_E f(E,I)\rho(E)m^*(E)\Delta E} = \varepsilon_\infty - \frac{Nq^2}{\varepsilon_0 m^*_{avg}(I)}\frac{1}{\omega^2+i\omega\Gamma(I)} \quad (1)$$

where N is the carrier concentration, $f(E,I)$ is the Fermi-Dirac distribution, $\rho(E)$ is the density of states, $m^*(E)$ is the effective mass of an electron residing at energy E and ω_p is the plasma frequency. The effective mass and density of states are determined though calculations of the band structure, fit by a hyperbola. The non-parabolic nature causes the effective mass to be energy dependent [7]. As electrons are excited to higher energies through free-carrier absorption, the average effective mass increases, shifting the plasma frequency and causing a change in permittivity. Through calculation of the electron excitation, the change in material characteristics can be calculated for any fluence. The approach is found to match well to previous literature [8], where Figure 1a illustrates a comparison of the model versus experimental data for the index change of a 900 nm thick aluminum doped zinc oxide (AZO), with an ENZ wavelength near 1.3 μm is plotted versus the probe frequency for a 100 fs pump at 875 nm.

The efficiency of the effect is dependent upon the balance between the amount of energy absorbed (increases for high loss, low mobility, films) and how drastic the change in effective mass alters the refractive index (increases for low loss, high mobility, films). This balance is shown in Figure 1b for the same AZO film. The ideal mobility for this calculation falls between μ = 25 to 35 [cm²/V-s] where films are currently grown. As such, there is little to gain by seeking lower loss materials for ENZ-enhanced nonlinear interactions.

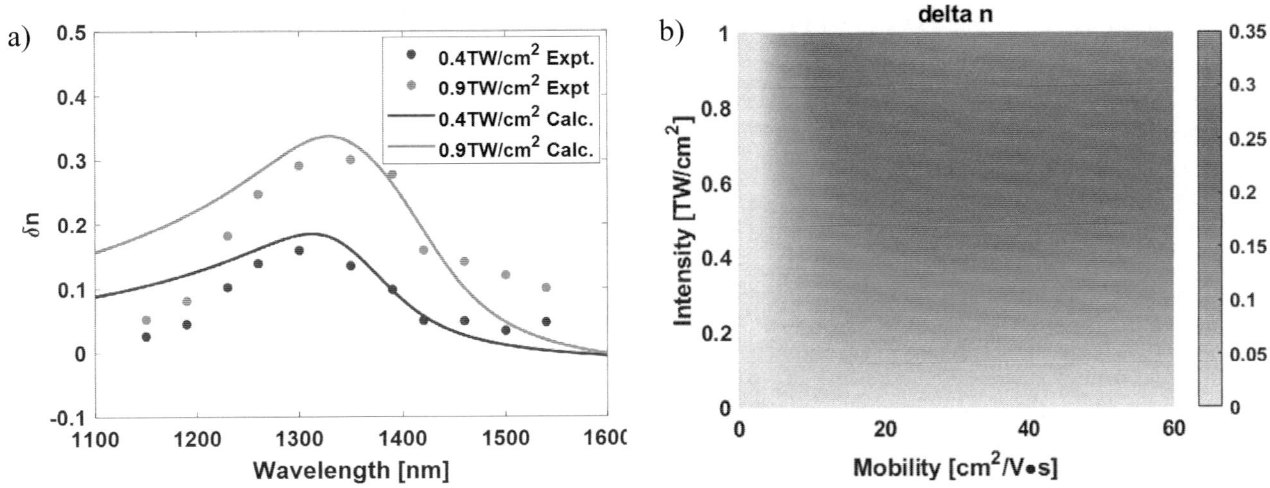

Fig. 1. a) δn for a 900 nm thick film of AZO with an epsilon-near-zero wavelength near 1.3μm pumped by a 100 fs laser pulse at 875 nm. The largest nonlinearities occur at mobilities between μ = 25 to 40 [cm²/V-s]. b) Nonlinear response spectrally compared between the experimental results from [8] and the calculations provided showing good overlap.

III. Figure of Merit

To examine the performance of various materials, optical properties, and excitations conditions, a figure of merit (FOM) was defined as:

$$FOM = A_{pump}\frac{1}{m_0 m_{CBM}^*}\frac{dm^*}{dE}\frac{dn_{probe}}{dm^*} \qquad (2)$$

where A_{pump} is the absorption at the pump wavelength, m_{CBM}^* is the effective mass at the conduction band minimum, and n_{probe} is the refractive index and the probe wavelength. From here it is straightforward to calculate the ideal loss for a given film through absorption, band curvature, and Drude permittivity calculations. An interesting finding of this formalism is that the driving factors of large $\frac{dn_{probe}}{dm^*}$ include low loss and a large ε_∞ (creating a steeper dispersion near ENZ) while the driving factor of A_{pump} is high loss. While this shows that loss requires balancing, it also shows that a large ε_∞ is prefereable for a large change. Further calculation, to compare to literature [8], illustrates that again, the ideal mobility falls between μ = 25 to 40 [cm²/V-s].

IV. Conclusions

Through analysis of band structures and electron kinetics we have developed a method for calculating the nonlinear index change for an arbitrary Drude epsilon-near-zero media as well as a figure of merit for simplified comparison of materials. These models rely on the non-parobolicity of the conduction band causing a change in effective mass due to excitation of electrons by a laser pulse. The aim of this analysis was to assist in optimizing the nonlinear process by applying a physical model to the system and provide a general framework for the comparison of different material classes.

V. References

[1] I. Liberal and N. Engheta, "Near-zero refractive index photonics," Nat. Photonics **11**, 149–158 (2017).

[2] R. W. Boyd, *Nonlinear Optics* (Academic Press, 2008).

[3] N. Kinsey, C. DeVault, A. Boltasseva, and V. M. Shalaev, "Near-zero-index materials for photonics," Nat. Rev. Mater. (2019).

[4] O. Reshef, I. De Leon, M. Z. Alam, and R. W. Boyd, "Nonlinear optical effects in epsilon-near-zero media," Nat. Rev. Mater. 1 (2019).

[5] M. Z. Alam, M. Z. Alam, I. De Leon, and R. W. Boyd, "Large optical nonlinearity of indium tin oxide in its epsilon-near-zero region," Science (80-.). **0330**, 0–5 (2016).

[6] J. B. Khurgin and N. Kinsey, "Adiabatic frequency conversion: it is all about group velocity," (2019).

[7] F. Ruske, A. Pflug, V. Sittinger, B. Szyszka, D. Greiner, and B. Rech, "Optical modeling of free electron behavior in highly doped ZnO films," Thin Solid Films **518**, 1289–1293 (2009).

[8] L. Caspani, R. P. M. Kaipurath, M. Clerici, M. Ferrera, T. Roger, J. Kim, N. Kinsey, M. Pietrzyk, A. Di Falco, V. M. Shalaev, A. Boltasseva, and D. Faccio, "Enhanced Nonlinear Refractive Index in ε-Near-Zero Materials," Phys. Rev. Lett. **116**, 233901 (2016).

Calculating Scattering Spectra using Time-domain Modeling of Time-modulated Systems

Adam Mock
School of Engineering and Technology
Central Michigan University
Mount Pleasant, MI, USA
mock1ap@cmich.edu

***Abstract*—Obtaining agreement between theoretical predictions that assume single-frequency excitation and finite-difference time-domain (FDTD) simulations that employ broadband excitation in the presence of time-varying materials is challenging due to frequency mixing. A simple solution is proposed to reduce artifacts in FDTD-calculated spectra from the frequency mixing induced by harmonic refractive index modulation applicable to scenarios in which second order and higher harmonics are negligible. Advantages of the proposed method are its simplicity and applicability to arbitrary problems including resonant structures.**

***Index Terms*—cavity resonators, finite-difference time-domain method, time-varying circuits.**

I. Introduction

The finite-difference time-domain method (FDTD) can generate entire scattering spectra in a single simulation run by exciting the system with a broadband source. The scattering parameters are calculated by dividing the scattered power spectrum by the incident power spectrum. However, in the case of time-modulated systems, one must exercise caution when calculating the scattering coefficients by dividing the scattered power by the incident power due to the frequency mixing caused by the modulation. Here, we explore the severity of this problem by comparing FDTD simulation results to theoretical predications, and we propose a simple solution to improve the agreement between theory and simulation in time-modulated systems. This problem has been previously addressed in the context of scattering from space-time modulated metasurfaces [1]; however, extension of that technique to resonant structures such as those analyzed here has not yet been reported. An advantage of the approach reported here is its simplicity, requiring only two executions of a standard pulse scattering simulation and minimal post-processing.

II. Coupled Mode Analysis of Modulated System

Fig. 1 (a) illustrates the coupling of two generic resonators that are each coupled to a waveguide. Fig. 1 (b) shows the system geometry that was simulated using FDTD. Of particular interest is the modulation of the refractive index via the electrooptic effect and an applied voltage. Modulating the refractive indices of the cavities introduces a small signal perturbation to the resonance frequency $\omega_0 + \delta\omega\cos(\omega_m t)$ where $\delta\omega$ is the change in resonance frequency due to the refractive index change. In another presentation [2] we show how the system can be designed to transmit near unity power at the resonance frequencies of the coupled cavities ($\omega_0 \pm \kappa$) when the modulation is off ($\delta\omega = 0$) and to reduce transmission to less than 1% when the modulation is applied as shown in Fig. 1 (b).

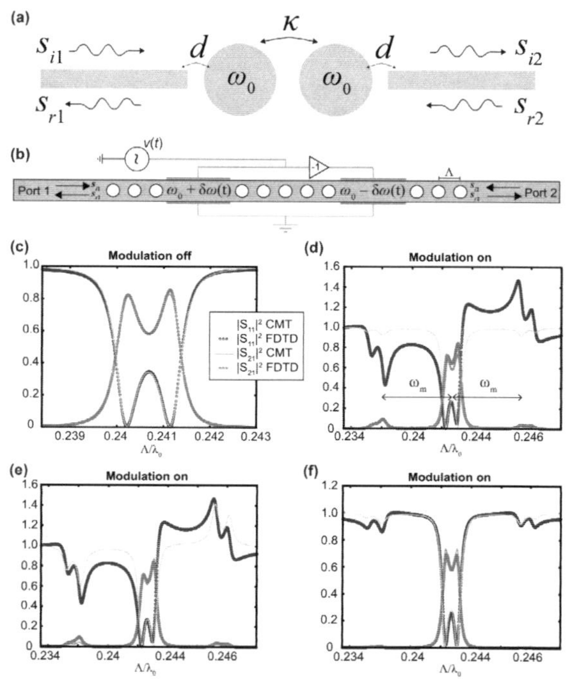

Fig. 1. (a) Generic depiction of two coupled resonant cavities each of which is coupled to a waveguide. ω_0 is the resonance frequency of an isolated resonator. κ is the coupling rate between the two cavities. d is the coupling rate between one cavity and one waveguide. (b) Depiction of the system modeled using FDTD. (c)-(f) Comparison between CMT and FDTD results: (c) when there is no applied modulation; (d) in the presence of modulation with normalized modulation frequency $\omega_m = 0.005$ and amplitude $\delta\omega = 0.0031$; (e) in the presence of modulation and a multi-frequency CMT model is used; (f) when the first order harmonics are canceled from the FDTD results.

Working in the coupled-cavity basis, the coupled mode theory (CMT) equations describing the dynamics of the system in Fig. 1 (a) are given by $\dot{\mathbf{a}} = [-i\mathbf{\Omega} - i\delta\mathbf{\Omega}(t) - \mathbf{\Gamma}]\mathbf{a} + \sqrt{2}\mathbf{D}^{\mathrm{T}}\mathbf{s}_{\mathrm{inc}}$ where $\mathbf{a} = \begin{bmatrix} a_+(t) & a_-(t) \end{bmatrix}^T$ represents the energy in the even

(+) and odd (−) coupled cavity modes, $\mathbf{\Gamma}$ is a diagonal matrix with γ on the diagonal, $\mathbf{\Omega}$ is given by:

$$\mathbf{\Omega} = \begin{bmatrix} \omega_0 + \kappa & 0 \\ 0 & \omega_0 - \kappa \end{bmatrix}, \tag{1}$$

and

$$\mathbf{D} = \frac{1}{\sqrt{2}} \begin{bmatrix} d & d \\ d & -d \end{bmatrix}. \tag{2}$$

d is the coupling rate between the cavity and the waveguide. $\mathbf{s}_{\text{inc}} = \begin{bmatrix} s_{i1} & s_{i2} \end{bmatrix}^{\text{T}}$ is a vector describing the incident field amplitudes in ports 1 and 2 [3]. In the presence of waveguide coupling, the loss rate decomposes into $\gamma = \gamma_i + \gamma_c$ where γ_i is the intrinsic cavity loss rate, and γ_c is the loss rate due to cavity coupling. The loss rate is related to the waveguide coupling parameter d via $d^2 = 2\gamma_c$. In the coupled-cavity basis $\delta\mathbf{\Omega}(t)$ is given by:

$$\delta\mathbf{\Omega}(t) = \begin{bmatrix} 0 & \delta\omega\cos(\omega_m t) \\ \delta\omega\cos(\omega_m t) & 0 \end{bmatrix}. \tag{3}$$

The scattered wave amplitude into ports 1 and 2 is determined using $\mathbf{s}_{\text{ref}} = -\mathbf{s}_{\text{inc}} + \mathbf{D}\mathbf{a}$ where $\mathbf{s}_{\text{ref}} = \begin{bmatrix} s_{r1} & s_{r2} \end{bmatrix}^{\text{T}}$ represents the amplitudes of the outgoing waves in ports 1 and 2 [3].

To solve the CMT equations, one must introduce the ansatz $a_{\pm}(t) = \sum_n a_{\pm,n} e^{-i(\omega + n\omega_m)t}$ and solve for the Fourier series coefficients $a_{\pm,n}$. The equations governing $a_{\pm,n}$ are:

$$[-i(\omega + n\omega_m - w_0 - \kappa) + \gamma]a_{+,n} + \frac{\delta\omega}{2}(a_{-,n+1} + a_{-,n-1}) = d s_{i1}\delta_{n,0}, \tag{4}$$

and

$$[-i(\omega + n\omega_m - w_0 + \kappa) + \gamma]a_{-,n} + \frac{\delta\omega}{2}(a_{+,n+1} + a_{+,n-1}) = d s_{i1}\delta_{n,0}, \tag{5}$$

assuming incidence from port 1. Exact solutions to these equations do not exist, so the Fourier series must be truncated. We discovered that the solution for $a_{\pm,n} \sim (\delta\omega)^n$. So if $\delta\omega \ll \omega_0$, then keeping only the first order harmonics $n = -1, 0, 1$ is justified.

III. Time-Modulated Cavities

Fig. 1 (c) displays the reflection ($|S_{11}|^2$) and transmission ($|S_{21}|^2$) coefficients determined using FDTD when no modulation is applied to the cavities ($\delta\omega = 0$). The system is excited by a broadband pulse in port 1. The incident and scattered powers are measured in ports 1 and 2. The plot shows significant power transmission at the coupled-cavity resonances ($\omega_0 \pm \kappa$) but little transmission at other frequencies. The agreement between the CMT results and the FDTD results is good. Fig. 1 (d) shows the scattering spectra when the modulation is applied, and less agreement between the CMT and FDTD results is observed. The reason for this disagreement is that the system is excited by a continuous range of frequencies; whereas, the CMT model assumes excitation by a single frequency. To confirm this hypothesis, we can remove

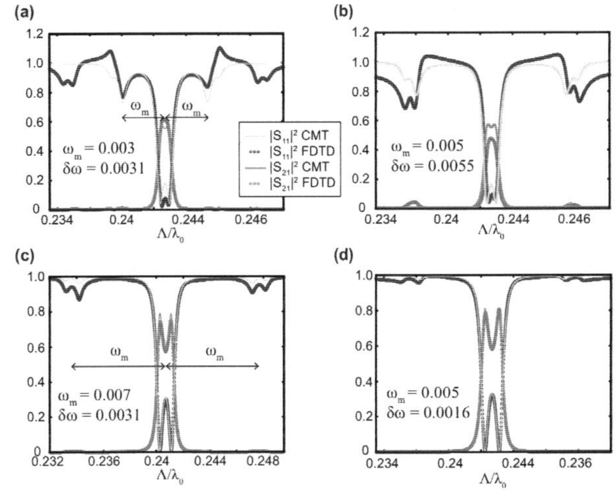

Fig. 2. Comparison between CMT and FDTD using the odd-order harmonic cancelation scheme. (a) and (c) change the modulation frequency while keeping $\delta\omega = 0.0031$. (b) and (d) change the modulation amplitude while keeping $\omega_m = 0.005$.

the delta functions in Eqs. 4 and 5 which introduces input energy at all harmonic frequencies $\omega + n\omega_m$. The result is shown in Fig. 1 (e) where the agreement between CMT and FDTD results is improved.

Returning to the observation that $a_{\pm,n} \sim (\delta\omega)^n$, we surmised that if two FDTD simulations are run where the first is run normally, and then a second is run with $\delta\omega \to -\delta\omega$ and the scattering spectra of the two are added, then the odd-order harmonics will be filtered out. Fig. 1 (f) depicts the comparison of FDTD results obtained in this manner with CMT calculations assuming single-frequency excitation showing good agreement.

The technique of running two FDTD simulations with the sign of the perturbation reversed is applicable only when the contributions from $a_{\pm,\pm1}$ are the dominant terms causing disagreement between single-frequency CMT and pulsed excitation FDTD. Fig. 2 explores regions of validity of this assumption. Figs. 2 (a) and (c) consider modulation frequencies $\omega_m = 0.003$ and 0.007. As the modulation frequency increases, the interference from uncanceled second order harmonics decreases and the agreement improves. Figs. 2 (b) and (d) consider $\delta\omega$ values 0.0055 and 0.0016. As the modulation modulation amplitude decreases, the interference from uncanceled second order harmonics decreases and the agreement improves.

References

[1] S. A. Stewart, T. J. Smy, and S. Gupta, "Finite-difference time-domain modeling of space?time-modulated metasurfaces," IEEE Transactions on Antennas and Propagation, vol. 66, pp. 281–292, 2017.

[2] A. Mock, "Time-modulated coupled-cavity system for optical switching," submitted to 2020 International Applied Computational Electromagnetics (ACES) Symposium, Monterey, CA, USA, March 2020, paper 1061.

[3] W. Suh, Z. Wang, and S. Fan, "Temporal coupled-mode theory and the presence of non-orthogonal modes in lossless multimode cavities," IEEE Journal of Quantum Electronics, vol. 40, pp. 1511–1518, 2004.

Complete Radiation Boundary Conditions for Maxwell's Equations

Thomas Hagstrom
Department of Mathematics
Southern Methodist University
Dallas TX, USA
thagstrom@smu.edu

John Lagrone
Department of Mathematics
Tulane University
New Orleans LA, USA
jlagrone@tulane.edu

***Abstract*—We describe the construction, analysis, and implementation of arbitrary-order local radiation boundary condition sequences for Maxwell's equations. In particular we use the complete radiation boundary conditions which implicitly apply uniformly accurate exponentially convergent rational approximants to the exact radiation boundary conditions. Numerical experiments for waveguide and free space problems using high-order discontinuous Galerkin spatial discretizations are presented.**

***Index Terms*—radiation boundary conditions, time-domain methods.**

I. Introduction

The radiation of energy to the far field is a central feature of electromagnetism. As such, efficient, convergent domain truncation algorithms are a necessary component of any software for simulating electromagnetic waves in the time domain. Complete radiation boundary conditions (CRBC), introduced for acoustics in [1], are, in our view, an ideal solution to this problem. In particular they have a number of advantages relative to the popular perfectly matched layers (PML) [2]. Most importantly:

i. They are provably spectrally convergent and the required parameters can be chosen automatically to guarantee any required accuracy;
ii. The computational boundary can be placed arbitrarily close to scatterers or other inhomogeneities.

In this paper we will outline the theory behind the method, discuss the auxiliary equations which must be solved, and show some results from simple numerical experiments using high-order discontinuous Galerkin (DG) discretizations [3].

II. Exact Radiation Conditions and Local Approximations

Consider Maxwell's equations in a uniform dielectric half-space, $x_1 > 0$:

$$\epsilon\frac{\partial E}{\partial t} = \nabla \times H, \quad \mu\frac{\partial H}{\partial t} = -\nabla \times E.$$

We imagine the computational domain to be located in $x_1 < 0$ with $x_1 = 0$ being the radiation boundary. The model used in $x_1 < 0$ may contain complex scatterers, dispersive media, and other complexities. It is possible to generalize our construction to the case of stratified media (see [4] for the acoustic case) and dispersive models [5] extending into the far field, but here we will restrict ourselves to the simplest case.

An exact radiation condition with $c = 1/\sqrt{\epsilon\mu}$ and $\alpha = \sqrt{\frac{\mu}{\epsilon}}$ is given by [6]:

$$\frac{2}{c}\frac{\partial}{\partial t}(E_2 - \alpha H_3) + \mathcal{R}(E_2 - \alpha H_3) = \alpha\frac{\partial H_1}{\partial x_3} - \frac{\partial E_1}{\partial x_2}, \quad (1)$$

$$\frac{2}{c}\frac{\partial}{\partial t}(E_3 + \alpha H_2) + \mathcal{R}(E_3 + \alpha H_2) = -\alpha\frac{\partial H_1}{\partial x_2} - \frac{\partial E_1}{\partial x_3}. \quad (2)$$

Here $\mathcal{R}$ is a nonlocal operator defined in terms of the spatial Fourier transform $\mathcal{F}$ on the hyperplane $x_1 = 0$ and a convolution in time with a Bessel kernel:

$$\mathcal{R}w = \mathcal{F}^{-1}\left(c|k|^2 K(c|k|t) * (\mathcal{F}w)\right), \quad K(z) = \frac{J_1(z)}{z}.$$

(A similar formula holds on a spherical boundary [6].)

It is possible to construct efficient, low-memory algorithms to evaluate these nonlocal operators [7], [8], which could be a useful alternative for waveguide geometries or scatterers which can be snugly fit by a spherical radiation boundary. With CRBC we approximate the nonlocal operator $\mathcal{R}$ using a sequence of auxiliary fields which satisfy hyperbolic equations on the radiation boundary. Advantages of the local approach are relative ease of implementation (no spatial transforms are required) and the possibility to use a rectangular cuboid or a more general polyhedron as the radiation boundary.

Fundamentally the local methods implement rational approximations in frequency space to the Laplace transform of the temporal convolution kernel K,

$$\hat{K}(s) = \frac{1}{s + (s^2 + c^2|k|^2)^{1/2}}.$$

We demand an accuracy τ uniformly on an inversion contour $\Re s = T^{-1}$ where T is the simulation time. Assuming a separation $\delta > 0$ from sources and scatterers we *guarantee* this accuracy with a CRBC using P auxiliary fields and [1]:

$$P \propto \ln\left(\frac{cT}{\delta}\right) \cdot \ln\left(\frac{1}{\tau}\right).$$

Optimal approximants are easily computed. They are defined via certain parameters a_j and a code for their computation given the error tolerance τ and the dimensionless parameter

$\eta = cT/\delta$ can be found at **www.rbcpack.org**. The approximations are extraordinarily efficient. For example, if we take $\tau = 10^{-4}$ and $\eta = 10^3$ then $P = 9$ suffices.

III. CRBC System

The CRBC system on a face with normal e_1 is defined via a collection of parameters a_j mentioned above. It is most easily understood using the normal characteristic variables, which we also note are what appear in (1)-(2). They are:

$$w^{\pm} = \begin{pmatrix} E_2 \pm \alpha H_3 \\ E_3 \mp \alpha H_2 \end{pmatrix}, \quad w^{\tan} = \begin{pmatrix} E_1 \\ \alpha H_1 \end{pmatrix}.$$

Written in terms of these variables Maxwell's equations take the form:

$$\begin{aligned} \frac{\partial w^+}{\partial t} + c\frac{\partial w^+}{\partial x_1} + cS^+\left(\frac{\partial}{\partial x_2}, \frac{\partial}{\partial x_3}\right) w^{\tan} &= 0 \\ \frac{\partial w^-}{\partial t} - c\frac{\partial w^+}{\partial x_1} + cS^-\left(\frac{\partial}{\partial x_2}, \frac{\partial}{\partial x_3}\right) w^{\tan} &= 0 \\ \frac{\partial w^{\tan}}{\partial t} + cS^{\tan}\left(\frac{\partial}{\partial x_2}, \frac{\partial}{\partial x_3}\right)(w^+, w^-) &= 0, \end{aligned}$$

where $S^{+,-,0}$ are linear partial differential operators. We now introduce auxiliary fields $(w_j^+, w_j^-, w_j^{\tan})$, $j = 0, \ldots, P$ and solve for $j = 1, \ldots, P$:

$$\begin{aligned} (1 + a_{2j})\frac{\partial w_j^+}{\partial t} + \frac{1 - a_{2j}^2}{T a_{2j}} w_j^+ + S^+ w_j^{\tan} &= \\ (1 - a_{2j-1})\frac{\partial w_{j-1}^+}{\partial t} - \frac{1 - a_{2j-1}^2}{T a_{2j-1}} w_{j-1}^+ + S^+ w_{j-1}^{\tan}, & \\ (1 + a_{2j-1})\frac{\partial w_{j-1}^-}{\partial t} + \frac{1 - a_{2j-1}^2}{T a_{2j-1}} w_{j-1}^- + S^- w_{j-1}^{\tan} &= \\ (1 - a_{2j})\frac{\partial w_j^-}{\partial t} - \frac{1 - a_{2j}^2}{T a_{2j}} w_j^- + S^- w_j^{\tan}, & \\ \frac{\partial w_j^{\tan}}{\partial t} + S^{\tan}(w_j^+, w_j^-) &= 0. \end{aligned}$$

Additionally we impose data from the interior related to w_0^+ and a termination condition on w_P^- - the precise choices of these may be implementation-dependent. The equations solved on faces with different normals are analogously defined. For our DG schemes we use $w_0^{+,-,\tan}$ as the outside states to define fluxes at the outer boundary of the mesh; full details will appear elsewhere.

For waveguide problems the auxiliary variables simply inherit the boundary conditions satisfied by the corresponding physical fields. For exterior problems we impose relations at edges and corners to close the system. These involve multiply-indexed auxiliary variables associated with the adjoining faces: P^2 at an edge and P^3 at a corner.

We note that a completely different approach to implementing the local boundary conditions is based on defining the auxiliary functions in a small layer. Termed the double absorbing boundary (DAB) formulation [9], the method has advantages for second order formulations of Maxwell's equations and for finite difference discretizations. In particular we have used to implement CRBC in conjunction with the Yee scheme [10], which we have made available at **www.rbcpack.org**. We have also used it for high order difference methods [11].

IV. Numerical Experiments

Here we demonstrate the accuracy of the method with DG discretizations of the TM system in two space dimensions. Further results, including computations in three space dimensions, will be presented in the talk. We consider initial value problems in a waveguide of width 1 and in free space. For the waveguide problem the computational domain is $(-1,1) \times (0,1)$ with PEC boundary conditions imposed at $x_2 = 0, 1$ and the CRBCs imposed at $x_1 = \pm 1$. Exact solutions are given by appropriate derivatives of solutions of the scalar wave equation produced by a point source centered near $(0, 0.1)$ with time amplitude $\exp\left(-125(t + .475)^2\right)$. For the free space problem the computational domain is $(-1,1) \times (-1,1)$ with CRBCs imposed at all four boundaries. This requires the corner closures alluded to above at the four corners of the domain. The exact solution is now produced, using the same prescription as above, with a free space solution of the wave equation produced by the point source centered near the origin.

We take $\epsilon = 0.8$, $\mu = 1.25$ and solve up to $T = 100$. Since the radiation boundaries are a distance 1 from the source we set $\eta = 100$. We use an upwind DG discretization with polynomial degree 9 and square elements of width $1/12$, time stepping using eighth order order Taylor series with $\Delta t = 1/600$. We compare results with $P = 5$ and $P = 9$. For these choices the *a priori* error bounds are 5.6×10^{-4} and 3.7×10^{-6} respectively. The actual maximum relative errors in the computations were approximately the same for each case and were below tolerance: 3.7×10^{-4} and 2.6×10^{-6}.

References

[1] T. Hagstrom and T. Warburton, "Complete radiation boundary conditions: minimizing the long time error growth of local methods," SIAM J. Numer. Anal., vol. 47, pp. 3678–3704, 2009.

[2] W. Chew and W. Weedon, "A 3-D perfectly matched medium from modified Maxwell's equations with stretched coordinates," Microwave Optical Technol. Lett., vol. 7, pp. 599–604, 1994.

[3] J. Hesthaven and T.Warburton, "High-order/spectral methods on unstructured grids. I. Time-domain solution of Maxwell's equations," J. Comput. Phys., vol. 181, pp. 186–221, 2002.

[4] T. Hagstrom, "High-order radiation boundary conditions for stratified media and curvilinear coordinates," J. Comput. Acoust., vol. 20, 2012.

[5] ——, "Extension of complete radiation boundary conditions to dispersive waves," in Waves 2017, 2017, pp. 175–176.

[6] T. Hagstrom and S. Lau, "Radiation boundary conditions for Maxwell's equations: A review of accurate time-domain formulations," J. Comput. Math., vol. 25, pp. 305–336, 2007.

[7] B. Alpert, L. Greengard, and T. Hagstrom, "Rapid evaluation of nonreflecting boundary kernels for time-domain wave propagation," SIAM J. Numer. Anal., vol. 37, pp. 1138–1164, 2000.

[8] ——, "Nonreflecting boundary conditions for the time-dependent wave equation," J. Comput. Phys., vol. 180, pp. 270–296, 2002.

[9] T. Hagstrom, D. Givoli, D. Rabinovich, and J. Bielak, "The double absorbing boundary method," J. Comput. Phys., vol. 259, pp. 220–241, 2014.

[10] J. Lagrone and T. Hagstrom, "Double absorbing boundaries for finite-difference time-domain electromagnetics," J. Comput. Phys., vol. 326, pp. 650–665, 2016.

[11] K. Juhnke, "High-order implementations of the double absorbing boundary," Ph.D. dissertation, Southern Methodist University, 2017.

A High-order Accurate Scheme for the Dispersive Maxwell's Equations and Material Interfaces on Overset Grids

Jeffrey W. Banks*, Benjamin B. Buckner*, William D. Henshaw*, Alexander V. Kildishev†, Gregor Kovačič*, Ludmila J. Prokopeva†, Donald W. Schwendeman*

* *Department of Mathematical Sciences*
Rensselaer Polytechnic Institute
Troy, New York USA,

†*Electrical and Computer Engineering*
Purdue University
West Lafayette, IN 47907, USA

***Abstract*—An efficient and high-order accurate scheme for solving the time-domain dispersive Maxwell's equations and material interfaces is described. Maxwell's equations are solved in second-order form for the electric field. A generalized dispersive material (GDM) model is used to represent a general class of linear dispersive materials and this model is implemented in the time-domain with the auxiliary differential equation (ADE) approach. Fourth-order accuracy is achieved with a single-step three-level scheme. High-order accuracy at interfaces is obtained using locally conforming grids and compatibility conditions. Composite overlapping grids are used to treat complex geometry with Cartesian grids generally covering most of the domain and local conforming grids representing curved boundaries and interfaces.**

Keywords*—*FDTD, dispersive Maxwell's equations, material interfaces, overset grids.

I. Introduction

We extend the high-order accurate scheme for dispersive Maxwell equations described in [1] to include high-order accurate treatment of material interfaces. The dispersive Maxwell equations in second-order form for the electric field $\mathbf{E}$ are solved using high-order finite difference approximations and Taylor (Lax-Wendroff type) time-stepping. A generalized dispersive material (GDM) model [2], with an auxiliary differential equation (ADE) approach, is used to represent arbitrary dispersive effects. Composite overset grids are used to represent complex geometry using structured body-fitted curvilinear-grids for boundaries and interfaces and Cartesian background grids to cover the majority of the domain [3]. The use of structured and Cartesian grids along with high-order accurate finite difference approximations leads to very efficient schemes. Conforming grids are used at planar and curved material interfaces and this allows a multivalued representation of the fields on the interface, see Fig. 1. Additional compatibility interface conditions are derived from the fundamental interface conditions and these are used to determine the values of the fields at ghost points adjacent to the interface. Second- and fourth-order accurate versions of the scheme have been developed and tested. At any order of accuracy the scheme is a single step scheme that uses three time levels and has a CFL-one time-step restriction. More details of the new approach are described in a forthcoming article [4].

This work was partially performed under DOE contracts from the ASCR Applied Math Program, and by the DARPA Defense Sciences Office.

II. The ADE-GDM Scheme With Interfaces

The second-order formulation of the governing equations using an ADE approach is

$$\partial_t^2 \mathbf{E} = c^2 \Delta \mathbf{E} - \epsilon_0^{-1}\, \partial_t^2 \mathbf{P} \tag{1}$$

$$\big(\partial_t^2 + b_{1,m}\partial_t + b_{0,m}\big)\mathbf{P}_m = \epsilon_0\big(a_{0,m} + a_{1,m}\partial_t\big)\mathbf{E}, \tag{2}$$

where $\mathbf{P} = \sum_{m=1}^{N_p} \mathbf{P}_m$, $c^2 = 1/(\epsilon_0\mu_0)$ is the nominal wave speed, and the total polarization vector, $\mathbf{P}$, is the sum of N_p component polarization vectors $\mathbf{P}_m$. Each $\mathbf{P}_m$ satisfies an ordinary differential equation whose coefficients $a_{0,m}$, $a_{1,m}$, $b_{0,m}$, and $b_{1,m}$ are chosen to fit a given dispersion model or spectroscopic data.

To achieve high-order accuracy at the interface we use conforming grids as shown in Fig. 1. By taking time derivatives of the usual interface jump conditions, and using the governing equations to replace time derivatives by spatial derivatives, we obtain interface compatibility conditions suitable for high-order finite difference schemes. For example, at second-order we use the jump conditions

$$\Big[\mathbf{n} \times \Big(c^2 \Delta_{2h} \mathbf{E}_{\mathbf{j}}^n - \epsilon_0^{-1}\, \partial_t^2 \mathbf{P}\big|_{\mathbf{j}}^{n}\Big)\Big]_I = 0, \qquad \mathbf{j} \in \Gamma_h, \tag{3a}$$

$$\big[\mu_0^{-1} \mathbf{n} \cdot \Delta_{2h} \mathbf{E}_{\mathbf{j}}^n\big]_I = 0, \qquad \mathbf{j} \in \Gamma_h, \tag{3b}$$

$$\big[\mu_0^{-1} \mathbf{n} \times \nabla_{2h} \times \mathbf{E}_{\mathbf{j}}^n\big]_I = 0, \qquad \mathbf{j} \in \Gamma_h, \tag{3c}$$

$$\big[\nabla_{2h} \cdot \mathbf{E}_{\mathbf{j}}^n\big]_I = 0, \qquad \mathbf{j} \in \Gamma_h, \tag{3d}$$

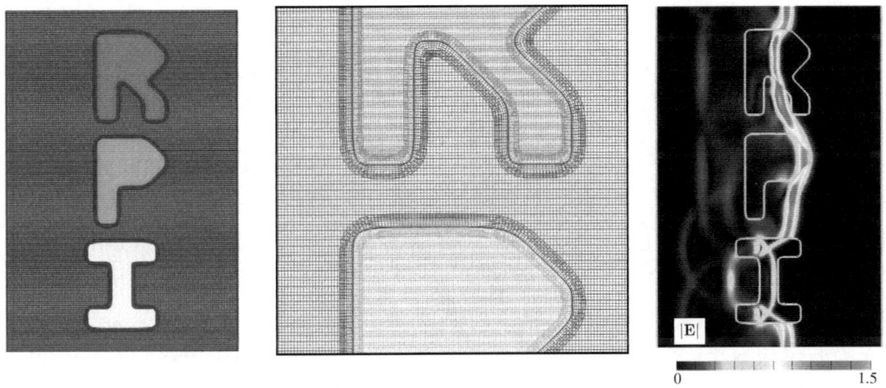

Fig. 1. Left and middle: composite grid for three dispersive objects. Two component grids, an interface-fitted grid and background grid (shown in same colour for each object), are used for each object. Right: Scattering of a Gaussian plane wave computed using the new high-order scheme.

where ∇_{2h} and Δ_{2h} denote second-order accurate approximations (with a three-point stencil in each coordinate direction) to the gradient and Laplace operators, respectively. The approximate set of interface conditions in (3) can be used to determine the ghost-point values for $\mathbf{E}_{\mathbf{j}}^{n}$ on both sides of the interface once a second-order accurate approximation to $\partial_t^2 \mathbf{P}\big|_{\mathbf{j}}^{n}$ in (3a) is defined. The key to obtaining a compact three-level approximation to $\partial_t^2 \mathbf{P}\big|_{\mathbf{j}}^{n}$ is to symbolically time-step the equations on the interface to obtain algebraic expressions for $\mathbf{E}^{n+1}$ and $\mathbf{P}^{n+1}$ at the new time which then leads to an approximation for $\partial_t^2 \mathbf{P}\big|_{\mathbf{j}}^{n}$ involving spatial derivatives of $\mathbf{E}^{n}$ at the current and previous time which can be used in (3a).

Similar ideas are used to develop fourth-order accurate interface compatibility conditions. Unfortunately, these high-order accurate conditions couple the unknown ghost point values along the interface and it would appear necessary to solve a system of equations involving all ghost points on the interface. Fortuitously, we have discovered an alternative approximation, of the same order of accuracy, that avoids this implicit solve. This new fourth-order accurate approximation is based on first obtaining second-order accurate values from the second-order accurate conditions (3), and then using these second-order accurate values in selected terms of the fourth-order conditions. This removes the coupling along the interface and thus provides an accurate and efficient approximation.

III. Numerical Results

For verification of the new scheme, several new exact solutions have been derived including scattering of a dispersive plane wave from a dispersive two-dimensional disk and from a dispersive solid sphere. These exact scattering solutions depend on the roots to a characteristic polynomial, and these different roots correspond to solutions that can be classified as resonant modes (dominated by dispersive effects) and non-resonant modes (perturbations of the non-dispersive scattering solutions). Fig. 2, for example, shows the maximum norm errors in computing resonant and non-resonant modes for the scattering from a dispersive solid sphere. The figure shows that the second-order accurate scheme (O2) and the fourth-order accurate scheme (O4) are converging at the expected order of accuracy. Note that the fourth-order scheme can be orders of magnitude faster than the second-order scheme to obtain similar accuracy.

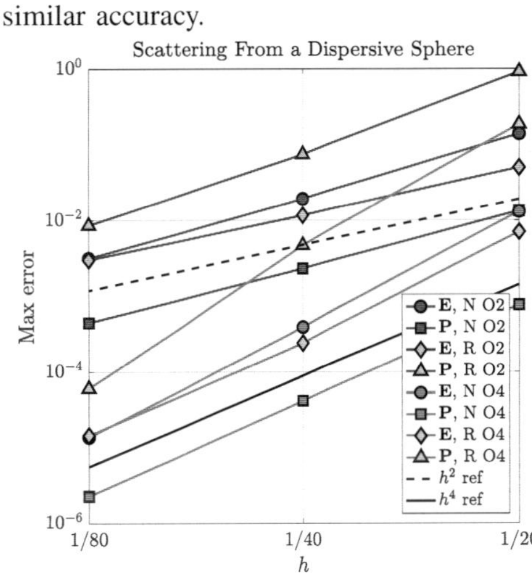

Fig. 2. Maximum errors versus grid spacing for scattering of a dispersive plane wave from a dispersive solid sphere. Results are shown for the second-order acccurate scheme (in blue) and the fourth-order accurate scheme (in red). Errors for a non-resonant mode (N) and a resonant mode (R) are given.

Fig. 1 illustrates the new approach for scattering of a Gaussian shaped plane wave from three dispersive objects. A closeup of the composite grid shows the conforming interface grids that follow the interface and allow a multi-valued representation of the fields. It is also seen that the majority of the domain is discretized with Cartesian grids where very efficient implementations of the scheme are used.

References

[1] J. Angel, J. W. Banks, W. D. Henshaw, M. J. Jenkinson, A. V. Kildishev, G. Kovačič, L. J. Prokopeva, and D. W. Schwendeman, "A high-order accurate scheme for Maxwell's equations with a generalized dispersion model," J. Comput. Phys., vol. 378, pp. 411–444, 2019.

[2] L. J. Prokopeva, J. D. Borneman, and A. V. Kildishev, "Optical dispersion models for time-domain modeling of metal-dielectric nanostructures," IEEE Transactions on Magnetics, vol. 47, pp. 1150–1153, 2011.

[3] G. S. Chesshire and W. D. Henshaw, "Composite overlapping meshes for the solution of partial differential equations," J. Comput. Phys., vol. 90, no. 1, pp. 1–64, 1990.

[4] B. Buckner, J. W. Banks, W. D. Henshaw, M. J. Jenkinson, , A. V. Kildishev, G. Kovačič, L. J. Prokopeva, and D. W. Schwendeman, "A high-order accurate scheme for maxwell's equations with a generalized dispersive material (gdm) model and material interfaces," Preprint, 2020, submitted for publication.

Nonlinear Light-Matter Interactions: Time-Domain Multiphysics Modeling

(invited)

Shaimaa I. Azzam[1], Ludmila J. Prokopeva[1], Qing Xia[2],
Gregor Kovačič[2], William D. Henshaw[2], and Alexander V. Kildishev[1]*
[1]Birck Nanotechnology Center, Purdue University, West Lafayette, IN 47907, USA
[2]Center for Modeling, Optimization and Computational Analysis, Rensselaer Polytechnic Institute, Troy, New York 12180, USA
*kildishev@purdue.edu

***Abstract*—Time-domain modeling of optical nonlinear responses is of utmost importance in the understanding and engineering of nonlinear photonic devices. Here, we overview our recent efforts in developing multilevel atomic models for simulating light-matter interaction for various nonlinear materials. Our multiphysics simulation framework couples the rate equations that model excitation and relaxation dynamics within a given material with the Maxwell equations. The framework covers many nonlinear phenomena (e.g., gain, saturable absorption, multi-photon absorption), while also accounting for plasmon-enhancement effects.**

Keywords* — *nonlinear materials, finite difference time domain, lasers, saturable absorption, multi-level atomic systems, multiphysics, rate equations.

I. Introduction

The simulation of the interactions between light and matter is highly relevant to the design and optimization of photonic devices. For linear materials, their optical response is represented by the refractive index. However, nonlinear interactions are significantly more complicated due to the dependence of the refractive index on the intensity of the incident light. Our approach in modeling the nonlinear interaction of light and matter is to employ a semi-classical approach where the nonlinear medium is described quantum-mechanically, and the light is described classically [1-5]. We utilize a set of rate equations to account for atomic relaxations and excitations within a nonlinear material through a multi-level system. Such multi-level atomic systems can track the carrier kinetics of numerous nonlinear photonic systems. Our multiphysics computational framework has several advantages. First, the framework provides material models for many nonlinear materials that were not previously available. Second, it allows for the full-wave simulation of complex nanophotonic devices coupled to nonlinear materials to accurately predict and optimize their performance. Moreover, it enables access to internal dynamics, such as the carrier population dynamics for each energy level. Additionally, access is available to the induced macroscopic polarization at each point of the computational domain, taking into account energy exchange between the atoms and fields, pumping, and nonradiative decays. Such access to internal dynamics enables a thorough understanding of the system. This approach allows for engineering devices that enhance their response based on the target application. Additionally, these models can be calibrated to dynamic parameters found in the experiment. Experimentally-fitted parameters allow for realistic device designs that adopt actual material characteristics [6]. We also discuss applications where our framework has played a critical role. Examples include nanolasing in all-dielectric metasurfaces and plasmon-enhanced optical limiting.

II. Multi-level Atomic Models

We developed multi-level atomic models to simulate different classes of nonlinear processes. Figure 1 shows three representative examples of our models. Figure 1(a) shows the Jablonski diagram of a four-level system describing the atomic transitions of active material. Similarly, figure 1(b) shows a Jablonski diagram of a two-photon absorbing material (TPA). Figure 1(c) illustrates a reverse saturable absorption material (RSA). Each figure shows the carrier population density N_i at each energy level i and the lifetimes of the different transitions τ_{ij}.

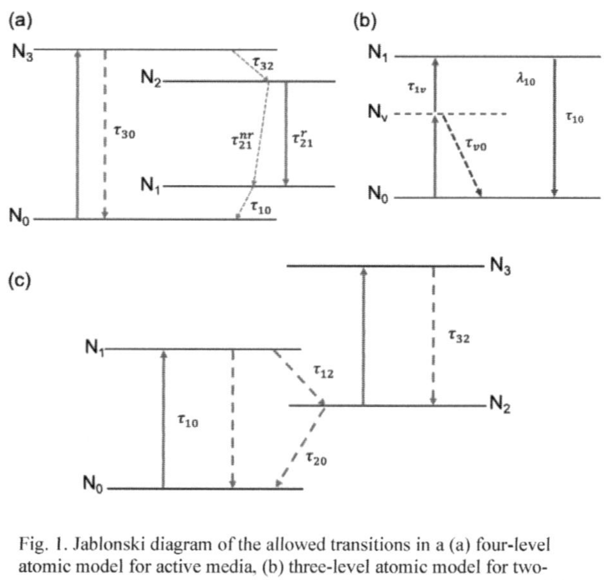

Fig. 1. Jablonski diagram of the allowed transitions in a (a) four-level atomic model for active media, (b) three-level atomic model for two-photon absorption, and (c) four-level atomic model for reverse saturable absorption.

The molecule of a nonlinear material is described quantum mechanically using a multi-level atomic model that incorporates all relevant radiative and nonradiative transitions

The authors acknowledge the financial support by DARPA/DSO Extreme Optics and Imaging (EXTREME) Program, Award HR00111720032.

[1-5]. Electromagnetic fields are treated classically using Maxwell's equations. Here we describe the system used to model the active medium as an example. The rate equations describing the transitions in the case of the active medium are given in eq. (1):

$$
\begin{aligned}
\frac{\partial N_3}{\partial t} &= -\frac{N_3}{\tau_{32}} + \frac{1}{\hbar\omega_{30}} \boldsymbol{E} \cdot \frac{\partial \boldsymbol{P}_{30}}{\partial t} \\
\frac{\partial N_2}{\partial t} &= \frac{N_3}{\tau_{32}} - \frac{N_2}{\tau_{21}} + \frac{1}{\hbar\omega_{21}} \boldsymbol{E} \frac{\partial \boldsymbol{P}_{21}}{\partial t} \\
\frac{\partial N_1}{\partial t} &= \frac{N_2}{\tau_{21}} - \frac{N_1}{\tau_{10}} - \frac{1}{\hbar\omega_{21}} \boldsymbol{E} \frac{\partial \boldsymbol{P}_{21}}{\partial t} \\
\frac{\partial N_0}{\partial t} &= \frac{N_1}{\tau_{10}} - \frac{1}{\hbar\omega_{30}} \boldsymbol{E} \cdot \frac{\partial \boldsymbol{P}_{30}}{\partial t}
\end{aligned}
\qquad (1)
$$

where ω_{ij} is the frequency of the transition from level i to level j, and $\boldsymbol{P}_{ij}$ is the induced macroscopic polarization vector associated with this transition. The macroscopic polarization vector is the average of the microscopic dipole moments of each molecule, and it takes the form of a Lorentzian ordinary differential equation, eq. (2):

$$\frac{\partial^2 \boldsymbol{P}_{ij}}{\partial t^2} + \gamma_{ij} \frac{\partial \boldsymbol{P}_{ij}}{\partial t} + \omega_{ij}^2 \boldsymbol{P}_{ij} = k_{ij}(N_j - N_i)\boldsymbol{E} \qquad (2)$$

where γ_{ij} is the damping coefficient of the ij transition, and k_{ij} is the coupling coefficient. Polarizations are coupled to Maxwell's equations through the electric flux

$$\nabla \times \boldsymbol{H}(\boldsymbol{r}, t) = -\varepsilon_0 \frac{\partial \boldsymbol{E}(\boldsymbol{r}, t)}{\partial t} + \sum_i \frac{\partial \boldsymbol{P}_i(\boldsymbol{r}, t)}{\partial t} \qquad (3)$$

where $i \in \{30, 21\}$. Equations 1 and 2 are modified to model other nonlinear processes.

III. Applications

We have applied the presented framework to analyzing a multitude of nonlinear nanophotonic systems, including lasing from hyperbolic metamaterials [7], lasing from a plasmonic nanohole array [8], plasmon-enhanced optical limiters [3], all-optical computing [9], and others. Here, we focus on two of the most recent problems, namely, lasing from an all-dielectric metasurface and plasmon-enhanced two-photon absorption. The time-domain kinetics of these systems is described in detail illustrating the insights possible with our multiphysics framework. These insights enable the accurate prediction of the performance of given systems and optimization of their metrics.

Implementation and SVE Approximation

The numerical implementation of the models is performed within a commercial FDTD solver (Lumerical) as *custom optical material models*. Additionally, we developed in-house FDTD codes where higher-order schemes are used for faster convergence [10]. Here, the multi-level system can have an arbitrary number of levels and transitions [11]. Also, in our codes, we exploit the slow varying envelope (SVE) formulation in order to reduce the computational cost by using a multiscale (in time) analysis of the processes.

Conclusion

Our approach to time-domain multiphysics models using carrier population kinetics for nonlinear nanophotonic systems is reviewed. We highlight the details of the computational framework, its numerical implementation in commercial software and in-house codes. We show that by using the SVE approximation the computational cost of the model can be significantly reduced. Also, we discuss some examples of applications that our framework is used to model, showing internal dynamics such as volumetric carrier population distributions and induced polarization that cannot be attained otherwise.

References

[1] S. Chang and A. Taflove, "Finite-difference time-domain model of lasing action in a four-level two-electron atomic system," Optics Express, vol. 12, pp. 3827-3833, 2004.

[2] A. Taflove and S. C. Hagness, Computational Electrodynamics: The Finite-Difference Time-Domain Method, Artech House, p. 394, 2005.

[3] S. I. Azzam, A. V. Kildishev, "Time-domain dynamics of reverse saturable absorbers with application to plasmon-enhanced optical limiters," Nanophotonics, vol. 8, pp. 145-151, 2018.

[4] S. I. Azzam, J. Fang, J. Liu, Z. Wang, N. Arnold, T. A. Klar, L. J. Prokopeva, X. Meng, V. M. Shalaev, A.V. Kildishev, "Exploring Time-Resolved Multiphysics of Active Plasmonic Systems with Experiment-Based Gain Models," Laser & Photonics Reviews, vol. 13, pp. 1800071-1800078, 2019.

[5] S. I. Azzam, A. V. Kildishev "Time-domain dynamics of saturation of absorption using multilevel atomic systems," Optical Materials Express, vol. 8, pp. 3829-3834, 2018.

[6] J. Trieschmann, S. Xiao, L. J. Prokopeva, V. P. Drachev, and A. V. Kildishev, "Experimental retrieval of the kinetic parameters of a dye in a solid film," Optics Express, vol. 19, pp. 18253-18259, 2011.

[7] R. Chandrasekar, Z. Wang, X. Meng, S. I. Azzam, M. Y. Shalaginov, A. Lagutchev, Y. L. Kim, A. Wei, A. V. Kildishev, A. Boltasseva, and V. M. Shalaev, "Lasing action with gold nanorod hyperbolic metamaterials," ACS Photonics, vol. 4, pp. 674–680, 2017.

[8] X. Meng, J. Liu, A. V. Kildishev and V. M. Shalaev, "Highly directional spaser array for the red wavelength region," Laser & Photonics Reviews, vol. 8, pp. 896–903, 2014.

[9] M. Miscuglio, A. Mehrabian, Z. Hu, S. I. Azzam, J. George, A. V. Kildishev, Matthew Pelton, V. J. Sorger, "All-optical nonlinear activation function for photonic neural networks," Optical Materials Express, vol. 8, pp. 3851-3863, 2018.

[10] J.B. Angel, et al. "A high-order accurate scheme for Maxwell's equations with a generalized dispersive material model." J. of Comp. Phys., vol. 378, pp. 411-444, 2019.

[11] L.J. Prokopeva, et al. "Numerical modeling of active plasmonic metamaterials." Optical Complex Systems: OCS11, vol. 8172, p. 81720B, International Society for Optics and Photonics, 2011.

Comparison of Different Ways of Extra Phosphorus Injection which Decrease the Threshold Voltage and On-resistance of UMOS

Xi Zhou
Institute of Microelectronics
Southwest Jiaotong University
Chengdu, China
myjoush@163.com

Quanyuan Feng
Institute of Microelectronics
Southwest Jiaotong University
Chengdu, China
fengquanyuan@163.com

***Abstract*—A method to decrease the threshold voltage and on-resistance is discussed in this paper, which is adding extra phosphorus injection into silicon. There are two ways to inject extra phosphorus without adding a mask. The first way is to inject extra phosphorus after the field oxide etching, and the second way is to inject extra phosphorus with the source region mask before the N+ implantation. Compare the results of the two ways to find their characteristics and choose the appropriate one.**

Keywords*—*extra phosphorus injection, on-resistance, threshold voltage, UMOS.

I. Introduction

Threshold voltage and on-resistance are important indexes to measure the performance of the device [1]. Under the premise of guaranteeing the anti-noise ability of the device, the low threshold voltage is conducive to the drive of the device [2], and the low on-resistance is conducive to decreasing the power consumption [3]. Extra phosphorus injection is an easy method to decrease threshold voltage and on-resistance. In order not to add a new mask and save costs, extra phosphorus injection can be carried out after field oxide etching or before N+ implantation [4]. Comparing these two ways can help to choose the one which is better to improve the performance of device from process.

II. Experiment

For UMOS with a breakdown voltage of 100V, in order to ensure the reliability of the device, the breakdown voltage is usually designed to exceed 100V. Extra phosphorus injection is carried out after field oxide etching and before N+ implantation respectively. The injection energy is 90KeV and 200KeV. The dose of extra phosphorus injection is the same, and choose the different dose to find the changing trend of the electrical parameter.

III. Simulation Results

The simulation software is TCAD Sentaurus. Furthermore, the DopingDependence model, Lackner model and some other models are used in the simulation. The resistivity of epitaxy is 1.425 Ω·cm and the thickness of epitaxy is 9 microns.

This work is supported by Key Project of the National Natural Science Foundation of China under Grant 61531016, 61831017 and the Sichuan Provincial Science and Technology Important Projects under Grant: 2018GZ0139, 2018GZDZX0001.

The structure is shown in Fig. 1 and the simulation results are shown in the Table I. When the injection energy is 90KeV, the threshold voltage and on-resistance can be decreased more by the first way which is injecting extra phosphorus after field oxide etching. However, the breakdown voltage will be sacrificed.

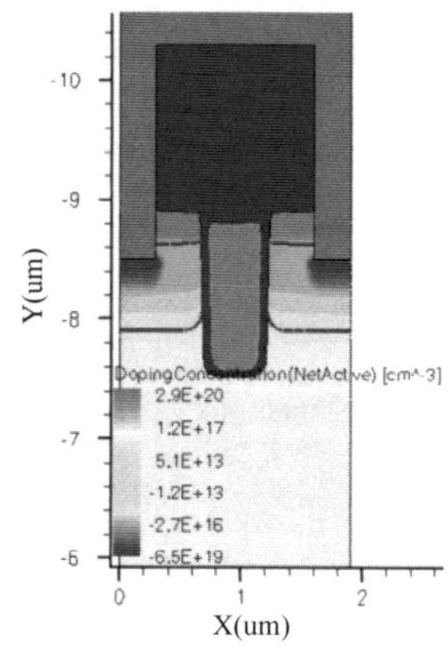

Fig. 1. Structure of the 100V UMOS.

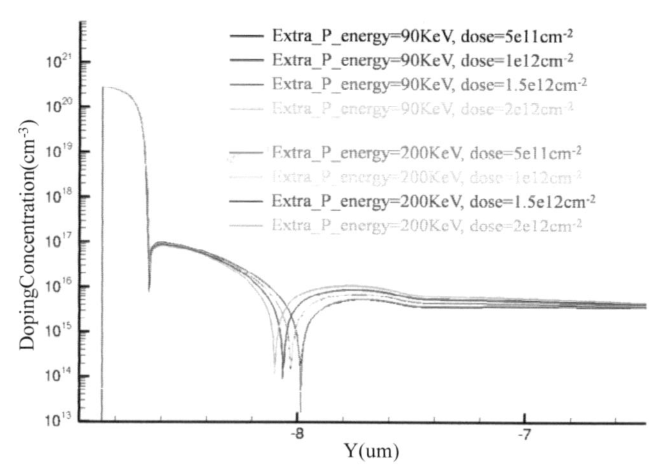

Fig. 2. Doping concentration curve of the 100V UMOS.

TABLE I. SIMULATION RESULTS OF DIFFERENT EXTRA PHOSPHORUS INJECTION DOSE AND ENERGY

Parameter \ Extra_P_imp_dose		Extra_P_imp_energy=90KeV					Extra_P_imp_energy=200KeV				
		0	5e11cm^{-2}	1e12cm^{-2}	1.5e12cm^{-2}	2e12cm^{-2}	0	5e11cm^{-2}	1e12cm^{-2}	1.5e12cm^{-2}	2e12cm^{-2}
After field oxide etching	Vth/V	2.11	2.04	1.95	1.86	1.78	2.11	2.03	1.95	1.88	1.76
	BV/V	112	110	108	105	102	112	110	107	104	101
	Vg=4.5V, Ron/mΩ	24.68	23.57	22.75	22.08	21.54	24.68	23.43	22.56	21.90	21.25
	Vg=10V, Ron/mΩ	22.05	21.09	20.41	19.90	19.48	22.05	20.99	20.24	19.69	19.18
Before N+ implantation	Vth/V	2.11	2.09	2.06	2.03	2.01	2.11	2.00	1.90	1.80	1.70
	BV/V	112	112	112	112	112	112	112	112	112	112
	Vg=4.5V, Ron/mΩ	24.68	24.64	24.59	24.51	24.49	24.68	24.46	24.27	24.11	23.97
	Vg=10V, Ron/mΩ	22.05	22.05	22.05	22.05	22.05	22.05	22.00	21.98	21.96	21.92

When the injection energy is 200KeV, the second way which is injecting extra phosphorus before N+ implantation can decrease more threshold voltage but on-resistance doesn't. At this time, the breakdown voltage is constant.

IV. ANALYSIS

In medium and low voltage devices, channel resistance occupies a large proportion, and the expression of channel resistance is shown in equation (1) [5]:

$$R_{\mathrm{CH,SP}} = \frac{L_{\mathrm{CH}} W_{\mathrm{Cell}}}{2\mu_{\mathrm{ni}} C_{\mathrm{OX}} \left(V_{\mathrm{G}} - V_{\mathrm{TH}}\right)}. \quad (1)$$

It can be found that when the threshold voltage decreases, the channel resistance decreases and the on-resistance decreases. For extra phosphorus injection carried out after field oxide etching, since both the epitaxy and phosphorus are n-type, the larger the phosphorus injection dose is, the higher the doping concentration at the top of the epitaxy will be, which will decrease the resistivity and breakdown voltage [6]. Meanwhile, the concentration distribution at the channel will be changed, which decrease the threshold voltage and on-resistance. In addition, it can be seen from Fig. 2 that the injection energy is different though, the concentration distribution curve of the same injection dose almost coincides. Which is the reason that the electrical parameters of the first way hardly change even the injection energy is larger.

For extra phosphorus injection carried out before N+ implantation, the phosphorus is compounded in the p-base region, which changes the distribution of impurities at the channel. However, if the injection energy is not large enough, the concentration distribution at the channel will not change significantly. Due to the second way doesn't change the resistivity, the breakdown voltage doesn't change, too.

V. CONCLUSION

Extra phosphorus injection can decrease threshold voltage and on-resistance. It is found that under the condition of the same extra phosphorus injection dose, if the designed breakdown voltage margin is large, the first way which is injecting extra phosphorus after field oxide etching is better. while if not, the second way which is injecting extra phosphorus before N+ implantation is better.

ACKNOWLEDGMENT

I want to express my gratitude to all those who have helped me during the writing of the paper. I gratefully acknowledge the help of my supervisor professor Quanyuan Feng. I do appreciate that he gives me a lot of theoretical guidance and help to solve some problems, which enables me to complete this subject study. I also acknowledge my partners who help me to complete this study and give me some good advices. My parents have given me great support in my life, which enable me to concentrate on my research. I am very grateful to my family for their care.

REFERENCES

[1] M. Shi and M. Li, Semiconductor Devices Physics and Technology, 3rd ed, Soochow University Press, 2014, pp. 176-180.

[2] L. Feng, "Threshold voltage model of short-channel MOSFETs," Changsha: National University of Defense Technology, 2006.

[3] D. Ma, "Study of novel structure and mechanism of trench type ultra-low specific on-resistance power device," Chengdu: University of Electronic Science and Technology of China, 2017.

[4] Q. Chen, "The characteristics research of 75V trench power MOSFET," Chengdu: Southwest Jiaotong University, 2013.

[5] B. J. Baliga, Fundamentals of Power Semiconductor Devices, Springer Science & Business Media, 2008, pp. 321-327.

[6] L. Zhao and Q. Feng, "A novel high voltage MOSFET with double trench gate," Microelectronics, vol. 49, no. 2, Apr. 2019.

Multi-Physical Study of the Effect of a Mobile Terminal in Proximity of Human Testicles

D. A. Agudelo, J.S. Chávez, J.S. Ramírez, and J.L. Araque
{daagudeloa, jschavezm, jusramirezgu, jlaraqueq} @unal.edu.co
Department of Electrical Engineering - Universidad Nacional de Colombia
Bogotá D.C - Colombia

***Abstract*—This contribution presents the results of a multi-physical study of the effect of the electromagnetic field generated by mobile on the human testicles, motivated by recent results that suggest negative effects for exposition values considered safe by standards. The software Sim4Life is used to compute the Specific Absorption Rate (SAR) when a simplified model of a mobile terminal operates close to a highly detailed anatomical model representing a situation in which the user ports the terminal in his pants pocket.**

***Index Terms*—Bio-heat, Multi-Physics, Sim4Life, Testicles, SAR.**

I. Introduction

The studies on the effects of electromagnetic fields generated by cellphone devices on the male reproductive system have been inconclusive. Even though cell phone radiation is of the non-ionizing type, animal studies with exposition to field intensities considered as safe have reported effects such as variations in testosterone level, semen quality and even indirect ionizing-like effects such as changes at the molecular level as a result of the cellular stress in physiological processes [1]–[4]. The widespread use of mobile communication terminals by young people generates concern of a possible generalized impact on the human reproductive processes and calls for further studies on humans, which can be initially tackled using high-resolution numerical simulation.

The male testicles are highly sensitive to temperature. Indeed, important affectations to sperm quality have been observed for a temperature increase of 1°C [5], which in turn may result from exposure to electromagnetic fields with a magnitude high enough to cause Specific Absorption Rates (SAR) over 4 W/kg [6]. Given that the most common exposition levels are well below this guideline, it should be noted that gaps in knowledge have been recognized [1], in particular on the cumulative impact of lower exposition levels on the physiological mechanisms of the body, therefore these guidelines could vary as more information is available.

Several works have studied numerically the interaction of the electromagnetic field with the human body. For instance [7] analyzes the natural electromagnetic resonance of various body organs using a 3-D anatomical model with resolution of 2mm. In [8], a similar study and model allowed analysis of the effect of limb placement on the interaction of the electromagnetic field and body. Most relevant for this work is [7], where the SAR for human testicles was computed; this study found a whole-body resonance frequency around 65MHz, and a testicle resonance around 600MHz. [8] found similar results, and demonstrated a significant impact of body posture on the interaction.

Unlike previous works, we present the electromagnetic-thermal analysis of the interaction of the electromagnetic field with the human testicles using a high-resolution 3-D anatomical model that accounts for all the tissue types in the neighboring zone, a consistent model of the cellular mobile terminal, and a realistic usage scenario. Results were obtained using Sim4life [9] and anatomical models from the Virtual Population (ViP 3.0) [10].

II. Simulation Setup

An Inverted F Antenna (IFA) coplanar to a 7cm x 15cm ground plane modeled the mobile terminal, while the ZMT model "Duke" [10] represented the human body with the correct constitutive parameters for all the body tissues at 850MHz (2G/3G communications), see Table I.

TABLE I
TISSUES AND CONSTITUTIVE PARAMETERS CONSIDERED IN THE SIMULATION.

Tissue	Source	Permittivity	Elec. Cond. (S/m)
Ductus	Blood Vessel Wall	4.47E+1	7.12E-1
Fat	Fat (Average Infiltrated)	1.13E+1	1.13E-1
Muscle	Muscles	5.49E+1	9.60E-1
Nerve	Nerve	3.24E+1	5.87E-1
Penis	Blood Vessel Wall	4.47E+1	7.12E-1
Prostate	Testis	6.04E+1	1.23E+0
SAT (Subcutaneous Fat)	Fat (Average Infiltrated)	1.13E+1	1.13E-1
Seminal vesicle	Testis	6.04E+1	1.23E+0
Skin	Skin (Dry)	4.12E+1	8.83E-1
Testis	Testis	6.04E+1	1.23E+0
Ureter / Urethra	Blood Vessel Wall	4.47E+1	7.12E-1

The Sim4Life package employs the Finite Difference Time Domain Method (FDTD) method; the computational platform used in the analysis is described in the Table II.

TABLE II
PARAMETERS OF THE COMPUTING PLATFORM USED FOR SIMULATION.

Processor	Intel Xeon X5690
GPU	NVIDIA Tesla C2050
Chipset	Intel 5520
RAM Memory	96GB
Simulation Time	37:12 min

The IFA was designed to irradiate a power level similar to that of a commercial cellphone (0.25 Watts), and resonates at

850MHz in free space; when it is in presence of the body model, the resonant frequency somewhat shifts but we still obtain a low reflection coefficient at the operating frequency. A quoted diagram of the antenna is seen in Figure 1.

Fig. 1. Antenna diagram with its dimentions

The gap of the feed port is 0.5 mm and the width of each branch is 3.470 mm. The antenna was positioned simulating the user holding it in his pants pocket considering the worst case, i.e. antenna feed closest to the reproductive organs (see Figure 2).

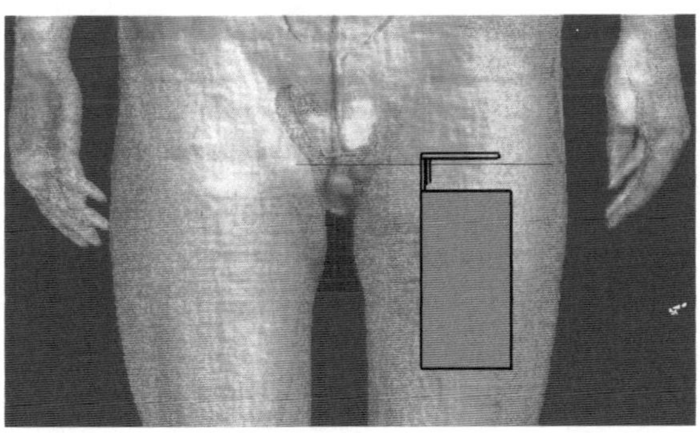

Fig. 2. Male human model with mobile terminal in front of the left leg.

III. Results

The SAR distribution was determined in the harmonic regime with the parameters described in the previous section. Results are shown in Figure 3. SAR is maximum in the leg, and only a marginal absorption is observed in the testicles, with a level well in conformance with the safety guidelines in [6].

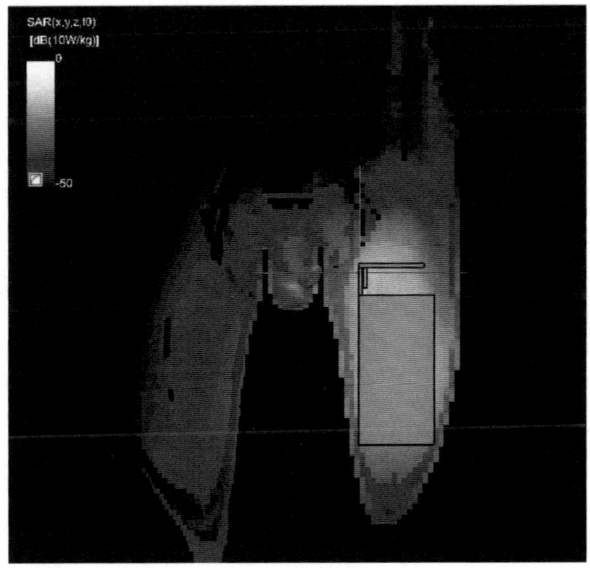

Fig. 3. SAR level due to cellphone excitation YZ plane

IV. Acknowledgement

This work was possible by a Sim4Life for Science License granted by ZMT [9].

References

[1] S. W, Mobile Phones and Health (The Stewart Report), GB, 2000, pp. 1–167, report. [Online]. Available: https://webarchive.nationalarchives.gov.uk/20100910162959

[2] H. Nisbet, C. Nisbet, A. Akaras, M. Cevik, and O. Karayigit, "Effects of exposure to Electromagnetic Field (1.8/0.9 GHz) on testicular function and structure in growing rats," Journal of Experimental and Clinical Medicine, vol. 30, pp. 275, Oct 2013.

[3] N. Falzone, C. Huyser, D. Leszczynski, and D. R. Franken, "The effect of non thermal 900 MHz mobile phone radiation on human spermatozoa," Ph.D. dissertation, University of Pretoria, 2008.

[4] J. C. Weaver, "Understanding conditions for which biological effects of nonionizing electromagnetic fields can be expected," Bioelectrochemistry, vol. 56, no. 1-2, pp. 207–209, 2002. [Online]. Available: http://citeseerx.ist.psu.edu/viewdoc/download?doi=10.1.1.483.2388&rep=rep1&type=pdf

[5] K. Kumar and A. Raju, "A review on male fertility," HYGEIA - Journal for Drugs and Medicines, pp. 20–28, 2011, ISSN=22293590 . [Online]. Available: http://oaji.net/articles/2017/4562-1487739225.pdf

[6] ICNIRP, "Icnirp (International Commission on Non-Ionizing Radiation Protection) guidelines for limiting exposure to time varying electric, magnetic and electromagnetic fields (up to 300 GHz)," Health Physics, vol. 74, no. 4, pp. 494–522, 1998.

[7] J. Wang, N. Mukaide, and O. Fujiwara, "FDTD calculation of organ resonance characteristics in an anatomically based human model for plane-wave exposure," Asia-Pacific Conference on Environmental Electromagnetics, 2003. CEEM 2003. Proceedings, 2003.

[8] R. P. Findlay and P. J. Dimbylow, "FDTD calculations of specific energy absorption rate in a seated and standing human voxel models of the human body from 10 MHz to 300 MHz," Physics in Medicine and Biology, vol. 51, no. 9, pp. 2339–2352, 2006.

[9] "Sim4life by zmt." [Online]. Available: www.zurichmedtech.com

[10] "Virtual population vip 3.0." [Online]. Available: https://itis.swiss/virtual-population/virtual-population/vip3/

A Frequency Selective Rasorber with Two Absorption Bands

Yuting Zhao and Yingsong Li*
College of Information and Communication Engineering, Harbin Engineering University, Harbin 150001, China
zhaoyt@hrbeu.edu.cn, *liyingsong@ieee.org

***Abstract*— In this paper, a frequency selective rasorber (FSR) with two absorption bands is proposed. The proposed FSR is a double-layer structure, which is composed of a resistive sheet and a bandpass frequency selective surface. By cascading a resistive sheet with a parallel LC resonator to a bandpass FSS (which has a passband coincides with that of resistive sheet), a transmission window in the two absorption bands can be achieved. The designed FSR also shows a dual-polarized character under normal incidence.**

Keywords—frequency selective rasorber, frequency selective surface, two absorption bands.

I. Introduction

The design of frequency selective surfaces (FSSs) goes back to the world war □, where FSSs were known for its application in radomes to reduce radar cross section (RCS) [1]. In a typical mono-station situation, RCS reduction was realized by the shaped radome with strong reflection outside its operating band, which shifted the strong reflection away from backscatter direction to reduce RCS, while it allow in-band signals to pass through. In order to ensure out-of-band RCS reduction of FSS-coated object in bi-station/multi-station situation, frequency selective rasorber (FSR) was recently reported [2]. According to the physical structure, the existing FSRs can be classified as two-dimensioned FSR and three-dimensioned FSR. Usually, 3-D FSR can readily achieve high selectivity and angular stability [3-5], but it is more complicated compared to 2-D FSR. Although it is difficult for 2-D FSR to obtain multiband absorption bands at both sides of the transmission window, [6-7] presented a 2-D FSR with two absorption bands by introducing a parallel LC resonator into the resistive sheet.

In this paper, a 2-D FSR with two absorption bands at both sides of transmission window is presented. By cascading a resistive sheet with the bandpass FSS, two absorption bands of 80% absorptivity in 2.18GHz-3.14 GHz, 6.38 GHz-9.2 GHz, and a 3 dB transmission band from 3.8GHz to 5.1GHz are obtained under the normal incidence.

II. The Design of FSR

The configuration of the FSR unit cell and side view of sheet 1 and sheet 2 are demonstrated in Fig. 1. The FSR unit cell is composed of a resistive sheet unit cell and a typical circular aperture element, which are separated by an air spacer of 12.4 mm. By introducing a parallel LC resonator, the resistive sheet unit cell is designed a combination element loaded four resistors R, which is supported by a 0.5 mm thick FR-4 substrate with relative permittivity of 4.2. The axe-shaped corner of the combination element can be equivalent to an inductance, while the parallel strip can be equivalent to a capacitor, which is parallel to the axe-shaped inductance. In this way, a parallel LC resonator is constructed. The bandpass FSS is a typical circular aperture element.

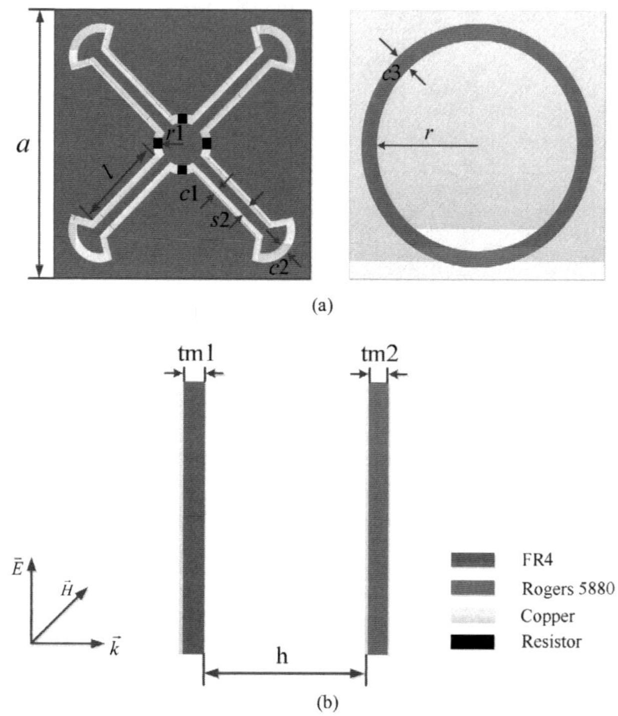

Fig. 1. Configuration of the proposed FSR unit cell: (a) front view of resistive sheet unit cell and bandpass FSS unit cell, and (b) side view of FSR.

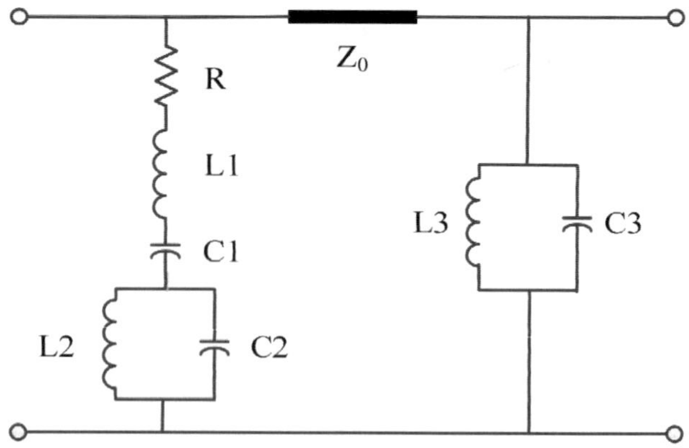

Fig. 2. Equivalent circuit model of the designed FSR.

In order to reduce the in-band loss, the bandpass FSS is supported by a 0.5 mm Rogers 5880 dielectric with permittivity of 2.2. The side view of the assembled FSR is depicted in Fig. 1 (b), the resistive sheet and bandpass FSS are separated by an air spacer h = 12.4 mm. The other key parameters are given as: a = 22 mm, l = 7.3 mm, c1 = 0.5 mm, c2 = 0.8 mm, c3 = 0.8 mm, s2 = 0.7 mm, r = 9.4 mm, r1 = 2 mm.

The equivalent circuit of the designed FSR is given in Fig. 2. By utilizing the equivalent circuit model, it is more directly to understand the mechanism of the designed FSR. In addition, the equivalent circuit can provide design guidelines.

III. The Simulation Results

The FSR is modeled and simulated in the full-wave simulation software CST, by using the Periodic Structures template in Microwave & RF/Optical studio. Its equivalent circuit model is simulated in Advanced Design System (ADS), and the optimized parameters are given as: R = 190 Ohm, L1 = 3.32 nH, C1 = 0.18 pf, L2 = 3.17 nH, C2 = 0.45 pf, L3 = 4.9 nH, C3 = 0.31pf. The electric length of transmission line is 67 degree, which represents the air spacer between two layers.

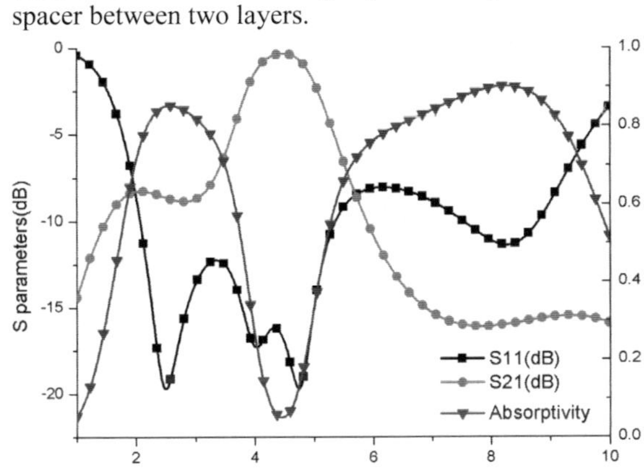

Fig. 3. Optimized S11/S21 and absorptivity of the FSR.

Fig. 3 shows the simulated reflection/transmission coefficient and absoptivity of the proposed FSR under normal incidence. The absorptivity is calculated by $A = 1 - |S_{11}|^2 - |S_{21}|^2$. It is shown that the FSR can provide a 3 dB transmission band from 3.8 GHz to 5.1 GHz and two absorption bands of 80% absorptivity at both sides of the transmission band. And the two absorption band with 80% absorptivity at both sides of transmission window are cover from 2.18 to 3.14 GHz and from 6.38 to 9.2 GHz, respectively.

The simulation results of full wave electromagnetic simulation and equivalent circuit model are compared in Fig. 4. It is shown that the S parameters simulated in CST agree well with that simulated in ADS, which demonstrated the accuracy of the equivalent circuit model and the effectivity of the design guideline provided by the equivalent circuit.

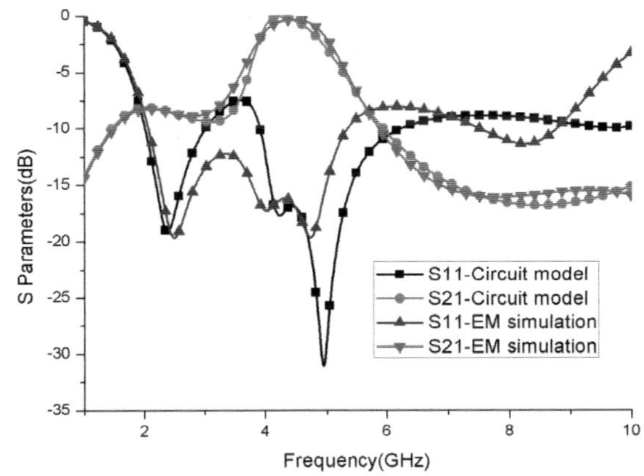

Fig.4. Simulated S parameters of EM simulation and equivalent circuit model.

IV. Conclusion

In this paper, a FSR with two absorption bands at both sides of the transmission window is developed, which is realized by cascading a resistive sheet with a bandpass FSS. The key to design is the resistive sheet, which can provide a transmission window coincides with that of the cascaded bandpass FSS, while it can also provide absorption characteristic out of the passband. By introducing a parallel LC resonator, which is realized by a well-designed combination element, the transmission window with low in-band loss performance is achieved. The designed FSR also performs a dual-polarized characteristic under normal incidence due to its symmetric structure.

Acknowledgment

This work was partially supported by the Key Research and Development Program of Heilongjiang (GX17A016).

References

[1] B. A. Munk. Frequency Selective Surface: Theory and Design. Hoboken, NJ. USA: Wiley, 2005.

[2] B. A. Munk. Metamaterial: Critique and Alternative. Hoboken, NJ. USA: Wiley, 2009.

[3] Z. Shen, J. Wang, and B. Li, "3-D frequency selective rasorber: concept, analysis, and design," IEEE Transactions on Microwave Theory and Techniques, 2016, vol. 63, no. 10, pp. 3087-3096.

[4] Z. Shen, A. Omar, and H. Huang, "Absorptive frequency-selective reflection and transmission structures," IEEE Transactions on Antennas and Propagation, 2017, vol. 65, no. 11, pp. 6173-6178.

[5] Y. Yu. Z. Shen, T. Deng, and G. Luo, "3-D frequency-selective rasorber with wide upper absorption band," IEEE Transactions on Antennas and Propagation, 2017, vol. 65, no. 8, pp. 4363-4367.

[6] Q. Chen, S. Yang, J. Bai, and Y. Fu, "Design of absorptive/transmissive frequency-selective surface based on parallel resonance," IEEE Transactions on Antennas and Propagation, 2017, vol. 65, no. 9, pp. 4897-4902

[7] Q. Chen, L. Liu, L. Chen, J. Bai, and Y. Fu, "Absorptive frequency selective surface using parallel LC resonance," Electron. Letter, 2016, vol. 52, no. 6, pp. 418-419.

3D Electromagnetic Particle-in-Cell Simulation of EMP Generated by Pulsed X-rays

Zhiqian Xu
Department of Engineering Physics
Tsinghua University
Beijing, China
xzq17@mails.tsinghua.edu.cn

Cui Meng
Department of Engineering Physics
Tsinghua University
Beijing, China
mengcui@mail.tsinghua.edu.cn

***Abstract*—Pulsed X-rays could cause significant cavity system-generated electromagnetic pulse (SGEMP) interference. A 3D electromagnetic particle-in-cell simulation approach is developed to calculate EMP generated inside a cylindrical cavity after X-ray illumination. The waveform, spatial distributions and resonant frequencies of cavity SGEMP are demonstrated by the computations. The peak value of cavity SGEMP main pulse is 72.88 kV/m. When farther away from the charge emitting face, the field strength decreases quickly and its polarity reverses; when the distance from symmetry axis increases, the field strength declines relatively slower. The cavity SGEMP would form a stable resonance and its frequency is dominated by the radius and length of cavity. The simulation method is verified and can be applied to the X-ray radiation hardness.**

Keywords—Cavity SGEMP, PIC, charge conservation, conformal mesh, X-rays.

I. Introduction

After X-rays penetrate metal surface, numerous electrons would be emitted to the internal vacuum region, forming transient current and emerging strong cavity system-generated electromagnetic pulse (SGEMP) in electronic equipment [1]. Previous studies have developed the 2D calculation ability under X-rays generated by nuclear explosion, like the ABORC code [2]. The influence of input parameters and geometry are also well discussed [3-4]. However, systematic research on the frequency and spatial characteristics and three-dimensional simulation of cavity SGEMP are still insufficient.

II. Calculation Method

A. Discrete Charge Conservation Theorem

The source term for Maxwell's equations is the current density $\boldsymbol{J}$ from emitting electrons:

$$\boldsymbol{J} = \sum Q_M \boldsymbol{v} N_S \,. \tag{1}$$

Where Q_M and $\boldsymbol{v}$ is charge and velocity of a macroparticle, while N_S is the assignment factor.

Conventional volume-based weight assignment method might not satisfy the Maxwell's divergence equations and require a very complex Poisson correction, which performs fairly complex iterations by SOR or other algorithms and cost a lot of memory resources and calculation time [5]. Chen et al. [6] proposed the discrete charge conservation by ensuring the continuity equation to automatically satisfy the Maxwell divergence equation. For example, the charge-conserving assignment for x component of the current density J_x is:

$$\begin{aligned} & J_x^{n+1/2}(i+\tfrac{1}{2},j,k)+J_x^{n+1/2}(i+\tfrac{1}{2},j+1,k)+J_x^{n+1/2}(i+\tfrac{1}{2},j,k+1) \\ & +J_x^{n+1/2}(i+\tfrac{1}{2},j+1,k+1)=\rho_M \cdot \frac{x_M^{n+1}-x_M^{n}}{dt}. \end{aligned} \tag{2}$$

Where ρ_M and x_M is charge density and position of a macroparticle.

B. Conformal Mesh Technique

Modelling irregular structures is an inevitable problem for three-dimensional simulation. "Staircased" approximation is broadly adopted to represent the curve with a polyline in conventional FDTD, inevitably generating some errors for complex structures. To accurately model the cylinder in three dimensions, conformal mesh is adopted, which is the internal part of conventional mesh at the boundary [7]. In this case, the magnetic field $\boldsymbol{B}$ is calculated by integrating the electric field $\boldsymbol{E}$ along the boundary of conformal mesh:

$$\oint_{C_l} \boldsymbol{E}\cdot d\boldsymbol{l} = -\frac{\partial}{\partial t}\iint_{S_l} \boldsymbol{B}\cdot d\boldsymbol{S}\,. \tag{3}$$

Where C_l and S_l is the edge and area of conformal mesh.

III. Computation Results

A vacuum cylindrical cavity, with a diameter of 50 cm and a length of 50 cm, is considered here to represent the typical metal shell of electronic device, as shown in Fig. 1. It is assumed that 10-keV-energy, 1-J/cm^2-fluence and 1-ns-duration X-rays illuminate one end of the cylinder uniformly along the direction of the symmetry axis. Therefore, the total number of electrons is calculated to be $N_0 = 2.38\times10^{12}$ by a Monte Carlo software. The waveform, frequency and spatial

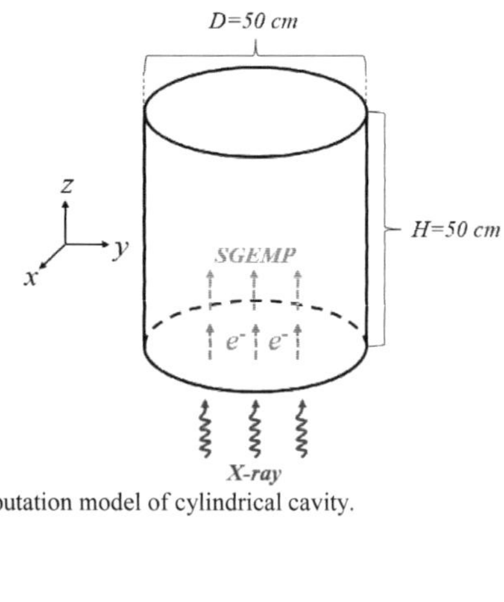

Fig. 1. Computation model of cylindrical cavity.

characteristics are calculated by the self-developed code 3Dcavitysgemp V1.0.

A. *Waveform of EMP*

There are four output positions which are 9 cm away from the axis of symmetry and 9 cm away from the emitting end, as well as 90 degrees apart from each other. They are marked as point A, B, C and D. The 10 ns waveforms of four output positions are illustrated in Fig. 2. Theoretically, they should be exactly the same for the geometric symmetry of cylindrical model. Numerically, these four waveforms do overlap each other qualitatively, with only slight distinctive caused by randomness of macroparticles' initial locations. The largest relative errors for Peak 1, Peak 2, Peak3 are 2.94%, 4.71%, 4.38% respectively. Therefore, it can be quantitatively concluded that simulation results have good hoop symmetry and agree well with the calculation model.

By averaging the data at four output positions, the peak value of cavity SGEMP main pulse is 72.88 kV/m.

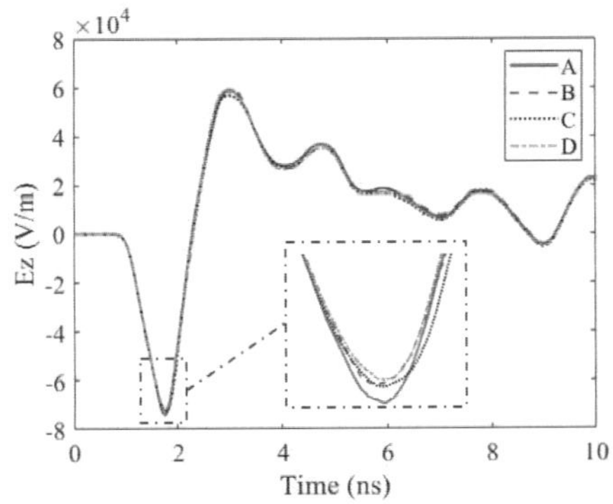

Fig. 2. Waveforms of four output positions.

B. *Spacial Distributions of Cavity SGEMP*

Fig. 3 depicts electric fields at locations 9 cm away from the axis of symmetry and leaving the emitting end with various distances from 1 cm to 40 cm. The space charge limited phenomenon at high X-ray fluence is clearly observed. Positive charges left on emitting end and emitting electrons excite a strong positive electric field that modifies the trajectories of electrons and returns majority of them back. A small amount of electrons can move beyond this lay, generating a relatively lower negative electric field. As a result, the field strength becomes smaller quickly when farther away from the emitting end and its polarity reverses when the distance is larger than 9 cm.

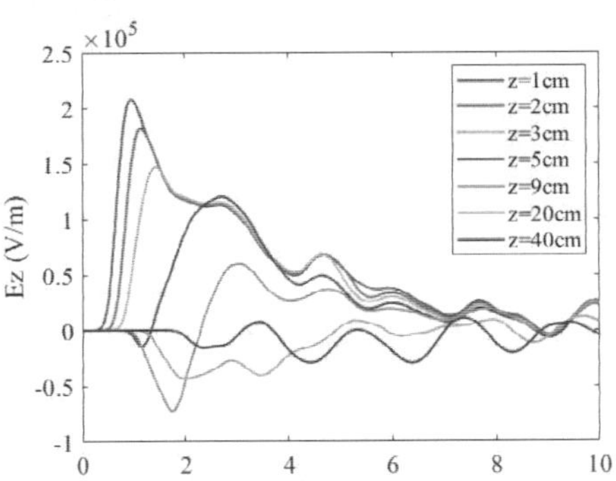

Fig. 3. Axial distribution of electric fields.

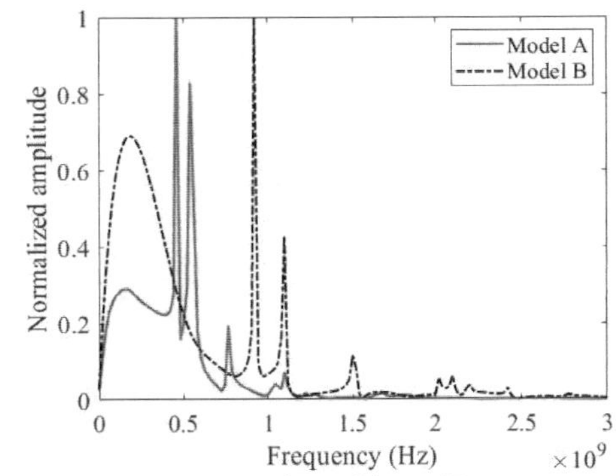

Fig. 4. Normalized spectrum under model A and B.

C. *Resonant Frequency*

To test the frequency characteristics of cavity SGEMP, two models of different size are established. The model used in above simulations are named as model A. Model B is a smaller cylindrical cavity with a diameter of 25 cm and a length of 25 cm. Fig. 4 demonstrates the normalized spectrum. Theoretically, resonant frequencies of a cylindrical waveguide are dominated by the radius and length. Numerically, discrete frequency centers under model A and B differ from each other as a factor of 2, exactly the same as prediction. Overall, the cavity SGEMP does form a stable resonance after reflections of the main pulse by metal walls.

IV. USING THE TEMPLATE

The 3D novel simulation approach is verified to be accurate within the error tolerance. The peak value, spatial distributions and resonant frequencies of cavity SGEMP are all demonstrated through 3D computations. These work could provide great help for solving the EMC problems in pulsed X-ray related physical experiments and applications.

REFERENCES

[1] C. L. Longmire, "State of the art in IEMP and SGEMP calculations," IEEE Trans. Nucl. Sci., vol. NS-22, no. 6, pp. 2340–2344, Dec. 1975, 10.1109/TNS.1975.4328130.

[2] R. Keyser and D. Swift, "Analysis and tests of a right circular cylinder in a photon environment," IEEE Trans. Nucl. Sci., vol. NS-24, no. 6, pp. 2445-2448, Dec. 1977, 10.1109/TNS.1977.4329234.

[3] E. P. Wenaas, S. Rogers and A. J. Woods, "Sensitivity of SGEMP response to input parameters," IEEE Trans. Nucl. Sci., vol. NS-22, no. 6, pp. 2362-2367, Dec. 1975, 10.1109/TNS.1975.4328134.

[4] A. J. Woods and E. P. Wenaas, "SGEMP geometry effects," IEEE Trans. Nucl. Sci., vol. NS-22, no. 6, pp. 2374-2380, Dec. 1975, 10.1109/TNS.1975.4328136.

[5] Y. Dong, Z. Dong, H. Zhou, and W. Yang, "Application of a novel charge-conservation method used in large-scale parallel computation for fully electromagnetic Particle-In-Cell simulation," Journal of Terahertz Science and Electronic Information Technology, vol. 14, no. 4, pp. 574-580, Aug. 2016.

[6] L. Chacón and G. Chen, "A curvilinear, fully implicit, conservative electromagnetic PIC algorithm in multiple dimensions," Journal of Computational Physics, vol. 316, pp. 578-597, July 2016, 10.1016/j.jcp.2016.03.070.

[7] M. R. Cabello, L. D. Angulo, J. Alvarez, A. R. Bretones, G. G. Gutierrez, and S. G. Garcia, "A new efficient and stable 3D conformal FDTD," IEEE Microwave and Wireless Components Letters, vol. 26, no. 8, pp. 553-555, Aug 2016, 10.1109/LMWC.2016.2588579.

Use of Dielectric Spectroscopy for the Study of Concentration of Glyphosate in Distilled Water

Camilo Mendivelso[1], John J. Pantoja[1,2], Felix Vega[1,2], Chaouki Kasmi[2], and Fahad Al Yafei[2]
[1]*Universidad Nacional de Colombia - Sede Bogota*
Bogotá, Colombia
[2]*Directed Energy Research Centre, Technology Innovation Institute*
Abu Dhabi, United Arab Emirates
john.pantoja@tii.ae

***Abstract*—In this paper, the capability of sensing low concentrations of glyphosate in water of two interdigital capacitive transducers are analyzed using numerical simulations and measurements. Each microwave sensor is analyzed using the surface electric field produced at the resonance frequency. In addition, the reflection coefficient of each transducer submerged in water with glyphosate is measured and compared with distilled water. Prepared samples with concentrations of 1ppm/L (1 part per million over a liter of distilled water) are used for the experimental tests.**

***Keywords*— dielectric spectroscopy, glyphosate, interdigital capacitor, microwave, sensor, water.**

I. Introduction

A direct application of dielectric spectroscopy is the characterization of materials. Dielectric spectrometry technique is commonly used to calculate the content of water in materials or liquids; however, it can be also used to determine different specific properties of materials. Dielectric properties of materials vary depending on the content on water but also on the content of other component such as salts [1]. For this reason, this technique has been proposed for monitoring glyphosate in water using interdigital transducers [2].

Glyphosate is a common component in a wide range of pesticide products used for the control of plantations and for intensive agriculture. However, some studies reveal that Glyphosate present health risk for amphibians and humans [3].

In this paper, the electromagnetic behavior of two interdigital capacitor (IDC) transducers is presented and the response of each transducer submerged in water with glyphosate is analyzed.

II. Transducer Selection

The intended transducer is especially designed to detect presence of glyphosate in water as a real time sensor. Small concentrations of glyphosate are required to consider. The IDC is a planar resonant structure, whose resonant frequencies and quality factors depend on the dielectric properties of the surrounding medium.

Two IDCs implemented in FR4 were analyzed to compare their behavior and to determine the geometric characteristics that increase the capability to determine concentration of glyphosate in water. IDCs of 5 and 20 digits, as shown in Fig. 1, were numerically simulated. The 5 digits IDC has a wider separation between digits, which could enable more interaction of the electric field and the material under test. On the other hand, the 20 digits IDC has a smaller separation between digits providing higher density of electric field between digits, as confirmed by the simulations shown in Fig. 2.

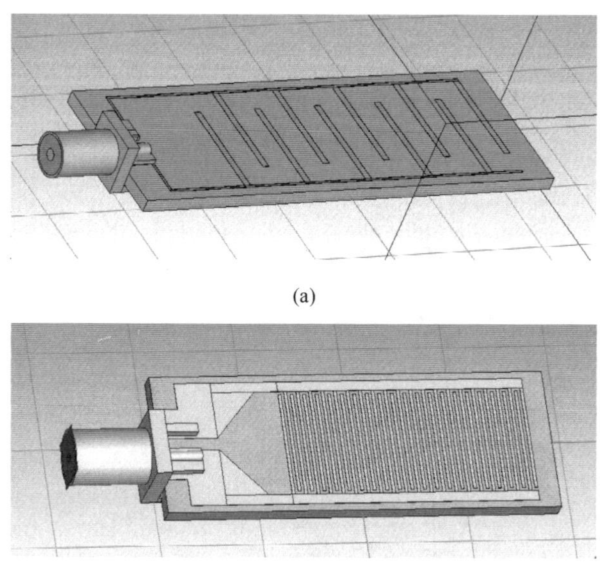

(a)

(b)

Fig. 1. Simulation models of IDCs with (a) 5 digits and (b) 20 digits.

(a)

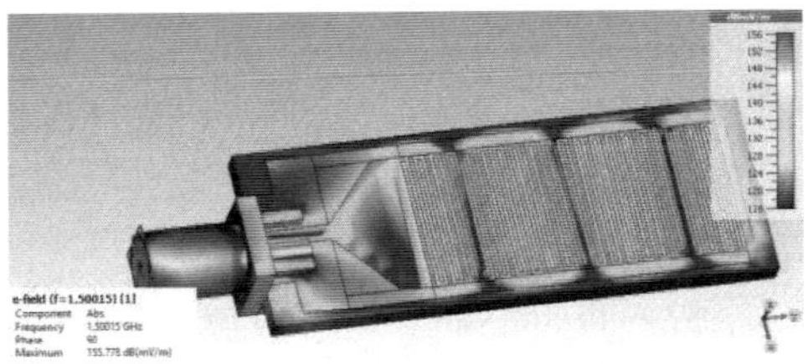

(b)

Fig. 2. Electric field simulated at the resonant frequency 1.5 GHz for the IDCs with (a) 5 digits and (b) 20 digits surrounded by air.

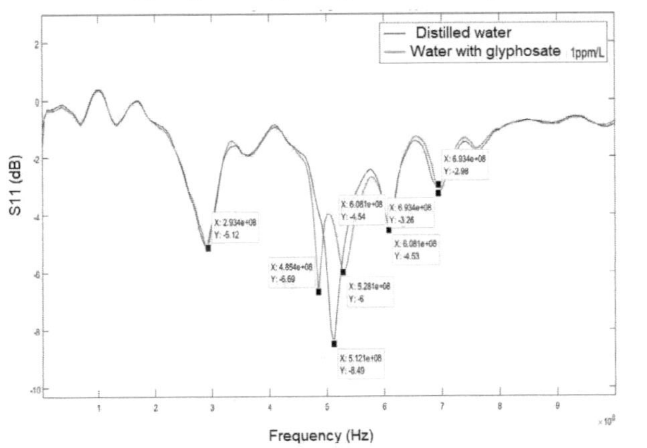

Fig. 3. Comparison of the S11 parameter of 5 digits IDC surrounded by water and water with glyphosate.

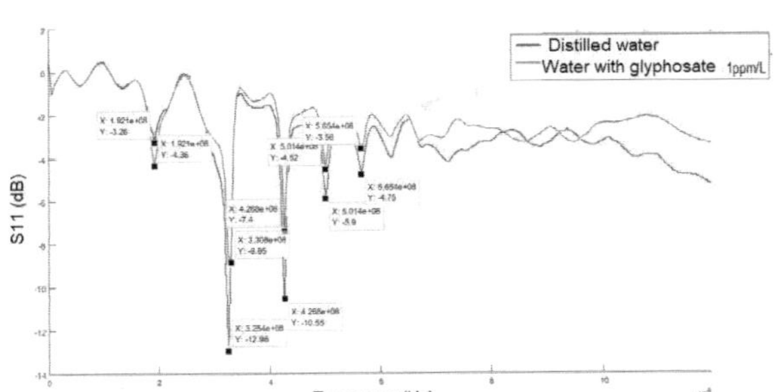

Fig. 4. Comparison of the S11 parameter of 20 digits IDC surrounded by water and water with glyphosate.

III. Experimental Results

In order to characterize the response of the considered IDCs, the S11 parameter was measured between 100 kHz and 1 GHz. Each IDC was submerged in previously prepared samples of distilled water and water with glyphosate with a concentration of 1 ppm/L (i.e., 1 part per million over a liter of distilled water). Each sample was prepared using microliter pipette.

Figs. 3 and 4 show the comparison of S11 parameter measured for both transducers surrounded by water and water with glyphosate. Experimental results show that both IDCs present a notable change of the response at the resonance frequencies. As mentioned before and verified with the electromagnetic simulations, the interaction of the electric field with the material under test in the sensor with 5 digits is higher than with the 20 digits sensor. This is expressed in Fig. 3, where the frequency response is modified and an additional minimum value in the S11 is presented for the test of water with glyphosate. On the other hand, the 20 digits IDC maintains the same number of minimums in the S11 and with almost the same frequencies for distilled water and water with glyphosate, as shown in Fig. 4. This indicates that the resonant structure is not strongly perturbed. However, the variation is obtained in the magnitude of the S11. Water with glyphosate case present magnitudes closer to zero dB with could be due to additional losses of the mixture.

IV. Conclusions

Two interdigital capacitive transducers used to detect glyphosate in water where analyzed with numerical simulations and experimental results. Two approaches for the design of the sensor were assessed. For one side, a 5 digits IDC showed lower concentration of electric field on the surface of the sensor which enable higher interaction of the electric field with the material under test. As a consequence, the frequency response is perturbed as the glyphosate is added to the water; for example, a minimum in S11 parameter at 512 MHz disappears but two new minimums at 485 MHz and 528 MHz are generated. For the other side, a 20 digits IDC, which presented a higher intensity of electric field on the surface, showed a more persistent frequency response as the glyphosate was added to the water. Nevertheless, experimental results showed that both approaches can be used to distinguish water from water with low concentrations of glyphosate from S11 measurements.

References

[1] K. Kupner, Electromagnetic Aquametry, Belin: Springer, 2005.

[2] O. Korostynska, A. Mason, and A. I. Al-Shamma'a, "Flexible microwave sensors for real-time analysis of water contaminants," J. of Electromag. Waves and Applications, vol. 27, issue 16, pp. 20752089, 2013. DOI: 10.1080/09205071.2013.832393.

[3] L. Mamy, B. Gabrielle, and E. Barriuso, "Comparative environmental impacts of glyphosate and conventional herbicides when used with glyphosate-tolerant and non-tolerant crops," Environmental Pollution, vol. 158, issue 10, p.p. 3172-3178, 2010.

Thermal Simulation of a Conductive Fabric Sheet Subjected to a Lightning-like Current

John J. Pantoja[1,2], Carlos Rivera[1], Jorge Cristancho[1], Jorge Rodriguez[1], and Francisco Román[1]
[1]Department of Electrical and Electronics Engineering, Universidad Nacional de Colombia - Sede Bogota
Bogotá, Colombia
[2]Directed Energy Research Center, Technology Innovation Institute
Abu Dhabi, United Arab Emirates
john.pantoja@tii.ae

Abstract— **A sample of electroconductive fabric subjected to a lightning-like current impulse is analyzed in this contribution. A multiphysics simulation is used to calculate the temperature distribution produced by a lightning-like current flowing through the material sample. A decoupled, electromagnetic (EM) and thermal, simulation was conducted for the analysis and is explained in the paper. The scaling factor calculation to represent the energy presented during current impulse tests is also detailed. Numerical results present patterns that agree with experimental tests reported in the literature and represent an additional tool for the phenomena insight.**

Keywords—Conductive fabric, electromagnetic simulation, impulse current, lightning, thermal simulation.

I. Introduction

Conductive fabrics have shown promising performance for different applications such as electromagnetic shielding, antennas, sensors, water treatment, and more recently lightning protection [1, 2]. Preliminary tests, in which different kinds of conductive fabrics are tested against lightning-like current impulses [1], show that the textiles can withstand high intense current impulses and provide a conductive path for lightning currents. However, the thermal stress produced in the electroconductive fabric materials during this kind of tests have not been studied in depth.

In this paper, a multiphysics simulation, including electromagnetic and thermal phenomena, is conducted in order to calculate and analyze the temperature produced in a sample of conductive fabric subjected to a high intensity current impulse.

II. Simulation Setup

The characteristics of the excitation signal and the samples under test are the same as the reported ones in previews experimental results [2].

A decoupled, electromagnetic (EM) and thermal, simulation was conducted for the analysis. The general steps for the simulation can be summarized as follows. First, the electromagnetic (EM) simulation is conducted. Then, power losses are calculated from the EM simulation. These losses are the source of the thermal simulation. Finally, thermal simulation is conducted and temperature distribution is obtained.

A. Conductive Fabric Samples

The selected samples of electroconductive fabrics tested in [2] are pieces of 10 cm x 10 cm of non-woven conductive fabrics. The main electrical characteristics of the samples are presented in Table I. Physical characteristics presented in the table are based in the manufacturer data. Simulation parameters, also included in the table, are based on experimental results reported in [2] and typical properties of the fabric's conductive materials.

B. Excitation Signal

The excitation signal used in [2] is a current impulse of 13,7 kA, 4/10 µs. The energy reported for this signal was with a time to half value of 10 µs. Since the used thermal simulator only imports power losses from EM simulation in frequency domain at one frequency and the excitation signal in the experimental tests is a pulse, different excitation signals were used in EM and thermal simulations. For the EM simulation, the excitation signal corresponds to a current signal injected in the sample. A Gaussian excitation covering the frequencies up to 20 MHz was used.

For the thermal simulation setup, a square pulsed excitation was used. The source in the thermal simulation corresponds to the imported losses from the EM simulation. For this reason, the average power of the pulse signal in the thermal simulations has to be calculated. The average power of a square pulse excitation can be estimated as:

$$P_{ave} = U/\tau, \tag{1}$$

where U is the delivered energy and τ is the pulse duration. In this case, it is assumed that the power is produced by a continuous wave signal. Therefore, if the power P_{ave} is produced by a continuous wave signal, the required current to obtain that power can be obtained from the power dissipated in a resistance. In our case, the conductive fabric is the resistance that dissipate this power into heat,

$$P_{ave} = \frac{I_{peak}^2}{2} R. \tag{2}$$

From (1) and (2), the equivalent current to produce the same energy used in the impulsive tests can be calculated. Using $U = 104$ J, $\tau = 10$ µs, and $R = 0.03\,\Omega$, a peak current of $I_{peak} = 26.3$ kA is obtained. This result provides the scaling factor used in the thermal simulation for the losses 26.3×10^3, which corresponds to the ratio between the desired peak current and the peak current used in the EM simulation that in this case was 1 A.

TABLE I. CHARACTERISTICS OF SIMULATED CONDUCTIVE FABRIC

Characteristic	Unit	Fabric	Simulation
Weave pattern	type	non-woven	Lossy conductive sheet
Conductive material	type	Ni-Cu	--
Weight	g/m^2	90±10	--
Sheet resistance	Ω/□	≤ 0.05	0.03
Resistivity	μΩ·m	≤ 4.0	1.17
Density	kg/m3	--	576.92
Thermal conductivity	W/K/m	--	50
Heat capacity	kJ/K/kg	--	0.385

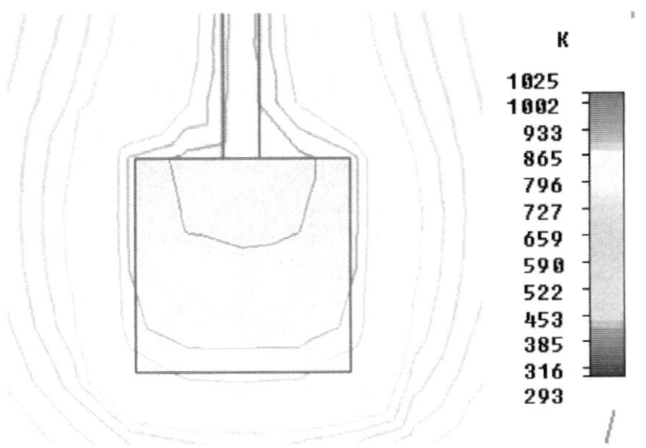

Fig. 1. Constant temperature lines calculated using the EM-thermal simulation.

C. Electromagnetic Simulation

The electromagnetic (EM) simulation included a box of air (normal) with thermal properties surrounding the conductive fabric, open boundary conditions in all directions, a current port defined in a straight line with a current of 1 A, a straight PEC wire used to connect the current port with the conductive sheet under test, and field monitors (e-field, h-field, loss) for the frequency that represent the desired energy distribution. The conductive fabric was modeled as a lossy conductive sheet with the thermo-electrical characteristics shown in Table I.

The EM simulation was performed using a finite element method (FEM) solver in frequency domain. To estimate the temperature increases, the power losses at 10 MHz were calculated after the EM was completed. At this frequency the sample is electrically small.

D. Thermal Simulation

The thermal simulation included isothermal boundary conditions in all directions, and a boundary temperature fixed at 293.1 K. To import the power dissipated in the sheet to the thermal simulator, the thermal loss distribution was calculated. The scaling factor deduced in the previous section equal to 26.3×10^3 was used to represent the energy used in the experimental tests reported in [2]. Due to the small duration of the impulse (i.e. several times lower than the thermal constant of the conductive sheet), heating can be considered adiabatic.

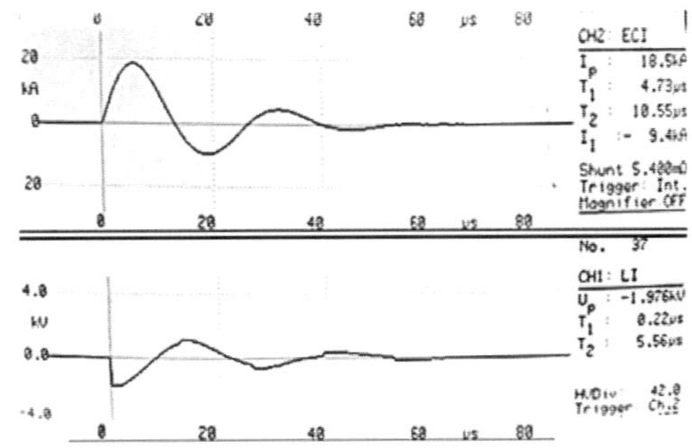

(a)

(b)

Fig. 2. (a) Current and voltage signals measured in the experimental test and (b) conductive fabric after impulsive test showing marks by overheating. Figure taken from [2].

III. RESULTS

Temperature distribution calculated in the conductive sheet is presented in Fig. 1. The highest temperature is presented around the electrode that injects the current. Similar results are obtained in experimental impulsive tests performed over conductive fabrics [2]. Material overheating produced by the lightning impulse current sublimates metallic layers around the electrodes contact area, as shown in Fig. 2. Particularly, circular patterns are formed around the electrodes, such as the isothermal lines suggested by the numerical simulation results presented in Fig. 1.

IV. CONCLUSIONS

Numerical simulations to calculate the temperature distributions produced by a lightning-like current in a conductive fabric are described in this paper. Numerical results agree with experimental tests previously reported in the literature. Particularly, patterns of melted conductive material observed in the non-woven fabric sheet follows the isothermal lines of high temperature numerically calculated. Work is in progress to numerically estimate thermal effects on conductive fabrics with higher current intensities and higher energy rates.

REFERENCES

[1] J. A. Cristancho C., J. E. Rodriguez M., C. A. Rivera G., F. Román, L. K. Herrera, and J. J. Pantoja, "Conductive Fabric Potential Rise due to Lightning Impulse Currents," in *2019 International Symposium on Lightning Protection (XV SIPDA)*, São Paulo, 2019.

[2] J. A. Cristancho C., J. E. Rodriguez M., C. A. Rivera G., F. Roman and J. J. Pantoja, "High Current Tests over Conductive Fabrics," *2018 International Conference on Electromagnetics in Advanced Applications (ICEAA)*, Cartagena des Indias, 2018, pp. 428-432, doi: 10.1109/ICEAA.2018.8520351.

Effective Design of Graphene Patch Arrays for Adjustable Plane-Wave Scattering

Stamatios Amanatiadis
Dept. of Electrical & Comp. Eng.
Aristotle University of Thessaloniki
Thessaloniki, Greece
samanati@auth.gr

Tadao Ohtani
1-17-134 Omachi
Asahikawa, Japan
bytcg100@ybb.ne.jp

Yasushi Kanai
Department of Engineering
Niigata Institute of Technology
Kashiwazaki, Japan
kanai@iee.niit.ac.jp

Nikolaos Kantartzis
Dept. of Electrical & Comp. Eng.
Aristotle University of Thessaloniki
Thessaloniki, Greece
kant@ece.auth.gr

***Abstract*—In this document, the scattering properties of graphene patches are investigated to design arrays that are able to control effectively plane wave propagation. Initially, single patches are examined in terms of their radar cross-section and surface wave generation. Moreover, an array of four identical elements is designed and thoroughly investigated indicating that electrostatic bias field has not a significant effect. However, the application of non-uniform biasing on the same setup reveals the fine adjustment of the scattered wave's main lobe direction.**

***Index Terms*—anisotropy, beam manipulation, chemical potential, surface waves.**

I. Introduction

Recently, technological advancements require efficiently adjustable devices such as radiators with beam manipulation features [1]. Moreover, the operation frequencies are continuously increasing, approximating THz regime, to support the demands of data rate transfer. However, conventional materials, such as metals, present degraded performance at this spectrum resulting in the consideration of alternative ones, such as the popular graphene [2]. Despite its negligible thickness, this truly two-dimensional carbon allotrope has gained significant recognition due to its exotic properties, such as the ability to support strongly confined surface plasmon polariton (SPP) waves at far-infrared frequencies.

This feature is exploited in this work to control the scattering properties of a graphene patch with finite dimensions. Specifically, our initial goal is the radar cross-section extraction of single square patches as well as the observation of surface wave generation onto graphene that are strongly connected to the application of electrostatic bias fields. To this end, the two-dimensional material is introduced in a properly modified Finite-Difference Time-Domain scheme as an equivalent surface current density that depends on graphene's surface conductivity [3]. Then, a 2×2 patch array setup is examined indicating that a non-uniform electrostatic biasing is able to rotate finely the main-lobes of both back and forward scattered waves.

II. Graphene Conductivity and Surface Waves

In our work, graphene is considered as infinitesimally thin layer, characterized via its surface conductivity $\sigma(\omega, \mu_c, \Gamma, T)$; where ω is the radian frequency, μ_c the chemical potential that is controlled via an applied electrostatic bias, Γ a phenomenological scattering rate assumed to be independent of energy, and T the temperature. Graphene's conductivity is evaluated by the compact expression resulting from the Kubo formula [4], involving only the dominant, at the far-infrared spectrum, intraband term:

$$\sigma_{\text{intra}}(\omega, \mu_c, \Gamma, T) = \frac{e^2 k_B T}{\pi \hbar^2 (j\omega + 2\Gamma)} \times \times \left[\frac{\mu_c}{k_B T} + 2 \ln(e^{-\mu_c / k_B T} + 1) \right]. \quad (1)$$

Moreover, the propagation properties of the surface wave onto graphene are evaluated via the complex wavenumber k_ρ of that depends on the material's conductivity and is extracted via [5]:

$$k_\rho = k_0 \sqrt{1 - \left(\frac{2}{\sigma_{\text{intra}} \eta_0} \right)^2}, \quad (2)$$

with k_0 and η_0 the free space wavenumber and wave impedance, respectively. An additional, more intuitive feature of the SPP wave is its wavelength λ_{SPP} that is promptly calculated in terms of:

$$\lambda_{SPP} = \frac{2\pi}{\Re\{k_\rho\}}. \quad (3)$$

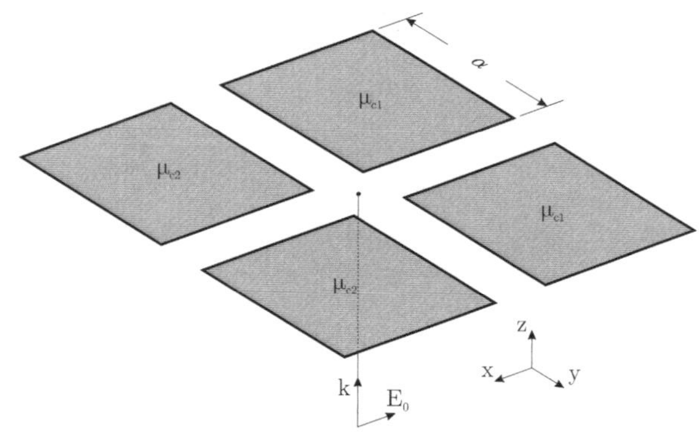

Fig. 1: Plane wave propagating towards a 2×2 graphene patch array.

III. Plane Wave Scattering on Graphene Patches

The general setup that is under investigation is depicted in Fig. 1, where graphene is on xy-plane and a plane wave is

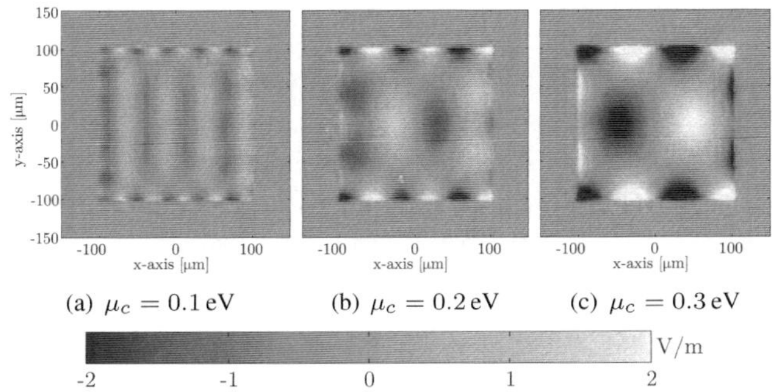

Fig. 2: Distribution of electric field component that is normal to graphene.

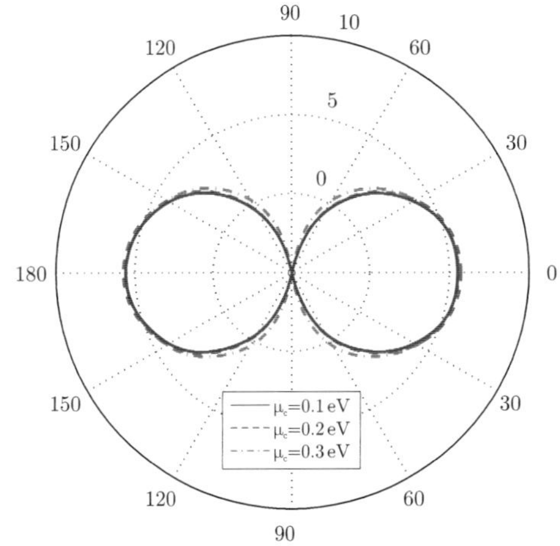

Fig. 3: Radar cross-section of a single graphene patch at a plane normal to plane wave direction and polarization.

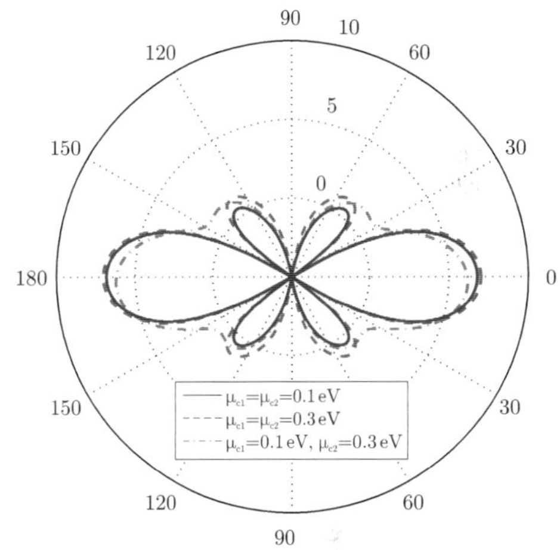

Fig. 4: Radar cross-section of a 2×2 graphene patch array at xz-plane that is normal to plane wave direction and polarization.

propagating towards positive z-axis, that is normal to graphene surface. Observe that the plane wave polarization is along negative x-axis. The computational domain for the subsequent analyses is divided into $300\times 300\times 300$ cells with $\Delta x = \Delta y = \Delta z = 2.5\,\mu\mathrm{m}$ and a time-step of $\Delta t = 4.5\,\mathrm{fs}$, while open boundaries are terminated with an 8-cell perfectly matched layer. The simulations are conducting at operating frequency 2 THz, where graphene SPP wave contribution is enhanced, while the dimension of square patches is selected $\alpha = 200\,\mu\mathrm{m}$. Finally, graphene parameters are set to $\Gamma = 0.33\,\mathrm{meV}$ and the chemical potential varies from low to moderate values, specifically $0.1 - 0.3\,\mathrm{eV}$.

A. Single Patch Scenario

Initially, a single graphene patch is placed into the computational domain and the generation of surface waves is investigated thoroughly. In particular, the distribution of the normal, to graphene, electric field component, namely E_z, is depicted in Fig. 2 for different chemical potential values. It is evident that as the latter increases, the SPP wavelength is larger, as expected through (3), where λ_{SPP} is 26.3, 50 and 70.2 μm for μ_c equal to 0.1, 0.2 and 0.3 eV, accordingly. Moreover, the stnading waves are appearing towards polarization, while electric field is stronger as chemical potential increases that can be explained due to the weaker matching of the propagating surface wave to the surface waves with decreased wavelength. Finally, the radar cross-section is evaluated at plane normal to plane wave direction and polarization and it is sketched in Fig. 3. Although, the surface waves onto graphene are influenced significantly due to chemical potential variation, the directivity is almost identical for the single patch case.

B. Array of Graphene Patches

In our second scenario, the 2×2 array of Fig. 1 is investigated. Firstly, graphene patches are uniformly biased with $\mu_{c1} = \mu_{c2} = 0.1\,\mathrm{eV}$ and $\mu_{c1} = \mu_{c2} = 0.3\,\mathrm{eV}$, while a final setup is designed, where the patches are distinguished in two groups along the polarization with $\mu_{c1} = 0.3\,\mathrm{eV}$ and $\mu_{c2} = 0.1\,\mathrm{eV}$. It is illustrated in Fig. 4 that for uniformly biased patches, radar cross-section is not influenced by chemical potential. However, the extracted results are more interesting for the final setup, where bias fields are distributed unevenly. Particularly, the main lobe of both back and forward scattered waves is rotating towards the lower chemical potential values due to the weaker matching with graphene surface. The measured angle is approximately 3° indicating the potential of fine beam manipulation utilizing graphene patch arrays.

REFERENCES

[1] L. Zhang, S. Mei, K. Huang, and C.-W. Qiu, "Advances in full control of electromagnetic waves with metasurfaces," Advanced Optical Materials, vol. 4, no. 6, pp. 818–833, 2016.

[2] A. K. Geim and K. S. Novoselov, "The rise of graphene," in Nanoscience and Technology: A Collection of Reviews from Nature Journals. World Scientific, 2010, pp. 11–19.

[3] G. D. Bouzianas, N. V. Kantartzis, T. V. Yioultsis, and T. D. Tsiboukis, "Consistent study of graphene structures through the direct incorporation of surface conductivity," IEEE Transactions on Magnetics, vol. 50, no. 2, pp. 161–164, 2014.

[4] V. Gusynin, S. Sharapov, and J. Carbotte, "Magneto-optical conductivity in graphene," Journal of Physics: Condensed Matter, vol. 19, no. 2, p. 026222, 2006.

[5] G. W. Hanson, "Dyadic Green's functions and guided surface waves for a surface conductivity model of graphene," J. Appl. Phys., vol. 103, no. 6, pp. 064 302(1–8), 2008.

Investigations of All Metal Heat Sink Dual Linear Polarized Phased Array Antenna for Ku-Band Applications

Rudraishwarya Banerjee[1], Satish K. Sharma[1], Philip Nguyen,[1]Jia-Chi S. Chieh[2], Randall Olsen[2]
[1]Antenna and Microwave Laboratory (AML), Department of Electrical and Computer Engineering
San Diego State University, San Diego, CA, 92182-1309, USA
[2]Advanced Integrated Circuits and Sensors Division, SPAWAR Systems Center Pacific
San Diego, CA, USA
Email: rbanerjee1202@sdsu.edu, ssharma@sdsu.edu

***Abstract*—A 4×8 dual linear polarized phased array antenna, comprised of all metallic radiators serving also as heat sink, is proposed for Ku-band applications. The single radiator, with a height nearly equal to λ/2, is shaped intuitively and fed by a stripline through a trapezium shaped balun. Two shaped radiators are placed orthogonally within a metal cavity of square cross section with overall dimension of λ/2 × λ/2, which constitutes the dual linear polarized radiating element. The surface waves generated due to multi-layered feed structure are supressed by using a number of vias, placed underneath each element cavity, with a period of nearly λ/6 and diameter 12 mils. This radiating element offers wideband performance and acceptable radiation pattern with wide beamwidth is observed over the entire bandwidth while the peak gain is varying between 3-5 dBi. Inter-element spacing is chosen according to expected beam scan range of ±45 degree.**

Keywords— Phased Array Antenna, Beamforming Board, Anokiwave RFIC, all metal, heat sink.

I. INTRODUCTION

The demand for antennas, that can supporting high data rate wireless network is increasing, which in turn, need wide impedance bandwidth, stable radiation pattern, high gain, and beam steering characteristics. Phased array antenna can radiate ample amount of microwave power in an intended direction to accomplish system link requirements. Conventional phased arrays use high power amplifiers which require cooling arrangement. In this work, all metal dual linear polarized antenna aperture for phased array is proposed, where radiators are shaped intuitively in such a way that the aperture can serve as a heat sink as well. In [1], a single linear polarized stepped notch antenna at Ku-band is presented to provide a thermal heat sink for active arrays. In this paper, the radiator is derived from the concept of Vivaldi antenna, but modified depending on the heat sink requirement [2]. The radiating element is designed for Ku-band application which covers 12-15 GHz. Solid thick metal structure is employed for the radiator to fulfil the purpose of heat sink with overall reduced height. Therefore, although the radiator is derived from the basic concept of Vivaldi, it has taken the form of a completely new radiator.

II. DUAL POLARIZED RADIATING ELEMENT

The dual linear polarized radiating element is shown in Fig 1(a) and (b) respectively. The single radiator, with a height nearly equal to λ/2, is shaped intuitively and fed by a stripline through a trapezium shaped balun. Two shaped radiators are placed orthogonally within a metal cavity of square cross section with overall dimension of λ/2 × λ/2, which constitutes the dual linear polarized radiating element. The design frequency is 13.5 GHz for λ calculation. The radiating element is simulated with a multi-layered feed structure to accommodate the stripline feed for two radiators. The surface waves generated due to multi-layered substrate is supressed by using a number of vias, placed underneath each element cavity, with a period of nearly λ/6 and diameter 12 mils. The reflection coefficient magnitude and radiation pattern at 13GHz is shown in Fig 2(a-c), respectively. Impedance matching bandwidth for this radiating element is between 10.5 GHz to 14.5 GHz which equates to 32% fractional bandwidth with respect to S_{11} =10 dB criteria. Acceptable radiation pattern is obtained over the entire bandwidth with gain varying from 3 dBi to 5 dBi range.

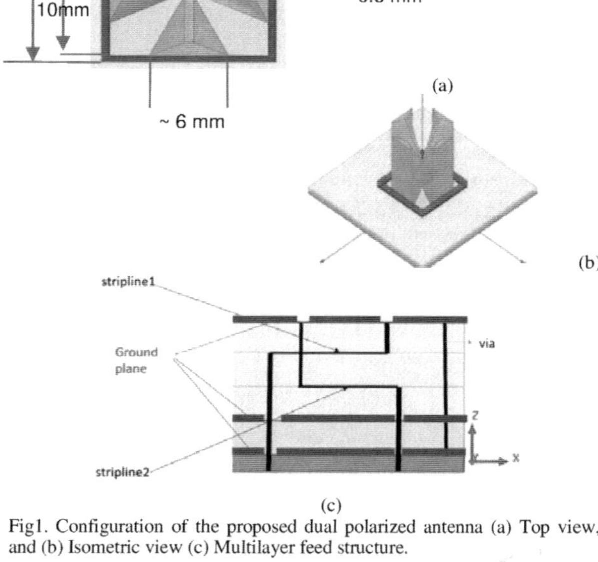

Fig1. Configuration of the proposed dual polarized antenna (a) Top view, and (b) Isometric view (c) Multilayer feed structure.

Design Guideline developed to design the radiating element are: 1) The height of each arm of the new radiator is nearly is λ/2 × λ/2 at 13.5 GHz. 2) The dimension of the cavity is λ/4 at 13.5GHz. 3) The thickness of each arm is nearly quarter wavelength. 4. The separation between two arms of the new radiator is 0.04 λ. 4) Thickness of the cavity wall is 0.04 λ.

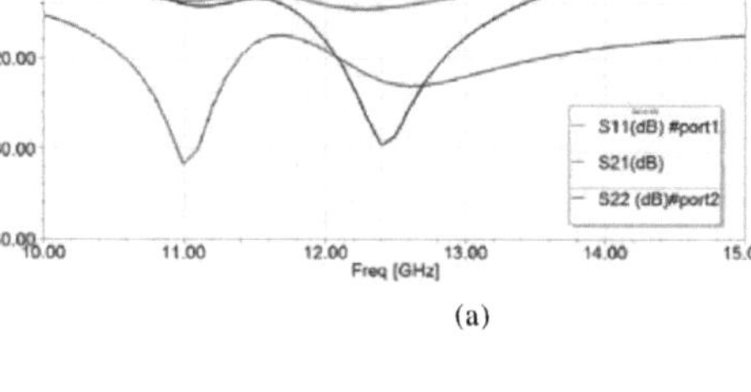

(a)

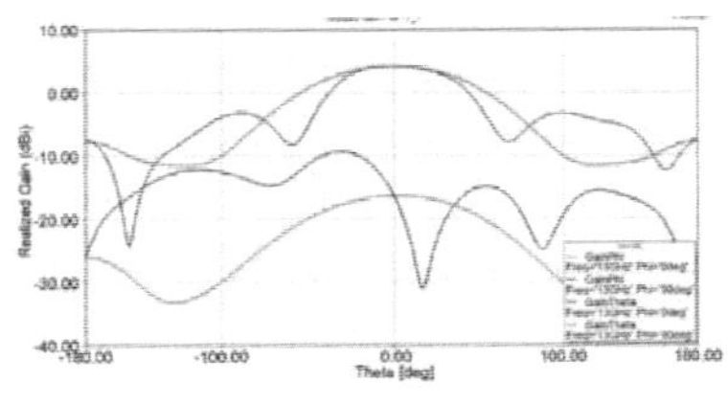

(b)

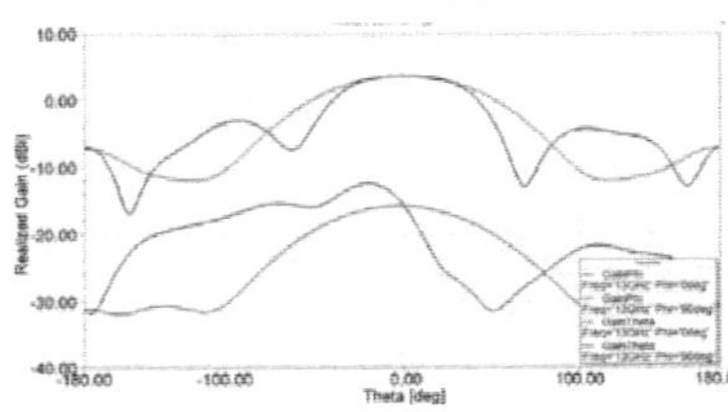

(c)

Fig2: (a) Simulated reflection coefficient; Simulated radiation patterns of the proposed antenna at 13 GHz for (b) X-polarization, and (c) Y-polarization.

III. 4X8 PHASED ARRAY ANTENNA

The 4x8 phased array antenna with connected configuration is designed as shown in Fig3. For the connected configuration, each cavity is connected with the adjacent cavities with a metal connector, which is easier for fabrication if 3D metal printing is considered. There are 32 ports for each polarization. The overall dimension of the 4x8 array is (2 λ x 4 λ). The inter-element spacing is λ/2. The beam scanning performance at 13 GHz is shown in Fig. 4(a-d) for different progressive phase shifts along x-axis and y-axis for X-polarized and Y-polarized array. The array offers a bandwidth of 12-14 GHz and beam scans upto ±45°.

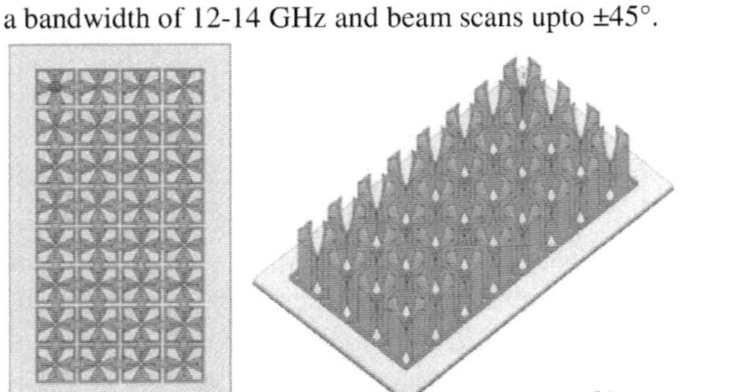

(a) (b)

Fig3. Configuration of the proposed connected phased array antenna array (a) Top view, and, (b) Isometric view.

IV. THERMAL ANALYSIS

The main motivation of this work is to build a radiator that can serve as heat sink as well. Ansys Icepack is used for heat sink analysis which is shown in Fig5 . There is no air flow or no forced cooling arrangement. It is assumed that chip generates approximately 0.25 watts power underneath each radiator and there is opening all around. The simulated temperature of the array is nearly 165° Celsius.

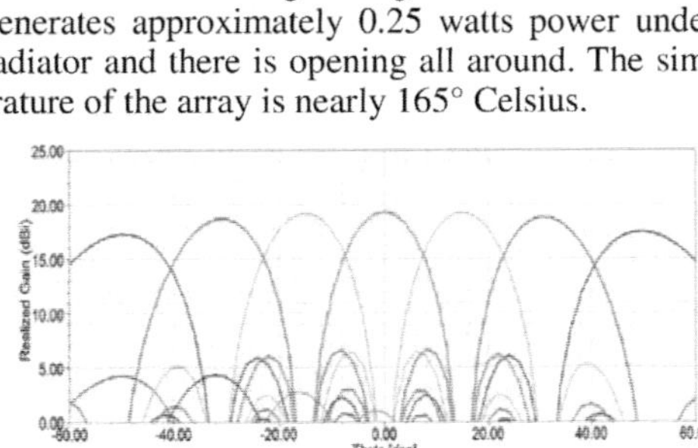

(a)

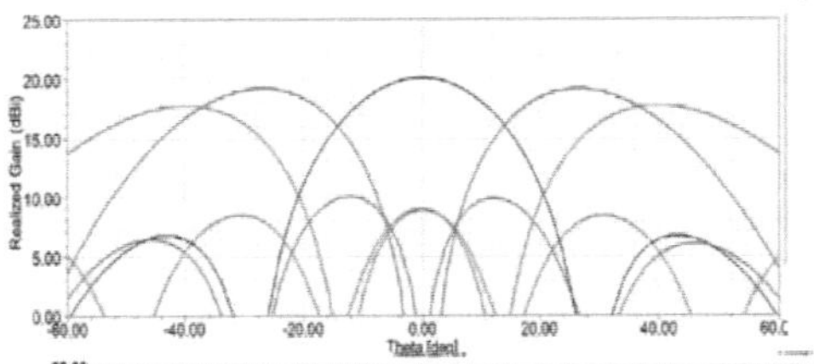

(b)

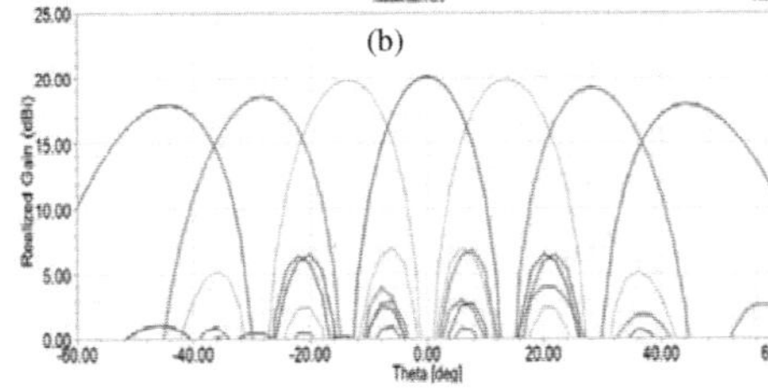

(c)

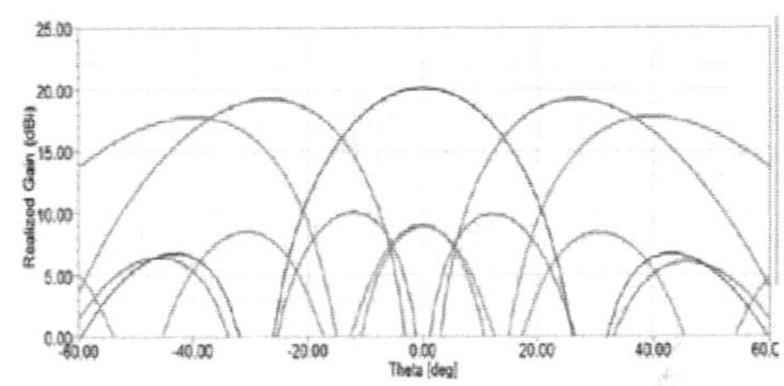

(d)

Fig4: Beam Steering Performance at 13 GHz by Controlling Progressive Phase differences (a) along x-axis for X-polarized array, (b) along y-axis for X-polarized array, (c) along x-axis for Y-polarized array, and (d) along y-axis for Y-polarized array.

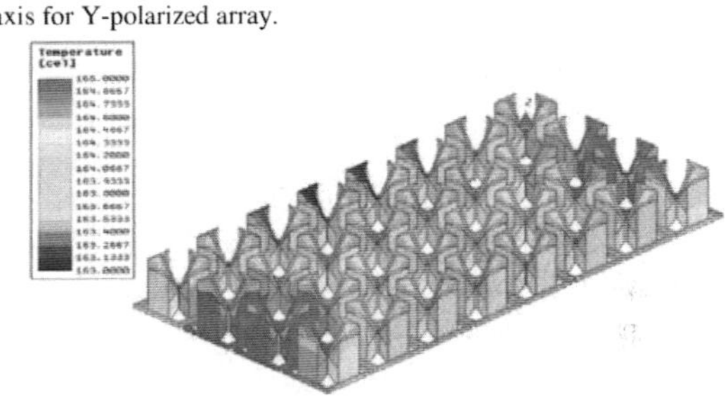

Fig5: The Thermal Analysis of the 4x8 Array: 0.25Watts power/radiator develops 165° C in 4x8 array

V. CONCLUSION AND FUTURE WORK

The array aperture will be 3D metal printed. Beamforming Board will be employed and Anokiwave chips will be incorporated within the board to achieve beam steering characteristics. The fabricated antenna will be measured and simulated results will be validated with experimental results.

REFERENCE

[1] S. M. Duffy, G. A. Brigham, K. B. Newman and J. S. Herd, "Stepped notch antenna array used as a low thermal resistance heat sink," *2013 IEEE Antennas and Propagation Society International Symposium (APSURSI)*, Orlando, FL, 2013, pp. 622-623.

[2] Rudraishwarya Banerjee, Satish K. Sharma, Jia-Chi S. Chieh, Randall Olsen, " Investigations of a Heat Sink All Metal Dual Linear Polarized Phased Array Antenna for Ku-Band Applications", IEEE *Antennas and Propagation Society International Symposium (APSURSI)*, 7-12 July,2019 at the Atlanta, Georgia, USA (*Abstract*).

Non Ideal Cylindrical Monopole Antenna Array

Carlos M. Martínez
Universidad Industrial de Santander
Bucaramanga, Colombia
carlos.martinez@radiogis.uis.edu.co

Ernesto Aguilera
Universidad Industrial de Santander
Bucaramanga, Colombia
eaguiler@uis.edu.co

Jesus Bonilla-Neira
Universidad Industrial de Santander
Bucaramanga, Colombia
jesus.bonilla@radiogis.uis.edu.

***Abstract*—This paper presents a study of a Two Monopole Antenna Array. The design takes into account considerations of non sinusoidal current distribution of each monopole antenna approximated by the three term theory developed by King et al. in 1966 and effects of mutual coupling between the two radiating elements. Numerical integration was done using Simpson's Method. A physical implementation was done to verify the simulated results with good accuracy.**

***Index Terms*—Antenna array, Monopole antenna, Non ideal current distribution.**

I. Introduction

An antenna is the transitional structure between free-space and a guiding device [1], in other words an antenna is used to propagate signals through electromagnetic fields in free-space in order to accomplish wireless communication.

For some applications, a single antenna elements, may not be adequate to meet some technical requirements for high gain, narrow and/or steerable beams, pattern nulls, and low sidelobes. An array of discrete elements can, however, cover most of these constraints [2], the simplest wire array is the two wire elements array. Nevertheless, the design of single wire antennas and antenna arrays is often done by making ideal assumptions of wire parameters as: radius, conductivity of the material among others. In 1966, King et al. [3] developed a whole theory related to the non ideal wire antennas by making considerations of a complex propagation constant which is relates the current distribution in the antenna with the real characteristics of the wire.

In this paper the idea of the Imperfectly Conducting Cylindrical is taken into account to design a two monopole antenna array, making considerations of non ideal conductors, in order to contribute to the theory of non ideal antenna arrays.

II. Current in Cylindrical Conductors

The antenna characteristics like driving point impedance and field pattern can be determined by knowing the current in the cylindrical conductor. The current in an ideal wire antenna is assumed to be sinusoidal, thus, this consideration ignores as an example, the effect of the ohmic resistance along their lengths, which is used in some applications in the designing of broadband antennas.

A well aproximated expression for the current on a non ideal wire antenna has been developed for a non ideal dipole antenna [3], the proposed expression for a half length dipole antenna is shown in 1. Where T_U, T_D, Φ_{dR} are complex constants, β is the complex propagation constant which depends on the impedance per unit legth of the conductor $z^i = r^i + jx^i$, ζ_0 is the characteristic impedance of the radiation media, in this case vacuum:

$$\begin{aligned} I_z(z) = \frac{2j\pi V_0^e \beta_0}{\zeta_0 \Phi_{dR} cos(\beta h)\beta}[(sin(\beta(h-|z|)) \\ +T_U(cos(\beta z) - cos(\beta h)) \\ +T_D(cos(\frac{1}{2}\beta_0 z) - cos(\frac{1}{2}\beta_0 h))], \end{aligned} \quad (1)$$

$$\beta = \beta_0 \left[1 + \frac{4\pi x^i}{\beta_0 \zeta_0 \Phi_{dR}} - j\frac{4\pi r^i}{\beta_0 \zeta_0 \Phi_{dR}}\right]^{1/2}, \quad (2)$$

$$z^i = \frac{1}{\pi a^2 \sigma_1}\left(\frac{\kappa a}{2}\right)\frac{J_0(\kappa a)}{J_1(\kappa a)}, \kappa = \sqrt{\omega \mu_1 \sigma 1} e^{-i\pi/4}. \quad (3)$$

These equations have been evaluated by King giving several examples [4].

III. Array of Cylindrical Antennas

Since the distance between elements is short, the currents of the antennas interact between them. Thus, the current distribution depends not only on the radius, conductivity, length and driving point voltage, but also on the other current distribution of all the elements in the array. The driving point impedances and radiation field are computed from these currents, they cannot be assumed to be identical.

A. Mutual Coupling

The interaction of two radiating elements near alters the currents of each element and therefore their respective impedance. This interaction is called mutual coupling and changes the current magnitude, phase and distribution on each element from their free-space counterparts [6].

For two monopole antennas, let $I_{1z}(z)$ and $I_{2z}(z)$ be their respective current distributions. It has been shown that, for a coupled array the expression in 4 is valid; $I_z^{(0)}$ and $I_z^{(1)}$ are found by shifting the V_{20} driving point voltage 180° respect the V_{10} voltage:

$$\begin{aligned} I_{1z}(z) = I_z^{(0)} + I_z^{(1)} = V_{10}v(z) + V_{20}w(z), \\ I_{1z}(z) = I_z^{(0)} + I_z^{(1)} = V_{10}v(z) + V_{20}w(z). \end{aligned} \quad (4)$$

Where $v(0) = Y_{s1} = Y_{s2}$ being Y_{s1} the self admittances of each element, and $w(0) = Y_{12} = Y_{21}$ the mutual impedance of the two element array [5].

The last has been developed for ideal cylindrical conductors. Thus, by combining the results on the current distribution of (1), making the same considerations and including the complex propagation constant that takes into account the surface impedance per unit length (3), it is possible to get an even more accurate expression for the currents and admittances of (4):

$$v(z) = \frac{j2\pi\beta_0}{\zeta_0\beta_0\Phi_{dR}cos(\beta h)}[sin(\beta(h-|z|)) + \frac{1}{2}(T_U^{(0)} + T_U^{(1)})(cos(\beta z) - cos(\beta h)) + \frac{1}{2}(T_D^{(0)} + T_D^{(1)})(cos(\frac{1}{2}\beta z) - cos(\frac{1}{2}\beta h))], \quad (5)$$

$$w(z) = \frac{j\pi\beta_0}{\zeta_0\beta_0\Phi_{dR}cos(\beta h)}[(T_U^{(0)} - T_U^{(1)})(cos(\beta z) - cos(\beta h)) + (T_D^{(0)} - T_D^{(1)})(cos(\frac{1}{2}\beta z) - cos(\frac{1}{2}\beta h))]. \quad (6)$$

IV. Implementation of a Two Monopole Array

A Monopole array of copper wires($\sigma_1 = 5.96\text{x}10^7[S/m]$, $\mu_1 = \mu_o\mu_{copper} \approx \mu_o[H/m]$) was used, both elements with a heigth of 5 [cm], diameter 2a = 0.81 [mm], it is expected a resonance frequency of about 1.363 [GHz] and, the model for the surface impedance is as shown in (3). The monopoles are two parallel wires prolonged from their respective transmission line over an aluminum squared ground of length $3\lambda/2 = 30[cm]$ of sides, separated $\lambda/2 = 10[cm]$.

A. Calculating Mutual Impedance from the Implemented Array

In [6] there is a procedure used to find the mutual impedance of an array, which is cited up-next:

- Open circuit (or remove antenna 2. Measure $Z_{oc} = Z_{11}$ at the terminals to antenna 1. For identical antennas, $Z_{22} = Z_{21}$.
- Short circuit antenna 2. Measure Z_{sc} at the terminals to antenna 1.
- Comute Z_{12} using $Z_{12} = \sqrt{Z_{oc}(Z_{oc} - Z_{sc})}$.

Using a *Vector Network Analyzer* it is possible to measure the respective impedances in terms of the total reflection coefficient Γ, next, the mutual impedance is then measured in terms of the reflection coefficients using (7), the monopoles were feed using a signal splitter to divide the signal of the VNA into two coaxial transmission lines of the same length (15 [cm]), thus guaranteeing both monopoles were feed at the same phase:

$$S_{12} = \frac{2Z_oZ_{12}}{(Z_{11} - Z_o)(Z_{22} - Z_o) - Z_{12}^2}. \quad (7)$$

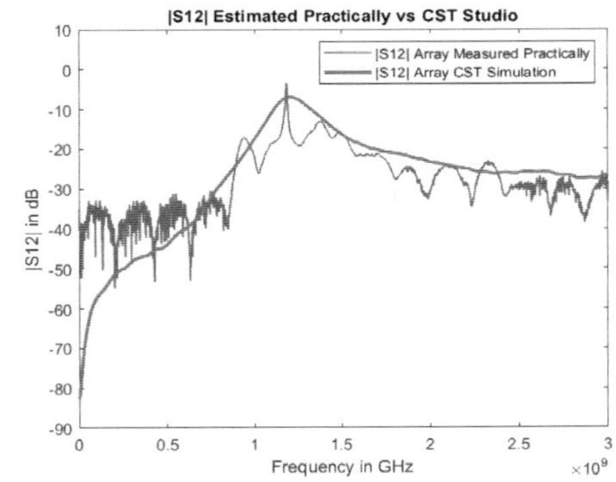

Fig. 1. Comparison between the method described in [6] and the results from CST Studio for two quarter wavelength monopoles separated $\lambda/2$ to obtain the $|S_{21}|$ in dB.

The previous procedure was done comparing experimental process with the mutual coupling in CST Studio assuming a transmission line of $Z_o = 50$ [Ω].

In the Fig. 1, the result of estimating practically the mutual impedance and a comparison of the results obtained by CST studio is shown. Using Kings method the driving point impedance magnitude was found to be 35.1299 [Ω] at the resonance frequency, by CST Studio was 36.981 [Ω] and practically 37.42 [Ω]. The model in CST Studio didn't take into account the effects on the phase of the feeding transmission line coaxial cable type.

V. Conclusion

Several methods to determine the effects of non ideal conductors in a two monopole antenna array were presented, it is shown that there is a difference between the procedures in order to find the magnitude of the mutual impedance, this because the effects of the imaginary part which in the Kings method is not accurate, nevertheless, the procedures were evaluated and tested, proposing tools for future work related to Non-Ideal Cylindrical Conductors.

References

[1] C. Balanis, Antenna Theory. New Jersey: John Wiley & Sons, Inc, pp. 285-360, 2016.

[2] J. Volakis, Antenna Engineering Handbook. McGraw-Hill, 4th Edition, pp. 326-327, 2007.

[3] R. W. P. King and T. T. Wu, "The imperfectly conducting cylindrical transmitting antenna," IEEE Trans. Antennas Propag., vol. 14, no. 5, pp. 524–534, Sep. 1966.

[4] R. W. P. King and T. T. Wu, "The imperfectly conducting cylindrical transmitting antenna: Numerical Results," IEEE Trans. Antennas Propag., vol. 14, no. 5, pp. 5235–542, Sep. 1966.

[5] R. W. P. King, G. J. Fikioris, and R. B. Mack, "Cylindrical Antennas and Arrays," Cambridge University Press, pp. 31-42, 2002.

[6] W. L. Stutzman and G. A. Thiele, Antenna Theory and Design, John Wiley and Sons, pp. 217-311, 2012.

Isolation Improvement between Closely-Spaced Antennas Using EBG

Ahmad H. Abdelgwad and Mohammod Ali
Department of Electrical Engineering
University of South Carolina, Columbia, SC USA
ahmedha@email.sc.edu, alimo@cec.sc.edu

***Abstract*—Isolation improvement between two closely spaced antennas using a single column EBG is proposed for compact wireless devices. The proposed design developed for the 2.4 GHz WLAN band achieves more than 17 dB isolation improvement between two planar inverted-F antennas (PIFAs) compared to the no-EBG case. As a result, improved MIMO capacity is also achieved. The proposed design can be scaled up or down in frequency and may be implemented for small devices such as, smart watches, Wi-Fi routers, internet of things (IoT) devices etc.**

Keywords—EBG structure, MIMO, mutual coupling, PIFA.

I. Introduction

Multiple antenna placement and operation are essential for multiple-input multiple-output (MIMO) communication systems. It is well known that such system can significantly improve wireless capacity and quality [1]. For small devices, such as, mobile phones, Wi-Fi routers, smart watches, and IoT devices placing multiple antennas within a small platform inevitably leads to higher mutual coupling between them. Excellent MIMO performance demands low mutual coupling or high isolation between antennas.

Electromagnetic band gap (EBG) structures have been proposed to reduce or suppress the mutual coupling between antennas [2]. Such structures act like bandstop filters if properly designed [3].

In this paper, a single column mushroom EBG is introduced that can significantly improve the isolation between two closely spaced PIFAs. Each PIFA and the EBG are designed to operate at 2.4 GHz. Thus, the concept can be implemented in applications and services that utilize the 2.4 GHz frequency band. The design can be scaled up or down in frequency to make suitable for other applications as well.

II. Antenna and EBG Configuration

The proposed antenna plus EBG configuration is shown in Fig. 1. There are two PIFAs at the two ends of a printed circuit board (PCB). In between the PIFAs resides a single column mushroom EBG structure. A single column EBG is proposed here to allow its application in compact structures. The PCB is made of FR4 substrate ($\varepsilon_r = 4.4$, and $\tan\delta = 0.02$). An additional FR4 substrate was used to create the EBG structure. All dimensions for 2.4 GHz operation can be seen in Fig. 1. For comparison, a second configuration with no EBG was also considered. For this case, a rectangular slot was etched on the ground plane of the PCB as shown in Fig. 1 (b).

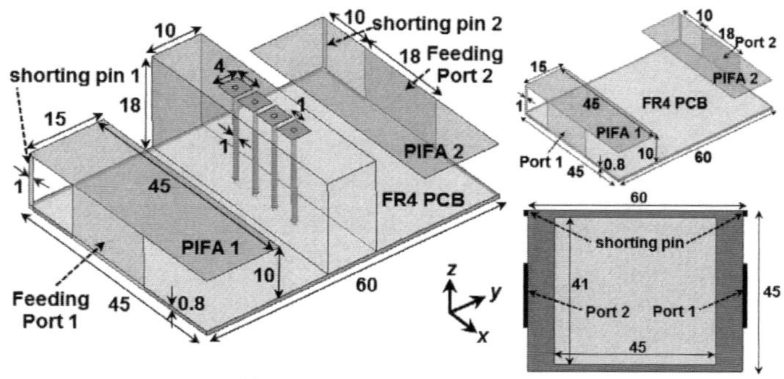

Fig. 1. (a) Antenna and EBG configuration (b) no EBG design, (upper) structure (lower) ground plane. (Dimensions are in mm).

III. Results

The design and analyses of the proposed structures were performed using Ansys HFSS. Simulated S-parameters for cases with and without EBG are compared in Fig. 2. For either case, the antenna exhibits operation from about 2.2 to 2.6 GHz within $S_{11} < -10$ dB. The mutual coupling, S_{21}, without EBG is -8.5 dB at 2.4 GHz. The mutual coupling with EBG is -26 dB at 2.4 GHz. Thus, more than 17 dB isolation improvement is achieved between the antennas using only a single column mushroom EBG at 2.4 GHz. The two antennas have over 20 dB isolation for a bandwidth of 10% which is greater than the bandwidth required for WLAN. Fig. 3 compares the efficiencies of the two configurations. The EBG structure improves the efficiency of each antenna by 11% at 2.4 GHz.

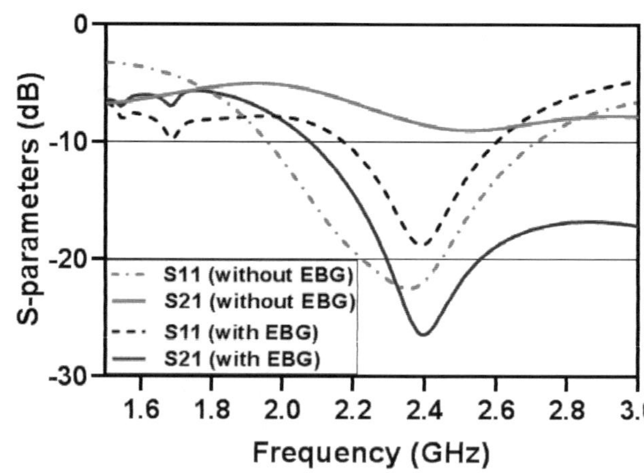

Fig. 2. Simulated S-parameters with and without EBG.

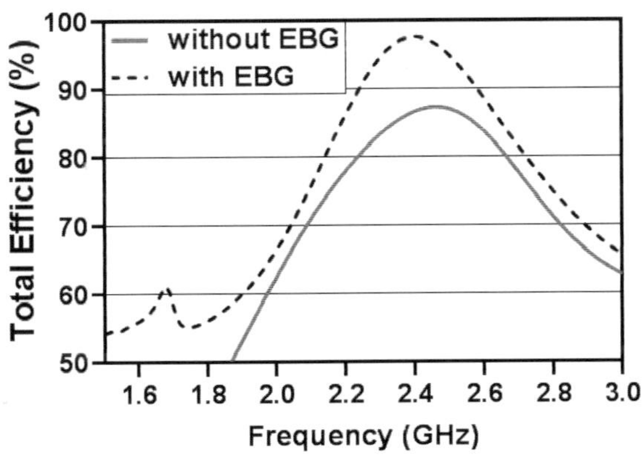

Fig. 3. Antenna efficiency with and without EBG.

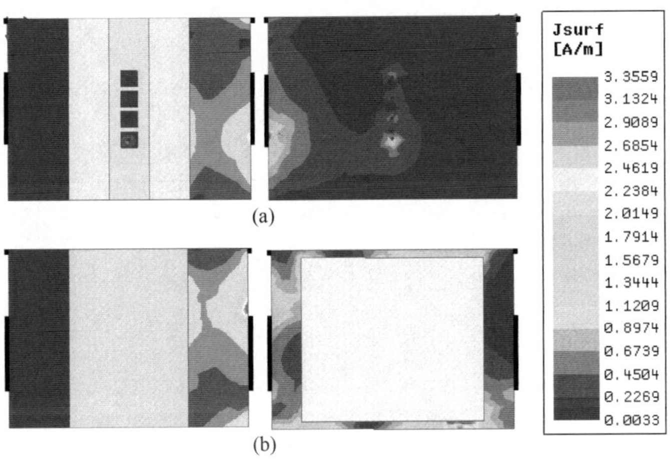

Fig. 4. Surface current distributions (port 2 excited), patches on the left and ground plane on the right (a) with EBG (b) without EBG.

Simulated current density distributions for the two studied configurations are shown in Fig. 4. Clearly the EBG significantly inhibits the flow of current between the two antenna ports, thus reducing the mutual coupling between them.

In order to evaluate the diversity and MIMO performance of the two configurations, the mean effective gain (MEG) and the envelope correlation coefficient (ECC) were calculated assuming a uniform propagation environment [4]. The cumulative density function (CDF) data as function of the relative signal to noise ratio (SNR) computed using a maximum ratio combining (MRC) scheme have been plotted in Fig. 5. For comparison, the Rayleigh distribution is also added as a reference. The effective diversity gain (EDG) values at 1% outage probability are 8.33 and 8.90 dB, respectively for the cases with and without EBG. Thus, as seen, the EBG allows improvement in the EDG as well. The capacity of the antennas was also estimated using the equations presented in [5]. The capacities of the antennas with and without EBG are compared in Fig. 6 which clarifies that the EBG allows higher ergodic capacity compared to the one without the EBG. This improvement is attributed to the reduced mutual coupling and the ECC the former of which is also reflected in the efficiencies.

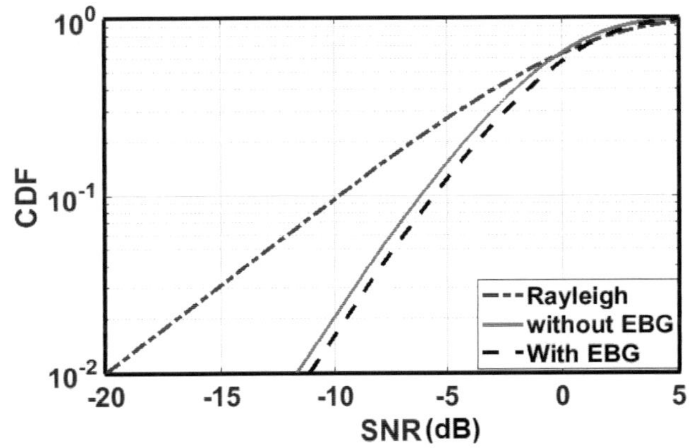

Fig. 5. CDF as function of relative SNR for configurations with and without EBG.

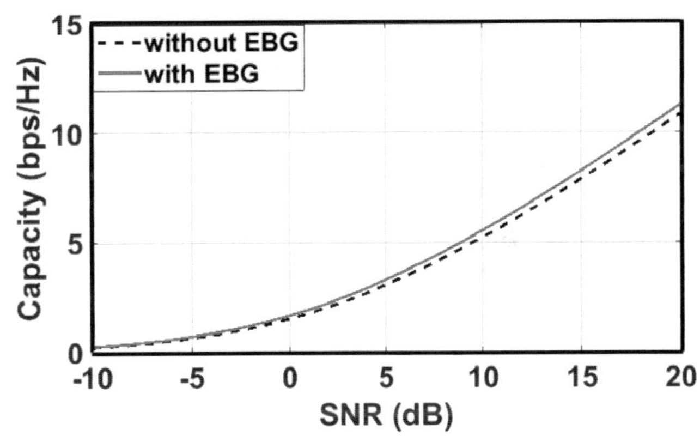

Fig. 6. The Ergodic MIMO capacity with and without EBG.

IV. Conclusion

A single column mushroom EBG structure is proposed to improve the isolation between two closely spaced PIFAs. The designed EBG can improve the isolation between the PIFAs by as much as 17.5 dB compared to the no-EBG case. As a result, the EBG also improves MIMO capacity due to improved antenna efficiencies.

References

[1] A. H. Radhi, R. Nilavalan, Y. Wang, H. S. Al-Raweshidy, A. A. Eltokhy, and N. Ab-Aziz, "Mutual coupling reduction with a novel fractal electromagnetic band gap structure," IET Microw., Antennas Propag., vol. 13, no. 2, pp. 134–141, 2019.

[2] A. H. Abdelgwad and M. Ali, "Isolation improvement of a two-port PIFA for MIMO using a planar EBG ground," Microw. Opt. Technol. Lett., pp. 1–6, 2019. https://doi.org/10.1002/mop.32059

[3] F. Yang and Y. Rahmat-Samii, "Microstrip antennas integrated with electromagnetic band-gap (EBG) structures: a low mutual coupling design for array applications," IEEE Trans. Antennas Propag., vol. 51, no. 10, pp. 2936-2946, Oct. 2003.

[4] M. Karaboikis, V. Papamichael, G. Tsachtsiris, C. Soras, and V. Makios, "Integrating compact printed antennas onto small diversity/MIMO terminals," IEEE Trans. Antennas Propag., 56, no. 7, pp. 2067–2078, July 2008.

[5] X. Chen, P. Kildal, and J. Carlsson "Simple calculation of ergodic capacity of lossless two-port antenna system using only S-parameters – comparison with common Z-parameter approach," IEEE Int. Symp. Antennas Propag., Spokane, USA, 2011.

Babinet's Principle Applied to Distributed Arrays

Kristopher Buchanan, Carlos Flores-Molina, Sara Wheeland, Drew Overturf, and Timi Adeyemi
Naval Information Warfare Center Pacific (NIWC Pacific), San Diego CA, USA

***Abstract*—This work investigates Babinet's Principle as applied to distributed arrays such that solving for one characteristic function is tantamount to solving its complement. Simulated results using triangular and complementary triangular distributions end this paper.**

***Index Terms*—Antenna array and distributed beamforming.**

I. INTRODUCTION

It has been shown from [1-3] that taking the expected value of the array factor across the unit interval [-1, 1] for a random variable x in any volumetric distribution provides the characteristic functions (1), which are orthogonal in all three axis and uncorrelated.

In other words, [3] has determined that the main beam and first sidelobe level of the characteristic function have deterministic properties. Therefore, the same methods used in aperture theory may be applied to distributed arrays [4]. To analyze this methodology a simplified expected pattern is used from (1) in terms of *Psi space* (Ψ) where Ψ is taken over all angular space (θ, ϕ),

$$\begin{aligned} \bar{U} &= \frac{1}{N}+\left(1-\frac{1}{N}\right)\Lambda|u|^2\Lambda|v|^2\Lambda|w|^2=\frac{1}{N}+\left(1-\frac{1}{N}\right)\Lambda\left|\vec{\Psi}\right|^2, \\ \vec{\Psi} &= \cos^{-1}\left(kA\left(\hat{r}(\theta,\phi)-\hat{r}(\theta_0,\phi_0)\right)\right)=\cos^{-1}[u \quad v \quad w] \quad .(1) \\ u &= \hat{x}\cdot\cos\vec{\Psi}, v=\hat{y}\cdot\cos\vec{\Psi}, w=\hat{z}\cdot\cos\vec{\Psi}, 1=\sqrt{u^2+v^2+w^2} \end{aligned}$$

II. BABINET'S PRINCIPLE

A. Green's Function of an Infinite Planar Screen

In free space the Dirichlet Green's function is provided by the well-known greens function of (1) and by that of (2) when placed over an infinite planar screen:

$$G(\vec{r},\vec{r}\,')=\exp\left(jk\left|\vec{r}-\vec{r}\,'\right|\right)/\left|\vec{r}-\vec{r}\,'\right|, \qquad (2)$$

$$G(\vec{r},\vec{r}\,')=\frac{e^{jk|\vec{r}-\vec{r}_2\,'|}}{\left|\vec{r}-\vec{r}_2\,'\right|}-\frac{e^{jk|\vec{r}-\vec{r}_1|}}{\left|\vec{r}-\vec{r}_1\right|},\ \begin{matrix}\vec{r}_2=(x',y',+z')\\ \vec{r}_1=(x',y',-z')\end{matrix} \qquad (3)$$

Illustrated in Fig. 1, the location $\vec{r}_2$ is in V, and generated from a monochromatic point source S (the image point at $\vec{r}_1$ is not in V). This satisfies the homogenous wave equation $\left(\nabla^2+k^2\right)G(\vec{r},\vec{r}\,')=-4\pi\delta(\vec{r}-\vec{r}\,')$ in V, such that it vanishes at infinity ($r'\rightarrow\infty$ since $1/r'^2\rightarrow 0$) and the boundary plane z'=0.

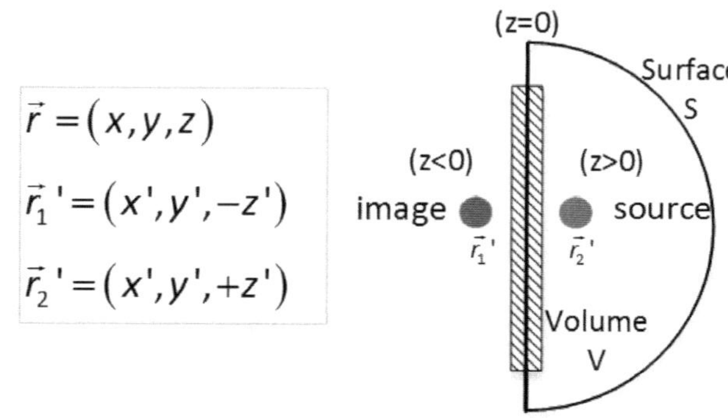

Fig. 1. Volume of a source and infinite planar screen.

The characteristic amplitude $\varphi(\vec{r})$ for a monochromatic point source S, observed at the observation point O on the opposite side of the screen becomes the Kirchhoff integral such that:

$$\varphi(\vec{r})=-1/(4\pi)\int_S d^2r'\vec{n}'\cdot\left(\varphi(\vec{r}\,')\nabla'G(\vec{r},\vec{r}\,')\right). \qquad (4)$$

B. Radiation from a Finite Source

If a slit is cut into the screen, the wave amplitude $\varphi(\vec{r}\,')$=0 on the screen as well as on the boundary of the screen results in a nonzero contribution from the opening of the screen:

$$\varphi(\vec{r})=-1/(4\pi)\int_{Opening} d^2r'\vec{n}'\cdot\left(\varphi(\vec{r}\,')\nabla'G(\vec{r},\vec{r}\,')\right), \qquad (5)$$

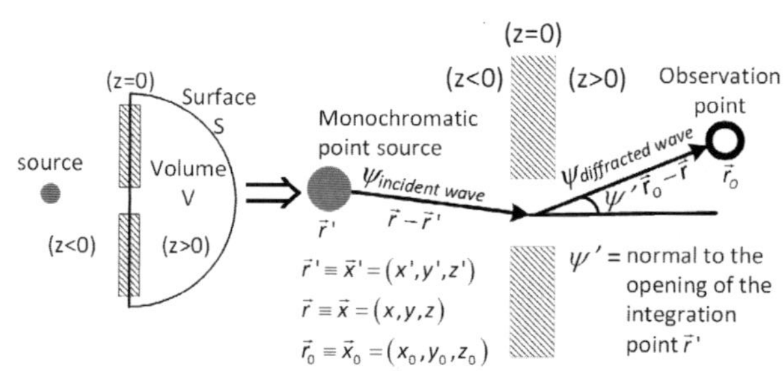

Fig. 2. Aperture excitation from an isotropic point source.

where $\vec{n}'$ is the direction in the opening of the slit of the volume V. Thus, $\nabla'G(\vec{r},\vec{r}\,')$ in the $\vec{n}'$ or outward normal direction, becomes:

$$\begin{aligned} &-\frac{d}{dz'}G(\vec{r},\vec{r}\,')\approx\frac{jk(z-z')}{\left|\vec{r}-\vec{r}_2\,'\right|}\frac{e^{jk|\vec{r}-\vec{r}_2\,'|}}{\left|\vec{r}-\vec{r}_2\,'\right|}+\frac{jk(z+z')}{\left|\vec{r}-\vec{r}_1\,'\right|}\frac{e^{jk|\vec{r}-\vec{r}_1\,'|}}{\left|\vec{r}-\vec{r}_1\,'\right|} \\ &\neg d\left|\vec{r}-\vec{r}_2\,'\right|^{-1}/dz\wedge d\left|\vec{r}-\vec{r}_1\,'\right|^{-1}/dz\approx 0\ (\text{denominator } \textit{neglible}) \ (6) \\ &\vec{r}\,'_{Isotropic}=\vec{r}_1\,',\ \vec{r}\,'_{Finite\,Source}=\vec{r}_2\,'. \end{aligned}$$

Equation (5) further reduces at the plane of the screen to:

$$-\frac{d}{dz'}G(\vec{r},\vec{r}\,')\Big|_{z=0} \approx \frac{2jkz}{|\vec{r}-\vec{r}\,'|}\frac{e^{jk|\vec{r}-\vec{r}\,'|}}{|\vec{r}-\vec{r}\,'|}, \neg\, \vec{r}_2 = \vec{r}_1 \text{ at } z=0\,. \quad (7)$$

Hence, the Kirchhoff approximation yields the following expression for the wave amplitude of the field observed at $\vec{r}$:

$$\varphi(\vec{r}) = -1/(4\pi)\int_{\sigma} d^2r'\vec{n}'\cdot\left(\varphi(\vec{r}\,')\nabla' G(\vec{r},\vec{r}\,')\right)$$

$$= -jk/(2\pi)\int_{opening} d^2r\, e^{jk|\vec{r}_1{}'-\vec{r}_2{}'|} e^{jk|\vec{r}-\vec{r}_2{}'|} \Big/ |\vec{r}_1{}'-\vec{r}_2{}'||\vec{r}-\vec{r}_2{}'|\cos(\psi_2{}') \quad (8)$$

since $\cos(\psi_2{}') = \hat{r}_2{}'\cdot\hat{r} = z/|\vec{r}-\vec{r}_2{}'|$.

This integral demonstrates three distinct terms of the Huygens-Fresnel principle. The first term represents field strength received at the point $\vec{r}_2{}'$ transmitted the point source located and reradiated from the slit. The second term represents field from the aperture excitation at $\vec{r}_2{}'$ and received at the observation point $\vec{r}$. The third and final term is the inclination factor.

Moreover, it can be easily shown the characteristic function in the Fraunhofer region becomes (8), which is nothing more than pattern multiplication of a point source and sinc function generated from a uniform aperture excitation. Finally, the aperture reaches a maximum when $\hat{\psi}_{IncWave} - \hat{\psi}_{Diff\,Wave} = 0$, similar to a phased array analysis,

$$\Lambda(r,\Psi)_{N\to\infty} = \left(-jk/(2\pi)\right)\left(e^{jkr_1}/r_1\right)\left(\text{sinc}\left(kA\vec{\Psi}\right)e^{jkr_2}/r_2\right)$$

$$\overset{Normalized}{\approx} \left(e^{jkr}/r\right)\left(\text{sinc}\left(kA\vec{\Psi}\right)\right), \vec{\Psi} = \left(\hat{\psi}_{IncWave} - \hat{\psi}_{Diff\,Wave}\right) \quad (9)$$

$$\neg \frac{e^{jk|\vec{r}_1{}'-\vec{r}_2{}'|}}{|\vec{r}_1{}'-\vec{r}_2{}'|}\frac{e^{jk|\vec{r}-\vec{r}_2{}'|}}{|\vec{r}-\vec{r}_2{}'|} \approx \frac{e^{jk(r+\vec{r}_1{}')}}{|r|}e^{jk(\vec{\Psi})\cdot\vec{r}_2{}'}, \cos(\psi)\approx 1.$$

C. Babinet's Priniciple

First consider two different screens which are complementary as illustrated in Fig 3 [5].

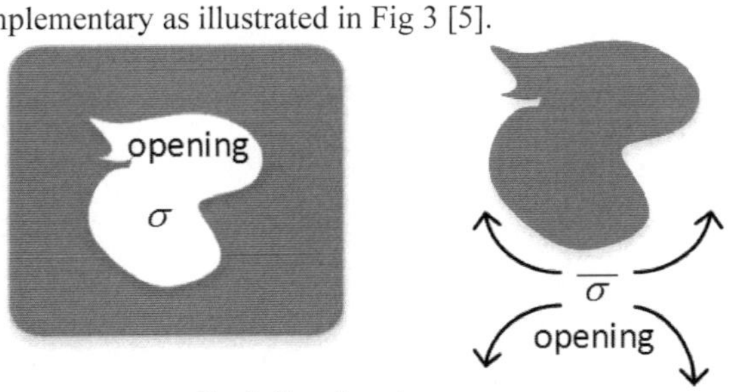

Fig. 3. Complimentary screens.

The figure labeled σ has an opening through the center, while the complementary image is just a disk with the entire z = 0 plane as its opening, denoted $\bar{\sigma}$. Hence the characteristic amplitude of two complementary cases becomes:

$$\begin{aligned}\varphi(\vec{r}) &= -1/(4\pi)\int_{\sigma} d^2r'\vec{n}'\cdot\left(\varphi(\vec{r}\,')\nabla G(\vec{r},\vec{r}\,')\right) \\ \overline{\varphi(\vec{r})} &= -1/(4\pi)\int_{\bar{\sigma}} d^2r'\vec{n}'\cdot\left(\varphi(\vec{r}\,')\nabla G(\vec{r},\vec{r}\,')\right)\end{aligned}, \quad (10)$$

where $\sigma +\ \bar{\sigma}$ represents the entire plane z = 0 and its characteristic function, $\varphi(\vec{r}) + \overline{\varphi(\vec{r})}$ at the observation point $\vec{r}$ includes no diffraction. To interpret this, note that $\varphi(\vec{r})$ may be written as:

$$\varphi(\vec{r}) = f\exp\left(jk|\vec{r}-\vec{r}_1{}'|\right)/|\vec{r}-\vec{r}_1{}'| + \psi_{diff}(\vec{r}), \quad (11)$$

where f is denoted as its ray optic amplitude. If f =1, line-of-sight exists from the observer to the source, and if f = 0, no line-of-sight exists. The second term represents the diffraction of the wave. Moreover, the sum for f =0 and f = 1 includes the term $\exp\left(jk|\vec{r}-\vec{r}_1{}'|\right)/|\vec{r}-\vec{r}_1{}'|$ representing Babinet's principle: solving one diffraction problem is tantamount to solving its complement [5].

D. Babinet's Principle using Complementary Topolgy

The superposition of a triangular distribution $f(x)$ in (11) and complementary inverted triangular distribution $\overline{f(x)}$ represents a square distribution in the entire z = 0 plane. Thus $\Lambda(\Psi)+\overline{\Lambda(\Psi)}$ represents the aggregated Fourier transform pair of (11) and (12), which provide the well-known sinc (Ψ). For this example, (13) describes the unnormalized characteristic function. Accordingly, this is Babinet's Principle as solving for one characteristic function solves its complement,

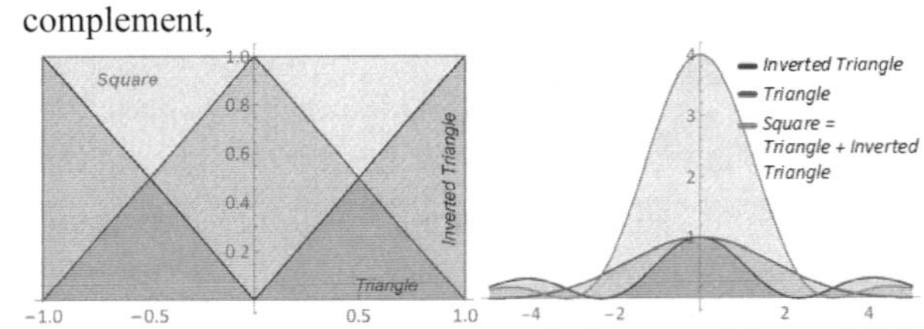

Fig. 4. Complementary triangular topologies (top) and characteristic functions (bottom).

$$f(x) = 1-|x|, \quad \overline{f(x)} = 1+|x|, \quad (12)$$

$$\Lambda(\Psi)_{Triangle} = \int_{-1}^{1} f(x)e^{j\Psi x} = 2h_0(\Psi)/\Psi, \quad (13)$$

$$\Lambda(\Psi)^{Inverted}_{Triangle} = \overline{\Lambda(\Psi)}_{Triangle} = \int_{-1}^{1}\overline{f(x)}e^{j\Psi x} = -2h_1(\Psi)+1, \quad (14)$$

$$\overset{Square}{\Lambda(\Psi)} = \Lambda(\Psi)_{Triangle} + \overline{\Lambda(\Psi)}_{Triangle} = 2j_0(\Psi) = 2\text{sinc}(\Psi). \quad (15)$$

REFERENCES

[1] K. R. Buchanan, "Theory and applications of aperiodic (random) phased arrays," Ph.D. dissertation, Dept. Elect. & Com. Eng., Texas A&M University, TX, 2014.

[2] H. Ochiai, "Collaborative beamforming for distributed wireless ad hoc sensor networks," IEEE Trans. Signal Process., vol. 53, pp. 4110, Nov. 2005.

[3] K. Buchanan and G. Huff, "A stochastic mathematical framework for the analysis of spherically bound random arrays," *IEEE Trans. Antennas Propag.*, vol. 62., pp. 3002-3011, June 2014.

[4] B. D. Steinberg, Principles of Aperture & Array System Design, New York: Wiley, 1976.

[5] M. Jarrell. (2001) "Radiation," in Lecture Notes [Online]. Available: http://www.phys.lsu.edu/~jarrell/COURSES/ELECTRODYNAMICS/Chap9/chap9.pdf

An Examination of the Even and Odd Characteristic Superposition of Circularly Tapered Antenna Arrays

Kristopher Buchanan, Carlos Flores-Molina, Sara Wheeland, Drew Overturf, and Timi Adeyemi
Naval Information Warfare Center Pacific (NIWC Pacific), San Diego CA, USA

***Abstract*—This work investigates circularly distributed antenna arrays of even and odd characteristic modal superpositions as it applies to a Hardy space. Examples are provided using a family of even (Sinc) and odd (Cosinc) modal tapers of the L^2 norm. Furthermore, this space has unique properties as it causes the negative spatial Fourier coefficients to vanish. This paper concludes with simulated results of newly defined modes within a Hardy space utilizing Sinc and Cosinc modes with and without amplitude tapering.**

***Index Terms*—Collaborative beamforming, distributed beamforming, and wireless sensor networks.**

I. Introduction

It has been shown from [1 – 4] that taking the expected value of the array factor across the unit interval [-1, 1] for a random variable x in any volumetric distribution provides the characteristic functions (1), which are orthogonal in all three axes and uncorrelated. In addition, [3 – 4] have determined that the main beam and first sidelobe level of the characteristic function have deterministic properties. Therefore, the same methods used in aperture theory may be applied to distributed arrays [3 – 4]. To analyze this methodology a simplified expected pattern is used from (1) in terms of *Psi space* (Ψ) where Ψ is taken over all angular space (θ, ϕ).[1]

$$\bar{U}=\frac{1}{N}+\left(1-\frac{1}{N}\right)\Lambda|u|^2\Lambda|v|^2\Lambda|w|^2=\frac{1}{N}+\left(1-\frac{1}{N}\right)\Lambda|\vec{\Psi}|^2,$$
$$\vec{\Psi}=\cos^{-1}\left(kA\left(\hat{r}(\theta,\phi)-\hat{r}(\theta_0,\phi_0)\right)\right)=\cos^{-1}[u \quad v \quad w] \qquad (1)$$
$$u=\hat{x}\cdot\cos\vec{\Psi}, v=\hat{y}\cdot\cos\vec{\Psi}, w=\hat{z}\cdot\cos\vec{\Psi}, 1=\sqrt{u^2+v^2+w^2}$$

The overbar in equation 1 is used to represent the mean valued radiation pattern, N is the number of radiators, A is the radius of the aperture, and k is the wavenumber.

The circular element population distribution (2) generalizes the expected radiation pattern for an arbitrary array and can be extended for two sets of characteristic functions: an even set of sum beams (Λ_E), (3) and an odd set for difference (Λ_O) beams (4) [5].

$$f_E(x;n)=\frac{\left(1-x^2\right)^{\frac{n-1}{2}}\Gamma(1+n/2)}{\sqrt{\pi}\Gamma\left((n+1)/2\right)} \qquad \neg(n\geq -1) \quad \textit{Even Distribution} \qquad (2)$$

[1] *Psi* space is also commonly referred to u space [1] and [4].

$$\Lambda_E(\Psi;n)=\int_{-1}^{1} f_E(x;n)e^{jx\Psi}=\mathrm{Sinc}_n(\Psi),$$
$$\neg\mathrm{Sinc}(\Psi;n)=\Gamma(n/2+1)J_{n/2}(\Psi)/(\Psi/2)^{n/2} \qquad (3)$$

$$\Lambda_O(\Psi;n)=\int_{-1}^{1} f_E(x;n)\,\mathrm{sgn}(x)e^{jx\Psi}=\mathrm{CoSinc}_n(\Psi;n)$$
$$\neg\mathrm{CoSinc}(\Psi;n)=\Gamma(n/2+1)H_{n/2}(\Psi)/(\Psi/2)^{n/2} \qquad (4)$$
$$\mathrm{sgn}(x)=x/|x|$$

II. Hardy Disttribution

The Hardy space $H^2(\Psi)$ consists of the even (Sinc) and odd (Cosinc) modes on L^2 function space. This space has unique properties as it causes the negative spatial Fourier coefficients to vanish. An example of the first n=12 modes are provided in Fig.1, which shows the peak of the odd modes approximates beamwidth. Moreover, these modes are similar to Euler's identity when added and are denoted the EulerSinc modes (5) as illustrated in Fig. 1.

$$\mathrm{EulerSinc}_n(\Psi)=\mathrm{Sinc}_n(\Psi)+j\,\mathrm{Cosinc}_n(\Psi) \qquad (5)$$

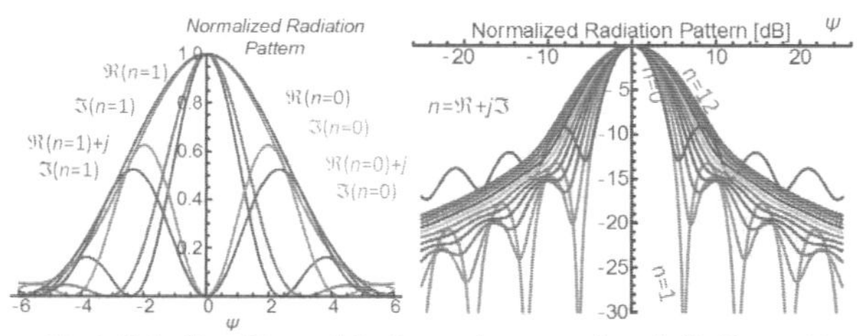

Fig 1. EulerSinc, Sinc and Cosinc modes comparison (left). First n=12 EulerSinc modes (right).

III. Orthogonal Sets and Amplitude Distributions

The Gegenbauer (Ultraspherical) Polynomials are shown below and will be utilized in the following section for their unique ability to orthogonalize circular topologies.

$$f_X(x)=\alpha\left(1-x^2\right)^{\lambda-1/2}C_n^{\lambda}(x) \qquad (6)$$

1) RingTapers; λ=0

Chebyshev polynomials form an orthonormal basis on the appropriate Sobolev space bounded between -1≤x≤1. Hence, they are an orthogonal polynomial set with respect to the weighting function $(1-x^2)^{-1/2}$. Moreover the pdf of (6) is slightly modified such that its normalization provides the characteristic modes of increasing Bessel order for even distributions as provided in (8). This is done to provide the odd and normalized Weber Characteristic functions (9) shown in Fig.2.

$$f_X(x) = (-j)^n T_n(x) \big/ \left(\pi\sqrt{1-x^2}\right) \tag{7}$$

$$\Lambda(\Psi)_{even} = J_n(\Psi) = \int_{-1}^{1} f_X(x) GF \tag{8}$$

$$\Lambda(\Psi)_{Odd} = E_n(\Psi) = \int_{0}^{1} f_X(x) GF - \int_{-1}^{0} f_X(x) GF \tag{9}$$

Similar to the EulerSinc (Ψ) modes one can determine the superposition of the Bessel-Weber modes (8) and (9) respectively as:

$$\text{BesselWeber}_n(\Psi) = J_n(\Psi) + jE_n(\Psi) \tag{10}$$

2) Line tapers; $\lambda=1/2$

The Legendre polynomials orthogonal to the L^2 inner product on the interval $-1 \leq x \leq 1$ are the eigenfunctions of the Hermitian differential operator. Moreover, they arise naturally in multipole expansion analogous to the monopole, dipole and higher moments of the spherical harmonic solutions yielding similar characteristic functions. The pdf of (6) is slightly modified such that (11) provides normalization to the characteristic modes of increasing spherical Bessel order for even distributions as provided in (12). This is done since it provides the normalized spherical Weber functions for odd modes (13).

$$f_X(x) = j^{-n} P_n(x)/2 \tag{11}$$

$$\Lambda(\Psi)_{Even} = j_n(\Psi) = \int_{-1}^{1} f_X(x) GF dx \tag{12}$$

$$\Lambda(\Psi)_{Odd} = e_n(\Psi) = \left(\int_{0}^{1} f_X(x) GF - \int_{-1}^{0} f_X(x) GF\right) dx \tag{13}$$

Similar to Bessel-Weber, the Spherical Bessel-Weber modes in Fig.3 are defined as:

$$\text{SphericalBesselWeber}_n(\Psi) = j_n(\Psi) + je_n(\Psi). \tag{14}$$

IV. Discussion

A hyperbolic analogy follows a similar analysis, but instead uses a *Sobolev space*. Moreover, the unit disc is considered within the complex plane. Transforms in this plane admit a reproducing kernel and are called *Bergman spaces*[2]. A comparison of the resulting radiation patterns is shown in Fig.4.

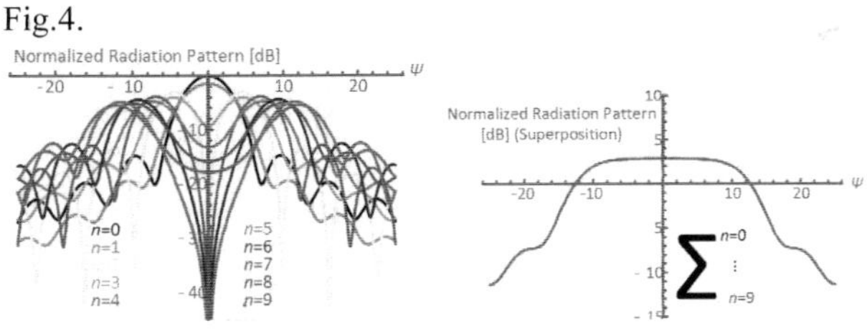

Fig 2. BesselWeber modal comparison, using equation (6) and λ=1 (left). First ten modes superimposed (right).

[2] *Bergman spaces* are also commonly known as reproducing *kernels* in a *Hilbert space* or *Szegõ kernels* in a *Hardy space*

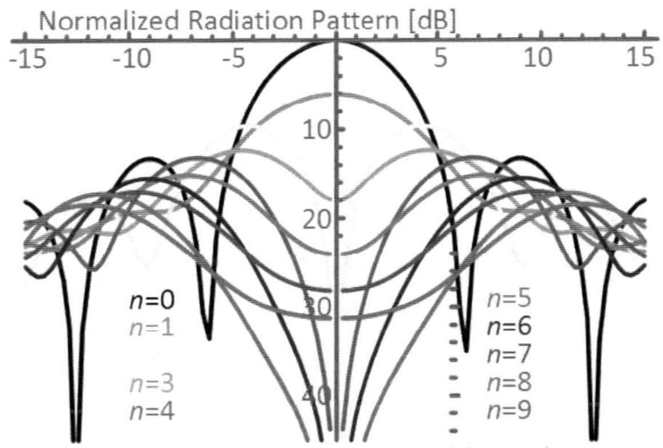

Fig 3. SphericalBessel-Weber (14) modal comparison.

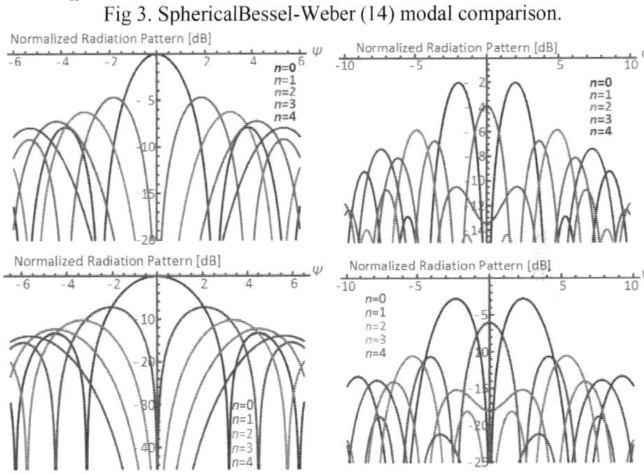

Fig 4. Comparison of (8), top left; (9), top right; (12), bottom left; and (13), bottom right.

References

[1] K. R. Buchanan, "Theory and applications of aperiodic (random) phased arrays," Ph.D. dissertation, Dept. Elect. & Com. Eng., Texas A&M University, TX, 2014.

[2] K. Buchanan and G. Huff, "A stochastic mathematical framework for the analysis of spherically bound random arrays," *IEEE Trans. Antennas Propag.*, vol. 62., pp. 3002-3011, June 2014.

[3] B. D. Steinberg, Principles of Aperture & Array System Design, New York: Wiley, 1976.

[4] H. Ochiai, "Collaborative beamforming for distributed wireless ad hoc sensor networks," IEEE Trans. Signal Process., vol. 53, pp. 4110, Nov. 2005.

[5] K. Buchanan, J. Rockway, O. Sternberg and N. Mai, "Sum-difference beamforming for radar applications using circularly tapered random arrays," *IEEE Radar Conference (RadarConf)*, Philadelphia, PA, 2016, pp. 1-5.

Reconfigurable Balanced Dualband Bandstop Filter

Dubari Borah
Dept. of Electrical and Computer Engineering
University of Colorado, Colorado Springs
Colorado Springs, USA
dborah@uccs.edu

Thottam S. Kalkur
Dept. of Electrical and Computer Engineering
University of Colorado, Colorado Springs
Colorado Springs, USA
tkalkur@uccs.edu

***Abstract*— This paper introduces a novel architecture of reconfigurable balanced (differential) dualband bandstop filter (BSF). In differential mode (DM), each symmetrical bisection of the filter incorporates in-series cascade of two tunable dualband bandstop sections whereas high CMRR is achieved by loading open stubs to the symmetry plane of the branch line structure. To validate the proposed topology, a microstrip prototype is designed and fabricated. Both simulation and measured results show a good agreement with each other.**

***Keywords*— Branchline structure, CM noise, CMRR, non-resonating node (NRN), tunable.**

I. Introduction

Bandstop filter (BSF) is an important building block of modern communication system as it protects the transceiver from unwanted interference [1]. Recent development of communication systems with multiband services is attracting much attention for notch filters capable of producing multiple stopbands [2]. Furthermore, electronic industry is continuously striving for compact size for which reconfigurable circuitry is getting popular in both digital [3],[4] and analog applications [5],[6]. Because of this, the demand of multiband BSF with tunable response is growing rapidly for research and development.

Meanwhile, balanced topology is being widely employed in constructing microwave circuits and systems because they are more immune to signal noise than their single-ended counterparts. So far, researchers have investigated a variety of differential bandpass filter topologies [5] whereas significantly less work has been done in the field of differential BSF. In [1] and [7], CM noise of a single-band tunable balanced BSF has been suppressed by using magnetic field property of Substrate Integrated Waveguide (SIW) resonator and balanced property of double-sided parallel-strip line (DSPSL), respectively. In [8] and [9], two balanced BSF structures employing one or more coupled line sections terminated with different loads are reported. In [6], a single-ended reconfigurable multiband BSF is reported. However, to the best of the author's knowledge, no work has been published yet which applies differential topology to a dualband tunable BSF structure.

In this paper, a tunable balanced dualband BSF structure is proposed by integrating tunable dualband sections in a branch line structure. The high CMRR is obtained by using the properties of stepped impedance resonator (SIR).

II. Proposed Design

Fig. 1 (a) shows the schematic of the proposed balanced dualband tunable BSF structure. This four-port branchline structure is symmetric about the horizontal central plane and each symmetrical bisection consists of two dualband sections connected in series through immittance inverter K_{12}. In each dualband section, (θ_{L1}, Z_{L1}) and (θ_{L2}, Z_{L2}) are two quarter-wavelength lines at resonant frequencies f_1 and f_2 respectively and they are connected to the NRN (or NRN') through inverters K_{01} and K_{02}, respectively. Both symmetrical bisections of the differential design are connected through tunable capacitors C_1 and C_2 in the central plane. Both NRN-NRN' pairs share the open stubs (θ_{os1}, Z_{os1}) and (θ_{os2}, Z_{os2}) in the horizontal symmetry plane using K_{os} inverters for the flexible control of CM response. All the inverters are designed at the center frequency of the entire frequency spectrum, $(f_1 + f_2)/2$.

A. Differential mode (DM) operation

When the circuit in Fig. 1 (a) is excited by a differential signal, the horizontal symmetry plane acts as a perfect electric wall (Fig. 1 (b)). Therefore, the open stubs are short-circuited and have no effect on differential resonant frequencies. Note that the capacitor values C_1 and C_2 in Fig. 1 (a) become $2C_1$ and $2C_2$, respectively in DM operation.

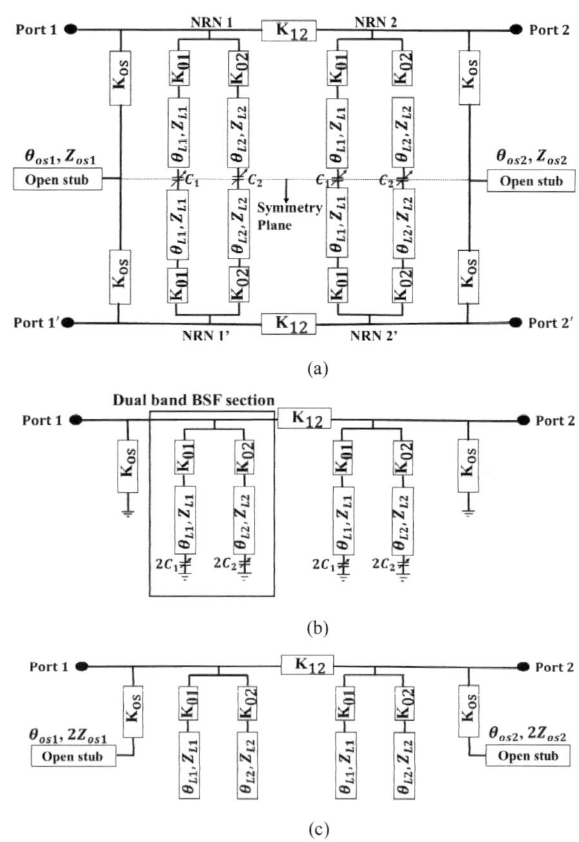

Fig. 1. (a) Schematic of the proposed topology, (b) DM equivalent circuit, and (c) CM equivalent circuit.

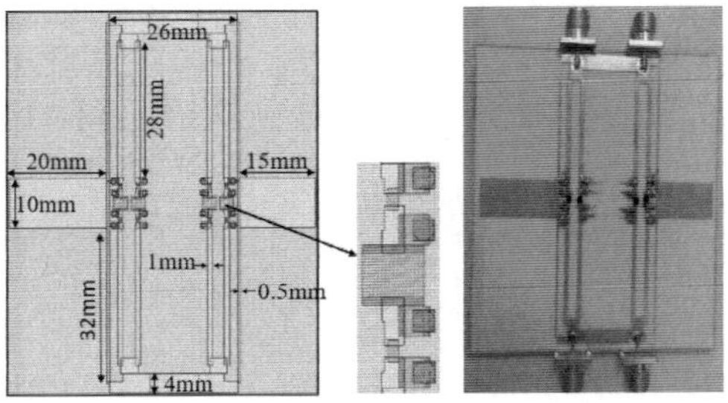

(a) (b)

Fig. 2. (a) Layout of the design with zoomed version of the lumped element section and (b) Fabricated prototype.

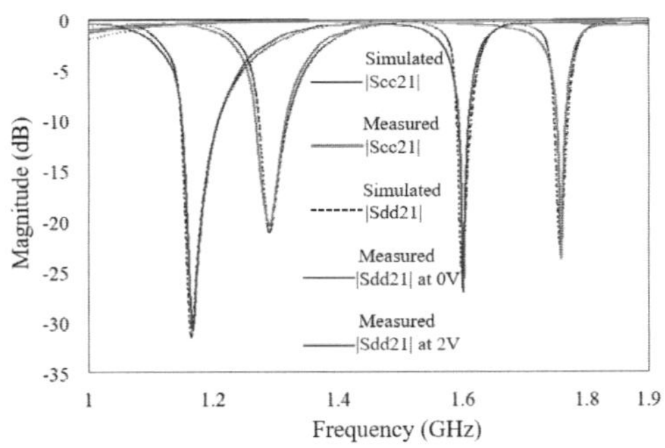

Fig. 3. DM insertion loss (Sdd21) and CM insertion loss (Scc21) plots of the proposed design.

B. Common mode (CM) operation

Under CM operation, the horizontal symmetry plane behaves as a perfect magnetic wall (Fig. 1 (c)). Therefore, the open stubs loaded in the symmetry plane cause extension and reconstruction of their corresponding couplings from the NRNs to form two SIRs. At resonance, each SIR produces two transmission zeros (TZs) [10]. By adjusting length and impedance of each open stub, the locations of the TZs can be controlled so that a flat CM bandpass response is achieved for each differential stopband, maintaining high CMRR.

III. Results and Discussion

To validate the proposed topology, a microstrip line prototype is fabricated on Rogers RO4003 substrate with relative dielectric constant 3.38, dielectric thickness 1.52mm and dielectric loss tangent 0.0027 (Fig. 2). The two line-sections (θ_{L1}, Z_{L1}) and (θ_{L2}, Z_{L2}) are replaced by their equivalent low-pass π networks [11]. The π network for (θ_{L1}, Z_{L1}) consists of a series inductance of 3.6 nH (Coilcraft 0402CS series) and two shunt capacitances of 3 pF (ATC 100A series) each. Similarly, the π network for (θ_{L2}, Z_{L2}) consists of a series inductance of 1.4 nH (Coilcraft 0402CS series) and two shunt capacitances of 2 pF (ATC 100A series) each. Dimensions of the other line sections are presented in Fig. 2 (a). For both C_1 and C_2, Skyworks SMV1233 model is used.

Fig. 3 shows that the measured response is in good agreement with the simulated response. The design is simulated using NI/AWR microwave office and the fabricated model is characterized with the help of Keysight N5224A 4-port network. From the Sdd21 plot, the tuning ranges of the lower and upper stopbands are 1.16 GHz- 1.29 GHz and 1.6 GHz-1.76 GHz, respectively. The attenuation level of the lower stopband varies in the range of 20.5dB-30.7dB whereas for the upper stopband, it varies from 24dB to 26.7dB. The 3dB FBW of the lower band changes from 9% to 12% whereas the same for the upper band varies from 2.4% to 3.2%. Also, the Scc21 plot shows a flat 0 dB passband response which results in the minimum CMRR values of 20.5 dB and 24 dB for the lower stopband and the upper stopband, respectively.

IV. Conclusion

A novel topology of tunable balanced dualband BSF is proposed in this paper. Each DM bisection of this branch line structure consists of two dualband BSF sections separated by an impedance inverter. The CM noise is eliminated by loading the four-port differential structure with open stubs in the horizontal symmetry plane. Finally, the simulated response and the measured response are compared to show a good match with each other.

References

[1] M. F. Hagag, M. Abdelfattah, and D. Peroulis, "Balanced octave-tunable absorptive bandstop filter," 2018 IEEE 19th Wireless and Microwave Technology Conference (WAMICON), Sand Key, FL, 2018, pp. 1-4.

[2] D. Borah and T. S. Kalkur, "A Planar Multiband Balanced Bandstop Filter," 2018 IEEE MTT-S Latin America Microwave Conference (LAMC 2018), Arequipa, Peru, 2018, pp. 1-3.

[3] S. N. Shahrouzi, "Optimized Embedded and Reconfigurable Hardware Architectures and Techniques for Data Mining Applications on Mobile Devises," Ph.D. Dissertation, University of Colorado Colorado Springs, December 2018.

[4] S. N. Shahrouzi, and D. G. Perera, "Dynamic partial reconfigurable hardware architecture for principal component analysis on mobile and embedded devices," EURASIP Journal on Embedded Systems, Springer Open, vol. 2017, article no. 25, February 2017.

[5] D. Borah and T. S. Kalkur, "A balanced dual-band tunable bandpass filter," 2018 International Applied Computational Electromagnetics Society Symposium (ACES), Denver, CO, 2018, pp. 1-2.

[6] D. Psychogiou, R. Gomez-Garcia, and D. Peroulis, "A class of fully-reconfigurable planar multi-band bandstop filters," 2016 IEEE MTT-S International Microwave Symposium (IMS), 2016.

[7] J. Cai, Y. J. Yang, W. Qin, and J. X. Chen, "Wideband Tunable Differential Bandstop Filter Based on Double-Sided Parallel-Strip Line," in IEEE Transactions on Components, Packaging and Manufacturing Technology.

[8] M. Kong, Y. Wu, Z. Zhuang, and Y. Liu, "Narrowband balanced absorptive bandstop filter integrated with wideband bandpass response," in Electronics Letters, vol. 54, no. 4, pp. 225-227, February 22 2018.

[9] J. Sorocki, I. Piekarz, S. Gruszczynski, and K. Wincza, "Low-Loss Directional Filters Based on Differential Band-Reject Filters With Improved Isolation Using Phase Inverter," in IEEE Microwave and Wireless Components Letters, vol. 28, no. 4, pp. 314-316, April 2018.

[10] M. Sagawa, M. Makimoto, and S. Yamashita, "Geometrical structures and fundamental characteristics of microwave stepped-impedance resonators," IEEE Transactions on Microwave Theory and Techniques, vol. 45, no. 7, pp. 1078-1085, July 1997.

[11] M. M. Elsbury, P. D. Dresselhaus, N. F. Bergren, C. J. Burroughs, S. P. Benz, and Z. Popovic, "Broadband Lumped-Element Integrated N-Way Power Dividers for Voltage Standards," in IEEE Transactions on Microwave Theory and Techniques, vol. 57, no. 8, pp. 2055-2063, Aug. 2009.

Frequency Selective Surface Network for In-Phase Ground Plane Reflections in Tightly Coupled Dipole Arrays

Maxence Carvalho, Alexander D. Johnson, Elias A. Alwan, and John L. Volakis
Electrical & Computer Engineering Dept., Florida International University
Miami, FL USA, mcarvalh@fiu.edu

***Abstract*—There is strong interest in improving the performance of Perfectly Electric Conductor (PEC) backed arrays to achieve wider bandwidths and near theoretical gain. This is challenging due to the well-known size-gain-bandwidth compromise. Indeed, the presence of a ground plane has limited antenna bandwidth until the development of Tightly Coupled Dipole Arrays (TCDA). TCDAs have allowed optimal bandwidth by reducing the Bode-Fano limits. In this paper, we introduce an approach to further increase the bandwidth using Frequency Selective Surfaces (FSS). The integration of such FSS network within a dual-polarized TCDA led to a 29:1 impedance bandwidth and scanning up to 60° at VSWR $<$ 3 (E-Plane) with an average efficiency of 80%. This large bandwidth was achieved by suppressing ground plane resonances.**

***Index Terms*—TCDA, Phased Array, FSS**

I. Introduction

The main challenge in using FSS to enhance performance of broadband arrays was addressed in the early 2000's [1]. Preliminary work for improving the bandwidth of arrays was introduced in 2002 using a computational approach [2]. Computational methods like the Finite Element Method (FEM) and Method of Moment (MoM) were used for design optimization [3]. However, as expressed in [4] conformal arrays have the fundamental bandwidth limit of:

$$B_{\infty} \leqslant \frac{\pi \mu k_0 h cos^p \theta}{log \frac{1}{|\Gamma_{max}|}} \tag{1}$$

Here Γ_{max} is the maximum allowed reflection coefficient, h the thickness of the ground plane, θ scanning angle, μ the relative permeability of the array and $k_0 = \frac{2\pi}{\lambda}$ the free space wavenumber. To further improve TCDAs bandwidth, resistive loading can be placed between the ground plane and the dipole to counter resonances. Periodic ground plane reflections cause wave cancellation when placed $\frac{p\lambda}{2}$ ($p \in \mathbb{N}$) from the radiator. This loading can have several implementations depending on the desired effect. In [5], the resistive loading was coated on a dielectric substrate. Loadings using FSS are realized using this same coating to control and have a targeted effect on a particular frequency band [6]. However, cancellations are the result of reducing the amplitude of the reflected waves through resistive loading. Therefore, while this method improves the bandwidth, it significantly reduces efficiency and doesn't exceed 73% on average. In this paper we present an alternative approach which consists of first shifting ground plane resonances then reducing them to keep an optimum efficiency in desired bands. Figure 1 depicts ground plane resonances rejection.

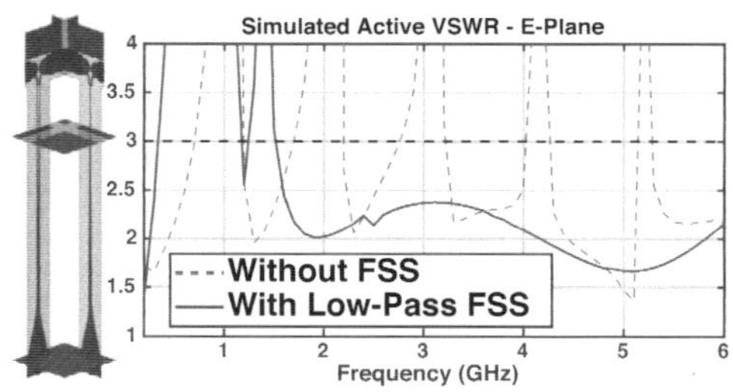

Fig. 1: Simulated active VSWR plot showing periodic ground plane rejection to a lower frequency band.

II. FSS Network Design

A. Non Resistive Low-Pass FSS

The first approach to increase bandwidth is to emulate different dipole heights by introducing a low-pass FSS. In other words, above a certain cut-off frequency the FSS becomes the ground plane itself. This leads to ground plane distance control, and therefore improved bandwidth and resonance suppression. At low frequency, the wave propagates through the low-pass FSS and acquires additional transmission delay $\phi_{FSS}(f)$. Subsequently, the wave continues to the ground plane and is reflected with a reflection phase of π. In its return, it passes again through the FSS and gets an additional phase delay. Further, since the wave propagated a distance of $2h$, a phase of $2k_0h$ is also added. In total, the overall phase delay becomes:

$$\Delta\phi = 2k_0h + \underbrace{2tan^{-1}(\frac{f}{f_0})}_{2\phi_{FSS}(f)} + \pi \tag{2}$$

In the above, h is the height of the ground plane, $k_0 = \frac{2\pi}{\lambda}$ the free space wavenumber, and f_0 is the cut-off frequency of the FSS. At higher frequencies, the wave is reflected by the low-pass FSS. Therefore, it is important to choose the FSS location carefully to cause the reflected and direct wave to be added coherently for frequencies above f_1 and f_0, where f_1 is the frequency of the highest existing ground plane resonance. Indeed, if the distance between the FSS and the dipole is $\frac{\lambda_1}{4}$, and considering the frequencies above the FSS cut-off, the first ground plane resonance will occur when $\frac{\lambda_{res}}{2} = \frac{\lambda_1}{4}$. In other words, $f_{res} = 2f_1$. It was found that this method only improves the high frequency TCDA performance. The lower band frequency signals are delayed by the FSS. That is, the above approach significantly reduces the TCDA profile it also presents a disadvantage. Specially, lower frequencies exhibits a delay between 0 and $\frac{\pi}{2}$.

B. Semi-Resistive Approach

As a trade off, we chose to keep the higher band TCDA performance as efficient as possible while introducing some loss in the lower band to suppress the remaining resonance. As the low-pass FSS acts as a ground plane at high frequencies, it is now possible to consider the TCDA as semi-resistive. That is, higher frequencies are not affected by the resistive loading. As depicted in Figure 2, one or more resistive sheets are

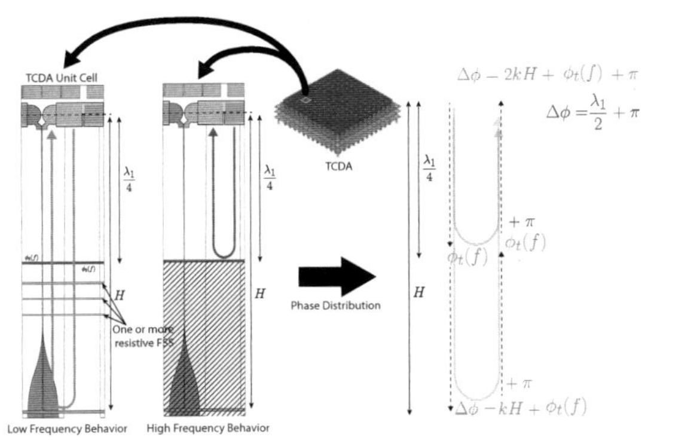

Fig. 2: FSS Network operation leading to different phase distribution in the dipole plane.

now introduced below the TCDA. Notably, the loading values and heights of the resistive screens are optimized to attenuate low-frequency resonances.

III. Full-Wave Simulation

Using this method, we were able to achieve a very high efficiency at the higher band ($\geqslant$ 90%) and maintain an acceptable efficiency for the lower band. Preliminary results in Figure 4 shows extremely wide bandwidth (29:1) from 0.2 to 5.8 GHz with impressive scanning capabilities up to 60° at VSWR $<$ 3 (E-Plane). The proposed design uses a single non-resistive FSS at the top and two other resistive sheets placed below the non-resistive FSS at different heights to suppress different resonances. As depicted in Figure 3, the array is $\frac{\lambda_{Low}}{13}$ tall. Notably, each dipole is fed by a Klopfenstein tapered balun $\frac{\lambda_{Low}}{18}$ tall.

IV. Conclusion

We presented an alternative method to increase the bandwidth of dual-polarized TCDAs leading to a 29:1 impedance bandwidth with scanning up to 60° at VSWR $<$ 3 (E-Plane) and an average efficiency of 80%. This technique also reduced aperture depth. Key to the design were the introduction of FSS to introduce phase delay and artificially increase the electrical profile of the array. It is therefore appropriate to state that the FSSs provide for an artificial magnetic structure. Design

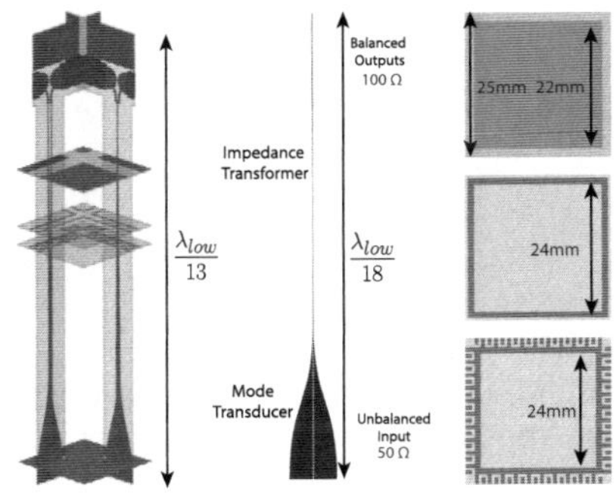

Fig. 3: TCDA unit cell showing FSS dimensions and Ultra Wideband Klopfenstein Tapered Balun.

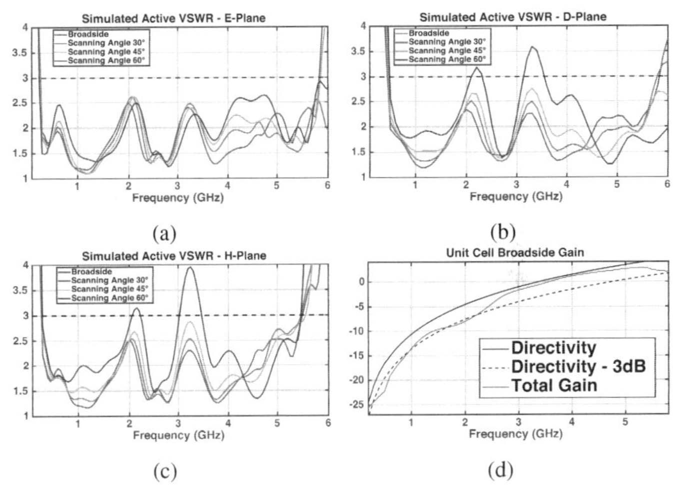

Fig. 4: (a) : E-Plane, (b) : D-Plane, (c) : H-Plane,(d) : Simulated broadside gain versus frequency showing near theoretical radiation for most of the band

formalization and measurements will be presented during the meeting.

V. Acknowledgement

The authors would like to acknowledge AFOSR grant FA9550-19-1-0290.

References

[1] B. A. Munk, *Frequency Selective Surfaces*. John Wiley & Sons, Inc., 2000.

[2] Y. E. Erdemli, K. Sertel, R. A. Gilbert, D. E. Wright, and J. L. Volakis, "Frequency-selective surfaces to enhance performance of broad-band reconfigurable arrays," *IEEE Transactions on Antennas and Propagation*, vol. 50, pp. 1716–1724, Dec 2002.

[3] E. A. Alwan, K. Sertel, and J. L. Volakis, "A simple equivalent circuit model for ultrawideband coupled arrays," *IEEE Antennas and Wireless Propagation Letters*, vol. 11, pp. 117–120, 2012.

[4] J. P. Doane, K. Sertel, and J. L. Volakis, "Bandwidth limits for lossless, reciprocal pec-backed arrays of arbitrary polarization," *IEEE Transactions on Antennas and Propagation*, vol. 62, pp. 2531–2542, May 2014.

[5] N. J. . Smith, D. K. Papantonis, and J. L. Volakis, "Bandwidth reconfigurable metamaterial arrays," *International Journal of Antennas and Propagation*, vol. 2014, pp. 325–328, June 2014.

[6] W. F. Moulder, K. Sertel, and J. L. Volakis, "Superstrate-enhanced ultrawideband tightly coupled array with resistive fss," *IEEE Transactions on Antennas and Propagation*, vol. 60, pp. 4166–4172, Sep. 2012.

Novel Compact Microstrip Monopole Antenna for UWB Wireless Applications

Hussein H. M. Ghouz
Department of Electronics and Communications Engineering.
Arab Academy for Science Technology and Maritime Transport
Cairo, Egypt
Hussein.ghouz@aast.edu

Mohamed F. Abo Sree
Department of Electronics and Communications Engineering.
Arab Academy for Science Technology and Maritime Transport
Cairo, Egypt
eng_m_fathey@hotmail.com

Hesham A. Mohamed
Department of Microstrip
Electronics Research Institute (ERI)
Giza 12622, Egypt
Hesham_280@eri.sci.eg

Muhammad A. Ibrahim
Department of Electronics and Communication Engineering
Ain Shams University
Cairo, Egypt
Muhammedalyibrahim@hotmail.com

***Abstract*— A novel microstrip monopole antenna with enhanced characteristic has been proposed and presented for UWB applications. It has an Elliptical Triangle Patch resonator "ETP" mounted on a compact FR-4 substrate. Parametric study of the ETP Monopole dimensions has been performed for optimization. Simulation resulted in an UWB of 14.5 GHz, compared to only 7.0 GHz for the conventional rectangular monopole with the same dimensions (Rect_Monopole). In addition, the ETP offers multi-resonances, a VSWR that is less than 1.5, high average gain of 6.75 dB, and good average efficiency of 75%. Reasonable agreement has been achieved between simulated and measured parameters over the entire frequency band.**

Keywords*— *Compact UWB antennas, Elliptical patch, Fractal patch, Microstrip antennas, Monopole antennas.

I. INTRODUCTION

In 2002, Federal Communication Commission (FCC) released an ultra-wideband (UWB) spectrum of 7.5 GHz band starting from 3.1GHz to 10.6 GHz. Since then great attention has been given to UWB systems for high data rate, accuracy, position tracking, imaging and remote sensing, with specific characteristic to cover the required UWB spectrum [1-3]. Several antenna structures were proposed and analyzed, including UWB MIMO antennas, UWB filters, and UWB signal processing, satisfying the requirements to cover many applications such as indoor communication including microstrip and coplanar structures with band-notched rejection in WiMax band (5-6 GHz) [4-10].

II. PROPOSED ANTENNA DESIGN

Two monopole antenna structures are presented to design and analyze a novel compact UWB antenna. The first antenna is a conventional UWB antenna having the configuration shown in Figs. 1 (a) and (b) and mounted on a single FR-4 substrate of 1.6 mm height, tangential loss of 0.02, $\varepsilon r=4.4$ and a conductor thickness of 0.035mm. The optimized monopole dimensions are listed in Table I. The resonance is based on the dimensions of the patch, and it's calculated using $fL=7.2/(Wp + Lp/2\pi)$ [3]. Secondly, a novel monopole antenna having a fractal patch shape, mounted on the same substrate is illustrated in Figs. 1 (c) and (d). The proposed ETP monopole antenna patch consists of a horizontal ellipse "HE", a vertical ellipse "VE" and two triangle patches "UT" and "DT, shown in Fig. 1 (e). The aspects of the "ETP" antenna are shown in Table I.

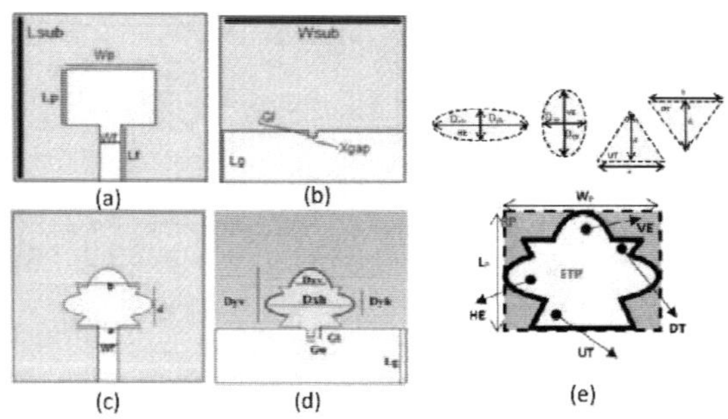

Fig. 1. (a) Rect top view, (b)Rect bottom view, (c) ETP top view, (d) ETP bottom view, and (e) proposed patch "ETP".

TABLE I. DIMENSIONS (IN MM) OF RECT AND ETP MONOPOLE

Parameter	*Value*	*Parameter*	*Value*
Lsub = Wsub	30	Lp = Lf	10
Wp	14	Wf	3.28
GL	1.2	Xgap = Gw	1.28
Lg	9.2	a = b	10
d	6.75	Rxy	3.6
Dyy = Lp	10	Dxh = Wp	14
Ryh	2.5	GL	1.5
Gw	1.15	Lg	9.5

III. SIMULATION RESULTS AND EXPERIMENTAL VALIDATION

A. Simulation and Parametric Study

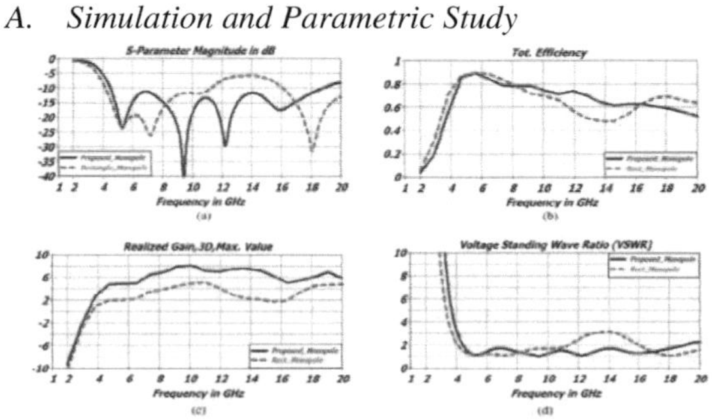

Fig. 2. Simulated parameters of "Rect" and "ETP": (a) |S11|, (b) Efficiency, (c) Gain, and (d) VSWR versus frequency.

The antennas are simulated using CST Microwave Studio, where the results are presented in Fig. 2 (a) through Fig. 4 (d). It can be concluded that the proposed "ETP" monopole achieved a larger bandwidth (14.5 GHz (230%), higher average gain (6.75dBi), and average VSWR (1.75), compared to the "Rect". The radiation patterns in E-and H plane of the proposed "ETP" for different frequencies (4.5 up to 19 GHz) are shown in Fig.3. As illustrated, Omni-directional patterns have been obtained almost over the whole band.

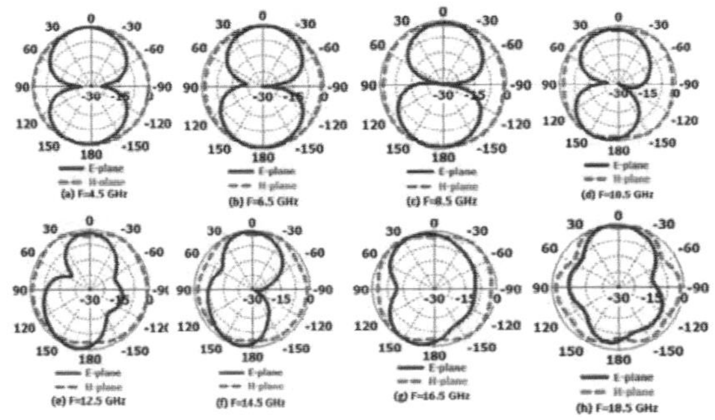

Fig. 3. UWB Radiation pattern of the proposed ETP_Monopole for different frequencies.

B. Comparison

Performance of the proposed "ETP" is compared to other published monopole antennas as presented in Table II.

TABLE II. COMPARISON WITH OTHER WORK

Ref	*Size (mm)*	*Dielectric Constant*	*Bandwidth (GHz)*	*Gain (dBi)*
[9]	45 x 50 x 0.41	3.38	3.0 – 11.57	6.91
[10]	58 x 24 x 1.6	4.4	3.29 -6.9 , 8.76 - 13.27 GHz	8
[11]	27 x 29 x 1.0	2.2	2.8 – 11.97	4.34
[12]	60 x 40 x 1.6	4.3	1.6 – 10	1.5
[13]	33 x 30 x 1.5	4.4	3.25 – 11.36	4.7
Rect	30 x 30 x 1.6	4.4	4.3 – 11.3	4.75
ETP	30 x 30 x 1.6	4.4	4.5 – 19.0	6.75

C. Fabrication Results

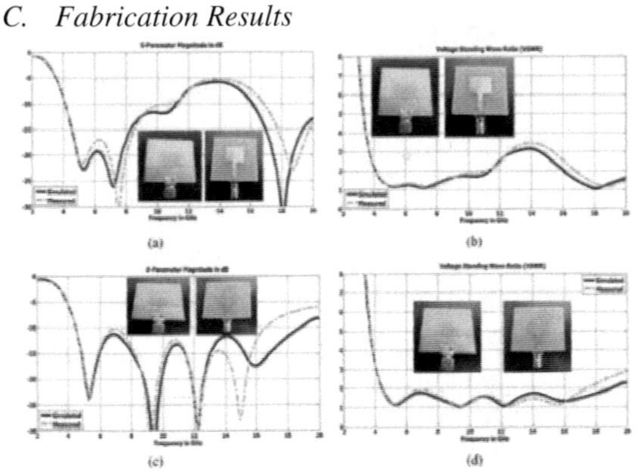

Fig. 4. Simulated and Measured parameters of ETP and Rect: (a) Rect |S11|, (b) Rect VSWR, (c) ETP |S11|, and (d) ETP VSWR.

Finally, the proposed "ETP" and "Rect" antennas have been fabricated and measured. The parameters were measured using R&S ZVA-67. A comparison between measured and simulated S-parameters and VSWR is represented in Figs. 5 (a) to 5 (d). Simulation results are in a good agreement with the measured.

IV. CONCLUSION

A compact UWB microstrip monopole antenna of enhanced characteristic has been proposed, designed and simulated. The presented antenna satisfies the UWB characteristic as well as the extended future use (4.5 GHz up to 19.0 GHz). The proposed ETP achieved a larger bandwidth (230%), higher average gain (6.75dBi), better average efficiency (75%), and lower average VSWR (1.75) relative to the Rect and other published antennas [4–6 and 16–18] over the entire bandwidth. These parameters are in good agreement through fabrication and measurement of the presented monopoles. The proposed monopole antenna can be used for many current and future short range UWB wireless applications (4G/5G).

REFERENCES

[1] Revision of Part 15 of the Communication's Rules Regarding Ultra-Wideband Transmission Systems, Federal Communications Commission, ET-Docket 98 153, FCC 02-48, 2002.

[2] J. H. Reed, "Introduction to Ultra Wideband Communication Systems," Prentice Hall PTR, 2012.

[3] A. A. R. Saad and H. A. Mohamed, "Conceptual design of a compact four-element UWB MIMO slot antenna array," IET Microwaves, Antennas & Propagation, vol. 13, no. 2, pp. 208-2015, 2018..

[4] D. Chen and C. H. Cheng, "A Novel Compact Ultra-Wideband (UWB) wide slot antenna with VIA hole," Progress In Electromagnetics Research, PIER, vol. 94, pp. 343-349, 2009.

[5] A. A. Shaheen and H. Al-Rizzo, " An Ultra Wide Band Antenna Design for Indoor Geolocation Applications," World Applied Sciences Journal, vol. 12, no. 8, pp. 1321-1326, 2011.

[6] Z.-H. Wu, et al., "A compact qaud band-notched UWB monopole antenna loaded one lateral L-Shaped solt," Progress In Electromagnetics Research, vol. 139, pp. 303-315, 2013.

[7] M. Susila and T. R. Rao, "A Novel Smiley Fractal Antenna (SFA) Design and Development for UWB Wireless Applications," Progress In Electromagnetics Research C, vol. 54, pp. 171–178, 2014.

[8] A. Reha, et al., "CPW-Fed KOCH SNOWFLAKE Fractal Antenna for UWB Wireless Applications," Trans. On Networks and Communications, vol.2, no.4, 2014

[9] M. E. Yassin, H. A. Mohamed, E. A. Abdallah, and H. S El-Hennawy, "Circularly Polarized Wideband-to-Narrowband Switchable Antenna," IEEE Access, vol. 7, pp. -36010-36018, 2019.

[10] M. A. Ibrahim, et al, "Ultra-wide band microstrip antenna for 4G applications," IOP Conference Series: Materials Science and Engineering, vol. 610, no. 1, IOP Publishing, 2019.

[11] W. Ahmad, A. Tarczynski, and D. Budimir, "Design of monopole antennas for uwb applications," 2017 IEEE International Symposium on Antennas and Propagation and USNC/URSI National Radio Science Meeting, IEEE, 2017.

[12] A. A. Deshmukh, et al., "Printed Monopole Antenna Using Modified Elliptical Shape Patches for UWB Response," 2017 International Conference on Computing, Communication, Control and Automation (ICCUBEA), IEEE, 2017.

[13] R. A. Lituma-Guartan, et al., "A Novel Hybrid Fractal Antenna Design for Ultra-Wideband Application," 2018 IEEE 10th Latin-American Conference on Communications (LATINCOM), IEEE, 2018.

Design and Implementation of Multiband Metamaterial Antennas

Mohamed F. Abo Sree
Department of Electronics and Communications Engineering.
Arab Academy for Science Technology and Maritime Transport
Cairo, Egypt
eng_m_fathey@hotmail.com

A.M.M.A. Allam
Faculty of Information Engineering and Technology
German University in Cairo
Cairo, Egypt
abdelmegid.allam@guc.edu.eg

Hesham A. Mohamed
Department of Microstrip
Electronics Research Institute (ERI)
Giza 12622, Egypt
Hesham_280@eri.sci.eg

***Abstract*— This article emphasizes the design, analysis and fabrication of conventional and multiband metamaterial antennas. The benefits of employing composite right/left-handed structure on bandwidth and gain are emulated. The structures with metamaterial properties handle multiple bandwidths of operation. The antennas are simulated by the CST microwave studio, fabricated on FR4 and measured using network analyzer. The measured and simulated results have fair match.**

Keywords— Metamaterial antennas, Multiband antennas.

I. INTRODUCTION

Metamaterials (MTM) are materials which are manufactured from available substrate or any bulky conventional structure, which results in a new artificial material with some new features added to the designed radio frequency or optical passive or active elements fabricated from those structure [1]. They were formed form three-dimensional unit cells as "Macroscopic composites" which may enhance the properties of the traditional elements like coupler, antennas…etc. with different responses [2]. It's applied for antennas to enhanced its performance [3-11].

This paper presents both conventional and metamaterial-inspired multiband antennas to illustrate the effect of utilizing CRLH structure on gain, bandwidth and beam steering characteristics.

II. DESIGN AND RESULTS

A. Antenna Design

The geometry and the dimensions of the proposed conventional double U-shape antenna is illustrated in Fig. 1 The antenna is printed on a FR4 substrate with a relative permittivity of 4.3 and thickness of 1.6 mm.

The coupling between the two U patches makes them combined to realize Wide Band (WB). The array is fed capacitively by a microstrip line. The width of the microstrip line is equal 1.57 mm in order to achieve 50Ω characteristic impedance. Fig. 2 shows the top &bottom view of fabricated version of the antenna structure.

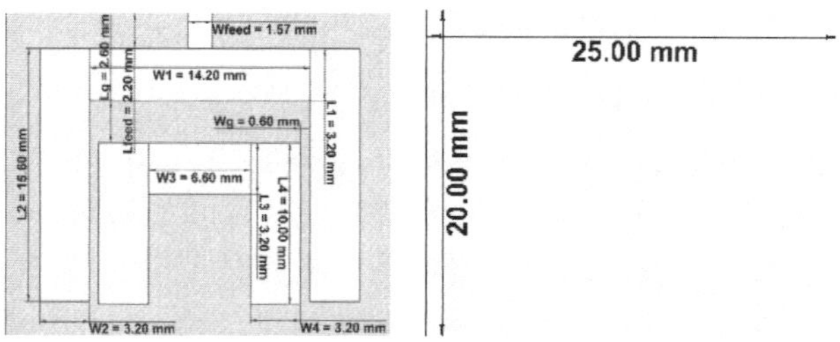

(a) (b)

Fig. 1. Proposed conventional antenna: (a) top view and (b) bottom view.

To investigate the performance of the proposed antennas in terms of achieving wideband operations, the commercially available simulation software CST STUDIO SUITE ver.2017 was used for numerical analysis.

(a) (b)

Fig. 2. Conventional antenna: (a) top view and (b) bottom view.

B. Antenna Results

The proposed conventional antenna is simulated and measured. The simulated and measured return loss is presented in Fig. 3 and it can be read that the antenna operates in a wide frequency range from 16.25 GHz to 22 GHz when -10 dB criteria is applied for bandwidth evaluation. The maximum gain of the antenna is 5 dB.

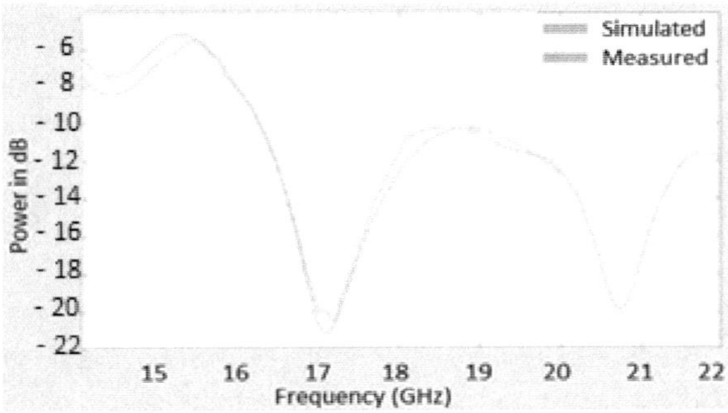

Fig. 3. The return loss of the proposed conventional antenna.

In order to enhance the gain of the antenna proposed in section II while obtaining multiband instead of wideband, a MTM model was designed and simulated. MTM is obtained by making an air slot in the ground following the concept of split ring resonator (SRR). This slotted element will add a series capacitance and coupling to the upper surface contributing a parasitic parallel coil which adding the left hand behavior for the structure. The geometry and dimensions of the MTM double U-shape multiband antenna are presented in Fig. 4. The fabrication presented in Fig. 5.

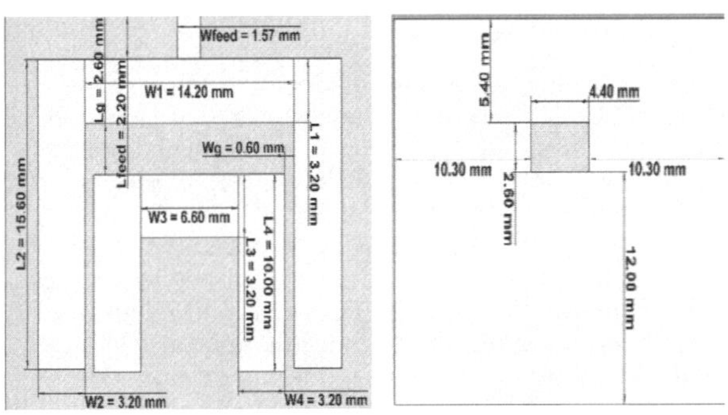

(a) (b)

Fig. 4. Proposed MTM antenna: (a) top view and (b) bottom view.

(a) (b)

Fig. 5. Fabricated MTM antenna: (a) top view and (b) bottom view.

In order to optimize the bandwidth and gain of the antenna, a tuning has been done by changing the grounded air slot's size; filling the whole coupling gap's length and changing the width symmetrically. The return loss is depicted in Fig. 6 and the maximum gain of the antenna is 8 dB.

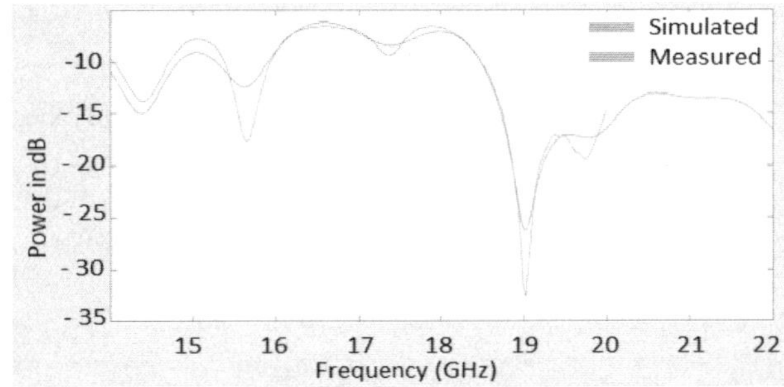

Fig. 6. The return loss of the optimized tuned grounded air slot proposed antenna.

III. CONCLUSION

This paper illustrates the design and implementation of both conventional wideband and MTM multiband antennas. By optimizing the air slot in the ground which follows the concept of SRRs (Split ring resonators), multiple bandwidths and better gain were attained in section III. Thus, the antennas discussed in this paper give great potential for future communications' applications.

REFERENCES

[1] T. J. Cui, D. R. Smith, and R. Liu, Metamaterials: Theory, Design, and Applications. 12 Springer. New York, 13, 2010.

[2] A. K. Singh, et al., "Design and simulation of metamaterials using star shape fractal antenna," 2017 2nd IEEE International Conference on Recent Trends in Electronics, Information & Communication Technology (RTEICT), IEEE, 2017.

[3] X. Wang, et al., "Experimental and numerical study of a magnetic resonance wireless power transfer system using superconductor and ferromagnetic metamaterials," IEEE Transactions on Applied Superconductivity, vol. 28, no. 5, pp. 1-6, 2018.

[4] V. G. Veselago, "The Electrodynamics of Substances with Simultaneously Negative Values of Img Align= Absmiddle Alt= ϵ Eps/Img and μ," Physics-Uspekhi, vol. 10, no. 4, pp. 509-514, 1968.

[5] R. A. Shelby, D. R. Smith, and S. Schultz, "Experimental verification of a negative index of refraction," Science, vol. 292, no. 5514, pp. 77-79, 2001.

[6] A. A. R. Saad and H. A. Mohamed, "Printed millimeter-wave MIMO-based slot antenna arrays for 5G networks," AEU-International Journal of Electronics and Communications, vol. 99, p.p 59-69, 2019.

[7] S. Zhang, et al., "Experimental demonstration of near-infrared negative-index metamaterials," Physical Review Letters, vol. 95, no. 13, p. 137404, 2005.

[8] V. I. Slyusar, "60 years of electrically small antennas theory," 2007 6th International Conference on Antenna Theory and Techniques, IEEE, 2007.

[9] Y. Li and N. Bowler, "Analysis of double-negative (DNG) bandwidths for metamaterials composed of three-dimensional periodic arrays of two different magnetodielectric spheres arbitrarily arranged on a simple tetragonal lattice," IEEE Antennas and Wireless Propagation Letters, vol. 10, pp. 1484-1487, 2011.

[10] A. S. Elkorany, G. Ahmed, D. Saleeb, and H. A. Mohamed, "Tunable elliptical split ring resonator using single varactor diode," Advanced Electromagnetics, vol. 7, no. 1, pp. 7-12 , 2018.

[11] W. A. Ali, H. A. Mohamed, A. A. Ibrahim, and M. Z. Hamdalla, " Gain improvement of tunable band-notched UWB antenna using metamaterial lens for high speed wireless communications," Microsystem Technologies, vol. 25 , no. 11 , pp. 4111-4117, 2019.

Experimental Realization of Full-parameter Transformation Optics Media

Xiaojun Hu, Ran Li, Zhouyi Wu, Chao Ma, Jiangtao Huangfu, and Dexin Ye*

Laboratory of Applied Research on Electromagnetics, Zhejiang University, Hangzhou 310027, China

desy@zju.edu.cn

***Abstract*—By engineering the spatial dispersion of metamaterial, we demonstrate the experimental realization of full-parameter transformation optics (TO) media. Such a medium allows near 100% transmission for all TE polarized incident waves from free space, regardless of both incidence and polarization angles. Its constitutive parameters tensor has a diagonal form diag(a, a, $1/a$), which exactly satisfies the model of uniaxial perfectly matched layer (UPML). The omnidirectionally reflectionless transparency is well explained by the model of UPML and TO media, verified by both simulation and experimental measurement. Such a universal approach can be easily extended from microwave to terahertz wave frequencies.**

Keywords—Omnidirectional transparency, transformation optics media, uniaxial perfectly matched layers.

I. INTRODUCTION

When electromagnetic waves are incident on a medium from free space, reflection generally occurs due to the mismatching impedance, which is mostly undesirable. Therefore, achieving reflectionless transmission has become the subject of extensive studies in both physics and engineers for decades. Frequency selective surface (FSS) [1], composed of periodic subwavelength structure, can strongly suppress reflection in a specific frequency band. However, the conventional FSS only has a reflectionless transmission effect for a single incident angle, e.g., normal incidence. Recently, the theory of transformation optics [2], shows that some lossless anisotropic media can achieve perfect transparency in principle, possessing an omnidirectional impedance matching. Such a class of media has a constitutive parameter tensor as diag(a, a, $1/a$), which is exactly the same with that of uniaxial perfectly matched layer (UPML) [3]. These uniaxial media are the bases of various exotic devices and applications of transformation optics, such as invisibility cloak [4].

In this letter, based on the spatial dispersion engineering of metamaterial, we propose a universal approach to realize full-parameter TO medium regardless of polarization angles. Retrieved results indicate that its constitutive parameters exactly satisfy the model of UPML, full-wave simulation and experimental results show the omnidirectional reflectionless transmission.

II. DESIGN AND SIMULATION

Without loss generality, we consider a plane wave incident on a TO medium from free space, as shown in Fig. 1. The TO medium has a diagonal tensor form as diag(a, a, $1/a$) in a Cartesian coordinate system, identical for both relative permittivity and relative permeability, the incident wave will fully transmit through the medium without any reflection independent of incident angles [3]. For a TE polarized (with electric field in the y direction), the involved constitutive parameters of TO medium are tangential permittivity and permeability, and normal permeability. Consequently, the omnidirectionally transparency only requires $\mu_y=\varepsilon_x=1/\mu_z=a$, where a is a real number.

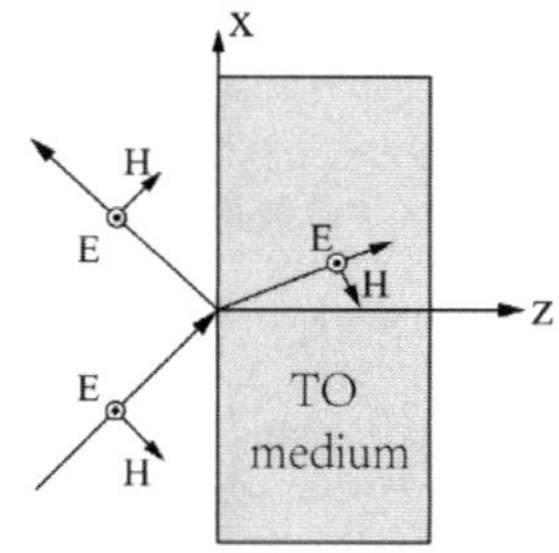

Fig. 1. Reflection and transmission of a TE polorized plane wave incident on the boundary of TO medium.

In the following, the theory of metamaterial is used to realize previous TO medium. The unit cell is designed as shown in Fig. 2 (a). Each unit contains a triangular copper ring and a copper cylinder, and the unit is surrounded by a dielectric medium. Here, the dielectric used is F4B, whose relative permittivity is 3.5 with a loss tangent of 0.001. In this design, the continuous thin copper strip will couple strongly to parallel electric fields (E_x and E_y) and slightly to magnetic fields, inducing a strong electric resonance to tune effective permittivity. Meanwhile, the copper cylinder is introduced to control the magnetic moments in xy plane and z direction. Due to the asymmetry, its xy component and z component of effective permeability can be tuned independently. Aimed to operate at 4.5 GHz, the dimensions of the unit cell are optimized as a=12 mm, b=1.2357 mm, r=2.33 mm, h_1=6 mm, h_2=10.035mm.

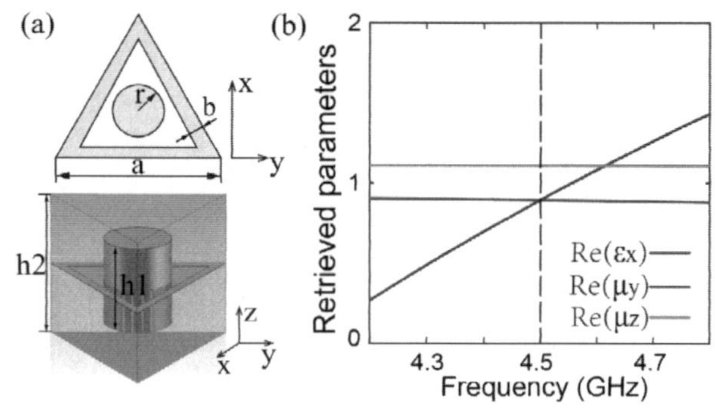

Fig. 2. Schematic of unit cell (a) and its retrieved consititutive parameters (b). Retrieved constitutive parameters: $\mu_y=\varepsilon_x$=0.8953, μ_z=1.108.

Fig. 2 (b) shows the retrieved relative permittivity and permeability from the simulated S-parameter based on the algorithms in [5]. At 4.5 GHz, we have: $\mu_y=\varepsilon_x$=0.8953, μ_z=1.108, satisfying the diag(a, a, $1/a$) form. Due to the negligible loss of dielectric and copper in microwave, the imaginary parts of all constitutive parameter are near zero.

Thus, the reflection coefficient can well represent the transmission of electromagnetic wave.

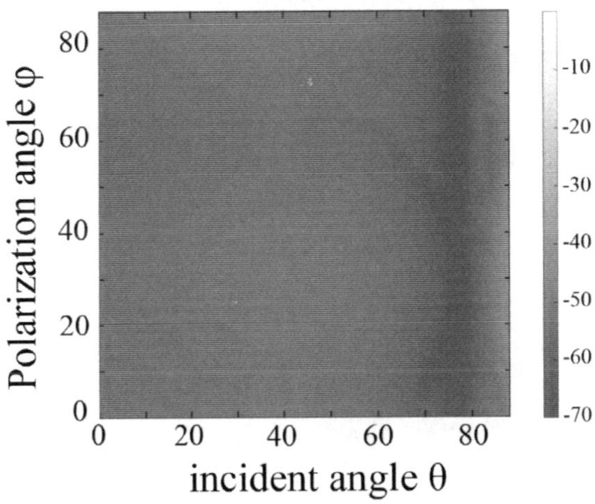

Fig. 3. Simulated reflection dependent of incident and polarization angles at 4.5 GHz.

To verify its reflectionless transmission independent of incidence and polarization angles, the angle scanning for transmission were performed at 4.5 GHz for TE wave. The results, shown in Fig. 3, indicate that the reflection coefficient is below -50 dB for all incidence and polarization angles, in accordance with our theoretical analysis.

III. Experiments and Discussion

To verify its performance experimentally, one layer of TO medium sample was fabricated according to the simulation model, as shown in Fig. 4. In the fabrication process, two F4B cover layers were firstly machined with circular openings by 3D sculpture technology, one of which was coated with copper strips. Then, all copper cylinders were embedded tightly inside the circular openings and sandwiched by two F4B covers. The final dimension of sample is $500\times500\times10.035$ mm^3.

Fig. 4. Experiment setup. The inset shows the fabrication process of sample.

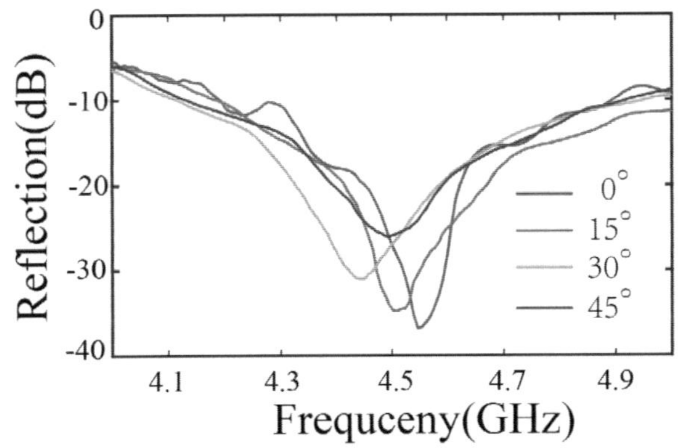

Fig. 5. Measured reflection dependent of incident angles.

The experimental setup we used to measure the reflection of sample is depicted in Fig. 4. Two identical horn antennas acted as receiver and transmitter with absorbing materials placed between two antennas to isolate the direct couple.

The measured results are shown in Fig. 5. We can see that at normal incidence, the reflection coefficient reaches -36 dB at 4.548 GHz, which means the reflection is smaller than 0.1%. Increasing incident angle, the nadir of reflection will be slightly shifted, but the reflection is always below -25 dB, indicating the transmission is still above 99%. Although the imperfections of fabrication and experiment setup inevitably degrade the performance, the measurement results agree with our analytic and numerical results.

IV. Conclusion

In conclusion, based on the spatial dispersion engineering of metamaterial, full-parameter TO medium was experimentally studied. Theoretical analysis, simulation, and experimental results are all in accordance with each other. The proposed approach is easily extended to high frequencies. We expect several applications of this general principle of spatial dispersion control in the realization of various anisotropic metamaterials, such as absorptive PML.

Acknowledgment

This research was supported by the NSFC under grants 61771422, the ZJNSF under grant LR18F010001.

References

[1] B. A. Munk, Frequency Selective Surfaces: Theory and Design, New York: Wiley, 2000.

[2] Y. A. Urzhumov and D. R. Smith, "Transformation optics with photonic band gap media," Phys. Rev. Lett., vol. 105, issue 16, pp. 163901-163905, Oct. 2010.

[3] Z. S. Sacks, D. M. Kingsland, R. Lee, and J. F. Lee, "Performance of an anisotropic artificial absorber for truncating finite element meshes," IEEE Trans. Antennas Propag., vol. 43, no. 12. pp. 1460-1463, Dec. 1995.

[4] J. B. Pendry, D. Schuring, and D. R. Smith, "Controlling electromagnetic fields," Science. vol. 312, issue 5781, pp. 1780-1782, Jun. 2006.

[5] D. R. Smith, S. Schultz, P. Markoš, and C. M. Soukoulis, "Determination of effective permittivity and permeability of metamaterials from reflection and transmission coefficients," Phys. Rev. B, vol. 65, no. 19, pp. 195104-195108, Apr. 2002.

Resonant Characteristics of Split Ring Resonator And Unit Cell for Periodic Metamaterial Devices

Brinta Chowdhury, Thisara Walpita, B. Yang, and A. Eroglu
Department of Electrical and Computer Engineering, North Carolina A&T State University, US

Abstract— **The resonant characteristics of single split ring resonator-based metamaterial devices with single gap are presented using the analytical formulation developed for the lumped element equivalent circuit model. The characteristics of the metamaterial resonators have been investigated for different ring sizes, gap widths and substrate permittivity. Equivalent circuit model is developed for two ring structures. The analytical, and simulation results are compared and verified. The prototype has been then built and measured. It has been observed that all the results agree. The results presented in this paper can be used to develop devices at the THz range that can operate as sensors, antennas or tuning elements.**

Keywords—RESONANT, SPLIT RING, RESONATOR, THZ, SENSOR, METAMATERIALS, RING, GAP.

I. INTRODUCTION

Split ring Resonator (SRR) is a conducting ring with a split printed on a dielectric substrate. This structure creates characteristics of metamaterial which can generate desired magnetic response up to 200 terahertz [1]. Split ring resonator structures are also called artificial left-handed materials which was primarily discovered in the seventies [2]. In [3], researchers examined split ring structures for negative permittivity and permeability.

Split ring resonators can be modeled as LC circuit as reported in [4]. In [5], authors formulated circular split ring resonator with two rings and showed the accuracy of the formulation. In last two decades, different types of split ring resonator are being proposed. Edge-coupled SRRs (EC-SRR) are proposed in [6]. This structure is also formulated with simple closed form equations in [5]. Another type of SRR is the broadside-coupled SRR (BC-SRR) which was proposed in [7]. Difference between these two structures is that EC-SRR has two rings on the same side of the substrate whereas in BC-SRR two rings are on the opposite side. Multiple split ring resonators are formulated and designed to increase the capacitance without increasing the size [8]. Periodic structures are being studied recently because of their higher symmetric property than the unit cells [9].

In this paper, characteristics of a single gap ring resonator are analyzed for different parameters such as ring radius, gap width and substrate permittivity. A unit cell (with two rings) is proposed to form a periodic structure. An equivalent circuit model is developed for the proposed design. Prototype is built and measured which gave similar results obtained in simulation. Novelty of this work is simplified analytical model based on physical dimension for one ring SRR and equivalent circuit model for two ring unit cell.

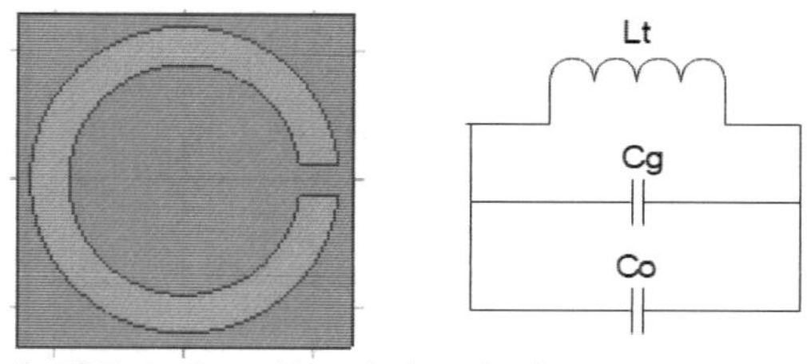

Fig. 1. SRR structure with equivalent circuit .

II. CHARACTERISTICS OF SRR RESONANCE

The dimensions of geometry of single gap split ring resonator and equivalent circuit are shown in shown in Fig. 1. Circuit parameters are calculated from,

$$L_T = 0.002\,(\ln\frac{4l}{c} - \gamma)\ \mu H \qquad (1),$$

$$C_{eq} = C_g + C_o = \varepsilon_o\frac{ct}{g} + l_{avg} \times \frac{\sqrt{\varepsilon_e}}{c_o Z_o} \qquad (2).$$

The resonant frequency of the total structure is,

$$f_o = \frac{1}{2\pi\sqrt{L_T C_{eq}}} \qquad (3),$$

where, t= ring thickness, h= substrate height, rext=ring external radius, g=gap, and ε_r = substrate permittivity.

Effect of changing ring parameters on the resonant frequency is studied. The resonant frequency decreases with the increasing the value of the external ring radius as shown in Fig. 2. It is observed that to get higher resonating frequency ring radius should be decreased.

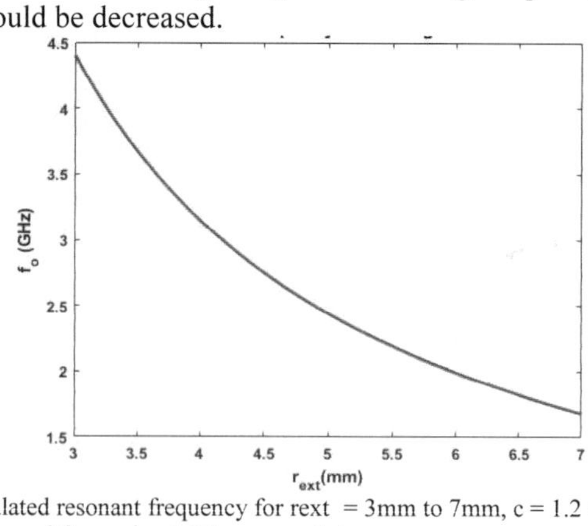

Fig 2. Calculated resonant frequency for rext = 3mm to 7mm, c = 1.2 mm, t = 0.0175 mm, g = 0.8 mm, h = 1.27mm, εr = 4.4.

The resonant frequency is also dependent on the gap size. With increasing the gap, capacitance increases, hence the resonant frequency decreases as shown in Fig. 3. Substrate material permittivity also has effect on the resonant frequency. Higher substrate permittivity gives lower capacitance and so increases the resonant frequency as illustrated in Fig. 4.

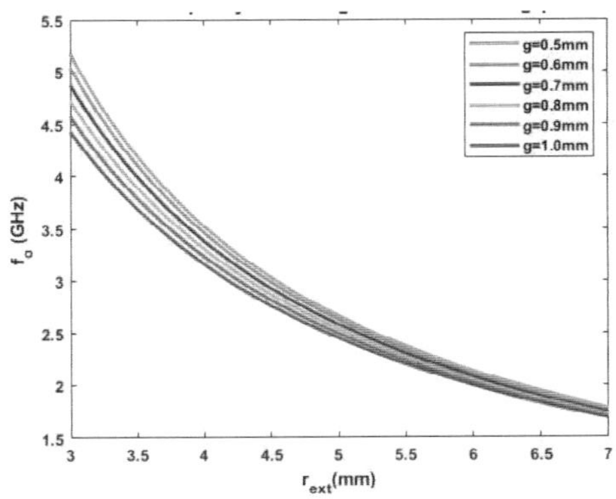

Fig. 3. Calculated resonant frequency for rext = 3mm to 7mm, c = 1.2 mm, t = 0.0175 mm, h = 1.27mm, εr = 4.4 with different gap.

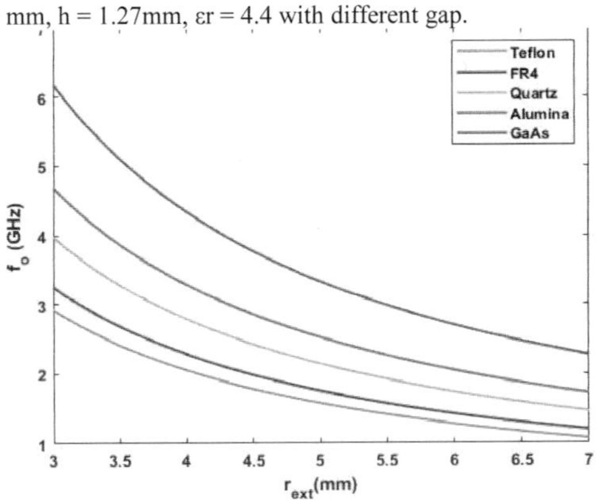

Fig. 4. Calculated resonant frequency for different substrate with rext = 3mm to 7mm, c = 1.2 mm, t = 0.0175 mm, g = 0.8mm, h = 1.27 mm.

III. Two Rings Unit Cell

We developed a unit cell with two rings for infinite periodic structures. Two magnetically coupled rings are considered as unit cell as shown in Fig.5(a) for the periodic structure [10]. Equivalent circuit is shown in Fig.5(b). Mutual inductance between two rings is considered for intra-unit cell and inter-unit cell. ABCD matrix is also developed.

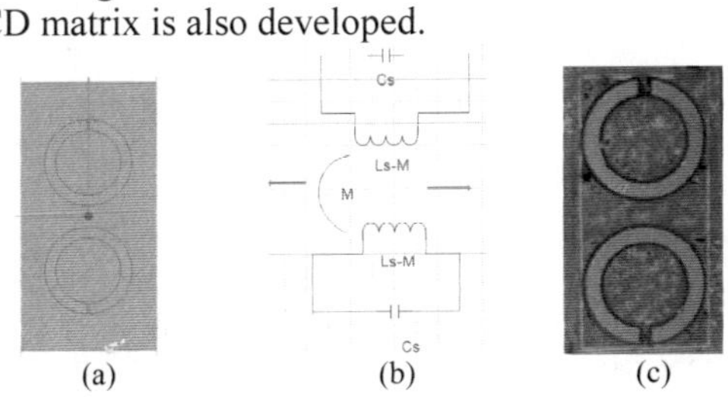

Fig. 5. (a) Two rings as a Unit Cell, (b) Equivalent Circuit of unit cell, and (c) Fabricated structure

ABCD parameters of the unit cell are,

$$ABCD = \begin{bmatrix} 1 & -j\frac{\omega^3(L_S-2M)C_SL_S-\omega(L_S-M)}{\omega^4(L_S-2M)C_S^2L_S-1} \\ 0 & 1 \end{bmatrix} \quad (4).$$

IV. Measurement

We built a prototype for two ring unit cell using PCB milling machine with FR4. Due to milling machine capability, the prototype is built at the milli meter scale. To get THz frequency, resonators must be built at the micrometer scale. To measure the prototype, rectangular waveguide is used. Measured results shown in Fig. 6 are aligned with the EM simulation and circuit simulation.

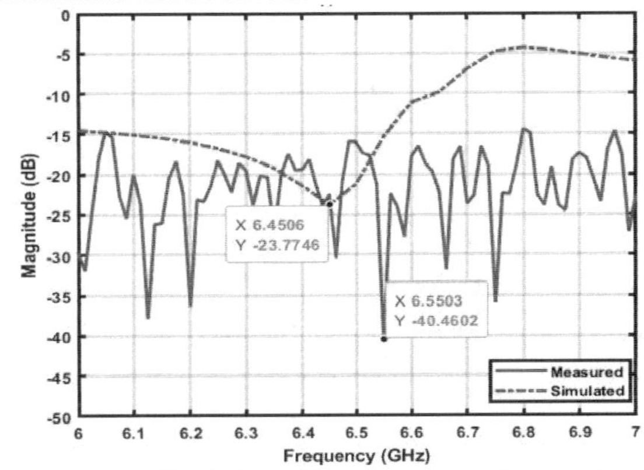

Fig.6. Comparison of Simulation and Measured resonant frequency for two ring unit cell with rext = 5mm, c = 1.2 mm, t = 0.0175 mm, g = 0.8 mm, h = 1.27 mm , εr = 4.4.

V. Conclusion

In this paper, we analyzed resonant characteristics of SRR with varying parameters like ring radius, gap width and substrate permittivity. A two rings unit cell is developed with network parameters which can be used to build infinite periodic structure. Our measurement results agree with the EM and circuit simulation results. This unit cell can be used to build periodic structure for sensors operating at the THz range.

References

[1] W. Contributors. "Split-ring Resonator", Wikipedia, The Free Encyclopedia. https://en.wikipedia.org/w/index.php?title=Split-ring_resonator&oldid=930942325 (accessed January 1, 2020).

[2] V. Veselago, "Electrodynamics of substances with simultaneously negative and," *Usp. Fiz. Nauk,* vol. 92, p. 517, 1967.

[3] D. R. Smith, W. J. Padilla, D. Vier, S. C. Nemat-Nasser, and S. Schultz, "Composite medium with simultaneously negative permeability and permittivity," Physical review letters, vol. 84, no. 18, p. 4184, 2000.

[4] J. D. Baena *et al.*, "Equivalent-circuit models for split-ring resonators and complementary split-ring resonators coupled to planar transmission lines," IEEE Transactions on Microwave Theory and Techniques, vol. 53, no. 4, pp. 1451-1461, 2005, doi: 10.1109/tmtt.2005.845211.

[5] C. Saha and J. Y. Siddiqui, "Theoretical Model for Estimation of Resonance Frequency of Rotational Circular Split-Ring Resonators," Electromagnetics, vol. 32, no. 6, pp. 345-355, 2012, doi: 10.1080/02726343.2012.701540.

[6] J. B. Pendry, A. J. Holden, D. J. Robbins, W. J. I. t. o. m. t. Stewart, and techniques, "Magnetism from conductors and enhanced nonlinear phenomena," vol. 47, no. 11, pp. 2075-2084, 1999.

[7] R. Marqués, F. Medina, and R. J. P. R. B. Rafii-El-Idrissi, "Role of bianisotropy in negative permeability and left-handed metamaterials," vol. 65, no. 14, p. 144440, 2002.

[8] F. Bilotti, A. Toscano, L. J. I. t. o. a. Vegni, and propagation, "Design of spiral and multiple split-ring resonators for the realization of miniaturized metamaterial samples," vol. 55, no. 8, pp. 2258-2267, 2007.

[9] A. Hessel, C. Ming Hui, R. C. M. Li, and A. A. Oliner, "Propagation in periodically loaded waveguides with higher symmetries," Proceedings of the IEEE, vol. 61, no. 2, pp. 183-195, 1973, doi: 10.1109/PROC.1973.9003.

[10] J.-S. Hong, M. J. J. I. T. o. M. t. Lancaster, and Techniques, "Couplings of microstrip square open-loop resonators for cross-coupled planar microwave filters," vol. 44, no. 11, pp. 2099-2109, 1996.

Non-physical Impedance Matching

William D. May
Raytheon/Applied Signal Technology
william.d.may@raytheon.com

***Abstract*—Non-physical matching (NPM) is a method for transforming the impedance of a CEM modeled device into a target impedance using algebraic methods. NPM is a useful tool for replicating existing devices in CEM models.**

***Index Terms*—impedance matching; EM modeling; commutative algebra; Gröbner basis**

I. Introduction

Although rarely mentioned in the CEM literature, it is not unusual to incorporate models of existing devices (such as antennas) into larger computational EM models. Most of the modeling challenges are the same as for developing new devices, but some are quite different.

Perhaps the most interesting difference is that the model need not resemble the actual device. It only needs to replicate the measured electrical characteristics of the original. If, for example, a simple wire dipole can be made to match the important characteristics in simulation then there is no need to develop a more accurate model.

Non-physical matching (NPM) is a method for transforming the impedance of a modeled device into a target impedance. The target might be the measured impedance of a physical device, or it might be a predetermined value, such as 50 ohms. The name comes from the fact that the method is algebraic, not physical.

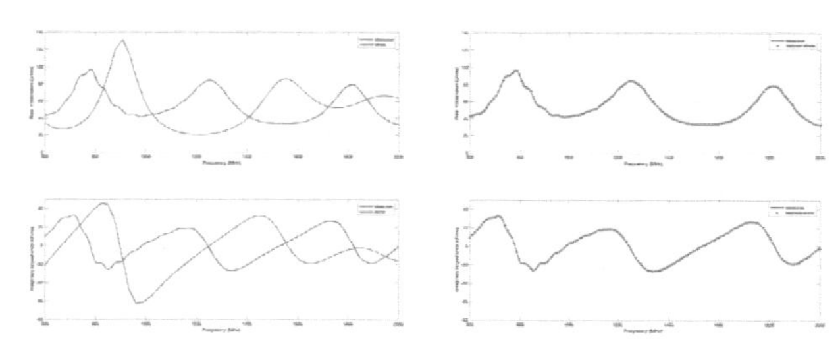

Fig. 1. Before and after of non-physical matching. The simulated impedance is clearly different from measurements in the left figure, it is indistinguishable from measurements in the right figure.

The data plotted in Figure 1 illustrates NPM. The left-hand plots show the measured real and imaginary measured impedance for a commercial UHF antenna (plotted in blue) versus simulated impedance (plotted in red, simulations were performed using FEKO [1]). Measured and simulated values are clearly different.

The results after applying NPM are shown on the right-hand side. Simulation and measurements are now indistinguishable.

II. The Single Antenna Solution

The NPM solution for a single antenna is a very useful result in its own right, and the derivation is a template for developing a general solution.

The measured (target) impedance, Z_m, and simulated impedance, Z_s, are known. These are complex scalar values with strictly positive real parts.

The NPM solution will be a 2-port network (impedance matrix Z) that transforms Z_s into Z_m. For matching to work for both transmit and receive the matrix Z must be symmetric. The network should also be lossless, so Z is pure imaginary.

The starting point is the 2-port impedance relationship [2]

$$\begin{pmatrix} V_m \\ V_s \end{pmatrix} = i \begin{pmatrix} z_{11} & z_{12} \\ z_{12} & z_{22} \end{pmatrix} \begin{pmatrix} I_m \\ -I_s \end{pmatrix}$$

where V_m and V_s are measured and simulated voltage respectively, I_m and I_s are measured and simulated current, and the z_{ij} are unknowns (real).

The NPM solution follows after using $Z_m = V_m/I_m$ and $Z_s = V_s/I_s$ to eliminate voltage and current, substituting $Z_m = x + iy$, $Z_s = u + iv$ (with $x > 0$ and $u > 0$), then separating into real and imaginary parts. The result is 2 equations in 3 unknowns, so it is a family of solutions with a single parameter.

If z_{22} is chosen to be the parameter, then the NPM solution is

$$Z = i \begin{pmatrix} y + \frac{x(v+z_{22})}{u} & \sqrt{\frac{x(u^2+(v+z_{22})^2)}{u}} \\ \sqrt{\frac{x(u^2+(v+z_{22})^2)}{u}} & -v \end{pmatrix}.$$

The results shown in Fig. 1 were obtained using this solution.

It is possible for Z to be poorly conditioned, especially for electrically small antennas (where x and/or u are very close to 0). A search over the range of z_{22} will locate well-conditioned Z matrices, so this is a not a problem in practice.

III. The General Solution

The solution to the general k-antenna problem follows in a similar manner to the single antenna solution, with scalars replaced by square matrices. Z_m and Z_s are known $k \times k$ complex matrices, with the real parts of diagonal elements strictly greater than 0. The impedance relationship is

$$\begin{pmatrix} V_m \\ V_s \end{pmatrix} = i \left(\begin{array}{c|c} Z_{11} & Z_{12} \\ \hline Z_{12}' & Z_{22} \end{array} \right) \begin{pmatrix} I_m \\ -I_s \end{pmatrix}$$

where V_m, V_s, I_m, I_s are $k \times 1$ complex vectors and the Z_{mn} are real $k \times k$ matrices. Since Z is symmetric both Z_{11} and Z_{22} are symmetric.

Substituting $V_m = Z_m I_m$, $V_s = Z_s I_s$, $Z_m = X + iY$, and $Z_s = U + iV$, separating into real and imaginary parts, the result is

$$X = -Z_{12}(U^2 + (V + iZ_{22})^2)^{-1} U Z_{12}'$$
$$Y = iZ_{11} + Z_{12}(U^2 + (V + Z_{22})^2)^{-1}(V + Z_{22}))Z_{12}'$$

This can be simplified by letting $Z_{11} = Y$ and $Z_{22} = -V$ to eliminate the equation in Y:

$$X = Z_{12} U^{-1} Z_{12}'$$

This simple expression is deceptive. Solving it is challenging, even for two antennas.

IV. The Two Antenna Solution

The two-antenna solution begins with the general solution

$$\Re(Z_m) = Z_{12} \Re(Z_s)^{-1} Z_{12}'.$$

expanded to

$$\begin{pmatrix} x_{11} & x_{12} \\ x_{12} & x_{22} \end{pmatrix} = \begin{pmatrix} a & b \\ c & d \end{pmatrix} \begin{pmatrix} -u_{22} & u_{12} \\ u_{12} & -u_{11} \end{pmatrix} \begin{pmatrix} a & c \\ b & d \end{pmatrix} / K$$
$$= \begin{pmatrix} a^2 u_{22} - 2abu_{12} + b^2 u_{11} & bdu_{11} - (bc + ad)u_{12} + acu_{22} \\ bdu_{11} - (bc + ad)u_{12} + acu_{22} & u_{22}c^2 - 2du_{12}c + d^2 u_{11} \end{pmatrix} / K$$

where $K = u_{11}u_{22} - u_{12}^2$, and a, b, c and d are the unknowns (real). This corresponds to a system of quadratic equations

$$a^2 u_{22} - 2abu_{12} + b^2 u_{11} - Kx_{11} = 0$$
$$bdu_{11} - (bc + ad)u_{12} + acu_{22} - Kx_{12} = 0$$
$$c^2 u_{22} - 2cdu_{12} + d^2 u_{11} - Kx_{22} = 0$$

With 3 equations and 4 unknowns one variable will be a parameter. By letting d be the parameter the third equation can be solved for c. The problem is to find a and b in terms of d.

Solving systems of polynomial equations falls within commutative algebra [3]. A major development in computational commutative algebra was the introduction of Gröbner bases in 1965. Gröbner bases are used to solve systems of polynomial equations in a manner similar to solving linear systems using Gaussian elimination.

The Gröbner basis for the two equations in a and b (c and d are treated as knowns) can be calculated using Mathematica [4]:

$$g_1 = b^2 K(c^2 u_{22} - 2cdu_{12} + d^2 u_{11}) - 2bdK^2 x_{12}$$
$$+ K(Ku_{22}x_{12}^2 - x_{11}(du_{12} - cu_{22})^2)$$
$$g_2 = -acu_{22} + adu_{12} + bcu_{12} - bdu_{11} + Kx_{12}$$
$$g_3 = abu_{22}(du_{11} - cu_{12}) - K(au_{22}x_{12} - cu_{22}x_{11} + du_{12}x_{11})$$
$$+ b^2(-(cu_{11}u_{22} - 2cu_{12}^2 + du_{11}u_{12})) + 2bKu_{12}x_{12}$$
$$g_4 = abcKu_{22} - Ku_{12}(au_{22}x_{12} - cu_{22}x_{11} + du_{12}x_{11})$$
$$+ b^2 K(du_{11} - 2cu_{12}) + bKx_{12}(2u_{12}^2 - u_{11}u_{22})$$
$$g_5 = a^2 u_{22} - 2abu_{12} + b^2 u_{11} - Kx_{11}$$

It isn't unusual for a Gröbner basis to have more elements than the polynomial system (one of the many ways polynomial systems differ from linear systems).

The solution follows by solving the first basis element for b:

$$b = \frac{dKx_{12} - \frac{1}{2}\sqrt{4(c^2 u_{22} - 2cdu_{12} + d^2 u_{11})\left(x_{11}(du_{12} - cu_{22})^2 - Ku_{22}x_{12}^2\right) + 4d^2 K^2 x_{12}^2}}{c^2 u_{22} - 2cdu_{12} + d^2 u_{11}}$$

and the fifth basis element for a:

$$a = \frac{bu_{12} - \sqrt{K(u_{22}x_{11} - b^2)}}{u_{22}} \tag{1}$$

It is essential to know the possible values for d. This is easily determined:

$$d = x_{12}\sqrt{\frac{u_{22}}{x_{11}}} \qquad G < 0 \wedge x_{12} \neq 0$$
$$-\sqrt{u_{22}x_{22}} \leq d \leq \sqrt{u_{22}x_{22}} \qquad G \geq 0 \vee x_{12} = 0$$

where $G = x_{11}x_{22} - x_{12}^2$.

The end result, Z, is then

$$Z = i \begin{pmatrix} y_{11} & y_{12} & a & b \\ y_{12} & y_{22} & c & d \\ a & c & v_{11} & v_{12} \\ b & d & v_{12} & v_{22} \end{pmatrix},$$

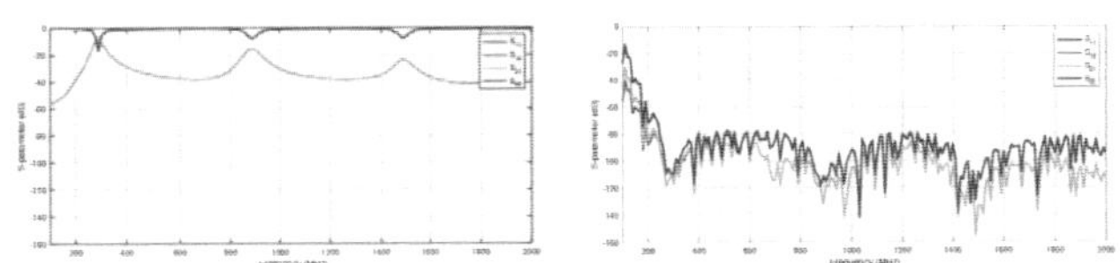

Fig. 2. Before and after of applying NPM to 2 dipole antennas. The vertical scale is 0 to -100 dB for both plots.

As an example, the plot on the left side of Figure 2 shows the S-parameters (S_{11}, S_{22} and S_{12} in dB) of two dipole antennas referenced to a 50-ohm impedance. The antennas perform well in narrow frequency bands around resonant frequencies, and there is coupling at all frequencies. The right-hand plot shows the S-parameters after applying NPM. The antennas now perform extremely well over a wide frequency range and coupling is negligible.

V. Conclusions

NPM is an easily used method to match simulated to measured impedance in CEM models with one or two antennas. It would be quite difficult to precisely match simulation to measurements, such as shown in Figure 1, using traditional matching methods.

References

[1] FEKO. (2019) Altair Engineering. [Online]. Available: www.altairhyperworks.com/feko

[2] J. Pozar, *Microwave Engineering*. John Wiley & Sons, 2012.

[3] D. Cox, J. Little, and D. O'Shea, *Ideals, Varieties and Algorithms*, 3rd ed. Springer-Verlag New York, 2007.

[4] Wolfram Research, Inc., *Mathematica*. Champaign, Illinois: Wolfram Research, Inc., 2019.

A High Gain Lens-Coupled On-Chip Antenna Module for Miniature-Sized Millimeter-Wave Wireless Transceivers

Milad Moosavifar and David Wentzloff
Electrical Engineering and Computer Science Department
University of Michigan
Ann Arbor, USA
moosavi@umich.edu

***Abstract*—This paper presents high gain and compact Transmit/Receive (TX/RX) integrated antennas in a standard BiCMOS 130nm technology for millimeter-scale millimeter-wave (mm-wave) applications, including high data rate radios and high resolution radars. The proposed TX/RX antenna module utilizes an integrated dipole antenna for the receiver and a slot antenna for the transmitter, placed orthogonally. The achieved gain and radiation efficiency are 5.7dBi and 41.3% for the slot antenna, respectively, and 6dBi and 39% for the dipole antenna. The link budget is improved by 16dB by optimization on the geometry as well as application of a high resistivity hemispheric silicon dielectric lens.**

Keywords*— 5G, antenna efficiency, dielectric lens, dipole, energy efficiency, high-speed communication, isolation, low-power, mm-wave, radar, receiver, silicon integrated circuits, slot, transmitter, wireless communication.

I. Introduction

The demand for high data rate wideband wireless links is higher than ever, especially with the definition of 5G communication with high data-rates (>1Gb/s), autonomous vehicles, and smart homes. However, the scalability of these systems is limited due to their large form factors, which is dominated by antennas. Thus, miniature antennas can improve system integration and scalability and pave the way for massive numbers of connected devices. Utilizing on-chip antennas can reduce the system form factor to millimeter scale, but there are a few challenges. A major impediment is maintaining the radiation efficiency, comparable to off-chip antennas. At low frequencies, the miniature size significantly reduces radiation efficiency, as low as 1% [1], [2] for mm-scale system on chips [3], due to the use of electrically-small antennas. Nevertheless, smaller wavelength at mm-wave frequency bands is a key enabler of efficient on-chip antennas for mm-scale, mm-wave wireless systems. Among the mm-wave frequency bands, the unlicensed 60GHz band has increasingly gained attraction due to its wide bandwidth, providing 7GHz in the spectrum, making it a great fit for high resolution radars and high data rate point-to-point wireless communications, which could be utilized in smart cities, surveillance, security, smart homes, autonomous vehicles, and wireless high definition video streaming.

Despite the miniature size of mm-wave on-chip antennas and their superior performance compared with sub-10GHz on-chip antennas, they suffer from low radiation efficiency and gain, limiting a wireless links' range. In this work, we have mitigated this problem and maintained the mm-scale form factor simultaneously by optimal design of the antennas at 60GHz and utilizing a high resistivity dielectric lens to minimize substrate losses.

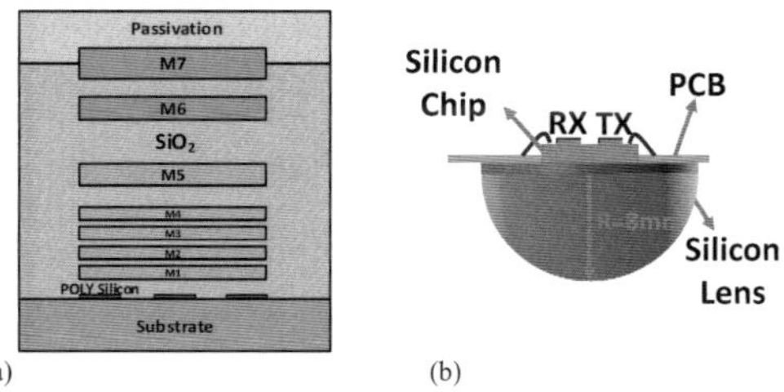

Fig. 1. (a) High resistivity silicon dielectric lens attached to chip backside (b) BiCMOS 130nm technology stack cross section.

II. High Efficiency Transceiver Antenna Design

According to state of the art, a typical on-chip antenna operating at 60GHz achieves only 10% efficiency and -4.4dBi gain [4], due to the low electric resistivity (~10Ω.cm) and high dielectric constant (ε_r=11.9) of the doped silicon substrate. In this work, we have designed a dipole and a slot antenna for a single chip transceiver. A dipole antenna has been used for the receiver because of its low input impedance at resonance frequency (~75 Ω) and differential feed, which is suitable for low-noise differential receivers with small input impedance. Similarly, slot antenna has been opted for the transmitter due to its compact size, compared to patch antennas, and single-ended feed, to be simply fed by a single-ended power amplifier stage. In Fig. 1 (a) the cross section view of the 130nm BiCMOS technology metal stack is shown. The slot antenna is designed

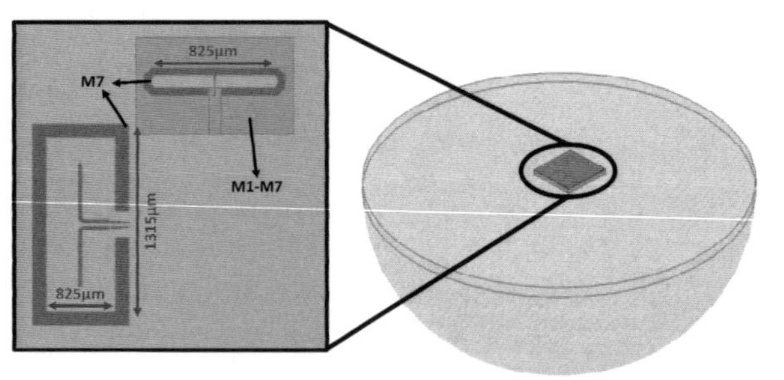

Fig. 2. HFSS geometry 3D model including the chip and silicon lens.

using M1-M7 and occupies 1030μm×630μm, including the surrounding ground plane. The RF feed is composed of M7, while M1-M7 are utilized and connected using arrays of metal vias in the optimally-sized ground plane to maximize radiation efficiency. The dipole antenna occupies 1315μm×624μm and only uses the top metal layer (M7). Furthermore, in order to suppress the undesirable coupling between TX and RX, the dipole antenna is shielded with a ground plane using the top metal layer. Dipole antenna is horizontally polarized, while slot antenna is vertically polarized. Thus, the TX and RX antennas should be placed orthogonally in order to maintain their polarization matching. Moreover, in order to suppress the lossy substrate modes, we have attached the silicon substrate to a high resistivity silicon dielectric lens, Fig. 1 (b). Finally, in order to maximize the gain of both antennas and the isolation between TX and RX antennas simultaneously, the position of TX and RX antennas on the chip has been optimized in HFSS. The overall 3D geometry, including the on-chip antennas and the silicon lens is shown in Fig. 2.

III. RESULTS AND DISCUSSIONS

ANSYS Electronics Desktop is used for the design and optimization of the antennas. Using the aforementioned dimensions, resonant frequency of the slot antenna is found to be 60GHz with approximately 6.75GHz bandwidth (11.25%). The proposed geometry provides 150Ω input impedance (at the resonant frequency), which can be matched to a power amplifier stage. Similarly, dipole antenna's resonant frequency is obtained to be 60GHz with 17 GHz bandwidth (28.33%) and an input impedance of 70Ω. Fig. 3 summarizes the simulated S-parameters for the TX/RX antennas. As can be observed, the proposed antenna geometry provides a minimum of 21dB isolation between TX and RX across the band.

Fig. 4 depicts the simulated radiation pattern and the gain of TX/RX antennas. The slot antenna offers 6dBi gain, while the dipole antenna's gain is around 5.7dBi. The radiation gain in each antenna has been improved more than 10dB compared to prior work in [4].

Based on simulation results, the slot antenna and dipole antenna provide 41.3% and 39% radiation efficiency, respectively, which is improved more than twice compared to previous on-chip antennas [4]. Additionally, the achieved gain is improved more than 1dB compared to those reported in [5] and [6], using a dielectric resonator antenna and off-chip antenna with plastic lens, respectively.

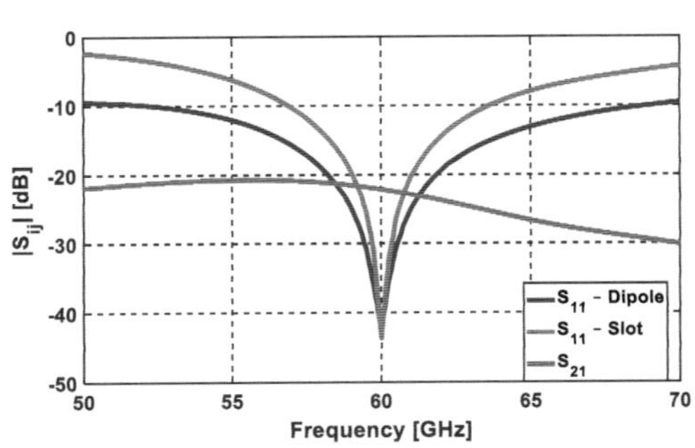

Fig. 3. Simulated S-Parameters of the antennas.

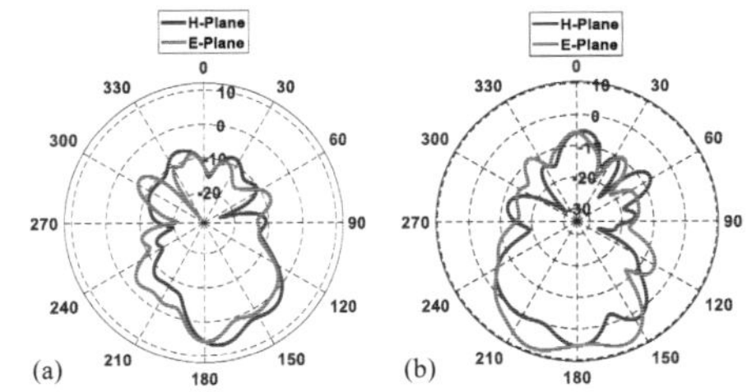

Fig. 4. Simulated radiation pattern (a) Dipole antenna (b) Slot antenna.

IV. CONCLUSION

A slot antenna and a dipole antenna, providing 11.7dB TX/RX gain, are designed in a standard 130nm SiGe process for fully integrated, mm-scale wireless systems. By design optimization and utilizing a high resistivity silicon lens, the gain is improved >8dB in each of the antennas, through suppressing the lossy modes in the low-resistivity doped silicon substrate. The designed antennas can be efficiently integrated with mm-wave wireless communication and sensing circuits and are suitable for low-power applications such as short-range IoT.

TABLE I. SUMMARY AND COMPARISON OF THE STATE-OF-THE-ART

	Frequency	*Type*	*Gain*	*Technology*
This Work	60GHz	lens coupled on-chip dipole	6dBi	130nm BiCMOS
[4]	60GHz	On-chip AMC based	-4.4dBi	0.18μm CMOS
[5]	60GHz	Dielectric resonator antenna	5dBi	65nm CMOS SOI
[6]	60GHz	Off-chip antenna with plastic lens	4dBi	HDI organic sub

ACKNOWLEDGMENT

This work is supported by US Department of Energy, Office of Energy Efficiency and Renewable Energy, under award number DE-EE0008225.

REFERENCES

[1] V. V. Kulkarni, M. Muqsith, K. Niitsu, H. Ishikuro and T. Kuroda, "A 750 Mb/s, 12 pJ/b, 6-to-10 GHz CMOS IR-UWB Transmitter With Embedded On-Chip Antenna," *IEEE Journal of Solid-State Circuits*, vol. 44, no. 2, pp. 394-403, Feb. 2009.

[2] A. Kosari, M. Moosavifar and D. D. Wentzloff, "A 152μW −99dBm BPSK/16-QAM OFDM Receiver for LPWAN Applications," *2018 IEEE Asian Solid-State Circuits Conference (A-SSCC)*, Tainan, 2018, pp. 303-306.

[3] R. Dreslinski et al., "Fully autonomous SoC synthesis using customizable cell-based synthesizable analog circuits," *press GOMACTech*, 2019, pp. 1111-1116.

[4] X. Bao, Y. Guo and Y. Xiong, "60-GHz AMC-Based Circularly Polarized On-Chip Antenna Using Standard 0.18-μm CMOS Technology," *IEEE Transactions on Antennas and Propagation*, vol. 60, no. 5, pp. 2234-2241, May 2012.

[5] J. P. Guzman *et al.*, "Silicon integrated dielectric resonator antenna solution for 60GHz front-end modules," *2012 IEEE 12th Topical Meeting on Silicon Monolithic Integrated Circuits in RF Systems*, Santa Clara, CA, 2012, pp. 53-56.

[6] A. Bisognin *et al.*, "3D printed plastic 60 GHz lens: Enabling innovative millimeter wave antenna solution and system," *2014 IEEE MTT-S International Microwave Symposium (IMS2014)*, Tampa, FL, 2014, pp. 1-4.

Investigation of Antennas for Car-to-Car Communications

Christian Winkler and Adalbert Beyer
Department of Electrical Engineering and Informatics
Duisburg-Essen University Campus Duisburg, Germany
a.beyer@ieee.org

Winfried Simon, Rüdiger Follmann, and Peter Waldow
IMST GmbH Kamp-Lintfort, Germany
simon@imst.de

Dominique Schreurs
Department of Electrical Engineering (ESAT)
KU Leuven, Leuven, Belgium
dominique.schreurs@kuleuven.be

***Abstract*—In this work the influence of a car shape on the radiation characteristics of a roof mounted antenna is examined. Simplified roof geometries are designed to study the radiation characteristics of dipoles and a monopole at different positions. It is shown that the electromagnetic waves are only slightly diffracted by the roof, and that there can be strong shading in the radiation direction. Simulations with a true-to-scale vehicle model were able to achieve comparable results and thus demonstrate the applicability of the proposed technique.**

Keywords—car-to-car communication, EM Simulation, roof antenna, shading.

I. Introduction

Car-to-Car Communication refers to the exchange of information between vehicles at a frequency of 5.9 GHz, as defined by IEEE standard 802.11p [1]. An important aspect is the antenna. Antennas can be so small that installation is possible on multiple points on the car. It has been shown that a roof antenna is in general the more robust position [2]. It turned out though that the performance strongly depends on the mounting and the car roof [3]. Furthermore, the presence of a glass roof influences the radiation characteristics [4]. Since a connection to other vehicles is to be established, an omnidirectional radiating antenna with a high antenna gain in the x, y plane is desirable (Fig. 1). As this fit with the radiation characteristics of dipole- and monopole antennas, the simulation results in Section III are based on these antennas. In this work, the car roof impact on the radiation characteristics is examined in detail using FDTD (Finite Difference Time Domain) method.

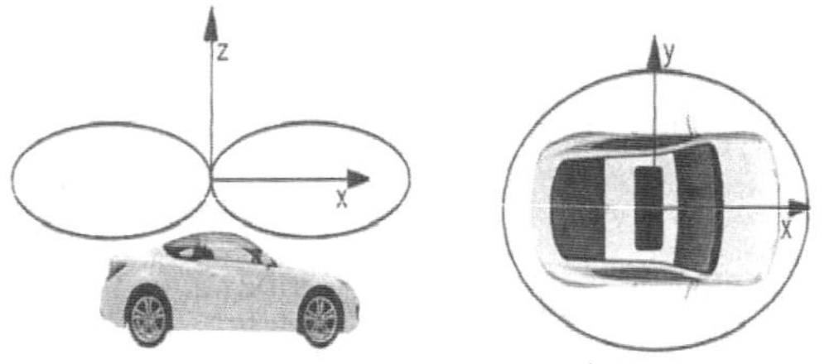

Fig. 1. Definition of the coordinate system and ideal radiation characteristics.

II. Simulation of the Radiation Characteristics

To carry out the numerical investigations, the FDTD based EMPIRE XPU™ simulation program [5] is selected. The complete car has to be included in the simulation domain to achieve most accurate results for the radiation pattern. A smaller simulation area is used for the first investigations while the verification is done with a complete car model. The correct selection of the simulation mesh is important. The smallest wavelength should be reproduced properly by the mesh while a too fine mesh leads to extremely long simulation time and huge memory usage. Nearby the antenna, 0.5 mm mesh steps are used, whereas other areas can be resolved with a coarser mesh. An energy decay of 40 dB is set as termination condition for the time domain simulations.

The system is excited with a Gaussian pulse. Proper care is taken to select the pulse duration n_{Puls} and number of time steps N [5]:

$$N = 2\left(\frac{t}{t_1} + n_{Puls}\right) \tag{1}$$

with t_1 the duration of the time step, which is 321.071 fs here.

III. Results and Discussion

In this section, simulation results for various configurations are shown and discussed. All far-field diagrams (Section III) are normalized to the gain.

A. Influence of Roof Curvature and Antenna Position

The roof structure varies greatly depending on model and manufacturer. For limousines and small cars, the curvature is in general evenly distributed over the surface, with a typical value of 10°. Within EMPIRE XPU™ an area is generated that has a diffraction of approx. 10° in the x-direction. Fig. 2 compares a $\lambda/4$ monopole positioned in the center of the curved surface with one near the edge (-x direction). To be noticed is shadowing in the x-direction of up to 10 dB. The solid line, drawn at an angle of 1.12° represents the angle which the antenna tip sees the vertex of the curved surface. Radiation below this line (1.12°) is due to diffraction effects. Also noticeable is the less distinct minimum in the z-direction, caused by edge proximity.

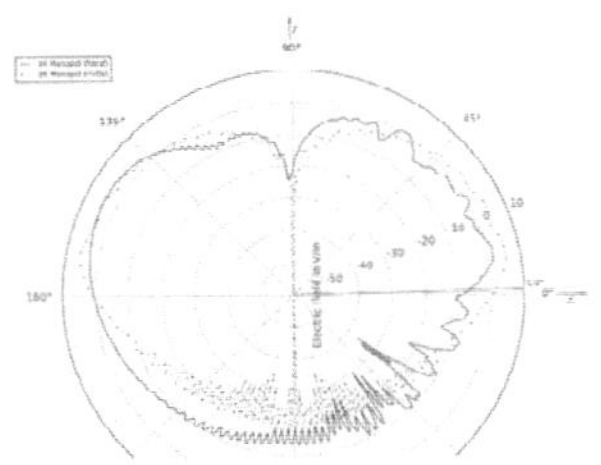

Fig. 2. Radiation pattern of $\lambda/4$ monopole on curved surface. (Solid line: near edge; dashed line: center)

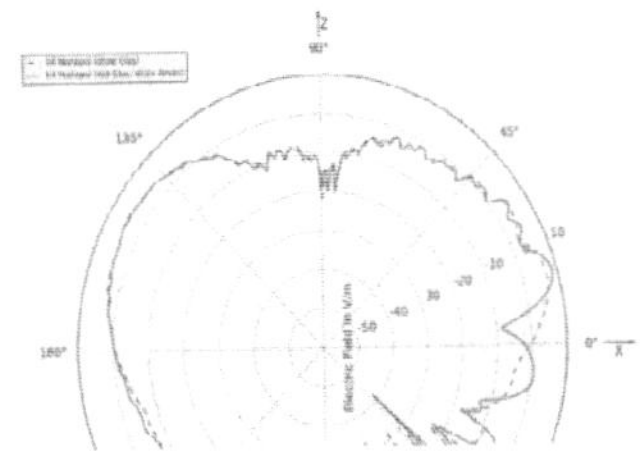

Fig. 3. Radiating pattern: Comparison with glass (solid line) and without glass (dashed line).

B. Influence of a Glass Sunroof

Next, a piece of the roof in the front part was replaced by glass. The simulations were performed with a straight roof structure, since the shading effect dominates as soon as the glass surface is out of the antenna's line of sight. The thickness of the glass is 6 mm. Fig. 3 clearly shows how part of the radiation is coupled into the glass layer and exits again at the lower end. This causes an attenuation of about 10 dB at an angle of 4° and a local maximum at an angle of about -5°, compared to a roof without glass. To determine the influence of glass thickness, different glass thicknesses are simulated. The results show that thinner glass with a thickness of 2 mm ($<\lambda/16$) hardly affects the radiation pattern, whereas a thickness of 12 mm (about $\lambda/4$) results in significant coupling of electromagnetic (EM) waves.

C. Influence of a Coated Glass Sunroof

An approach to reduce the penetration into the glass roof, is coating the glass sheet with a thin, electrically conductive sheet. The mechanism that plays a role is the so-called skin effect.

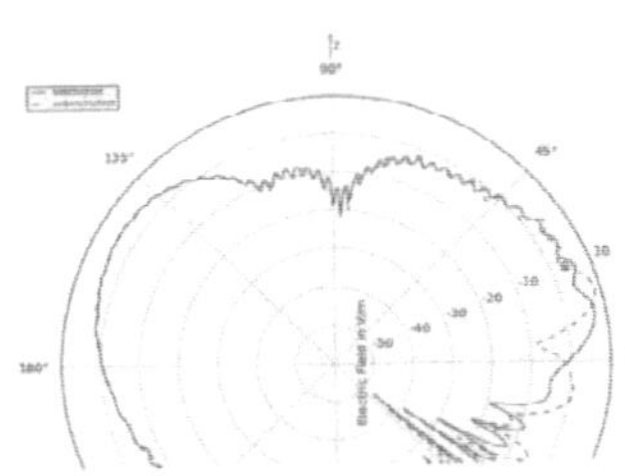

Fig. 4. Comparison of glass plane coated (solid)/uncoated (dashed).

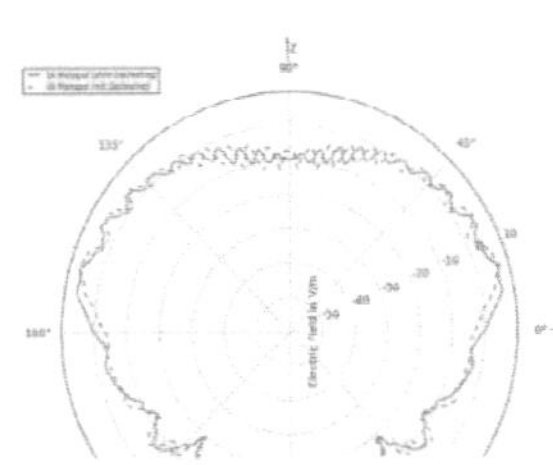

Fig. 5. Radiating pattern: Influence of a roof support

If an EM wave strikes the surface of an electrically conductive layer, it is damped in the interior of the layer according to an e-function. With Cu material parameters, one obtains a penetration depth of 0.86 µm at 5.9 GHz. In Fig. 4 one can see that the radiation in the x-direction is improved compared to an uncoated glass panel. There is no coupling of EM waves into the glass layer.

D. Influence of Roof Mounts on the Radiation Characteristics

Another factor is the side-mounted roof supports. Fig. 5 shows the radiation pattern for a $\lambda/4$ monopole for lateral radiation in the y-direction. The damping is 4 dB compared to no roof mounts. Radiation below the angle of 1° is due to diffraction effects. The x-direction radiation remains unchanged.

G. Field Simulation with a True-to-Scale Vehicle Model

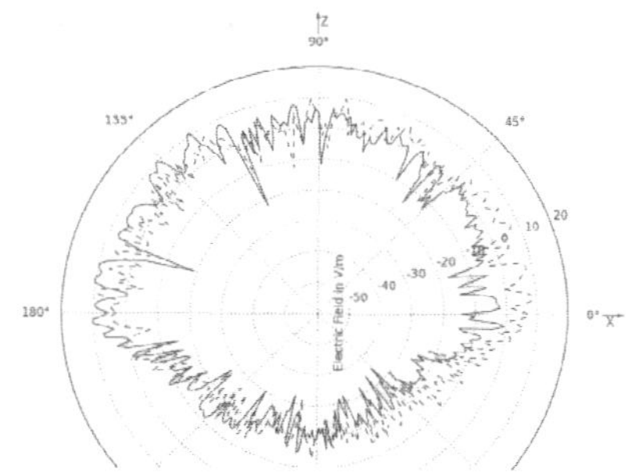

Fig. 6. Radiating pattern: Audi A6 (solid line: monopole on roof edge, dashed line: dipole on back mirror).

Finally, a true-to-scale vehicle model (Audi A6) is studied. Compared to sub-section *A*, the roof differs, it is about half the length in the x-direction and has a larger curvature. Due to the larger structure, also the computational effort increases. The antenna is located further below the vertex than before, causing the shadow region to begin at an angle of about 9° (see Fig. 6).

Fig. 7. E-Field distribution Audi A6 (roof antenna).

Fig. 7 shows the electric field distribution. Blue/red regions are weak/high field strength, resp. It can be clearly seen that EM waves are shadowed to the front of the vehicle by the roof curve. A certain amount of energy is coupled through the windows to the inside of the car. Investigating the EM exposure of a person sitting inside may be an interesting future work.

IV. CONCLUSION

This work shows the influence of the roof curvature and glass roof on the radiation pattern of a car-to-car communication antenna. The 3D EM simulator EMPIRE XPU™ was used to simulate a reduced model as well as a full-scale car model. A shadowing effect towards the front of the car is clearly visible.

REFERENCES

[1] D. Jiang and L. Delgrossi, IEEE 802.11p: Towards an International Standard for Wireless Access in Vehicular Environments/Mercedes-Benz R & D North America Inc. - Research Paper - 2008.

[2] L. Reichardt, T. Fuegen, and T. Zwick, "Influence of Antennas Placement on Car-to-Car Communications Channel," Institute for M. T. and E., University of Karlsruhe - Research Paper - 2012.

[3] O. Klemp, "Performance Considerations for Automotive Antenna Equipment in Vehicle-to-Vehicle Communications," Institute for M. T. and R. S., Leibnitz University Hannover, - Research Paper -, 2010.

[4] M. M. Weiner, Monopol Antennas. 1. CRC Press, 2003.

[5] IMST GmbH, "User and Reference Manual for the 3D EM Time Domain Simulator Empire-XPU" - http://www.empire.de/empire.pdf

Simulation of Creeping Wave Propagation in Electrically Large Curved Surface Using HFSS

Shahid Ahmed

ANSYS EBU, San Jose, California, USA, email: shahid.ahmed@ansys.com

Abstract—**A creeping wave propagating through a curved convex surface may contribute to electromagnetic scattering, which could be critical for potential applications such as RCS prediction and autonomous vehicles where many antennas are mounted. ANSYS HFSS provides a robust and reliable computer simulation for addressing such an important issue. The comprehensive solver utilizes the shooting and bouncing ray (SBR) plus creeping wave (CW) approach, which ideally suited for the faster solution of electrically large electromagnetic problems. Moreover, it facilitates the multi-variable parametric optimization – desirable to achieve the mission objective.**

Keywords—creeping wave, shooting and bouncing ray method

I. Introduction

Creeping wave (CW) plays an important role in the analysis of electromagnetic scattering from electrically large structures with closed curved surfaces [1]. An accurate prediction of the creeping wave may be crucial in designing potential systems such as stealth missiles and antennas mounted on vehicles, and aircraft. With the increased complexity due to wide selections of materials, different shapes and sizes – accurate and robust computer simulations become the pathway to the mission success. ANSYS HFSS provides a unique solver - shooting and bouncing ray (SBR) method combined with the creeping wave for solving such large structures accurately.

In this paper, a comprehensive simulation showing the effect of a creeping wave due to a sphere mounted with a monopole antenna has been illustrated. The sphere is made of PEC, however, the more complex scenario such as dielectric coating, frequency-dependent material coating, and different structures will be presented in the symposium. The distinctive feature of CW addition in the SBR solver (SBR+CW) has been compared and discussed in the paper. It is important to note that the SBR method is computationally suitable for the electrically large systems; the highly accurate and predictable solution can be achieved in a much faster time scale using the SBR+CW solver of HFSS.

II. Model Description

For illustration, the computational model used in the simulation consists of a monopole antenna mounted on a solid sphere (radius r=5m) made of a PEC – illustrated in Fig. 1. In this illustration, the monopole antenna has been excited at the frequency f=130 MHz. A comparison of the two methods: SBR and SBR+CW are illustrated in Fig. 2. Clearly, the SBR+CW method shows a distinctive feature in the vicinity of the shadow region around θ=±180, which, cannot be otherwise captured by the SBR method. The significance of CW will be discussed with examples at the conference. The traces of CW emanating from the dipole antenna and recirculating around the curved surfaces of the sphere are depicted in Fig. 3. A detailed study of these traces due to the creeping wave for different material layers coated onto the different region of the sphere will be presented.

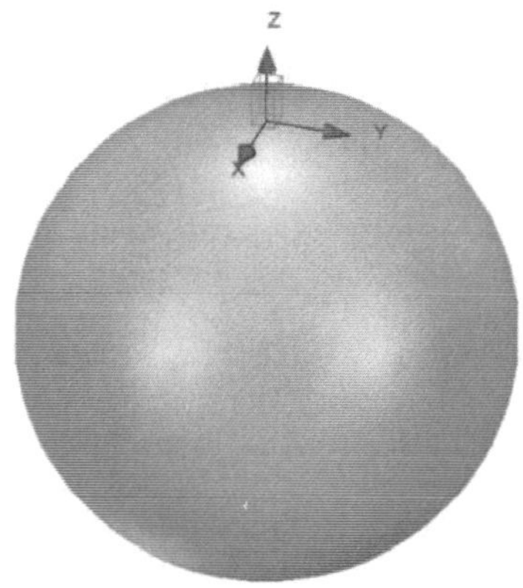

Fig. 1. Model configuration comprised of a monopole antenna (f=130 MHz) mounted on the top of a perfectly conducting sphere (r=5 m).

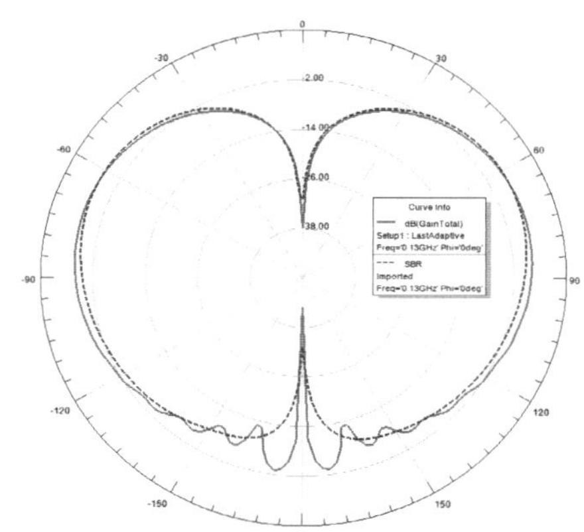

Fig. 2. A comparison of total gain (dB) for φ=0, -180≤θ≤180 obtained by the SBR (blue dashed line) and the SBR+CW (red solid line) methods. The significance of creeping wave (CW) is distinctive in the vicinity of θ=±180, which is expected due to the shadow region.

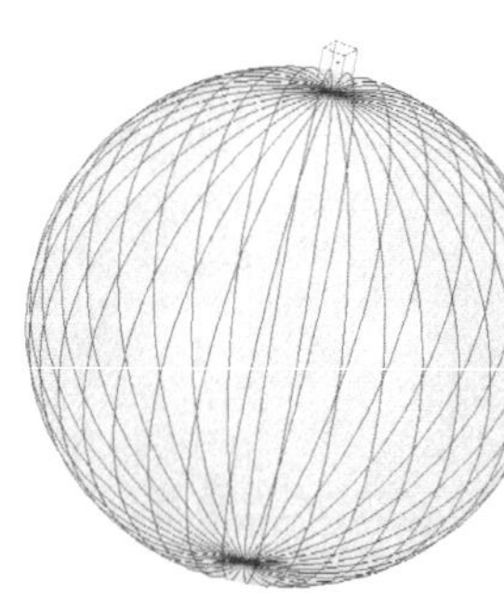

Fig. 3. Ray tracing view of creeping wave generated from the antenna current excitation at f = 130 MHz. As shown, the creeping wave traverses around the surface.

III. RESULTS AND CONCLUSIONS

In this paper, the novelty of the creeping wave has been demonstrated. For potential applications as discussed in the introduction of this paper, it is significantly important to understand the contributions of the creeping wave. HFSS simulations provide unique capabilities in terms of optimization by changing the frequency range, material properties, shapes, and sizes, etc. Also, the in-built HPC capabilities make such studies practical. The details of the parameter space will be discussed.

ACKNOWLEDGMENT

The author would like to thank the development team of ANSYS, Inc. for their efforts in enhancing the capabilities of HFSS.

REFERENCES

[1] P. H. Pathak, W. D. Burnside and R. J. Marhefka, "A uniform GTD analysis of the diffraction of electromagnetic waves by a smooth convex surface," in IEEE Trans. on Antennas Propag., vol. 28, no. 5, pp. 631-642, Sep. 1980.

Shooting-Bouncing-Rays Technique to Model Mine Tunnels: Algorithm Acceleration

Stephen Kasdorf, Blake Troksa, Jake Harmon, Cam Key, and Branislav M. Notaroš
Colorado State University, Electrical & Computer Engineering Department, Fort Collins, CO
skasdorf@rams.colostate.edu, blake.troksa@gmail.com, J.Harmon@colostate.edu, camkey@rams.colostate.edu, notaros@colostate.edu

***Abstract*—We present and discuss acceleration of a shooting and bouncing rays (SBR) algorithm for ray-tracing electromagnetic analysis of electrically very large structures such as underground mine tunnels at modern wireless communication frequencies. The acceleration is based on the parallelization of the SBR technique on NVIDIA GPUs using the OptiX application programming interface. The results show dramatic speedups of the parallel SBR algorithm compared with serial implementation.**

Keywords—wireless communications, computational electromagnetics, high-frequency techniques, ray tracing, high performance computing, parallelization, graphics processing units, GPU acceleration, signal propagation, waveguides.

I. Introduction

In the field of computational electromagnetics (CEM), the necessity of acceleration of simulation techniques is becoming more and more apparent. At high frequencies especially, acceleration of CEM algorithms becomes vital for practicality of CEM solutions. Ray tracing (RT) [1]–[4] is an asymptotic high-frequency CEM methodology that demonstrates significant potential to efficiently characterize extremely large structures with computation times that are orders of magnitude shorter when compared to traditional full-wave CEM techniques, such as the finite element method and method of moments. When coupled with high-performance computing (HPC) strategies such as general-purpose computing on graphics processing units (GPGPU), simulations which would otherwise requires days or weeks can be condensed into minutes or hours. Moreover, with proper memory allocation and management, even low-end computing hardware can be leveraged for extremely rapid electromagnetic simulations and post-processing.

This paper presents and discusses acceleration of a CEM algorithm based on shooting and bouncing rays (SBR) method for RT analysis of electrically very large structures such as underground mine tunnels at modern wireless communication frequencies. It highlights the parallelization of the SBR technique on NVIDIA GPUs using the OptiX application programming interface.

II. Acceleration of SBR Ray-Tracing Algorithm for CEM Modeling

The SBR ray-tracing algorithm [3], [4] involves spawning, and propagating millions of rays. These rays are traced geometrically through the environment, and the electric field is tracked as this propagation occurs. The memory and time requirements of tracking the information of each ray can be substantial on a CPU when implemented in series. The field contribution from each ray is linear, and thus ray tracing algorithms are perfect candidates for parallel computations on a GPU. Geometric ray propagation calculations are independent from one another. This means that rays can be traced through the environment in parallel without the need for synchronization. Additionally, the electric field at observation points is linear, meaning that the electric field calculations can be carried out independently per ray.

We perform parallelization and acceleration of our SBR RT algorithm using the compute unified device architecture (CUDA) parallel computing platform as the primary language for parallel programming on NVIDIA GPUs. The GPUs are used as a tool to parallelize the core ray-tracing algorithm and also to provide access to the NVIDIA OptiX ray-tracing application programming interface (API) [5]. The OptiX API efficiently traces rays within complex structures. Using OptiX, we are able to generate information about the closest hit point of a ray with the geometric environment and use this information to reflect rays and adjust their power according to Fresnel's coefficients. The combination of OptiX and CUDA enables quick and efficient simulations to optimize the placement of communication nodes within the structures under consideration.

The memory requirements of the ray tracing can still be cumbersome due to the large number of rays and information associated with the simulation. The problem is alleviated by breaking up the ray spawning into batches. Rays are launched by inscribing an icosahedron into a unit sphere. The faces of the icosahedron are subdivided according to the nth triangular number so that the desired number of rays is achieved. The nth triangular subdivision of a face of the icosahedron is shown in Figure 1.

This helps to ensure an even distribution of rays used to cover the radiation pattern. The icosahedron also proves useful for batching. The subdivided rays on each face of the icosahedron make up each batch of the algorithm. Again the geometric and electric field ray contributions are independent, so splitting the algorithm into batches is not problematic. The algorithm is performed on each batch individually, and the electric field contribution of this batch at the observation

This work was supported by the National Science Foundation under grant ECCS-1646562.

points is recorded. Once the batch has finished, the memory from these rays can be cleared before moving to the next. This alleviates the memory bottleneck associated with launching millions of rays simultaneously. If enough rays are launched such that these batches also experience bottlenecks, they can be subdivided into sub-batches and the memory bottleneck is again alleviated. This process can be used to launch and trace extremely large numbers of rays quickly and efficiently.

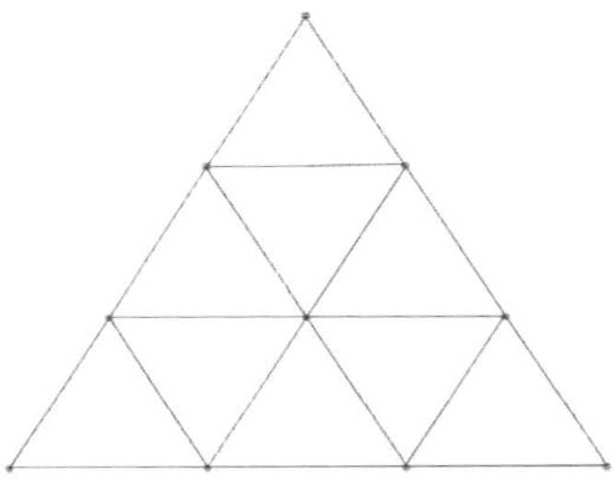

Fig. 1. Subdivision of the icosahedron face into the *n*th triangular number ($n = 4$). The face is used as a batch of rays, where $N = n(n+1)/2$.

This helps to ensure an even distribution of rays used to cover the radiation pattern. The icosahedron also proves useful for batching. The subdivided rays on each face of the icosahedron make up each batch of the algorithm. Again the geometric and electric field ray contributions are independent, so splitting the algorithm into batches is not problematic. The algorithm is performed on each batch individually, and the electric field contribution of this batch at the observation points is recorded. Once the batch has finished, the memory from these rays can be cleared before moving to the next. This alleviates the memory bottleneck associated with launching millions of rays simultaneously. If enough rays are launched such that these batches also experience bottlenecks, they can be subdivided into sub-batches and the memory bottleneck is again alleviated. This process can be used to launch and trace extremely large numbers of rays quickly and efficiently.

III. Results and Discussion

The acceleration of this method is tested by comparing run time of the accelerated parallel algorithm against a serial CPU implementation. The algorithm steps remain the same, so the comparison gives a true comparison of the speedup. Table 1 shows the results of this comparison. The results are generated from a tunnel environment detailed in [6].

When launching 10,000 rays we see a speedup of 12.36, which is not as substantial. Due to the fairly significant fixed cost associated with GPU usage, the performance of the parallelized code scales rapidly with increasing number of rays relative to the serial realization of the code. With a high ray count, we expect to see extremely high speedup because the algorithm can fully take advantage of the threads in the GPU. Indeed, at one million rays and 100 million rays, respectively, we see a speedup of over 130 times.

Table 1: Speedup of the parallel SBR algorithm compared with serial implementation for a RT simulation of a tunnel environment.

Number of rays	Number of reflections	Sequential code	Parallelized code	Speedup
10,000	20	4.251 s	0.344 s	12.36 ×
1,000,000	80	24 m 40.096 s	11.125 s	133.04 ×
100,000,000	40	21 h 14 m 17 s	9 m 46 s	130.47 ×

IV. Conclusions

This paper has presented acceleration of an SBR RT algorithm for CEM analysis based on the parallelization of the SBR technique on NVIDIA GPUs using the OptiX application programming interface. Accurate simulations in electrically large and complex geometric environments, such as underground mine tunnels and galleries in wireless communication applications, will certainly necessitate the use of extremely large numbers of rays to adequately sample the environment. Based on the results presented in this paper, the presented algorithm proves to be very beneficial for these types of simulations.

References

[1] M. F. Cátedra and J. Perez, Cell Planning for Wireless Communications. Norwood, MA, USA: Artech House, 1999.

[2] Z. Yun, M. F. Iskander and Z. Zhang, "Development of a new shooting-and-bouncing ray (SBR) tracing method that avoids ray double counting," *IEEE Antennas and Propagation Society International Symposium. 2001 Digest.* Boston, MA, USA, 2001, pp. 464-467.

[3] B. Troksa, C. Key, F. Kunkel, S. V. Savic, M. M. Ilic, and B. M. Notaros, "Ray Tracing Using Shooting-Bouncing Technique to Model Mine Tunnels: Theory and Verification for a PEC Waveguide," *Proceedings of the 2018 International Applied Computational Electromagnetics Society (ACES) Symposium – ACES2018*, March 25–29, 2018, Denver, Colorado, USA.

[4] C. Key, B. Troksa, F. Kunkel, S. V. Savić, M. M. Ilic and B. M. Notaroš, "Comparison of Three Sampling Methods for Shooting-Bouncing Ray Tracing Using a simple Waveguide Model," *2018 IEEE International Symposium on Antennas and Propagation & USNC/URSI National Radio Science Meeting*, Boston, MA, 2018, pp. 2273-2274.

[5] S. G. Parker, J. Bigler, A. Dietrich, H. Friedrich, J. Hoberock, D. Luebke, D. McAllister, M. McGuire, K. Morley, A. Robison, and M. Stich, "OptiX: a general purpose ray tracing engine," *ACM Trans. Graph.*, Vol. 29, No. 4, Article 66, July 2010.

[6] D. Didascalou, "Ray Optical Wave Propagation Modelling in Arbitrarily Shaped Tunnels", *Forschungsberichte aus dem Institut für Höchstfrequenztechnik und Elektronik der Universität Karlsruhe*, Vol. 24, Institut für Höchstfrequenztechnik und Elektronik, Universität Karlsruhe, 2000.

High Performance Computing in Parallel Electromagnetics Simulation Code suite ACE3P

Lixin Ge
SLAC National Accelerator Laboratory
Menlo Park, CA 94025 USA
lge@slac.stanford.edu

Zenghai Li
SLAC National Accelerator Laboratory
Menlo Park, CA 94025 USA
lizh@slac.stanford.edu

Cho-Kuen Ng
SLAC National Accelerator Laboratory
Menlo Park, CA 94025 USA
cho@slac.stanford.edu

Liling Xiao
SLAC National Accelerator Laboratory
Menlo Park, CA 94025 USA
liling@slac.stanford.edu

***Abstract*— A comprehensive set of parallel finite-element codes suite ACE3P (Advanced Computational Electromagnetics 3D Parallel) is developed by SLAC for multi-physics modeling of particle accelerators running on massively parallel computer platforms for high fidelity and high accuracy simulation. ACE3P enables rapid virtual prototyping of accelerator and RF component design, optimization and analysis. Advanced modeling capabilities have been facilitated by implementations of novel algorithms for numerical solvers. Code performance on state-of-the-art high performance computing (HPC) platforms for large-scale RF modeling in accelerator applications will be presented in this paper. All the simulations have been performed on the supercomputers at National Energy Research Computer Center (NERSC).**

Keywords— Finite element method, high performance parallel computing, hybrid MPI+OpenMP, multi-physics modeling, particle accelerator

I. Introduction

High energy accelerators are complex multi-million dollar scientific instruments. Successful design and operation of an accelerator has to satisfy RF, thermal, mechanical and beam requirements. Through the support of Department of Energy (DOE), SLAC has developed a comprehensive set of conformal, higher-order, parallel finite element electromagnetics modelling code suite ACE3P (Advanced Computational Electromagnetics 3D Parallel) for accelerator cavity and structure design including integrated multi-physics effects in electromagnetic, thermal, and mechanical characteristics with two unique features: (1) Based on higher order curved finite elements for high-fidelity modelling and improved solution accuracy; (2). Implemented on massively parallel computers for increased memory and speed. The codes are capable of using massively parallel supercomputers for modelling large accelerator structures with higher accuracy and speed.

II. ACE3P Modules

The electromagnetics codes in ACE3P solves Maxwell equations in the frequency and time domains using unstructured grids with elements represented by Nedelec basis functions. Together with the conventional nodal finite element methods used in solving thermal and mechanical equations, ACE3P has six multi-physics parallel simulation modules to address different physics aspects of accelerator applications [1-7], and the modules are (1) Omega3P, an electromagnetic eigensolver for finding resonator modes and their damping in RF cavities; (2) S3P, a frequency-domain solver for calculating scattering parameters of RF components; (3) TEM3P, a multi-physics code in frequency domain for calculating integrated electromagnetic, thermal and mechanical effects; (4) Track3P, a particle tracking code for calculating dark current and multipacting in the presence of external fields; (5) T3P, a time-domain solver for calculating transient responses of driven systems and for wakefields due to charged particle beams; and (6) Pic3P, a particle-in-cell code for self-consistent simulation of particle and RF field interactions in space-charge dominated devices.

In a typical accelerator cavity simulation, the electromagnetic modules discretize the vacuum region inside the accelerator cavity, while the thermal and mechanical solvers are formulated in the frequency domain for the computational volume of the cavity walls and their surroundings. Relevant physical data are transferred at the interface of the two computational domains for integrated multi-physics simulation.

Several direct and iterative linear solvers have been implemented in ACE3P for the solution of a linear system of equations arising from the finite element formulations [5]. The eigensolver Omega3P can solve linear and quadratic eigenproblems for cavities with and without energy loss. Recently, in collaboration with applied mathematicians, a nonlinear eigensolver based on the CORK algorithm has been added to determine resonant mode external quality factor for cavities equipped with external waveguides [6].

III. Parallelization Strategy and Software Design

ACE3P code suite is written in C++ and uses MPI for inter process communication. It takes a tetrahedral mesh in NetCDF format as input for the geometry of a cavity. The parallelization in ACE3P with the exception of Track3P is done using domain decomposition, where the mesh is partitioned into P subdomains

Work supported by the Department of Energy under Contract No. DE-AC02-76SF00515.

using ParMetis and Zoltan, where P is the number of the MPI tasks. The mesh region at each subdomain boundary is replicated for data communication with adjacent subdomains. The hierarchical basis functions are employed for representing the electric field. The edge, face and volume degrees of freedom are located and the matrices assembled in parallel for each subdomain. Due to the nature of the resulting linear system, direct solvers are used in the frequency domain for fast solution convergence, and iterative solvers in the time domain for its parallel scalability for large-scale problems.

The particle tracking module Track3P is essentially embarrassingly parallel. Each compute node owns the whole finite element mesh and the associated external fields while particles are uniformly distributed among the compute cores, and thus no communication between the cores is required. High computational efficiency is achieved if the mesh and fields can fit into the shared memory of each processor. For large problems, the total size of the mesh and fields exceeds the shared memory of each processor, and therefore some processors are left idle by reducing the number of MPI tasks within a compute node. To improve the computational performance on state-of-the-art computing facilities with multi cores at NERSC, a hybrid MPI+OpenMP parallel programing model has been implemented for the particle tracking algorithms in Track3P.

IV. HPC Performance Study

The use of HPC enables the solution of large-scale problem at the system level which is not readily achieved on desktop computers. The strong scalability of Omega3P solver running on supercomputers has been presented in [5]. Fig. 1 shows an Omega3P calculation using the nonlinear eigensolver to calculate the damping factors of resonant modes in a structure coupled with waveguides with different mode cutoff frequencies. Using second order basis functions, we obtained a discretized problem with 20 million degrees of freedom (DOFs). The computation was completed within 10 wall clock minutes on the NERSC Edison computer employing 960 processors for 16 trapped modes. Fig. 2 shows a TEM3P calculation for the lowest longitudinal mechanical modes profiles in PIP-II 650 MHz cryomodule (CM) consisting of six superconducting RF (SRF) cavities. The problem was solved using 10 nodes, 320 processors on Cori at NERSC and took less than 1 minute per mode calculation. For SRF cavity thermal simulations, thermal conductivity, surface resistance, and Kapitza conductance are temperature dependent. Due to the strong nonlinearity, care must be taken in the solution of nonlinear thermal equation. TEM3P uses Newton method for solving the nonlinear thermal equation, which needs robust implementation for strongly nonlinear problems. We use an inexact Newton method for solving the nonlinear equations, each of which requires the solution of a system of linear equations. The resulting linear equations are solved using the iterative preconditioned Krylov space methods, such as GMRES

Fig. 1. Electric field amplitude profile for the highest external Q mode in the 3rd dipole passband in an ideal LCLS-II cryomodule.

Hybrid MPI+OpenMP programing performance study has been carried out on the NERSC Edison supercomputer for a Track3P simulation on dark current simulation in a chain of 8 LCLS-II SRF cavities. 4 times speedup has been achieved for one tracking cycle compared with pure MPI implementation.

Fig. 3 shows the strong scalability of T3P running on the NERSC Cori. The test problem was solving electromagnetic wave propagation in human body. The computer model has 2.5M tetrahedral elements. As a comparison, the perfect linear scalability is also plotted as the black line. It is evident that T3P scales very well for this problem up to 10k processors. In the case using 4096 processors, each processor on average has less than 650 tetrahedral elements.

Fig. 2. The longitudinal cavity mechanical mode displacement profile at longitudinal plane in PIP-II 650 MHz SRF CM.

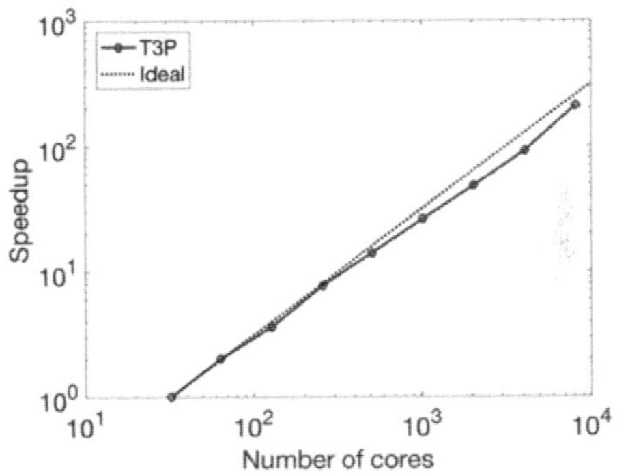

Fig. 3. Strong parallel scaling of T3P on NERSC Cori.

Acknowledgments

This research used resources of the National Energy Research Scientific Computing Center (NERSC), which is supported by the Office of Science of the U.S. Department of Energy (DOE) under Contract No. DE-AC0205CH11231.

References

[1] https://confluence.slac.stanford.edu/display/AdvComp/Materials+for+CW18

[2] K. Ko, A. Candel, L. Ge, A. Kabel, L-Q. Lee, Z. Li, C. Ng, V. Rawat, G. Schussman, and L. Xiao, "Advances in Parallel Electromagnetic Codes for Accelerator Science and Development," LINAC2010, Tsukuba, Japan, 2010.

[3] L. Ge, K. Ko, O. Kononenko, Z. Li, C.-K. Ng, L Xiao, and J. Qiang, "Advances in Parallel Finite Element Code Suite ACE3P," Proc. of 6th International Particle Accelerator Conference, Richmond, VA, USA May 3-8, 2015.

[4] Z. Li, L. Ge, C.-K. Ng, L. Xiao, "Recent Developments and Applications of Parallel Multi-Physics Accelerator Modeling Suite ACE3P", Proc. NAPAC2019, September 1-6 2019, Lansing, MI.

[5] L.-Q. Lee, Z. Li, C-K. Ng, and K. Ko, "Omega3P: A Parallel Finite-Element Eigenmode Analysis Code for Accelerator Cavities", SLAC-PUB-13529.

[6] R. Beeumen, et al., "Computing Resonant Modes of Accelerator Cavities by Solving Nonlinear Eigenvalue Problems via Rational Approximation", J. Comput. Phys. 374 (2018) 1031-1043.

[7] Liling Xiao , Lixin Ge, Zenghai Li, and Cho-Kuen Ng, "Advances in Multiphysics Modeling for Parallel Finite-Element Code Suite ACE3P", IEEE Journal on Multiscale and Multiphysics Computational Techniques. 21 November 2019

Magnetic Resonance Imaging using Optimized 2D Non-Uniform FFTs

A. Capozzoli, C. Curcio and A. Liseno
Dipartimento di Ingegneria Elettrica e delle Tecnologie dell'Informazione
Università di Napoli Federico II
via Claudio 21, I 80125 Napoli (Italy)
a.capozzoli@unina.it

***Abstract*—We propose optimized 2D Non-Uniform FFT (NUFFT) algorithms and apply them to Magnetic Resonance Imaging under radial acquisitions.**

***Index Terms*—Filtered Backprojection, MRI, NUFFT.**

I. Introduction

In MRI, much effort has been devoted to acquisition methods using non-Cartesian grids [1], such as radial [2] and spiral [3] scannings, to achieve fast data acquisition. Spiral scans are motivated by the simpler generation of field gradients which do not require high-speed, abrupt changes [3] as compared to the Cartesian one. Radial scans are also less prone to residual motion and changes of the imaging plane during interactive scanning making them attractive tools for image-guided interventions [4].

However, the use of standard FFTs to process non-Cartesian data breaks down under radial or spiral scans so that MRI imaging under alternative collection procedures requires more involved data processing to properly balance accuracy and computational burden. Fortunately, Non-Uniform FFT (NUFFT) provide a convenient trade-off between accuracy and complexity [1], [5]–[8].

Recently, an optimized approach, based on a general and new perspective, has been presented in [8] for all the three types of NUFFTs. The choice of the window function has been optimized to obtain more accurate results than those available in the literature. The computational costs and the memory requirements of the proposed schemes have been theoretically analyzed and their very convenient performance assessed, theoretically and numerically, by comparisons with a number of relevant and popular approaches. The proposed method has proved to be more accurate than the confronted schemes without burdening the computational and memory requirements. However, the approach has been limited to 1D. The purpose of this paper is twofold: 1) extend the approach presented in [8] to 2D; 2) apply the "optimized" 2D NUFFT to non-Cartesian k-space acquisitions; in particular, radial MRI processing is considered.

II. NUFFT-based MRI Reconstruction

The signal r acquired by the coils of an MRI system is related to the spin density ρ by the following relation

$$r(k_x(t), k_y(t)) = \iint_O S(x,y)\rho(x,y)e^{-j2\pi[k_x(t)x+k_y(t)y]}dO, \tag{1}$$

where S is the receiving coil sensitivity map, $\underline{k}(t) = (k_x(t), k_y(t))$ denotes the k-space trajectory and O is the Region of Interest (ROI), having considered, for the sake of simplicity, a 2D case.

Using a pixel-based approximation for ρ and sampling the signal r at the time instants t_n, eq. (1) is regarded as a system of linear equations:

$$\underline{\underline{A}}\,\underline{\rho} = \underline{r}, \tag{2}$$

where $\underline{r}$ is the data vector whose generic element is $r_n = r(k_x(t_n), k_y(t_n))$, $\underline{\rho}$ is the unknowns vector containing the pixel values $\rho_s = \rho(x_s, y_s)$, with (x_s, y_s) the pixel centers. We assume that the pixel centers (x_s, y_s) are arranged on a Cartesian grid, namely, $(x_s, y_s) = (x_p, y_q)$, with $s = s(p,q)$.

The generic element A_{ns} of $\underline{\underline{A}}$ is provided by:

$$A_{ns} = S(x_s, y_s)e^{-j2\pi[k_x(t_n)x_s+k_y(t_n)y_s]}\Delta x\Delta y, \tag{3}$$

with $\Delta x \Delta y$ the pixel size.

A pseudosolution to the system (2) is typically searched for by solving the associated Euler equation:

$$\underline{\underline{A}}^\dagger\,\underline{\underline{A}}\,\underline{\rho} = \underline{b}, \tag{4}$$

where $\underline{b} = \underline{\underline{A}}^\dagger\,\underline{r}$ and $\underline{\underline{A}}^\dagger$ is the adjoint matrix of $\underline{\underline{A}}$ whose generic element is:

$$A^\dagger_{s\,n} = S^*(x_s, y_s)e^{j2\pi[k_x(t_n)x_s+k_y(t_n)y_s]}\Delta x\Delta y, \tag{5}$$

where * denotes complex conjugation. Eq. (4) is then solved by using iterative techniques minimizing the following error functional:

$$\Phi(\underline{\rho}) = ||\underline{\underline{A}}^\dagger\,\underline{\underline{A}}\,\underline{\rho} - \underline{\underline{A}}^\dagger\,\underline{r}||^2, \tag{6}$$

for example, the conjugate gradient method.

The matrix-vector multiplications involving matrices $\underline{\underline{A}}$ and $\underline{\underline{A}}^\dagger$ can be computed by 2D NUFFTs of Non-Equispaced

Results (NER) and Non-Equispaced Data (NED), respectively. We now briefly recall the NER and NED Non-Uniform DFTs in the 1D case, for the case of simplicity. However, the results in the next Section will regard the 2D case.

In the 1D case, the NER NUDFT of uniform samples $\{z_k\}_{k=-N/2}^{N/2-1}$, evaluated at non-equispaced grid points $\widetilde{x}_l \in \left[-\frac{N}{2}, \frac{N}{2}\right]$, is defined as:

$$\hat{z}_l = \sum_{k=-\frac{N}{2}}^{\frac{N}{2}-1} z_k e^{-j2\pi \widetilde{x}_l \frac{k}{N}}, \quad l = 1, \ldots, M. \tag{7}$$

On the other side, the 1D NED NUDFT of samples $\{z_l\}_{l=1}^{M}$, located at non-equispaced points $\{\widetilde{x}_l\}_{l=1}^{M}$ and evaluated on an equispaced grid, is defined as:

$$\hat{z}_k = \sum_{l=1}^{M} z_l e^{-j2\pi \widetilde{x}_l \frac{k}{N}}, k = -N/2, \ldots, N/2-1. \tag{8}$$

III. Numerical Results

We now focus the attention on the extensions of the NER- and NED-NUFFT algorithms developed in [8] to the 2D case.

The accuracy of the NER-NUFFT is quantitatively assessed in the case of 12×12 non-uniformly and randomly distributed sampling points generated in the $[-6, 6]m^{-1} \times [-6, 6]m^{-1}$ spectral region. The data to be transformed have been assumed complex, with real and imaginary parts uniformly distributed in $[-0.5, 0.5]$. Tabs. I and II illustrate the accuracy in terms of Root Mean Square (RMS) errors and maximum errors as compared to the respective NER-NUDFT for single and double precision arithmetics, respectively. In both the cases, the accuracy of the optimized NUFFT is compared to the scheme in [5]. For single precision, the optimized NUFFT is compared also with that in [1] which is available for single precision only. As it can be seen, our approach outperforms the compared ones.

The performance of the NED-NUFFT is illustrated by showing the result of the computation of $\underline{\underline{A}}^{\dagger}\underline{\underline{A}}\rho$ which amounts at the so-called Filtered Backprojection (FPB) algorithm for radial MRI acquisitions. Fig. 1 illustrates the radial spectral sample locations, while Fig. 2 depicts the reconstruction of the Shepp-Logan phantom. Accuracies similar to those in Table I are achieved.

TABLE I: RMS and Maximum Errors: Single Precision

	Type-2 NUFFT Algorithm		
	KB	*Optimized*	*Fessler*
RMS	$6.23 \cdot 10^{-4}$	$1.11 \cdot 10^{-4}$	$122 \cdot 10^{-4}$
MAX	$6.93 \cdot 10^{-5}$	$1.12 \cdot 10^{-5}$	$140 \cdot 10^{-5}$

TABLE II: RMS and Maximum Errors: Double Precision

	Type-2 NUFFT Algorithm	
	KB	*Optimized*
RMS	$5.40 \cdot 10^{-10}$	$8.87 \cdot 10^{-11}$
MAX	$7.92 \cdot 10^{-10}$	$1.73 \cdot 10^{-10}$

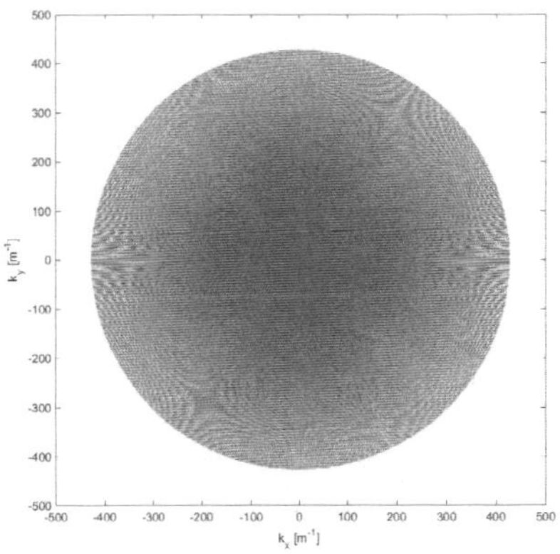

Fig. 1: Radial sample locations.

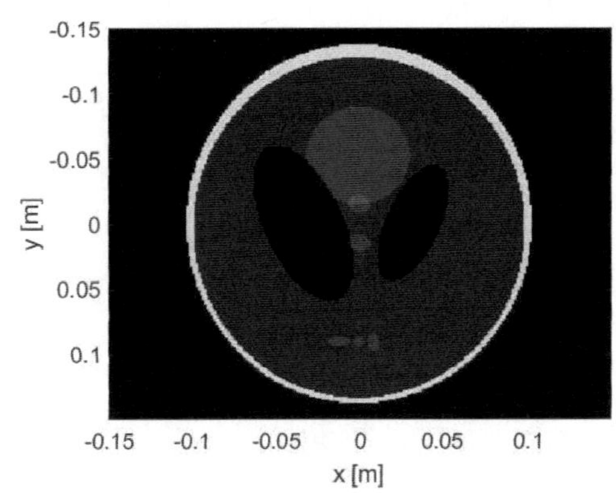

Fig. 2: Phantom reconstruction.

References

[1] J.A. Fessler, "On NUFFT-based gridding for non-Cartesian MRI," J. Magn. Res., vol. 188, no. 2, pp. 191–195, Oct. 2007.

[2] S. Konstandin, A. M. Nagel, P. M. Heiler and L. R. Schad, "Twodimensional radial acquisition technique with density adaption in sodium MRI," Mag. Res. Med., vol. 65, no. 4, pp. 1091–1097, Apr. 2011.

[3] R. K. Robison, A. Devaraj and J. G. Pipe, "Fast, simple gradient delay estimation for spiral MRI," Mag. Res. Med., vol. 63, no. 6, pp. 1683–1690, Jun. 2010.

[4] M. Uecker, S. Zhang, D. Voit, K.D. Merboldt and J. Frahm, "Real-time MRI: recent advances using radial FLASH," Imaging in Medicine, vol. 4, no. 4, pp. 461–476, 2012.

[5] K. Fourmont, "Non-Equispaced Fast Fourier Transforms with applications to tomography," J. Fourier Anal. Appl., vol. 9, no. 5, pp. 431-450, Sept. 2003.

[6] A. Capozzoli, C. Curcio, A. Di Vico and A. Liseno, "NUFFT-& GPU-based fast imaging of vegetation," IEICE Trans. Commun., vol. E94-B, no. 7, 2092–2103, Jul. 2011.

[7] A. Capozzoli, C. Curcio, A. Liseno and A. Riccardi, "Parameter selection and accuracy in type-3 non-uniform FFTs based on Gaussian gridding," Progr. Electromagn. Res., vol. 142, pp. 743–770, 2013.

[8] A. Capozzoli, C. Curcio and A. Liseno, "Optimized Non-Uniform FFTs (NUFFTs) and their application to array factor computation," IEEE Trans. Antennas Prop., vol. 67, no. 6, pp. 3924–3938, Jun. 2019.

Simulating Improved Antenna Performance using Measured Data of Electrically Thin Antennas

Steven Weiss
US Army Research Lab
Adelphi, MD
steven.j.weiss14.civ@mail.mil

***Abstract*—This paper gives an in-depth analysis of the measured performance of a pair of low-profile antennas. One antenna is linearly polarized with two radiating elements while the second antenna and is circularly polarized having four radiating elements. The linearly polarized antenna is fed in a balanced configuration using a 180-degree hybrid splitter. The circularly polarized antenna uses a 90-degree hybrid splitter cascaded into two 180-degree hybrid splitters to achieve orthogonal fields in phase quadrature. The ports of the antennas are coaxial inputs and connect to the hybrids using coaxial cables. Each antenna has been fully characterized in terms of S-parameters at their input ports, after the hybrid splitters, in an effort to determine the power reflected back into the dummy loads of the hybrids. Active reflection coefficients are determined from measured data. Accordingly, an adjustment to the radiation efficiency is obtained knowing both the insertion loss of the hybrids as well as the percentage of power absorbed into the dummy port of the hybrids. The dependence of the active reflection coefficient in terms of the mutual coupling between elements is quantified giving insight into possible improvements for the antennas.**

Keywords—S-parameters, Active Reflection Coefficient, Realized Gain.

I. Introduction

The advent of engineered magnetodielectric materials has made it possible to realize antennas of thicknesses approaching 1/50th of a wavelength while maintaining performance over an octave of frequency. Although electrically thin, such antennas are not electrically small as the cross-sectional dimensions are on the order of 1/4th of a wavelength or greater at the lowest frequency of operation. Accordingly, the radius of the smallest sphere enclosing the antenna as multiplied by the wavenumber is greater than one. Therefore, the antennas are not small from the standpoint of the Chu limit. Fabrication of these antennas is generally comprised of a shallow conductive cavity with magnetodielectric materials sandwiched between the bottom (ground plane) and the upper planar radiating elements. Although the antennas have measured data to verify that they maintain a positive realized gain over the desired frequency range, some further gain improvements can be made to mitigate internal losses. The improvement of these antennas from the standpoint of simulations and measurement of actual performance is discussed in subsequent sections of this paper.

II. Performance of a Linearly Polarized Antenna

The broadband, low-profile UHF/VHF antenna shown in Fig. 1 was measured to determine its gain over the frequency range of 200 MHz to 500 MHz. As gain accounts for power loss within the antenna (i.e., as quantified by the radiation efficiency) it is important to minimize such losses in an effort to improve the performance of the antenna.

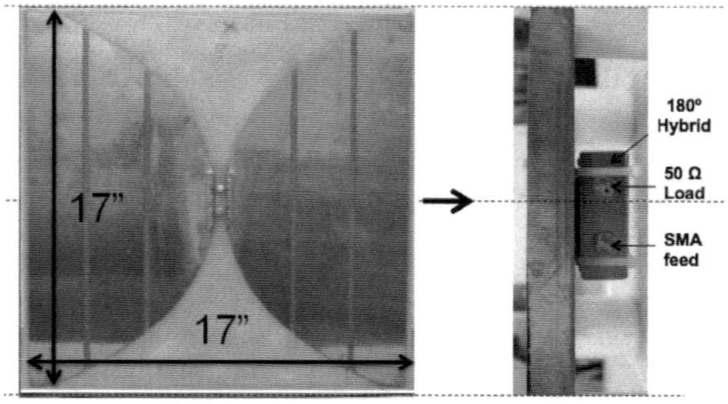

Fig. 1. A low-profile, broadband linearly polarized antenna.

The internal losses of the antenna shown in Fig. 1 occur for three reasons: losses due to the materials used to construct the antenna, losses due to the insertion loss of the 180-degree hybrid splitters, and losses due to the energy reflected from the ports of the antenna back into the hybrid which are then dissipated in heat into the dummy load of the hybrid. It is the reflected losses that can be mitigated by re-engineering the feed ports of the antenna to create better matches to the 50 Ohm feed line connecting the hybrids to the antenna ports.

The measured s-parameters are the subjected to excitation coefficients +1 and -1 as shown in (1) accounting for the 180-degree phase shift of the hybrid. The active reflection [1] and [2] (using the measured s-parameters) is then found using (2).

$$\begin{bmatrix} b_1 \\ b_2 \end{bmatrix} = \begin{bmatrix} s_{11} & s_{12} \\ s_{21} & s_{22} \end{bmatrix} \begin{bmatrix} a_1 \\ a_2 \end{bmatrix} \qquad (1)$$

$$\begin{bmatrix} b_1 \\ b_2 \end{bmatrix} = \begin{bmatrix} s_{11} & s_{12} \\ s_{21} & s_{22} \end{bmatrix} \begin{bmatrix} +1 \\ -1 \end{bmatrix}$$

$$\Gamma_1 = \frac{b_1}{+1} = s_{11} - s_{12} \qquad (2)$$

$$\Gamma_2 = \frac{b_2}{-1} = -s_{21} + s_{22}$$

The measured gains of the antenna are shown in Fig. 2. Note that the absolute gain backs out the reflection coefficient at the input port to the hybrids. It does not account for the active reflection coefficients causing heat to be dissipated into the terminated load of the hybrid. Fig. 3 shows the possible increase in gain is the loss of power into the terminated port of the hybrid could be reduced to zero. It is noted that just using the reflection coefficients S_{11} and S_{22} would give an improper adjustment. The proper adjustment to the measured data is:

$$G_{abs} = \left(1 - \frac{1}{2}|\Gamma_1|^2 - \frac{1}{2}|\Gamma_2|^2\right) G_0. \tag{3}$$

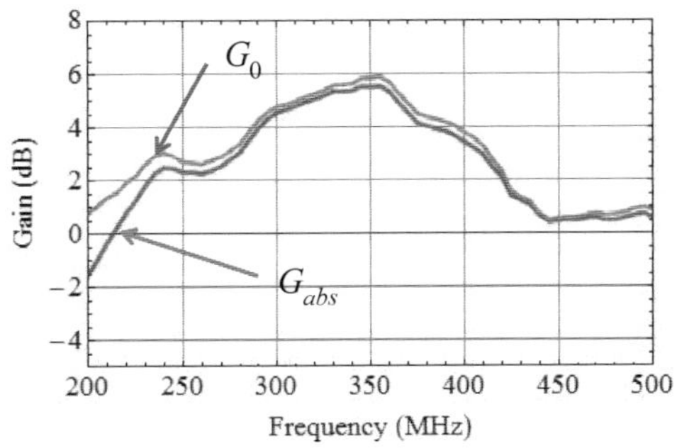

Fig. 2. Measured gains of the linearly polarized antenna.

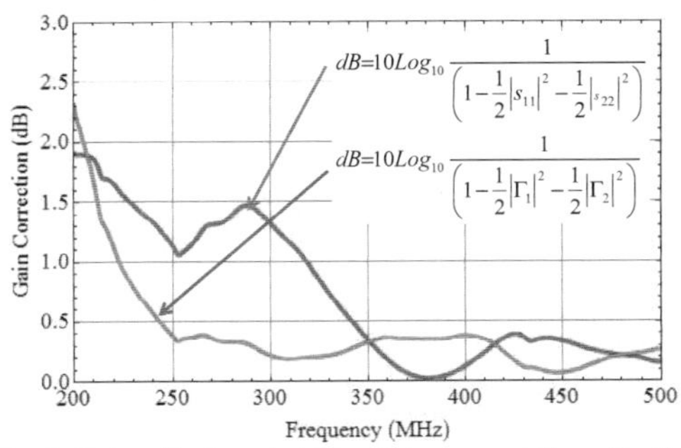

Fig. 3. Gain adjustments taking into account the reflection coefficients for the linearly polarized antenna.

III. Performance of a Circularly Polarized Antenna

The circularly polarized antenna is a 4-port device as shown in Fig. 4. A 90-Degree hybrid is cascaded into two 180-Degree hybrids which then feed the ports of the antenna. As with the linearly polarized antenna, one can make adjustments for the power dissipated into the terminations of the hybrids with knowledge of the measured s-parameters.

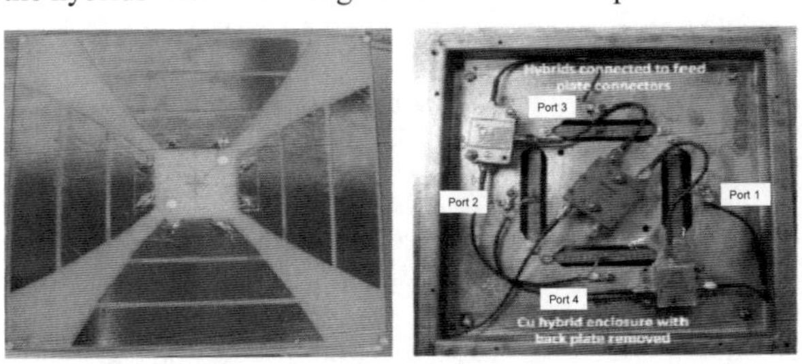

Fig. 4. Feed details for the circularly polarized antenna.

The adjustment for the actual gain closely follows the procedure for the linearly polarized antenna. The excitation weights in (4) are modified to account for the phase shifts and then the active reflection coefficients - also shown in (4). The active reflection coefficients are found by (5). The final adjustment to the gain is given by (6). Gain adjustments using the measured data are shown in Fig. 5.

$$\begin{bmatrix} b_1 \\ b_2 \\ b_3 \\ b_4 \end{bmatrix} = \begin{bmatrix} s_{11} & s_{12} & s_{13} & s_{14} \\ s_{21} & s_{22} & s_{23} & s_{24} \\ s_{31} & s_{32} & s_{33} & s_{34} \\ s_{41} & s_{42} & s_{43} & s_{44} \end{bmatrix} \begin{bmatrix} a_1 \\ a_2 \\ a_3 \\ a_4 \end{bmatrix}$$
$$\begin{bmatrix} b_1 \\ b_2 \\ b_3 \\ b_4 \end{bmatrix} = \begin{bmatrix} s_{11} & s_{12} & s_{13} & s_{14} \\ s_{21} & s_{22} & s_{23} & s_{24} \\ s_{31} & s_{32} & s_{33} & s_{34} \\ s_{41} & s_{42} & s_{43} & s_{44} \end{bmatrix} \begin{bmatrix} +1 \\ -1 \\ -j \\ +j \end{bmatrix} \tag{4}$$

$$\Gamma_1 = \frac{b_1}{+1} = s_{11} - s_{12} - js_{13} + js_{14}$$
$$\Gamma_2 = \frac{b_2}{-1} = -s_{21} + s_{22} + js_{23} - js_4$$
$$\Gamma_3 = \frac{b_3}{-j} = js_{31} - j\,s_{32} + s_{33} - s_{34}$$
$$\Gamma_4 = \frac{b_4}{+j} = -js_{41} + j\,s_{42} - s_{43} + s_{44} \tag{5}$$

$$G_{abs} = \left(1 - \frac{1}{4}|\Gamma_1|^2 - \frac{1}{4}|\Gamma_2|^2 - \frac{1}{4}|\Gamma_3|^2 - \frac{1}{4}|\Gamma_4|^2\right) G_0 \tag{6}$$

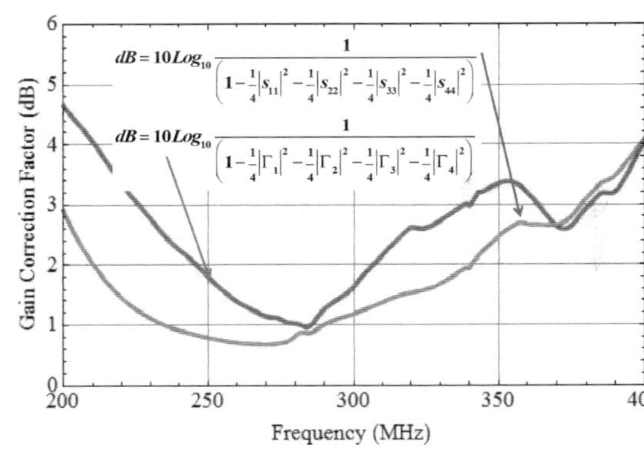

Fig. 5. Gain adjustments taking into account the reflection coefficients for the circularly polarized antenna.

As seen in the analysis of the two antennas, the actual gain of both antennas can be improved with better engineering improving the impedance match to the input of the ports of the antennas. Improvements on the order of 0.5 to 2 dB could be realized.

References

[1] D. Pozar, Microwave Engineering. Wiley, 4th ed. 2005s.

[2] S. Weiss, notes for Antenna Systems class, Johns Hopkins University.

A Comparison of Error Estimators for the Method of Moments

Charles W. Braddock
School of ECE
Georgia Institute of Technology
Atlanta, GA
cbraddock6@gatech.edu

Andrew F. Peterson
School of ECE
Georgia Institute of Technology
Atlanta, GA
afpeterson@gatech.edu

***Abstract*—Local error estimators are investigated for use with numerical solutions of the electric field integral equation. Three-dimensional test targets include a sphere, disk, NASA almond, and a Lockheed Martin Expedite aircraft model. Visual plots and correlation coefficients are used to assess the accuracy of the estimators. It is shown that the inexpensive discontinuity estimators are usually as accurate as the residual estimators.**

Keywords—A posteriori error estimation, Integral equations, Method of moments, Residuals.

I. Introduction

The goal of a numerical approach is to be reliable and efficient [1]. To that aim, a posteriori error estimation has been used as a key method to assess the accuracy of computational solutions and to determine high error cells for *h*- and *p*-refinement [2]. For integral equations, the most widely used estimators are based on residual equations, which have a high computational cost. Error estimation schemes that take advantage of the discontinuity of the tangential current and charge density in the Rao-Wilton-Glisson (RWG) have been introduced that are as useful but much less computationally costly than a residual based error estimate [3], [4]. Strydom and Botha introduced charge and current recovery methods for the RWG that used smoothing procedures to determine more accurate solutions [5], [6]. In this work, modified versions of the discontinuity error estimators in [4], the recovery methods of [5] and [6], and a magnetic field tangential residual method are compared on PEC surfaces of a sphere, disk, almond, and Expedite model.

II. Error Estimator Equations

A. Tangential Current Discontinuity Estimator

The tangential current discontinuity error at the ith cell is based on the average discontinuity of the surface current density at the midpoint of the three surrounding edges divided by two, normalized to twice the absolute value of the incident magnetic field:

$$LE_{Jtan}^{i} = \frac{\frac{1}{3}\sum_{m=1}^{3}\frac{1}{2}|\hat{t}_m\cdot(\bar{J}^{i}-\bar{J}^{n(i,m)})|}{2|\bar{H}^{inc}|}\frac{A_i}{A_{avg}}, \tag{1}$$

where $\hat{t}_m$ is a unit vector tangential to the mth edge of the ith cell, $n(i,m)$ is the adjacent cell that shares the mth edge with the ith cell, A_i is the area of the ith cell, and A_{avg} is the average cell area of the mesh. The factor of one half in the numerator of (1) is motivated by the assumption that the true value of the tangential current is the average of the two calculated values. The normalization factor was chosen due to it being the theoretical maximum value of the current on a sphere. The maximum value of the discontinuities was not used so that large discontinuities from cells along edges do not overwhelm the calculations of other cells.

B. Charge Discontinuity Error Estimator

The charge discontinuity error estimate at the ith cell is of the form:

$$LE_{\rho}^{i} = \frac{\frac{1}{3}\sum_{m=1}^{3}\frac{1}{2\epsilon}|\rho^{i}-\rho^{n(i,m)}|}{2|\bar{E}^{inc}|}\frac{A_i}{A_{avg}}, \tag{2}$$

where the same superscripts of i and $n(i,m)$ are used as the tangential current discontinuity estimator. Each difference of the charge densities along an edge is divided by the epsilon of the surrounding space. The normalization constant, twice the absolute value of the incident electric field, is chosen because it is the theoretical maximum value of the charge density on a smooth surface. The additional division by two comes from the same assumption as that in the tangential current discontinuity estimator.

C. Current Weighted Charge Discontinuity Estimator

The current weighted charge discontinuity (CWCD) error estimator was introduced in [3] and uses the current density to modify the charge discontinuity estimator to obtain:

$$LE_{CWCD}^{i} = \frac{\frac{1}{3}\sum_{m=1}^{3}\frac{1}{2}||k\eta\langle\bar{T}_m,(\bar{J}^{i}+\bar{J}^{n(i,m)})\rangle|+\frac{1}{2\epsilon}|\rho^{i}-\rho^{n(i,m)}|}{2|\bar{E}^{inc}|}\frac{A_i}{A_{avg}}. \tag{3}$$

The same superscripts of i and $n(i,m)$ are used as the current discontinuity estimator. $\bar{T}_m$ is the razor-blade test function across edge m from the ith cell to the $n(i,m)^{th}$ cell. The normalization constant of twice the magnitude of the incident electric field was chosen due to the common units being V/m.

This project was supported by the Lockheed Martin Corp.

D. Magnetic Field Tangential Residual

The tangential H-field residual estimator is defined as:

$$LE^{i}_{HtanRes} = \frac{\sqrt{\sum_{m=1}^{2}(\hat{t}\cdot\{\hat{n}\times(\bar{H}^{inc}+\bar{H}^{s})-\bar{J}_s\}_{cell\,i})^2}}{2|\bar{H}^{inc}|} * \frac{A_i}{A_{avg}}, \quad (4)$$

where $\hat{t}_1$ and $\hat{t}_2$ are orthogonal unit tangent vectors at the center of cell i, and the fields and current density are sampled at the center of cell i. The scattered field $\bar{H}^s$ is computed from:

$$\bar{H}^s = \nabla\times \iint \bar{J}_s(u',v')G(u,v,u',v')du'dv', \quad (5)$$

which is imposed an infinitesimal distance outside the target surface. The estimator is limited to closed targets.

III. Test Problems

The error estimators in Section II and the recovery methods introduced in [5] and [6] were tested with perfectly conducting targets including a sphere, a disk, a NASA almond, and an Expedite model (Fig. 1). The sources were uniform plane waves and the targets were modeled with triangular facets.

A. Sphere

The first test problem is a PEC sphere of radius λ with 648 fairly uniform and symmetric cells.

B. Disk

The disk is of approximate radius 1.6λ with 516 cells. The incident plane wave is normally-incident to the disk plane.

C. NASA Almond

The NASA almond is of width 2.5λ and length 6λ with 640 cells. The incident plane waves used were horizontally (y) and vertically (z) polarized along the midline of the almond.

D. Expedite Model

The Expedite model, shown in Fig. 1, was provided by Lockheed Martin Corporation. It was of length 6λ and width 5λ with 676 cells. The incident plane waves horizontally (y) and vertically (z) polarized.

IV. Results

For each test problem, visual models, global error estimates, scatter plots, and correlation coefficients as defined in [4] were generated. For the sphere and disk meshes, the results were compared to the true error values obtained from exact solutions. For the NASA Almond and Expedite meshes, the results were compared to the error values found by comparing to extrapolated values from much finer meshes. The local error is computed using using:

$$LE^{i}_{ref} = \frac{\frac{1}{3}\sum_{m=1}^{3}|\hat{n}_m(\bar{J}^{i}_{ref}-\bar{J}^{i}_{MoM})|}{2|H_{inc}|}\frac{A_i}{A_{avg}}. \quad (6)$$

A. Global Error Estimate

The two-norm global error estimate was computed for each estimator. The two-norm global estimate was of the form:

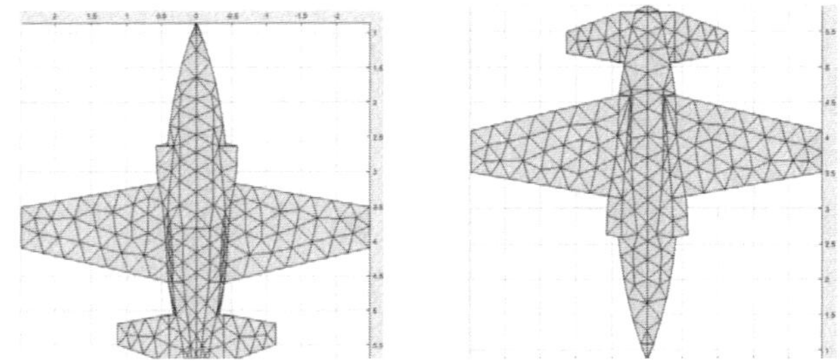

Fig. 1. 676 cell Expedite mesh viewed from the top and bottom of the mesh.

$$GE_{2\,Norm} = \sqrt{\frac{\sum A_n(LE_n\frac{A_{avg}}{A_n})^2}{\sum A_n}}, \quad (7)$$

where A_n is the area of the nth cell and LE_n is the local error at the nth cell.

B. Correlation

The correlation coefficients between each estimator and the exact or reference error for each mesh are shown in Table I, following the definition in [7].

TABLE I. Correlation Coefficients

Geometry	Pol.	J_t	ρ_e	$CWCD$	J_{rec}	ρ_{rec}	Res H_t
Sphere	x	0.95	0.59	0.63	0.95	0.56	0.95
Disk	y	0.85	0.74	0.74	0.79	0.72	(*NA*)
Almond	y	0.85	0.88	0.89	0.84	0.87	0.87
Almond	z	0.29	0.26	0.33	0.16	0.24	0.30
Expedite	y	0.76	0.67	0.73	0.59	0.59	0.74
Expedite	z	0.47	0.43	0.49	0.44	0.39	0.75

C. Discussion

Based on the results shown above, it can be seen that for most cases the computationally cheaper discontinuity error estimation methods are just as accurate as the "industry standard" residual method.

References

[1] A. F. Peterson, S. L. Ray, and R. Mittra, Computational Methods for Electromagnetics, New York, NY, USA: IEEE Press, 1998.

[2] M. Ainsworth and J. T. Oden, A Posteriori Error Estimation in Finite Element Analysis, Hoboken, NJ, USA: Wiley, 2000.

[3] J. Wang and J. P. Webb, "Hierarchal vector boundary elements and p-adaption for 3-D electromagnetic scattering," IEEE Trans. Antennas Propag., vol. 45, no. 12, pp. 1869-1879, Dec. 1997.

[4] S. K. Kim and A. F. Peterson, "Evaluation of local error estimators for the RWG based EFIE," IEEE Tans. Antennas Propagat., vol. 66, no. 2, pp. 819-826, Feb. 2018.

[5] W. J. Strydom and M. M. Botha, "Charge recovery for the RWG-based method of moments," IEEE Tans. Antennas Propagat. Letters, vol. 14, pp. 305-308, Oct. 2014.

[6] W. J. Strydom and M. M. Botha, "Current recovery for the RWG-based method of moments," IET Science, Measurement & Technology, vol. 10, no. 8, pp. 831-838, Nov. 2016.

[7] S. K. Kim, "Error estimation and adaptive refinement technique in the method of moments," Ph.D. dissertation, Dept. Elect. Comput. Eng., Georgia Inst. Technol., Atlanta, GA, USA, May 2017.

On the Accuracy of Flexible Antennas Simulations

Sima Noghanian
Simulation Support
PADT Inc.
Tempe, AZ
sima_noghanian@ieee.org

Michael Griesi
Simulation Support
PADT Inc.
Tempe, AZ
michael.b.griesi@ieee.org

***Abstract*— The performance of wearable and flexible antennas can be greatly affected by bending and crumpling. While these effects have been studied in the literature, the accuracy of simulation in these conditions should be considered. In this paper, the effects of accurate modeling of the excitation, and the supporting structures are investigated.**

Keywords—bending effects, flexible antennas.

I. Introduction

Flexible electronics have been of interest due to their applications in wearable and the Internet of Things (IoT) [1]-[7]. In this context, many researchers have investigated various types of planar antennas on flexible substrate materials, e.g. textile [1]-[7], flexible 3D printed materials [6], and Liquid Crystal Polymer (LCP) [7]. There are multiple challenges in designing flexible antennas, e.g. material characterization, durable structural designs, feeding structures and matching network designs, and prediction of the effects of bending and crumpling.

To understand the antenna's behavior under various conditions such as bending and crumpling, electromagnetics simulation tools are used, however, it is often difficult to design a simulation setup that exactly mimics the details of measurement setups. In this paper, we intend to show the effects of some of the often missed details that can affect the accuracy of the simulation results.

II. Antenna Model and Analysis

A. *Antenna Model*

To show the effects of excitation modeling, we chose an antenna described in [7]. This antenna has a very thin layer of LCP (thickness 0.1 mm) as its substrate and is fed through a Co-Planar Waveguide (CPW) line. The overall size of the antenna is 20 mm × 32 mm in its flat shape. The other dimensions are mentioned in Table 2 of [7]. All the measurement results are taken from this reference are referred to as "Measured_Ref".

B. *Excitation Model Effects*

All the simulations in this paper are performed using ANSYS HFSS 2019 R3 [8]. There are various excitation models available in HFSS. The most common ones used for planar antennas are wave-port and lumped-port. We do not show the lumped-port model in the paper for brevity. The Lumped-port requires an additional structure to connect two ground planes of CPW that can lead to deviation from the measurements without careful consideration. We considered three types of Wave-ports, as shown in Fig. 1. This figure clearly shows the differences between the current distributions on the planar monopole for these three feeding methods. To investigate further one can examine the impedance seen by the port. Fig. 2 shows the real part of port impedance for various cases. While SMA (SubMiniature version A) model maintains the 50 Ω impedance, even after bending the antenna in H-plane, the other wave-port models show a variation of impedance. Fig. 3 shows how these can affect the accuracy of the reflection coefficient compared to measured values for a flat antenna.

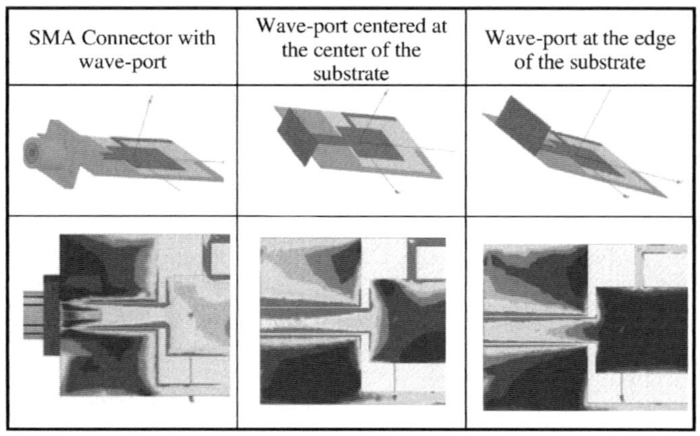

Fig. 1. Comparison of three different excitation models in HFSS and the current distribution generated by them.

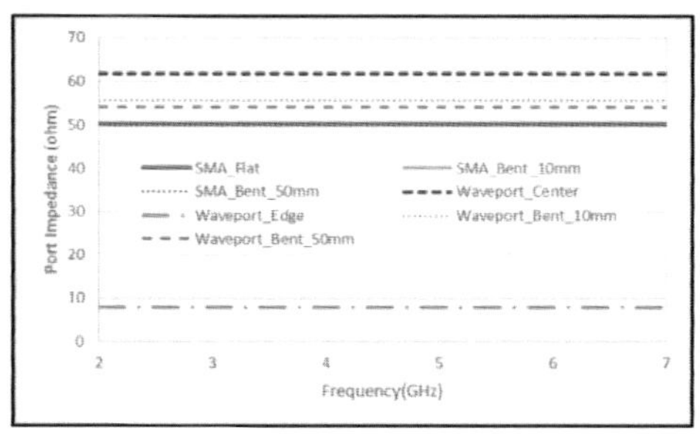

Fig. 2. The real part of the port impedance of different types of excitation for flat and bent antenna models.

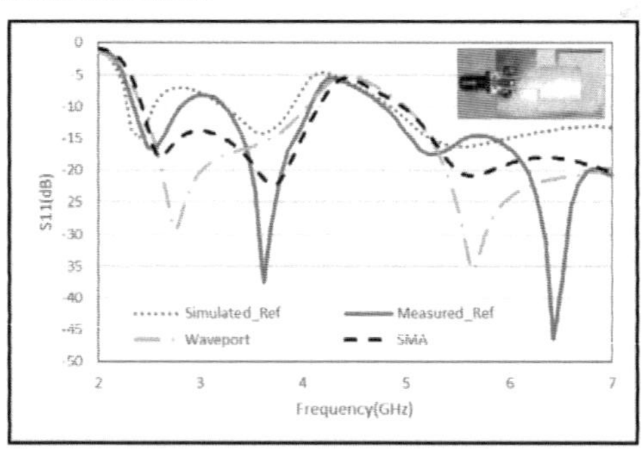

Fig. 3. Reflection coefficient comparison for SMA and waveport fed antennas with the measured values (Measured_Ref) and simulated values (Simulated_Ref) obtained from [7].

This work is supported financially by PADT Inc.

C. *Bending and Support Material Effects*

Fig. 4 shows the simulation results of bending the antenna on a cylindrical surface with a radius of 10mm in the H-plane. We considered the H-plane bending since it has more effects on the feeding structure. Although the SMA model maintains very good matching to 50 Ω (Fig. 1), the simulation results do not match the measurement (Fig. 4 (a)). In the initial attempt, we investigated the effects of conductor thickness or the CPW gap (parameter g in Table 2 of [7]) that could have been affected by the physical bending, however, these had a negligible effect on the results. A closer look at the photograph of the measurement setup in [7] shows that the antenna was bent on a supporting cylindrical structure (Fig. 4 (b)). The reference does not provide information about this material. Two different materials were used for 10 mm and 50 mm bending. In many situations, the effect of the supporting structure is neglected to simplify the simulation. This antenna has a very thin substrate and the support structure has affected the matching. By including a 0.7 mm thick support structure (Fig. 4 (b)) of Plexiglas ($\varepsilon_r = 3.4$) we found that the simulation better represents the measurements (Fig. 4 (c)). In this simulation first, we used a complete cylinder of Plexiglas, but it is also seen that the support structure is not exactly aligned at the SMA location. An estimated ring of vacuum was added to represent this misalignment. A similar investigation for bending with a 50 mm radius showed a support structure such as foam ($\varepsilon_r = 1.6$) with 2.5 mm thickens can represent the support material (Fig. 5).

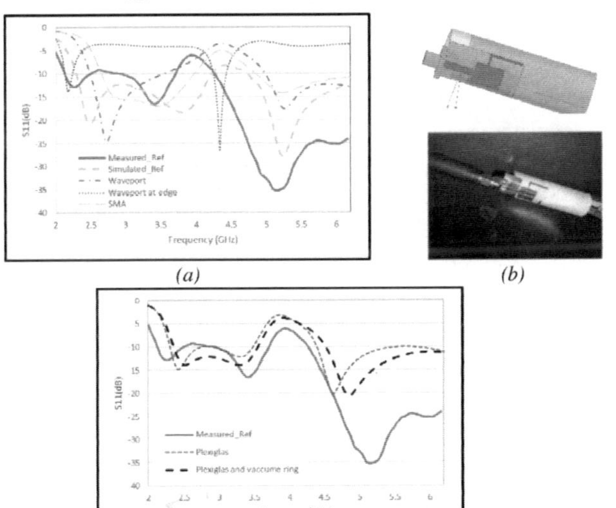

Fig. 4. (a) Reflection coefficient comparison for SMA fed bent antenna on a 10 mm radius without a support structure, (b) support structure, (c) reflection coefficient with a support structure, measurement data from [7].

D. *Surface Curvature Transition Effects*

Another detailed effect is the transition from the planar surface to the bent shape. Due to the rigidity of the SMA connector, it is not possible to get a complete bent surface closer to the SMA connection. To include this effect, we connected a bent part to the planar part using a transition area, as shown in Fig. 6. A support structure of Polyester ($\varepsilon_r = 3.2$) with 1.15 mm thickness was used.

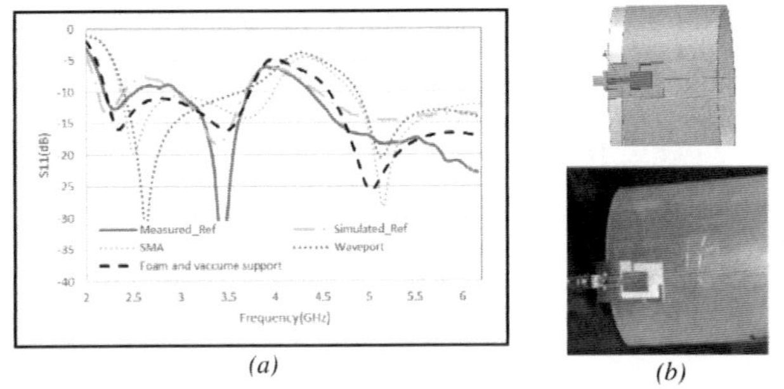

Fig. 5. (a) Reflection coefficient comparison for SMA fed bent antenna on a 50 mm radius (b) support structure, measurement data from [7].

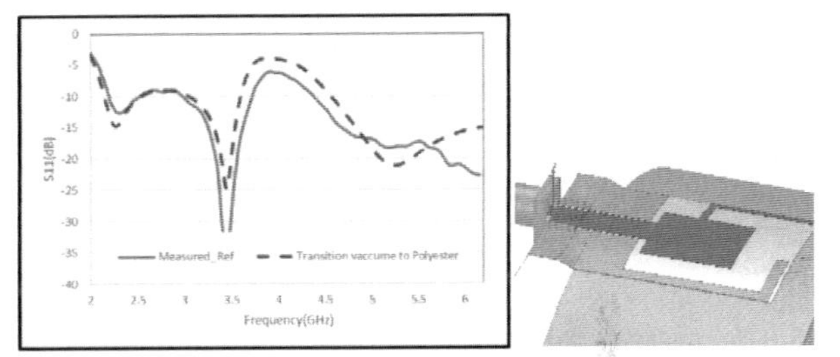

Fig. 6. Reflection coefficient comparison for SMA fed bent antenna on a 50 mm radius with the transition from planar to the cylinder.

III. CONCLUSIONS

The accurate simulation of flexible antennas requires attention to include details of measurement such as support structure, shape deformation, and accurate model of excitation. Due to the length of the paper, detailed examples will be provided in the presentation.

REFERENCES

[1] B. Hu, G. Gao, L. He, X. Cong and J. Zhao, "Bending and on-arm effects on a wearable antenna for 2.45 GHz body area network," in *IEEE Antennas and Wireless Propagation Letters*, vol. 15, pp. 378-381, 2016.

[2] Y. Sun, S. W. Cheung and T. I. Yuk, "Design of a textile ultra-wideband antenna with stable performance for body-centric wireless communications," in *IET Microwaves, Antennas & Propagation*, vol. 8, no. 15, pp. 1363-1375, 9 12 2014. doi: 10.1049/iet-map.2013.0658

[3] L. Song and Y. Rahmat-Samii, "A systematic investigation of rectangular patch antenna bending effects for wearable applications," in *IEEE Transactions on Antennas and Propagation*, vol. 66, no. 5, pp. 2219-2228, May 2018.

[4] A. Alemaryeen and S. Noghanian, "Crumpling effects and specific absorption rates of flexible AMC integrated antennas," in *IET Microwaves, Antennas & Propagation*, vol. 12, no. 4, pp. 627-635, 28 3 2018. doi: 10.1049/iet-map.2017.0652

[5] A. Alemaryeen and S. Noghanian, "On-body low-profile textile antenna with artificial magnetic conductor," in *IEEE Transactions on Antennas and Propagation*, vol. 67, no. 6, pp. 3649-3656, June 2019.

[6] K. Nate and M. M. Tentzeris, "A novel 3-D printed loop antenna using flexible NinjaFlex material for wearable and IoT applications," 2015 *IEEE 24th Electrical Performance of Electronic Packaging and Systems (EPEPS)*, San Jose, CA, 2015, pp. 171-174. doi: 10.1109/EPEPS.2015.7347155

[7] C. Du, X. Li and S. Zhong, "Compact Liquid crystal polymer based tri-band flexible antenna for WLAN/WiMAX/5G applications," in *IEEE Access*. doi: 10.1109/ACCESS.2019.2941212.

[8] https://www.ansys.com/products/release-highlights, visited Oct. 2019.

Benchmark of Acceleware vs XFdtd for Field Simulations of Microstrip Patch Antenna

Tendayi Kamucheka[1], Zhijun Gui[2], Miaoqing Huang[1], Hugh Churchill[3], and Magda El-Shenawee[2]
[1]Department of Computer Science Computer Engineering, University of Arkansas, Fayetteville, AR 72701
[2]Department of Electrical Engineering, University of Arkansas, Fayetteville, AR 72701
[3]Department of Physics, University of Arkansas, Fayetteville, AR 72701
tfkamuch@uark.edu

***Abstract*—We benchmark the accuracy and the speed of the Acceleware FDTD library vs XFdtd in simulating a microstrip patch antenna. The benchmark is based on the sampled electric and magnetic fields. The results show that Acceleware performs almost three times faster than XFdtd. The relative mean error is less than 2.0%.**

***Index Terms*—Acceleware, Microstrip antenna, XFdtd**

I. Introduction

The finite-difference time-domain (FDTD) method is a well-established and widely used technique in solving electromagnetic (EM) problems [1]. Fast FDTD computations including those in many FDTD commercial solvers were achieved by utilizing graphics processing units (GPUs) [2]–[5]. However, it is necessary to verify the accuracy of the simulation of the electric (E) and magnetic (H) fields before fabricating real devices. In this work, the simulations on two established software packages are presented, Acceleware FDTD library and Remcom's XFdtd. The Acceleware FDTD library is a bundle of C/C++ functions that can be used to build applications to solve EM problems [6]. In contrast, Remcom's XFdtd is a full-featured EM simulation solver software package [7]. In this paper, the Acceleware FDTD library is benchmarked against XFdtd regarding the simulation of the electric (E) and magnetic (H) fields of a patch antenna. The hardware and implementation are described below.

II. Design and Simulations

For the benchmark, a rectangular microstrip patch antenna is simulated in both the XFdtd software and the Acceleware application. Fig. 1 shows the dimensions of the antenna in yee-cells. The dimensions of each yee-cell are $\Delta x = 1 \times 10^{-3}$, $\Delta y = 9.9 \times 10^{-4}$, and $\Delta z = 9.41 \times 10^{-4}$ meters. Since XFdtd presents a more polished interface and features, the modeling effort starts in the XFdtd package. The antenna design and material properties are provided in [8]. Initially, a voltage source with a Gaussian time pulse of a frequency range from 0 to 20 GHz is implemented. The S-parameters are extracted from the package to identify the antenna resonant frequency at 6.564 GHz. Then the excitation is substituted for a sinusoid with frequency 6.564 GHz. Once the design is completed in XFdtd, the same antenna specification is modeled in Acceleware C/C++. A custom voltage source with the same frequency and sinusoidal time signal is implemented. Convolutional perfectly matched layer (CPML) is modeled based on [9], [10]. Uniform kappa and alpha values are used as 1 and 0, respectively, over seven layers of CPML. The matching layer covers all sides except the bottom one (in the z-direction), which is set to be a Perfect Electrical Conductor (PEC) and is used as the ground plane. Following the work in [1], [11], the time-step value Δt is calculated as:

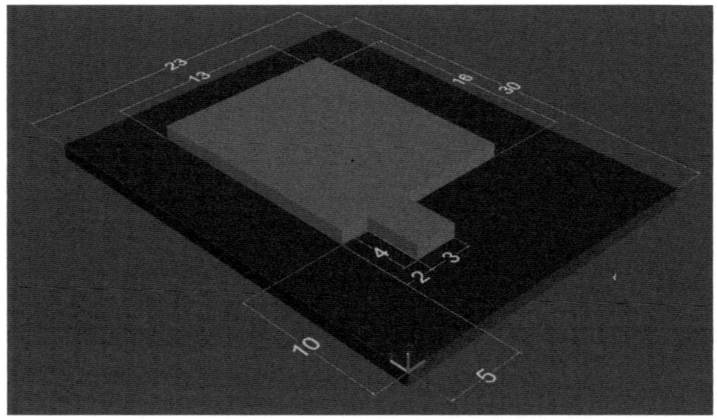

Fig. 1. Microstrip patch antenna model. All dimensions are given in yee-cells ($\Delta x = 1 \times 10^{-3}$, $\Delta y = 9.9 \times 10^{-4}$, and $\Delta z = 9.41 \times 10^{-4}$ meters).

$$\Delta t \leq \frac{1}{c\sqrt{\frac{1}{\Delta x^2} + \frac{1}{\Delta y^2} + \frac{1}{\Delta z^2}}}, \tag{1}$$

where c is the speed of light and Δx, Δy, and Δz are the yee-cell dimensions for free space in metres.

A key part of the benchmark is to compare the E- and H-field data at the same yee-cell vertices in these two simulations. A 1:1 mapping between spatial coordinates of the yee-cells is ensured in both models between XFdtd and Acceleware. In XFdtd, the near-field sensors are used to record the field data from the selected locations. The same locations are used in the Acceleware C/C++ code to extract the E- and H-field data at those locations. In total, there are three sets of locations, each set containing at least four spatial coordinates. Each coordinate

This work is partially supported by NSF grant No. 1408007 and the University of Arkansas Chancellor's Discovery, Creativity, Innovation, and Collaboration Fund Program.

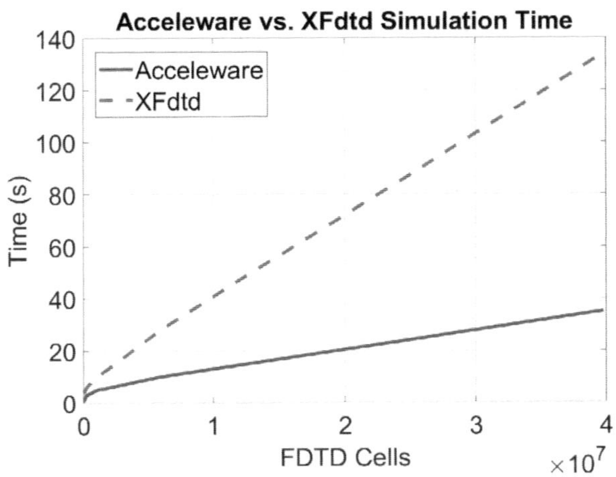

Fig. 2. Simulation times vs the number of FDTD cells.

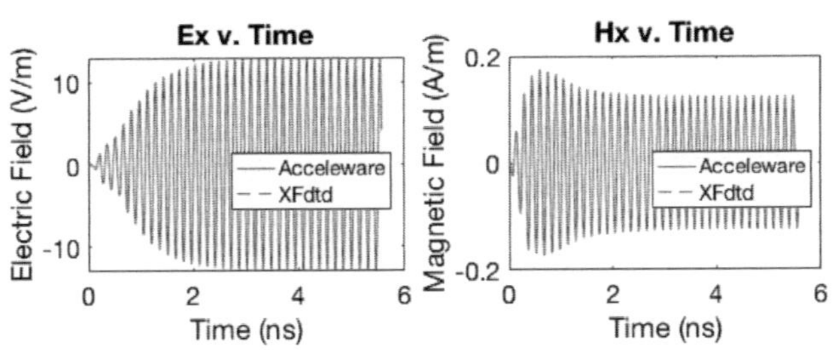

Fig. 3. Accuracy of the simulated E-x & H-x fields at yee-cell coordinates (13, 11, 3).

yields six data points, three for the E-field components and three for the H-field components in x-, y-, and z-directions.

All XFdtd simulations are run on an AMD Ryzen Threadripper 2990WX 32-core CPU with 128 GB system memory and an Nvidia GTX 1050 GPU, running on Windows 10. The Acceleware application was tested on an Intel Xeon Silver 4110 8-core CPU with 128 GB system memory and an Nvidia Tesla V100 GPU, running on CentOS 7. Field recording instruments are disabled in all simulation time tests.

III. Simulation Results

Fig. 2 shows the performance achieved by the Acceleware code vs XFdtd package. Upon increasing the number of cells in the FDTD simulation, the execution times were measured for the time-marching loop. Each test was executed five times and the mean execution time was recorded. The results show that the Acceleware code performs significantly faster. However, this could be due to the use of the Tesla V100 compared with the GTX 1050 in XFdtd simulation.

It should be noted that when benchmarking field data, data recorded in XFdtd is used as the reference. Furthermore, to observe the difference between the two datasets, we calculated percentage error following Equation 2:

$$Error = \frac{|A - X|}{X} \times 100\%, \tag{2}$$

where X is the peak values of $|XFdtd|$ and A is the peak values of $|Acceleware|$, respectively. Fig. 3 shows E- and H-field simulation data in the x-direction at yee-cell with x, y, and z coordinates of (13, 11, 3) in space. The results show that the Acceleware code is in good accuracy agreement with the XFdtd package. The highest error calculated for all locations is less than 5%. Table I shows the mean and standard deviation of error at twelve locations in space for each field component averaged over 3000 time-steps.

TABLE I: Summary of Mean and Standard deviation of error

Field	E[x]	E[y]	E[z]	H[x]	H[y]	H[z]
Mean	0.46%	1.09%	0.55%	1.37%	0.28%	1.00%
Stdev	0.36%	0.58%	0.45%	0.71%	0.27%	0.60%

IV. Conclusion

We have shown that the Acceleware FDTD library-based code results are in good accuracy agreement with the commercial package XFdtd. The cases presented here demonstrate a mean error less than 2.0%. Furthermore, we have also demonstrated that with a state-of-the-art GPU, the Acceleware code achieves high-performance simulations. The Acceleware code is almost three times faster than the XFdtd simulation. However, it should be noted that the hardware platform is not the same across the comparison. In the future, we plan to use identical hardware configurations in similar benchmarks. We are also working on modeling more complex configurations using the Acceleware FDTD library package.

References

[1] A. Taflove and S. C. Hagness, Computational electrodynamics: the finite-difference time-domain method, 3rd ed. Norwood: Artech House, 2005.

[2] S. Krakiwsky, L. Turner, and M. Okoniewski, "Acceleration of finite-difference time-domain (FDTD) using graphics processor units (GPU)," in 2004 IEEE MTT-S International Microwave Symposium Digest (IEEE Cat. No.04CH37535), vol. 2. IEEE, pp. 1031–1034. [Online]. Available: http://ieeexplore.ieee.org/document/1339160/

[3] T. P. Stefański, S. Benkler, N. Chavannes, and N. Kuster, "Parallel implementation of the finite-difference time-domain method in open computing language," in Proceedings - 2010 12th International Conference on Electromagnetics in Advanced Applications, ICEAA'10, 2010, pp. 557–560.

[4] S. Adams, J. Payne, and R. Boppana, "Finite difference time domain (FDTD) simulations using graphics processors," in Department of Defense - Proceedings of the HPCMP Users Group Conference 2007; High Performance Computing Modernization Program: A Bridge to Future Defense, DoD HPCMP UGC, 2007, pp. 334–338.

[5] D. L. Markovich, K. S. Ladutenko, and P. A. Belov, "Performance of FDTD method CPU implementations for simulation of electromagnetic processes," Progress in Electromagnetics Research, vol. 139, pp. 655–670, 2013.

[6] Acceleware, "Acceleware FDTD Library." [Online]. Available: https://www.acceleware.com https://www.acceleware.com/fdtd-solvers

[7] Remcom, "XFdtd 3D Electromagnetic Simulation Software." [Online]. Available: https://www.remcom.com/xfdtd-3d-em-simulation-software

[8] ——, "XFdtd User Guide," Tech. Rep., 2018.

[9] Acceleware, "Convolutional Perfectly Matched Layer Whitepaper," Tech. Rep., 2007.

[10] A. Elsherbeni and V. Demir, "The finite-difference time-domain method for electromagnetics with matlab simulations, aces series on computational electromagnetics and engineering," 2015.

[11] Remcom, "XFdtd Reference Manual," Tech. Rep., 2018.

Adding a Reproducible Airplane Model to the Austin RCS Benchmark Suite

Jon T. Kelley[1], Andrew Maicke[1], David A. Chamulak[2], Clifton C. Courtney[2], and Ali E. Yilmaz[1]
[1]The University of Texas at Austin
[2]Lockheed Martin Aeronautics Company

***Abstract*—A full-size airplane model (the EXPEDITE-RCS model) was developed as part of a benchmark suite for evaluating radar-cross-section (RCS) prediction methods. To generate accurate reference data for the benchmark problems formulated using the model, scale-model targets were additively manufactured, their material properties and RCS were measured, and the measurements were validated with a surface-integral-equation solver. To enable benchmarking of as many computational methods as possible, the following data are made available in a version-controlled online repository: (1) Exterior surface (outer mold line) of the CAD model in two standard file formats. (2) Triangular surface meshes. (3) Measured and predicted monostatic RCS data.**

I. Introduction

The radar cross section (RCS) of realistic airplane models—complex models that cannot be described sufficiently with a few equations, drawings, or pictures—is used frequently to motivate advances in computational electromagnetics as well as to demonstrate capabilities of new methods (e.g., see [1]-[5]). Unfortunately, the published RCS data for such airplane models found by numerically solving the scattering problem—even if the computed results correlate well with independent physical measurements as in [1]-[3]—are generally impossible to replicate or corroborate [6]. It is also generally impossible to use the published data for such models to objectively compare the performance of a new algorithm, software, or hardware for predicting RCS to existing or future alternatives [7]. This is in part because complex models are almost never available to anyone but the authors of the study that used them—even the authors can lose access to the models and the ability to reproduce their published data over time. This article introduces a high-fidelity airplane model to the Austin RCS Benchmark Suite [7]-[11], a publicly available suite that is being developed to verify, validate, and benchmark modern and future computational methods for predicting RCS. It also describes various difficulties encountered when developing such models and the steps the authors followed to increase the likelihood that the model and its RCS patterns can be reproduced precisely and used independently to judge different RCS prediction methods.

II. Development of the EXPEDITE-RCS Model

The benchmark airplane model is based on a test platform created by Lockheed Martin Aeronautics and collaborators as part of the ongoing expanded multidisciplinary analysis and design optimization for effectiveness based design technologies (EXPEDITE) program [12]. The major elements of the EXPEDITE program are structured to be as open as possible with a minimal amount of proprietary information [12], thus enabling public release of precise CAD models derived from the test platform. Thanks to this exceptionally favorable setup for collaboration, an airplane model could be rapidly developed for RCS benchmarking.

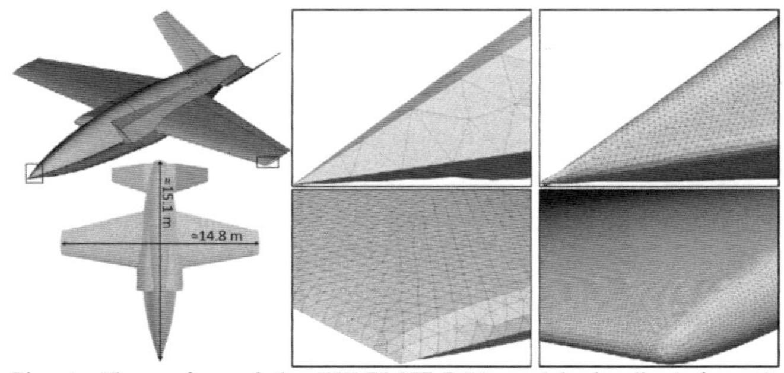

Fig. 1. The surface of the EXPEDITE-RCS model visualized from the defeatured IGS file (left) and triangular meshes of the model's nose and wingtip using an average edge length of ~2 in (middle) and ~0.25 in (right).

Because of a lack of precedents for sharing geometrically-complex targets, the authors faced numerous major choices during the development of the benchmark model. While aiming to maximize the model's utility, the authors also had to manage the uncertainty in the RCS computations and measurements, in the amount/type/format of data to be shared, and in the process of releasing the model and building benchmark problem sets. This led to four major decisions: (i) While the EXPEDITE program's test platform is architected as a fully parameterized geometry that enables multidisciplinary trade-off studies, a particular realization—referred to as the EXPEDITE-RCS model—was selected rather than an ensemble of potential designs (Fig. 1). (ii) The engine intake and exhaust cavities of the selected model would be closed at first (but can be opened in the future). (iii) Simple materials would be used at first. (iv) Scale-model targets would be additively manufactured and their RCS patterns would be measured carefully. Following these decisions, the model was developed in five steps.

Step 1: Initial evaluation. The surface of the EXPEDITE-RCS model was meshed in the same CAD software used to design the test platform [12]. The model's RCS was computed assuming it was perfectly electrically conducting (PEC). The simulations were used to verify that the model was closed, its surface could be meshed properly, its RCS patterns were symmetric, and the results converged as the mesh was refined.

Step 2: Preparation for manufacturing. The suitability of the original model for additive manufacturing was evaluated by

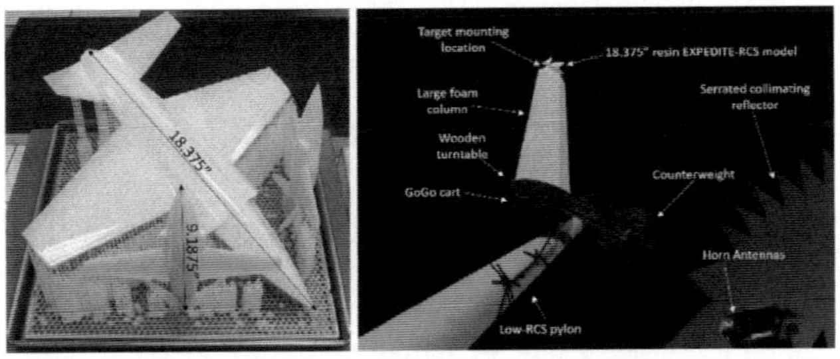

Fig. 2. Left: The additively manufactured scale models before their support structures were removed and they were sanded and metallized. Right: The measurement of the ~18.4-in long model in the compact chamber.

specialists. Various geometrical features (e.g., sharp wing tips) of the scaled model were deemed too small for accurate printing and the design was modified accordingly to respect the minimum feature sizes and tolerances of the 3D printing process, e.g., the airfoils' trailing edges were thickened and the surface joints were blended. The modified design's computed RCS patterns were also tested for symmetry and convergence.

Step 3: Manufacture and measurement of scale models. Proportionally scaled resin targets of length ~18.4-in and ~9.2-in were printed and their RCS were measured (Fig. 2) using the facilities and methodology detailed in [10],[11]. The targets were then coated with a highly conductive silver paint and their RCS were measured again. The measured data were post-processed and validated with simulations just as in [11]. A sample result is shown in Fig. 3; additional data and accompanying simulations, for both the metallized and resin targets at 2.58 GHz, 5.12 GHz, 7 GHz, and 10.25 GHz are available as part of the problem sets IV-A and IV-B in [9].

Step 4: Preparation for public release. To facilitate replicability of the model, its surface description was exported in STL and IGS file formats. The STL file was the one used in 3D printing of the scale models. The IGS file was imported to a second more widely available meshing software to test the relative ease of independent mesh development. This revealed that there were 220 surfaces in the IGS file; many were artifacts from the test platform, including minute surfaces with edges that are smaller than 1 in. These could be merged easily with neighbors while ensuring tangential (C^1) continuity with the help of a CAD tool. Other surfaces had to be first split into smaller sub-surfaces using iso-curves along edges shared with a neighbor; this also helped align edges of neighboring surfaces, resulting in a model composed of 108 surfaces that can be relatively easily meshed. While this defeaturing process led to minute differences between the old and new model surfaces, computations using the two models converged to visually identical RCS patterns. In addition to the STL and IGS files, a series of increasingly finer triangular surface meshes (coarsest-finest: $\sim 2 \times 10^3 - \sim 5 \times 10^7$ elements) are also shared in [9].

Step 5: Publication and presentation. The model was first described in this article, shown at the conference, and made available in [9] at the time of the conference presentation.

III. Conclusion

A realistic airplane model was developed to serve as a publicly available reproducible RCS benchmark target. To increase the utility of the model, metallized and non-metallic

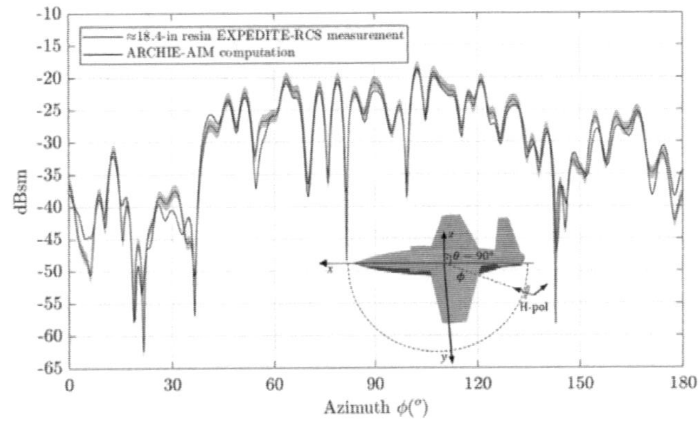

Fig. 3. Measured and computed HH-polarized monostatic RCS at 7 GHz for the ~18.4-in long uncoated-resin model. The measured data are shown with a ±1 dB uncertainty band [10]. The computed data were generated using the resin material properties in [11].

scale-model targets were additively manufactured, RCS measurements supported by simulations were performed and documented, and model files, meshes, measured RCS data, and computed RCS data were shared on an online repository [9].

Acknowledgment

The authors are grateful to LMA staff members S. Cox, W. Harwood, R. Heinstadt, E. Kuang, E. Lagos, E. Smith, Z. Teitelbaum, and M. Levy. The development, meshing, measurement, and public release of the model would not have been possible without their help and expertise.

References

[1] L. Gurel *et al.*, "Validation through comparison: Measurement and calculation of the bistatic radar cross section of a stealth target," *Radio Sci.*, vol. 38, no. 3, 1046, 2003.

[2] J. Song, C. C. Lu, and W. C. Chew, "Multilevel fast multipole algorithm for electromagnetic scattering by large complex objects," *IEEE Trans. Antennas Propag.*, vol. 45, no. 10, pp. 1488-1493, Oct. 1997.

[3] F. Wei and A. E. Yilmaz, "A hybrid message passing/shared memory parallelization of the adaptive integral method for multi-core clusters," *Parallel Comp.*, vol. 37, no. 6-7, pp. 279-301, June-July 2011.

[4] Z. Peng, X.-C. Wang, and J.-F. Lee, "Integral equation based domain decomposition method for solving electromagnetic wave scattering from non-penetrable objects," *IEEE Trans. Antennas Propag.*, vol. 59, no. 9, pp. 3328-3338, July 2011.

[5] S. Hughey *et al.*, "Parallel wideband MLFMA for analysis of electrically large, nonuniform, multiscale structures," *IEEE Trans. Antennas Propag.*, vol. 67, no. 2, pp. 1094-1107, Feb. 2019.

[6] D. G. Feitelson, "From repeatability to reproducibility and corroboration," *ACM SIGOPS Oper. Sys. Rev.*, vol. 49, no. 1, pp. 3-11, Jan. 2015.

[7] J. W. Massey, J. T. Kelley, C. Courtney, D. A. Chamulak, and A. E. Yilmaz, "A benchmark suite for quantifying RCS simulation performance on modern computers," in *Proc. USNC/URSI Rad. Sci. Meet.*, July 2018.

[8] J. T. Kelley *et al.*, "Austin RCS benchmark suite developments," in *Proc. USNC/URSI Rad. Sci. Meet.*, July 2019, pp. 19-20.

[9] "Austin Benchmark Suites for Computational Electromagnetics", 2018. [Online]. Available: https://github.com/UTAustinCEMGroup/AustinCEMBenchmarks

[10] J. T. Kelley, D. A. Chamulak, C. C. Courtney, and A. E. Yılmaz, "EM programmers notebook-Rye Canyon RCS measurements of benchmark almond targets" to appear in *IEEE Ant. Prop. Soc. Mag.*, Feb. 2020.

[11] J. T. Kelley, D. A. Chamulak, C. C. Courtney, and A. E. Yılmaz, "Measurements of non-metallic targets for the Austin RCS Benchmark Suite," in *Proc. Ant. Meas. Tech. Assoc.*, Oct. 2019.

[12] C. Davies, "Lockheed Martin overview of the AFRL EXPEDITE program," in *Proc. AIAA Scietech*, Jan. 2019, pp. 1-12.

Improving Precision of RCS Measurement Based on Spectral Extrapolation Method

Chufeng Hu, Nanjing Li, Weijun Chen, and Shuxia Guo
Science and Technology on UAV Laboratory
Northwestern Polytechnic University, NWPU
Xi'an, Shaanxi, China
huchufeng@nwpu.edu.cn, linanjing76@163.com, ajie@nwpu.edu.cn, guoshuxia0223@sina.com

***Abstract*—This paper proposes a spectral extrapolation method for measuring the RCS at two ends of band more exactly. The measured data are extrapolated to obtain the unknown value out of band with an auto-regressive model (AR model). The parameters in AR model are calculated by using maximum entropy spectral estimation algorithm. Therefore, the span of original band is extended, and the both ends of frequency on original band are inside the range of new band. If a time gating is adding to the new band, the precision at both ends of frequency on original band can be greatly improved. The simulation and experimental results show that about 25% extended data for each ends of original band can be obtained after spectral extrapolation, and even if a time gating reduces the effective frequency domain data, but the maximum error at the ends of band is less than 1dB. Moreover, RCS values near the out of band can be predicted by using spectral extrapolation method. The method can also be applied to broadband RCS measurement.**

Keywords—auto-regressive model, RCS, spectral estimation

I. INTRODUCTION

The values of the radar cross section (RCS) of the weapon system directly affect its survivability in modern electronic warfare [1,2]. With the development of modern stealth technology, accurate measurement especially for low scattering target can be taken full advantage in developing scientific research and improving models [3,4]. The stepped-frequency RCS measurement method is widely used in indoor [5,6], which can obtain broadband information with a wide band. Combined with the Inverse Fast Fourier Transform (IFFT), the clutter out of target area can be eliminated by a time gating, and that may improve the measurement accuracy. However, the time gating only intercepts a part of time domain information, so the effective frequency domain data is reduced, especially at the both ends of frequency domain data. After using the spectral extrapolation method, the span of original band is extended, and the two ends of frequency on original band are inside the range of new band. So even if a time gating reduces the effective data, the precision at both ends of frequency on original band will be greatly improved. The results of experiment show that the spectral extrapolation technique can ensure accuracy of RCS measurement at full frequencies.

II. SPECTRAL ESTIMATION ALGORITHM

In the stepped-frequency RCS measurement, the time gating intercepts a part of time domain information. The clutter out of target area can be eliminated by a time gating, but the effective frequency domain data is also reduced [7,8], and the narrower width of the time gating, the less effective frequency domain data can be obtained. Therefore, the method of the spectrum estimation extrapolation is used to extend the original band without increasing the stepped-frequency data.

Parametric model method in the spectral estimation is used to obtain the AR model of band data [9,10]. The parameters in AR model are calculated by using maximum entropy spectral estimation algorithm (Burg algorithm),

$$x(n) = -\sum_{i=1}^{m} a_m(i)x(n-i) + e(n) \tag{1}$$

Where, $a_m(i)$ is the coefficient of data, e(n) is estimation error.

It is assumed that the error of forward prediction and the error of backward prediction are $e^f(n)$ and $e^b(n)$ in linear prediction AR model. The sum of forward and backward forecasting errors is:

$$P_{fb} = \frac{1}{2}\left[P_f + P_b\right] = \frac{1}{2(N-m)}\sum_{n=m}^{N-1}\left|e^f(n)\right|^2 + \frac{1}{2(N-m)}\sum_{n=m}^{N-1}\left|e^b(n)\right|^2 \tag{2}$$

$e^f(n)$ and $e^b(n)$ have the following recursive relations:

$$\begin{aligned} e_m^f(n) &= e_{m-1}^f(n) + k_m e_{m-1}^b(n-1) \\ e_m^b(n) &= e_{m-1}^b(n-1) + k_m^* e_{m-1}^f(n) \end{aligned} \tag{3}$$

According to the maximum entropy method, when the sums of forward and backward forecasting errors are minimum, estimating equation of k_m can be obtained as follow:

$$k_m = \frac{-2\sum_{n=m}^{N-1} e_{m-1}^f(n)e_{m-1}^{b*}(n-1)}{\sum_{n=m}^{N-1}\left|e_{m-1}^f(n)\right|^2 + \sum_{n=s}^{N-1}\left|e_{m-1}^b(n-1)\right|^2} \tag{4}$$

Then, the parameters of the m-order AR model can be calculated by Levinson-Durbin recursive algorithm:

$$\begin{aligned} a_m(i) &= a_{m-1}(i) + k_m a_{m-1}^*(m-i) \\ a_m(m) &= k_m \end{aligned} \tag{5}$$

The steps of obtaining extrapolated data using original data are as follows:

Step 1: Given the initial condition $e_0^f(n) = e_0^b(n) = x(n)$, then k_1 is estimated by equation (4);

Step 2: the model coefficient $a_1(1) = k_1$ is obtained for m = 1;

Step 3: $e_1^f(n)$ and $e_1^b(n)$ are obtained by k_1, then k_2 is estimated;

Step 4: The model coefficients $a_2(1)$ and $a_2(2)$ for m = 2 are calculated by equation (5);

Step 5: Repeat the step 2 to step 4 until m = p, all of model coefficients are obtained. Then the forward and backward prediction data can be calculated by the coefficients.

This work was supported by the National Natural Science Foundation of China (No. 61871323; 61571368).

III. EXPERIMENTAL RESULTS

Metal ball with diameters of 150 mm and 75 mm are measured by using the stepped-frequency RCS measurement method respectively, see Fig. 1 and Fig. 2. The 150mm metal ball is used as the calibration body, and the 75mm metal ball is measured in the experiment. The measuring frequency band is 8000-12000MHz and there are 801 frequency points.

Fig.1. Φ150mm metal ball.

Fig.2. Φ75mm metal ball.

After adding a time gating, the RCS at all frequency points of 8000MHz to 12000MHz can be obtained. As shown in Fig. 3, the maximum error compared with the theory values at most of frequency points is less than 1dB, but the RCS error at the ends of 8000MHz and 12000MHz is larger, which can reach ±2dB.

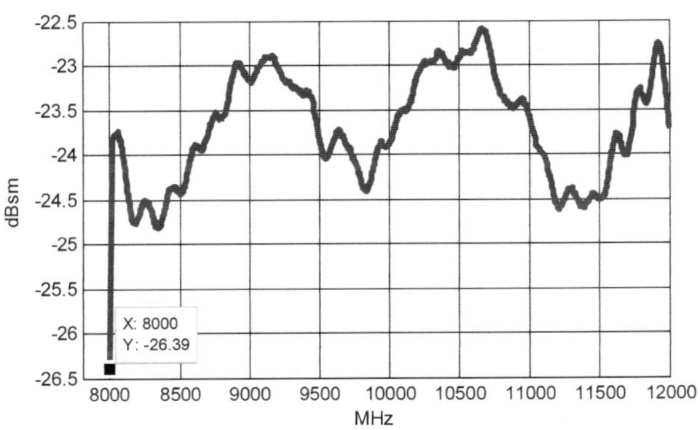

Fig.3. The RCS of 8000MHz to 12000MHz.

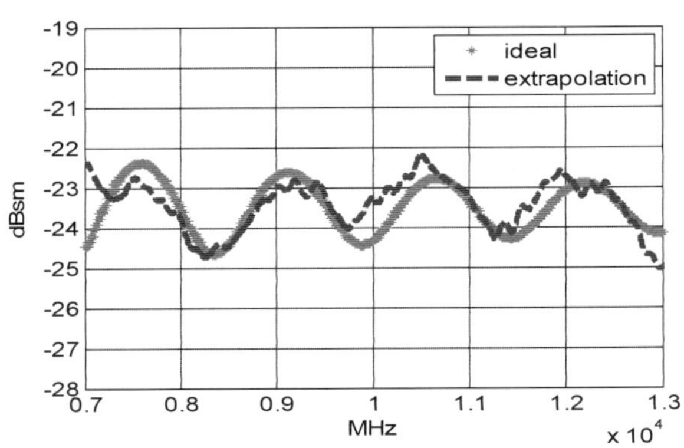

Fig.4. The RCS results after the extrapolation.

The measured data are extrapolated by using spectral extrapolation technique, then adding the same time gating to the new band of 7000MHz to 13000MHz, so the precision at both ends of frequency 8000MHz and 12000MHz on original band can be greatly improved, as shown in Fig. 4, the maximum error is less than 1dB.

It can be seen that the precision on both ends of frequency can be greatly improved by using spectral extrapolation technique, and the RCS values near the out of band can be predicted in some extent.

IV. CONCLUSION

The stepped-frequency RCS measurement method has high measurement efficiency and accuracy, but it has a low measurement precision on both ends of frequency. This paper presents a method of spectral extrapolation technique which is experimentally demonstrated to be effective. The both ends of frequency on original band are inside the range of new band by using this method, so that the measurement precision at the original band can be improved. Moreover, RCS values near the out of band can be predicted by using spectral extrapolation technique. The method can also be applied to broadband RCS measurement, and it can be used in engineering application.

REFERENCES

[1] E. Kemptner, D. Klement, and H. Wagner, "RCS determination for DLR stealth design F7," The ROT SCI Symposium on Non-Cooperative Air Target Identification Using Radar, Mannheim, Germany, RTO MP-6, 1998.

[2] B. Persson, and M. Norsell, "On modeling RCS of aircraft for flight simulation," IEEE Antennas and Propagation Magazine, vol. 56, no. 4, pp. 34-43, Oct. 2014.

[3] C. Corbel, C. Bourlier, N. Pinel, and J. Chauveau, "Rough surface RCS measurements and simulations using the physical optics approximation," IEEE Transactions on Antennas and Propagation, vol. 61, no. 10, pp. 5155-5165, Oct. 2013.

[4] C. H. Fang, X. X. Cheng, and F. Ding, "The prediction study of composite scattering from the ship on the surface via simulation and experiment," IEEE Asia-Pacific Conference on Antennas and Propagation, Kuta, Indonesia, 2015.

[5] A. Bati, L. To, and D. Hilliard, "Advanced radar cross section clutter removal algorithms," IEEE Conference on Antennas and Propagation, Barcelona, Spain, 2010.

[6] M. Potgieter, J. W. Odendaal, C. Blaauw, and J. Joubert. "Bistatic RCS Measurements of Large Targets in a Compact Range," IEEE Transactions on Antennas and Propagation, vol. 67, no. 4, pp. 2847-2852, 2019.

[7] R. A. M. Mauermayer, and T. F. Eibert, "Time gating based on sparse time domain signal reconstruction from limited frequency domain information," Symposium of the Antenna Measurement Techniques Association, Texas, USA, 2016.

[8] R. Phumvijit, P. Supanakoon, and S. Promwong, "Measurement scheme of radar cross section with time gating," International Conference on Electrical Engineering/Electronics, Computer, Telecommunications and Information Technology (ECTI-CON), Phuket, Thailand, 2017.

[9] S. M. Alessio, "Digital signal processing and spectral analysis for scientists: Concepts and applications", Springer, Berlin, Germany, 2016.

[10] P. Sukhacheuski, "Spectral metod analysis of radio-frequency pulse signal scattering from cylindrical and conical shapes object in the VHF band," International Conference on Ultra-wideband and Ultra-short Impulse Signals, Odessa, Ukraine, 2018.

Nonlinear Supra-Electroporation in Realistic Stem Cell Morphologies

Somen Baidya
Department of Computer Science and Electrical Engineering
University of Missouri–Kansas City
Kansas City, MO, 64110, USA.
sbg58@mail.umkc.edu

Ahmed M. Hassan
Department of Computer Science and Electrical Engineering
University of Missouri–Kansas City
Kansas City, MO, 64110, USA.
hassanam@umkc.edu

***Abstract*— Exposing cells to ultrashort electric field pulses can lead to the permeabilization of the membranes of the internal cell organelles, such as the nucleus, which is termed as supra-electroporation. In this paper, we study the supra-electroporation of stem cells with realistic morphologies under nanosecond electrical pulse stimulation. For such short pulses, the cell and the nucleus membranes exhibit non-linearity in their conductance. Therefore, we used a non-linear model for the cells' membranes, coupled with a quasi-static electromagnetic solver, and obtained the solution using a commercial Finite Element Method (FEM) solver. The results show that the outer shape of the cell has a strong effect on the magnitude and the spatiotemporal patterns of the electric field inside the cell, which affects the rate of the supra-electroporation of the nucleus. These variations in the rate of the supra-electroporation of the nucleus can guide the selective targeting of desired cells with specific shapes.**

Keywords—Supra-Electroporation, Stem Cells, Nonlinear.

I. Introduction

Cell membrane presents an insulating barrier to several molecules and foreign objects and it regulates the ion exchange between the extracellular and intracellular mediums. The semipermeable nature of the cell membrane can be changed by using external electrical excitation of different pulse width and amplitude, allowing the intake of chemotherapeutic drugs, proteins, gene transfection, extraction of molecules from cell, or even cell death for certain excitations [1]. When the excitation pulse width is in the nanosecond range, which is smaller than the membrane charging time, the induced electric field can manipulate the membrane permeability of intracellular components as well (i.e. the nucleus or the endoplasmic reticulum) [1]. This phenomena of regulating the intracellular organelles by engineering the excitation field parameter is known as Supra-Electroporation.

The goal of this study is to quantify the effect of cell morphology on the rate of supra-electroporation. Realistic cell shapes were obtained from the stem cell database developed by the National Institute of Standards and Technology (NIST) [2]. The database is divided into ten families and exhibits a wide range of variations in cell morphology, nucleus morphology, and the relative location of the nucleus inside the cell. In the following section, we will describe the nonlinear model used to simulate the supra-electroporation of these stem cells with realistic morphologies.

II. Methodology

In this study, we have used one cell map from each of the ten families and used a symmetrical 2D cross-section of the cells and embedded nuclei to incorporate in our model. Each cell cross-section from all the ten families are identified

This work is supported in part by the NIST Grant 70NANB15H28 and by the University of Missouri-Kansas City, SGS Research Award.

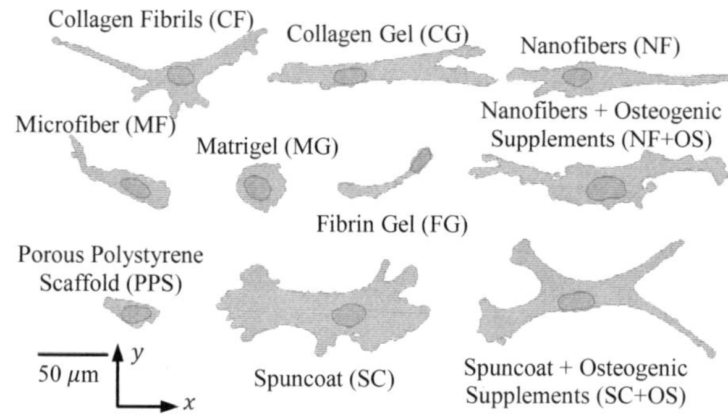

Fig. 1. 2D cross-sections of the ten different cell shapes and embedded nucleus used in this study.

according to their microenvironment name as depicted in Fig. 1. Using the known material properties (i.e., conductivity, permittivity) of the extracellular medium, the intracellular medium, and the cell membrane, we can solve Laplace Equation (1) to derive the electric field distribution and voltage inside and outside of the object. At any point on the cell membrane, a different value of the intracellular and extracellular voltage can exist based on the cell's shape. The difference of these voltages, at a point (i, j) is referred to as the transmembrane voltage of the cell membrane (V_m^{ij}). Under the effect of a sufficiently large electrical excitation, the transmembrane voltage induced on the membrane reaches its threshold for permeabilization (V_{ep}). The physical representation of this phenomenon is depicted by the density of pores formed on the cell and nucleus membrane (N_{ij}), which follows a nonlinear relationship with the transmembrane voltage (2). Initially, the cell and nucleus membranes have an equilibrium pore density (N_0). As the transmembrane voltage reaches its threshold, the pore density also saturates, resulting in a significant increase in the membrane conductivity (σ_m^{ij}) , hence increasing the membrane's permeability (3):

$$\nabla^2 V = 0, \tag{1}$$

$$\frac{dN_{ij}(t)}{dt} = \alpha e^{\left(\frac{V_m^{ij}}{V_{ep}}\right)^2}\left(1 - \frac{N_{ij}(t)}{N_0 e^{q\left(V_m^{ij}/V_{ep}\right)^2}}\right), \tag{2}$$

$$\sigma_m^{ij}(t) = \sigma_{m0} + N_{ij}(t)\sigma_p * \pi r_p^2 * K. \tag{3}$$

In (3), r_p and σ_p are the pore radius and pore conductivity, respectively. The nonlinearity of the physics arises from the correlation between the pore density and the membrane conductivity (3), which eventually effects the field distribution around the membrane (1). For our study, we have designed and implemented the aforementioned physics on both cell and nucleus membrane using COMSOL Multiphysics, a commercial finite element method solver. We have incorporated the Electric Current (Time Domain) solver

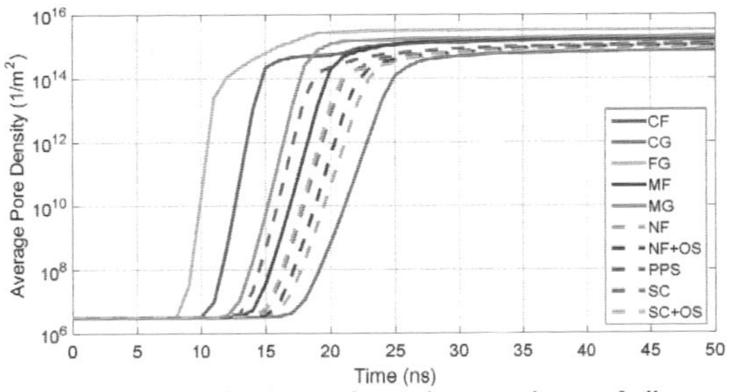

Fig. 2. Average pore density on the nucleus membrane of all ten cell sections in Fig. 1 versus time.

to solve (1) and a weak form PDE solver to solve (2) in the Multiphysics domain. The external excitation field used in this study was a 16 kV/cm pulse with 71 ns pulse duration accompanied by 6 ns rise time and 10 ns fall time. Since we are interested in electroporation of the internal organelles in this study, we modelled our excitation field in the supra-electroporation region of the pulse strength-duration map reported in [3]. The excitation field strength in this observation was in the range of "*cell survival*" as reported in [3]. To the best of our knowledge, the exact electrical properties of the stem cells reported in the NIST database were not characterized and therefore we used the electrical parameters of a general cell model [4]. In the subsequent results, we highlight only the characteristics of the nucleus membrane, although the nonlinear membrane was implemented on both the cell and nucleus membrane.

III. Result and Discussion

The induced transmembrane voltage is largely impacted by the orientation and location of cell with respect to direction of electric excitation. To maintain consistency in this regard, we diagonalized the cell with embedded nucleus along their largest gyration tensor, using their respective polarizability matrix information [5], then we translated the cell and the nucleus such that center of mass of the nucleus coincides with the origin before taking the 2D cross-section at the center of the cell (Fig. 1).

A. Average Pore Density on Stem Cell Sections

The pore density profile of all the ten nuclei from the cell sections considered in this study is depicted in Fig. 2. The average pore density is calculated by taking a line integral of the pore density along the perimeter of the nucleus ($\int N_{ij(t)} . dl \,/ \int dl$). As can be observed, CG nucleus demonstrates the slowest response, since the cell shape distribution is larger along the electric excitation direction. The slanted alignment of the FG cell and embedded nucleus results in faster pore density saturation under identical electrical excitation. There is also a significant difference in the saturated pore density, depicting the variation in cell shape is a major contributor to supra-electroporation characteristics.

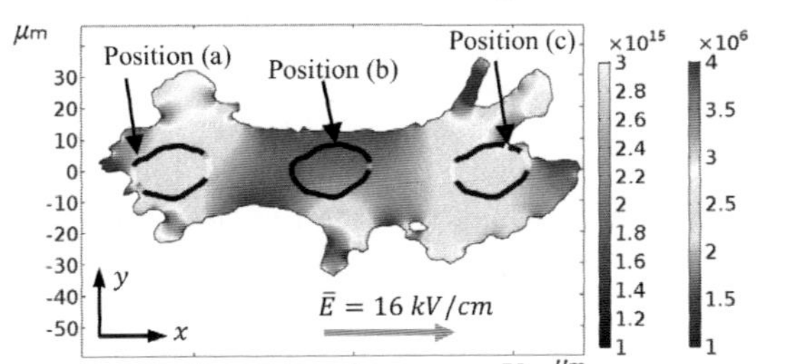

Fig. 3: Electric field distribution of SC cell section at $t = 25\ ns$ as the nucleus location is varied; *rainbow* color bar represents the electric field distribution (*V/m*) and *grayscale* color bar represents the pore density (*$1/m^2$*) at the nucleus membrane at the same instant for various nucleus location.

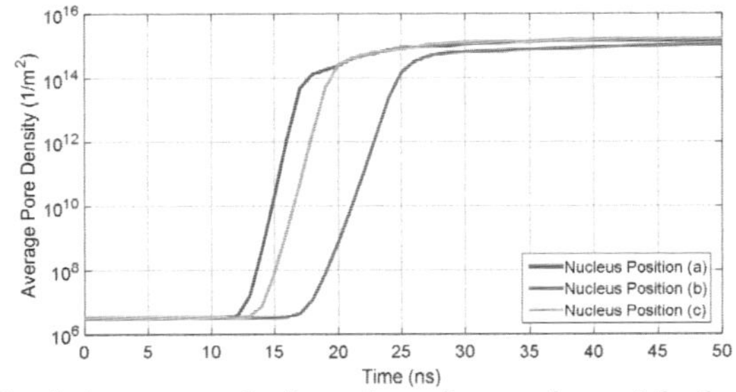

Fig. 4. Average pore density on the nucleus membrane at the three positions depicted in Fig. 3.

B. Variable Nucleus Location

To illustrate the effect of relative position of the nucleus inside the cell, we performed a parametric study by varying the nucleus location inside SC cell section, as depicted in Fig. 3 and Fig. 4. For simplicity, we have combined simulation from three different nucleus position and only demonstrated the field distribution at time $t = 25\ ns$ after the excitation starts as shown in Fig. 3. The internal electric field strength due to external excitation remains unperturbed by the position of the nucleus. As shown in Fig. 3, the presence of protrusions in the membrane creates a non-uniform electric field distribution inside the cell. As a result, the nucleus at position (a) experiences the fastest rate of electroporation, as shown by the blue curve in Fig. 4, because it experiences the largest electric field as shown in Fig. 3 (refer to nucleus at position (a)). The nucleus at position (b) experiences the slowest rate of electroporation since it is at the location where the internal electric field is minimum. Therefore, by controlling the electroporation time, the results in Fig. 2-Fig. 3 can be used for the selective supra-electroporation of cells with specific morphologies and nucleus positions. Moreover, the rate of supra-electroporation was found to vary with the direction of the field excitation which can also be leveraged for the selective targeting of specific cell shapes and orientations.

IV. Conclusion

In this paper, the supra-electroporation behavior of realistic cell morphologies was studied using a nonlinear computational model. The findings of this study draw the conclusion that, the morphology and the relative location of the cell's nucleus, play a significant role on the rate of electroporation of the nucleus membrane and can be used to guide the targeting of specific cells.

References

[1] L. Rems and D. Miklavčič, "Tutorial: Electroporation of cells in complex materials and tissue," Journal of Applied Physics, vol. 119, no. 20, p. 201101, May 2016, doi: 10.1063/1.4949264.

[2] https://isg.nist.gov/deepzoomweb/fileBrowsing/3D/.

[3] Weaver, James C., *et al.* "A brief overview of electroporation pulse strength–duration space: A region where additional intracellular effects are expected," Bioelectrochemistry, vol. 87, pp. 236–243, Oct. 2012, doi: 10.1016/j.bioelechem.2012.02.007.

[4] K. C. Smith and J. C. Weaver, "Active mechanisms are needed to describe cell responses to submicrosecond, megavolt-per-meter pulses: cell models for ultrashort pulses," Biophys. J., vol. 95, no. 4, pp. 1547–1563, Aug. 2008, doi: 10.1529/biophysj.107.121921.

[5] Baidya, Somen, *et al.* "Analysis of Different Computational Techniques for Calculating the Polarizability Tensors of Stem Cells with Realistic Three-Dimensional Morphologies," IEEE Transactions on Biomedical Engineering, vol. 66, no. 7, pp. 1816–1831, Jul. 2019, doi: 10.1109/TBME.2018.2876145.

On the Report of Performance Analysis of Electrospun Carbon Nanofibers based Strain Sensor for Applications in Human Motion Monitoring

Ahsan Aqueeb[1], Sayan Roy[1,*], Yichun Ding[2], Obiora Onyilagha[2], and Zhengtao Zhu[2]
Department of Electrical Engineering[1], *Department of Chemistry Biology and Health Sciences*[2]
South Dakota School of Mines and Technology
Rapid City, SD-57701, USA
Corresponding author*: sayan.roy.us@ieee.org

***Abstract*—Flexible and wearable sensors are currently being extensively used in versatile applications including wireless body area network. Specifically, such sensors are mostly incorporated to yield a linear response within their range of operations. A recently developed flexible and wearable resistive strain sensor made of electrospun carbon nanofibers has been reported with a gauge factor up to 72. In this paper, the performance of the strain sensor embedded in a polyurethane matrix was studied at first. A linear region of operation of such sensor was defined from direct measurements for wireless body area network applications. The equivalent analytical expressions were established and reported.**

***Index Terms*—resistivity, strain sensor, wireless body area network.**

I. INTRODUCTION

Strain sensors have been a very popular choice by scientists and engineers due to its low-cost, simplicity, and versatility. Currently they are being used for applications, like human monitoring where various motion (bending finger, arms or legs) require high stretch ability and sensitivity. Recently, various methods of fabrication such as electrospun carbon nanofibers [1], graphite-based strain sensors by pencil-trace drawn on flexible printing paper [2] and commercial plain weave carbonized cotton fabric [3] were reported. As reported in [4], prior studies of such sensors did not explore the change of resistance based on the amount of angle created by applied stress.

The objective of this paper was to study the change of resistance followed by the applied stress due to wireless body area network applications in determining a region of linear operation of such a sensor. As shown in Fig. 1 (a), a highly stretchable and sensitive strain sensor composed of free-standing electrospun carbon nanofibers (CNGs) embedded in a polyurethane (PU) elastomer with gauge factor up to 72 [1] was incorporated here to perform a study on finger movements for wireless body area network applications. In particular, the linear region of the strain limit was identified of the CNG based sensor where a change of angle within the specific linear region would produce a linear change of resistance.

II. METHODOLOGY

Initially, a single CNG based strain sensor was placed on the index finger to analyze the strain performance. Using a glove, the sensor was electrically separated and evenly distributed over the finger, as illustrated in Fig. 1 (b).

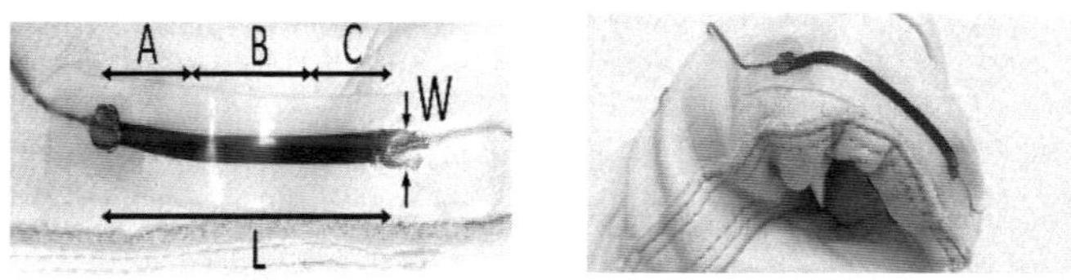

(a) (b)

Fig. 1. (a) Highly stretchable strain sensor based on electrospun carbon nanofibers and distribution of the Strain Sensor (Dimensions (in mm): A = 1.31, B = 27.6, C = 0.99, W = 2.86 and L = 29.9). (b) Distribution of the strain sensor over the finger using a glove.

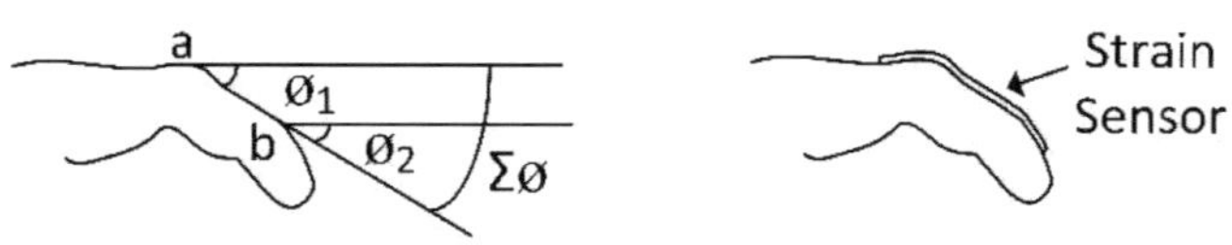

(a) (b)

Fig. 2. (a) Point a and b on a finger where the bend angles are $\emptyset_1$, $\emptyset_2$ and the summation of both the angle is defined as $\Sigma\emptyset$. (b) Sideview: CNG based strain sensor is placed on a finger.

Typically, a finger bends at two interphalangeal joints as shown in Fig. 2 (a). These two points of bending can be identified as points a and b, where the respective bend angles have been defined as $\emptyset_1$ and $\emptyset_2$. It can be observed that even though such joints bend at two different locations with different angles, in terms of the equivalent total applied stress on a strain sensor placed on the finger, they can be analytically represented using a single angle, $\Sigma\emptyset$ where,

$$\Sigma\emptyset = \emptyset_1 + \emptyset_2. \quad (1)$$

III. RESULT and DISCUSSION

a) Measurement of bending angles and resistances: An extensive study on most possible combinations of bending angles was taken into consideration here. In a few cases, measurements of the resistances (R) using various possible combinations of $\emptyset_1$ and $\emptyset_2$ yielded identical values of $\Sigma\emptyset$ and R where an average resistance value was considered. Next, a voltage divider circuit was used to generate an equivalent change in voltage for change in resistance for variable applied stress. Changes of per unit resistance ($\Delta R/R$) and per unit voltage ($\Delta V/V$) were then measured for a possible range of $\Sigma\emptyset$, as shown

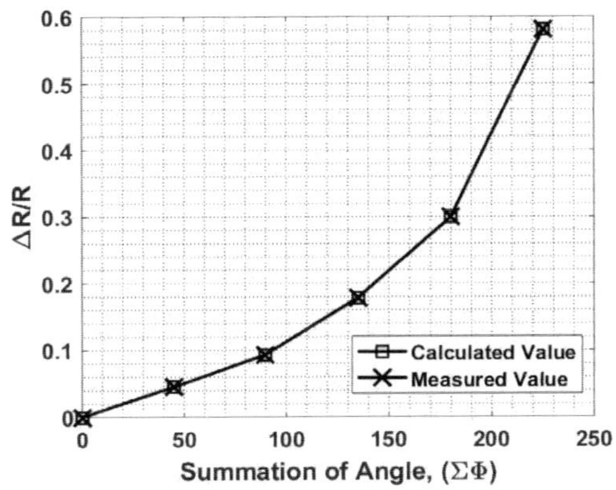

Fig. 3. Comparison between measured and calculated per unit resistance $\Delta R/R$ with change of angle $\Sigma\emptyset$.

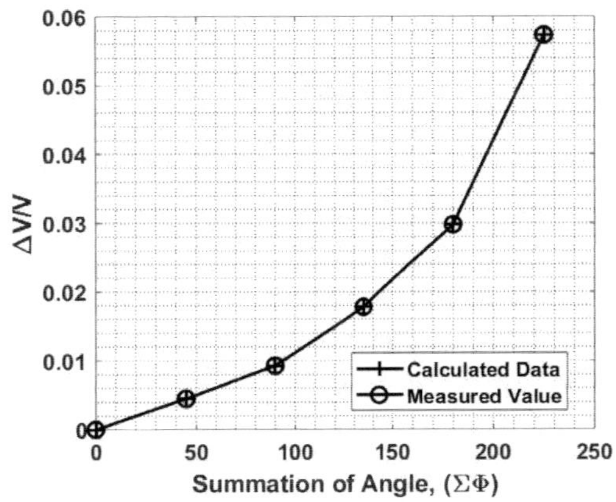

Fig. 4. Comparison between measured and calculated per unit voltage $\Delta V/V$ with change of angle $\Sigma\emptyset$.

in Figs. 3 and 4. Based on the measured data, a linear relation between $\Delta R/R$ and $\Sigma\emptyset$ was analytically approximated,

$$y_1 = 0.0019x_1 - 0.0733\,, \quad (2)$$

where y_1 and x_1 represents $\Delta R/R$ and $\Sigma\emptyset$, respectively. Similarly, a linear relation was analytically approximated between $\Delta V/V$ and $\Sigma\emptyset$,

$$y_2 = 0.00018767x_1 - 0.0072\,, \quad (3)$$

where, y_2 represents ΔV/V. Next, the accuracy of equations (2) and (3) was analyzed by calculating equivalent total bend angle ($\Sigma\emptyset_{calc}$) directly from measured per unit resistances and voltages using the above two equations. The error (in percentage) were then measured using equation 4 and reported in Table I.

$$\text{Error (in \%)} = \frac{\Sigma\emptyset - \Sigma\emptyset_{\text{calc}}}{\Sigma\emptyset_{\text{calc}}} \times 100\ \%. \quad (4)$$

TABLE I

MEASUREMENT OF PERCENTAGE ERROR

$\Sigma\emptyset$ (degrees)	$\Delta R/R$	$\Delta V/V$	$\Sigma\emptyset_{calc}$ (degrees)	error (%)
45	0.0452	0.0045	62.3435	38.54
90	0.0935	0.0093	87.9203	-2.31
135	0.1784	0.0178	133.2126	-1.32
180	0.3	0.0298	197.1546	9.53

Now, the relations between per unit components ($\Delta R/R$ and $\Delta V/V$) with the total bend angle $\sum\emptyset$, as can be seen in Figs. 3 and 4, are non-linear and equations (2) and (3) are only linear approximations with the reported error in Table I. For further accuracy, an exponential equation is analyzed if the CNG based sensor is needed to be operated beyond its linear region. The following parameters a and z are then defined analytically and Table II summarizes their values using curve fitting techniques.

$$a = ln(x + 1). \quad (5)$$

$$z = e^{a} - 1. \quad (6)$$

TABLE II

CALCULATION OF EXPONENTIAL OUTPUT

$\Sigma\emptyset$ °	$\Delta R/R$	a	z	$\Delta V/V$	a	z
45	0.0452	0.0442	0.0452	0.0045	0.0045	0.0045
90	0.0935	0.0894	0.0935	0.0093	0.0093	0.0093
135	0.1784	0.1638	0.1780	0.0178	0.0176	0.0178
180	0.3	0.2624	0.3	0.0298	0.0294	0.0298

b) Result: The CNG based sensor yields an approximately linear response between 90° to 180° region of operation with percentage error of less than 10%. The sensor can also be used from 0° to 225° with non-linear approximations, as reported.

IV. CONCLUSION

A study on the performance of CNG based strain sensor was reported. Specifically, relations between the bend angles caused by the movement of fingers and its equivalent changes in resistance and voltage were established. Finally, it was concluded that CNG based strain sensor reported in [1] could be used between 90° to 180° which is the sum of bend angles at two interphalangeal joints of a finger for linear operations.

ACKNOWLEDGMENT

This research is supported by the National Aeronautics and Space Administration (NASA) of the United States. (Grant Number – 80NSSC18M0022).

REFERENCES

[1] Y. Ding, J. Yang, C. R. Tollebc, and Z. Zhu, "A highly stretchable strain sensor based on electrospun carbon nanofibers for human motion monitoring" RSC Adv., vol. 8, no. 26, Aug. 2016.

[2] X. Liao, Z. Zhang, Q. Liao, Q. Liang, Y. Ou, M. Xu, M. Li, G. Zhanga, and Y. Zhang, "Flexible and printable paper-based strain sensors for wearable and large-area green electronics" Nanoscale, vol. 8, no. 26,June 2016.

[3] M. Zhang, C. Wang, H. Wang, M. Jian, X. Hao, and Y. Zhang, "Carbonized Cotton Fabric for High-performance Wearable Strain Sensors," Advanced Functional Materials, vol. 27, no. 2, Nov. 2016.

[4] M. Sanati, A. Sandwell, H. Mostaghimi, and S. S. Park, "Development of Nanocomposite-Based Strain Sensor with Piezoelectric and Piezoresistive Properties," Sensors (Basel), vol. 18, no. 11, Nov. 2018.

Numerical Analysis of an Applicator for Hyperthermia Treatment of Melanoma

J. L. Duque Muñoz
Dept.of Electrical Engineering
Universidad Nacional de Colombia
Bogotá D.C., Colombia
jlduquem@unal.edu.co

N. García Ramirez
Dept.of Electrical Engineering
Universidad Nacional de Colombia
Bogotá D.C., Colombia
nigarciara@unal.edu.co

J. L. Araque Quijano
Dept.of Electrical Engineering
Universidad Nacional de Colombia
Bogotá D.C., Colombia
jlaraqueq@unal.edu.co

***Abstract*—This document presents the design and validation of an applicator conceived for hyperthermia treatment of the melanoma in the human male torso and female leg. The applicator consists of an antenna array operating in the 5.8GHz ISM band immersed in an interface layer. The resulting device is comfortable to wear by the patient, low-cost and easy to store and handle. Simulation is carried out using Sim4Life and the ViP 3.0 human model, and the results demonstrate correct energy delivery to the tissue under treatment.**

***Index Terms*—Cancer, hyperthermia, melanoma, multi-physics simulation, tissue, Sim4Life.**

I. Introduction

Hyperthermia is a therapy for the treatment of tumors that operates by raising the temperature of affected tissue above the body average temperature in a selective manner, typically in the range 42°C-45°C. By combining hyperthermia with radiotherapy and chemotherapy, the effectiveness of these conventional treatments may reach five-fold and ten-fold improvements respectively [1]. Nonetheless, hyperthermia is still under scrutiny as there is no evidence that it induces increased survival rates, while side effects such as burns, blisters, pain and nausea have been reported [2].

In order to improve the effectiveness of hyperthermia and avoid its negative side effects, several works have been carried out recently. In [3] it is presented an improvement to the magnetic heat induction technique consisting in the insertion of nanoparticles in the affected tissue. The work in [4] proposes a metamaterial structure operating at the 2.4GHz ISM band to improve focusing of electromagnetic energy in the zone of interest. At lower frequencies, [5] propose a metamaterial antenna array at 434 MHz to heat uniformly tissue areas of considerable size. In [6], the FDTD method is used to evaluate the temperature increase induced by the electromagnetic field with a graded grid for improved accuracy in the geometrical representation.

The work in [7] presents a realistic model of space-dependent blood perfusion in a multi-physics simulation to understand the perfusion features of the tumor, with a circular patch antenna with slotted ground operating at 434 MHz as applicator. In [8] the authors design an applicator for hyperthermia treatment specifically targeted at not causing the patient any pain, using a transmitarray lens and a distilled water interface. [9] proposes a 3-D antenna array operating at 4.2GHz for the treatment of breast cancer that avoids hot spots outside the treated area.

Throughout the literature revised we see a variation of: applicator type (antenna), interface layer, illness targeted, tissue location, level of detail anatomical model. In this work, we present the design and numerical validation of an antenna array applicator for hyperthermia treatment of melanoma that is compact, robust in view that antennas are immersed on a solid interface layer and cost-effective thanks to a simple design. The validation process considers a detailed model of the affected zone and its environment within the body to assess the performance in terms of energy focusing and power delivery. The computation is carried out with Sim4Life [10], and results in quantitative data that provide a very accurate prediction of the performance.

II. Simulation Scenario and Applicator Design

The anatomical model employed is extracted from the Virtual Population (ViP 3.0) [11], which is a group of computable human models that describe the multi-physics and physiological behavior of body tissues with great accuracy in high resolution, and allow postural manipulation. In the anatomical model employed, no differentiation in tissue characteristics for healthy/ill tissue is analyzed.

The applicator consists of a planar antenna array operating in the 5.8GHz ISM band, designed to attain energy focusing in the zone of interest and low return loss. An interface layer favors energy delivery to the affected tissue by avoiding the free-space/body impedance mismatch and preventing the generation of hot spots in or near the body, thus preventing discomfort and unintended tissue heating, while favoring focusing for better control of the temperature profile. The resulting design is compact, such that the patient can wear it comfortably, and robust in view that the 3D radiating structures are backed by a ground plane and are embedded in a solid dielectric interface medium. The elemental radiators are elevated patch antennas fed with an L-feed, which are directive and very broadband (even more so thanks to the 2x2 broadside array configuration), hence making the device robust against patient-to-patient variations. Furthermore, the ground plane prevents radiation in unwanted directions and provides a solid support for connector/handles to operate the device. The details of this design are illustrated in Fig. 1.

The array applicator is embedded in an interface with transverse dimensions 15cm x 15cm and height 10 cm. In order to minimize reflections with actual tissue, this material is chosen with parameters very similar to muscle: dielectric constant 48.4846 and loss tangent 0.0227.

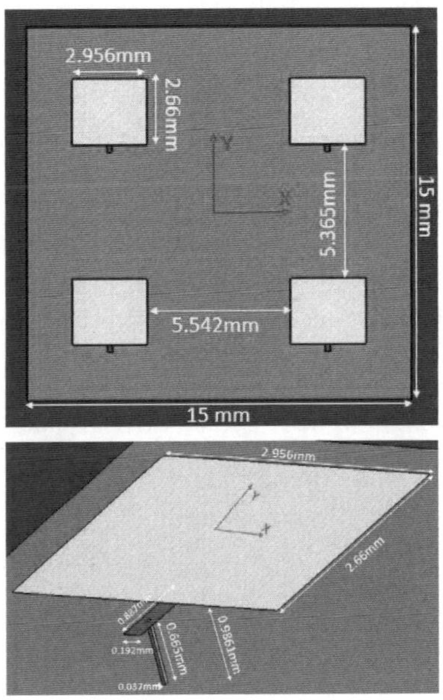

Fig. 1: Detail of the antenna array used as applicator.

III. Results

We report results on the initial validation of the applicator, as shown in Fig. 2 in the form of cuts of the Specific Absorption Rate (SAR) in three orthogonal cuts inside the interface. The first aspect to notice from the first two cuts in Fig. 2 is the favorable role played by the interface, that buffers the unfavorable field distribution present near the array elements (broad and multiple high-intensity lobes). It is clear from the last cut in Fig. 2 that 9cm above the ground plane, near the end of the interface, the field distribution is well suited for the treatment of melanoma (3dB diameter of about 2cm).

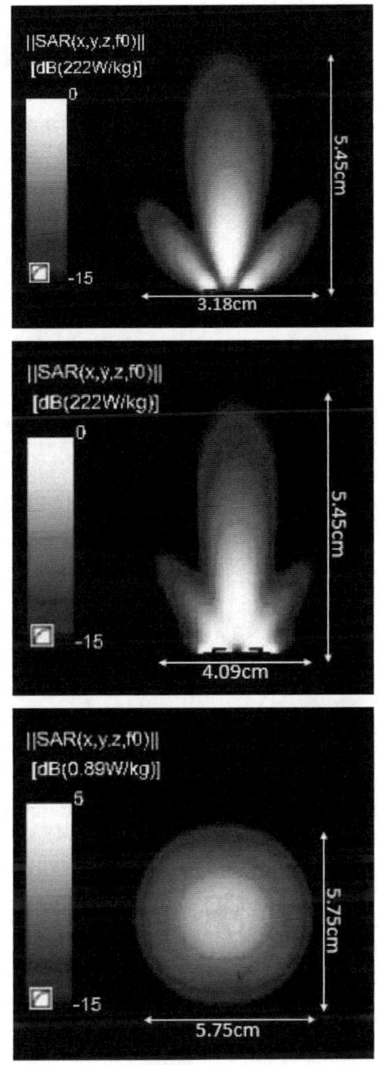

Fig. 2: SAR results for three orthogonal cuts: XZ (top), YZ (center) and XY, 9cm above the ground plane (bottom).

Acknowledgment

This work was possible by a Sim4Life for Science License granted by ZMT [10].

References

[1] J. van der Zee, "Heating the patient: A promising approach?," Annals of Oncology, vol. 13, no. 8, pp. 1173-1184, 2002.

[2] "Hyperthermia in Cancer Treatment," National Cancer Institute. [Online]. Available in: https://www.cancer.gov/about-cancer/treatment/types/surgery/hyperthermia-fact-sheet.

[3] L. Zhang, Y. Du, and D. Wu, "FDTD simulation of magnetic heat induction on Human Body Subject," ACES Conference Paper, 2015.

[4] Y. Gong and G. Wang, "Superficial Tumor Hyperthermia with Flat Left-Handed Metamerial Lens," Progress in Electromagnetic Research, PIER 98, 389-405, 2009.

[5] D. Vrba, D. B. Rodriguez, J. Vrba, and P. R. Stauffer, "Metamaterial Antenna Arrays for Improved Uniformity of Microwave Hyperthermia Treatments," Progress in Electromagnetic Research, vol. 156, 1-12, 2016.

[6] N. Chavannes, E. Neufeld, and N. Kuster, "Recent Advances in Biomedical Modeling: Hyperthermia Treatment Planning," 23rd Annual Review of Progress in Applied Computational Electromagnetics, March 19-23, 2007 - Verona, Italy, 2007, ACES.

[7] G. Muntoni, A. Fanti, G. Montisci, and M. Muntoni, "A Blood Perfusion Model of a RMS Tumor in a Local Hyperthermia Multi-Physic Scenario: A Preliminary Study," IEEE Journal of Electromagnetics, RF, and Microwaves in Medicine, vol. 3, no. 1, pp. 71-78, March 2019.

[8] W. C. Choi, S. Lim, and Y. J. Yoon, "Design of Noninvasive Hyperthermia System Using Transmit-Array Lens Antenna Configuration," IEEE Antennas and Wireless Propagation Letters, vol. 15, pp. 857-860, 2016.

[9] P. T. Nguyen, A. Abbosh, and S. Crozier, "Three-Dimensional Microwave Hyperthermia for Breast Cancer Treatment in a Realistic Environment Using Particle Swarm Optimization," IEEE Transactions on Biomedical Engineering, vol. 64, no. 6, pp. 1335-1344, June 2017.

[10] Sim4Life by ZMT, www.zurichmedtech.com.

[11] https://itis.swiss/virtual-population/virtual-population/vip3/

Wireless Body Area Networks

UWB Antenna Design and Channel Modeling

Mona Elhelbawy
Department of Electrical Engineering
California Polytechnic State University
San Luis Obispo, CA, USA
melhelba@calpoly.edu

Abstract— **Ultrawideband (UWB) technology is considered a key technology for Wireless Body Area Networks (WBANs) due to its unique characteristics: high-bandwidth, low-power consumption, less sensitivity to fading, and low interference probability. This paper presents a review of the IEEE 802.15.6 standard, UWB antenna designs and channel models.**

Keywords— ***BAN; WBAN; UWB; LOS; NLOS***

I. INTRODUCTION

A Wireless Body Area Network (WBAN) is a wireless network comprised of low power computing devices or nodes that may be implanted inside, mounted on, or placed in close proximity to the human body. Applications of WBANs include healthcare, sports and fitness, military and public safety [1]. In WBAN applications, operation in and/or close proximity to the human body brings several challenges. Wireless links between BAN nodes are often formed by on-body creeping waves and signal components reflected, diffracted and scattered from other body parts [2]. Factors such as mobility, body shape and composition, and physiological processes, make BAN channels susceptible to time-varying received signal characteristics [3], [4]. Channel characteristics in a given scenario can be determined using analytical, measurement or electromagnetic simulation based channel models [5]. WBAN channel simulation methods include asymptotic techniques such as ray tracing (RT) and Uniform Theory of Diffraction (UTD), and full-wave numerical techniques such as the Method of Moments (MoM), Finite Element Method (FEM), Finite-Difference Time-Domain (FDTD), and Finite Integration Technique (FIT). In WBAN, performing a full-wave numerical simulation at millimeter wave frequencies can be computationally demanding. A hybrid of asymptotic and full-wave can be used to enhance simulation speed at the cost of accuracy. This paper is organized as follows: Section II describes the IEEE 802.16.5 channel models. In Section III provides the key design requirements. Section IV provides a review of few UWB antenna designs. Section V provides a brief summary.

II. THE IEEE 802.15.6 STANDARD

The IEEE 802.15.6 standard [6] identified three different types of BAN nodes based on their physical position: (1) *Implant* node: placed inside the human body, immediately below the skin or deeper inside the body tissue; (2) *Body surface* node: placed on the surface of the human skin; and (3) *External* node: not in contact with human skin.

WBAN Communication links, shown in Fig.1, can be divided into three categories: on-body, off-body, and in-body communications. The on-body link describes communication between two *body surface* nodes. The off-body link describes communication between a *body surface* node and an *external* node. The in-body link is used to describe communication involving at least one implant node, i.e., communication between two *implant* nodes, an *implant* node and a *body surface* or between an *implant* node and an *external* node.

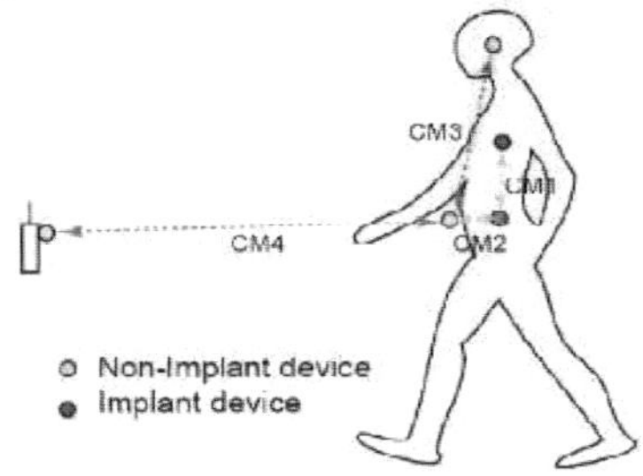

Fig 1. IEEE Channel Models [7]

A number of scenarios were identified by the IEEE 802.15.6 based on the communication link, the frequency of interest, and on whether there is a Line-of-Sight (LOS) or Non-Line-of-Sight (NLOS) between the nodes. The scenarios were grouped into categories that may be represented by the same channel model (CM) as shown in Table 1.

TABLE I. LIST OF SCENARIOS AND THEIR DESCRIPTION [8]

Scenario	Description	Frequency Band	Channel Model
S1	Implant to Implant	402-405 MHz	CM1
S2	Implant to Body Surface		CM2
S3	Implant to external		CM2
S4	Body surface to body surface (LOS)	13.5, 50, 400, 600, 900 MHz, 2.4, 3.1-10.6 GHz	CM3
S5	Body surface to body surface (NLOS)		CM3
S6	Body surface to external (LOS)	900 MHz, 2.4, 3.1-10.6 GHz	CM4
S7	Body surface to external (NLOS)		CM4

III. WBAN Design Requirements

The key design requirements for WBAN nodes include: small size, reliability, wireless communication ability, and low power consumption. Antenna Design for WBANs is essential for the reliability of communication. The shape and size of a WBAN antenna depends on the location of the node and on the radio technology used for transmission. Antenna's characteristics such as input impedance, resonant frequency and radiation patterns, are affected by the human body's weight, skin type, and posture [9]. The dielectric properties of human body tissues are dependent on the operating frequencies [10]. At UWB frequencies, the high absorption, and hence attenuation, prevents transmission through the human body. One important design consideration is the Specific Absorption Rate (SAR) [7]. The Federal Communications Commission (FCC) recommends a maximum SAR value of 1.6 W/kg averaged over a 1g of human body tissue. SAR values above the prescribed limit can lead to considerable tissue heating and damage [11].

IV. UWB WBAN Antenna

The FCC allocated the 3.1–10.6 GHz frequency band for UWB communications [12]. In [13], a compact antenna for on-body communications at UWB frequencies was proposed; the antenna consisted of mono-cone and a ring patch with four shorting pins, and had overall dimensions of $64 \times 64 \times 7$ mm^3. The antenna's performance was simulated and measured in free space and on a homogeneous human equivalent phantom. The radiation pattern in free space was similar to that on the phantom. In [14], a compact size four-leaf clover shaped antenna for on-body communication was proposed. The proposed antenna consisted of four antenna elements, made for omnidirectional radiation parallel to the surface of the human body. The proposed antenna was built on the Flame Retardant (FR-4) substrate, a popular material for UWB antennas, with the size of $46 \times 46 \times 0.6$ mm^3 and a bandwidth of 6 to 10.6 GHz. Results show an omnidirectional gain of 2.44 dBi at 7 GHz and 3.44 dBi at 9 GHz. In [15], a high-fidelity all-textile UWB antenna with full-ground plane for operation within the FCC UWB bandwidth of 3.1-10.6 GHz was introduced. A multilayered structure was implemented to meet the requirements of WBANs backward radiation reduction and high-fidelity for UWB pulse transmission/reception. The structure consisted of two patches and a ground plane implemented on two layers of 2-mm-thick substrate. The full ground plane on the lower layer is designed as a shield against on-body radiation. Results showed high on-body system fidelity values of between 95% and 97% measured at a distance of 1 m. In [16], a 0.1 mm thick planar monopole antenna for WBAN wearable applications was presented. The design was fabricated on flexible liquid crystalline polymer (LCP) substrate and the antenna was fed by a uni-planar coplanar waveguide transmission line of 51×22 mm^2 total size. The highest SAR values of 0.96676 W/kg at 3 GHz and 2.5961 W/kg at 7 GHz (exceeding the FCC 1.6 W/kg limit) occurred with simulated power of 0.1 W. It was determined that the maximum permissible feeding power with this antenna design is limited to 60 mW for compliance with the FCC SAR recommendations. A number of novel antenna designs and characterization methodologies for medical applications were presented in [17].

V. Conclusion

This paper provided an overview of WBANs and investigated some of the research challenges in this field. Channel modeling for UWB is currently in the research phase due to the complex environment of the human body. There is no standard antenna design for WBANs. Antenna's directionality, gain and SAR values continue to be investigated.

References

[1] S. Movassaghi, M. Abolhasan, J. Lipman, D. Smith, and A. Jamalipour. "Wireless Body Area Networks: A Survey," IEEE Communications Surveys and Tutorials, vol. 16, no. 3, pp. 1658–1686, 2014.

[2] G. R. Tsouri, A. Sapio and J. Wilczewski, "An investigation into relaying of creeping waves for reliable low-power body sensor networking," IEEE Transactions on Biomedical Circuits and Systems, vol. 5, no. 4, pp. 307-319, 2011.

[3] G. A. Conway, W. G. Scanlon, C. Orlenius and C. Walker, "In situ measurement of UHF wearable antenna radiation efficiency using reverberation chamber," IEEE Antennas Wireless Propagation Letters, vol. 7, pp. 271-274, 2008.

[4] R. D'Errico and L. Ouvry, "Time-variant BAN channel characterization," IEEE 20th International Symposium on Personal, Indoor and Mobile Radio Communications, pp. 3000-3004, 2009.

[5] M. Säreströniemi, M. Hämäläinen and J. Iinatti, "An Overview of the Electromagnetic Simulation-Based Channel Modeling Techniques for Wireless Body Area Network Applications," in IEEE Access, vol. 5, pp. 10622-10632, 2017.

[6] IEEE 802.15: Standard for local and metropolitan area networks – part 15.6: Wireless Body Area Networks, www.ieee802.org/15/pub/TG6.html

[7] K. Yazdandoost and K. Sayrafian, "Channel Model for Body Area Network (BAN)," IEEE 802.15-08-0780-12-0006, 2010.

[8] S. L. Cotton, R. D'Errico and C. Oestges, "A review of radio channel models for body centric communications," Radio Science, vol. 49, pp. 371-388, 2014.

[9] B. Antonescu and S. Basagni, "Wireless Body Area Networks: Challenges, Trends and Emerging Technologies," BodyNets '13 Proceedings of the 8th International Conference on Body Area Networks, pp. 1-7, 2013.

[10] X. Qing, Z. N. Chen, T. S. P. See, C. K. Goh and T. M. Chiam, "RF transmission characteristics in/through the human body," *2010 IEEE Conference on Cybernetics and Intelligent Systems*, Singapore, pp. 20-23, 2010.

[11] FCC policy on human exposure to radio frequency electromagnetic fields, https://www.fcc.gov/general/radio-frequency-safety-0

[12] Federal Communications Commission. "Resvision of Part 15 of the Commissions's rules regarding ultra-wideband transmission system from 3.1 to 10.6 GHz," ET-Docket, Federal Communications Commision, FCC, 98-153, Washington, DC, 2002.

[13] W. Jeong, J. Tak and J. Choi, "A Low-Profile IR-UWB Antenna With Ring Patch for WBAN Applications," *IEEE Antennas and Wireless Propagation Letters*, vol. 14, pp. 1447-1450, 2015.

[14] K. Chen, N. Liu and J. Tarng, "A compact size four-leaf clover shaped antenna for on-body communications," *2016 IEEE International Symposium on Antennas and Propagation (APSURSI)*, pp. 1775-1776, Fajardo, 2016.

[15] L. A. Yimdjo Poffelie, P. J. Soh, S. Yan and G. A. E. Vandenbosch, "A high-fidelity all-textile UWB antenna with low back radiation for off-body WBAN applications," *IEEE Transactions on Antennas and Propagation*, vol. 64, no. 2, pp. 757-760, Feb. 2016.

[16] S. R. Zahran, M. A. Abdalla, and A. Gaafar, "New Thin Wide-band Bracelet-like Antenna with Low SAR for On-arm WBAN Applications." IET Microwaves, Antennas & Propagation 13.8, pp. 1219-225, 2019.

[17] D. H. Werner; Z. H. Jiang, "Novel Antenna Designs and Characterization Methodologies for Medical Diagnostics and Sensing," in Electromagnetics of Body Area Networks: Antennas, Propagation, and RF Systems , IEEE, pp.87-134, 2016.

Antenna cased bias of polarimetric variables obtained by Electromagnetic simulations

Djordje Mirkovic
Cooperative Institute for Mesoscale Meteorological Studies (OU)
The National Severe Storms Laboratory (NOAA)
Norman, OK
djordje.mirkovic@noaa.gov

Dusan S. Zrnic
The National Severe Storms Laboratory (NOAA)
Norman, OK
dusan.zrnic@noaa.gov

***Abstract*—A roadmap for polarimetric weather radar antenna modeling is presented. Validation of the model, as well as comparison of multiple solvers, is presented in determining the most optimal research tool for large polarimetric array modeling. The application of the infinite array approximation is investigated in terms of polarimetric calibration requirements. Finally, a set of antenna caused biases is examined for a mobile radar.**

Keywords*— *polarimetric calibration, weather radar calibration.

I. Introduction

Polarimetric phased array weather radars are making their first steps into weather observations. The first full-size S-band polarimetric radar, Advanced Technology Demonstrator (ATD), has been deployed in Norman, OK. Yet the study of the ATD's Ten Panel Demonstrator (TPD) is an ongoing project. Here, we present the roadmap of the computational electromagnetic (CEM) study of the TPD. The study includes modeling of the TPD's antenna from the single element to the full array with and without radar's radome. Of special interest is a comparison of CEM solvers applied to the single panel, shared between the ATD and TPD, in terms of numerical complexity and solving time.

II. Problem of Calibration

The modeling process can be subdivided into three stages. First is the modeling of a single radiator, second is modeling of the single panel and finally the full radar array modeling. Naturally, complexity of the model increases with the number of elements. As the modeling of three-layer stacked patch differentially fed antennas is well documented we will skip the single element model and start with the single panel.

The single panel consists of 64 radiating elements arranged in 8 by 8 array. This array was measured and modeled with only one of the central elements active, while the others were load-matched. We measured and compared both copolar and cross-polar radiation patterns for E, H, and D cuts. For brevity only the H and D cuts are presented. In collaboration with the OU ARRC, we simulated the array using the same computing capabilities in WIPL-D, CST, and HFSS. As it is obvious in Fig. 1 HFSS had some convergence issues on our machine, however these results are comparable as we recorded the overall simulation time. For simulating both polarizations WIPL-D took 3 h and 20 mins, CST about 5 h and 30 mins, while HFFS achieved partial convergence ($\Delta_S = 0.027$) after 6 hours of simulation. It is important to note that simulation on our machine failed at this point.

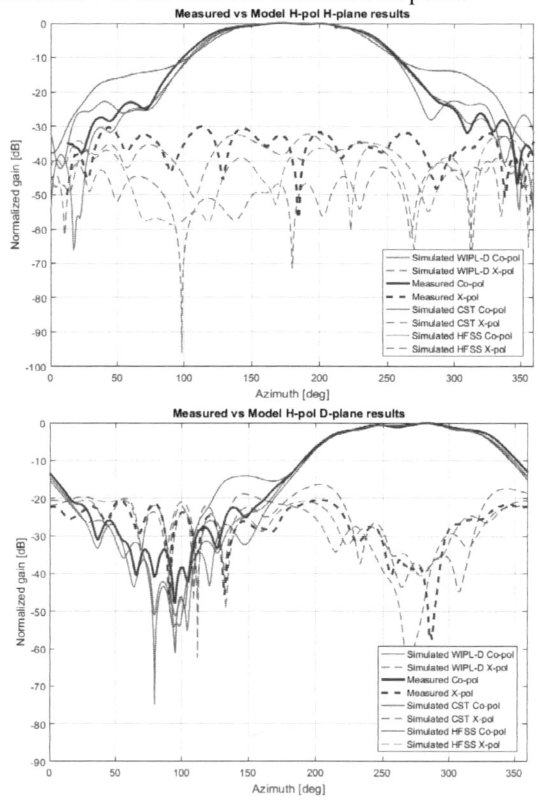

Fig. 1. – Measured and simulated patterns of the single panel array with only one central element excited and others load matched. Compared are simulations using WIPL-D, CST and HFSS solver for H-polarization, H-plane (up) and D-plane (down).

Analyzing the results in Fig. 1 (up) we see that all simulated patterns agree quite well with the measurement in the 100° to 250° region although the measured main lobe is slightly wider. CST and WIPL-D main lobe patterns between 50° and 150° match well but the measured main lobe is a bit larger. The pattern computed with HFSS misses the sidelobes, due to convergence problems. On the opposite side of the main lobe (200° to 275°), the pattern computed with CST falls off quicker compared to the measured and WIPL-D patterns. The computed cross-polar patterns by the CST solver are about 15 to 20 dB lower than the measured and WIPL-D patterns, while the pattern computed with the HFSS is in-between the patterns from these two simulators.

For the D-plane cut (Fig. 1. down) within the main lobe, the shape of the sidelobes computed by WIPL-D is in better agreement with measurement than the shapes computed by the other two solvers. This is important because the cross-polar lobes of an antenna populated with the same elements determine the biases in the polarimetric variables. For example, if the sidelobes within the main lobe exhibit four symmetric peaks, the bias in polarimetric variables caused by coupling is significantly reduced [1], [2]. The ones computed with CST agree almost as well except at angles 0° to 50°. The D-plane has the strongest cross-polar radiation and is typically used as a benchmark for cross-pol simulation results.

III. Full Array Modeling

Encouraging results in single panel measurement comparisons set the bar quite high for modeling of the full TPD array. This array consists of ten panels arranged in 2 by 5 configuration. The array has 640 elements with an area of about 2 m^2.

In terms of CEM, this array is considered to be quite large as the problem would yield about 1.2 million unknowns. However this number could be decreased if the (a)symmetry option in the WIPL-D solver is employed. The (a)symmetry argument applies to the full topological structure while all excitation remains independent of each other. Using the (a)symmetry we were, for the first time, able to model this size of an array and implement beam steering capability into the model. The complete model is driven by 2560 excitations, for H and V polarization, that are separately controlled.

Implementing the full 3D CEM model is of specific importance, as approximate techniques, such as infinite array method, may fail to provide necessary precision in cross-polar radiation modeling.

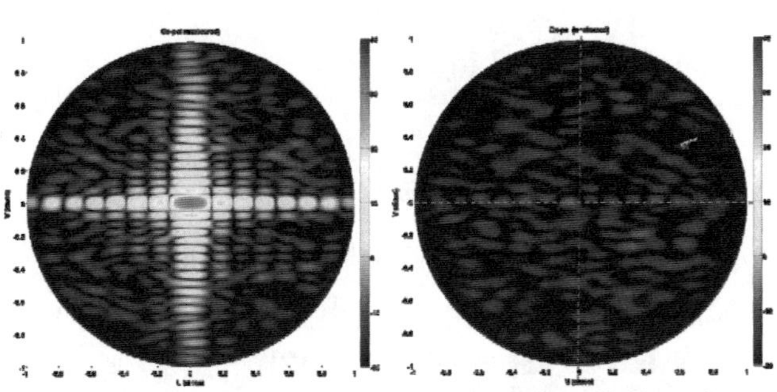

Fig. 2. – Ten Panel Demonstrator copolar (left) and cross-polar (right) radiation pattern at broadside calculated using the infinite array method in HFFS software. The color bar is dBi and the red dotted lines are added to the cross-polar pattern to facilitated reading.

Comparing the results in Fig. 2 with WIPL-D broadside results in Fig. 3. we see that the copolar main lobe and sidelobes in the principal planes are well approximated. However, out of the principal plane, copolar far sidelobes in Fig. 2 (left) are not symmetric as in Fig. 3 (left). A more significant deficiency of the approximate technique is evident in the cross-polar pattern. The symmetry of the cross-polar pattern is absent in the results in Fig. 2 (right). Furthermore, the results do not predict four symmetrical cross-polar lobes. This is especially important as the phases of adjacent lobes differ by 180°. This cancels the first order bias terms in the polarimetric variables which would otherwise be produced by the cross-polar voltage patterns.

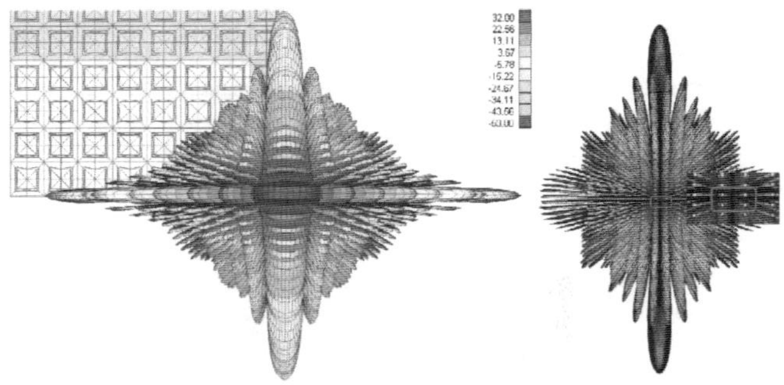

Fig. 3. - Antenna patterns of the ten-panel demonstrator, (left) copolar $f_{hh}(\theta, \phi)$, (right) cross-polar $f_{vh}(\theta, \phi)$ and its enlarged values within the main beam (encompassed with the rectangle). The beam is pointing broadside. The peak to peak isolation within the main lobe is over 50 dB while the cross-polar minimum is aligned with the copolar peak. The color bar indicates values in dBi.

IV. Conclusion

CEM tools had very limited use in quantifying the performance of phased array antennas meant for weather observations. Herein we examined the precision of the WIPL-D and other tools in modeling polarimetric phased array weather radar antenna and compared their simulation times and accuracy. Furthermore we considered application of the infinite array approach in modeling the antenna and isolated possible issues that may result in offsetting polarimetric calibration. The weather radar array modeled here is most likely among the largest polarimetric weather radars that can be fully modeled and thus represents an important milestone in developing hybrid techniques to address larger antenna arrays.

References

[1] D. S. Zrnic, G. Zhang, and R. J. Doviak, "Bias correction and doppler measurement for polarimetric phased-array radar," *IEEE Trans. On Geosci. and Remote Sensing,* I 2, vol. 49. pp. 842-853, 2010.

[2] Galletti, M., and D. S. Zrnic, 2011: Bias in copolar correlation coefficient caused by antenna radiation patterns. *IEEE Trans. Geosci. Remote Sens.,* **49,** 2274-2284.

Circularly Polarized Antenna Array Based on Open End Waveguide

Milos M. Jovicic
School of Electrical Engineering, University of Belgrade
Belgrade, Serbia
jm195050p@student.etf.bg.ac.rs

Branko M. Kolundzija
Department of General Electrical Engineering
School of Electrical Engineering, University of Belgrade
Belgrade, Serbia
kol@etf.rs

***Abstract*—Proposed type of the waveguide 2-D array combines simplicity of the design and manufacturing of the waveguide components with its good performances. Comparing it to the commonly used waveguide slot antennas, they offer stable main beam direction at wide frequency range. In addition, simple method of forming a linear array is easily applicable here, which leads to high gain antenna system. The whole process of modeling and simulations is performed using WIPL-D Pro CAD EM simulation software.**

Keywords—2-D array, high gain, waveguide, WIPL-D software.

I. Introduction

Nowadays, wireless communications become one of the most popular topics for engineers around the world. Whether in satellite communications, point-to-point communication, or point-to-multipoint communications, etc., microwave region offers wide bandwidths and so very high data rates along to compact devices [1].

Compared to linear polarized antennas, circularly polarized antennas offer much more robustness in terms of polarization efficiency [2]. With the system of the two linear polarized antennas, one has to match the polarization of the antennas (set both antennas in the same manner, to be parallel to each other) in order to obtain the maximum of the link budget. With the system of circularly polarized antennas, the maximum of the polarization efficiency is inherently achieved. Moreover, system with the circularly polarized antennas offers elimination of the ground reflected wave at the receiver because the wave reflected from the ground changes its polarization (RHCP to LHCP and vice versa) and thus it cannot be received.

Very popular type of circularly polarized antennas is waveguide slot antenna. It offers very low axial ratio, along with pretty good return loss. One of the characteristics of the waveguide slot antenna is low gain, so it should be set into a serial fed array with high number of cells to achieve higher gain. The problem with serial fed array is variation of the angle of the main beam over the frequency range [3]. With more elements, beamwidth decreases, so pointing of the antenna becomes difficult, especially over the frequency range.

Compared to serial fed array, parallel fed array offers frequency stable main beam direction. Along with the high gain open end waveguide radiator, it seems that parallel fed network could be used for proposed antenna system.

In order to obtain high gain antenna array with circular polarization the polarizer is employed at the end of the feeding network. This approach enables to adjust matching of the antenna system and axial ratio of the array separately.

II. Polarizer

Polarizer is the microwave component which transform polarization of the wave. In this particular case, polarizer is used to make circular polarized wave from the linear one. Model of the polarizer is created using WIPL-D Pro CAD software [4] and can be seen in Fig. 1.

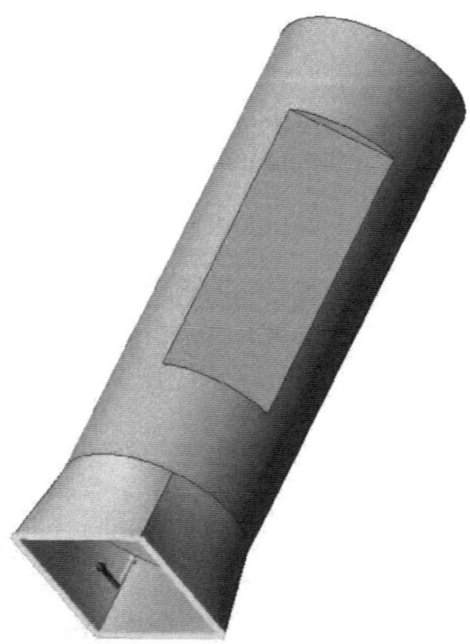

Fig. 1. Model of the polarizer obtained in WIPL-D Pro CAD software.

Polarizer consists of circular waveguide, pinched on both sides, rotated for 45 degrees relative to liner polarization. Incoming wave can be decomposed to two orthogonal components, one parallel and one normal, relative to side walls. Circular polarization is simply obtained using different group velocity of the orthogonal components of the linearly polarized wave. At the output of the pinched area, two orthogonal components differ for 90 degree in phase one from another and make circular polarization.

Feeding network is realized using square waveguide, so taper, obtained using *loft* operation, is used to transient from square to circular waveguide. It is also presented in the Fig. 1.

III. FEEDING NETWORK

Feeding network is realized as parallel feeding network, using combination of square and rectangular waveguide (it could be realized using rectangular waveguide only). First, every row of four antenna element is fed from one point, using matched dividers, making 1-D array. Further, those array cells are set into another four elements array configuration, to achieve 2-D array (16 elements in total). The idea is to use the same template of feeding network of 1-D array to feed 2-D array. Physically, those feeding networks are mutually rotated for 90 degrees, so twister element had to be employed. Twister element should physically rotate linear polarization for 90 degrees. Square waveguide twister is not able to do this rotation, so rectangular waveguide is employed. Full model of the feeding network and polarizers is presented in the Fig. 2.

Fig. 2. Model of the feeding network along with polarization open end radiated elements, obtained in WIPL-D Pro CAD software.

IV. RESULTS

The proposed model is designed to operate at central frequency of 10.75 GHz. It is not optimized, just designed to present possibilities and capabilities of the proposed 2-D array topology. At the Fig. 3, it is presented antenna gain for LHCP (blue line) and RHCP (redline) at central frequency. One can see that isolation between orthogonal polarizations is around 10 dB in the main direction.

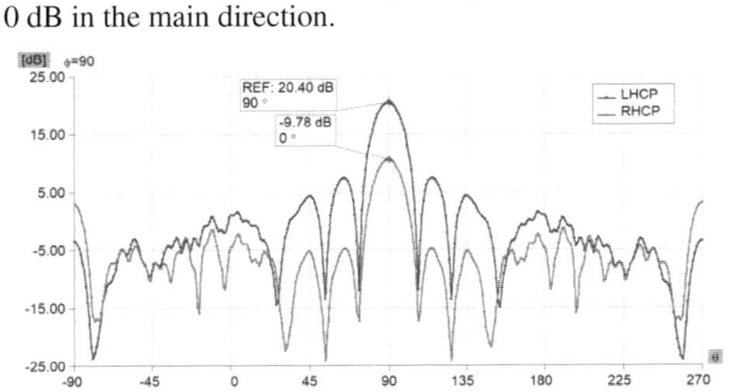

Fig. 3. Antenna system gain given for the LHCP (blue) and RHCP (red).

The Fig. 4 illustrates axial ratio of the antenna system. Proposed system provides low axial ration, below 2.25, over the given frequency range.

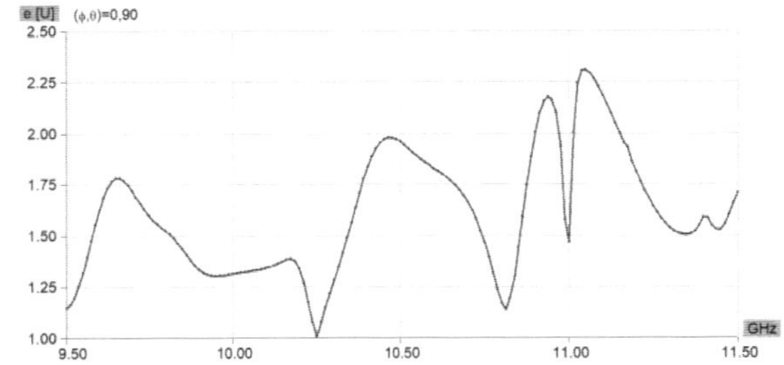

Fig. 4. Antenna system axial ratio.

The weakest part of the system is its return loss, which is presented in Fig. 5. The design is not optimized for low return loss, but it could be done using advanced techniques for waveguide component design. Corrugations at some stages could improve the return loss, but it would be done in the future work.

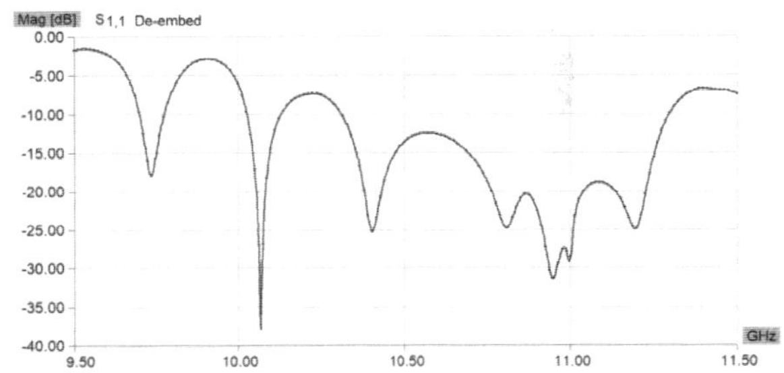

Fig. 5. Antenna system return loss.

V. CONCLUSION

The proposed model shows good capabilities in terms of circular polarization, as well as acceptable return loss. Even not optimized, the system has low axial ratio, high orthogonal isolation and return loss below 10 dB. Also, high gain is achieved. Different radiation patterns and higher gain could be obtained by increasing the number of radiation elements. Changing of the polarization, from LHCP to RHCP could be easily obtained by rotating polarizers for 90 degrees.

At the end, it can be concluded that proposed design offers a few degrees of freedom in the design process, which makes it suitable for different applications.

ACKNOWLEDGMENT

This paper was supported by WIPL-D company, which provided license for the software.

REFERENCES

[1] D. M. Pozar, Microwave Engineering, 3rd edition, John Wiley & Sons, Inc.

[2] C. A. Balanis, Antenna Theory Analysis and Design, 3rd edition, John Wiley & Sons, Inc.

[3] Hamadallah, M., Frequency limitation on broad-band performance of shunt slot array, *IEEE Trans. Antennas and Propagat.*, Vol. 37, 817-823, 1989

[4] WIPL-D Team, WIPL-D Pro CAD 2018 User's Manual.

Cavity-Backed Dual-Sinuous Antenna Modeling

Ruben P. Ortega
NAWCAD
Radar, Antennas and Sensor Fusion Division
Patuxent River, MD, USA
ruben.ortega1@navy.mil

Nicholas M. Christensen
NAWCAD
Radar, Antennas and Sensor Fusion Division
Patuxent River, MD, USA
nick.christensen@navy.mil

Saad N. Tabet
NAWCAD
Radar, Antennas and Sensor Fusion Division
Patuxent River, MD, USA
saad.tabet@navy.mil

Abstract—**Recently, for Radio Frequency (RF) signal identification on air vehicles, it has become critical to not only be able to detect the direction and angle of arrival of signals, but to also properly identify the polarization of such signals. For decades, cavity-backed dual-spiral antennas were heavily used for this purpose. However, that required the placement of both right-hand and left-hand elements to perform this function. Due to limited space and other issues, an alternative type of broadband antenna had to be identified. The Cavity-Backed Dual-Sinuous (CBDS) antenna makes an excellent replacement for this function. With its elements rotated 45° about its center, each element exhibits slant linear performance. Such an antenna, paired with proper connections and detection hardware, allows the detector to determine the polarization of arriving RF signals. A CBDS antenna was developed in the WIPL-D CEM code. Its RHCP and LHCP performance was studied over a broad range of frequencies. Results did prove that CBDS antennas have excellent broadband performance and polarization extraction.**

Keywords— Angle of Arrival, Cavity-Backed, Dual-Sinuous, Dual-Spiral, Polarization, RF Signal, WIPL-D.

I. Introduction

Sinuous type antennas are very attractive for many applications due to their broadband performance, polarization agility and miniaturized size. A sinuous antenna belongs to the log-periodic antenna family. However, its arms (made up of arcs and bends) are etched on PC-boards, which miniaturizes their size. Two sinuous asymmetric arms form a very broadband log-periodic dipole. The smallest and largest arcs and bends dictate its highest and lowest frequencies of operation, respectively. The number of arcs and bends allows the designer to better control a sinuous antenna's Radiation Pattern (RP) at intermediate frequencies.

A crisscrossed four-arm sinuous antenna [1] is one of the more commonly used versions of the antenna. The four arms form a cross-dipole antenna. Similar spiral antennas, sinuous antennas radiate in both directions, normal to the plane of the antenna. However, in most uses, the RP needs to be directed to one side only. Due to its broadband performance, one cannot place a ground plane at ¼-wavelength from one side of the antenna that will achieve the required performance at all operating frequencies. Therefore, a square or circular cylindrical conductive cavity, filled with absorbing materials, is customarily used to eliminate or significantly reduce the unwanted radiation. In this effort, a circular cylinder cavity, whose interior is laced with thin layers of magnetically loaded absorbing materials, is considered. Sources for such absorbing materials are Laird's Emerson Cuming and PPG Aerospace's Cuming Microwave Corporation.

II. Modeling Effort Details

A. Cavity-Backed Dual-Sinuous Antenna Design

The sinuous antenna described in this effort is capable of three-octave frequency coverage 2-18 GHz). The number of arcs/bends per arm was set to nine. Due to the lack of antenna software (such as Antenna Magus) to generate the arm models, an alternate approach was used. A web-search identified [2] as a source for sinuous arm design. Following the design procedures in [2], a MATLAB script was used to generate a single sinuous line with nine arcs/bends. The dense number of points forming one bound of the sinuous line were then imported into a CAD tool, where a Non-Unifrom Rational B-Spline (NURB) line containing those points was generated. The other bound, required to form the metalized arms, was created by copying the first sinuous line and rotating it to fit a sample physical antenna's footprint.

The two created nurb lines were then connected to form nurb surfaces representing a single sinuous arm's metallization. The sinuous arm was then copied three times, using a 90° rotational copying command, to form the antenna's four arms. Once that was completed, the four arms were rotated by 45° to form two slant linear sinuous dipoles. This model was then meshed in CAD and the mesh was exported into WIPL-D [3]. The feed region, all with feed wires were added in WIPL-D. The cylindrical cavity, including all absorbing materials, was then created using WIPL-D's Canonical Shape generators, to produce the WIPL-D model shown in Fig. 1.

Due to the frequency dependent nature of the absorbing materials used, a relatively new feature in WIPL-D was utilized. This feature allows for the frequency dependent absorbing materials characteristics to be read directly from files, for each frequency of interest. If an exact frequency match is not available in the materials' table, WIPL-D interpolates the available data to produce an approximate set of absorbing materials' electrical properties to use for that frequency.

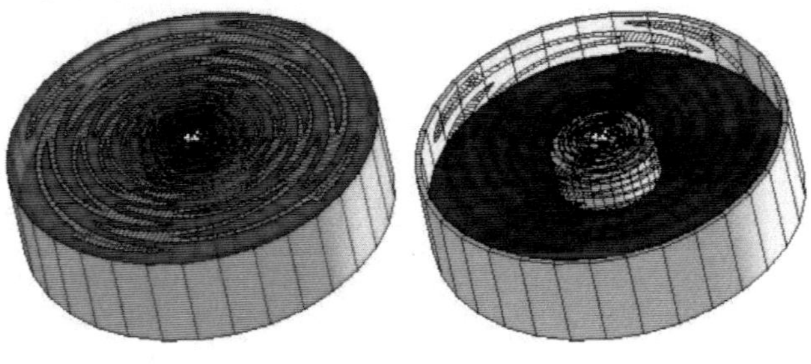

(a) (b)

Fig. 1. CBDS Antenna WIPL-D Model. (a) Full; (b) Absorbing Materials.

B. Cavity-Backed Dual-Sinuous Antenna Performance

The two slanted dipole elements of the CBDS antenna in Fig. 1 were driven using quadrature phasing to produce RHCP and LHCP RPs. Overlays of the broadband peak gain and beamwidth (BW), over the 2-18 GHz frequency range, for RHCP and LHCP is provided in Fig. 2 (a, b), respectively.

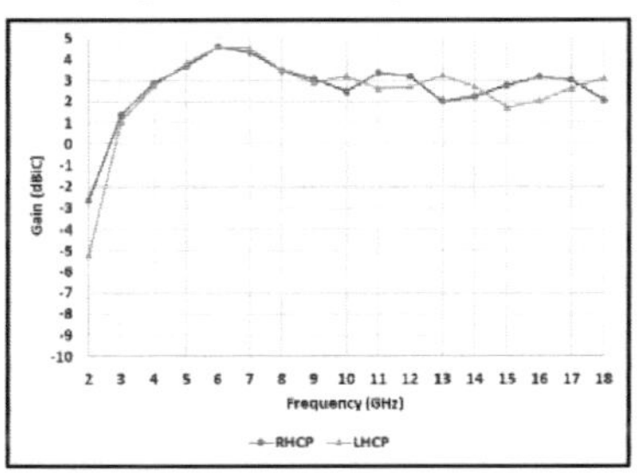

(a)

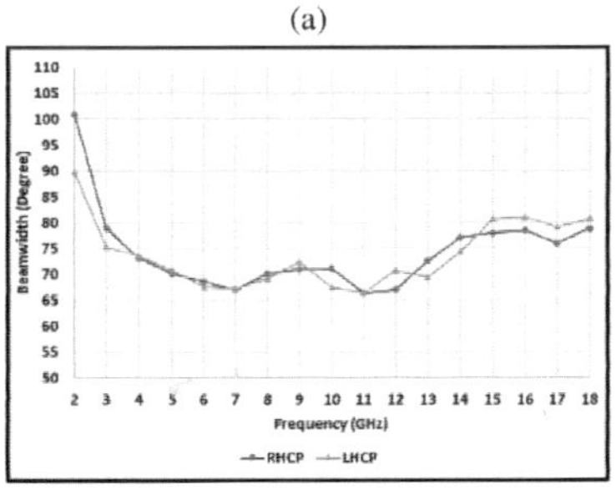

(b)

Fig. 2. CBDS Antenna Broadband RHCP and LHCP Overlays. (a) Peak Gain; (b) Beamwidth.

Overlays of RHCP and LHCP principal plane RPs at 2, 6, 10, 14 and 18 GHz are provided in Fig. 3.

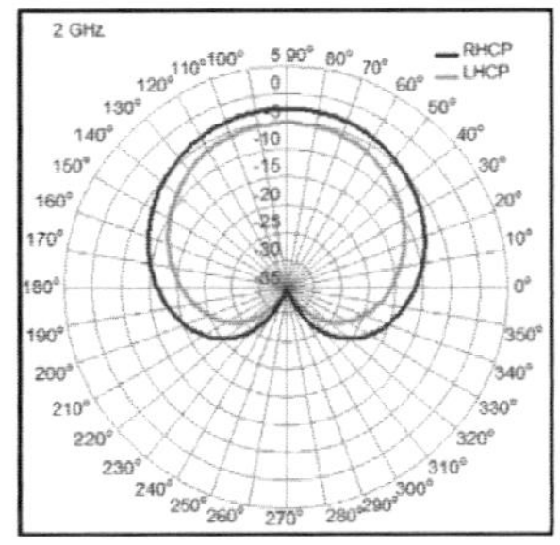

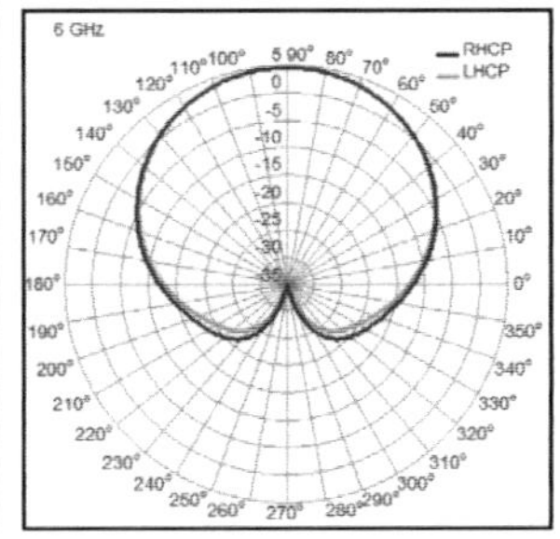

(a) (b)

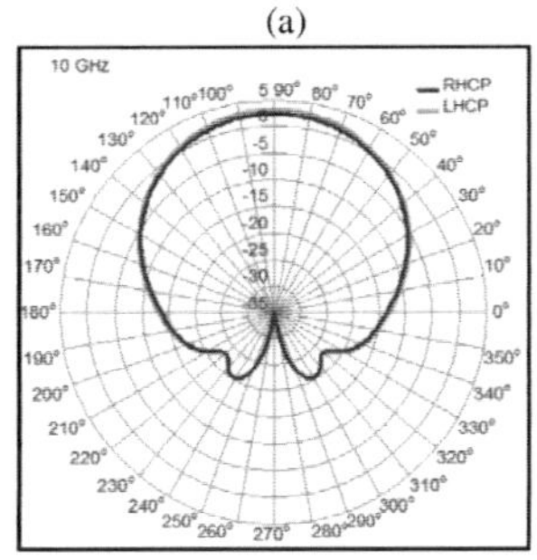

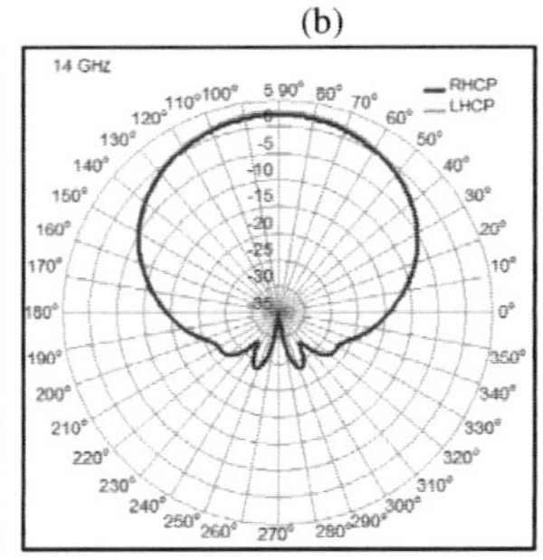

(c) (d)

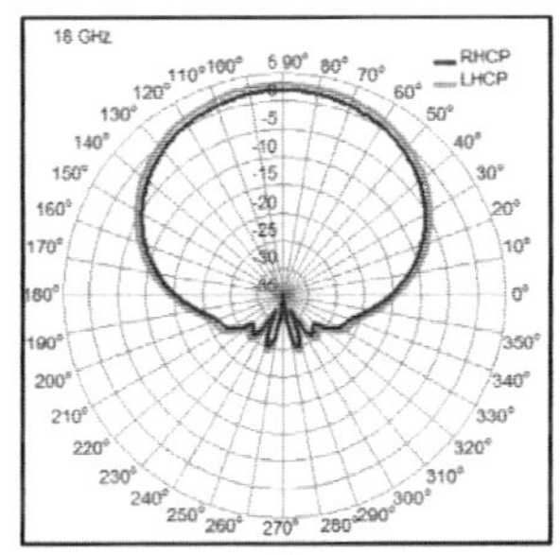

(e)

Fig. 3. CBDS Antenna RHCP and LHCP Overlays. (a) 2 GHz; (b) 6 GHz; (c) 10 GHz; (d) 14 GHz; (e) 18 GHz.

III. Analysis of Results

Figs. 2 and 3 provide ample proof that CBDS antennas possess excellent performance, similar to the previously commonly used Cavity-Backed Dual-Spiral antenna, over a three-octave range. This is evident on two fronts: Peak gain exceeds 0 dBiC, except at 2 GHz; BW of 67° to 100°, across the 2-18 GHz range. Such gain and BW performance is critical in quadrant angle-of-arrival determination.

The most significant difference in the RHCP and LHCP RP and BW performance of the CBDS antenna occurs at 2 GHz. Inexplicably, the LHCP peak gain and BW are more than 2 dBiC and 10° lower than those for RHCP, respectively.

References

[1] K. S. Saini, R. F. Bradley, "The Sinuous Antenna – A Dual Polarized Element for Wideband Phased Array Feed Application," Electronics Division Internal Report No. 301, National Radio Astronomy Observatory, Green Bank, WV 1996.

[2] D. S. Filipovic, T. Cencich, "Frequency Independent Antennas, Chapter 13 in Antenna Engineering Handbook/J. L. Volakis, Editor-4th Edition," 2007, pp 58-63.

[3] WIPL-D Pro, Software and User's Manual, WIPL-D d.o.o., Belgrade, Serbia, 2019.

Optimal Range of Coupling Coefficient of Loosely Coupled Transformer Considering System Resistance

Jiawei Ge[1], Hassan H. Eldeeb[2], Kun Liu[1], Jinping Kang[1], Haisen Zhao[1,2], and Osama Mohammed[2]
[1] School of electrical and electronics engineering, North China Electric Power University, Changping District, Beijing, 102206
[2] ESRL, Dept. of Electrical and Computer Engineering, Florida International University, Miami, FL33174, USA
15733290456@163.com; helde002@fiu.edu; 1362815547@qq.com; hbdlkjp@163.com; hzhao@fiu.edu; mohammed@fiu.edu

***Abstract*—Accurate system resistance may lead to an obvious error between the simulated and the real efficiency of the system. This paper proposes an optimal range of coupling coefficient, for ensuring the effiencency and the sufficient output power of the WPT. A 3-kW prototype WPTS is manufactured and the effectiveness of optimal range of coupling coefficient is validated.**

***Index Terms*—Wireless power transfer system (WPTS), system resistance, system efficiency.**

I. Introduction

There are many studies focused on electric vehicles [1], and on improving the performance of WPTS. For efficiency improvement, the square coils were considered to be more suitable [2], moreover, the wide variation of output voltage and coupling coefficient were also optimized [3] and a compensation topology named as LC/S was also proposed [4]. For reducing the iron losses of LCT, the multi-coil LCT which uses wires and air as the carrier and medium for the transmission of energy were proposed [5], and a misalignment-tolerant series-hybrid wireless EV charging system was also proposed [6].

During the design of them, they all followed the step that the experimental verification after the simulation. However, these LCTs neglected the system resistance during the design, which may lead to an error between the simulated and the real efficiency of the system.

In this paper, an optimal range of coupling coefficient is proposed to reduce the error between the simulated and the real system efficiency, as well as, to ensure the sufficient system output power. The optimal range of coupling coefficient at 85 kHz is also identified. Finally, a 3-kW WPT prototype is manufactured and related experimental validations are also carried out. The results show that the optimal range of coupling coefficient can reduce the error to around 5%.

II. Efficiency Error Between the Simulated and the Real System

A. Model of WPTS

The model of the resonant WPTS with the series-series (SS) topology is introduced and drawn in Fig. 1, where, U_t is the high-frequency supply, L_t and L_r are the self-inductances of the transmitting and the receiving coils, respectively, R_t and R_r are the resistances of the transmitting and the receiving system, respectively, C_t and C_r are the compensate capacitors of the transmitting and the receiving system, respectively, R_{eq} is the equivalent load resistance, and M_{tr} is the mutual inductance between the transmitting and the receiving coils.

Since the WPT is in resonance, the equations of the system output power and efficiency can be given by (1) and (2):

$$P_{out} = \frac{U_t^2 \omega^2 M_{tr}^2 R_{eq}}{\left[R_t\left(R_r+R_{eq}\right)+\omega^2 M_{tr}^2\right]^2}. \quad (1)$$

$$\eta = \frac{\omega^2 M_{tr}^2 R_{eq}}{\left[R_t\left(R_r+R_{eq}\right)+\omega^2 M_{tr}^2\right]\left(R_r+R_{eq}\right)}. \quad (2)$$

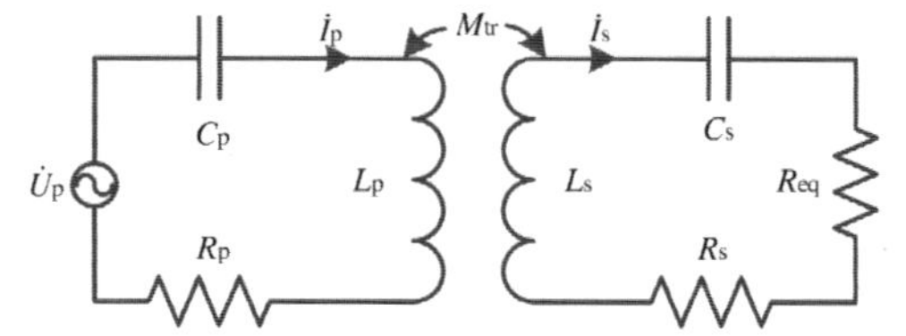

Fig. 1. Equivalent circuit of resonate two-coil WPT system.

B. Effects of neglecting resistance on system efficiency

With the case of WPTS which parameters are shown in Table I, where, k_{tr} is the coupling coefficient between the transmitting and the receiving coils. The variation of system efficiency with the R_t and R_r is obtained in Fig.2. It can be seen that the system efficiency can drop to 90% when the R_t and R_r are up to 1 Ω. It is assumed that when the system resistance is neglected and the real system resistance is a random value in 0 to 1 Ω, the maximum error can reach 10% between the simulated and the real system efficiency.

Table I Parameters of a resonant WPTS

Parameters	Value
Transmitting voltage U_t (V)	318
Equivalent load resistance R_{eq} (Ω)	28.65
Operating frequency f (kHz)	85
Self-inductance of transmitting coil L_t (μH)	272.07
Self-inductance of receiving coil L_r (μH)	205.6
Resonant capacitor of transmitting coil C_t (nF)	12.89
Resonant capacitor of receiving coil C_r (nF)	17.05
Coupling coefficient k_{tr}	0.16

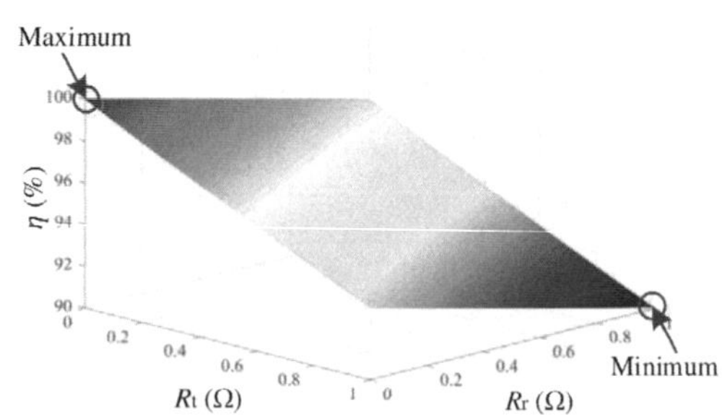

Fig. 2. Variation of efficiency with R_t and R_r

III. Optimal Range of Coupling Coefficient

With the case shown in Table I, the variations of system output power and efficiency with the k_{tr} under the different R_s are given in Fig. 3, where, the k_{tr} is the coupling coefficient between the transmitting and the receiving coils of WPTS, the R_s is the system resistance, $R_s=R_t+R_r$, the R_{s2} is the real system resistance, the R_{s1} and R_{s3} are the assumed system resistance, $R_{s2}=1.36R_{s1}$, $R_{s3}=1.265R_{s2}$.

It can be seen that, with the increases of k_{tr}, the system efficiency gradually approaches 100%, and the output power of system firstly increases and then gradually decreases to around 0 kW. For avoiding the insufficient output power of WPT, the k_{tr} should not be too large, and the optimal range of coupling coefficient can be introduced. With (1) and (2) as the objective functions and (3) and (4) as the constraints, the optimal range of coupling coefficient of the case at 85 kHz can be obtained, which is 0.15 to 0.23, as shown in the green area of Fig. 3. Within this range, the error between the simulated and the real system efficiency is reduced by not more than 5%, and the system output power is always not less than 3.3 kW:

$$\frac{\eta_{R_{p1}} - \eta_{R_{p3}}}{\eta_{R_{p1}}}\times 100\% \le 5\% \,. \tag{3}$$

$$P_{out} \ge 3.3 \,. \tag{4}$$

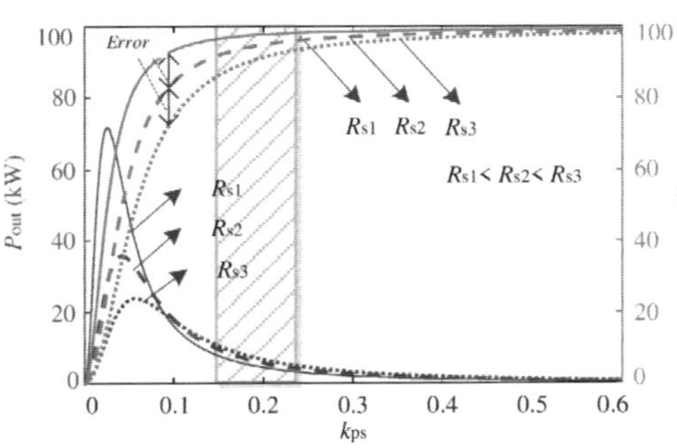

Fig. 3. Variations of system output power and efficiency with coupling coefficient under different R_s

IV. Experimental Validations

A 3-kW prototype WPTS is manufactured, as shown in Fig. 4. The efficiencies and output power of prototype can be measured under different k_{tr} when the R_s changes from 1.3Ω to 1.6Ω, the results are shown in Fig. 5. It can be seen that:

1) When R_s =1.3Ω, with the increases of k_{tr}, the system efficiency increases gradually, but the output power of prototype decreases gradually. When the R_s are 1.6Ω and 1.7Ω, the variations of the system efficiency and output power with the increases of k_{tr} are same as that when the R_s is 1.3Ω.

2) When the k_{tr} is equal to 0.118 (less than the lower limit of the optimal coupling coefficient range), the decline of the system efficiency is 19.065%, when the k_{tr} rises to 0.165, the decline of the system efficiency can sharply reduce to 5.264%; when the k_{tr} is equal to 0.232 (more than the upper limit of the optimal coupling coefficient range), the decline of the system efficiency can be further suppressed by 3.968%.

3) When the k_{tr} is equal to 0.118, the output power of the prototype is gradually decreased with the increases of R_s. However, when the k_{tr} is 0.165 and 0.232, respectively, with the increases of R_s, the output power of the prototype is gradually increased.

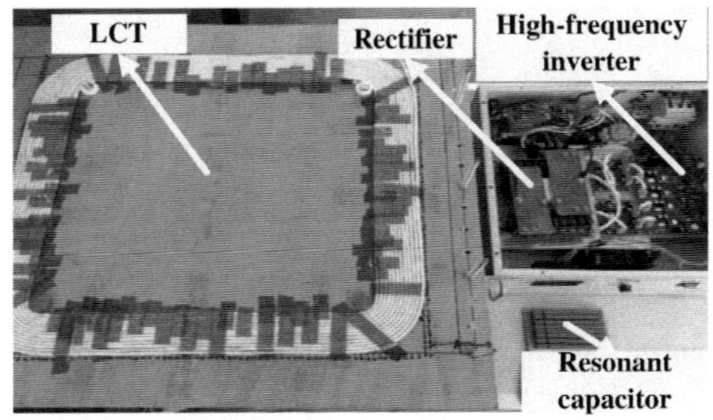

Fig. 4. Prototype WPTS.

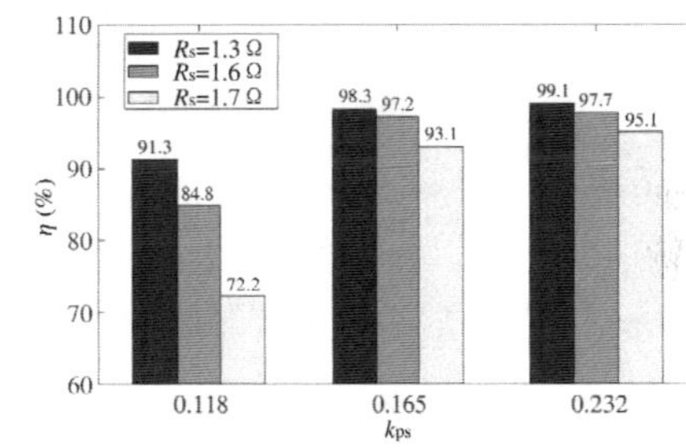

Fig. 5. Experimental results of system efficiency under different k_{tr} and different R_s.

V. Conclusion

This paper focuses on the influence of the inaccurate estimation of system resistance on efficiency of WPTS. An optimal range of coupling coefficient is proposed, by which the error between the simulated and the real system efficiency can be reduced to not more than 5%, and the system output power can be sufficient. A 3-kW prototype WPT is manufactured, and the effectiveness of optimal range of coupling coefficient is validated.

References

[1] H. H. Eldeeb etal., "Hybrid Energy Storage Sizing and Power Splitting Optimization for Plug-In Electric Vehicles," in *IEEE Trans on Ind Appl*, vol. 55, no. 3, pp. 2252-2262, May-June 2019.

[2] Z. Luo, and X. Wei, "Analysis of square and circular planar spiral coils in wireless power transfer system for electric vehicles," IEEE Trans. Ind. Electron., vol. 65, no. 1, pp. 331-341, Jan. 2018.

[3] M. Kim, D. M. Joo, and B. K. Lee, "Design and control of inductive power transfer system for electric vehicles considering wide variation of output voltage and coupling coefficient," IEEE Trans. Power Electron., vol.34, no. 2, pp. 1197-1208, Feb. 2019

[4] Y. J. Wang, Y. S. Yao, X. S. Liu, D. G. Xu, and L. Cai, "An LC/S compensation topology and coil design technique for wireless power transfer," IEEE Tran. Power Electron., vol.33, no.3, pp.2007-2025, Mar. 2018.

[5] D. H. Tran, V. B. Vu, and W. Choi, "Design of a high-efficiency wireless power transfer system with intermediate coils for the on-board chargers of electric vehicles," IEEE Trans. Power Electron., vol. 33, no. 1, pp. 175-187, Jan. 2018.

[6] L. Zhao, D. J. Thrimawithana, U. K. madawala, A. P. Hu, and C. C. Mi, "A misalignment-tolerant series-hybrid wireless EV charging system with integrated mangetics," IEEE Trans. Power Electron., vol.34, no. 2, pp. 1276-1285, Feb. 2019

Taguchi-EM-AI Design Optimization Environment for SynRM Drives in Traction Applications

A.A. Arkadan[1], N. Al Aawar[2]

[1]Colorado School of Mines, Dept. of Electrical Engineering, Golden CO 80401, USA
[2]Marquette University, Dept. of Electrical and Computer Engineering, Milwaukee WI, 53233, USA
aaarkadan@mines.edu

***Abstract*—Multi-objective design optimization environments are used for electric vehicles and other traction applications to arrive at efficient motor drives. Typically, the environment includes characterization modules that involve the use of Electromagnetic Finite Element and State-Space models that require large number of iterations and computational time. This work proposes the utilization of a Taguchi orthogonal arrays method in conjunction with a Particle Swarm Optimization search algorithm to reduce computational time needed in the design optimization of electric motors for traction applications. The effectiveness of the Taguchi method in conjunction with the optimization environment is demonstrated in a case study involving a prototype of a Synchronous Reluctance Motor drive system.**

Index Terms— Design Optimization, Taguchi Algorithm.

I. Introduction

Internal combustion engines (ICEs) running on fossil fuel and powering vehicles are major contributors to carbon emissions. In traction applications, hybrid and electric vehicles (EVs) utilizing electric motors are increasingly used as viable alternatives to ICE driven systems. As such, the development of reliable efficient electric motors is receiving attention and design optimization environments are utilized by researchers in this field. In this work, we consider Axially Laminated Anisotropic (ALA) Rotor Synchronous Reluctance Motor (SynRM) drives, that possess ideal characteristics for traction applications [1, 2].

This paper presents a design optimization environment that includes a module comprised of an electromagnetic Finite Element (EM) and state space (SS) models of the motor drive system. The EM-SS module is used as a system identifier in the design optimization process. The block diagram of a prototype EV drive system modeled in this work is shown in Fig. 1 and it includes a SynRM motor, the drive power electronics, and associated controllers. As can be appreciated, it is critical that the characterization module of the drive system properly accounts for effects of magnetic saturation and nonlinearities, as well as effects of space and time harmonics when predicting the system performance.

II. Motor Drive System Characterization Module

This paper presents a Multi-objective design optimization environment that includes an EM-SS characterization module. The objective of the design optimization environment implemented in this work is to maximize the developed torque while minimizing the torque ripple and total (Ohmic, core, and switching) losses of an ALA SynRM drive system, Fig, 1. This system utilizes a decoupled d- and q-axis current control and a flux controller in the inner loop that are implemented with PI controllers [3]. In addition, the power converter implemented in this case study is of the full wave, 3-phase, PWM Inverter type. The motor is designed for traction applications, Fig. 2, and is rated at 100 KW and 6000-rev/min. The motor stator is constructed from nonlinear magnetic material that holds poly-phase windings similar to a conventional AC machine. The rotor is made of axially laminated anisotropic magnetic silicon steel laminations interleaved with thin insulation layers that form the rotor composite flux path segments.

The integrated EM-SS module used for the characterization of the ALA rotor SynRM generates data required by an artificial intelligence (AI) particle swarm optimization (PSO) based design optimization search algorithm. The SS model that governs the performance of the SynRM is expressed as:

$$\begin{bmatrix} i_a \\ i_b \\ i_c \\ \dot{\omega}_m \\ \dot{\theta}_m \end{bmatrix} = \begin{bmatrix} & A & & 0 & 0 \\ & & & 0 & 0 \\ & & & 0 & 0 \\ 0 & 0 & 0 & 0 & 0 \\ 0 & 0 & 0 & 1 & 0 \end{bmatrix} \begin{bmatrix} I_a \\ I_\partial \\ I_c \\ \omega_m \\ \theta_m \end{bmatrix} + \begin{bmatrix} V_a \\ V_b \\ V_c \\ F \\ 0 \end{bmatrix} \quad (1)$$

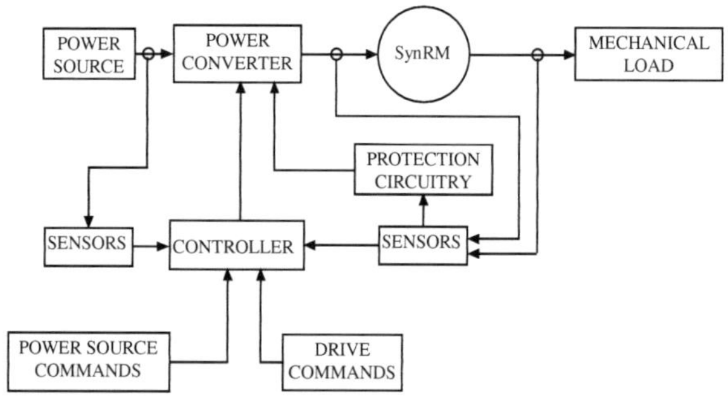

Fig. 1. SynRM Drive System

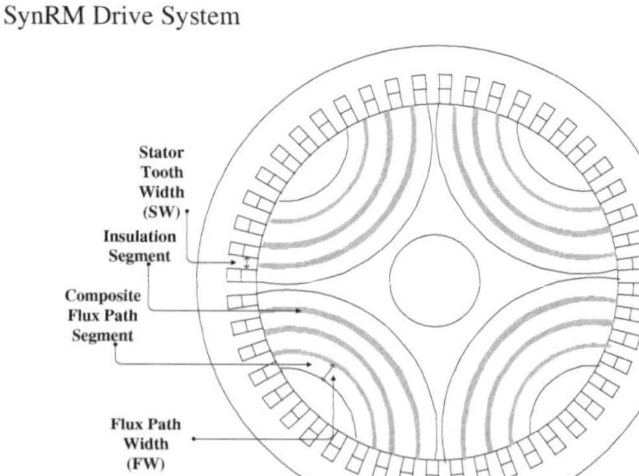

Fig. 2. ALA Rotor SynRM Cross-section

In equation (1), matrix A is given as:

$$A = -inv(L) \cdot \left(R + \omega_m \cdot \frac{dL}{d\theta_m} \right) \qquad (2)$$

where L and R are the motor inductance and resistance matrices, respectively, and ω_m is the rotor speed. In addition, the voltages V_a, V_b, and V_c represent the system input voltage vector, which accounts for the drive power electronics and associated controllers [1-3].

III. THE TAGUCHI-EM-PSO DESIGN ENVIRNOMENT

The objective of the design optimization environment is to maximize the developed torque while minimizing torque ripple as well as Ohmic and core losses of the SynRM drive system of Fig. 1. The Input Design Vector, I_{Design}, for the optimization problem consists of the number of flux paths, the stator tooth width (SW), and the rotor flux path width (FW), shown in Fig. 2. The optimization objective function, OF, is defined as the weighted sum of the performance indicators that include torque ripple, T_r, the total losses in the machine, T_L, and the developed torque average, T_{avg}, constrained at a desired load, T_d:

$$OF = \alpha \cdot T_r + \beta \cdot T_L + \lambda \cdot |T_{ave} - T_d| \qquad (3)$$

where α and β are the weights of T_r and T_L, respectively and λ is the Lagrangian multiplier.

The EM-PSO optimization environment of Fig. 3 was implemented where the finite element based EM-SS characterization module described above was used to generate needed data to train offline a Fuzzy Logic (FL) model, which is used in turn in a Particle Swarm Optimization (PSO) search algorithm [4]. The input vector of the FL model is the design vector, I_{Design}, and the output is a set of performance indicators. The PSO uses the FL model to evaluate the objective function corresponding to any values of the design vector in the search space. The SynRM drive system was implemented with both Urban and Highway Federal Driving Schedules, Fig, 4. The application of the EM-PSO design environment to the prototype SynRM drive of Fig. 1, operating at 50 Nm and 3000 rpm load conditions, resulted in optimized design performance indicators values, which are compared in Table 1 to corresponding initial design values. An inspection of Table 1 reveals the excellent improvement in the values of the performance indicators.

As can be appreciated from above, a large number of EM and PSO iterations are required to find an optimum design. As such, a Taguchi orthogonal arrays algorithm [5] was employed to reduce computational time needed to reach an optimum design. The Taguchi algorithm was integrated with the EM-PSO design environment of the Fig. 3 and resulted in the Taguchi-EM-PSO design optimization environment of Fig. 5. This algorithm reduces the computational requirements by determining the minimum number of input design parameter's combinations required to cover the whole search space of the optimization problem [5]. The application of the algorithm shown in Fig. 5 to the prototype traction SynRM drive, Fig. 1, operating at the same conditions noted above, resulted in similar performance indicator values as shown in Table 1 and about 80% reduction of needed computational time.

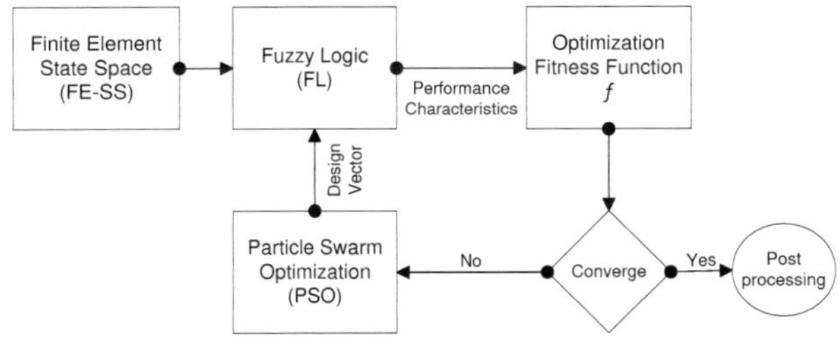

Fig. 3. EM-PSO Design Optimization Environment

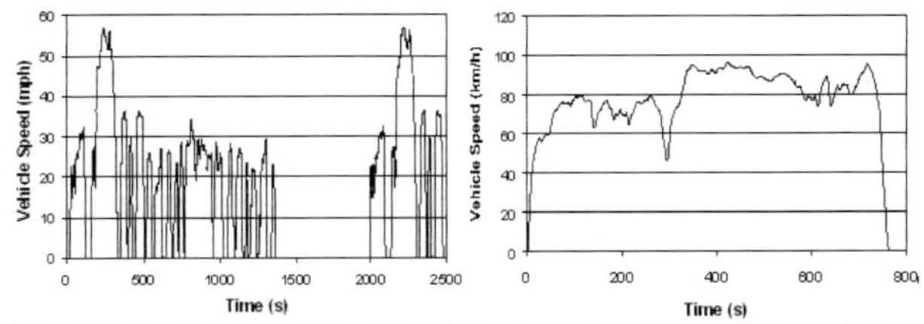

Fig. 4. Federal Driving Schedules (a) Urban "FUDS", (b) Highway "FHDS"

TABLE I
INITIAL AND OPTIMAL DESIGN

DESIGN	INITIAL	OPTIMAL	IMPROVEMENT
LOSSES (W)	6,260	2,400	61%
TORQUE RIPPLE	52%	30%	42%
AVG. TORQUE	90 N.M.	90 N.M.	N/A

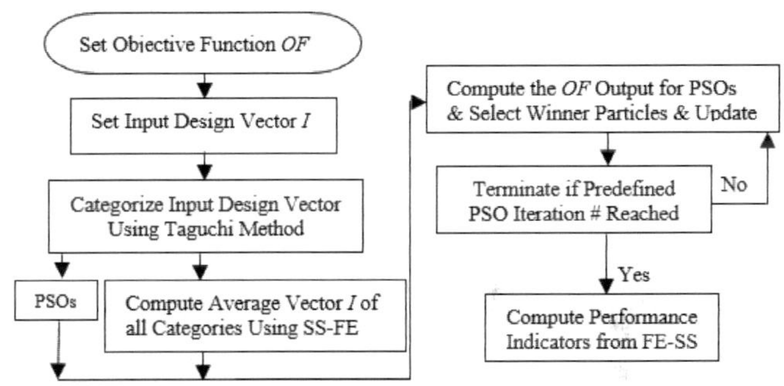

Fig. 5. Taguchi-EM-PSO Design Optimization Environment

IV. CONCLUSION

This work demonstrates the effectiveness of including a Taguchi algorithm in reducing computational time requirements in design optimization environments for traction applications.

V. REFERENCES

[1] Arkadan, A.A., Isaac, F. and Mohammed, O.A., "Parameters Evaluation of Axially Laminated Anisotropic Synchronous Reluctance Motor Drives," *IEEE Trans. on Magnetics*, Vol. 36, pp. 1950 - 1955, Jul. 2000.

[2] Arkadan, A.A., Hanbali, A., Al-Aawar, N., "Characterization and Design Optimization of ALA Rotor Synchronous Reluctance Motor Drives for Traction Applications," 22nd Annual Review of Progress in Applied Computational Electromagnetics (ACES), pp. 249-256, Florida, U.S., March 2006.

[3] Boldea I., and Nasar, S.A., "Vector Control of AC Drives", *CRC Press*, Boca Raton, FL, pp. 167-200, 1992.

[4] Kennedy J., and Eberhart, R., "Particle Swarm Optimization," *Proc. IEEE Int. Conf. on Neural Networks*, pp. 1942-1948, 1995.

[5] Arkadan, A.A., Al-Aawar, N., and Hariri A.O., "EM-Taguchi Identifier for PSO Design Optimization Environment," Presented at the 30th Applied Computational Electromagnetics Society, ACES, Symposium, Jacksonville FL, March 23-27, 2014.

Beyond LOS Detection of Hypersonic Vehicles

Randall L. Musselman and Stephan H. Chastain

US Air Force Academy, Department of Electrical and Computer Engineering, Colorado Springs, CO, USA
randall.musselman@usafa.edu; stephan.chastain@usafa.edu

***Abstract*—RCS modeling of a typical hypersonic vehicle and its plasma sheath was investigated. The plasma parameters were analyzed to determine which were most dominant for accurate RCS prediction. HF was determined to provide BLOS detection and good conductivity of the plasma, for optimum RCS.**

***Index Terms* – HF, Hypersonic, Over-the-Horizon Radar, plasma, RCS.**

I. Introduction

RF propagation to and from hypersonic vehicles has been studied since the early years of the US and Soviet space programs. Primarily, this interest concentrated on techniques to mitigate the communication "blackout" that occurred during spacecraft reentering the atmosphere, due to the extreme temperature. Molecular oxygen and nitrogen would dissociate into atomic oxygen (2000K), atomic nitrogen (4000K), as well as ions and free electrons [1]. This generation of positive ions and negative free electrons would have formed a plasma, shielding the spacecraft from RF communication [2].

The electrical properties of the plasma generated by hypersonic travel depend on parameters such as the charge densities, masses, velocities, and collision frequency of the ions and free electrons. These parameters depend on speed, altitude, and temperature. Furthermore, these parameters fluctuate rapidly during flight [3]. The statistical-mechanic and thermodynamic characterizations of these parameters is an area of ongoing research that is beyond the scope for our purposes. Rather, our goal is to contrive a modeling technique, in order to characterize the radar cross section (RCS) that would provide a reliable and practical detection method for hypersonic vehicles.

II. Plasma Model

Plasma densities ranging from 10^{15} to 10^{19} m^{-3} are typical for hypersonic vehicles [4]. Since the mass of the free electrons is orders of magnitude less than that of the ions, we will assume that the plasma conductivity is dominated by the electrons, thus ignoring the contribution from the ions. The plasma frequency can be calculated by:

$$\omega_p = q_e\sqrt{\frac{N_e}{\varepsilon_0 m_e}}\,, \qquad (1)$$

where q_e is electron charge (C), m_e is electron mass (Kg), and N_e is the electron density (m^{-3}). Using the aforementioned range of plasma densities, the plasma frequency ranges from 284 MHz to 28 GHz. From the Drude model, the real component of permittivity, $Re\{\varepsilon = \varepsilon' - j\varepsilon''\}$ is:

$$\varepsilon' = \varepsilon_0\left(1 - \frac{\omega_p^2}{\omega^2+\gamma^2}\right), \qquad (2)$$

where γ is the electron collision frequency [5]. At frequencies above the plasma frequency, ε' will be positive, asymptotically approaching unity. The radio waves will transmit through the plasma as a lossy dielectric,

$$e^{-\omega\varepsilon'' x} e^{-j\omega\sqrt{\mu_0\varepsilon'}\cdot x}. \qquad (3)$$

Below the plasma frequency (assuming $\omega_p^2 \gg \gamma^2$ in the upper atmosphere), ε' will be negative, and the radio waves will reflect as from a conductor. Based on an empirically derived formula for plasma frequency vs temperature, the collision frequency at 3000K is approximately $\gamma = 5$ MHz [6]. To detect the features of the vehicle itself, one would need to choose a radar frequency above the plasma frequency. Unless the radar is agile enough to adapt to varying plasma densities, collision frequencies, etc., an operational frequency well above 28 GHz would be necessary, since the plasma would tend to be absorptive near the plasma frequency.

A major disadvantage of the Ka radar band is that it suffers from relatively high absorption, due to water droplets. Furthermore, for a terrestrial-based radar to detect a hypersonic vehicle traveling horizontally, a Ka-band radar would provide very little detection range. A vehicle flying at Mach 8 at an altitude of 70 km, would have a maximum line-of-sight (LOS) range of 1000 km. At Mach 8, it would close this distance in 7 minutes. It would be more advantageous to use a frequency below the plasma frequency and detect the plasma sheath, instead of the actual vehicle that would be shielded within the sheath. This also eliminates the need to precisely predict the various plasma parameters, as the sheath would appear to be relatively conductive, over a broad range of varying parameters. Fig. 1 demonstrates beyond-LOS (BLOS), by refracting from the ionosphere, using 30 MHz [7].

A first-order approximation for plasma sheath is to assume a conical shape, with a blunt vertex at the leading tip of the vehicle. The half angle of this conical sheath can be visualized in Fig. 2 and calculated by:

$$\alpha = \sin^{-1}(1/M)\,, \qquad (4)$$

where $M = u/s$ is the Mach number, u is the vehicle speed, and s is the speed of sound, i.e., the speed of the outwardly propagating shockwave. At Mach 8, which is sufficient for plasma generation, the half angle is $\alpha = 7.2^{\circ}$.

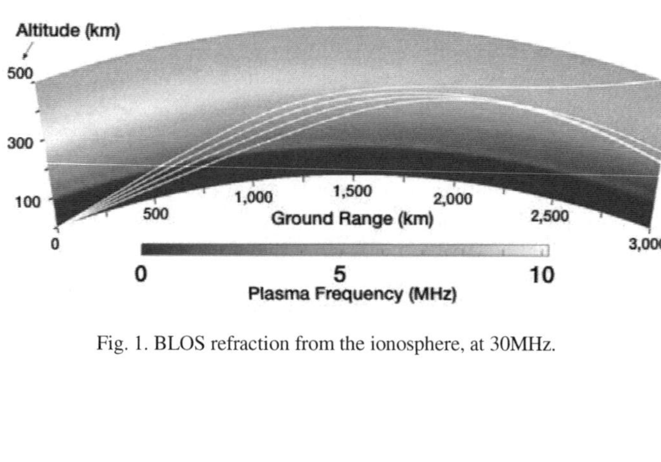

Fig. 1. BLOS refraction from the ionosphere, at 30MHz.

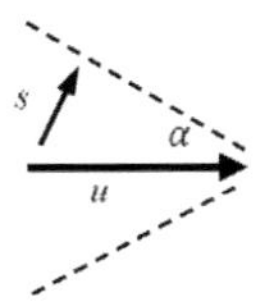

Fig. 2. Plasma sheath angle, $\sin\alpha = s/u$

The DC conductivity can be calculated from:

$$\sigma_0 = \frac{N_e q^2}{m_e v}\,, \tag{5}$$

and the AC conductivity from:

$$\sigma(f) = \frac{\sigma_0}{1+(2\pi f/v)^2}\,. \tag{6}$$

Fig. 3 shows a simulated plasma sheath, constructed around a 2m-diameter and 2m-long reentry-shaped vehicle, simulated as a PEC in HFSS. The radiation propagation space ("air box") was a cube, 32 m on side, with the vehicle in the center. Curvilinear meshing was applied in the initial setting, and was done automatically. The nose of the plasma used a conductivity of $38\,\Omega^{-1}\mathrm{m}^{-1}$, corresponding to $N_e = 10^{19}\ \mathrm{m}^{-3}$, at a thickness of 20% of the nose radius [5]. The rest of the cone/cylinder section used $0.38\,\Omega^{-1}\mathrm{m}^{-1} \Rightarrow N_e = 10^{17}\ \mathrm{m}^{-3}$. These parameters yielded penetration depths of 1.4 cm and 14 cm, respectively, at 30MHz. While the penetration depth is affected by the plasma density, it is not significantly affected by the temperature-dependent collision frequency.

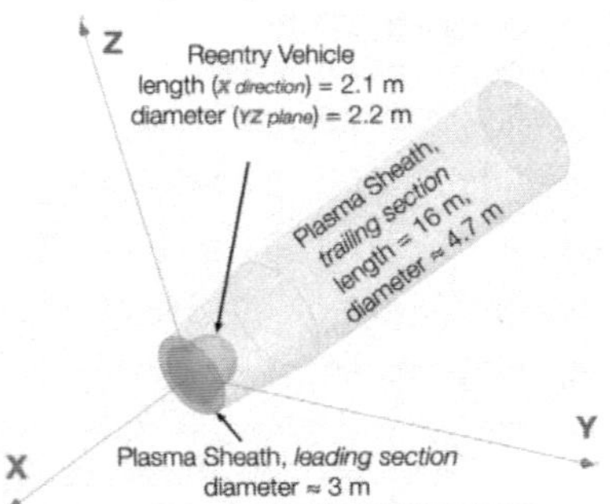

Fig. 3. HFSS model of reentry vehicle shrouded by plasma sheath.

III. RCS RESULTS

The RCS of the vehicle alone (red, smaller) and the plasma sheath alone (green, larger) are superimposed in Fig. 4, at 30MHz. Equal θ and ϕ polarization was used, to mimic circular polarization. The broadside RCS (90°) from the plasma sheath is almost 16 dB higher than the RCS of the PEC vehicle alone. The RCS of the PEC vehicle engulfed in the plasma is shown in Fig. 5, depicting the vehicle completely shielded by the plasma. These results confirm the efficacy of an over-the-horizon radar (OTHR) for BLOS detection of hypersonic vehicles.

IV. CONCLUSION

A plasma sheath was constructed around a capsule-shaped reentry vehicle, in HFSS, to simulate the plasma generated at Mach 8. This sheath was made of two representative plasma densities, with the higher density at the leading edge of the vehicle, where the temperature would be the most extreme. The RCS of the vehicle and plasma sheath were simulated at upper HF, to show the capabilities of BLOS detection, using the ionosphere, from an OTHR. The HFSS simulations showed that the RCS is dominated by the plasma sheath, rather than the vehicle shape and material. These results demonstrate that the RCS is enhanced at HF, as it is well below the plasma frequency of the plasma sheath.

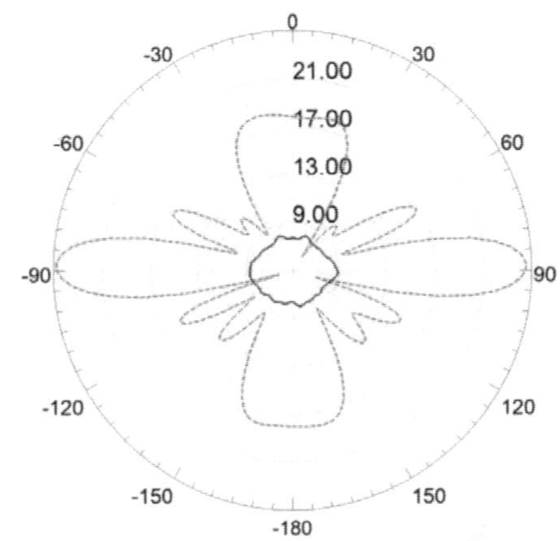

Fig.4. HFSS RCS simulations of the PEC reentry vehicle, without plasma sheath (red), and RCS of the plasma sheath (green), without the vehicle, values expressed in dBsm.

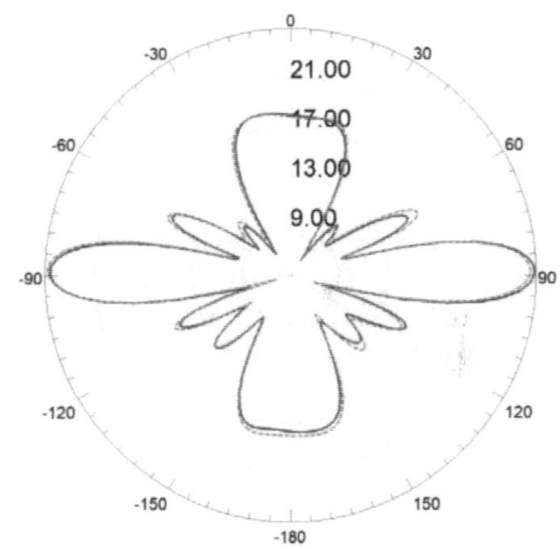

Fig.5. HFSS RCS simulations of the PEC reentry vehicle engulfed in the plasma sheath (red) compared to the plasma sheath alone (green).

REFERENCES

[1] J. D. Anderson Jr., Hypersonic and High-Temperature Gas Dynamics, 3rd ed., AIAA, Inc., Reston, VA, 2019.

[2] R. S. Savino, et al., "Plasma-Radiofrequency Interactions Around Atmospheric Re-Entry Vehicles: Modelling and Arc-Jet Simulations," The Open Aerospace Engineering Journal, 2010.

[3] B. Yao, et al., "A layered fluctuation model of electron density in plasma sheath and instability effect on electromagnetic wave at Ka band," Aerospace Science and Technology, 78, 2018.

[4] M. Keidar, et al., "Electromagnetic Reduction of Plasma Density During Atmospheric Reentry and Hypersonic Flights," Journal of Spacecraft and Rockets, vol. 45, no. 3, May-June 2008.

[5] P. Andre, et al., "Air Plasma Key Param for EM Wave Prop at and out of Therm Eq: Appl to EMC," ACES Journal, vol. 33, no. 12, Dec. 2018.

[6] U. Inan, et al., Principles of Plasma Physics for Engineers and Scientists, Cambridge Univ. Press, Cambridge, UK 2011.

[7] PHaRLAP, Manuel Cervera, Defence Science and Technology Group, Australia (manuel.cervera@dsto.defence.gov.au).

Electromagnetic Susceptibility of COTS Control Systems

Randall L. Musselman and Brian J. Neff

US Air Force Academy, Department of Electrical and Computer Engineering, Colorado Springs, CO, USA
randall.musselman@usafa.edu; brian.neff@usafa.edu

***Abstract*—COTS control systems used on small UAVs were investigated for EMC vulnerabilities. Electronic speed controllers, autopilots, and inertial measurement units were electromagnetically disrupted, by modulating RF signals with waveforms that were rectified by nonlinearities. These disruptions had catastrophic effects on the functionality of the devices, without physically damaging them.**

***Index Terms* – COTS, EMC, susceptibility, UAV.**

I. INTRODUCTION

Both the commercial and hobbyist communities make use of common off-the-shelf (COTS) control systems for robotics applications. These devices can range from Arduinos to more purpose built embedded systems. While COTS equipment is typically tested for electromagnetic compatibility (EMC), many of these inexpensive devices were not designed to be robust to harsh electromagnetic environments, and therefore have electromagnetic susceptibilities that can alter their functionality [1]. These vulnerabilities are exacerbated when subjected to intentional electromagnetic interference (IEMI) [2], which has been an emerging threat in recent years [3]. Characterizing these electromagnetic vulnerabilities can lead to more robust electromagnetic compatibility design techniques.

Specifically, the electromagnetic susceptibilities of COTS control systems were investigated, that are commonly found on small unmanned aerial vehicles (sUAV). These sUAVs are ubiquitous in society, and are commercially available, as well as custom built by hobbyists. Some of the COTS components typically found on these platforms include electronic speed controllers, autopilots, and inertial measurement units.

II. ELECTRONIC SPEED CONTROLLER

Electronic Speed Controllers (ESC) are typically brushless DC motors, which consist of electronics that convert a pulse-width-modulation (PWM) control signal into three-phase voltage for a delta or wye-wound motor. Two ESC examples are shown in Fig. 1, i.e., the DJI 420 Lite (bottom) and a BL Heli (top). The wires entering the right side of the ESCs are power and PWM control-signal wires. The three conductors on the left side of the ESDs in Fig. 1 provide the motors with their three-phase power. Increasing the pulse width increases the three-phase voltages, speeding up the propeller motors.

By modulating an RF signal with PWM, the radiated signal can couple into the ESC, where it can be rectified to baseband, by the various nonlinearities that all electronics possess, if driven hard enough. If this rectified PWM voltage is great enough, the ESCs will respond by speeding up or slowing down, depending on the pulse width.

Fig. 1. Electronic speed controllers (ESC), BL Heli (top) and: DJI 430 Lite (middle and bottom).

The DJI ESC in Fig. 1 was connected directly to a function generator that provided a 400-Hz PWM signal to the ESC, with a 1.55-ms pulse width (46% duty cycle). This control signal fixed the propeller to a steady speed that was used as a reference. Then a 1.581-GHz signal was modulated with a similar PWM signal and transmitted with an EIRP of 19W, using the setup in Fig. 2. As the pulse width of the modulated RF signal was increased/decreased, the propeller speed increased/decreased proportionally, as would be expected if the wired PWM controlling signal had been varied.

III. PIXHAWK AUTOPILOT

The Pixhawk PX4 autopilot, shown in Fig. 3 was similarly disrupted by modulating a 2.001-GHz signal with a 300-Hz PWM waveform, and a pulse width of 1.3 ms (52% duty cycle). The autopilot was configured to control the ailerons of a fixed-wing sUAV, using servos that were attached to the ailerons. As soon as the modulated RF signal began to transmit onto the autopilot, the servos snapped the ailerons to their neutral positions, preventing control by the autopilot. As soon as the RF transmission was turned off, the autopilot regained control.

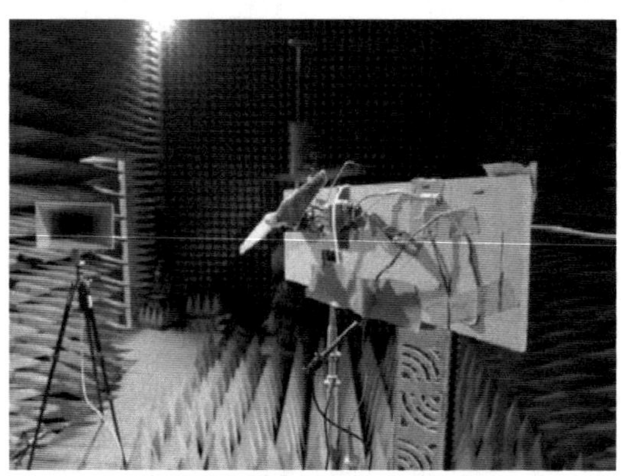

Fig. 2. DJI ESC experimental setup.

Fig 3. Pixhawk, PX4 autopilot.

IV. Waveform Determination

This same technique could be used to disrupt several makes and models of autopilots and ESCs. The relatively low power levels that were required to disrupt these devices was achieved by finding resonances on their respective PCBs. As a first-order approximation, the fundamental resonant frequency can be estimated by:

$$f = \frac{n * c}{2 * \sqrt{\varepsilon} * (Length\ OR\ Width)}, \tag{1}$$

where ε is the effective permittivity. Since 'n' represents an infinite number of half wavelengths, (1) can lead to several convenient resonant frequencies. The challenge is predicting ε. Ansys SIwave provided several resonant frequencies, as illustrated in Fig. 4. However, a detailed CAD model was required for this simulation, which may not always be available. Another method is to probe for unintentional emissions. It was discovered that radiating frequencies often led to electromagnetic susceptibilities at those same frequencies. Furthermore, some system-level emissions data can often be found in FCC EMC reports, simply by searching for the FCC ID number. Known resonant frequencies can lead to many more susceptibilities from intermodulation products, such as the third-order product:

$$2f_1 \pm f_2 \quad \text{and} \quad 2f_2 \pm f_1 \,. \tag{2}$$

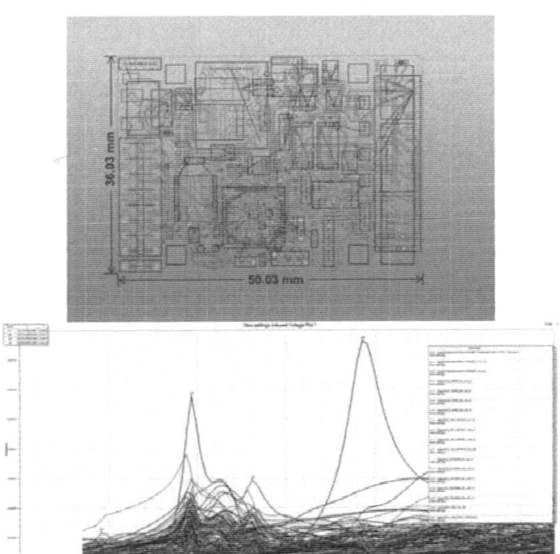

Fig 4. SIwave simulation (bottom) of a Pixhawk PCB (top).

V. Inertial Measurement Unit

Many sUAVs use an inertial measurement unit (IMU) for stability control, as well as a navigational supplement to GPS. Several IMUs are commercially available for less than $100. They consist of accelerometers and three-axis gyros, on integrated circuits, mounted to a PCBs, exemplified in Fig. 5. The gyros are made of arrays of micro-electromechanical systems (MEMs). As inherently mechanical devices, each gyro axis has an acoustic resonant frequency. By modulating an RF signal to the same frequency as the acoustic resonant frequency, the rectified electrical signal is transduced to a mechanical wave on the MEMs array. The result can be seen in the Betaflight software display in Fig. 5. The actual IMU was stationary but appeared to be shaking violently every time the modulated RF signal transmitted. Each axis could be individually disrupted, by selecting the corresponding modulating frequency.

VI. Conclusion

COTS control systems that are commonly found on sUAVs were disrupted by modulated low-power RF signals, using selected waveforms. These COTS control systems included electronic speed sensors, autopilots, and inertial measurement units. A variety of techniques were used to determine the modulating waveforms and resonant RF frequencies that had the most disruptive effect on these devices. Understanding these vulnerabilities could lead to more robust EMC protection.

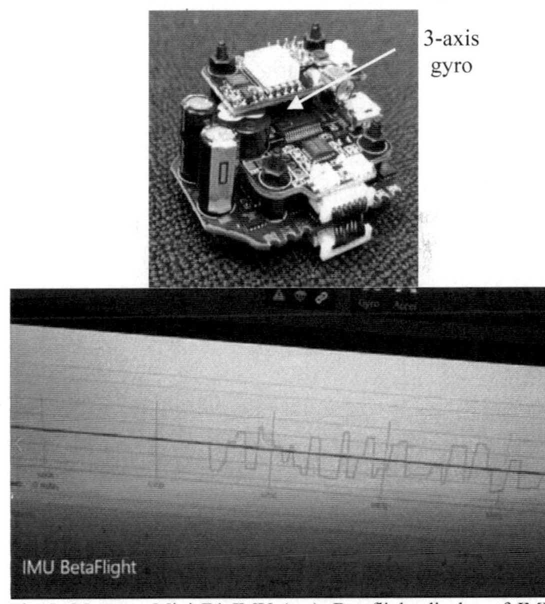

Fig 5. Magnum Mini F4 IMU (top). Betaflight display of IMU appearing to be shaking violently, even though it was stationary.

References

[1] E. L. Kirchner and B. D. Salati, "An EMC Design Approach for Integrating COTS Equipment into an Existing Military Aircraft," IEEE International Symposium on EMC, Seattle, 1999.

[2] R. Thottappillil and M. Backstrom, "Intentional Electromagnetic Interference and Critical Infrastructure," URSI AP-RASC, New Delhi, 2019.

[3] C. K. Kasmi and J. L. E. Lopes-Esteves, "Functional Susceptibility of COTS devices to IEMI at local and large-scale levels," Int. Conf. on Electromagnetics in Advanced Applications (ICEAA), Cairns, 2016.

Multi-Physical Analysis of the Corrosion of Buried Pipes due to Nearby High Voltage Transmission Lines

Dario Mateo Arango Angarita
Dept. of Electrical Engineering
Universidad Nacional Colombia
Bogotá, Colombia
dmarangoa@unal.edu.co

Daniel Vargas Medina
Dept. of Electrical Engineering
Universidad Nacional Colombia
Bogotá, Colombia
davargasme@unal.edu.co

Javier Leonardo Araque Quijano
Dept. of Electrical Engineering
Universidad Nacional Colombia
Bogotá, Colombia
jlaraqueq@unal.edu.co

***Abstract*—In this contribution we present the multi-physical analysis of the induction-corrosion process undergone by a buried pipe that experiences electromagnetic induction from a nearby High Voltage Transmission Line (HVTL). The scenario analyzed models a typical situation found in Colombia by using realistic characteristics of the pipe, the HVTL, and environmental parameters such as soil resistivity. The results presented provide a quantitative view of the corrosion process and constitute a useful tool for the analysis and design of the increasingly common situation of pipelines running near HVTLs.**

1

***Index Terms*—Buried pipelines. Corrosion. Electromagnetic fields. HVTL. Multi-physics.**

I. Introduction

The rise in the energy demand, the high cost of rights-of-ways and environmental regulations have led many companies to use the same pathways for both high voltage transmission lines and pipelines, which has increased the parallelism between these structures through long distances. Such extended parallelism is known to increase the corrosion rate of pipelines, hence the present trend will likely increase the risk of negative environmental, health and economical impacts due to the leak of pipe contents. Due to the relevance of the phenomenon of corrosion, its study remains an area of active research [1]–[11], though to the best of our knowledge, these deal separately with the electromagnetic and corrosion phenomena.

Characteristics of the line such as geometry, nominal voltage/current level, environmental factors such as ground resistance and temperature [5], [10], and pipeline material and coating [1], are variables of interest that affect the underlying mechanism of electromagnetic induction. The complex interplay of parameters in several physical domains, and the need of an accurate prediction tool for analysis and design makes this problem very well suited for numerical multi-physical analysis.

In this work, the COMSOL package, based on the Finite Element Method (FEM), was used to perform an integrated analysis of the induction-corrosion phenomenon by coupling the electromagnetic and electrochemical domains in the analysis of a realistic scenario. The simulation parameters are based on a case study that includes the geometry of HVTLs used typically in Colombia and the corresponding soil parameters. Results show the material loss (corrosion) due the electromagnetic induction in the pipeline.

II. Scenario under Analysis

The scenario analyzed consists of a simplified 2-D representation of a HVTL tower, its corresponding power and guard lines, its grounding, and the pipe buried in soil in close proximity, as shown in Fig.1. The Table I summarizes the characteristics of the materials considered in the simulation.

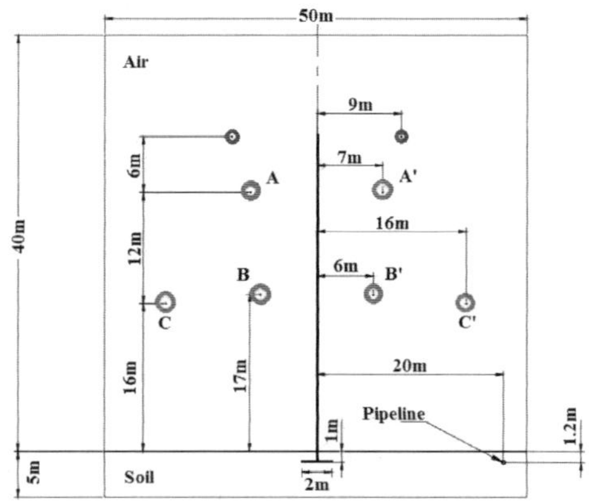

Fig. 1. Quoted diagram of the scenario analyzed.

TABLE I
MATERIAL VALUES FOR SIMULATION

Material	$\sigma[Sm^{-1}]$	μ_r	ϵ_r	$E_{eq}[V]$
Air	0	1	1.0006	-
Soil	0.01	1	40	-
Copper	5.998e7	1	1	-0.38
Pipeline	8.33e6	250	1	-0.859

III. System Equations

A. Induction Analysis

The excitation consists of a standard three-phase sinusoidal voltage of 500kV at 60Hz (see Figure 1). Given the small electrical dimensions of the scenario, one may perform an analysis is based on a time-stepped static approximation of the electric field:

$$E = -\nabla V \quad (1)$$

$$\nabla \cdot (\epsilon_0 \epsilon_r E) = \rho_v \quad (2)$$

where E is the electric field, V is the electrostatic potential, $\epsilon_0 \epsilon_r$ is the electrical permittivity of the medium, and ρ_v is the free charge density. The initial conditions were assumed as $0V$ for all elements. Also, the boundary of the domain and the tower are considered as ground.

B. Corrosion Analysis

The voltage induced in the pipeline affects the corrosion mechanism as follows:

$$\eta = \phi_{ext} - \phi_l - E_{eq} \quad (3)$$

where ϕ_{ext} is the external potential (the one induced in the electrode), ϕ_l is the electrolyte potential, and E_{eq} is the equilibrium potential. The Tafel equations were employed to model the anodic (i_a) and cathodic (i_b) current of the electrodes.

$$i_c = i_{oc} 10^{\frac{\eta}{b_c}} \quad (4)$$

$$i_a = i_{oa} 10^{\frac{\eta}{b_a}} \quad (5)$$

$$\frac{\partial c_{d.j}}{\partial t} = \sum_m R_{d,j,m}. \quad (6)$$

with $i_{oa} = 2.35mA/m^2$, $ioc = 14,57mA/m^2$,$b_a = 0.118V$ and $b_c = -0.207V$. Equation (6) shows how the material concentration $c_{d.j}$ changes due to the reaction rate R, which satisfies the following relation in the electrodes:

$$R_{d,j} = \frac{-v_{d,j} i_{el}}{2F} \quad (7)$$

Where F is the Faraday constant, i_{el} is the current of the electrode (i_a or i_c) and $v_{d,j}$ is the stoichiometric coefficient in the reduction reaction.

IV. Results

The voltage induced in the pipeline is sinusoidal with an RMS value of $176V$. The corrosion current density in the pipeline surface shows a maximum value of $3.76A/m^2$ and a average value of 1.2 A/m^2. The material loss after 10,000 hours is between 0.8mm and 1.4mm as shown in Figure 2.

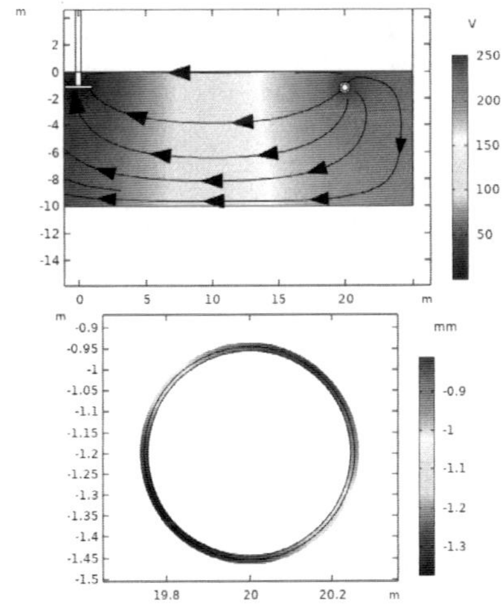

Fig. 2. Voltage induced in the soil around the pipeline and illustration of the flow of corrosion current (top) and surface displacement in the pipeline after 10.000 h (bottom).

References

[1] M. Ouadah, O. Touhami, R. Ibtiouen and, M. Zergoug, "Method for diagnosis of the effect of AC on the X70 pipeline due to an inductive coupling caused by HVPL," IET Science, Measurement & Technology, vol. 11, 2017.

[2] O. M'hamed et. al.,"AC Corrosion Induced by High Voltage Power Line on Cathodically Protected Pipeline," CEIT'14.

[3] O. M'hamed, O. Touhami, R. ibtiouen and, A. Bouzida, "Diagnoses and Mitigation of the Corrosion due to the Electromagnetic Coupling Between the HVPTL and Buried Pipeline", Large Electrical Network Conference (CAGRE) 2019 Algerian, pp. 1-5, 2019.

[4] Adedeji Kazeem, Ponnle Akinlolu , Jimoh Abdul-Ganiyu Abe B.T., Abu-Mahfouz Adnan, Hamam Yskandar. (2018). "GUI-Based AC Induced Corrosion Monitoring for Buried Pipelines near HVTLs," Engineering Letters. 26, 489-497.

[5] G. C. Christoforidis, D. P. Labridis, and P. S. Dokopoulos, "Inductive interference on pipelines buried in multilayer soil due to magnetic fields from nearby faulted powerLines," IEEE Transactions on Electromagnetic Compatibility, vol. 47, no. 2, pp. 254-262, May 2005.

[6] K. B. Adedeji, A. A. Ponnle, B. T. Abe, and A. A. Jimoh, "Effect of increasing energy demand on the corrosion rate of buried pipelines in the vicinity of high voltage overhead transmission lines," 2015 Intl Aegean Conference on Electrical Machines & Power Electronics (ACEMP), 2015 Intl Conference on Optimization of Electrical, Side, 2015, pp. 299-303.

[7] T. H. Shabangu, P. Shrivastava, B. T. Abe, K. B. Adedeji, and P. A. Olubambi, "Influence of AC interference on the cathodic protection potentials of pipelines: Towards a comprehensive picture," 2017 IEEE AFRICON, Cape Town, 2017, pp. 597-602.

[8] M. S. A. Rahman and H. Hasbullah, "Early detection method of corrosion on buried steel gas pipeline using wireless sensor network," 2010 The 2nd International Conference on Computer and Automation Engineering (ICCAE), Singapore, 2010, pp. 553-556.

[9] Y. He, G. Tian, L. Cheng, H. Zhang and P. Jackson, "Parameters influence in steel corrosion evaluation using PEC thermography," The 17th International Conference on Automation and Computing, Huddersfield, 2011, pp. 255-260.

[10] T. H. Shabangu, A. A. Ponnle, K. B. Adedeji, B. T. Abe, P. A. Olubambi, and A. A. Jimoh, "Effects of soil properties on corrosion of buried steel pipeline: A case study of rand water pipeline, South Africa," AFRICON 2015, Addis Ababa, 2015, pp. 1-5.

[11] A. M. Qabazard and M. A. Elhirbawy, "Corrosion and Electromagnetic Field Coupling in the State of Kuwait," ESMO 2006 - 2006 IEEE 11th International Conference on Transmission & Distribution Construction, Operation and Live-Line Maintenance, Albuquerque, NM, 2006.

Mixed-Mode Effect on Motor Common Mode Current

Vefa Karakasli, Gerd Griepentrog and Danil Drozhzhin
Institute of Power Electronics and Control of Drives
Technical University Darmstadt
Darmstadt, Germany
vefa.karakasli@lea.tu-darmstadt.de

Junsheng Wei
Research and Technology Center
ZF Friedrichshafen AG
Friedrichshafen, Germany

***Abstract*—This paper presents the mixed-mode effect on motor common mode current (CMC) in an adjustable speed drive (ASD). It is expected that the motor CMC is lower than inverter output CMC. However, the measurement result of the ASD shows that the AC motor input CMC is higher than the inverter output CMC in a frequency range. By using a mixed-mode (MM) 6-port networks, it is proven that the AC motor input CMC is higher due to an MM CMC which is generated from differential mode current.**

***Index Terms*—AC drive, CM, frequency domain model, mixed-mode, six-port network.**

I. Introduction

Wide-bandgap (WBG) semiconductors, such as silicon carbide (SiC), has a trending to be used for application of adjustable speed drives (ASDs), since they have great operational advantages such as switch higher current and voltage, faster switching and higher operational temperature [1], [2]. This allows to the designer to increase the frequency of power converter to achieve a lower size. Meanwhile, the fast rise and fall time transient of SiC semiconductors cause electromagnetic interference (EMI) challenges which are EMI effect to the neighbour devices, higher bearing current and deterioration of motor winding insulations [3], [4]. There are some international EMC standards which define limitations to minimize EMI problems. Therefore, it is important to predict the generated EMI noise accurately and use a suitable solution to minimize the aforementioned problem.

In a simplified equivalent common mode (CM) circuit of the ASDs, the common mode current (CMC) is induced by the high switching patterns ($\frac{\mathrm{d}v}{\mathrm{d}t}$) between the converter and ground terminals [5]. The CMC at AC side flows through the parasitic capacitances of inverter, EMI filter, 3-phase shielded cable and motor to ground, as shown in Fig. 1. Considering the simplified CM circuit, the summation of cable and motor CMCs are equal to filter output CMC as expressed in (1):

$$I_{\mathrm{CM_o}} = I_{\mathrm{CM_{cab1}}} + I_{\mathrm{CM_{cab2}}} + I_{\mathrm{CM_{mot}}}. \quad (1)$$

However, the measurements show that $I_{\mathrm{CM_{mot}}}$ is higher than $I_{\mathrm{CM_o}}$ in the frequency range (0.5-25MHz), as shown in Fig. 2. The main reasons for this phenomenon are the coupling between CM and differential mode (DM) caused by asymmetry of the three-phase system and non-linear operation of inverter [6], [7]. This phenomenon is called mixed-mode (MM) effect. In this paper, the MM in motor CMC will be considered.

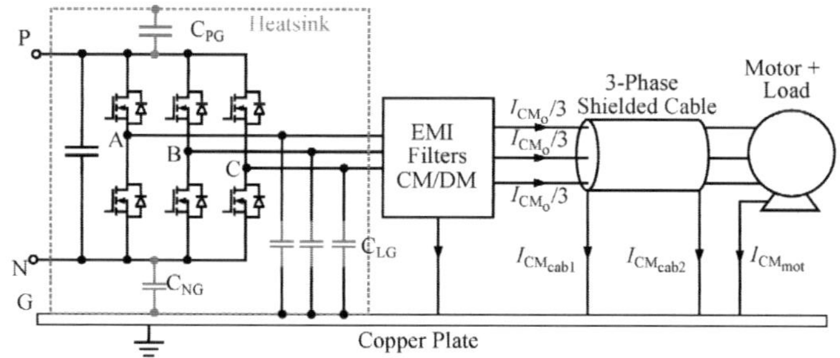

Fig. 1: The detailed model of AC side of ASD.

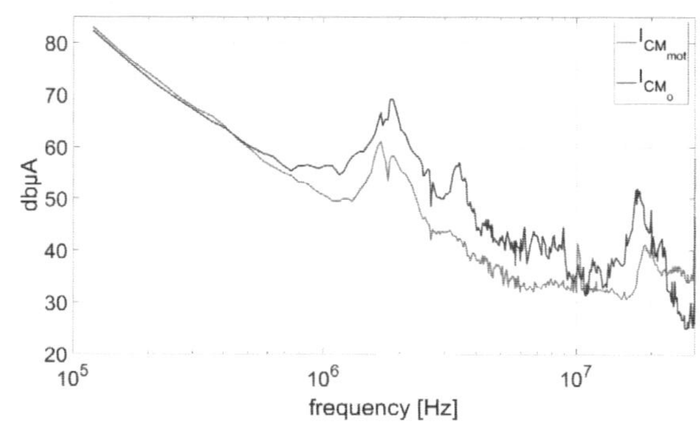

Fig. 2: Output side CMC measurements.

II. Model Description and Results for Motor Common Mode Current

A 6-port MM behavioral frequency domain model is used to model the effect of DM on CM which is explained in deeply in [6]. Here, the DC side of ASD, which influences pure CMC and induced CMC due to MM, is also added as given in Fig. 3. The CM voltage in (2) is coupled with two DM voltages in (3) by 6-port MM impedance ($\mathbf{Z}_{\mathrm{MM}}$) which is obtained 6-port single-ended impedance ($\mathbf{Z}_{\mathrm{SE}}$) measurement by using the transformation matrix in (4):

$$U_{\mathrm{CM}} = \frac{U_{\mathrm{A}} + U_{\mathrm{B}} + U_{\mathrm{C}}}{3}, \quad (2)$$

$$
\begin{aligned}
U_{\mathrm{DM}_1} &= U_{\mathrm{A}} - U_{\mathrm{B}}, \\
U_{\mathrm{DM}_2} &= U_{\mathrm{B}} - U_{\mathrm{C}},
\end{aligned} \tag{3}
$$

$$
\mathbf{Z}_{\mathrm{MM}} = \mathbf{T}\mathbf{Z}_{\mathrm{SE}}\mathbf{T}^{-1}. \tag{4}
$$

The DC side equivalent circuit of CM ($Z_{\mathrm{CM_i}}$) is calculated from the impedance parameter analysis of terminated 2-port based on Fig. 3(a). The 2-port input CM and two DM chain parameters matrices which are calculated from (5) and (6) are coupled to get the input 6-port chain parameters matrix ($\mathbf{ABCD}_{\mathrm{in}}$). 6-port $\mathbf{Z}_{\mathrm{MM}}$ of EMI filter, AC cable and motor are transferred to 6-port chain parameters for cascade connection of system. Then, all 6-port chain matrices are cascade connected to obtain a total 6-port system chain matrix ($\mathbf{ABCD}_{\mathrm{tot}}$):

$$
\begin{bmatrix} A_{\mathrm{CM_{in}}} & B_{\mathrm{CM_{in}}} \\ C_{\mathrm{CM_{in}}} & D_{\mathrm{CM_{in}}} \end{bmatrix} = \begin{bmatrix} 1 + Z_{\mathrm{CM_i}} Y_{\mathrm{CM_i}} & Z_{\mathrm{CM_i}} \\ Y_{\mathrm{CM_i}} & 1 \end{bmatrix}, \tag{5}
$$

$$
\begin{bmatrix} A_{\mathrm{DM_{k,in}}} & B_{\mathrm{DM_{k,in}}} \\ C_{\mathrm{DM_{k,in}}} & D_{\mathrm{DM_{k,in}}} \end{bmatrix} = \begin{bmatrix} 1 & Z_{\mathrm{DM_{k,in}}} \\ 0 & 1 \end{bmatrix} \qquad k = 1, 2. \tag{6}
$$

In order to find the input currents and motor output currents, $\mathbf{ABCD}_{\mathrm{tot}}$ is transferred to a admittance matrix $\mathbf{Y}_{\mathrm{tot}}$ and admittance matrix equation is used as given (7). $\mathbf{ABCD}_{\mathrm{in}}$, 6-port chain parameters matrices of output cable ($\mathbf{ABCD}_{\mathrm{cab}}$) and output filter ($\mathbf{ABCD}_{\mathrm{fil}}$) are cascade connected to calculate the motor input current from the inverse chain parameters equation in (8):

$$
\begin{bmatrix} I_{\mathrm{CM_u}} \\ I_{\mathrm{DM_{1u}}} \\ I_{\mathrm{DM_{2u}}} \\ I_{\mathrm{DM_{3mot,o}}} \\ I_{\mathrm{DM_{1mot,o}}} \\ I_{\mathrm{DM_{2mot,o}}} \end{bmatrix} = \mathbf{Y}_{\mathrm{tot}} \begin{bmatrix} U_{\mathrm{CM}} \\ U_{\mathrm{DM_1}} \\ U_{\mathrm{DM_2}} \\ 0 \\ 0 \\ 0 \end{bmatrix}, \tag{7}
$$

$$
\begin{bmatrix} U_{\mathrm{CM_{mot,i}}} \\ U_{\mathrm{DM_{1mot,i}}} \\ U_{\mathrm{DM_{2mot,i}}} \\ I_{\mathrm{CM_{mot,i}}} \\ I_{\mathrm{DM_{1mot,i}}} \\ I_{\mathrm{DM_{2mot,i}}} \end{bmatrix} = \mathbf{ABCD}^{-1}_{\mathrm{in,cab,fil}} \begin{bmatrix} U_{\mathrm{CM}} \\ U_{\mathrm{DM_1}} \\ U_{\mathrm{DM_2}} \\ I_{\mathrm{CM_u}} \\ I_{\mathrm{DM_{1u}}} \\ I_{\mathrm{DM_{2u}}} \end{bmatrix}. \tag{8}
$$

The motor CMC input ($I_{\mathrm{CM_{mot,i}}}$) consists of pure CMC and MM CMC. It is possible to find these two CMCs separately. If $U_{\mathrm{CM_{mot,i}}}$ is assigned by 0, the MM CMC of motor will be obtained. In case of $U_{\mathrm{DM_{1mot,i}}} = U_{\mathrm{DM_{2mot,i}}} = 0$, the pure CMC of motor is calculated. The simulated CMC of motor is compared with measured result in Fig. 4. It can be observed that the simulated result matches very well with measured results except for the HF resonance peak (18MHz) because of the difficulties of HF impedance prediction. The MM $I_{\mathrm{CM_{mot,i}}}$ is more dominant than the pure one in 0.55-22MHz frequency range. This is reason why $I_{\mathrm{CM_{mot,i}}}$ is higher then $I_{\mathrm{CM_o}}$.

III. Conclusion

In this paper, a fast prediction method is proposed to model the effect of MM current on motor CMC. The simulation results are also proven by measurement results. This research will help ASD designers to take precautions against CMC effect on bearing current and deterioration of motor windings.

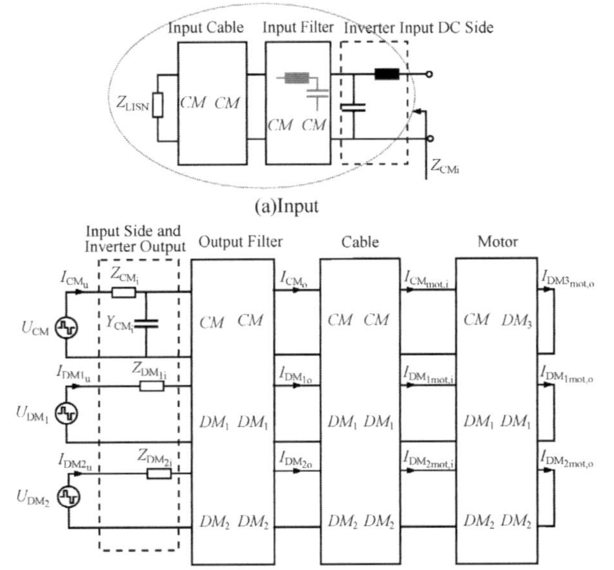

(b)Input and output

Fig. 3: 6-port MM EMC prediction model .

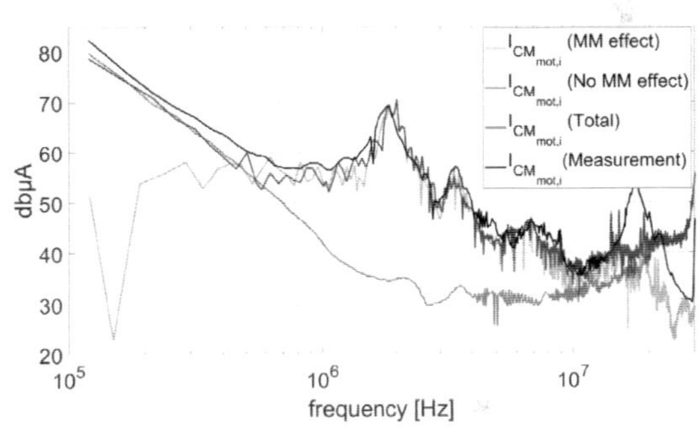

Fig. 4: The simulation result of motor CMC are compared with measurement results.

References

[1] S. Tanimoto and K. Matsui, "High junction temperature and low parasitic inductance power module technology for compact power conversion systems," IEEE Trans. Electron Devices, vol. 62, no. 2, pp. 258-269, Feb. 2015.

[2] X. Ding, et al., "Analytical and experimental evaluation of SiC-inverter nonlinearities for traction drives used in eletric vehicles," IEEE Trans. Veh. Technol., no. 99, pp. 1, 2017.

[3] G. Vidmar and D. Miljavec, "A Universal High-Frequency Three-Phase Electric-Motor Model Suitable for the Delta- and Star-Winding Connections," IEEE Transactions on Power Electronics, vol. 30, pp. 4365-4376, 2015.

[4] H. Chen, Y. Yan and H. Zhao, "Extraction of common-mode impedance of an inverter-fed induction motor," IEEE Trans. Electromagn. Compat., vol. 58, no. 2, pp. 599-606, Apr. 2016.

[5] J. Luszcz, High Frequency Conducted Emission in AC Motor Drives Fed By Frequency Converters: Sources and Propagation Paths. John Wiley & Sons, 2018.

[6] D. Drozhzhin and G. Griepentrog, "Simulation of Conducted Noise of an AC Drive by Means of Mixed Mode 6-Port Networks," In 2018 International Symposium on Electromagnetic Compatibility (EMC EUROPE), pp. 1-6, Aug. 2018.

[7] J. Xue and F. Wang, "Mixed-mode EMI noise in three-phase DC-fed PWM motor drive system," in 2013 IEEE Energy Conversion Congress and Exposition, pp. 4312–4317, Sep. 2013.

Polyethylene Pipeline Detection and Visualization Using the Method of Auxiliary Sources

Ömer Faruk Güner
Informatics Institute
Istanbul Technical University
Istanbul, Turkey
guner16@itu.edu.tr

Vasil Tabatadze
Informatics Institute
Istanbul Technical University
Istanbul, Turkey
vasilitabatadze@gmail.com

Sebahattin EKER
Informatics Institute
Istanbul Technical University
Istanbul, Turkey
sebahattin.eker@itu.edu.tr

***Abstract*— Pipelines maintaining and upgrading are the most important undertakings for utility companies. Excavation work is required to reach the pipe for possible maintenance works that may occur on the pipelines. It is possible to detect the pipeline using the electromagnetic waves because there exists the frequency range for which the ground is transparent. Pipeline gives resonance response for some frequencies and makes it easily detectable. In this work, the Method of Auxiliary Sources (MAS) is used for direct scattering problem solution of the electromagnetic waves by the ground with pipeline inside. Some interesting results are obtained and analyzed.**

***Keywords*— Method of Auxiliary Sources, ground-penetrating radar, detection of polyethylene pipe-lines, buried object recognition**

I. Introduction

Investigation of infrastructure using electromagnetic radiation to detect infrastructure systems buried in the soil is a very typical problem. It is widely used in the detection and mapping of infrastructure systems with different material properties and different transmission lines that are underground with electromagnetic waves [1-2].In big cities, where the infrastructure is dense and complicated in terms of transmission lines, it is really difficult to detect the pipes by the non-destructive testing method. To find and distinguish between transmission lines such as natural gas, water, fiber optic, electrical cables within the infrastructure employing the non-destructive testing method and tried to differentiate them from each other has been tried and obtained fast and healthy data. For this reason, the resonance frequency of a pipeline made of polyethylene material was determined by using a different method, and the detectability of the pipe was investigated by using a source sent from outside without excavation. The auxiliary source is a method that is based on the distribution of singularities. With this method, the basic functions found in scattering objects are concentrated by the property of the analytical progress of a scattered field. As a result, the collision coefficient was determined and proved by the sequencing technology to solve the external and internal problems of electrodynamics[2-4].

II. Theory and Numerical Simulation Experiments

The Method of Auxiliary Sources (MAS) is a numerical technique for the analysis of electromagnetic radiation and scattering problems. MAS can explain an external scattering problem. The sources of the scattered field are selected as separate sources such as Hertzian dipoles and line currents. These spread fields are given in closed-form expressions. The auxiliary sources are placed on an auxiliary surface and placed in the scatter. Allow the auxiliary resources to be disseminated in the free space. Their excitations are then determined by matching the boundary condition on the surface of the scattering. Thus we can resolve the linear system of equations in this way. Consider object perfectly conductor scatterer with surface C. Incident field excites current on the C, and we get the scattered field. To find the scattered field, we have to determine currents excited on the surface. For this, we have to require boundary condition satisfaction on the scatterer's surface.

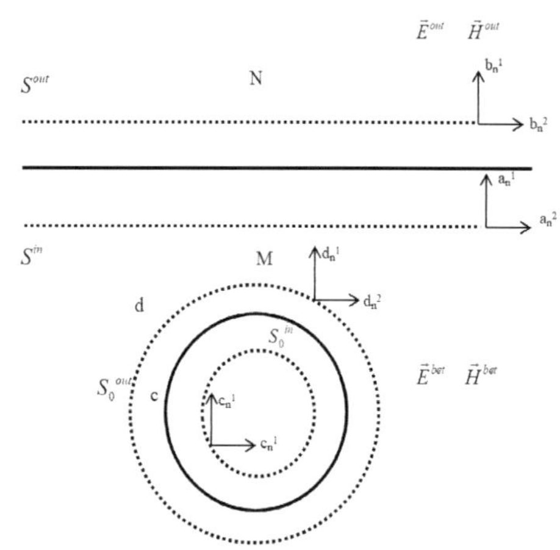

Fig. 1. The geometry of the auxiliary surfaces fields.

If we now examine the part of the polyethylene pipeline means that the surface among S and S0. Surfaces with dielectrics complex permittivity losses $\varepsilon_c = (\varepsilon', \varepsilon'')$. The area above the surface and inside the PE pipeline permittivity which ε_0, μ_0. We can think about the *S* plane part of the surface, a mass of the cylindrical polyethylene pipeline S_0 is placed (Figure 2). EM wave, which includes time-harmonic $\vec{E}_{inc}$, $\vec{H}_{inc}$ affect to *S* surface. The purpose in this section is to detect reflected field which $\vec{E}^{out}$, $\vec{H}^{out}$ above the area, the field among surface and polyethylene pipeline $\vec{E}^{bet}$, $\vec{H}^{bet}$ and area inside layer in $\vec{E}^{in}$, $\vec{H}^{in}$. We define the inner with S^{in} and outer S^{out}. The selected auxiliary surfaces must be parallel to the S surface, and they must be placed at equal intervals on the S surface. The auxiliary surfaces S_0^{in} and S_0^{out} are must build inner and outer of the polyethylene pipeline Figure 1. The polarization vectors come from the tangent vectors of the main surface and the polyethylene pipeline surface. The total area on the surface includes $\vec{E}_{inc}(\vec{r})$, $\vec{H}_{inc}(\vec{r})$. And the same area also has reflected $\vec{E}_{S^{in}}(\vec{r})$, $\vec{H}_{S^{in}}(\vec{r})$. The reflected is defined by the auxiliary sources deploy on the area S_0^{in}. The area between S and S_0 also include $\vec{E}_{S^{out}}(\vec{r})$, $\vec{H}_{S^{out}}(\vec{r})$ fields. The fields reflected the surface is $\overrightarrow{E}_{S_0^{in}}(\vec{r})$, $\overrightarrow{H}_{S_0^{in}}(\vec{r})$.

The fields are located on S^{out} and S^{in} have been identified regarding auxiliary sources.

III. Simulation and Experimental Results

We have created a user-friendly program package for performing numerical experiments with the mathematical algorithm mentioned above. With this program package, we have gained the ability to select ground and polyethylene pipeline parameters, welding position, and other parameters to calculate field distributions. We can create frequency properties for different situations, and we can compare the

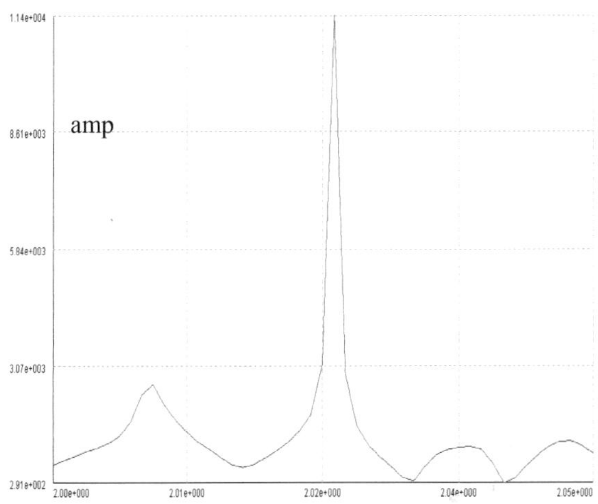

Fig. 2. Result of the ka range (1.95 - 2.05).

results with each other. The principal idea of these experiments is to formulate the methodology of the given problem. The User-friendly Program provides the ability to administrate some parameters; configure the problem with material characteristics (cylindrical polyethylene pipeline), select the type of source, the frequency range of the EM wave and the reflected area. If can we compose a library of these properties, we can compute the measurement results with the values we have previously determined in the library. In this way, we can easily decide that the polyethylene pipeline that we searched for by real experiment is in the dry soil.

The program package we have created allows us to examine the dynamics in the 3D field. It is also possible to create a wider library by making additional calculations for all infrastructure assets. First of all, it is necessary to obtain the resonance frequency of the polyethylene pipe to perform this study. To find the resonance frequency of the polyethylene The graph obtained as a result of the scanning of the frequency range 1.95 to 2.05 in Figure 2.

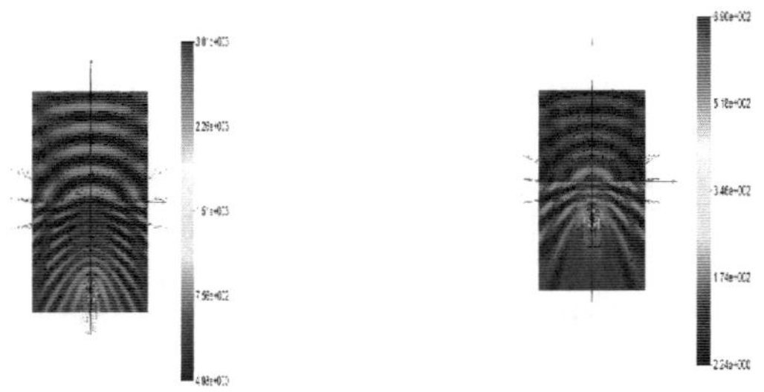

Fig. 3.(a) 1 meter depth Ø32mm PE X-Z coordinate, (b) 1 meter depth Ø63mm PE X-Z coordinate

IV. Conclusion

In this study, resonant properties of polyethylene pipelines of different sizes (Ø32mm, Ø63mm, Ø125mm) and different depths (1 - 1.5 m) in dry soil were investigated. The main objective of the study was to determine the presence, size, and direction of the polyethylene pipeline in dry soil by using electromagnetic wave radiation with MAS. In this case, some numerical results have been proposed for the source to show different polarizations. With this program, we changed the radius and depth coordinates of the polyethylene pipeline, and we calculated the soil conductivity and the frequency characteristic for different conditions according to the environment we selected.

References

[1] V. Tabatadze, D. Kakulia (2011) "Development of a New Efficient Numerical Approach for Buried Object Recognition", Sensing and Imaging: An International Journal: Volume 12, Issue 1 (2011), Page 35-56,

[2] V. Tabatadze, B. Baratashvili "Tunnel Detection and Visualization Using the Method of Auxiliary Sources " Iv. Javakhishvili Tbilisi State University Chavchavadze Av. 3, 0176, Tbilisi, Georgia

[3] D. Karkashadze R. Zaridze (1995) "The method of auxiliary sources in applied electrodynamics, in Computational Electrodynamics," Latsis Symposium ETH, Zurich, 1995, pp. 163-180.

[4] Larry G. Stolarczyk, Robert Troublefield (2005)"Detection of Underground Tunnels with a Synchronized Electromagnetic Wave Gradiometer" Proc. of SPIE Vol. 5778

[5] Karamehmedovic, Mirza; Sørensen (2008) " Progress in Industrial Mathematics at ECMI 2008 Application of the method of auxiliary sources in optical diffraction microscopy".

[6] R.S.Zaridze, D.D.Karkashadze (2004) Tbilisi State University, Tbilisi, USSR Conference Paper "A Method Of Auxiliary Sources In Applied Electrodynamic

Effect of Stator's Insulation Failure on the Performance of Motor Drive system

Hassan H. Eldeeb[1], Haisen Zhao[1,2], and Osama Mohammed[1], *Fellow, ACES*

1. Energy System Research Laboratory, ECE Department, Florida International University, Miami, FL33174, USA
2. School of Electrical and Electronics Engineering, North China Electric Power University, Beijing, 102206

helde002@fiu.edu; hzhao@fiu.edu; mohammed@fiu.edu

***Abstract*— This study investigates the influence of the stator's turn-to-turn failures (TTFs) on the electromagnetic (EM) fields, such as air gap flux density, flux density in stator and rotor iron core, as well as, current density in rotor bars, inside of a direct self control (DSC) driven induction machines (IMs). The purpose of the investigation is to capture the fault signatures in the air gap EM flux for detecting the stator's fault at its embryonic stage**

***Index Terms*—Fault detection, Induction machine, Inverter-fed IM, Inter-turn short-circuit, FEA co-simulation.**

I. Introduction

URN-to-turn fault (TTF) is the second most common fault in induction motors (IMs) [1]. That's why it has been investigated extensively for direct online (DOL) connected IMs and for open loop driven ones from voltage source inverters (VSI) [2]. Although most of the IMs in high performance industry applications are driven by closed-loop controllers, very few studies investigated the TTF fault detection (FD) in closed loop drive systems. The direct self-control (DSC) technique has the merit of being robust and easy to implement. Moreover DSC has an advantage over the other closed loop drive techniques, that it is independent on the IM parameters. Consequently, DSC is the most implemented technique among all the vector control ones. However, the FD of TTFs in DSC controlled IM is the least studied in literature [1].

The studies investigated the TTF effect on the DSC driven IMs focused on the impacts of the fault on the stator's current (i_s) and the developed torque, as in [1] and [3], or on the radiatted electromagnetic (EM) flux from the IM, as in [4]. However, the impacts of the TTF on the EM of the air gap and iron core of the motor was not futher investigated before. Nethertheless, those impacts are the first step toward the invasive FD, via inserting search coils in the machine's air gap. Therfore, this study present a comprehensive investigation to the impacts of the stator's turn-to turn faliure on the internal EM field of a DSC driven IM for the purpose of FD.

II. IM Drive System under Study

The co-simulation platform of the vector driven IM under study is shown in Fig.1. The drive system algorithm is based on two hysteresis controllers , the first is to control the developed torque (T_e), while the other is to control the magnitude of the flux-linkage ($|\boldsymbol{\lambda}_s|$).The switching frequency ($f_s = 10$ kHz). The DSC algorithm procedure could summarized in the following steps:

Measurement of VSI signals': The first step is the measurement of the DC-link voltage (V_{DC}) and the motor's line current($\boldsymbol{i}_s$).

Transformation into $\alpha\beta$ coordinates: The measured values are transformed from abc into $\alpha\beta$.

Stator's voltage estimation: The space-vector (SV) output voltage of the VSI ($\hat{\boldsymbol{v}}_s$) could be estimated through the knowledge of V_{DC} and the switching sequence

Estimation of T_e and $\boldsymbol{\lambda}_s$: T_e and $\lambda_s$are estimated by (1) and (2), respectively. R_s is the stator resistance.

$$\hat{T}_e = \frac{3}{2}\frac{P}{2}\frac{L_m}{L_s}\left(i_{s\beta}\hat{\lambda}_{s\alpha} - i_{s\alpha}\hat{\lambda}_{s\beta}\right) \quad (1)$$

$$\hat{\boldsymbol{\lambda}}_s = \int(\boldsymbol{v}_s - R_s\boldsymbol{i}_s)dt \quad (2)$$

Controllers action: The error between the estimated and reference values of T_e and $\boldsymbol{\lambda}_s$ are the inputs to the controllers. The output indicate the switching requirements.

Sector detection: Based on τ and ψ, the sector (S_x, where$x = \{1-6\}$) where the flux-linkage lies is determined.

The TTF inserts inter-harmonics in i_s as in (3), where p is number of pole pairs. The DSC react to the TTF through insertion of $3f$ harmonic component in i_s [1].

$$f_{TTF} = f\left[\frac{m}{p}(1-s) \pm l\right],\ m = 0,1,2\ldots, l = 0,1,3,5\ldots \quad (4)$$

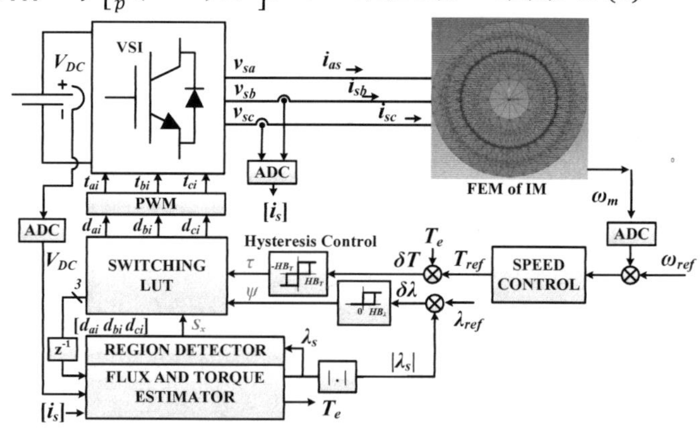

Fig. 1. FEA Co-simulation platform of the DSC driven IM under study

III. FEA Model Results

A. Details of the Motor

With a 1-hp induction motor, the electromagnetic fields, such as air-gap flux density, flux density in stator and rotor iron core and current density in rotor bars, are investigated systematically. The 3-D structure of the motor and fault setting are given in

This work was partially supported by grants from the Office of Naval Research. Authors are with the Energy Systems Research Laboratory, Florida International University, Miami, FL 33174, USA. email: mohammed@fiu.edu

Fig.2, which is made out of iron core M19 USS with 36 slots, while the rotor The rotor bars are made of aluminum 3.8e7 Siemens/m and there are 44 of them (R=44). The air gap is 0.31 mm. Each phase has 6 coils connected in series, with total number of turns per phase is N_{sa}=510. Four taps were done on the physical IM and the FEA model to study the ITSC. The fault severity factor (μ_f) is a ratio (in percentage) between the number of turns short-circuited and N_{sa}.

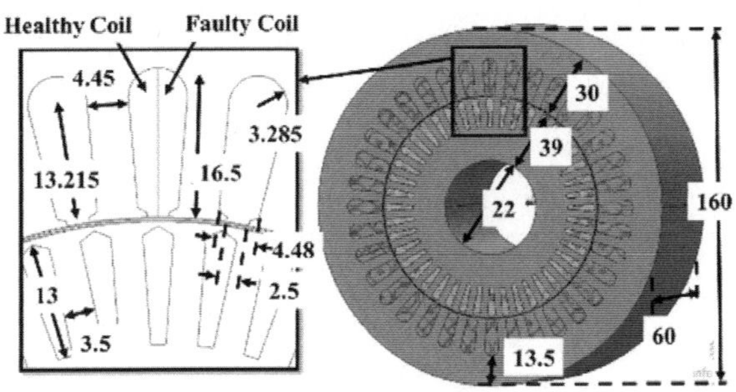

Fig.2 Structure of 1 hp motor and fault setting

TABLE I: DETAILS OF THE MOTOR.

Rating	Value	Param.	Value
Pr (W)	750	Stator outer diameter	160
U (V)	460	Stator inner diameter	100
I (A)	1.47	Rotor inner diameter	22
f (HZ)	60	Air-gap length	0.31
n (rpm)	1730	Parallel branch	1
J (kgm^2)	0.053	Slot numbers (Z1/Z2)	36/44

B. FEA Results

The different faulty cases, including μ_f=1.08%, 2.68%, 3.98%, and 4.7%, are computed, respectively. The fault resistance is $R_f = 0.67\ \Omega$. The faulty case of μ_f= 2.68% is analyzed in this digest, as it could be detected from i_s signatures. Comparisons of current and air-gap flux density with healthy and faulty conditions are given in Fig.3. It can be found that.

1) With the healthy condition, three phase currents are balance and the amplitude is 1.93A. However, with the faulty condition, the phase-A current increase to 2.02A, which is obviously higher than the other ones. It is the reason that the turn-to-turn fault can lead to the unbalance MMF and the current in faulty winding may increase correspondingly.

2) As seen from in Fig.3 (b), it can be found that, comparing with the healthy condition, there are more abrupt variations (dot circled area) in air-gap's flux density waveform with faulty condition. Beside the slot opening effect, the inter-action between the additional EM flux introduced by the short-circuited windings and main rotating field caused those abrupt changes. The aforementioned effect is influenced by the relative position between the faulty windings and the main rotating flux.

IV. CONCLUSION

The Study presented the impacts of the TTFs on the magnetic field harmonics and power loss componentsof a DSC driven IM. The FEA co-simulation results showed the air gap's magnetic field sensitivity to the TTF more than i_s . The results demonstrate that FD based on air gap flux density can detect TTFs at their incipient stages.

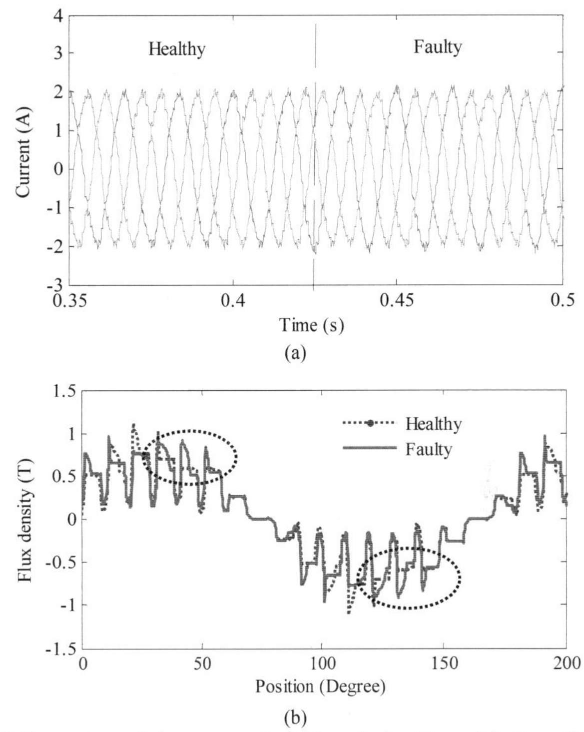

Fig.3 Comparison of electromagnetic fields under healthy and fault conditions. (a). Stator current. (b). Air-gap flux density.

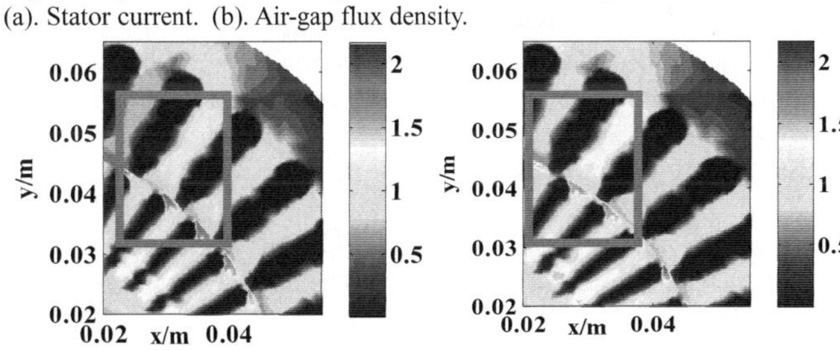

Fig.4. 2D distribution of $|B|$ under 50% loading: (a) healthy, (b) 2.6 % TTF

REFERENCES

[1] H. H. Eldeeb, A. Berzoy and O. Mohammed, "Comprehensive Investigation of Harmonic Signatures Resulting from Inter- Tum Short-Circuit Faults in DSC Driven IM Operating in Harsh Environments," *2018 XIII International Conference on Electrical Machines (ICEM)*, Alexandroupoli, Greece, 2018, pp. 2579-2585

[2] A. Berzoy, A. A. S. Mohamed and O. Mohammed, "Impact of Inter-Turn Short-Circuit Location on Induction Machines Parameters Through FE Computations," in *IEEE Transactions on Magnetics*, vol. 53, no. 6, pp. 1-4, June 2017

[3] A. Berzoy, O. A. Mohammed and J. Restrepo, "Analysis of the Impact of Stator Interturn Short-Circuit Faults on Induction Machines Driven by Direct Torque Control," in *IEEE Transactions on Energy Conversion*, vol. 33, no. 3, pp. 1463-1474, Sept. 2018.

[4] H. H. Eldeeb, A. Berzoy and O. Mohammed, "Stator Fault Detection on DSC Driven IM via Magnetic Signatures aided by 2DFEA Co-simulation," in *IEEE Transactions on Magnetics*, in Press.

Composite Materials Development for Fused Filament Fabrication of RF Systems

Paul Parsons
DeLUX Advanced Manufacturing
Newark, DE, 19713, USA
p.parsons@delux-engineering.com

Zachary Larimore
DeLUX Advanced Manufacturing
Newark, DE, 19713, USA
larimore@delux-engineering.com

Mark Mirotznik
Department of Electrical Engineering
University of Delaware
Newark, DE, 19716, USA
mirotzni@udel.edu

Gregory Mitchell
Antennas and Technology Integration Branch
U.S. Army Research Laboratory
Adelphi, MD, 20783, USA
gregory.a.mitchell1.civ@mail.mil

***Abstract*—In this paper we present the development of feedstock materials, specifically tailored permittivity materials used in fused filament fabrication (FFF), for microwave applications. One of the major bottlenecks in utilizing additive manufacturing for useful radiofrequency (RF) applications is the lack of suitable materials. Flexible, high-dielectric constant and low dielectric loss tangent composite materials, consisting of a mixture of polymer and ceramic nanoparticles in controlled volume fractions, are manufactured. Effective medium approximations (EMA) to predict composite properties, such as Bruggeman approximations, are validated with measurements between 18 – 40 GHz and are presented.**

Keywords—additive manufacturing, composite materials, dielectric characterization, fused filament fabrication, antennas.

I. INTRODUCTION

To reduce size, weight, power and cost (SWaP-c), military platforms have been evolving towards a more integrated design approach that efficiently utilizes all available space. In fact, to accommodate limited space constraints many commercial off-the-shelf (COTS) systems will need to be replaced by custom designed and fabricated systems. In the case of RF antennas and electronic systems, this will require exploring innovative design methods, new materials and novel manufacturing approaches to realize cost-effective, customizable and conformal radar and communication systems that do not rely on standard COTS technologies.

An attractive solution to this challenge is offered by the field of additive manufacturing (AM). While the current AM market has been growing rapidly, it is still built primarily around single material based systems, where the applicability of these systems to RF applications is limited. While very good progress has been made on the development of general multi-material AM printers less progress has been made on the development of materials designed specifically for use in RF applications, where the typical dielectric properties at RF or microwave frequencies of base materials are shown in Fig. 1 [1]. In many cases, the lack of suitable materials is the bottleneck that is preventing the applicability of this technology towards real-world applications.

In this paper we present our methods of addressing the material development concerns for AM-RF applications, by demonstrating flexible, high-dielectric constant and low dielectric loss tangent composite filaments feedstock materials that have been characterized between 18 – 40 GHz.

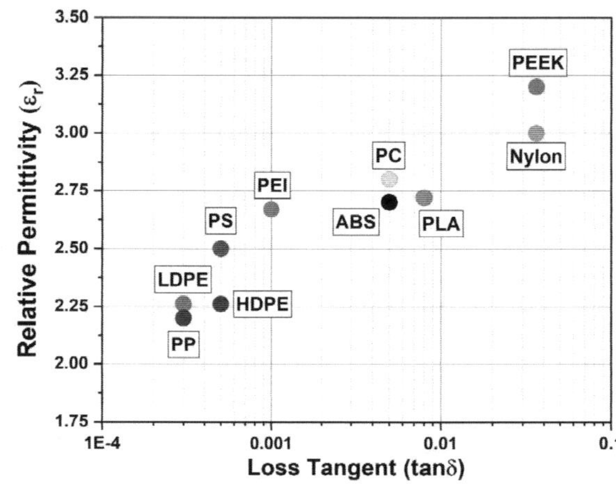

Fig. 1. Reported electrical properties of various commercially available polymer filament materials used in FFF processes. These materials offer a relatively narrow range in dielectric constant.

II. FABRICATION OF FLEXIBLE FILAMENTS AND SAMPLES

Composite materials were prepared using mixing techniques used by other research groups [2, 3]. Pellets of acrylonitrile butadiene styrene (ABS) were dissolved using acetone, afterwards a plasticizer, dibutyl phthalate (DBP), and a surfactant, octyl gallate (OG) were added in small concentrations. These additives are necessary, as the plasticizer acts as a lubricant between molecular chains in the polymer, enabling flexibility even with loading of ceramic powders; however, the addition of too much plasticizer negatively affects the composite by rendering it too elastic. The surfactant is used to prevent aggregation between the ceramic particles.

Ceramic nanoparticles, (diameter < 800 nm) of $BaTiO_3$, $SrTiO_3$, or $Ba_{0.67}Sr_{0.33}TiO_3$ are added in controlled amounts to the mixtures, in volume fractions between 15 – 30%, and allowed to homogenize within the matrix. We specifically selected nanoparticles over microparticles owing to their lower

Work supported by U.S. Army Research Laboratory, Adelphi.

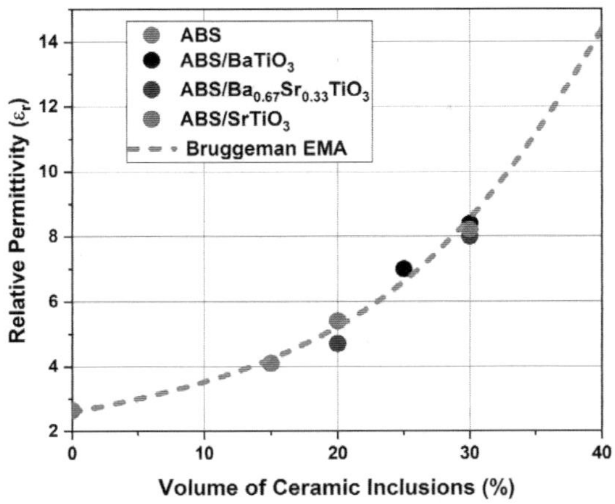

Fig. 2. Mean relative permittivity of the ABS-ceramic composite samples as a function of volume loading compared to EMA predictions (dashed line).

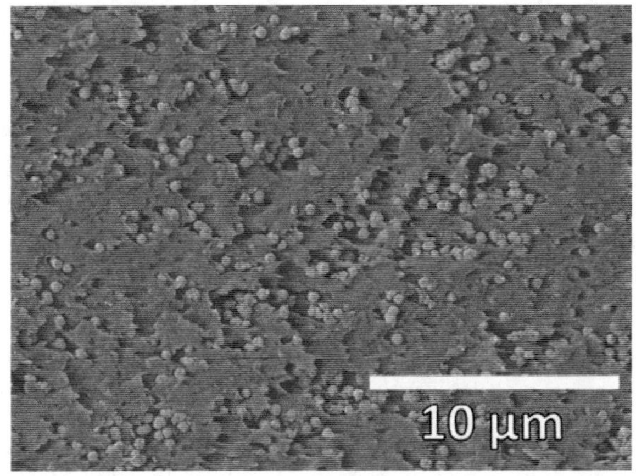

Fig. 3. SEM image of a ceramic nanoparticle-loaded ABS-composite filament showing well-dispersed particles within the polymer matrix.

dielectric loss tangents at the expense of a reduced maximum relative permittivity. The suspension was spread onto a chemically inert tray where the acetone was allowed to evaporate. After fully evaporating, the composite slab was cut into pieces and then ground into approximately 2 mm pellets. The composite pellets were extruded into 1.75mm diameter filaments using a single screw extruder at 190°C. We found that adding more than 40% ceramic powder resulted in a filament that was too brittle for use, even with the addition of plasticizer. To address this, we utilize a hopper-fed approach to printing samples, which we will expand in the future.

These filaments were then printed into 150 mm x 150 mm x 1-2 mm samples for dielectric characterization using an nScrypt 3Dn-300 multi-material platform. Print head and build plate temperatures during deposition were set to 240°C and 110°C, respectively. We also observed that as the loading of ceramic inclusions increases, so too does the viscosity of the material. Care needs to be exercised as these viscous materials are prone to printing defects, such as voids, and we found that use off an overlapping fill pattern minimizes such defects.

III. Material Characterization and Results

The composite sample plates were characterized using a free-space focused beam system (VNA model E8364B) between 18 – 40 GHz, with the mean relative permittivity and dielectric loss tangents summarized in Table I.

TABLE I. Dielectric Properties of ABS-Composite Filaments

Ceramic Inclusion	Vol. Loading (%)	Permittivity	Loss Tangent
$BaTiO_3$	25	7.01	0.011
	30	8.39	0.016
$Ba_{0.67}Sr_{0.33}TiO_3$	20	4.72	0.029
	30	8.02	0.069
$SrTiO_3$	15	4.10	<0.01
	20	5.39	< 0.01
	30	8.18	< 0.01

The relative permittivity and dielectric loss tangent increase as the loading of ceramic increases. Surprisingly, all of the ceramic materials measure similar values of permittivity ($\varepsilon_r \approx 5$ at 20% and $\varepsilon_r \approx 8$ at 30% loading) and is shown in Fig. 2 compared to Bruggeman predictions. However, out of all the ceramic nanoparticles, ABS-$SrTiO_3$ shows the most promise as a low-loss tangent candidate.

Scanning electron microscope (SEM) images of a composite filament sample is presented in Fig. 3. These images are useful to determine the relative dispersion of ceramic nanoparticles within the polymer matrix. We observe that this mixing approach provided well-dispersed materials.

IV. Conclusions

We have produced flexible filament composite materials for AM platforms that contain high dielectric constants and low dielectric loss tangents that are attractive for RF applications. These composites incorporate ceramic nanoparticles into an ABS matrix, aided by a plasticizer and surfactant. Sample plates using these materials were fabricated using an AM platform, and then characterized with a free-space focused beam system between 18 – 40 GHz, where predictions using EMA have been experimentally validated.

Acknowledgment

This work was supported by the U.S. Army Research Laboratory, under the Phase I SBIR Topic "Additive Manufacturing for RF Materials and Antennas", topic number A18-020.

References

[1] P. Parsons, Z. Larimore, F. Muhammed, and M. Mirotznik, "Fabrication of Low Dielectric Constant Composite Filaments for use in Fused Filament Fabrication 3D Printing," Additive Manufacturing, **30**, 2019.

[2] F. Castles, et al., "Microwave dielectric characterisation of 3D-printed BaTiO3/ABS polymer composites," Scientific Reports, **6**, 2016.

[3] J. Castro, E. Rojas-Nastrucci, A. Ross, T. Weller, and J. Wang, "Fabrication, Modeling, and Application of Ceramic-Thermoplastic Composites for Fused Deposition Modeling of Microwave Components," IEEE Transactions on Microwave Theory, **65**, 2017.

Additive Manufacturing of a Dual Band, Hybrid Substrate, and Dual Polarization Antenna

Gregory Mitchell
Army Research Laboratory
Adelphi, USA
gregory.a.mitchell1.civ@mail.mil

Zachary Larimore
DeLUX Engineering
Newark, USA
larimore@delux-engineering.com

Paul Parsons
DeLUX Engineering
Newark, USA
p.parsons@delux-engineering.com

***Abstract*—We describe the results of additive manufacturing pertaining to a multi-function antenna aperture. The antenna consists of customized high dielectric and low loss feedstocks as the enabling technology. The 3D printed prototype shows agreement with simulation while providing excellent performance. State of the art electromagnetic materials for additive manufacturing of antennas is the future of realizing complex antenna designs not realizable by traditional manufacturing methods.**

Keywords*—*additive manufacturing, dual band antenna, dual polarization, high dielectric hybrid feedstocks, 3D printing.

I. Introduction

Recent interest in multi-function antenna applications necessitates the investigation of multi-band antenna approaches. Currently, a host of antenna functions are performed utilizing a suite of different antennas that are challenging to upgrade, costly to maintain, and difficult to network for realizing multi-function capabilities. A single multi-function antenna could replace current disparate antenna technologies. Additive manufacturing (AM) allows engineers to re-think the RF design space. AM facilitates complex designs that required properties not achievable by current manufacturing methods. The 3D and hybrid-material approaches needed to achieve these designs makes AM critical to the future of radio frequency (RF) systems.

Strides in AM produce robust structural and mechanical parts, but industry has yet to develop and characterize electromagnetic properties of AM feedstocks for antennas. Low dielectric constants of commercial feedstocks limit current antenna designs. Recent research into the composition of high dielectric feedstocks for AM opens the design space for printed hybrid material antennas [1-3]. Space filling algorithms paired with extruding high dielectric filaments allow customized dielectric constants not previously achievable [4].

We propose a dual band antenna utilizing hybrid dielectric substrates to shrink the footprint of the low frequency antenna element. For this investigation, we design the dual-band antenna for S-band and X-band respectively. Each of these elements achieves both vertical and horizontal polarization via a pair of orthogonal pin feeds for each element. We perform all simulations using the finite difference time domain (FDTD) solver of CST Studio Suite 2019.

II. Dual Band Antenna Design

We base the hybrid substrate shared aperture antenna on a previously documented shorted annular ring and concentric patch antenna [5-9]. Fig. 1 (left) shows the geometry of the dual band antenna on the hybrid substrates, and Fig. 1 (right) shows the layout of the concentric hybrid substrates themselves. Table I shows the dimensions of the geometries given in Fig. 1. Using a substrate of ε_{r2}=6.15 instead of ε_{r1}=2.65 under the S-band element allows us to shrink the footprint of the antenna by 32%.

Orthogonal microstrip pin feeds achieve either vertical or horizontal polarization at both S- and X-bands. Fig. 2 shows the locations of the orthogonal pin feeds for both the annular ring and the concentric patch. We use a shorting wall shown in Fig. 2 to short the annular ring at its inner perimeter. This cancels surface waves on the dielectrics by suppressing the dominant mode, and helps increase isolation between both the cross polarization ports in the same frequency band and the isolation between the ports in the S- and X-bands.

Fig. 3 shows a to-scale 3D printed prototype of the antenna shown in Fig. 2. The antenna shown in Fig. 3 utilizes a microstrip stack of a silver ink layer, hybrid custom dielectric layer, and a copper ground layer. All conductive layers are 0.1 mm thick. The hybrid substrate layer is 5.05 mm thick. The total profile of the antenna is 5.25 mm.

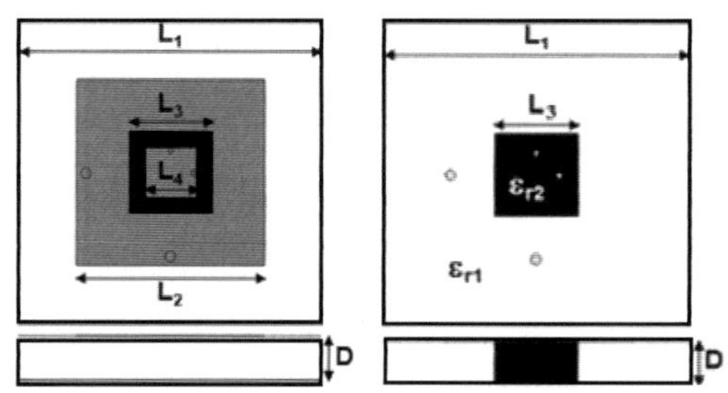

Fig. 1. Top view geometry of the dual band antenna (left) and layout of the hybrid substrates (right).

TABLE I. Antenna Dimensions in Millimeters of Fig. 1

Fig.	L_1	L_2	L_3	L_4	*D*	ε_{r1}	ε_{r2}
1	36.7	22.57	10.23	7.08	5.05	2.65	6.15

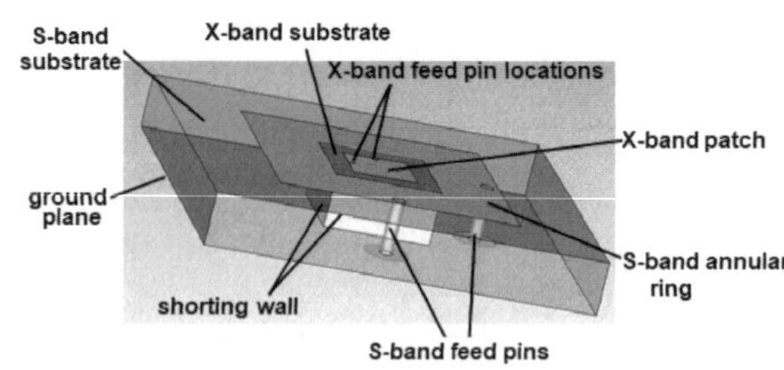

Fig. 2. 3D view of the antenna and pin feed network.

Fig. 3. 3D printed dual band and hybrid dielectric antenna.

III. Measured and Simulated Results

We show the measured versus simulated return loss and realized gain of the dual band antenna at S-band in Fig. 4 and Fig. 5 as well as at X-band in Fig. 6 and Fig. 7. We measured all realized gain versus frequency measurements at boresight to the antenna. We see general agreement at both bands for all measurements. One discrepancy is in the S-band realized gain where measurements show a drop out at resonance of 6 dB. We believe this is due to poor isolation between the orthogonal ports at S-band at resonance, but this warrants further investigation. We attribute measured differences in the return loss to manufacturing tolerances since the pin fed patch is an extremely resonant type of feed. This is more apparent at X-band frequencies where tolerances become electrically larger.

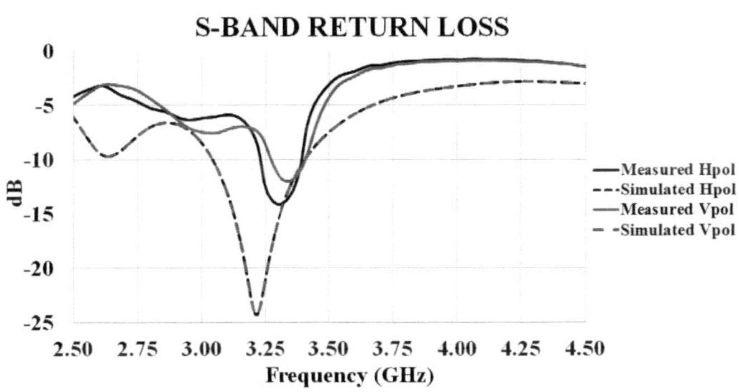

Fig. 4. Measured and simulated return loss at each orthogonal S-band port.

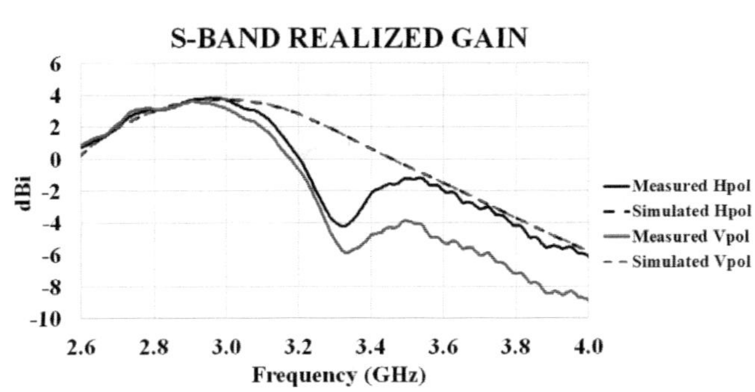

Fig. 5. Measured and simulated gain at each orthogonal S-band port.

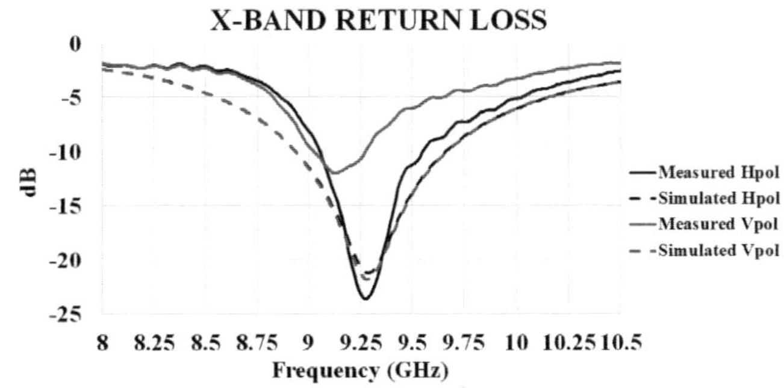

Fig. 6. Measured and simulated return loss at each orthogonal X-band port.

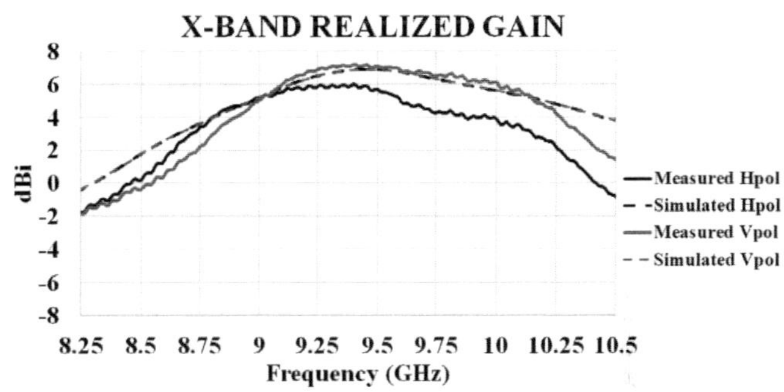

Fig. 7. Measured and simulated gain at each orthogonal X-band port.

IV. Conclusions and Future Work

This article shows that AM customizes dielectric properties to optimize antenna designs, and achieves robust measured data compared to simulation. AM enables complex antenna designs combining multi-functionality into a single aperture that would be expensive and cumbersome using traditional methods. Future work includes researching conductivity of AM inks, increasing achievable dielectric constants of AM materials, researching coupling issues, and broad banding the multi-function antenna through future AM advances.

References

[1] A. Moulart, et al., "Polymeric composites for use in electronic and microwave devices," Polymer Eng. and Sci., vol. 44, pP. 588–597, 2004.

[2] F. Castles, *et al.*, "Microwave Dielectric Characterization of 3D-printed $BaTiO_3$/ABS Polymer Composites," US National Library of Medicine, PMC4778131, 2016.

[3] Y. Rao, *et al.*, "Novel polymer-ceramic nanocomposite based on high dielectric constant epoxy formula for embedded capacitor application," Journal of Applied Polymer Science, 2001.

[4] Z. Larimore, *et al.*, "Additive Manufacturing of Luneburg Lens Antenas Using Space Filling Curves and Fused Filament Fabrication," IEEE Transa. on Ant. and Prop., Vol. 66 (6), June 2018.

[5] W. Dorsey and A. Zaghloul, "Dual-polarized dual-band antenna element for ISM bands," Proc. IEEE Ant. and Propagat. Society Int. Symp., APS/URSI, June 2009.

[6] W. Dorsey and A. Zaghloul, "Dual-band dual-circularly polarized antenna element," IET Microw. and Ant. Propagat., vol. 7, 2013.

[7] G. Mitchell and A. Zaghloul, "Increased Bandwidth and Reduced Footprint of a Dual-band Microstrip Antenna," *Proc. of NRSM* (URSI 2015), Jan. 2015.

[8] G. Mitchell and A. Zaghloul, "Reduced Footprint of a Dual-Band Dual-Polarization Microstrip Antenna," *Proc. of Int. ACES Symposium*, March 2015.

[9] G. Mitchell and A. Zaghloul, "Design of a Multi-band, Dual Substrate Concentric Annular Ring Antenna," *Proceedings of the IEEE APS International Symposium*, June 2016.

Modelling and Impact of 3D Print Inaccuracies on the Performance of Circular Waveguide Hybrid Coupler

Amrita Bal
Department of Electrical and Computer Engineering
Texas A&M University
College Station, TX, USA
abal@tamu.edu

Gregory H. Huff
Department of Electrical Engineering
The Pennsylvania State University
State College, PA, USA
ghuff@psu.edu

***Abstract*— Circular waveguide hybrid coupler operating over a frequency range of ISM 57-64 GHz, additively printed and metal plated using electroless technique is introduced. Effects of orientation of print and thickness of intricate structures on the performance of circular waveguide hybrid coupler are presented. The structure is printed using commercially available stereolithographic (SLA) printer. Circulatory system operated by a peristaltic pump is used for selective silver deposition of the hybrid coupler.**

Keywords—3D printing, circular waveguide hybrid coupler and electroless silver deposition.

I. INTRODUCTION

Different 3D printing processes are used for fabrication of microwave and millimeter-wave components in lesser time and cost. These techniques are stereolithography (SLA), polyjet, digital light processing (DLP), selective laser melting (SLM) and various others. Various structures fabricated using these additive manufacturing techniques are discussed in [1]. Print inaccuracies can lead to degraded performance. Inaccuracies introduced during printing and their impact on the performance of the structure is analyzed in [2]. Waveguide components are often modified for ease of fabrication and metal deposition [3]. Metal deposition is an important step that follows 3D printing. Metal deposition using electroless methods is discussed in [4].

This article aims to draw attention on the 3D printing inaccuracies and their effects on the performance of the structure. Fig. 1 shows the CAD model and the fabricated model of the circular waveguide hybrid coupler. Fig. 2 focusses on the intricate structures of the coupler. The group of ridges at the center of the structure and the vertical posts are prone to inaccurate prints. The authors aim to focus on the deviation between measured and simulated results due to print inaccuracies. HFSS is used for carrying out simulations of the hybrid assuming perfectly conducting electric walls.

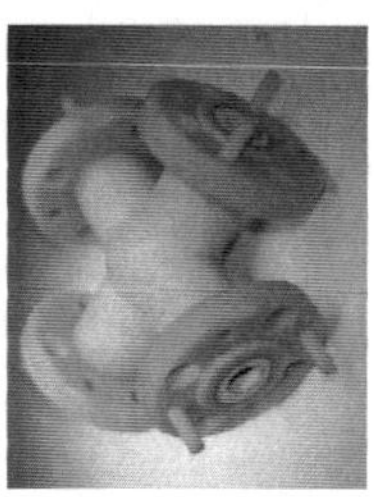

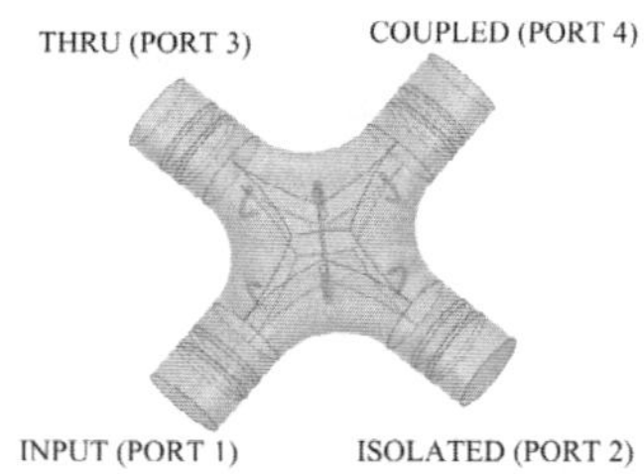

Fig. 1. Fabricated model (top) and CAD model (bottom) of coupler.

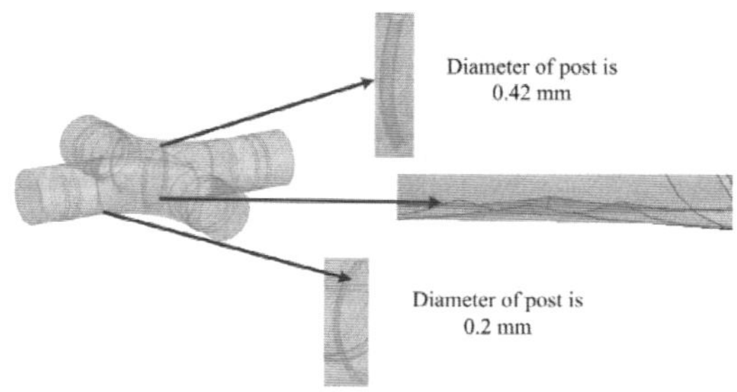

Fig. 2. Delicate structures inside the circular waveguide hybrid coupler.

II. 3D PRINTING OF THE HYBRID COUPLER

The hybrid coupler is printed in different orientations along x- and y-axis on the build plate for accurate prints of the group of ridges. On printing the hybrid horizontally on the build plate, two among the four ridges supported by the internal post in the structure are printed accurately while, the other two unsupported ridges get deformed. In the next iteration the structure is printed at incremental angles from 10 to 30 degrees with respect to x- and y-axis. Fig. 3 compares the printed ridges at the center of the structure for angle of print 10 and 30 degrees respectively. Clearly the ridges are printed accurately at higher elevation.

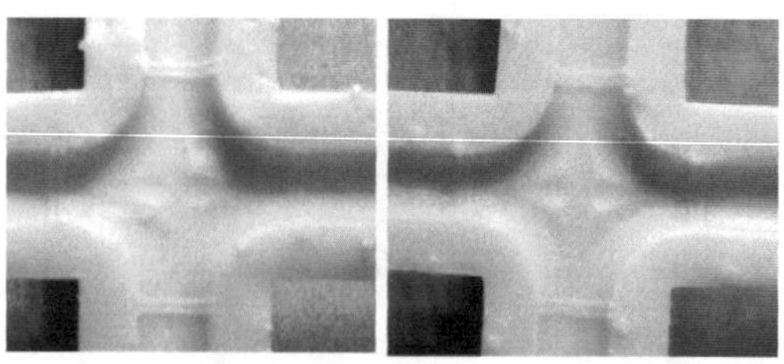

Fig. 3. Printed structure at 10 degree (left) and 30 degree (right) elevation along x- and y-axis.

A comparison of the printed posts of diameter 0.2 mm and 0.42 mm for similar curvature are shown in Fig. 4. Clearly, the 0.42 mm diameter post is printed accurately than the 0.2 mm diameter post.

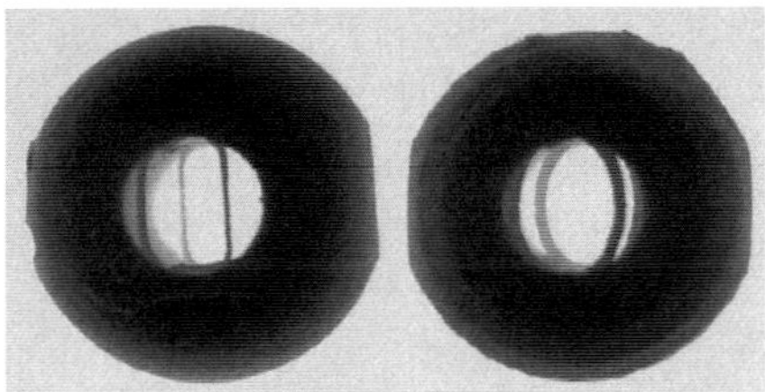

Fig. 4. Printed post of diameter 0.2 mm (left) and 0.42 mm (right).

III. MEASURED RESULTS

This section discusses the effects of printing inaccuracies on the performance of the structure. The measured structure has inductive post of diameter 0.2 mm, printed at an elevation of 10 degrees to x- and y-axis. The hybrid coupler is metal plated using electroless silver deposition technique discussed in [4]. Figs. 5 and 6 shows the measured and simulated results. Fig. 7 shows the error encountered in path length between input and output due to fabrication inaccuracies.

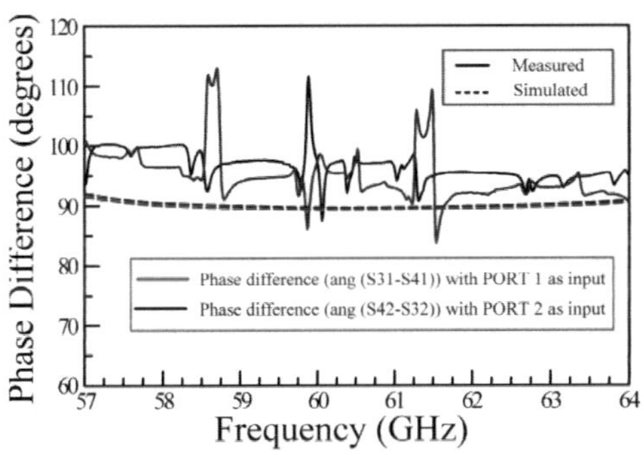

Fig. 5. Measured and simulated phase difference between output ports.

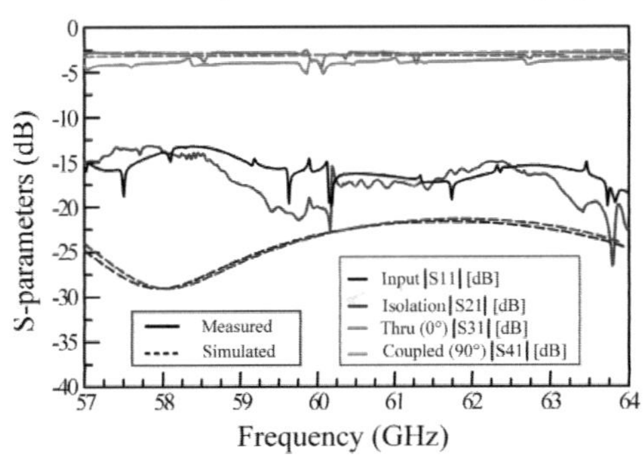

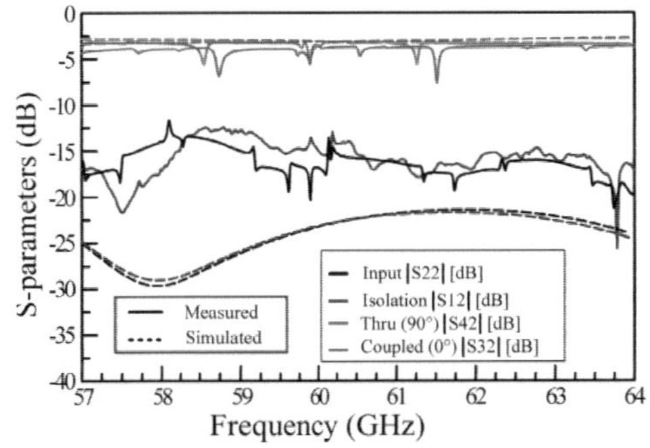

Fig. 6. Measured and simulated magnitude distribution at output ports when PORT 1 (top) and PORT 2 (bottom) are excited.

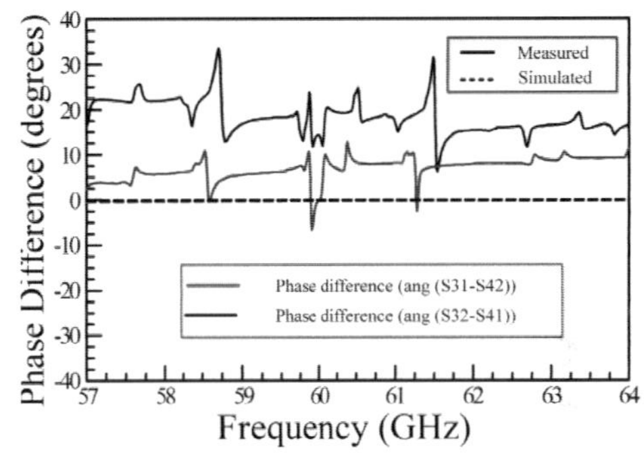

Fig. 7. Difference in path length between input and output ports.

IV. CONCLUSION

This paper summarizes the performance variations observed in a hybrid coupler due to printing inaccuracies. The variation between simulated and measured results can be attributed to the dissimilar path lengths introduced between input and output ports due to print inaccuracies. The discussion in this paper can be used to understand print inaccuracies in any 3D printed structure in general.

REFERENCES

[1] A. Bal., A. Tiwari and G. H. Huff, "Electroless Silver Plating of Additive Manufactured Trough Waveguide Mode Transducer and Antenna Structure," IEEE International Symposium on Antennas and Propagation and USNC-URSI Radio Science Meeting, 2019.

[2] J. Shen and D. S. Ricketts, "Additive Manufacturing of Complex Millimeter-Wave Waveguides Structures Using Digital Light Processing," IEEE Transactions on Microwave Theory and Techniques, 2019.

[3] K. Lomakin, L. Klein, et al., "3D Printed E-Band Hybrid Coupler," IEEE Microwave and Wireless Components Letters, 2019.

[4] A. Bal, D. G. Carey, F. A. Espinal and G. H. Huff, "Electroless silver plating of 3D printed waveguide components by peristaltic pump driven system," Electronics Letters, vol. 55(2), pp. 100-102, 2018.

Shape Synthesis of Multi-mode Dielectric Resonator Antennas Using Characteristic Modes

Binbin Yang and Abdullah Eroglu
Department of Electrical and Computer Engineering
North Carolina Agricultural and Technical State University
Greensboro, United States
byang1@ncat.edu, aeroglu@ncat.edu

Jacob J. Adams
Department of Electrical and Computer Engineering
North Carolina State University
Raleigh, United States
jacob.adams@ncsu.edu

***Abstract*—This paper demonstrates a shape synthesis technique for multi-mode dielectric resonator antennas using binary genetic algorithm and characteristic mode analysis. The cost function for the synthesis process is defined from characteristic modal parameters, such as modal quality factors and self-resonance frequencies. Since only modal parameters are involved in the cost function, the shape synthesis process is made independent of feeds. In the paper, we demonstrate the shape synthesis of a DRA with three self-resonant modes at 3 GHz.**

***Index Terms*—characteristic modes, dielectric resonator antennas, multi-mode antennas, shape synthesis.**

I. Introduction

Due to their compactness and high radiation efficiency at microwave and milimeter wave frequencies, dielectric resonator antennas (DRAs) have attracted a lot of attention since their initial investigation by Long [1]. However, most of the analysis and designs in literature are limited to DRAs of canonical geometries, such as cylindrical, spherical and rectangular blocks, partially because of the readily available analytical design formulas [2]. While the analytical and empirical design formulas serve the purpose for simple DRA designs, it limits the form factor and the search space of the design. Exploring DRAs of non-canonical geometries could provide new possibilities for DRA miniaturization, multi-mode DRAs and broadband DRAs. With recent advances in the 3D printing of high dielectric constant materials that can be applied to DRA design [3], there are opportunities to investigate novel 3D DRA geometries. Several unconventional DRA designs can be found in [4], [5]. However, the designs are still based on slight modification of the canonical geometry using a combination of intuition and parametric study. A more methodical search algorithm for the desirable DRA geometries would provide a more uniform approach to DRA design and potentially yield performance improvements.

In this paper, we introduce a feed-independent shape synthesis technique for dielectric resonator antennas, as an expansion of our prior work on planar metallic antennas [6]. Though one interesting work on shape synthesis of DRAs has been reported in [7], our approach takes into account of the bandwidth of individual modes in optimization and also has fewer constraints on allowable geometry.

II. Shape Synthesis Technique and Implementation

The shape synthesis technique we adopt relies largely upon characteristic mode analysis in order to first create a resonator shape that supports modes with the desired properties. Characteristic mode theory (CMT) [8], a theory for the modal analysis of an antenna/scattering structure, solves the following eigenvalue equation:

$$\mathrm{XJ_n} = \lambda_\mathrm{n} \mathrm{RJ_n}, \tag{1}$$

where X and R are the imaginary and real parts of the method of moments (MoM) Z matrix, and λ_n and $\mathrm{J_n}$ are the eigenvalue and eigencurrent of the $n-$th mode. Depending on the way dielectric objects are modeled, the MoM Z matrix could be based on surface integral euqation (SIE) or volume integral equation (VIE).

As pointed out in [9], the VIE, though computationally heavier than the SIE, avoids the issue of non-physical modes in characteristic mode analysis of DRAs. Furthermore, the eigencurrents calculated from the VIE can be directly used to calculate Q factors from the source formulation as demonstrated in [9]. We therefore choose the VIE for our analysis here.

An important parameter we will use in our optimization is the quality factor of each individual characteristic mode. Once having solved the characteristic eigenvalue equation, the characteristic modal Q factors of DRAs can be calculated from the characteristic modal current and charge distribution, as shown in [9].

A. *Shape Synthesis Framework for Multi-mode DRAs*

Our shape synthesis of DRAs is based on a binary genetic algorithm, where the binary gene in the chromosome represents the presence or absence of a tetrahedron in the mesh. For the multi-mode DRA synthesis problem studied here, the goal is to search for an antenna geometry with multiple modes resonating at the same frequency, which could be useful for MIMO applications. To facilitate the optimization of broadband self-resonant DRAs, the cost function for the shape synthesis is defined from characteristic modal parameters as:

$$\mathrm{cost} = \sum_{\mathrm{n}=1}^{\mathrm{N}} \mathrm{C_n} + w_2 \mathrm{V}, \tag{2}$$

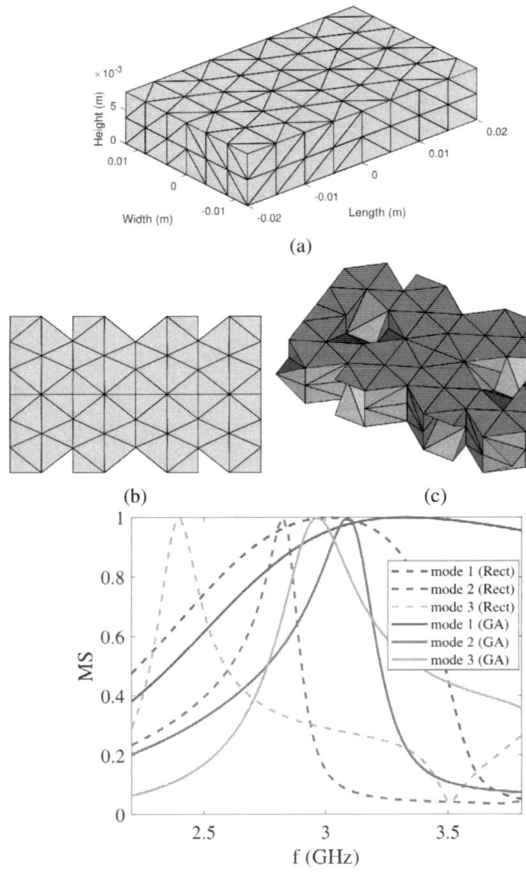

Fig. 1: (a) The complete antenna geometry (Rect), (b) top view and (c) isometric view of the optimized antenna geometry (GA), (d) the modal significance before (dash) and after (solid) optimization.

TABLE I: Comparison of Modal Significance and Modal Q Factors Before and After Optimization at 3 GHz

Modes	MS (Before)	MS (After)	Q (Before)	Q (After)
Mode 1	1	0.95	2.2	1.7
Mode 2	0.15	0.85	118	8
Mode 3	0.29	0.97	11	9.6

where $C_n = w_1(1 - MS_n) + Q_n$ represents the contribution from the n−th mode. $MS_n = \frac{1}{|1+j\lambda_n|}$ is the characteristic modal significance, and reaches the maximum of 1 at self resonance ($\lambda_n = 0$). Q_n is the modal Q factor, the minimization of which maximizes the bandwidth. V is the volume of the search geometry normalized to that of the complete geometry, the inclusion of which in the cost function removes unnecessary tetrahedra in the mesh while reducing size and weight. w_1 and w_2 are the weighting coefficients to be selected depending on the problem.

III. Design Example

Following the shape synthesis technique explained in Section II, we demonstrate the shape synthesis process using an example. The complete structure before optimization has a dimension of $40 \times 25 \times 7.7\text{mm}^3$, as shown in Fig. 1 (a). The dielectric constant of the material is chosen as 23. The characteristic modal significance for the first three modes of the complete geometry are calculated and shown as dashed lines in Fig. 1 (d). The self-resonant frequencies correspond to the frequencies where $MS_n = 1$, and we observe from Fig. 1 (d) that the three modes are resonant at 3 GHz, 2.8 GHz and 2.4 GHz respectively.

For demonstration, we optimize the antenna geometry so that three modes are resonant at 3 GHz. The shape synthesis is conducted using a binary genetic algorithm with the cost function in (2) with three modes, a mutation rate of 10%, and the number of generations as 200. The weighting coefficients are selected as $w_1 = 200$, and $w_2 = 20$ after several trials. In order to simplify the optimized geometry and expedite the convergence, we force geometric symmetry in x, y and z dimensions. Fig. 1 (b) and (c) show the top view and isometric view of the final optimized geometry. The modal significance of the first three modes of the optimized geometry is shown as solid lines in Fig. 1 (d). Comparing with the dashed lines, we notice that the resonance frequency of mode 2 has shifted from 2.8 GHz to 3.09 GHz and that of mode 3 has shifted from 2.4 GHz to 2.97 GHz, while the resonance frequency of mode 1 has slightly shifted up (3.3 GHz) as a trade-off. Table I compares the modal significance and the modal Q factors of the three modes before and after optimization. It is obvious from the modal significance that all three modes are very close to resonance at 3 GHz after shape synthesis. It is also worth noting that the Q factors of the three modes are optimized as well, with that of mode 2 being significantly reduced from 118 to 8 after optimization.

References

[1] S. Long, M. McAllister, and Liang Shen, "The resonant cylindrical dielectric cavity antenna," IEEE Transactions on Antennas and Propagation, vol. 31, no. 3, pp. 406–412, May 1983.

[2] K. M. Luk, "Dielectric resonator antennas," Research Studies Pr., 2003.

[3] Y. Oh, V. Bharambe, B. Mummareddy, J. Martin, J. McKnight, M. A. Abraham, J. M. Walker, K. Rogers, B. Conner, P. Cortes, E. MacDonald, and J. J. Adams, "Microwave dielectric properties of zirconia fabricated using nanoparticle jetting™," Additive Manufacturing, vol. 27, pp. 586 – 594, 2019.

[4] G. Almpanis, C. Fumeaux, and R. Vahldieck, "Comparison of various non-canonical rectangular dielectric resonator antennas for enhanced bandwidth," in 2008 IEEE Antennas and Propagation Society International Symposium. IEEE, 2008, pp. 1–4.

[5] X. Liang and T. A. Denidni, "H-shaped dielectric resonator antenna for wideband applications," IEEE Antennas and Wireless Propagation Letters, vol. 7, pp. 163–166, 2008.

[6] B. Yang, J. Zhou, and J. J. Adams, "A shape-first, feed-next design approach for compact planar mimo antennas," Progress In Electromagnetics Research, vol. 77, pp. 157–165, 2019.

[7] H. Alroughani, The Shape Synthesis of Dielectric Resonator Antennas for Wireless Communication Systems. The Pennsylvania State University, 2018.

[8] R. Harrington and J. Mautz, "Theory of characteristic modes for conducting bodies," IEEE Trans. Antennas Propag., vol. 19, no. 5, pp. 622–628, 1971.

[9] B. Yang and J. J. Adams, "Quality factor calculations for the characteristic modes of dielectric resonator antennas," in Radio Science Meeting (USNC-URSI NRSM), 2017 United States National Committee of URSI National. IEEE, 2017, pp. 1–2.

On the Crosstalks between a Pair of Transmission Lines in the Presence of a 3D Printed Electrifi Trace

Dipankar Mitra[1], Kazi Sadman Kabir[2], Jerika Clevelenad[1], Ryan Striker[1], Benjamin D. Braaten[1], Shengrong Ye[3], and Sayan Roy[2*]
*: Corresponding Author, email: sayan.roy@sdsmt.edu
[1]*Department of Electrical & Computer Engineering, North Dakota State University, Fargo, ND, USA*
[2]*Department of Electrical Engineering, South Dakota School of Mines & Technology, Rapid City, SD, USA*
[3]*Multi3D, Cary, NC, USA*

***Abstract*—The technology of additive manufacturing results in 3D printing of conductive traces in radio frequency circuits. This creates a plethora of possibilities in realizing flexible and wearable electronics. While the prototypes of microstrip transmission lines and antennas have been recently reported, there is now a need of Electromagnetic Compatibility based study of such 3D printed conductive traces. This paper presents a comparative study on the near end and far end unintentional crosstalk components between a pair of microstrip transmission lines made of Copper in the presence of a 3D printed conductive trace made of a commercially available conductive filament, *Electrifi*. Any physical contact with the 3D printed trace has been purposefully averted to discard the high contact resistance between the trace and such contact.**

Keywords—Additive Manufacturing, EMC analysis, Electrifi, Transmission Lines.

I. Introduction

Additive manufacturing (AM) technology has been gaining popularity among researchers [1] - [3] in realizing radio frequency (RF) circuits for applications such as Internet of Things (IoT), health monitoring, sports monitoring, and consumer electronics. Researchers have recently demonstrated that it is now possible to develop printed microstrip transmission lines (TLs) [1] – [2] and simple microstrip antennas [3] by incorporating the economic fused filament fabrication (FFF) method of AM technology. Specifically, a commercially available conductive filament [4], *Electrifi*, was used in designing such RF circuits. Now, it is imperative to perform an electromagnetic compatibility (EMC) analysis on such a material to better understand its suitability for use in the proximity of other RF circuitry. One of the major aspects of EMC analysis is to find out the crosstalk or noise coupling components of the printed transmission lines. To the best of the authors' knowledge, this paper presents for the first time an EMC analysis of a 3D printed *Electrifi* based trace in the proximity of a pair of copper-based microstrip TLs. Specifically, the pair of copper-based microstrip TLs was initially prototyped ("setup a") and validated by comparing the measured near-end and far-end crosstalk elements with the full wave simulation model. Next, the *Electrifi* based trace was placed in between the copper-based TL ("setup b") and the measurement was again

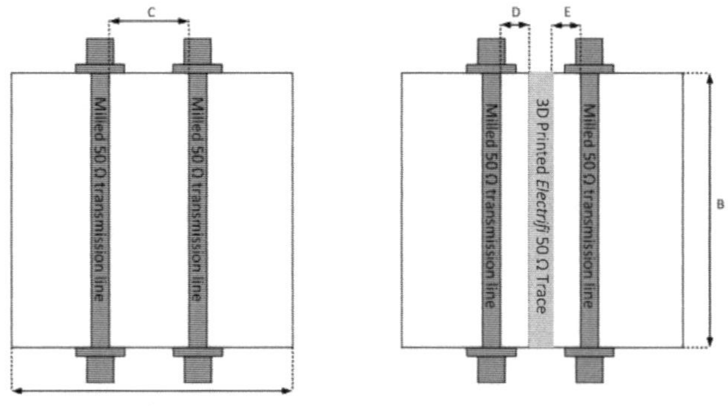

Fig. 1. Diagram of the two test setups on a 1.57 mm thick Rogers TMM4 substrate (bottom plane → grounded), involving (a) only a pair of 50 Ω microstrip TLs and (b) with a presence of the 3D printed *Electrifi* 50 Ω trace in-between. Dimensions: A = B = 50 mm, C = 8 mm and D = E = 2.6mm.

taken. Finally, an equivalent full-wave simulation model was designed and presented for comparison. It must be noted here that to prevent any error in the study due to reported high resistive contact between the *Electrifi* based trace and connectors [1], the authors purposefully avoided usual study cases which might involve a physical contact between the *Electrifi* trace and connector(s).

II. Methodology and Fabrication of Prototype

Two test setups were considered in order to test the interaction of the 3D printed Electrifi 50 Ω trace, when placed between two standard 50 Ω microstrip TLs, as shown in Fig 1. Both the setups (a) and (b) were prototyped on Rogers TMM4 [5] (ε_r = 4.5 and tan δ = 0.0020) with a thickness of 1.52 mm with 35μm copper cladding on the bottom (i.e., grounded substrate). The Electrifi trace in setup (b) was fabricated using a Creality CR-10 printer by FFF process. The 3-D printing settings mentioned in [2] were followed. The manufactured prototypes are shown in Fig 2. The fabricated prototypes were also full wave modeled in Ansys HFSS [5].

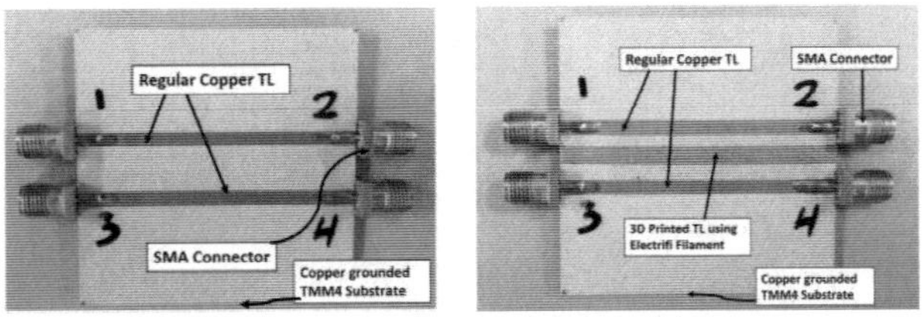

(a) (b)

Fig. 2. Prototype of the two test setups on a 1.57 mm thick Rogers TMM4 substrate (bottom plane → grounded), involving (a) only a pair of 50 Ω microstrip TLs and (b) with a presence of the 3D printed Electrifi 50 Ω trace in-between.

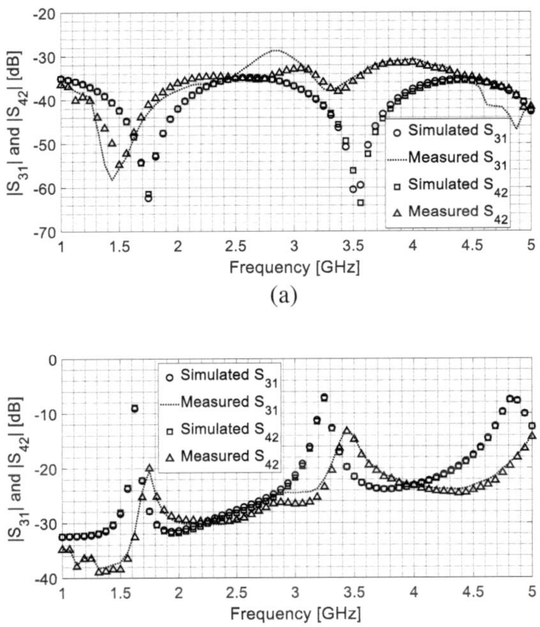

(a)

(b)

Fig. 3. Near End Coupling components (a) without 3D printed trace and (b) with 3D printed trace.

III. SIMULATION AND MEASUREMENT VALIDATION RESULTS

All the measurements were performed using a Keysight E5071C 100 KHz – 8.5 GHz ENA series network analyzer. The network analyzer was set from 1GHz to 5GHz with 1601 points before calibration. The prototypes of setups (a) and (b) are shown in Figs. 2 (a) and (b), respectively. The ports not being measured were terminated each time with a 50 Ω load. Followed by a two-port (SOLT) calibration in the network analyzer, the magnitudes of the near-end coupling components (S_{31} and S_{42}) and the far-end coupling components (S_{32} and S_{41}) were measured for both setups. Fig. 3 demonstrates the near end coupling components (S_{31} and S_{42}) for both setups. It was observed that in the presence of *Electrifi* trace between the two regular copper TLs, the near end coupling voltage changes significantly at the resonant frequencies. Fig. 4 shows the far end coupling voltages (S_{31} and S_{42}) for both the cases. A significant change in the far end coupling components was also observed with the addition of 3D printed trace between the two regular copper TLs. Overall, agreement between measurements and full-wave simulation can be observed.

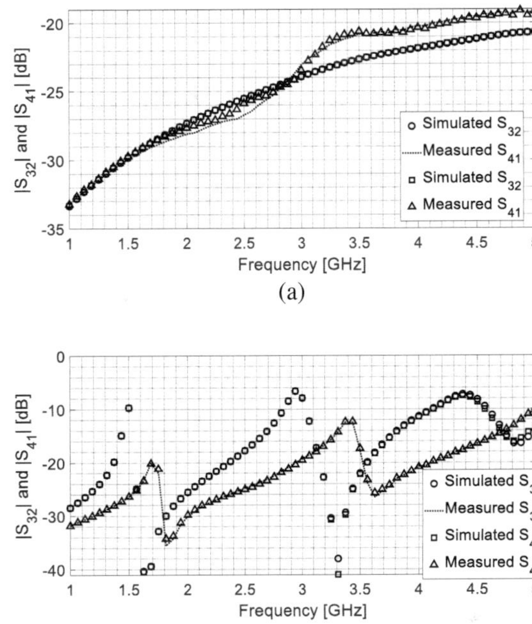

(a)

(b)

Fig. 4. Far End Coupling components (a) without 3D printed line (case 1) and (b) with 3D printed line (case 2).

IV. CONCLUSION

An analysis of the unintentional noise crosstalk between two regular copper TLs in the presence of a conductive *Electrifi* filament based 3D printed trace is presented in this paper. Two prototypes were tested for both "without 3D printed trace" and "with 3D printed trace" cases. The full-wave simulated and measured near and far end noise coupling S parameters for both the cases were presented for validation and overall agreement between simulations and measurements were observed. The authors like to thank Dr. Ahmed Hassan in the Department of Computer Science Electrical Engineering at University of Missouri-Kansas City for sharing valuable inputs in this paper.

REFERENCES

[1] S. Roy, M. B. Qureshi, S. Asif and B. D. Braaten, "A Model for 3D Printed Microstrip Transmission Lines using Conductive Electrifi Filament," *2017 IEEE International Symposium on Antennas and Propagation*, California, USA, Jul. 9 - 14, 2017.

[2] D. Mitra, R. Striker, B. D. Braaten, A. Aqueeb, K. S. Kabir and S. Roy, "On the Design of An Improved Model of Additively Manufactured Microstrip Transmission Lines for Radio Frequency Applications," *2019 IEEE International Conference on Electro Information Technology (EIT)*, Brookings, SD, USA, 2019, pp. 182-184.

[3] F. Pizarro, R. Salazar, E. Rajo-Iglesias, M. Rodríguez, S. Fingerhuth and G. Hermosilla, "Parametric Study of 3D Additive Printing Parameters Using Conductive Filaments on Microwave Topologies," in *IEEE Access*, vol. 7, pp. 106814-106823, 2019.

[4] Multi3D. [online] Available: www.multi3dllc.com

[5] Rogers Corporation [online] Available: www.rogerscorp.com.

[6] 2016 Ansys, Inc. Available: https://www.ansys.com

Antennas and RF Components Designed with Graded Index Composite Materials

Roberto Rojas, Patrick Bluem, Idahosa Osaretin, and Bradley Duncan
MIT Lincoln Laboratory
Lexington, MA 02421-6426
roberto.rojas@ll.mit.edu, patrick.bluem@ll.mit.edu, idahosa.osaretin@ll.mit.edu, and bradley.duncan.@ll.mit.edu

***Abstract*—Antennas and RF components in general, can greatly benefit with the recent development of low-loss 3D print graded index materials. The additional degrees of freedom provided by graded index materials can result in the design of antennas and other RF components with superior performance than currently available designs based on conventional constant permittivity materials. Here we discuss our work designing flat lenses for antennas and RF matching networks as well as filters based on graded index composite materials.**

Keywords—3D Printing, Antennas, Composite Materials, Graded Index, RF Components.

I. Introduction

The increased use of sensors in unmanned airborne systems (UAS) as shown in Fig. 1 and CubeSats has increased the demand for small size, weight and power (SWaP) RF components with large frequency bandwidths. In some specialized applications, low radar cross section (RCS) is also a requirement. Unfortunately, the SWaP of devices currently available for RF systems exceeds the typical requirements of UAS and CubeSats. Methods to miniaturize RF systems while maintaining typical performance by replacing several narrow bandwidth systems with one wideband system is of interest. The incorporation of low loss, graded index (GRIN) materials with controllable electrical properties (spatially variable permittivity and permeability) provides additional degrees of freedom that can result in wideband, conformal, low-volume, and low-profile apertures with comparable or superior performance metrics to larger existing antenna systems.

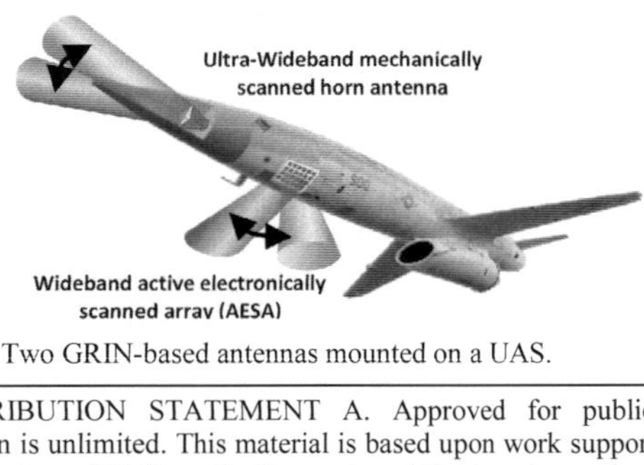

Fig. 1. Two GRIN-based antennas mounted on a UAS.

DISTRIBUTION STATEMENT A. Approved for public release. Distribution is unlimited. This material is based upon work supported by the Under Secretary of Defense for Research and Engineering under Air Force Contract No. FA8702-15-D-0001. Any opinions, findings, conclusions or recommendations expressed in this material are those of the author(s) and do not necessarily reflect the views of the Under Secretary of Defense for Research and Engineering.

The work presented here discusses design methodologies to improve the performance of antennas and RF components by taking advantage of two key recent developments that facilitate the use of GRIN materials in RF systems design: first is the development of a generalized block copolymer-based strategy to incorporate ceramic, magnetic, and conductive materials into 3D-printable inks [1-2] for printing low loss GRIN materials, especially in the K_a frequency band (26.5-40 GHz); and second, the development of metamaterial concepts and cloaking techniques that theoretically show that anisotropic, varying dielectric/magnetic materials can precisely control the propagation of electromagnetic waves [3-4]. 3D-printing of graded index dielectric, magnetic, and conductive materials enables increased frequency bandwidth and reduced volume of antenna systems as well as RF/microwave components, such as filters, feeding networks, and matching networks. It also makes possible to properly control electromagnetic scattering from antennas and other structures.

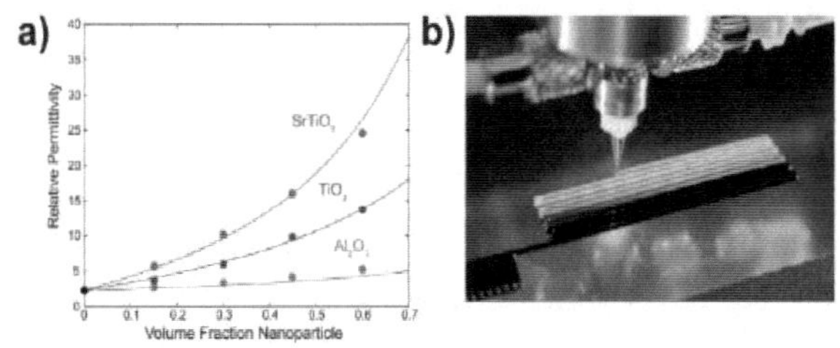

Fig. 2. MIT-LL dielectric deposition technology. a) Range of relative permittivity that can be generated. Measured data are the dot-dot curves while the solid lines represent the model used to fit the measured data b) Active mixing nozzle printing a graded filament.

II. Composite Materials

Our work has focused on tailoring the dielectric constants of printable materials while maintaining their low-loss characteristics. Our hypothesis was that by varying the ceramic nanoparticle content of our composite inks, we should be able to tune the relative permittivity of our printed structures. Hydrophobic (styrene-isoprene-styrene) triblock polymers served as our model low dielectric polymer with a measured dielectric constant of 2.2 and loss tangent of 1.6 x 10^{-3}. We selected Al_2O_3, TiO_2, and $SrTiO_3$ nanoparticles due to their higher relative permittivities and low-loss tangents. The surface of ceramic nanoparticles were functionalized to facilitate improved blending into the polymer matrix. With these materials we have been able to print and test structures with median relative permittivities from 2 – 24.5 and loss tangents on the order of 10^{-4} - 10^{-2} over the 26.5 to 40 GHz range as shown in Fig. 2 (a). Magnetic materials, such as iron carbonyl particles, have also been added into printable inks for applications at lower frequencies (L/S bands) and measured data will be presented at the conference.

We have also established a methodology that allows both sequential and gradient deposition of our low-loss composite inks to generate novel RF assemblies using custom direct-write 3D printing dispensing nozzles. We are able to direct the dielectric constant of the final printed structure via programmably controlling the serial deposition of multiple materials or by varying the polymer-to-nanoparticle ratio within the ink on-the-fly using an active mixing nozzle. This active mixing nozzle eliminates the sharp transitions from individual inks allowing for both geometric and compositional control over printed structures (see Fig. 2 (b)).

III. Flat Lens for Conventioal Ka-Band Horn Antenna

The availability of low-loss GRIN materials can have a great impact on the design of antennas and phased arrays. Here we consider the design of a flat GRIN lens to increase the gain of a conventional Ka band pyramidal horn antenna (see Fig. 3). As it is well-known, the flat lens has to be designed to focus the fields and thus decrease the beamwidth in the far-zone. Keeping in mind that horn antenna considered here has different beamwidths in the E and H planes, the dielectric profiles of the flat lens are not the same in the E and H planes. Furthermore, the dielectric profile along the axis of the antenna/lens has to be carefully designed to impedance matched the lens to the fields of the horn at its aperture and to free-space. Otherwise, the impedance mismatch losses will increase and consequently, decrease the realized gain of the antenna.

IV. Design of Matching Networks

Another important application of GRIN materials is in the design of matching networks (MN) and low- and band-pass filters. Although these components are designed using microstrip transmission lines, the lines, as depicted in Fig. 4, have constant width while the permittivity of the substrate varies along the axis of the device. For reference purposes, the performance of a conventional variable-width transmission line is also considered, Fig. 4. It can be observed that both designs have similar performance where the reflection coefficient is less than -20dB for frequencies about 10 GHz. These MN are currently being built and measured results will be shown to access the performance of these devices.

V. Impact

Important areas where this work will have a great impact are with small UAS and other airborne and space borne structures such as CubeSats. Small UAVs and CubeSats require low mass, conformal, and low cost antenna systems for sensors (radars/radiometers). The resulting wideband (or multi-band) system will replace several narrow band systems, resulting in lower overall mass and volume. Another application where this work is relevant is in the ability to control the scattering of electromagnetic waves from antennas and other structures. Adding GRIN materials to currently available materials enables the RF designer to better control and shape the fields scattered by airborne and spaceborne structures.

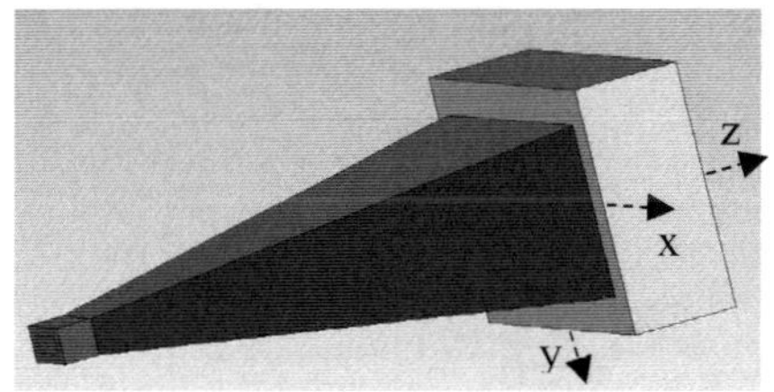

Fig. 3. Conventional Ka-band pyramidal horn antenna with flat GRIN lens.

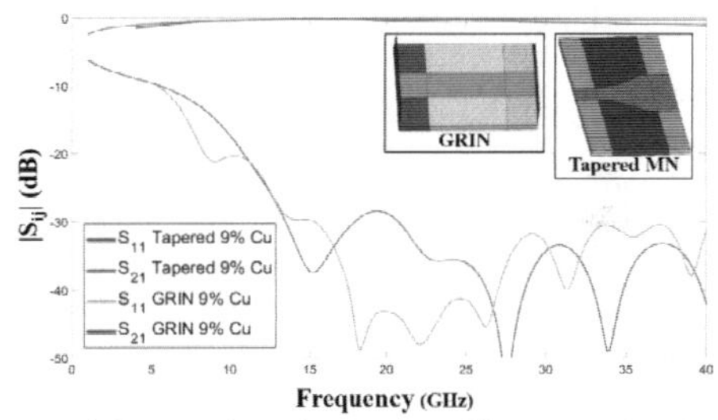

Fig. 4. Simulated S-parameters for two matching networks. One MN is implemented with a GRIN substrate and the second one with a conventional tapered transmission line where the substrate has a fixed dielectric value.

VI. Summary and Conclusions

This work demonstrates the use of a flat GRIN lens designed to increase the realized gain of conventional Ka band pyramidal horn antenna. These composite materials are tailored for 3D printing of custom microwave components. Sub-millimeter precision allows for printing of high frequency components to improve on classical microwave techniques in both SWaP and performance. The programmability and precise control of the permittivity as a function of position allow us to control the behavior of electromagnetic waves, enabling the direct realization of new technologies benefitting the commercial and military sectors. However, further work is necessary to develop techniques to measure the permittivity and/or permeability of graded index materials. Most current techniques are not applicable to GRIN materials.

References

[1] B. Duncan. *et al.*, "Development of 3D Printable Composite Inks for Millimeter Wave Applications," 2018 IEEE Int. Symp. on Antennas and Propagation, July 2018.

[2] B. Duncan, "Materials Development for 3D Printing RF Devices," 2019 MITRE Symposium on AM Antennas, May 2019.

[3] U. Leonhardt, "Optical Conformal Mapping," Science, vol. 312, pp. 1777-1780, June 2006.

[4] J.B. Pendry, *et al.*, "Controlling Electromagnetic Fields," Science, vol. 312, pp. 1780-1782, June 2006.

Efficient Jacobian Matrix Determination for H^2 Representations of Nonlinear Electrostatic Surface Integral Equations

John C. Young
Depatrment of Electrical & Computer Engineering
University of Kentucky
Lexington, KY USA
john.c.young@uky.edu

Robert J. Adams
Depatrment of Electrical & Computer Engineering
University of Kentucky
Lexington, KY USA
robert.adams@uky.edu

Stephen D. Gedney
Department of Electrical Engineering
University of Colorado-Denver
Denver, CO USA
stephen.gedney@ucdenver.edu

***Abstract*—In this paper, a nonlinear electrostatic surface integral equation is presented that is suitable for predicting corrosion-related fields. Nonlinear behavior arises due to electrochemical reactions at polarized surfaces. Hierarchical H^2 matrices are used to compress the discretized integral equation for the fast solution of large problems. A technique based on randomized linear algebra is discussed for the efficient computation of the Jacobian matrix required at each iteration of a nonlinear solution.**

Keywords—corrosion-related fields, hierarchical matrices, nonlinear integral equation, randomized linear algebra.

I. INTRODUCTION

The prediction of corrosion-related fields is an important problem in various areas such as ships in marine environments. Knowledge of the corrosion-related fields is useful in the design of various systems to mitigate corrosion. Due to the electrochemical reactions that may occur at polarized conducting surfaces in an electrolyte, the electromagnetic integral equations that describe the relevant physics are often nonlinear, and Newton-Raphson techniques are commonly used in the solution of these nonlinear problems. However, for large problems, the Jacobian matrix that arises in the Newton-Raphson solution of a nonlinear integral equation can be expensive to compute in terms of memory and time. The determination of the Jacobian matrix becomes even more challenging when using fast methods since the system matrices are not fully computed but are represented in a compressed form.

In this paper, the basic electrostatic surface integral equation [1] for predicting corrosion-related (CR) fields is presented. For large problems, the integral equation discretization is compressed using Hierarchical (H^2) matrices [2]. An overview is then provided of the appropriate Jacobian matrix that arises in the nonlinear solution. Finally, an efficient method for determining the Jacobian matrix using randomized linear algebra [3] is discussed.

This work was supported in part by Office of Naval Research Grant N00014-16-1-3066.

II. THEORY

A. Nonlinear Integral Equation

Consider an unbounded electrolytic region V with a homogeneous conductivity σ. The region V is bound by a surface $\Gamma = \Gamma_\infty \cup \Gamma_b$ where Γ_∞ is an unbounded surface and Γ_b is a bound surface. The electrostatic potential in the electrolytic region V is:

$$\Phi(\mathbf{r}) + \oint_\Gamma \Phi(\mathbf{r}')\hat{\mathbf{n}}'\cdot\nabla' G(\mathbf{r},\mathbf{r}')d\Gamma' = \oint_\Gamma G(\mathbf{r},\mathbf{r}')\hat{\mathbf{n}}'\cdot\nabla'\Phi(\mathbf{r}')d\Gamma', \tag{1}$$

where $\mathbf{r}\in V$, $\hat{\mathbf{n}}$ is the unit normal to Γ oriented out of V, and $G = 1/\left(4\pi|\mathbf{r}-\mathbf{r}'|\right)$ is the static Green's function. Restriction of $\mathbf{r}\in\Gamma_b$ leads to the integral equation:

$$\frac{1}{2}\Phi(\mathbf{r}) + \oint_{\Gamma_b} \Phi(\mathbf{r}')\hat{\mathbf{n}}'\cdot\nabla' G(\mathbf{r},\mathbf{r}')d\Gamma' - \Phi_\infty = \oint_{\Gamma_b} G(\mathbf{r},\mathbf{r}')\hat{\mathbf{n}}'\cdot\nabla'\Phi(\mathbf{r}')d\Gamma', \quad \mathbf{r}\in\Gamma_b, \tag{2}$$

where $\Phi_\infty = -\oint_{\Gamma_\infty}\Phi(\mathbf{r}')\hat{\mathbf{n}}'\cdot\nabla' G(\mathbf{r},\mathbf{r}')d\Gamma'$ is a possible constant potential offset that must be determined as part of the nonlinear solution. The nonlinear problem admits a one-dimensional null space that is eliminated by requiring that the total flux through the bound surface be zero:

$$0 = \oint_{\Gamma_b}\hat{\mathbf{n}}'\cdot\nabla'\Phi(\mathbf{r}')d\Gamma' . \tag{3}$$

A pure Neumann problem is assumed, and the normal flux on Γ_b is specified as $\hat{\mathbf{n}}\cdot\nabla\Phi(\mathbf{r}) = f(\Phi)$. For insulating surfaces, $f(\Phi)=0$, and, for non-insulating surfaces, $f(\Phi)\neq 0$. If on any part of Γ_b, $f'(\Phi)\neq 0$, then that portion of the surface is polarized, and the integral equation is nonlinear.

For polarized surfaces, $f(\Phi)$ is called a *polarization curve*. For a nonlinear problem, the locally-corrected-Nyström discretized integral equation is [4]:

$$[H]\bar{\Phi} = [G]f(\bar{\Phi}) , \quad (4)$$

where $[H]$ and $[G]$ are the discretized forms of the left and right (of the equal sign) parts of (2) and (3), respectively, and $[\bar{\Phi}]_j = \Phi(\mathbf{r}_j)$ where $\mathbf{r}_j$ is the *j*th quadrature point in the Nyström discretization. Note that for a linear problem, $f(\bar{\Phi})$ in (4) does not depend on $\bar{\Phi}$ and is known everywhere *a priori*; hence, $[G]f$ reduces to a single excitation vector.

Application of the Newton-Raphson method to (4) gives the update equation at the *k*th iteration as:

$$\bar{\Phi}_{k+1} = \bar{\Phi}_k - [J_k]^{-1} \bar{F}(\Phi_k) , \quad (5)$$

where the residual $\bar{F}$ is:

$$F(\bar{\Phi}) = [G]f(\bar{\Phi}) - [H]\bar{\Phi} \quad (6)$$

and the Jacobian matrix is:

$$[J_k] = [G]\text{diag}[f'(\bar{\Phi}_k)] - [H]. \quad (7)$$

Here, $\text{diag}[f'(\bar{\Phi}_k)]$ is a diagonal matrix whose diagonal entries are taken from the vector $f'(\bar{\Phi}_k)$.

B. *Efficient Jacobian Matrix Determination*

When the matrices $[G]$ and $[H]$ in (7) are represented as dense matrices, the determination of $[J_k]$ is straight-forward. Furthermore, when only a small portion of the bound surface is polarized, an efficient update using the Schur complement has been presented [4]. On the other hand, if $[G]$ and $[H]$ are represented in a compressed form, the operations in (7) are more difficult since it is desired that all intermediate operations and the final $[J_k]$ remain in compressed form. In this work, $[G]$ and $[H]$ are represented using Hierarchical H^2 matrices [2], and, so, $[J_k]$ should also be represented in H^2 form. Efficient computation of (7) requires being able 1) to compute $[G]\text{diag}[f'(\bar{\Phi}_k)]$ directly with the result in an H^2 representation and 2) to subtract two H^2-represented matrices directly with the result in an H^2 representation.

In general, the required operations fall into the general form:

$$[C] = [A]\text{diag}(\bar{a}) \pm [B]\text{diag}(\bar{b}) , \quad (8)$$

where $\text{diag}(\bar{x})$ indicates a diagonal matrix constructed from the vector $\bar{x}$ and $[A]$, $[B]$, and $[C]$ are H^2 matrices. It is further assumed that all H^2 matrices are built using the same tree structure. The necessary algorithm to implement (8) is constructed by noting that H^2 matrices are usually formed by compressing sub-blocks of the matrix using techniques such as the Adaptive Cross Approximation (ACA) to efficiently sample rows and columns of the sub-block and then compressing the sub-block ACA approximation using an SVD [5]. Direct use of the ACA+SVD method to sample the rows and columns of the $[A]\text{diag}(\bar{a}) \pm [B]\text{diag}(\bar{b})$ would be inefficient, although it does produce the desired H^2 representation of $[C]$.

Randomized linear algebra methods, on the other hand, provide a simple method to generate the SVD compressed sub-blocks in the H^2 representation without resorting to the row and column sampling required in an ACA technique. For example, an efficient randomized sampling method to generate the SVD of a matrix is detailed in [3]. Such methods enable the construction of controllably accurate outer-product representations of the sub-matrices of (8) through left and right multiplication with sets of random vectors. Because the matrices in (8) are represented using H^2 data structures, the required matrix-vector products encountered when using random projection methods (RPMs) can be rapidly evaluated.

This presentation will discuss the details associated with using an RPM to construct the H^2 representation of $[C]$ in (8). These details include the re-use of random matrix-vector product data at different levels of the nested H^2 data structure, as well as rank and convergence estimation for the blocks of $[C]$. The presentation will also review how such random projection methods can be modularly fitted within an existing software framework that constructs the original H^2 representations of $[A]$ and $[B]$ using ACA-based methods.

REFERENCES

[1] N. G. Zamani, J. M. Chuang, and J. F. Porter, "BEM Simulation of Cathodic Protection Systems Employed in Infinite Electrolytes," *International Journal for Numerical Methods in Engineering,* vol. 45, pp. 605-620, 1987.

[2] W. Hackbusch, Hierarchical Matrices Algorithms and Analysis, Heidelberg: Springer, 2015, p. 1 online resource. [Online]. Available: http://dx.doi.org/10.1007/978-3-662-47324-5 MIT Access Only.

[3] N. Halko, P. G. Martinsson, and J. A. Tropp, "Finding Structure with Randomness: Probabilistic Algorithms for Constructing Approximate Matrix Decompositions," vol. 53, no. 2, pp. 217-288, 2011.

[4] R. A. Pfeiffer, J. C. Young, R. J. Adams, and S. D. Gedney, "Higher-order simulation of impressed current cathodic protection systems," *Journal of Computational Physics,* vol. 394, pp. 522-531, 2019/10/01/ 2019.

[5] M. Bebendorf and S. Kunis, "Recompression Techniques for Aadaptive Cross Aapproximation," *The Journal of Integral Equations and Applications,* vol. 21, no. 3, pp. 331-357, 2009.

Shooting-Bouncing-Rays Technique to Model Mine Tunnels: Theory and Accuracy Validation

Stephen Kasdorf, Blake Troksa, Jake Harmon, Cam Key, and Branislav M. Notaroš
Colorado State University, Electrical & Computer Engineering Department, Fort Collins, CO
skasdorf@rams.colostate.edu, blake.troksa@gmail.com, J.Harmon@colostate.edu, camkey@rams.colostate.edu, notaros@colostate.edu

***Abstract*—We present a shooting-bouncing rays technique for electromagnetic modeling of wireless propagation in long tunnels focusing on the accuracy of ray-tracing computation. The examples demonstrate excellent agreement with the traditionally more accurate but less efficient alternative ray-tracing approach using path corrections based on image theory and with a commercial solver.**

Keywords—wireless communications, computational electromagnetics, high-frequency techniques, frequency-domain analysis, microwaves, ray tracing, signal propagation, waveguides.

I. Introduction

Electromagnetic (EM) modeling and simulation of wireless signal propagation in underground mines presents extraordinary challenges since the mine tunnels and galleries at wireless communication frequencies are electrically extremely large, with mine tunnels spanning thousands of wavelengths in length in typical applications. Using traditional full-wave computational electromagnetics (CEM) solvers for such applications may prove impractical in most cases due to computation run time required, as well as memory requirements, depending on the particular technique employed. Asymptotic methods for numerically approximate high-frequency modeling, such as ray-based techniques, are less accurate but much faster than the full-wave methods for numerically rigorous field computation, such as integral-equation techniques, and provide a good approach to modeling of wireless propagation and received signal strength simulation in underground mines.

This paper addresses application of the ray-tracing (RT) approach [1] to CEM analysis of long real tunnels. It presents and validates our RT method based on a shooting-bouncing rays (SBR) approach. Most importantly, it shows that when all the major components of the SBR RT methodology are properly developed and implemented, the accuracy of the new technique is sufficient for realistic wireless propagation modeling of tunnels and matches or outperforms the accuracy of computationally slower but traditionally more accurate alternative RT simulations.

II. Shooting-Bouncing Rays Method

There are two broad classes of ray tracing techniques common in CEM. The first is known as image theory (IT), or the method of images. This technique finds exact ray paths between a transmitter and receiver by employing images from the transmitter across reflecting surfaces in the environment being modeled. This is advantageous because the exact paths determination completely eliminates any phase error. However, the computational complexity of IT is $O(N^R)$ [2], where N is the number of observation points, and R is the number of reflections. In situations where reflection is the dominant propagation phenomenon, the IT technique becomes impractical due to its complexity.

The SBR approach in RT involves launching a set of rays from a transmitter in every direction. Each ray represents an equiphase surface, which combine to cover the radiation pattern of an antenna. These rays are then geometrically traced through the scene according to Snell's law, and their complex amplitude is governed by Fresnel's coefficients [3]. Once the ray path has been determined, the paths are tested for intersections with receivers. If the ray is determined to intersect the receiver, its electric field is calculated and added to the total computed field at that point. These ray paths are not the exact paths from the source to the receiver, so phase error is introduced making it traditionally less accurate than IT. While SBR includes phase error, it offers much lower computational complexity than IT making it more flexible in different scenarios. For this reason, SBR is chosen as the technique for modeling mine structures and tunnels [4], [5] in the present study.

Within the SBR family, there are two common methods of tracing the rays. The phase fronts are represented either using a center ray approach, known as "cones", or rays are used to trace the edges of the phase front, i.e., "tubes." To accurately model the radiation pattern of a transmitting antenna, the cones approach necessitates the overlap of phase fronts on adjacent rays. This leads to the problem of double counting of this phase surface, leading to substantial error in the simulation. While these double counts can be identified and eliminated, this causes an increase in computational demand of the simulation [6]. The tubes approach uses rays along the edge of triangular or rectangular geometries, which can fill the radiation pattern without any overlap. This eliminates overlaps of the phase fronts but requires a minimum of 4 times the number of rays per tube. In complex environments, a high number of rays is necessary to accurately sample the environment, which puts this method at a disadvantage. The cones method is used in our approach for this reason.

This work was supported by the National Science Foundation under grant ECCS-1646562.

III. Results and Discussion

Testing of the ray tracing method we developed was conducted on a real rectangular tunnel. This scene was chosen because the reflection phenomenon is extremely important in tunnel environments and represents a difficult simulation case for SBR. The tunnel cross section dimensions are chosen to be 5 m × 8 m, and the tunnel walls are characterized by relative permittivity ε_r = 5.5 and conductivity σ = 0.03 S/m. The waveguide is excited with a vertically polarized half-wave dipole transmitter at a frequency of 1 GHz. Electric field measurements (simulations) are taken along the length of the tunnel from 30 m to 150 m.

This tunnel embodies a very challenging case for ray-tracing as reflections become very important for the electric field, and rays must be traced to very long distances. The rays propagating long distances can have a very large number of reflections before reaching a receiver, and they can, in turn, accumulate a large path length error, leading to significant inaccuracies in the electric field solutions.

The results of the tunnel are compared to an SBR/IT hybrid method developed in [7], where an SBR algorithm was improved with IT path corrections. Figure 1 shows the results of the two ray-tracing methods on this scene.

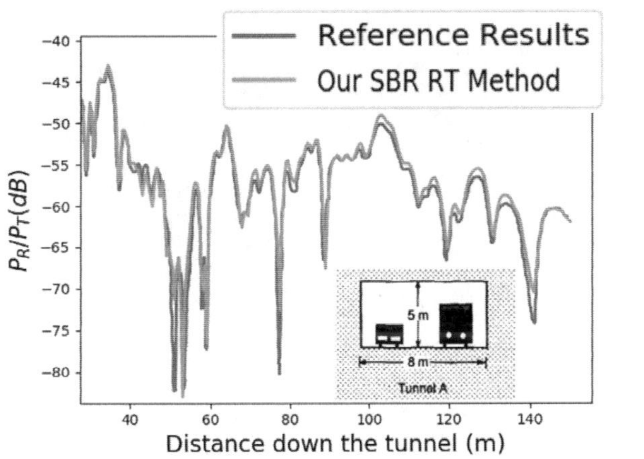

Fig. 1. Received/transmitted power along a rectangular tunnel (ε_r = 5.5, σ = 0.03 S/m) excited with a vertically polarized half-wave dipole transmitter at 1 GHz: comparison of our SBR RT method and an SBR algorithm with IT path corrections from [7].

We observe in Fig. 1 an excellent match of our SBR technique when compared to SBR/IT reference solution, at distances up to 150 m. This shows the accuracy of the SBR technique developed and its ability to very successfully eliminate the phase errors up to very long distances.

Additionally, we simulate a second real tunnel, now with a partly curved cross section to help verify the effectiveness of this model. Curved structures are traditionally difficult for ray-based techniques due to the images not being well defined.

We observe from Fig. 2 an excellent agreement of our SBR results with the hybrid SBR/IT solution from [7] for a tunnel with curved ceiling. Additionally, shown in Fig. 2 are the results obtained by the commercial software REMCOM Wireless InSite. We see that all three simulations agree very well.

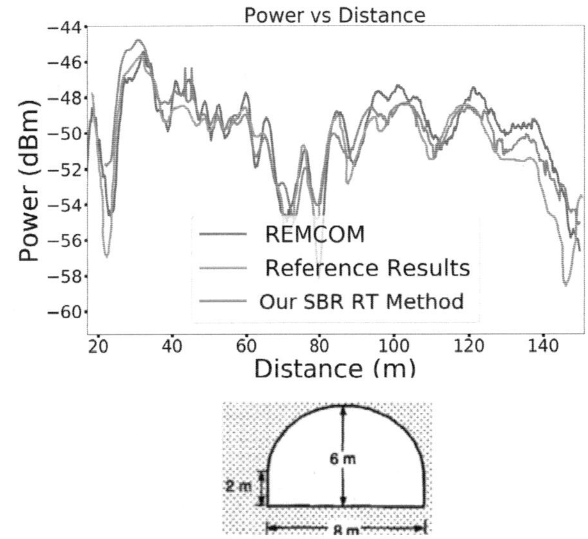

Fig. 2. Power [dBm] down the length of an arched tunnel (the tunnel cross section is shown; σ = 0.03 S/m, ε_r = 5.5; excitation: vertically polarized dipole antenna at 1 GHz): comparison of our SBR RT method with the results by the hybrid SBR/IT RT solution [7] and by the commercial REMCOM Wireless InSite solver.

IV. Conclusions

This paper has presented and validated the accuracy of our shooting-bouncing rays technique for ray-tracing modeling of long tunnels. The examples have demonstrated the excellent agreement of our method with the traditionally more accurate but less efficient hybrid SBR/IT ray-tracing approach, using image-theory path corrections, as well as with REMCOM Wireless InSite.

References

[1] M. F. Cátedra and J. Perez, Cell Planning for Wireless Communications. Norwood, MA, USA: Artech House, 1999.

[2] D. Didascalou, "Ray Optical Wave Propagation Modelling in Arbitrarily Shaped Tunnels", *Forschungsberichte aus dem Institut für Höchstfrequenztechnik und Elektronik der Universität Karlsruhe*, Vol. 24, Institut für Höchstfrequenztechnik und Elektronik, Universität Karlsruhe, 2000.

[3] B. M. Notaros, *Electromagnetics,* New Jersey: PEARSON Prentice Hall; 2010.

[4] B. Troksa, C. Key, F. Kunkel, S. V. Savic, M. M. Ilic, and B. M. Notaros, "Ray Tracing Using Shooting-Bouncing Technique to Model Mine Tunnels: Theory and Verification for a PEC Waveguide," *Proceedings of the 2018 International Applied Computational Electromagnetics Society (ACES) Symposium – ACES2018*, March 25–29, 2018, Denver, Colorado, USA.

[5] C. Key, B. Troksa, F. Kunkel, S. V. Savić, M. M. Ilic and B. M. Notaroš, "Comparison of Three Sampling Methods for Shooting-Bouncing Ray Tracing Using a simple Waveguide Model," *2018 IEEE International Symposium on Antennas and Propagation & USNC/URSI National Radio Science Meeting*, Boston, MA, 2018, pp. 2273-2274.

[6] Z. Yun, M. F. Iskander and Z. Zhang, "Development of a new shooting-and-bouncing ray (SBR) tracing method that avoids ray double counting," *IEEE Antennas and Propagation Society International Symposium. 2001 Digest.* Boston, MA, USA, 2001, pp. 464-467.

[7] S.-H. Chen and S.-K. Jeng, "SBR image approach for radio wave propagation in tunnels with and without traffic," *IEEE Transactions on Vehicular Technology*, vol. 45, no. 3, Aug. 1996, pp. 570-578.

Accelerating the Multilevel Fast Multipole Algorithm Using Machine Learning

Barışcan Karaosmanoğlu and Özgür Ergül

Department of Electrical and Electronics Engineering
Middle East Technical University
Ankara, Turkey
bariscan@metu.edu.tr

***Abstract*—We present a novel strategy to accelerate large-scale electromagnetic simulations with the multilevel fast multipole algorithm (MLFMA). The approach is based on a systematic reduction of electromagnetic interactions during an iterative solution such that both the number of iterations and time per iteration can be reduced. In order to eliminate matrix columns, errors in current coefficients are estimated via machine learning. The resulting implementation, namely trimmed MLFMA, provides significantly accelerated solutions without sacrificing the accuracy of results in comparison to high-frequency techniques.**

***Index Terms*—Machine learning, MLFMA, surface integral equations.**

I. Introduction

Machine learning (ML) techniques have extensively been studied in the last couple of decades for classification, regression, and prediction applications in a plethora of areas. Recently, they have also been employed in electromagnetics, such as for antenna optimization [1], visual result prediction [2], and enhancement of simulation efficiency [3]. In most of these applications, however, ML techniques and electromagnetic solvers are combined as black boxes, without truly benefiting from ML. In this paper, we present a novel approach to accelerate electromagnetic simulations with the multilevel fast multipole algorithm [4], [5] using ML techniques. Specifically, we integrate an ML-based interaction reduction technique into MLFMA to trim multilevel tree structures by eliminating insignificant interactions, leading to dynamically accelerated matrix-vector multiplications during iterative solutions. A remarkable speedup is obtained with the resulting implementation, namely the trimmed MLFMA (T-MLFMA), in comparison to MLFMA, without deteriorating the accuracy of simulations as opposed to high-frequency techniques.

II. Method and Numerical Results

Without losing generality, we consider scattering problems involving perfectly conducting objects formulated by using the combined-field integral equation (CFIE) and discretized with the Rao-Wilton-Glisson (RWG) functions [6]. The constructed dense matrix equations are solved iteratively, where the required matrix-vector multiplications (MVMs) are performed with MLFMA. Due to the nature of iterative solvers, unknown equivalent surface currents and the corresponding scattered

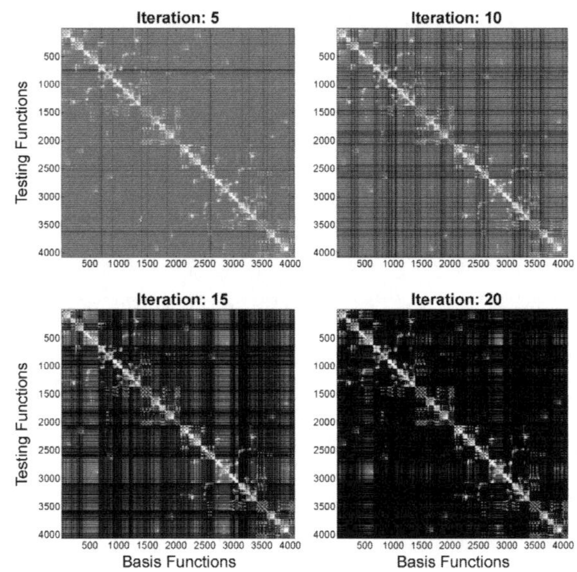

Fig. 1. Trimmed matrix layout for a 2λ PEC sphere at four different iterations during its solution.

fields on equivalence surfaces converge to true solutions as iterations proceed. On the other hand, after a number of iterations, some interactions in an MVM provide smaller contributions to the iteration updates. Since interactions cannot be checked one by one (otherwise, the complexity would be $\mathcal{O}(N^2)$), we employ ML to predict which interactions can safely be omitted. Specifically, during an iterative solution, the progress in equivalent surface currents are observed and the corresponding error levels are predicted at each iteration by a four-layer neural network. The network estimates the error in the surface currents so that the converged current coefficients (matrix columns) can be omitted in the far-zone interaction computations, leading to an increasingly sparser matrix as the iterations continue. In a more straightforward manner, the calculated scattered fields are also compared with the given right-hand-side vector and the matrix rows corresponding to sufficiently small error values are omitted. As a result, the MVM time can dramatically be reduced, while the number of iterations is also decreased.

To illustrate the concept and elaborate the proposed strategy, Fig. 1 depicts pictures of the impedance matrix related to a

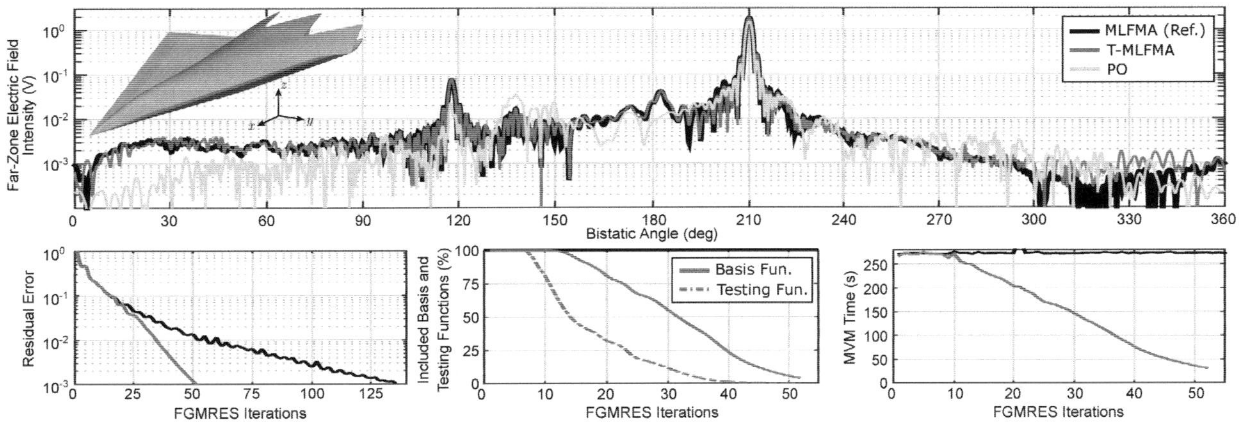

Fig. 2. Solutions of a scattering problem involving the Flamme geometry with an electrical size of 64λ.

perfectly conducting sphere of radius 300 mm. The geometry is illuminated by a plane wave at 1 GHz and it is discretized with $\lambda/10$ triangles, leading to a matrix equation involving 4080 unknowns. The generalized minimal residual (GMRES) algorithm is used as the iterative solver. For omitting interactions, the convergence threshold is set to 10%, i.e., a basis/testing function (and the related far-zone interactions) is dropped if the corresponding error (of current/field) is smaller than 10%. Fig. 1 presents the status of the impedance matrix at the intervals of five iterations. White and red regions correspond to near-zone and far-zone interactions, whereas the black regions (rows and columns) represent the omitted far-zone interactions. We observe that the matrix becomes increasingly sparse with the corresponding density values of $98.1\%, 84.2\%, 40.6\%$, and 12.9%.

To demonstrate the improved efficiency of T-MLFMA, we consider a scattering problem involving the Flamme geometry with an electrical size of 64λ. Using $\lambda/10$ triangles, the constructed matrix equation involves 811,080 unknowns. The object is illuminated by a horizontally polarized plane wave at 30° angle from the nose (x axis). Fig. 2 presents the bistatic far-zone electric field intensity on the x-y plane obtained by using the conventional MLFMA and the proposed T-MLFMA, as well as with the physical optics (PO) using the same discretization. The convergence thresholds in T-MLFMA are defined as 10% for surface currents (basis functions) and 5% for tested scattered fields (testing functions). The far-zone electric field intensity plots show good consistency between T-MLFMA and MLFMA, while the PO values significantly deviate from the MLFMA values (including the backscattering (30°) direction). The norm error in T-MLFMA with respect to MLFMA is found to be 3.36%. Fig. 2 also depicts the iterative solutions (residual errors with respect to flexible GMRES iterations), where the faster convergence of T-MLFMA is remarkable. Specifically, the number of iterations is reduced from 135 (MLFMA) to 51 (T-MLFMA) as a result of the sparsification. Fig. 2 further illustrates the ratios of the included basis/testing functions in MVMs by T-MLFMA (dropping as the iterations continue), as well as the processing time per MVM. We observe that MVM time is reduced from 267.7s (first iteration) to 30.8s (last iteration) as the residual error drops to below 0.001. As a result of both accelerated MVMs and the decreased number of iterations, the total solution time is reduced to 2.33 hours (T-MLFMA) compared to 10.25 hours (MLFMA).

III. Conclusion

We present an integration of an ML technique into MLFMA to accelerate solutions of large-scale electromagnetic problems. During an iterative solution, ML provides an estimation of errors in equivalent current coefficients such that converged coefficients can be omitted. This corresponds to a systematic deletion of matrix columns during the iterative solution. By also eliminating testing functions (matrix rows) based on more straightforward checks with the right-hand side, the impedance matrix becomes increasingly sparser as the iterations continue. The result is both reduced numbers of iterations and decreased MVM (per iteration) time, leading to significant accelerations in terms of overall solution times.

Acknowledgment

This work was supported by the Scientific and Technical Research Council of Turkey (TUBITAK) under the Research Grant 118E243 and by the Turkish Academy of Sciences (TUBA) in the framework of the YSA Program.

References

[1] B. Liu, et al., "An efficient method for antenna design optimization based on evolutionary computation and machine learning techniques," IEEE Trans. Antennas Propag., vol. 62, no. 1, pp. 7–18, Jan. 2014.
[2] B. Karaosmanoğlu and Ö. Ergül, "Visual result prediction in electromagnetic simulations using machine learning," IEEE Antennas Wireless Propag. Lett., vol. 18, no. 11, pp. 2664–2666, Nov. 2019.
[3] D. Yun, et al., "Improvement in computation time of the finite multipole method by using K-means clustering," IEEE Antennas Wireless Propag. Lett., vol. 18, no. 9, pp. 1814–1817, Sep. 2019.
[4] W. C. Chew, et al. Fast and Efficient Algorithms in Computational Electromagnetics. Norwood, MA, USA: Artech House, 2001.
[5] Ö. Ergül and L. Gürel, The Multilevel Fast Multipole Algorithm (MLFMA) for Solving Large-Scale Computational Electromagnetics Problems. Hoboken, NJ, USA: Wiley-IEEE, 2014.
[6] S. M. Rao, D. R. Wilton, and A. W. Glisson, "Electromagnetic scattering by surfaces of arbitrary shape," IEEE Trans. Antennas Propag., vol. 30, no. 3, pp. 409–418, Feb. 1982.

Deep Neural Network Inverse-Design for Long Wave Infrared Hyperspectral Imaging

Clayton Fowler[1], Sensong An[1], Bowen Zheng[1], Hong Tang[1], Hang Li[1], Wei Guo[2], and Hualiang Zhang[1]
[1]Electrical and Computer Engineering Dept.
[2]Physics and Applied Physics Dept.
University of Massachusetts Lowell
1 University Ave., Lowell, MA 01854, USA
hualiang_zhang@uml.edu

***Abstract*—This paper presents deep learning approaches for the inverse-design of metal-insulator-metal metasurfaces for hyperspectral imaging applications. Generative adversarial networks are able to compensate for the complex interactions between electromagnetic waves and metastructures to efficiently produce multiple design solutions that would be difficult to obtain using other methods.**

***Keywords*—generative adversarial networks, hyperspectral imaging, metasurface, metal-insulator-metal, narrowband filter.**

I. Introduction

Hyperspectral imaging introduces an additional dimensionality to conventional imaging by measuring many narrowband channels of electromagnetic radiation emitted from each point on an object. This additional information can help distinguish otherwise unseen features of an object and aid in applications such as identification, diagnosis, and spectroscopy.

One of the main challenges with hyperspectral imaging is producing these narrowband channels so that they are highly efficient over their specified bandwidth, but also strongly reject any signals outside this bandwidth. Metallic structures are useful for satisfying the rejection criteria, but their lossy characteristics at infrared and optical frequencies tend to prohibit the high-Q response needed to produce highly transmissive narrowband windows. Dielectrics, on the other hand, can support high-Q resonances, but it is difficult to create broad rejection bands, since they are naturally transmissive. Metal-insulator-metal (MIM) metamaterials [1] have shown potential for overcoming these trade-offs, but the complexity of the structures makes it difficult to satisfy the necessary conditions for hyper-spectral imaging.

Deep neural network (DNN) approaches have begun to emerge as viable solutions for engineering metamaterial structures to produce specified functionalities [2-4]. Generative Adversarial Networks [5] are especially promising for solving inverse-design challenges in that they can produce non-intuitive solutions. Specifically, we will demonstrate the use of DNNs to produce metasurface filters for hyperspectral imaging applications in the long wave infrared regime (9-11μm).

II. Proposed Metastructure and Design

Fig. 1 shows the basic design of the metamaterial filter. We use a uniform slab of GaAs with patterned layers of Au structures on the top and bottom of the slab to form an (MIM) metasurface. By altering the unit cell size and the shapes of the Au structures across the surface, we can create separate

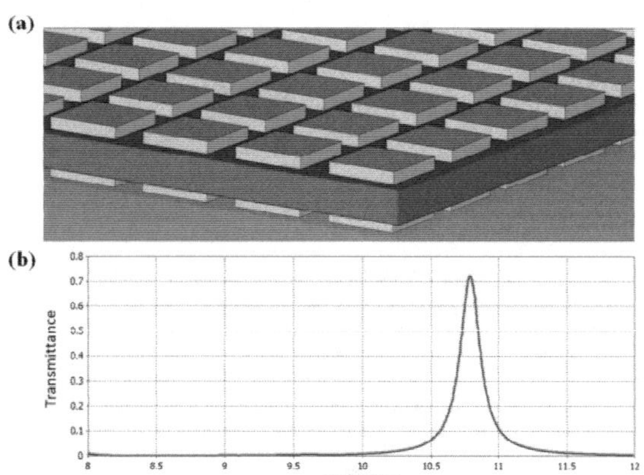

Fig. 1. (a) Metasurface filter composed of a slab of GaAs between layers of patterned Au structures. (b) Typical transmittance spectrum.

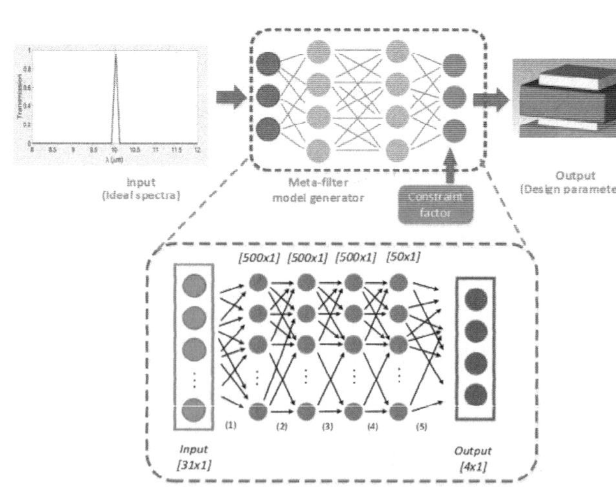

Fig. 2. Representative architecture for an inverse-design network for narrowband Au/GaAs/Au metal-insulator-metal filters. A target spectrum is used as input, and the network passes the spectrum through multiple hidden layers of neurons to determine the dimensional parameters for a metastructure that will produce a response close to the targeted spectrum.

passbands for different sections of the metasurface and form 20-40 channels spanning the 9-11 μm range. Additional shapes beyond squares, particularly freeform designs, can be considered to improve the transmittance and narrow the passband for better performance.

III. Deep Neural Network Approach

Fig. 2 shows representative architecture of a DNN for the inverse-design of narrowband transmissive filters. The network contains multiple hidden layers of connected neurons that pass the input at a specified number of frequencies (31 in this case) and outputs parameters for a structure whose response is close to the input spectrum. A constraint factor is introduced to prohibit designs that are outside of what can be physically manufactured. To further improve the performance of the proposed deep learning network, a generative adversarial network (GAN) can be employed.

A GAN is created by training two networks together, one is called the Generator and the other is called a Discriminator. The Generator is trying to produce "fake" samples that belong to a targeted distribution, while the Discriminator tries to distinguish "fake" samples from "real" ones that are known to belong to the targeted distribution. Through the training process, both networks get better at their respective tasks, which results in a Generator that can produce fake members that are indistinguishable from real ones. We choose the targeted distribution to consist of all the designs that meet our desired filter performance, and then a GAN is trained to produce multiple designs that will be as close to those specifications as allowed by constraints (physical laws, manufacturing tolerance, etc.). A GAN is especially useful in that it will be able to obtain freeform meta-structures that would likely not have been found by a human designer, who would be depending on intuition and/or trial-and-error methods.

IV. Discussion

The presented metal-insulator-metal design works by using the Au layers as diffraction gratings, which couple free space electromagnetic waves to surface plasmon polariton (SPP) resonance modes that occur at the GaAs/Au interfaces. These modes are less lossy than those that would occur in purely plasmonic structures and thus exhibit a higher-Q factor; as required for narrowband transmission. The dual gratings are essential, as wave vector conservation prohibits SPP modes from being directly excited by free space EM waves or from directly radiating into free space.

Given the complexity of this process, deep neural network techniques provide an efficient method for producing and realizing designs for complex metastructures, such as the MIM narrowband filter we have presented. A DNN can be trained by conducting full wave simulations ($\sim10^4$ structures will be simulated to provide the training dataset), whereas parameter sweeping methods would require several orders of magnitude more simulations to assemble a library of structures from which a matching design could be pulled. Such a design would likely require further optimization, whereas one produced by a fully trained DNN would already be optimal.

V. Conclusion

Hyperspectral imaging requires the creation of many narrowband channels to characterize the emission spectrum of an object. The channels can potentially be created by appropriate metamaterials, but the complex interactions between structures and electromagnetic waves make it difficult to satisfy the necessary criteria. We have proposed deep neural network approaches for the inverse-design of metal-insulator-metal narrowband filters to overcome these issues. Generative adversarial networks are particularly useful for generating multiple non-intuitive solutions to this problem so that an optimal design can be found.

References

[1] T. Xu, Y.-K. Wu, X. Luo, and L. J. Guo, "Plasmonic nanoresonators for high-resolution colour filtering and spectral imaging," Nature Communications, vol. 1, no. 1, p. 59, 2010/08/24 2010, doi: 10.1038/ncomms1058.

[2] S. An, *et al.*, "A Novel Modeling Approach for All-Dielectric Metasurfaces Using Deep Neural Networks," arXiv:1906.03387, 2019.

[3] S. An, *et al.*, "Generative Multi-Functional Meta-Atom and Metasurface Design Networks," arXiv:1908.04851, 2019.

[4] J. Jiang, D. Sell, S. Hoyer, J. Hickey, J. Yang, and J. A. Fan, "Free-Form Diffractive Metagrating Design Based on Generative Adversarial Networks," ACS Nano, vol. 13, no. 8, pp. 8872-8878, 2019/08/27 2019, doi: 10.1021/acsnano.9b02371.

[5] I. J. Goodfellow, *et al.*, "Generative Adversarial Nets," Advances in Neural Information Processing Systems, vol. 27, 2014.

Optimization and Inverse-design Techniques for Metalens Synthesis

Sawyer D. Campbell, Eric B. Whiting, Ronald P. Jenkins, Pingjuan L. Werner, and Douglas H. Werner
Department of Electrical Engineering
The Pennsylvania State University
University Park, PA 16802, USA
sdc22@psu.edu

***Abstract*—Phase-gradient metasurfaces enable designers to tailor the behavior of electromagnetic waves at surfaces by exploiting the generalized form of Snell's law. This ability has led to the investigation of metalenses which have the potential to significantly reduce the size, weight, and power (SWaP) of conventional optical systems. While traditional lenses are made from individual glasses, metalenses are comprised of patterned meta-atom unit cells which are arranged in such a way so as to give the metalens its desired behavior. Therefore, any metalens's performance is ultimately determined by that of its underlying unit cell components. However, designing meta-atoms that simultaneously achieve high performance over wide frequency bandwidths and fields-of-view is an extremely challenging problem that is best addressed with powerful optimization and inverse-design techniques.**

Keywords—nanoantennas; optimization; inverse-design; metasurfaces; metamaterials.

I. Introduction

Metasurfaces have garnered lots of attention in recent years for their potential ability to disrupt conventional optical systems. By exploiting the more general form of Snell's law [1] metasurfaces can achieve relatively arbitrary optical performance by manipulating a spatially-varying reflection and/or transmission phase profile along a surface. When used in imaging systems, metasurfaces are known as "metalenses" and have been investigated at a number of frequency bands including the visible [2], mid IR [3], and terahertz [4] regimes. One of the most promising aspects of metalenses is their ability to achieve optical power comparable to traditional spherical glass lenses albeit in a thin planar geometry [5]. Moreover, due to their unique dispersion behaviors, metalenses can be paired with conventional optical elements to provide color correction while significantly reducing the number of lenses required compared to conventional optical systems [6]. Regardless of their targeted frequency regime or application of interest, all metalenses can benefit from optimization. To this end, there exist a number of optimization techniques for meta-devices [7], such as metalenses, that include local, global, and multi-objective [8], [9] algorithms and new approaches such as surrogate-modeling, topology-optimization [10], and deep learning [7]. All of these techniques have seen success in the design of meta-atom unit cells and supercells for a variety of beam-steering and focusing applications. These meta-atoms are the building blocks used to synthesize large diameter metalenses and finding high performance meta-atoms is paramount to realizing metalenses with imaging performance comparable to conventional optical elements. With respect to performance, metalenses are typically judged by their focusing efficiency over a specified frequency bandwidth and field-of-view. This efficiency is ultimately determined by the available phase options and transmission magnitudes of the meta-atom building blocks. For this reason, dielectric-based meta-atoms have seen tremendous interest in the optical regime due to their low intrinsic losses [11]. This paper presents a brief introduction to the optimization of meta-atom unit cells for high-performance metalens synthesis.

II. Metalens Optimization

Nearly all meta-atom and metalens optimization strategies follow the same basic design flow which is summarized is Fig. 1. With the optimizer selected, an initial set of design parameters are generated which are then used to construct the unit cell

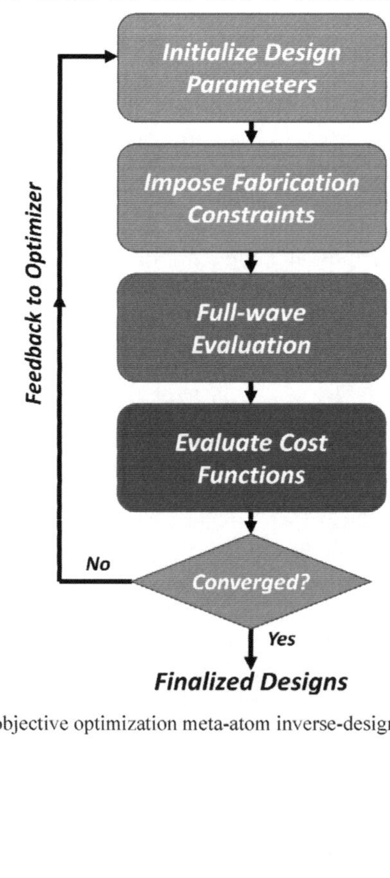

Fig. 1. Multi-objective optimization meta-atom inverse-design framework.

The work is supported in part by DARPA contract no. HR00111720032.

geometry. At this stage, any and all fabrication constraints are applied to the geometry to ensure its manufacturability. Note, this may require constraints being applied both before and after the unit cell is generated, depending on the complexity of the geometry generation techniques being employed. Next, a suitable full-wave forward solver (*e.g.*, Finite-Element Method, Finite-Difference Time Domain, or Discontinuous Galerkin Time Domain) is used to simulate the meta-atom(s) under plane-wave illumination across a pre-determined range of frequencies and incidence angles. When the simulation is complete, reflection and/or transmission (*i.e.*, S-parameter) data is extracted and used to evaluate one or more user-defined cost functions which are constructed in order to find meta-atom geometries that achieve the desired performance(s). After this stage, the optimizer generally checks if it has converged to the optimal solution(s); if not, it uses feedback gained from the most recent evaluations to choose another set of design parameters and the process repeats until convergence or a stopping criterion has been met. When the optimization is complete, the user is presented with a finalized design or set of designs depending on whether a single- [12], [13] or multi-objective [14] optimization algorithm, respectively, is employed.

The optimized meta-atoms can then be used to pattern a metalens to achieve a desired optical functionality. Figure 2 depicts an optimized metalens that has perfect focusing at a desired focal plane. The metalens is comprised of square unit cells that provide the requisite transmission phase at their individual locations. In addition to optimizing the meta-atoms themselves, the phase-profile of the metalens itself can be optimized to best exploit the properties of the available meta-atoms. For example, optical systems comprised of conventional glass elements and metasurfaces will have complex combinations of mono- and polychromatic aberrations that will require both the refractive lens geometrical parameters and the metalens phase profile to be optimized in concert to achieve the best possible optical performance of the combined system. Moreover, the requisite metalens phase profile can be used to drive the meta-atom optimization procedure and *vice versa* where a library of meta-atoms is used to constrain the metalens phase profile range. Interestingly, the same optimization algorithms and techniques can be used to optimize both the nano-scale meta-atoms and the centime-scale metalenses.

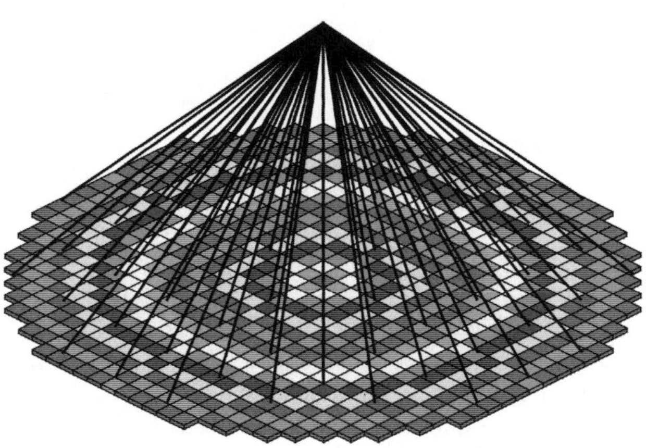

Fig. 2. Synthesized metalens comprised of optimized meta-atoms.

III. Future Work

High-performance meta-atoms should be robust to fabrication uncertainties, mechanical stresses, and thermal changes which may be experienced in real world operation. Thus, an inverse-design framework that enables the optimization of meta-atoms based on performance robustness is highly desirable. Future studies will investigate the potential for realizing robust meta-atoms and metalenses. Additionally, the ability to simultaneously simulate and optimize the meta-atoms and metalenses across all size scales is an active area of research.

References

[1] N. Yu, P. Genevet, M. A. Kats, F. Aieta, J.-P. Tetienne, F. Capasso, and Z. Gaburro, "Light Propagation with Phase Discontinuities: Generalized Laws of Reflection and Refraction," *Science, New Series*, vol. 334, no. 6054, pp. 333–337, 2011.

[2] M. Khorasaninejad, W. T. Chen, R. C. Devlin, J. Oh, A. Y. Zhu, and F. Capasso, "Metalenses at Visible Wavelengths: Diffraction-limited Focusing and Subwavelength Resolution Imaging," *Science*, vol. 352, no. 6290, pp. 1190–1194, Jun. 2016.

[3] H. Zuo, D.-Y. Choi, X. Gai, P. Ma, L. Xu, D. N. Neshev, B. Zhang, and B. Luther-Davies, "High-Efficiency All-Dielectric Metalenses for Mid-Infrared Imaging," *Advanced Optical Materials*, vol. 5, no. 23, p. 1700585, Dec. 2017.

[4] D. Jia, Y. Tian, W. Ma, X. Gong, J. Yu, G. Zhao, and X. Yu, "Transmissive Terahertz Metalens with Full Phase Control Based on a Dielectric Metasurface," *Optics Letters*, vol. 42, no. 21, p. 4494, Nov. 2017.

[5] N. Yu and F. Capasso, "Flat Optics with Designer Metasurfaces," *Nat. Mater*, vol. 13, no. 2, pp. 139–150, Feb. 2014.

[6] J. Nagar, S. D. Campbell, and D. H. Werner, "Apochromatic Singlets Enabled by Metasurface-augmented GRIN Lenses," *Optica*, vol. 5, no. 2, pp. 99–102, 2018.

[7] S. D. Campbell, D. Sell, R. P. Jenkins, E. B. Whiting, J. A. Fan, and D. H. Werner, "Review of Numerical Optimization Techniques for Meta-device Design [Invited]," *Opt. Mater. Express*, vol. 9, no. 4, pp. 1842–1863, Apr. 2019.

[8] S. D. Campbell, D. Z. Zhu, E. B. Whiting, J. Nagar, D. H. Werner, and P. L. Werner, "Advanced Multi-objective and Surrogate-assisted Optimization of Topologically Diverse Metasurface Architectures," in *Metamaterials, Metadevices, and Metasystems 2018*, vol. 10719, p. 107190U.

[9] S. D. Campbell, E. B. Whiting, D. H. Werner, and P. L. Werner, "High-Performance Metasurfaces Synthesized via Multi-Objective Optimization," in *2019 International Applied Computational Electromagnetics Society Symposium (ACES)*, pp. 1–2.

[10] D. Sell, J. Yang, S. Doshay, and J. A. Fan, "Periodic Dielectric Metasurfaces with High-Efficiency, Multiwavelength Functionalities," *Adv. Opt. Mater.*, vol. 5, no. 23, p. 1700645, Dec. 2017.

[11] A. Arbabi, Y. Horie, M. Bagheri, and A. Faraon, "Dielectric Metasurfaces for Complete Control of Phase and Polarization with Subwavelength Spatial Resolution and High Transmission," *Nat. Nanotechnol.*, vol. 10, no. 11, pp. 937–943, Nov. 2015.

[12] N. Hansen, S. D. Müller, and P. Koumoutsakos, "Reducing the Time Complexity of the Derandomized Evolution Strategy with Covariance Matrix Adaptation (CMA-ES)," *Evolutionary Computation*, vol. 11, no. 1, pp. 1–18, Mar. 2003.

[13] M. D. Gregory, Z. Bayraktar, and D. H. Werner, "Fast Optimization of Electromagnetic Design Problems Using the Covariance Matrix Adaptation Evolutionary Strategy," *IEEE Transactions on Antennas and Propagation*, vol. 59, no. 4, pp. 1275–1285, Apr. 2011.

[14] D. Hadka and P. Reed, "Borg: An Auto-Adaptive Many-Objective Evolutionary Computing Framework," *Evol. Comput.*, vol. 21, no. 2, pp. 231–259, May 2013.

Designing Large-Scale Metasurfaces with Parameterized Adjoint Optimization

(Invited Paper)

Mahdad Mansouree, Andrew McClung, Sarath Samudrala, and Amir Arbabi*
Department of Electrical and Computer Engineering
University of Massachusetts Amherst, Amherst, MA 01003, USA
*arbabi@umass.edu

***Abstract*—We present the details of a metasurface design method based on adjoint optimization and finite-difference time-domain simulation. Instead of meta-atom topology, our method optimizes parameterized meta-atoms that can be readily fabricated. As proof-of-concept, we design large, high-efficiency metalenses which outperform conventionally designed counterparts.**

***Index Terms*—Adjoint method, metasurfaces, optimization,**

I. Introduction

Metasurfaces are arrays of optical scatterers ("meta-atoms") with sub-wavelength dimensions that implement a desired transformation on incident light. The metasurface optics is a versatile and scalable platform that is attractive for implementing many components such as lenses, holograms, and beam splitters [1], [2]. However, designing efficient metasurfaces is challenging. In conventionally-designed [3] dielectric metasurfaces, losses are dominated by unwanted diffraction. These losses can be attributed to two implicit but inaccurate assumptions about the meta-atom's response: first, that it is localized and independent from its neighbors, and second, that it is the same at all deflection angles.

An alternative approach is to use optimization-based design methods. More specifically, adjoint optimization [4], [5] has been shown to be an efficient method to optimize optical structures. In this paper, we describe the details of a parameterized adjoint optimization technique based on finite difference time domain (FDTD) simulations. Unlike previously reported adjoint optimization methods [4], [6], which produce complex, free-form structures, our method uses parameterized square meta-atoms which can be fabricated easily.

II. Design

Our method treats metasurface design as an optimization problem. We begin with a simple initial state (in this work, a metasurface comprising uniform meta-atoms), evaluate an objective and obtain its gradient using an adjoint technique, and iteratively improve the design using gradient ascent.

The adjoint method requires simulating the response of a design to two different source fields. In the first simulation, referred to as the *forward* simulation, the structure is excited by a field incident from below (Fig. 1 (a)). This source realizes a field $\mathbf{E}_\mathrm{t}$ at an output plane Σ above the structure. In the second, *adjoint* simulation, the structure is excited by a surface current distribution $\mathbf{j}_s$ incident from above that generates the time-inversed desired field $\mathbf{E}_\mathrm{d}^*$ at Σ (dashed lines in Fig. 1).

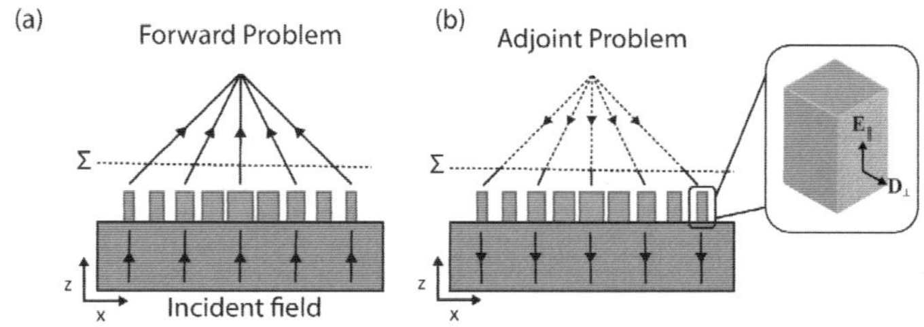

Fig. 1. Schematic representation of forward and adjoint problems. Dashed lines indicate the output plane Σ. (a) The forward problem simulates the response of the metasurface to a planned incident source. (b) The adjoint problem simulates the response of the metasurface to a source generating the time-reversed desired field. Inset shows the magnified version of a meta-atom and the field components used to estimate its derivatives.

We select as our objective function $I = |F|^2$, where F is the projection of $\mathbf{E}_\mathrm{t}$ and $\mathbf{E}_\mathrm{d}$ on the plane Σ: $F = \int_\Sigma \mathbf{E}_\mathrm{t} \cdot \mathbf{E}_\mathrm{d}^* \, \mathrm{d}s$. The derivative of F with respect to an arbitrary geometrical parameter w_i is given by [6]:

$$\frac{\partial F}{\partial w_i} = j\omega\left(\epsilon_\mathrm{p} - \epsilon_\mathrm{C}\right) \int_{S_i} \mathbf{E}_\parallel^\mathrm{f} \cdot \mathbf{E}_\parallel^\mathrm{a} + \frac{1}{\epsilon_\mathrm{p}\epsilon_\mathrm{C}} \mathbf{D}_\perp^\mathrm{f} \cdot \mathbf{D}_\perp^\mathrm{a} \, \mathrm{d}s \quad (1)$$

where ϵ_p (ϵ_C) is dielectric constant of the meta-atom (cladding), S_i the surface affected by changing w_i, $\mathbf{E}^\mathrm{f}$ and $\mathbf{D}^\mathrm{f}$ the electric and displacement fields from the forward simulation, and $\mathbf{E}^\mathrm{a}$ and $\mathbf{D}^\mathrm{a}$ the corresponding fields from the adjoint simulation. The derivative $\partial I/\partial w_i$ can thus be written:

$$\frac{\partial I}{\partial w_i} = 2\mathrm{Re}\left[F^* \frac{\partial F}{\partial w_i}\right]. \quad (2)$$

The derivatives for all meta-atoms are used to optimize the device via gradient ascent.

FDTD [7] is used for both simulations, which produces time-domain fields. However, equations (1) and (2) are valid in the frequency domain and we are interested in the metasurface results at a single wavelength. To efficiently convert from time to frequency domain, we use the two equations, two

This work is funded by Samsung Electronics.

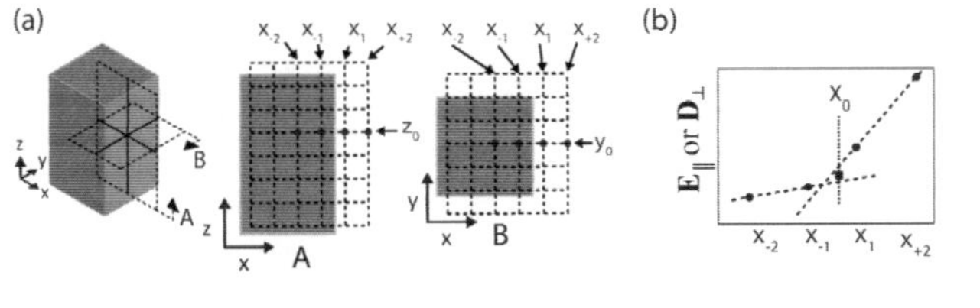

Fig. 2. Interpolation of boundary fields. (a) The boundary position relative to simulation grid. (b) Schematic of two-sided interpolation technique.

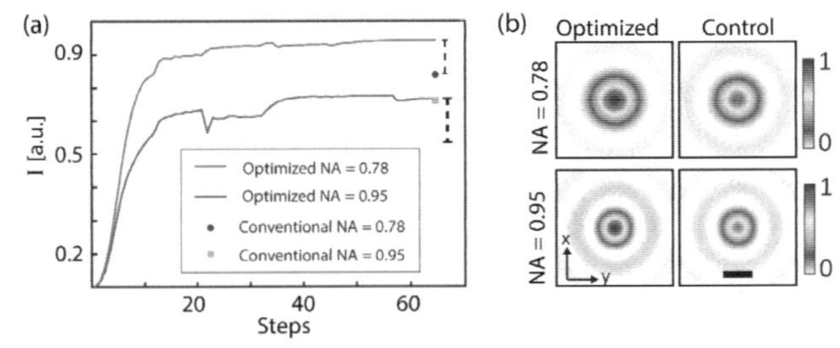

Fig. 3. Optimization of the lenses. (a) Improvement of efficiencies on the objective function I during optimization. (b) Simulated intensities at focal plane. Scale bar indicates 0.5 μm.

unknowns method described in [8]. Because the metasurface is excited by a single harmonic source, all the frequency domain information can be retrieved using only two time domain samples. The accuracy of $\partial I/\partial w_i$ depends on precise knowledge of the fields at the meta-atom boundaries, but FDTD simulations only determine these fields on a uniform grid. To calculate the boundary fields we must interpolate neighboring grid points. Maxwell's equations enforce continuity for $\mathbf{E}_\parallel$ and $\mathbf{D}_\perp$ at meta-atom boundaries, but their first derivatives may be discontinuous. Only grid points along the axis normal to the boundary (Fig. 2 (a)) are considered. We interpolate using a two-sided linear approach (Fig. 2 (b)): First, we interpolate the real and imaginary part of the fields both inside (x_{-2}, x_{-1}) and outside (x_1, x_2) the meta-atom. Next, we extrapolate the field at x_0 using inside and outside interpolants. Because the boundary does not necessarily fall at the intersection of these interpolants, we estimate the field at the boundary using a distance-weighted average (Fig. 2 (b)).

III. Results

We simulated metalenses with 50 μm diameter and focal distances of 20 μm and 8.33 μm (NA of 0.78 and 0.95 respectively) designed using both conventional and the proposed adjoint method. Metalenses comprise a rectangular array of square, amorphous silicon nanoposts resting on a fused silica substrate. The nanopost array has a lattice constant of 320 nm and uniform height of 420 nm; we select meta-atom width as the design parameter in our optimization. Conventionally designed metalenses with NA of 0.78 (0.95) showed focusing efficiencies of 68% (43%) within a 6 μm diameter in the focal plane, while optimized metalenses showed 78% (52%) efficiency after 64 iterations, demonstrating an improvement

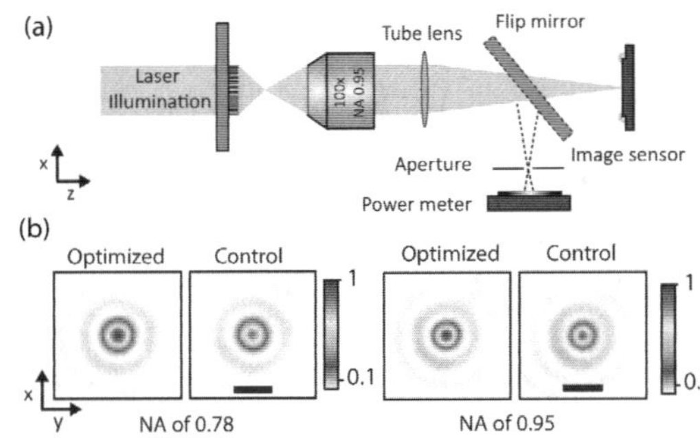

Fig. 4. (a) Schematic of measurement setup. (b) Measured intensities at focal plane. Scale bar indicates 1 μm.

of 14% (32%). Fig. 3 (a) shows the improving focusing efficiency as iterative optimization progresses.

To validate our approach, we fabricated and characterized both optimized and control lenses. Our measurement setup is schematically illustrated in Fig. 4a. We measured focal efficiencies using an effective aperture of 7 μm. The focal efficiency for optimized (control) lenses with NA of 0.78 (0.95) are 77% (58%), higher than those of the control lens 65% (51%). Fig. 4 (b) shows intensity profiles for all lenses.

IV. Conclusion

The performance of metasurfaces including simple building blocks is limited by the assumptions in the conventional method. As demonstrated, metasurfaces designed by parameterized adjoint optimization that outperform their conventionally designed counterparts. The approach is readily extendable to multi-wavelength objectives and to more complex structures (e.g., multilayer).

References

[1] S. M. Kamali, E. Arbabi, A. Arbabi, and A. Faraon, "A review of dielectric optical metasurfaces for wavefront control," *Nanophotonics*, vol. 7, no. 6, pp. 1041–1068, June 2018.

[2] H.-T. Chen, A. J. Taylor, and N. Yu, "A review of metasurfaces: physics and applications," *Reports on progress in physics*, vol. 79, no. 7, p. 076401, 2016.

[3] A. Arbabi, Y. Horie, A. J. Ball, M. Bagheri, and A. Faraon, "Subwavelength-thick lenses with high numerical apertures and large efficiency based on high-contrast transmitarrays," *Nature Communications*, vol. 6, no. 1, p. 7069, May 2015.

[4] S. Molesky, Z. Lin, A. Y. Piggott, W. Jin, J. Vucković, and A. W. Rodriguez, "Inverse design in nanophotonics," *Nature Photonics*, vol. 12, no. 11, p. 659, 2018.

[5] M. Mansouree and A. Arbabi, "Large-scale metasurface design using the adjoint sensitivity technique," in *Conference on Lasers and Electro-Optics*. Optical Society of America, 2018, p. FF1F.7.

[6] O. D. Miller, "Photonic design: From fundamental solar cell physics to computational inverse design," Ph.D. dissertation, UC Berkeley, 2012.

[7] A. F. Oskooi, D. Roundy, M. Ibanescu, P. Bermel, J. D. Joannopoulos, and S. G. Johnson, "Meep: A flexible free-software package for electromagnetic simulations by the FDTD method," *Computer Physics Communications*, vol. 181, pp. 687–702, 2010.

[8] C. M. Furse, "Faster than fourier: Ultra-efficient time-to-frequency-domain conversions for fdtd simulations," *IEEE Antennas and Propagation Magazine*, vol. 42, no. 6, pp. 24–34, 2000.

Adversarial Autoencoders for Metasurface Design Optimization *(invited)*

Zhaxylyk A. Kudyshev
School of Electrical and Computer Engineering and Birck Nanotechnology Center
Purdue University
West Lafayette, USA
zkudyshev@purdue.edu

Alexander V. Kildishev
School of Electrical and Computer Engineering and Birck Nanotechnology Center
Purdue University
West Lafayette, USA
kildishev@purdue.edu

Vladimir M. Shalaev
School of Electrical and Computer Engineering and Birck Nanotechnology Center
Purdue University
West Lafayette, USA
shalaev@purdue.edu

Alexandra Boltasseva
School of Electrical and Computer Engineering and Birck Nanotechnology Center
Purdue University
West Lafayette, USA
aeb@purdue.edu

***Abstract*— We have coupled adversarial autoencoder deep generative network with adjoined topology optimization technique for metasurface design optimization. We have demonstrated that such approach ensures not only efficient optimization search of highly efficient metasurface designs but also provides unparalleled control over compressed design space distribution. The latter fact assures scalability of the approach to highly-constrained optimization problems.**

Keywords*— *metamaterials, metasurfaces, topology optimization.

I. Introduction

With the recent progress of new plasmonic/photonic material platforms, as well as advances in fabrication techniques, nanophotonics can address different interdisciplinary challenges, e.g., energy [1], quantum information [2]. However, these types of problems require highly-constrained optimization of the device, due to inherent complexity and multi-disciplinary nature. Conventionally, adjoint [3] and genetic [4] optimization methods have been used to address such optimization tasks. Unfortunately, the computational power requirement of these methods scales up with the number of constraints of the problem. This fact substantially limits the applicability of conventional optimization techniques to such problems.

II. AAE assisted topology optimization

Within this work, we propose to merge the adjoint topology optimization technique with adversarial autoencoders (AAE) to achieve significant improvement in the optimization search of non-trivial nano-antenna designs [5]. Particularly we have demonstrated that such approach ensures not only efficient optimization search of highly efficient metasurface designs but also provides unparalleled control over compressed design space distribution. The latter fact assures scalability of the approach to highly-constrained optimization problems. Fig. 1 shows the proposed flow of the optimization process.

III. Conclusion

To showcase AAE assisted method, we optimize a metasurface thermal emitter for thermophotovoltaic (TPV) applications. Compared to an adjoint-based TO design with 92% efficiency of the thermal emission reshaping, the proposed method provides three times speedup and gives 98% efficiency. The proposed approach can be adapted to a broader scope of the problems in optics, chemistry, and mechanics.

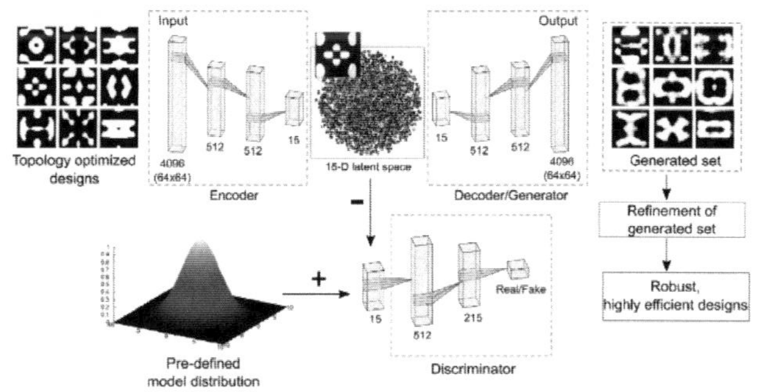

Fig. 1. AAE-assisted topology optimization. Starting from a discrete set of the topology optimized designs of nanoantenna that serves as the metasurface building block, the encoder compresses each nanoantenna design into a point in the latent space – compressed, continuous design space. The decoder reconstructs the design based on the input coordinate in the latent space. The discriminator forces the encoder to construct the latent space with a pre-defined distribution. The trained decoder is then used as a generator, which takes the latent space coordinate as an input and generates a large set of designs. The structure refinement procedure is applied to the generated set to eliminate unstable, low-efficient designs.

IV. Acknowledgment

Authors acknowledge support from AFOSR (FA9550-17-1-0243), NSF (0939370-CCF), DARPA/DSO Extreme Optics and Imaging (EXTREME) Program (HR00111720032).

References

[1] S. Linic, P. Christopher, and D. B. Ingram, "Plasmonic-metal nanostructures for efficient conversion of solar to chemical energy," Nature Materialsk, vol. 10, pp. 911-921, 2011.

[2] S. I. Bogdanov, A. Boltasseva, and V. M. Shalaev, "Overcoming quantum decoherence with plasmonics," Science, vol. 364, pp. 532-533, 2019.

[3] J. S. Jensen and O. Sigmund, "Topology optimization for nano-photonics," Laser and Photonics Reviews, vol. 5, pp. 308-321, 2011.

[4] C. Forestiere, et al., "Genetically engineered plasmonic nanoarrays," Nano Letters, vol. 12, pp. 2037-2044, 2012.

[5] Z. A. Kudyshev, A. V. Kildishev, V. M. Shalaev, and A. Boltasseva, "Machine-Learning-Assisted Metasurface Design for High-Efficiency Thermal Emitter Optimization," arXiv Preprint arXiv:1910.12741, 2019.

Topology-optimized Nanostructures for High-NA Lensing Optics

Zin Lin
Department of Mathematics
Massachusetts Institute of Technology
Cambridge, MA, USA
zinlin@mit.edu

Steven G. Johnson
Department of Mathematics
Massachusetts Institute of Technology
Cambridge, MA, USA
stevenj@math.mit.edu

***Abstract*— We demonstrate a large-scale computational approach, based on topology optimization, for designing high-NA large-area *single-piece* metalenses. We report on a variety of nanostructures with broadband and wide-angle functionalities.**

Keywords—topology optimization, nanophotonics, multi-layered nanostructures, metasurfaces

I. Introduction

Metasurface optics has been hailed as a breakthrough technology for 21st-century photonics, promising a new generation of ultra-compact ultra-lightweight photonic devices that would find important applications in numerous areas of science and technology [1]. However, many hurdles remain before the full promise of metasurfaces can be realized. For example, the current metasurface technology suffers from issues such as limited capability for realizing large-area/high-numerical-aperture (NA) designs, poor device efficiencies, or limited spectral and angular bandwidth control. We argue that these issues may be traced to a few common limitations of the standard design methodologies: adherence to single-layer designs, reliance on intuitive primitive geometries, and a common computational approach known as a locally periodic approximation (LPA) [2]. To successfully address the issues besetting the state-of-the-art LPA-based metasurface designs, we propose a novel computational approach with three key components: multiple interacting layers with deeply sub-wavelength separations (three-dimensional single-piece nanophotonics) [3] designed by large-scale optimization techniques (inverse design and topology optimization) [4], using more sophisticated overlapping domain-decomposition methods [5] superior to LPA. The combination of these ingredients allows us to utilize the full electromagnetic degrees of freedom (multiple-scattering full-vector Maxwell equations) — exploiting every fabrication "pixel" of a large-area multilayer metasurface — in order to obtain complete control over every aspect of light propagation: phase, amplitude, polarization, including angular and frequency dispersion, in an ultrathin device.

U. S. Army Research Office through the Institute for Soldier Nanotechnologies (W911NF-13-D-0001).

II. Chromatic and Angular Aberrations Correction

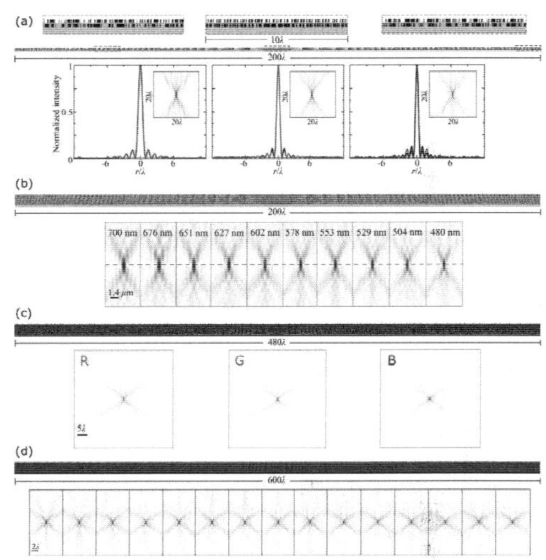

Fig. 1 High-NA two-dimensional cylindrical achromatic metalens designs with spectral dispersion control. (a) Bilayer TiO_2 metalens with NA=0.71 and lens width=200λ where λ=700nm. Achromatic aberration corrections at red (700nm), green (540nm) and blue (480nm) wavelengths. The normalized far-field profile at the focal distance (red, green or blue line) shows good agreement with that of an ideal monochromatic lens at the corresponding wavelength (black solid line). (b) 15-layer TiO_2 metalens with NA=0.71 and lens width=200λ. Broadband achromatic aberration corrections over the bandwidth 480-700 nm. (c) 10-layer polymer (n ~ 1.5) 3d-printable metalens with NA=0.92 and lens width=480λ. Achromatic aberration corrections at RGB. The lens has a minimum lateral feature size of 150 nm and a minimum vertical feature size of 350 nm consistent with the high-resolution nanoscale 3D-printing technologies such as Nanoscribe. (d) 25-layer polymer (n ~ 1.5) 3d-printable metalens with NA=0.95 and lens width=600λ where λ=1600nm. Broadband achromatic aberration corrections over the telecomm bandwidth 1300-1600nm. Note that we perform rigorous validations of all the optimized designs via full-wave FDTD simulations [6] of the entire structures without any approximation.

As a demonstration of our approach, we report on several high-NA large-area nanophotonic lens designs that exhibit broadband achromatic functionalities as well as wide-angle aberration corrections (Figs. 1-3). For example, as proofs of concepts, Fig. 1 shows a variety of two-dimensional (invariant along the out-of-page direction) cylindrical nanophotonic lens

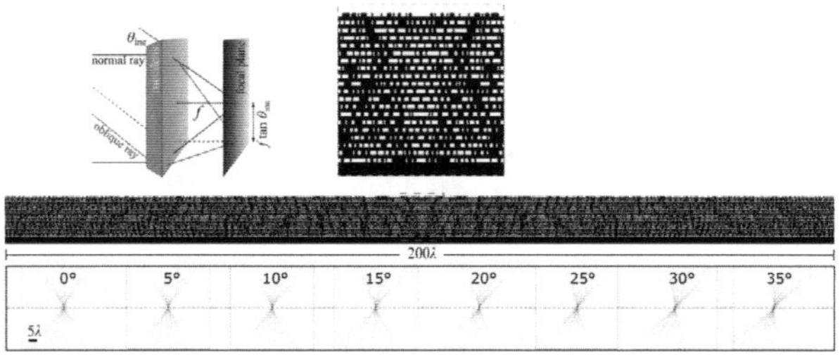

Fig. 2 High-NA 2D cylindrical metalens (NA=0.71) with angular dispersion control. The schematic illustrates how the lens corrects monochromatic angular aberrations (such as coma and Petzval field curvature, etc.) due to oblique incidence. The lens is 200λ wide and consists of 20 layers of 3D-printable polymer (n=1.53), where λ=1550nm. The lens has an average focusing efficiency of 40%.

designs with NAs ranging from 0.7 to 0.95 and spanning over visible and near-infra-red frequency ranges. While the lenses are designed under a domain decomposition approximation [5], the far-field focal intensity profiles are obtained from rigorous FDTD simulations [6] of the entire structures without any approximation, showing diffraction-limited focusing. Fig. 2 shows another lens design which seeks to correct off-axis angular aberrations (e.g. such as coma and Petzval field curvatures) at multiple incident angles. We emphasize that inverse design allows such corrections in a *single-piece* multi-layered design (at most, a few tens of microns in thickness) by fully exploiting the Maxwell's equations without resorting to the simplified ray optics picture as in the conventional *doublets* (typically, a few millimeters in thickness). We also note that some of the designs are developed with structural constraints imposed by nano-scale 3D printing such as direct laser writing. Finally, in contrast to most metalenses (which achieve aberration corrections either at multiple frequencies or under multiple incident angles but not both), we also present a proof-of-concept single-piece *plan-achromat* (Fig. 3) which achieves aberrations correction at multiple frequencies and angles simultaneously. The somewhat smaller NA and width is only limited by our current computational resources. The smeared broadened focal spot for 30° is due to the fact that the bundle of light at the 30° incident angle is almost exceeding the diffraction-limited field of view admitted by the lens aperture.

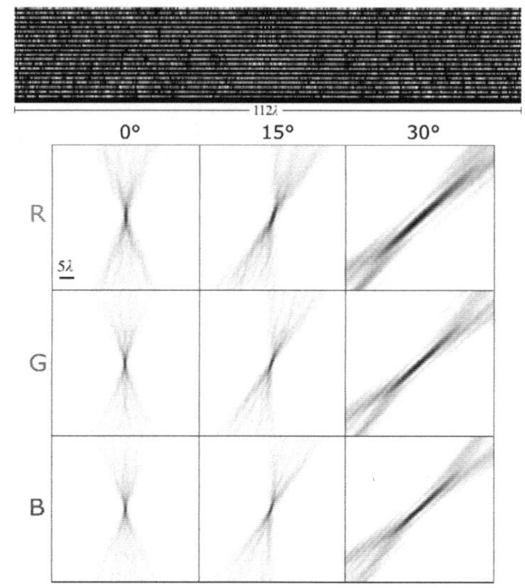

Fig. 2 Cylindrical metalens (NA=0.49) with both chromatic and angular aberration corrections at three discrete wavelengths (RGB) and three discrete incident angles (0°, 15°, 30°). The lens is 112λ wide and consists of 20 layers of 3D-printable polymer (n=1.53), where λ=700nm.

[1] Nanfang Yu and Federico Capasso, "Flat optics with designer metasurfaces," Nature Materials, 13(2) p. 139, 2014.

[2] Raphaël Pestourie, Carlos Perez-Arancibia, Zin Lin, Wonseok Shin, Federico Capasso, and Steven G. Johnson, "Inverse design of large-areametasurfaces," Optics Express, vol. 26, pp. 33732–33747, 2018.

[3] Zin Lin, Benedikt Groever, Federico Capasso, Alejandro W. Rodriguez, and Marko Lončar, "Topology-optimized multilayered metaoptics," Physical Review Applied, 9(4) p. 044030, 2018.

[4] Sean Molesky, Zin Lin, Alexander Y. Piggott, Weiliang Jin, Jelena Vucković, and Alejandro W. Rodriguez, "Inverse design in nanophotonics," Nature Photonics, 12(11) p. 659, 2018.

[5] Zin Lin and Steven G. Johnson, "Overlapping domains for topology optimization of large-area metasurfaces," Optics Express, vol. 27, pp. 32445-32453, 2019.

[6] Ardavan F. Oskooi, David Roundy, Mihai Ibanescu, Peter Bermel, John D Joannopoulos, and Steven G. Johnson, "MEEP: A flexiblefree-software package for electromagnetic simulations by the FDTD method," Computer Physics Communications, vol. 181, pp. 687 – 702, 2010.